Empirical Research for Futuristic E-Commerce Systems:

Foundations and Applications

Saurabh Bilgaiyan
Kalinga Institute of Industrial Technology (Deemed), Bhubaneswar, India

Jagannath Singh
Kalinga Institute of Industrial Technology (Deemed), Bhubaneswar, India

Himansu Das
Kalinga Institute of Industrial Technology (Deemed), Bhubaneswar, India

IGI Global
PUBLISHER of TIMELY KNOWLEDGE

A volume in the Advances in Electronic Commerce (AEC) Book Series

Published in the United States of America by
IGI Global
Business Science Reference (an imprint of IGI Global)
701 E. Chocolate Avenue
Hershey PA, USA 17033
Tel: 717-533-8845
Fax: 717-533-8661
E-mail: cust@igi-global.com
Web site: http://www.igi-global.com

Copyright © 2022 by IGI Global. All rights reserved. No part of this publication may be reproduced, stored or distributed in any form or by any means, electronic or mechanical, including photocopying, without written permission from the publisher. Product or company names used in this set are for identification purposes only. Inclusion of the names of the products or companies does not indicate a claim of ownership by IGI Global of the trademark or registered trademark.

Library of Congress Cataloging-in-Publication Data

Names: Bilgaiyan, Saurabh, 1990- editor. | Singh, Jagannath, 1979- editor. | Das, Himansu, editor.
Title: Empirical research for futuristic e-commerce systems / Saurabh Bilgaiyan, Jagannath Singh, and Himansu Das, editor.
Description: Hershey, PA : Business Science Reference, [2022] | Includes bibliographical references and index. | Summary: "This book offers contributions from various fields of machine learning, deep learning, nature-inspired computing, artificial intelligence to build intelligent systems for developing efficient e-commerce platforms"-- Provided by publisher.
Identifiers: LCCN 2022014829 (print) | LCCN 2022014830 (ebook) | ISBN 9781668449691 (hardcover) | ISBN 9781668449707 (paperback) | ISBN 9781668449714 (ebook)
Subjects: LCSH: Electronic commerce. | Electronic data interchange.
Classification: LCC HF5548.32 .E486 2022 (print) | LCC HF5548.32 (ebook) | DDC 381/.142--dc23/eng/20220328
LC record available at https://lccn.loc.gov/2022014829
LC ebook record available at https://lccn.loc.gov/2022014830

This book is published in the IGI Global book series Advances in Electronic Commerce (AEC) (ISSN: 1935-2921; eISSN: 1935-293X)

British Cataloguing in Publication Data
A Cataloguing in Publication record for this book is available from the British Library.

All work contributed to this book is new, previously-unpublished material. The views expressed in this book are those of the authors, but not necessarily of the publisher.

For electronic access to this publication, please contact: eresources@igi-global.com.

Advances in Electronic Commerce (AEC) Book Series

Mehdi Khosrow-Pour, D.B.A.
Information Resources Management Association, USA

ISSN:1935-2921
EISSN:1935-293X

Mission

The impact of information technology on commerce is a dynamic and perpetually evolving field of research, most notably as electronic approaches for business transactions shift to the Internet and other telecommunication networks. Given the rapid advancements in the field, research addressing e-commerce and its related areas needs an outlet to reach its audience.

The **Advances in Electronic Commerce (AEC) Book Series** provides comprehensive coverage and understanding of the social, cultural, organizational, and cognitive impacts of e-commerce technologies. The series provides accounts from both the consumer perspective and the organization perspective. **AEC** aims to expand the body of knowledge regarding e-commerce technologies and applications, thus assisting researchers and practitioners to develop more effective systems.

Coverage

- Commerce Strategy
- Mobile Banking
- E-Tailing
- Mobile Commerce
- Electronic Funds Transfer
- Electronic Banking
- Online Transaction Processing
- Social Media and E-Commerce
- B2B and C2C Technologies
- Virtual Storefronts

IGI Global is currently accepting manuscripts for publication within this series. To submit a proposal for a volume in this series, please contact our Acquisition Editors at Acquisitions@igi-global.com or visit: http://www.igi-global.com/publish/.

The Advances in Electronic Commerce (AEC) Book Series (ISSN 1935-2921) is published by IGI Global, 701 E. Chocolate Avenue, Hershey, PA 17033-1240, USA, www.igi-global.com. This series is composed of titles available for purchase individually; each title is edited to be contextually exclusive from any other title within the series. For pricing and ordering information please visit http://www.igi-global.com/book-series/advances-electronic-commerce/37141. Postmaster: Send all address changes to above address. Copyright © 2022 IGI Global. All rights, including translation in other languages reserved by the publisher. No part of this series may be reproduced or used in any form or by any means – graphics, electronic, or mechanical, including photocopying, recording, taping, or information and retrieval systems – without written permission from the publisher, except for non commercial, educational use, including classroom teaching purposes. The views expressed in this series are those of the authors, but not necessarily of IGI Global.

Titles in this Series

For a list of additional titles in this series, please visit: http://www.igi-global.com/book-series/advances-electronic-commerce/37141

Handbook of Research on Social Impacts of E-Payment and Blockchain Technology
P.C. Lai (University Malaya, Kuala Lumpur, Malaysia)
Business Science Reference • © 2022 • 561pp • H/C (ISBN: 9781799890355) • US $435.00

Moving Businesses Online and Embracing E-Commerce Impact and Opportunities Caused by COVID-19
Tereza Semerádová (Technical University of Liberec, Czech Republic) and Petr Weinlich (Technical University of Liberec, Czech Republic)
Business Science Reference • © 2022 • 275pp • H/C (ISBN: 9781799882947) • US $240.00

Handbook of Research on the Platform Economy and the Evolution of E-Commerce
Myriam Ertz (LaboNFC, University of Quebec at Chicoutimi, Canada)
Business Science Reference • © 2022 • 554pp • H/C (ISBN: 9781799875451) • US $325.00

Cross-Border E-Commerce Marketing and Management
Md. Rakibul Hoque (University of Dhaka, Bangladesh & Emporia State University, USA) and R. Edward Bashaw (Emporia State University, USA)
Business Science Reference • © 2021 • 349pp • H/C (ISBN: 9781799858232) • US $215.00

Handbook of Research on Innovation and Development of E-Commerce and E-Business in ASEAN
Mohammad Nabil Almunawar (Universiti Brunei Darussalam, Brunei) Muhammad Anshari Ali (Universiti Brunei Darussalam, Brunei) and Syamimi Ariff Lim (Universiti Brunei Darussalam, Brunei)
Business Science Reference • © 2021 • 738pp • H/C (ISBN: 9781799849841) • US $405.00

Impact of Mobile Services on Business Development and E-Commerce
Francisco Liébana (University of Granada, Spain) Zoran Kalinić (University of Kragujevac, Serbia) Iviane Ramos de Luna (Open University of Catalonia, Spain) and Inma Rodríguez-Ardura (Open University of Catalonia, Spain)
Business Science Reference • © 2020 • 280pp • H/C (ISBN: 9781799800507) • US $230.00

Internet Taxation and E-Retailing Law in the Global Context
Sana Moid (Amity University, India) and Shailja Dixit (Amity University, India)
Business Science Reference • © 2018 • 245pp • H/C (ISBN: 9781522537878) • US $195.00

User Innovation and the Entrepreneurship Phenomenon in the Digital Economy

IGI Global
PUBLISHER of TIMELY KNOWLEDGE

701 East Chocolate Avenue, Hershey, PA 17033, USA
Tel: 717-533-8845 x100 • Fax: 717-533-8661
E-Mail: cust@igi-global.com • www.igi-global.com

Table of Contents

Detailed Table of Contents

Technological advancement is evident especially after the internet has come into the market; it has revolutionized the way we do business. Electronic commerce has been largely benefitted by the technology. The chapter commenced with the introduction to commerce, a brief comparison between the business and commerce. Later the chapter will shed light on electronic commerce, its types, advantages, and drawbacks of e-commerce, followed by a few revenue-generation models. In this chapter, the authors will discuss the technological impact on e-commerce in supply chain management, value chain, customer relationship management, and many such propositions. The authors will also explore machine learning and the role of artificial intelligence in e-commerce. Later a few use cases/some live cases will be discussed at length for better clarity.

This chapter aims to study the development of futuristic e-commerce systems in rural China. This chapter will explore the current situation of the whole industrial chain in rural small and medium enterprises and their developing trends in B2C model. Why are rural agricultural small and medium-sized enterprises (SMEs) developing rapidly in China? What is the digital context for the development of rural SMEs in the agricultural sector? What digital transformations have rural SMEs experienced in terms of business models, especially in less developed areas, such as Tier 4 and Tier 5 areas, compared with international ones? Compared with the previous rural e-commerce, what are the advantages of optimizing the new system? This chapter will use CiteSpace to perform statistical and correlation analysis on Chinese agricultural e-commerce system, including the Web of Science (WOS) database and CSSCI database. Cases from China will be used for comparison. This chapter will provide suggestions for the development of futuristic e-commerce system in emerging economies.

Today's e-commerce is completely dependent on artificial intelligence. Whatever technology was used in the ancient days, there was a huge gap between a customer and a seller. From a seller's point of view, he wanted to sell the maximum product and a customer had to purchase the product whose price was lowest in the market but best in quality. In this situation, we need a system that can automatically recommend a suitable product to the customer so that we can buy his goods easily and at a low price. For this, artificial intelligence is the best method. Artificial intelligence recommendation system is a combination of machine learning algorithms that are used by developers to help users predict their choices and get related suggestions.Through this chapter, the authors show the different processes and uses of artificial intelligence that help the user for an accurate recommendation of a product such as search queries, past purchases, items placed in the shopping cart, viewing history, and the location of the customer or buyer.

Autonomous robots that operate objects within a limited workspace have wide applications in the e-commerce industry, which helps in overcoming the lack of flexibility and improves operation efficiency by minimizing material delivery and handling time. In this work, a model has been developed for an intelligent picking warehouse robot that independently conducts pick and place operations on payloads of up to 2.2 kgs and have a maximum size in any dimension up to 20 cm. It consists of robotic system and various sub-systems, including mechanical design and analysis, perception pipeline, sensor fusion, control architecture, trajectory planning, and grasp synthesis. Performance evaluation of the model has been done using software simulation for picking systems in various tasks in warehouse settings. It autonomously

Opinion mining and sentiment analysis help in extracting valuable information from the huge user data generated in the form of opinions and reviews from the customers and comments. Such a huge increase in data available on the electronic or social media has also increased interest in this field. Sentiment analysis helps in extraction of opinions of others (writer or speaker) from a given source (text) using different methods and techniques like NLP, text mining, and linguistic computation and classifying them into positive, negative, and neutral opinions. Decision making for both consumers as well as the seller becomes much easier with such type of classification. This chapter consists of survey report on different elements of sentiment analysis, its applications, and challenges involved. The chapter studies and compares some of the techniques used to evaluate the item's reputation using sentiment analysis. A number of tools and features for sentiment analysis are also included in this chapter that can later help to perform better sentiment analysis of data.

To abate the rapid spread of corona virus, most countries restricted social life. The primary purpose of this study is to look into the elements that influence online consumer sentiments regarding shopping during a pandemic. This research focuses on the study of different factors' significance and priority using strength, weakness, opportunity, threat (SWOT) analysis; interpretive structural modelling (ISM); and analytical hierarchy process (AHP) after extracting the different crucial factors using critical review of previous literature and expert opinions. The ISM methodology has helped to present a structural relationship among the key factors and helped to derive the short-term goals and long-term goals. Finally, the AHP model has ranked the existing three popular websites of India comparing their effectiveness using the factors such as product quality, customer satisfaction, low perceived risk, and social media. This chapter will be a strong vaccine for the Indian online shopping consumer sentiments during and post-pandemic scenario.

COVID-19 was first reported in December 2019 and has spread since then. Different vaccines are under development and digital technologies are used for contact tracing, vaccine monitoring, screening of infection, etc. But the healthcare providers are dealing with many challenges, such as cases of fake documents (i.e., test reports and vaccine certificates). Blockchain can help mitigate the challenges with its features, such as data transparency, accuracy, and decentralization. Even in general day purpose, the verification of the documents is required for booking of airline ticket, hotel room, etc. E-commerce deals with online selling and buying of products, which together with blockchain can fulfill the requirement. This chapter proposes a framework for verification of COVID-19 test reports and vaccine certificates with the help of blockchain technology and e-commerce. The aim of the proposed framework is to validate the details online so that the proper treatment and medication can be provided to the patient. IPFS is used to store the data.

The rapid growth in online purchases and product return pose challenges to the supply chain. The demography influences purchases. After an extensive literature review, the authors examine if the product return in online purchases depends on demographic factors and product categories. This online survey-based research analyzed the 619 responses and identifies that age, gender, profession, search intensity have a significant relationship with the return frequency. After using statistical analysis, findings suggest that the family income, payment method, purchase frequency, monthly spending do not have a significant influence on return frequency. Similarly, analysis indicated age, gender, profession, and search intensity to be significant. Textile and household goods showed a significant relationship with return frequency from the different categories. This research emphasizes the role of demography factors; however, online purchase and return is a complex process involving the role of product, retailer, website, and delivery.

With the advancement of the internet, the e-commerce sector has seen a tremendous opportunity in the field for e-healthcare, which has resulted in decrement of labor cost, faster insurance claims, and much more. Machine learning has paved various regimes, which the future of medical treatment and teaching could be based upon. Thereafter, with the advent of these methods, the timeline of extracting and segregating patients started to become a more straightforward process. The sorting process could be primarily based on symptoms, medical reports, and medical test results. Had this been based on human

E-commerce packaging has unique needs, and new robot technology is meeting those needs. These needs include handling mixed pallet loads, workforce problems, and a range of secondary packaging types. This chapter presents the trajectory tracking control of an industrial SCARA robot in a realistic simulated environment with the help of fractional order PID (FOPID) and PID controller. FOPID controller has two extra degrees of freedom, thereby providing added flexibility to the design over the PID scheme. The optimum parameters of these controllers are obtained using the genetic algorithm (GA) by minimizing a weighted sum of absolute errors as an objective. Further, a comparative study of the controllers is performed for set-point tracking and model parameter uncertainty based on settling time, rise time, overshoot, and integral absolute error (IAE). The results have proved that FOPID outperforms its integer-order counterpart under a variety of operating conditions.

Customers are riding a wave of social media growth, transforming the customer's journey to purchase and aspire to go social. Social networking is the driving factor behind the evolution of retail and customer behavior. Today's retailers' widespread usage of social media as a marketing strategy has never been seen before. The omnichannel market has been addressed in Marketing 4.0 as a brand commitment approach where retailers incorporate omnichannel retail through social networks in the consumer purchasing route (5 A's: be aware, appeal, ask, act, and advocate). Omnichannel retailing convergence is a transition rather than a change that has a pronounced effect on consumers and retailers. The omnichannel market is a process of combining various platforms to provide a smooth and reliable consumer experience. This chapter discusses how technology serves as propulsion and gives a significant impetus to social networks for omni-retailing in the coming years in India. It also discusses how network integration differs depending on geography and product segment.

Preface

INTRODUCTION

Massive use of Internet in the present society helps the mankind not only accessing the huge information available but also provides the solutions to acquire his/her day-to-day needs at a finger click. It helps the society in many ways which includes to broadcast the ideas, thoughts, online games, listen to music, video streaming, learning, selling and purchasing goods mainly through e-marketing. In the present situation, maximum number of internet users belong to social networking and e-commerce websites. E-commerce helps the people in shopping their required items by accessing unlimited product categories with time saving, convenience. The consumers can easily search, compare and select for a particular item from different e-commerce vendors. Due to increase in the number of users of e-commerce in recent days, the online shopping become a new and challenging market for e-commerce vendors. Apart from cheap and quality products, security, availability of products, reliability and performance of e-commerce website, interface design, etc. are the challenges.

Worldwide on daily basis millions of e-commerce transactions are taking place, which can be used to solve the challenges faced by e-commerce companies. In this scenario, new futuristic techniques such as artificial intelligence, machine learning, etc are becoming very popular now a day to solve such type of problems. Such advanced techniques can be effective in product search, security, testing, recommendation, etc. Advanced techniques such as Deep Learning, Data Analytics and Big Data can be used to develop more efficient solutions. Researchers, academicians, faculties, scientists and computer professional will find this book beneficial for their research work and set new ideas in the field of e-commerce. This book will cater research work in many fields related to e-commerce and it will provide an in depth knowledge of the fields covered.

ORGANIZATION OF THE BOOK

To achieve the objectives, this book contains 15 chapters contributed by promising authors that are organized as shown below.

Chapter 1 entitled "Study of E-Commerce and Impact of Machine Learning in E-Commerce" has presented a comprehensive study of the introduction to commerce and has presented a detailed comparative analysis between business and commerce. The chapter has also pointed out the various advantages, disadvantages, and various challenges in the application areas of e-commerce. Finally, the chapter has shown the probable role of modern-day technology such as AI in the betterment of e-commerce services.

Chapter 2 entitled "The Digital Transformation of Rural Agricultural Business Management: A Case Study of China" has presented a detailed study of the revolutionary e-commerce systems in rural China. The study is based on the present situation of industrial supply and production chains, ranging from small-scale to medium-sized enterprises. The study covers the future trends in the B2C model of the small-to-medium industries. The chapter has also suggested a future e-commerce system for next-generation emerging economies.

Chapter 3 entitled "Artificial Intelligence-Based Approaches for Product Recommendation in E-Commerce" has shown the importance of AI in the modern-day e-commerce system. The chapter has highlighted the key features and the revolutionary breakthrough of the application of different AI mechanisms in product recommendations for various e-commerce services.

Chapter 4 entitled "A Fuzzy-Based Intelligent Picking and Placing Warehouse Robot" has proposed an intelligent picking warehouse robot model for automation. The proposed model consists of an intelligent robotics system along with various other design and technological aspects for making it operational. It can autonomously identify the pick-up and drop locations for objects in its workspace using the combination of an onboard camera and other complementing sensors.

Chapter 5 entitled "Interpretive Structural Modelling of Critical Factors Influencing E-Commerce in India" has identified and shown a study on the nine most influential factors that may affect the e-commerce system to a greater extent. These factors are customer satisfaction, user interface, gender-related approach to the e-commerce platform, company's association with customers, data breach, digital literacy, localization of internet content, digital infrastructure, and government policy.

Chapter 6 entitled "A Collaborative Cloud Model of Auto-Scaling With Load Balancing for Effective E-Commerce" focuses on the load balancing problem in the cloud computing environment and hence, proposes a mechanism of collaborating auto-scaling and load balancing to achieve an equal distribution of load across the servers.

Chapter 7 entitled "Analytical Review on Techniques and Challenges in Sentiment Analysis" has presented a systematic survey on various sentiment analysis elements. The idea of the chapter is to understand and analyse the customer's opinions and improve them, which may be used for improving e-commerce and related sub-systems. The study also highlighted various tools and features for sentiment analysis that may be used for better sentiment analysis of data.

In Chapter 8 entitled "Consumer Sentiments About Online Shopping in the Indian Scenario During COVID-19," a study of various factors is presented that influence online consumer sentiments regarding shopping during a pandemic. This chapter focuses on the study of different factors' significance and priority using strength, weakness, opportunity, threat (SWOT) analysis, Interpretive Structural Modelling (ISM), and Analytical Hierarchy Process (AHP).

Chapter 9 describes "COVID-19 Test Report and Vaccine Certificate Verification Through Blockchain and E-Commerce". It emphasis that during the Covid-19, various digital technologies are used for contact tracing, vaccine monitoring, screening of infection, etc. This chapter proposes a framework for verification of Covid-19 test reports and vaccine certificates with the help of blockchain technology and e-commerce. The main aim of the proposed framework is to validate the online details of a person so that proper treatment and medication can be provided.

In Chapter 10, "Commerce Scenario in India," presents the challenges faced by the supply chain management due to the rapid growth in online purchases and product return. The author has examined if the product return in online purchases depends on demographic factors and product categories. After using statistical analysis, findings suggest that the family income, payment method, purchase frequency, monthly spending do not have a significant influence on return frequency.

Chapter 11 entitled "E-Healthcare System for Disease Detection Based on Medical Image Classification Using CNN" showcases the advantages of the internet in the field of e-commerce sector which also has seen a tremendous opportunity in the field for e-healthcare. In this chapter, the Convolution Neural Network (CNN) algorithm is applied on X-ray datasets to determine Brain Tumor and Corona-virus in patients. The author has provided a short snapshot of what the future could be for the medical industry with the incorporation of deep learning to access and cure various diseases.

Chapter 12 entitled "Consumer-Centric E-Commerce Systems" focuses on meeting the challenges such as security, reliability and performance of e-commerce. Bright opportunities for transformation in business models, aggregator, user interface, and vendor/customer recommendations are investigated utilizing deep learning technologies. The solutions provided and strategies explained in this chapter will be surely help e-commerce at least for the next ten years to have flawless and swift progress.

In Chapter 13, "Framework for Blockchain-Based Smart Healthcare System," a model has been proposed for healthcare system is Health 4.0 which is an Artificial Intelligence (AI) based intelligent devices enabled through the Internet of Medical Things (IoMT). The data collected from the patients are sensitive as it is crucial for diagnosis and to make critical decisions. This chapter present a framework for block chain-based smart health care system, in order to improve the security of the system.

Chapter 14, "Fractional Order PID Controller for Tracking Control of Scara Robot," has been considered for the need of new types of packaging robots for e-commerce.This chapter presents the trajectory tracking control of an industrial SCARA robot in a realistic simulated environment with the help of fractional order PID (FOPID) and PID controller.

Chapter 15 is entitled "Delineate Omnichannel Retailer and Consumer Engagement on Social Networks". It has been presented the importance of social media for e-commerce. This chapter discusses how technology serves as propulsion and gives a significant impetus to social networks for Omni-retailing in the coming years in India.

This book will cater the need of advance and futuristic techniques for handling the challenges in e-commerce business. The book presents the study of the importance of e-commerce in the day-to-day life of a common person as well as the contribution it makes to the world economy. This book has presented solutions to problems like security, usability, marketing, inventory management, etc. It also provides different upcoming fields where e-commerce can be extended such as e-healthcare.

Saurabh Bilgaiyan
Kalinga Institute of Industrial Technology (Deemed), Bhubaneswar, India

Jagannath Singh
Kalinga Institute of Industrial Technology (Deemed), Bhubaneswar, India

Himansu Das
Kalinga Institute of Industrial Technology (Deemed), Bhubaneswar, India

Acknowledgment

We would like to thank everyone who participated in this project and made this book into a reality. In particular, we would like to acknowledge the hard work of authors and their cooperation during the revisions of their chapters.

We would also like to acknowledge the valuable comments of the reviewers which have enabled us to select these chapters out of the so many chapters we received and also improve the quality of the chapters.

Lastly, we appreciate the IGI Global team for their continuous support throughout the entire process of publication. Our gratitude is extended to the readers, who gave us their trust, and we hope this work guides and inspires them.

Saurabh Bilgaiyan
Kalinga Institute of Industrial Technology (Deemed), Bhubaneswar, India

Jagannath Singh
Kalinga Institute of Industrial Technology (Deemed), Bhubaneswar, India

Himansu Das
Kalinga Institute of Industrial Technology (Deemed), Bhubaneswar, India

Chapter 1
Study of E-Commerce and Impact of Machine Learning in E-Commerce

Mukta Sharma
Trinity Institute of Professional Studies, India

Vinita Sharma
Amity International Business School, Amity University, Noida, India

Ritika Kapoor
Trinity Institute of Professional Studies, India

ABSTRACT

Technological advancement is evident especially after the internet has come into the market; it has revolutionized the way we do business. Electronic commerce has been largely benefitted by the technology. The chapter commenced with the introduction to commerce, a brief comparison between the business and commerce. Later the chapter will shed light on electronic commerce, its types, advantages, and drawbacks of e-commerce, followed by a few revenue-generation models. In this chapter, the authors will discuss the technological impact on e-commerce in supply chain management, value chain, customer relationship management, and many such propositions. The authors will also explore machine learning and the role of artificial intelligence in e-commerce. Later a few use cases/some live cases will be discussed at length for better clarity.

1. BUSINESS

Business is a broad phrase that can be divided into two categories, as seen in the diagram below: industry/trade and commerce. A business is an economic activity in which commodities and services are manufactured and distributed. A business includes planning, advertising, selling, buying, marketing, accounting, manufacturing, and other operations. Business is a subset of commerce (Koshal, 2011)

DOI: 10.4018/978-1-6684-4969-1.ch001

Copyright © 2022, IGI Global. Copying or distributing in print or electronic forms without written permission of IGI Global is prohibited.

that focuses mostly on purchasing and selling. Business interactions involving the exchange of services and goods are referred to as "commerce." In a word, e-commerce is the way of selling and distributing goods and services online.

Figure 1. **Business vs. Commerce** *(Koshal, 2011)*

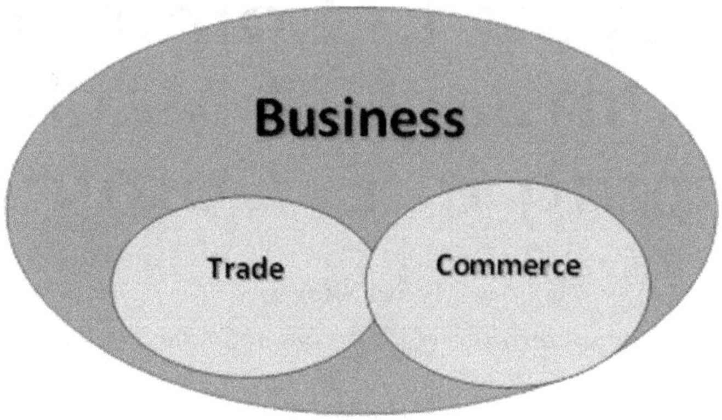

2. E-COMMERCE VS. E-BUSINESS

Electronic commerce refers to the process of conducting business through the internet using electronic technology, allowing consumers to electronically exchange products and services regardless of time or location (Imtiaz, M. A., November 2018; Zande, V.J., n.a).

E-Commerce is a modern business model that aims to meet the needs of businesses, merchants, and customers by quality enhancement of goods and services while lowering prices and speeding up service delivery. E-commerce has an extensive range of uses, comprising online ticketing, electronic banking, online shopping, social networking, and more.

E-business refers to a company's online presence and stands for electronic business. E-business comprises both e-commerce and other business activities, and it is not limited to commercial transactions; it also includes other services. The use of information technology and communication to conduct business, trade, and commerce is known as e-business. E-business encompasses more than just the purchase and selling of items; it also involves activities such as providing customer support, connecting with staff, and allowing clients or business partners to contact the company with any issues, difficulties with services, quality, or any other issue.

3. FEATURES OF E-COMMERCE

- **Debit and credit card payments:** E-commerce allows users to pay in a variety of ways other than cash. Some examples include debit cards, credit cards, smart cards, electronic funds transfer with a bank's website, and various digital payment methods (Imtiaz, M. A., November 2018; Multidev technologies, 2015; Zobrist, T., 2019).

Table 1. Traditional/ Conventional Commerce vs. E-Commerce (Thakur, M., n.a).

Traditional Commerce	E-Commerce
In conventional trade, established practices are difficult to create and sustain.	In e-commerce, a consistent strategy may be readily established and maintained.
Individual abilities play a role in corporate communication.	There is no human intervention in e-commerce.
Conventional business relies significantly on personal connection; there is a lack of a uniform platform.	E-commerce websites give users a platform where users can find information in one spot.
Synchronous communication/transactions are carried out. Each communication or transaction necessitates manual intervention.	Asynchronous communication or transactions are possible. The entire procedure is fully automated.
There is no standardized mechanism for sharing information because it is mainly reliant on personal communication.	E-commerce support corporate and commercial activity on a global platform.
There is a great deal of reliance on the conveyance of information from one person to the next.	Electronic communication channels make information sharing simple, reducing the reliance on face-face communication.

- **24*7:** E-commerce allows the users to access 24*7 and they can order anytime, anywhere. Services are provided through e-commerce, which may be accessed at any time and from anywhere 24*7.
- **Advertising/Marketing:** E-commerce expands the company's product and service marketing choices. It makes product/service marketing administration easier.
- **Increased Sales:** Customers can order things as per their convenience at any time, sitting at any location, without the requirement for any human intervention. Due to this there has been a significant increase in sales.
- **Support:** To serve customers in a better manner, pre-sales and post-sales support is provided by the e-commerce.
- **Inventory Management:** E-commerce automates inventory management. When reports are required, they have generated right away. Product inventory management becomes a lot easier and more efficient.
- E-commerce allows customers and partners to connect more quickly, efficiently, and reliably.

4. TRADITIONAL/ CONVENTIONAL WAY OF COMMERCE VS. ELECTRONIC COMMERCE

5. HISTORY OF E-COMMERCE

Ecommerce has a long history that dates back to the telephone's creation. Companies began exchanging commercial paperwork through Electronic Data Interchange in the 1960s, and e-commerce was born (EDI). In a nutshell, Electronic Data Interchange (EDI) was important in the development of e-commerce in the 1960s and 1980s (Maday, J., n.a).

- The American National Standards Institute produced ASC X12 in 1979 as a global standard for organizations to send documents via electronic networks.

Figure 2. Advantages of E-Commerce

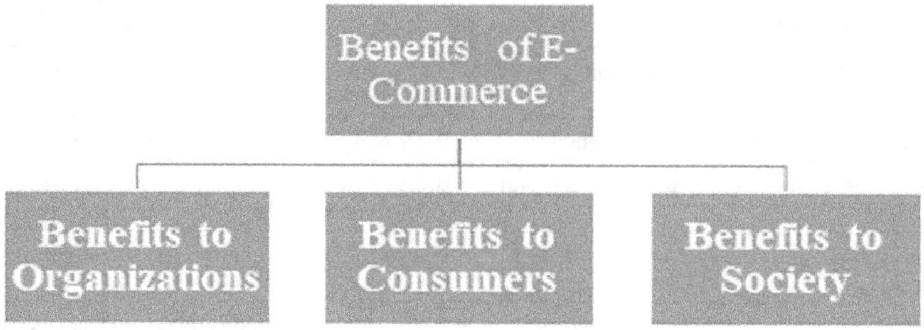

- In 1979, Michael Aldrich invented online shopping, which has since become a significant feature and an integral part of electronic commerce.
- In the 1990s, e-commerce saw the introduction of data collecting and Enterprise Resource Planning (ERP) technologies. The World Wide Web was invented about this time, providing the world with a daily communication method. Despite the Internet's popularity, security safeguards were not established until five years later. Since the early 2000s, people have utilized ecommerce to sell and buy goods and services.

6. BENEFITS OF E-COMMERCE

The benefits of e-commerce are divided into three general groups (Zande, V.J., n.a).

Benefits to Organizations

- Organizations can use e-commerce to grow their business in national and international markets with small investment. A company may easily locate extra clients, the greatest suppliers and business partners all around the world.
- E-commerce reduces the cost of handling paper based information in creating, processing, distributing and retrieving by digitizing it.
- Organizations gain from e-commerce because it reduces the cost of handling paper based information in creating, processing, distributing and retrieving by digitizing it.
- E-commerce aids in the enhancement of a company's brand image.
- E-commerce enables companies to provide better customer service.
- E-commerce facilitates the simplification and acceleration of company processes.
- E-commerce improves organizational productivity. It provides for supply control on a "pull" basis. A business process in "pull" supply management initiates only after the customer places an order, and just-in-time manufacturing is used.

Benefits to Society

- E-commerce reduces paperwork and provides customer service 24*7. Customers can obtain information anytime regarding the product or services and order can be placed from anywhere at any time.
- An e-commerce site will help the customer receives items promptly.
- An e-commerce program provides consumers with more options by allowing them to contrast and choose the best options.
- A consumer can share reviews for product and see what other people are buying before making a final purchase.
- In the world of e-commerce, virtual auctions are a viable option.
- It facilitates access to information. Consumers can see important information at a glance without having to wait days.
- E-commerce improves competition between businesses, which leads to significant discounts for customers.

Benefits to Consumers

- Customers don't have to drive to buy a product, which saves their time and leads to traffic control on the roads and less pollution in the air.
- Customers don't have to drive to buy a product, which helps save time, reduce road traffic congestion and air pollution.
- E-commerce provides access to services and products that can't reach rural populations.
- E-commerce allows governments to make public services such as health, education and social services cheaper and more efficient.

General Benefits

- Get Around Geographical Barriers
- Increase your search engine visibility to gain new customers
- Lower your costs
- Allows user to compare prices
- Enable Offers, Discounts, Coupons, and Group Buying
- Provide large amount of Information
- Create Targeted Communication
- Available 24*7
- Create Markets for Niche Products

7. SHORTCOMINGS OF E-COMMERCE

The disadvantages of e-commerce can be broadly categorized as follows:

Figure 3. Shortcomings of E-Commerce

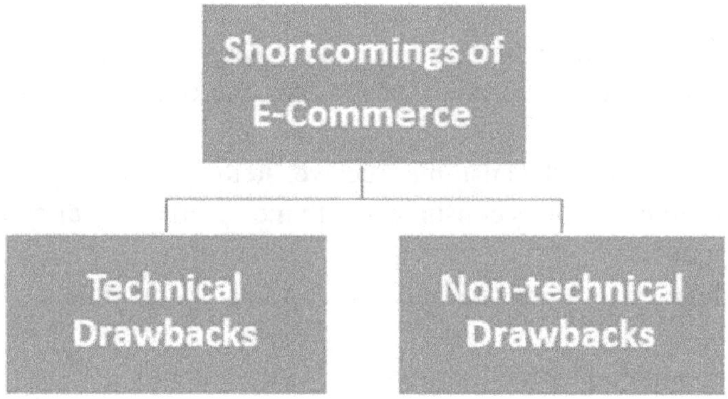

Technical Drawbacks

- There is a lack of system security, stability, or standards as a result of inadequate e-commerce implementation (Tutorials Point, n.a).
- The software industry is always changing and progressing.
- In many situations, network bandwidth is an issue.
- Separating your e-commerce environment from your network server requires a dedicated web server and application.
- Integrating an e-commerce website or software with an existing application or database can be difficult.

Non-Technical Drawbacks

- Initial investment: Building an e-commerce platform from scratch can be costly. There may be delays in deploying an e-commerce application due to errors and a lack of expertise.
- User skepticism: Because the site is run by an unknown vendor, users may be cautious to trust it. Because of this skepticism, convincing traditional clients to switch from physical to online stores is difficult.
- Security: Managing the security and privacy of Internet transactions is difficult.
- Buying products virtually without being able to touch or feel them is a disadvantage.
- Internet connectivity is costly and inconvenient for many potential customers, particularly those who live in rural locations.

General Drawbacks

- The startup costs for an e-commerce platform are fairly substantial. Setting up the equipment and software, as well as personnel training and regular maintenance and upkeep, are all important costs.

Figure 4. B2B

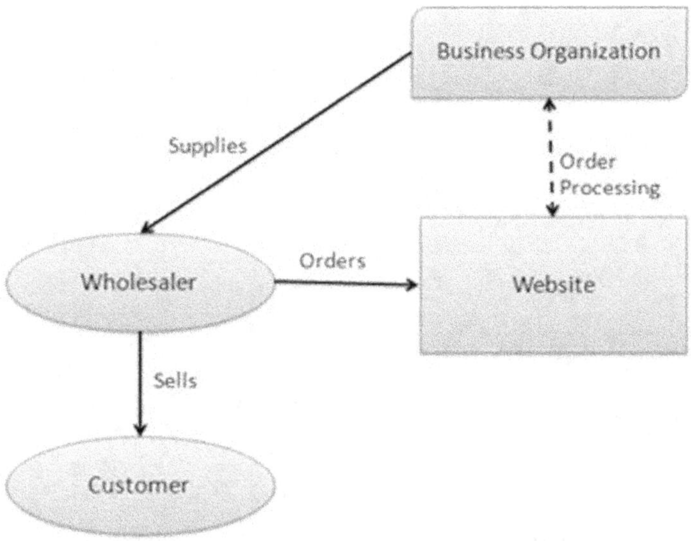

- While it may appear to be a sure thing, the e-commerce industry is on a huge risk of failure. As numerous enterprises tried to cash in on the dot com boom in the 1990s, they all failed terribly. There's still a good risk of failure today.
- E-commerce lacks human touch. As a result, it lacks the comfort of a human interaction, which many businesses and goods require. Many services and products, such as interior design or jewelry, may suffer from a lack of human interaction.

8. TYPES OF E-COMMERCE

E-commerce can generally be categorized into the following categories (Zande, V.J., n.a).

- **B2B (Business to Business)** –The B2B website sells its products to intermediaries, who sell them to their end customers.

For example, a wholesaler places an order on the company's website and sells the finished product to the end customer. The end customer will access one of the company's retail stores after receiving the shipment.

The following are examples of B2B. PeopleSoft, Oracle, Broadvision, SAP, Heatheon / Webmd, Commerce One, Technologies, Ariba, Aspect Development, Baan, BEA Systems and Internet Capital Group are the leading providers of e-commerce and B2B. solution.

- **Business to Consumer (B2C) -** A website that follows the B2C business model sells its items to customers directly. The products shown on the website are visible to customers. The customer can select a product and place an order for it.

Figure 5. B2C

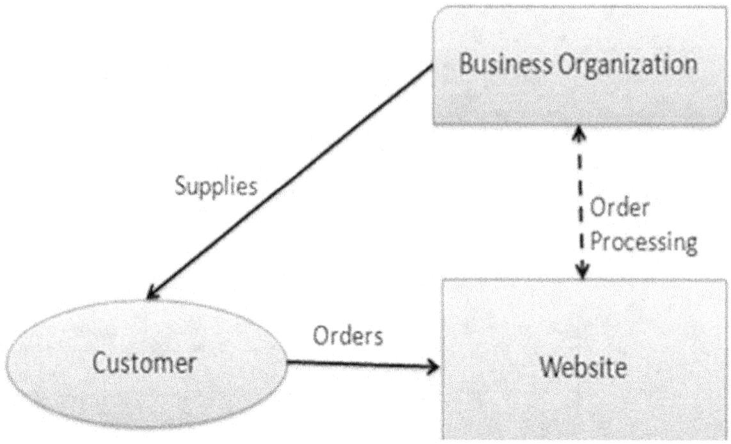

The website then sends an email message to the company, which ships the product to the customer.

Amazon.com, Dell, Wal-Mart, and other traditional corporations have established extensive websites and virtual storefronts to compete in the virtual economy. Adidas, Nike, Bata, Hush Puppies, Liberty, Allen Solley, Louis Phillips, Levis, Pepe Jeans, Wrangler, Tommy Hilfiger, Biba, Fab India, Global Desi, Rollex, Casio, Fossil, Titan, Lakme, Chamboor, NYX Professional Makeup, MAC, L'Oréal Paris, Michael Kors, Gucci, Tommy Hilfiger, Biba, Fab India, Global Desi, Jackie, Prada, Marc Jacobs, Lavie, and Caprese are just a few of the names that come to mind.

- **Consumer - to - Consumer (C2C)-** Customers can sell their assets, such as residential properties, cars, motorcycles, and other vehicles, or rent a room, by publishing their information on a website that follows the C2C business model.

Figure 6. C2C

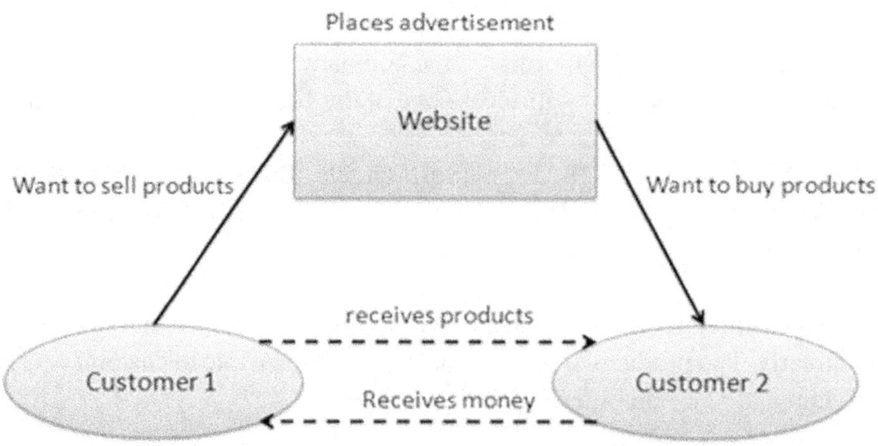

Website services may or may not be charged to the customer. After seeing an ad on your website, another buyer may choose to purchase the original customer's product.

A classified section of a newspaper or an auction is an example of C2C transactions. A customer sells goods or services to another customer in both circumstances. OLX, eBay, and other similar sites

- **Consumer - to - Business (C2B)** - C2B redefines the term by dealing with customers who have valuable items or services that can be consumed by businesses.

Instead of consumers investing money in anything, the organization invests in this model. It might be purchasing a tangible item. Shutter stock relies on user photographs, and Fiverr offers a variety of user-provided services such as copywriting and sound effects for businesses that need a little extra help in a specific area.

In a nutshell, C2B gives businesses something they need from customers, such as important feedback on a new product or an evaluation of their services.

§ Books, music CDs, gadgets, software, toys, video games, prescription medications, and electrical devices are all available on **Amazon.com.**

§ For credit card transactions, **American Express** successfully employs e-commerce.

§ **Apple Computer** is an online retailer of PCs and laptops.

§ **Auto-by-Tel** is a company that sells autos through the internet.

§ **Cisco Systems** is a company that sells data communication components over the internet.

§ **Dell Computer** and Gateway sell PCs and laptops via their websites, allowing users to configure and purchase their systems online.

§ **Online pharmacies** such as Drugstore.com and CVS.com stock and sell new drugs, vitamins and other health and beauty items.

§ **Epicurious** sells unusual cuisine over the Web.

§ **Peapod** is an online grocery store.

§ **Orders are placed** electronically by Proctor & Gamble and IBM.

Consumer to Government (C2G)-. Electronic transactions between individuals and the government are covered under the Consumer-to-Government e-commerce business model. Consumers can use this relationship to get information, pay invoices, and establish direct communication between the two governments.

Paying electronic taxes, bills, fines, health-care payments, and tuition to a government university are all examples of regular C2G transactions. This allows customers to transact business with major corporations in real-time, which was previously time-consuming and ineffective. Previously, this type of company was difficult and time-consuming, but since transactions are now handled through the internet, operations have dramatically improved. Both customers and the government have access to more resources as a result of this.

- **Business to Government (B2G)** - Business-to-Government transactions take place between businesses, government departments, and government agencies. The internet is used to conduct transactions between businesses and government agencies in this e-commerce business model.

B2G e-commerce, often known as business-to-government e-commerce, refers to transactions between enterprises and the government. This is related to government procurement, licensing, and the use of the Internet for other purposes. This sort of e-commerce ensures that the government takes the lead in building e-commerce, and it is believed that the government has the most compelling need to enhance its procurement system. The purchase process is more transparent with web-based purchasing policies. However, while government e-procurement systems continue to exist, B2G e-commerce remains a small part of total e-commerce. Business-to-Government transactions take place between businesses, government departments, and government agencies. The internet is used to conduct transactions between businesses and government agencies in this e-commerce business model.

Government to Business (G2B): The G2B approach significantly reduces paperwork and makes it easier for companies to handle legal processes such as payments and document updates. A government website where businesses can pay taxes is a typical example of G2B.

Government to Citizen (G2C): Find startup finance on the G2C marketplace, and get contracts on the G2C e-commerce platform.

§ **Education -** providing information, distance learning, etc.
§ **Social Security -** disseminating information, issuing payments, and so on are examples of applications.
§ **Taxes -** filing tax returns, making payments, and so on.
§ **Health -** appointments, disease information, and payment of health services, and so on.

Both public administration models (B2A and C2A) are intimately linked to the idea of government services providing citizens with effectiveness and ease of use, with the aid of information and communication technologies.

9. APPLICATIONS OF E-COMMERCE

E-commerce applications are utilized in a variety of industries, including retail, wholesale and manufacturing. The following are the some of the common E-commerce applications (Thakur, M., n.a; Tutorials Point, n.a).

- ***Online marketing and purchase***- Web and E-commerce allow for the collecting of data on consumer behavior, preferences, needs, and purchase patterns. This is useful for marketing tasks such as product pricing, negotiation, enhancements, and customer interactions.

- ***Retail and wholesale***- There are numerous retail and wholesale applications for e-commerce. Internet-based product sales from stores to consumers, including electronic catalogs and shopping carts, are known as e-tailing. Virtual mall is a website where you can buy and sell various products and services. Connect buyers and sellers in virtual space via a web browser.
- ***Finance***- Financial enterprises make extensive use of E-commerce. Customers can use online banking for routine bank transactions. E.g., to check their account balances, transfer the amount to another account, and settle their utility bills. Another E-commerce use is online stock trading. A variety of websites provide stock market news, share prices, company profiles, and ratings.

Figure 7. Online Marketing

- ***Manufacturing***- E-commerce is also used to manufacture supply chain activities. Some companies combine buying and selling goods with the provision of warehouse management information in the back office to create electronic exchanges. As a result, the flow of raw materials and finished items among company leaders is improved.
- ***Online Auction***- On the internet, electronic auctions with bidding are available. In a bidding auction, buyers place bids on various items. Customers can, for example, inquire about the cost of an airline ticket for a given route and time.
- ***E-Banking***- E-Banking is an electronic payment system that allows bank customers to conduct financial transactions via the bank's website. Internet banking, e-banking, and virtual banking are all terms used to describe online banking.
- O***nline publishing***- Online publishing includes the digital publication of e-books, digital magazines, the creation of web pages, and the maintenance of websites.
- ***The Internet Booking Engine*** (IBE) supports online booking (tickets, hotels, etc.) for tickets, hotels reservations and so on which is very helpful to the travel and tourism industry. It allows consumers to compare costs and book flights, hotels, holiday packages, and insurance online. These kinds of applications have a lot of potential in the aviation business, which has witnessed a lot of growth.

10. E-TECHNOLOGICAL COMMERCE'S IMPACT

Technology has always been at the heart of E-commerce. For ordering, monitoring, payment, returns, and other purposes, technology has connected vendors and purchasers via mobile phones/websites. All activities, including value chain, supply chain, recruitment, marketing, advertising, obtaining customer evaluations, and offering improved Customer relationship management, are heavily reliant on technology (Acquire, 2022; Bhagat, V., 2021; Big Commerce, n.a; IndustryWired, 2019; Meiryani, Y. W. 2019; Multidev technologies, 2015; Tutorials Point, n.a).

- ***Ubiquitous* e-commerce:** It has been noted that consumers have connected practically all of the time thanks to their mobile phones, which are driving online purchases (Acquire, 2022).
- ***AI-powered personalization:*** Chatbots are computer programs that mimic human interactions. Communicate with customers in real time and respond to customer concerns across multiple platforms 24/7. Artificial intelligence is used by chatbots to analyze customer preferences and provide a personalized shopping experience (Acquire, 2022).

Visual search and discovery technologies are used by Artificia, an AI company based in India, to match particular photographs with a user's preferences in order to offer things they are more likely to prefer. By communicating with people through messages and detecting and finding products based on photos, Infinite Analytics provides AI-powered personalization solutions.

- ***Cognitive supply chain management gains momentum:*** The concept of cognitive supply chain management is gaining traction: For e-commerce businesses, on-time delivery is an important difference. It is imperative for these companies to play an important role in optimizing supply chain management processes and ensuring effective and rapid delivery technologies. Technological improvements also enable other important areas of the supply chain, such as:
  § Warehouse management (anti-hacking RFID chip),
  § Protection of brand by using invisible digital tag to fight counterfeit goods,
  § warehousing (robot technology for joint automated picking),
  § infrastructure (bridge using drone) Surveillance, and delivery are all areas that the drone can use. Help (using a drone for broadcasting).
- ***Redefining the Consumer Shopping Experience:*** Using product videos on E-Commerce sites can enhance sales, redefining the consumer shopping experience. This is because when people view a video regarding a product, they have more faith in it. When done well, product movies can both educate and motivate customers to buy. Gamification makes online shopping more fun by incentivizing customers to shop in a certain way in exchange for additional rewards. Three popular gamification tactics are promotional quizzes, spin-to-win opportunities, and VIP loyalty programs. Customers can speak about their questions and search on Google, Amazon Echo, or other similar technology using voice search, which is gaining in popularity. Successful voice search methods for e-commerce businesses include implementing a sound SEO strategy, developing brand affinity through informational skills and activities, such as product features and review videos, and focusing on giving a superior customer experience. Platforms that allow e-commerce companies to sell directly through their social media sites are driving sales, and social media is a major source of revenue. Consumers are sent to a product page where they may make a purchase by clicking on a link within a social post. PWAs (Progressive Web Apps) are websites that can be accessed straight from a browser and provide many of the same functionality as native apps. These apps aren't available in the app store. These websites are intended to provide useful information to consumers.
- ***Online shopping becomes more interactive through augmented reality and virtual reality:*** E-commerce companies are using augmented reality (AR) and virtual reality (VR) to overcome one of the biggest hurdles. Earlier customers were not able to try things before making a purchase. Now customers can use AR and VR to virtually experiment with things. Like Asian Paints allow the customer to select the design, color and pattern for the wall with existing furniture. Companies like Lens Kart is enhancing the feature of trying the spectacles and shades at home or office using

Augmented Reality (Smartinsights, 2020). The customers have the flexibility to customize their shoes, dresses by using AR & VR.

- ***Customization gives products a distinct personality:*** Consumers expect personalized items, and recent improvements in digital and manufacturing technologies have enabled businesses to offer personalization and customization online. Brands improve the user experience by enabling customers to partner in the product manufacturing process, increasing customer satisfaction and loyalty, and increasing revenue.
- ***Personalized product recommendations promote upselling and cross-selling:*** One can increase their purchase potential by adjusting product recommendations to suit the tastes of existing consumers. According to marketers, personalization is important to shoppers, with 92% of customers expecting a customized experience. After personalizing the buying experience of prospects, 97% of marketers' report having a positive impact on their brand. Companies need to ensure that data from customers' past purchases and local searches provides the right product to enhance their personalized experience.
- ***E-Commerce subscription services are gaining popularity:*** Subscriptions are becoming a more popular way to purchase products and services online. The e-commerce subscription business is expected to increase by 68 percent by 2025, hitting $478.2 billion in sales, according to the Subscription Economy Index, which shows that subscription services have grown by 403 percent in the last eight years. Refillment, personalization, and access are the three forms of e-commerce subscription services. For greatest success, companies should establish their subscription model in one of these three services.
- ***Seamless Payment Process:*** E-value commerce's promise revolves around convenience. Faster, more efficient, and secure payment solutions have been critical in driving the e-commerce market's explosive expansion in recent years. E-wallet usage gives clients with simplicity of use and greater security, in addition to increasing sales and conversion rates for suppliers. They don't have to enter credit card information on websites or give cashiers their credit card details. Prior to transactions, many e-Wallets offer or require dual authentication. In most situations, the E-commerce business uses a purely digital payment method. These days, e-wallets and gift cards are in high demand.

The concern of non-transparency and the safety of money were eliminated thanks to technical advancements. As a result, technology plays an unavoidable and smooth role in e-commerce.

11. IMPACT OF TECHNOLOGY OR TECHNOLOGICAL ADVANCEMENTS IN THE FIELD OF E-COMMERCE

The use of technology in almost all domains has shown great results. From the use of AI, which helps in mimicking the humans the objective is to make the machines intelligent. Like Sophia, the human robot created by Dr. Hanson, Sophia has got citizenship in the year 2016 (Netscribes., 2018) Sophia uses AI, visual processing, voice and facial recognition. The algorithm records all conversation for further refining its response in the future. Let us discuss a few more examples of AI like Siri, Alexa- Virtual Assistants, Intelligent Cars like Tesla, Google Waymo, Numerous AI Games like Google DeepMind, Alpha Go, etc. Machine learning a subset of Artificial Intelligence, which gives an ability to automatically learn and improve from experience. It works on observing and recognizing patterns and designing rules rather than programming. Deep Learning is a part of ML. ML depends on Statistical Analysis to identify trends in the form of mathematical or data patterns. The E-commerce Supply Chain Management is used to predict the demand accurately using Neural Network and other Machine learning algorithms. Also it will allow to automate the everyday tasks, which allows the employees to focus on more strategic & significant tasks. AI and ML can help in planning the resources more properly, also by optimizing the product flow, can satisfy customers' needs by predicting the demands accurately, ensuring quality and safety, transportation cost can be reduced and also price can be determined. Top use cases of Machine Learning in supply chain are Predictive analysis, Automatic Quality Checks/Inspection, reducing errors in forecasting, Real time, Streamlining planning of production, reducing cost and response time, managing the warehouse, Tracking and Fraud Prevention. There are numerous companies like Amazon, P&G, Rolls Royce, etc. are using ML in managing SCM. According to a research by Gartner, 50% companies will be using AI & ML by 2023. Let us dive into some of the benefits of using technologies before moving further.

- Making decisions is an essential component of any business. Technology is a terrific way to make the decision-making process more efficient. It is critical to keep track of consumer and market information; technology allows for error-free reporting. You can be confident in the accuracy of KPIs collected by the finance, marketing, and customer engagement departments. It is technology that captures critical data and enables a corporation in detecting and strategizing about its weak places.
- In a manufacturing unit robots use deep reinforcement learning to identify a device from one box and put in a container, this is reinforcement ML, which will see later in the chapter.
- Manufacturers can look back at previous failures and estimate when to service equipment to avoid breakdowns in the future.
- Manufacturers can look back at previous failures and estimate when to service equipment to avoid breakdowns in the future.
- Marketers can look at their best accounts and build ads that target people who are similar to them in the hopes of attracting new, high-quality consumers.
- Credit card fraud analysis could help the banks or financial companies from bad debts.
- Airlines can analyze vacant seats and map flights accordingly to generate more profit.
- E-commerce websites helps the users viewing the site that what product they should purchase using predictive analysis. Predictive analysis is also used to infer what others users have purchased, also it will inform which products people are buying with what.
- Marketers can analyze and build campaigns to target people with similar interest to attract them in the hopes of attracting new, high-quality consumers.
- Data analysis is deriving new findings from the archived data, as it mainly focuses on aggregating table to find solutions in business.
- Sentiment Analysis allows businesses to get the feedback from customers (negative or positive attitudes about their product or service) with accuracy, allowing them to plan and make a strategy to handle the situation or to further cash the situation.
- In data-intensive systems, machine learning is commonly used. Sensors attached to various assets, for example, collect data for smart energy management systems. Machine-learning algorithms help your company's decision-makers understand energy usage and maintenance requirements by contextualizing enormous amounts of data.

12. MACHINE LEARNING

Arthur Samuel, an American pioneer in the fields of computer games and artificial intelligence, coined the term machine learning in 1959 and stated that it "provides the ability to learn without being explicitly taught by computers." (Shaw, N., N.A)

Tom Mitchell in 1997 defined a "well-posed" definition, "A computer program is said to learn from experience, related to task (T) and performance measurement (P); if its performance on T, as measured by P, increases with experience E."

Computers or machines follow the commands or instructions given by humans. Humans have the capability of learning through experience. Machine learning`s job is to figure out what role computers play in understanding instructions. Without being explicitly coded, machine learning allows a machine to learn from data, improve performance via experience, and predict things.

Machine learning algorithms use sample data, also known as training data, to create a mathematical model that aids in generating predictions or judgments. To create predictive models, machine learning combines computer science and statistics. Machine learning employs algorithms that learn from previous experience.

13. HISTORY OF MACHINE LEARNING

The major support to all applications of Artificial Intelligence is provided by machine learning. Due to machine learning, the machines start learning new tasks on their own and they learn more by doing. The main objective of machine learning is to create the ability in machines to learn new tasks automatically without any assistance from humans (Marr. B., 2016). Machine learning evolved over the period of many years. Year-wise development of machine learning can be shown as below –

- § **1950:** British mathematician and computer scientist Alan Turing invented the Turing test machine in the 1950s. The Turing test was designed to determine if a machine has human intelligence. Computers need to convince humans that they are different in order to pass the exam. No other successful attempt was made, except for a computer program that simulated a 13-year-old Ukrainian boy who passed the Turing test.
- § **1952:** Arthur Samuels, a computer games and an artificial intelligence pioneer, created the first computer learning software in 1952. The application was just a checkers' game. The IBM computer would first research which moves result in victory before incorporating them into its program.
- § **1957,** this year, Frank Rosenblatt invented the first neural network, the perceptron for computers. It successfully engaged the thinking processes of the human brain. It was this process that gave birth to today`s neural networks.

The first version of the nearest neighbor algorithm was published in the year, **1967**. It allows computers to recognize basic patterns. This way was used to propose the travel route for the salesman. Start anywhere and use the shortest route through all the cities salesman needs to visit. The KNN method, also known as the nearest neighbor algorithm, is used to classify data points according to how they are classified.

§ **1981:** "Explanation-based learning" was innovated by Gerald Dejong in 1981. The analysis is done with the help of training data through a general protocol that can be followed by rejecting data that does not appear to be significant.

§ **1985**: Terry Sejnowski developed the Net Talk tool, which allows users to learn to recite words in the same way as a baby does during the language acquisition process. The artificial neural network's purpose was to construct a simplified model that showed how difficult it is to learn human-level cognitive skills.

- During the **1990s**, machine learning research shifted from a knowledge-driven to a data-driven method. Scientists and researchers devised computer systems capable of analyzing huge data to get insights. IBM Deep Blue computer was the innovation of this period which defeated Garry Kasparov, the global chess champion, in 1997.

§ **2006:** Deep learning was introduced by Geoffrey Hinton this year. IT emerged as a brand-new class of algorithms that allowed computers to recognize objects or language in still photographs or videos (Net scribes, 2018).

§ **2010:** Microsoft Kinect was released this year which was able to track up to 20 human features, 30 times per second. Users might interface with devices through gestures and movements with Microsoft Kinect.

§ **2011:** Machine learning had an exciting year this year. For starters, Watson from IBM defeated human rivals on Jeopardy. In addition, Google Brain was created, which had a deep neural network that could learn to discover and categories items.

- Google's X lab was developed in the year **2012** using a machine learning algorithm that could automatically watch YouTube videos and distinguish those featuring cats.

§ **2014**: Deep Face is a software algorithm developed by Facebook that can recognize and verify people in photos on par with humans.

- Amazon established its own ML platform in **2015**, bringing machine learning to the forefront of software development and making it more accessible. The Distributed ML Toolkit was built by Microsoft to allow developers to competently partition machine learning work over multiple processors. In the same year, over 3,000 AI and robotics researchers signed an open letter warning about the hazards of autonomous weapons that can choose targets without human interference, including Elon Musk, Stephen Hawking, and Steve Wozniak.

§ **2016**: Google's artificial intelligence system has defeated the Chinese board game Go pro player. This game was widely considered to be the most difficult board game in the world. Google's Alpha Go software has won five of the five games in the contest, putting the spotlight on artificial intelligence.

§ **2020:** Open AI releases GPT3, a revolutionary natural language processing system that can generate human-like sentences accordingly. With 175 billion parameters, GPT3 was the world's largest and most powerful language model trained on Microsoft Azure AI supercomputers.

14. TYPES OF MACHINE LEARNING

Supervised Learning- Machine Leaning program is given the training data along with expected output to categories the data known as Labels. Data sets (Input and Output) is given to forecast the result for an unknown future input. Labeled data (Input+ Expected Data)-ML Algo-Learned Model. Classification

(SVM, KNN, Logistics, Trees) and Regression (Polynomial, Linear, Trees) are algorithms of Supervised algorithms

Unsupervised learning- The algorithm learns from unlabeled dataset and uses input data to train the model. This is used to find anomalies and patterns. Clustering is a good example of Unsupervised learning. Clustering (K-Means, PCA, SVD) and Association Analysis (Apriori, FP-Growth) are used for unlabeled learning.

Semi- Supervised Learning- It is a hybrid technique which is a combination of both supervised and unsupervised learning.

Reinforcement Learning- Observes the environment and learns the ideal behavior, selects and take certain actions, receives rewards in return, receives feedback and learn the strategy or policy that maximizes rewards.

15. MACHINE LEARNING ADVANTAGE

Machine learning has become omnipresent in almost all domains whether it is agriculture, traffic management, stock trading, the health care sector, etc. For instance, the role of machine learning in the agriculture domain is to predict weather forecasts and crop rotation. The following are some of the advantages of machine learning (Haponik. A., 2021):

1. ***Value Prediction for the Customer***-These days the marketers confront on two important issues; one is predicting the lifetime valuation and second is segmenting customers. Large volumes of data are available to businesses, which may be used to provide useful business insights. Machine learning and data mining can be used by businesses to predict customer behavior and purchase trends, as well as send the best potential offers to specific customers based on their browsing and purchase histories.
2. ***Predictive Maintenance***- On a regular basis, manufacturing organizations spend a lot of money on preventative and corrective maintenance approaches, which are usually useless. Thanks to the emergence of machine learning, companies in this field may now use it to identify valuable insights and patterns concealed in their production data. Predictive maintenance minimizes the likelihood of unexpected breakdowns while also minimizing unnecessary costs. ML architecture can be built using historical data, a process visualization tool, a flexible analytical environment, and a feedback loop.
3. ***Removes the need for data entering by hand***- Removes the necessity for data entering by hand- Erroneous, identical or duplicate data are two of the most common problems that businesses face today. Using predictive modelling and machine learning, manual data entry errors can be dramatically minimized. Machine learning programs improve these operations by leveraging freshly discovered data. As a result, employees can devote the same amount of time to tasks that benefit the organization.
4. ***Spam Detection***- Machine learning has long been proven to be effective in detecting spam. Previously, email service providers relied on already deployed rule-based spam filtering technology. Spam filters, on the other hand, have already used neural networks to establish new algorithms for detecting spam and phishing messages.

5. ***Product Recommendations-*** Recommendations for Products- The development of product-based recommendation systems is aided by unsupervised learning. The bulk of e-commerce sites now employ machine learning to offer product recommendations. Machine learning algorithms are used to compare a customer`s purchase history to a large product inventory in order to identify hidden commonalities and group comparable products together. Customers are then encouraged to purchase these products after being recommended them.
6. ***Analyzing the financial prospects:*** Thanks to the vast amount of quantitative and accurate historical data, ML can now be used for financial analysis. Machine learning is already used in finance in areas such as portfolio management, algorithmic trading, and lending fraud detection. Banking machine learning applications include chatbots and other conversational interfaces for security, customer service, sentiment analysis.
7. ***Computer Vision-*** well known as, Image recognition. It is a technique for extracting numerical and symbolic data from images and other high-dimensional data. Techniques used include data mining, pattern recognition, machine learning, and database knowledge discovery. Machine learning is used for image recognition by companies in a variety of industries, including healthcare and automotive.
8. ***Diagnosis of Medical Reports-*** ML in medical diagnosis has helped many medical institutions improve patient health and reduce medical costs through the use of improved diagnostic tools and effective treatment procedures. It is used in healthcare to make a near-complete diagnosis, predict readmissions, prescribe medications, and identify high-risk patients. Patient records and data sources, as well as patient symptoms, are used to create these predictions and insights.
9. ***Improved cyber security-*** ML can be utilized to improve an organization's security because cyber security is one of the primary concerns that machine learning solves. In this case, machine learning enables new-generation providers to develop better solutions that can detect unknown risks rapidly and effectively.
10. ***Improving Client Satisfaction-*** Machine learning can help increase customer loyalty and enhance the customer experience. This is done by looking at previous call logs for customer behavior and appropriately assigning customer requests to the most qualified account managers. This reduces the time and expense of managing customer relationships. As a result, large companies use predictive algorithms to serve their customers.

16. CASES - E-COMMERCE WITH MACHINE LEARNING

Netflix

There was a time when you were eagerly waited for your favourite TV show and it was really heart breaking when you missed your favourite show because you did not have any other source or method to watch it again. Now the time has come when we all are enjoying web streaming services which provide us online media due to which we are able to watch the episodes or documentary films on our own convenience.

Netflix is the pioneer in this field of online web streaming. Netflix is one of the most popular television networks, with more than 150 million paying subscribers worldwide.

Netflix began its operations in 1997 by renting out CDs, and in 2007, it launched its own streaming services. Customers could view TV shows on their phones, televisions, desktops, laptops, or gaming devices. It began competing with TV and cable networks for original content in 2013. Netflix was the largest online TV streaming service provider in 2019.

Now, the point is, what did Netflix do which was unique and was appreciated by millions of its customers all over the world? What did Netflix do that its competitors did not?

The simple answer to these queries is that Netflix understood and used the power of AI, Big data analytics and machine learning. It makes use of a content delivery network to store and broadcast movies and television programs.

Netflix provides content via negotiating licensing agreements with TV series and film producers. Netflix shows diverse content to its subscribers throughout the world based on their location, popularity, and purchasing privileges. That is why what you see in London differs from what you see in Hyderabad. However, there are some shows and movies that appeal to all viewers regardless of their geographical location, such as Netflix's original show House of Cards, which was a huge smash.

Netflix contains over 7000 movies and TV episodes, making it tough for viewers to decide what to watch at any one time. As a result, Netflix began a practice of recommending shows to its users.

Netflix uses the recommendation Engine for recommending shows to its subscribers. In the beginning, the customer has to fill out a survey form in which the choice of TV shows and movies are filled. After that Netflix fine-tunes these recommendations to provide a more personalized experience. This is the reason that all the subscribers will have a unique recommendation list. Because it leverages user data to create intelligent suggestions, machine learning is required for providing such a service to clients. Data such as what viewers have previously viewed, their search rate, show ratings, and so on. All of this information is gathered, analyzed, and a conclusion is reached.

What else is capturing your eye, besides these customized engines? It's a fingernail. Visually stunning thumb nail that catches our attention and prompts us to click. At thumbnails, Netflix does not usually use the show's original cover. It employs algorithms to extract high-quality photos from the corresponding videos. Netflix creates eye-catching thumbnails using aesthetic vision analysis and innovation.

Amazon

Amazon is a very well-known e market place and millions of people shop through amazon globally. Amazon takes the help of machine learning a few actions:

- **Product suggestion** - As you select any product on Amazon, it starts giving suggestions for purchasing more similar kinds of products of the same price or more prices. This recommendation system works due to machine learning. Also, when you purchase a product, Amazon starts recommending accessories or related products too for your next purchase which is done by machine learning. By this product recommendation, Amazon increases its revenue by 35%.
- **Dynamic Pricing** – The price of every product varies at different times due to changes in demand. This variation of price is done by the machine learning algorithm.

When the demand for the product is high in the market, machine learning increases the price of the product. Therefore, Amazon is always able to give competitive price in the market and generate more revenue.

Few machine learning algorithms also keep an eye on the prices of the same products offered by the competitors. If the price offered by Amazon are higher than machine learning automatically decreases the price on a suitable margin to increase the sale.

- **Customer Segmentation** – This is one of the most crucial things for all the e commerce platforms. Machine learning differentiates the customers based on their past purchase.

Figure 8. Amazon's Actions with Machine Learning

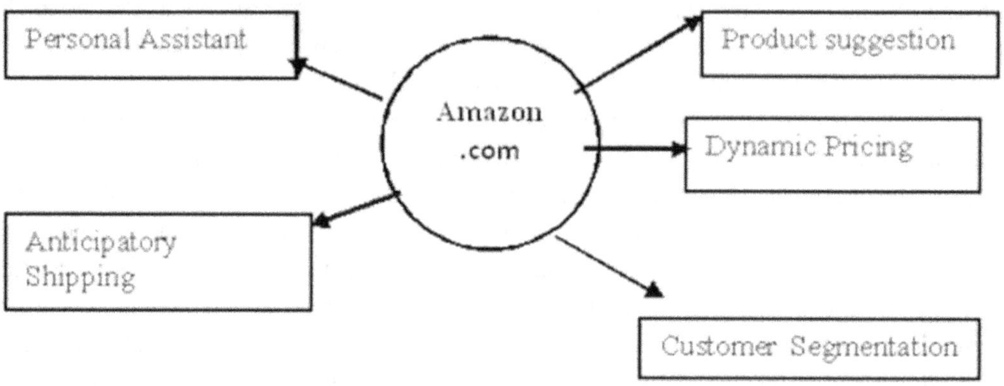

- **Personal Assistant** –Amazon Alexa is a personal assistant which is supported by machine learning. Through a personal assistant, amazons collect various keywords of customers' choice and recommend the related products in response and as a result, increase the total sale.
- **Anticipatory Shipping** – Amazon is using machine learning algorithms to increase customer engagement. There is an interesting fact about Amazon that it starts shipping the product to your city even before you order. This is called anticipatory shipping which Amazon uses. Now the question is, how Amazon knows which product you are planning to order or in other words, how Amazon is taking a big risk by shipping the products even before it gets the demand.

There are multiple machine learning algorithms that work together behind this game plan of Amazon which are identifying which are the products that you and other customers in your area or city are likely to purchase within 1-2 weeks, based on your past purchasing behaviour, your shopping cart, wish list, and your recent visits on the Amazon platform. This is why Amazon is able to deliver the product to its customers very fast.

- **Prime Customer** - The next unique Selling Point of Amazon is Amazon Prime in which machine learning is applied. If you are a prime member of Amazon, you will find different offers and prices of the products and a few other services too, like the quickest delivery promise. This quick delivery may be done within 8 hours or 10 hours too.

How Amazon is managing to provide such very quick deliveries to its prime customers? Machine learning algorithms make these estimations of quick deliveries due to which Amazon is able to inform its customers beforehand about the estimated delivery date. Based on the few factors like products already shipped in your city, quantity available in your city at your nearest Amazon Centre, availability of the delivery vehicle and delivery staff, machine learning estimates and decides when the product may be delivered to the customer.

17. CONCLUSION

E-Commerce industry is doing really well and has over powered the conventional business especially during pandemic it was well observed that all the daily household essential needs were also fulfilled by the Apps and websites. Companies are launching business online for food ordering, medicine ordering, booking online tickets and doing a video call with doctor, and many more.

Since the new oil is the data and companies are heavily relying on leveraging the data. The role of Machine learning is becoming an important technology that is organically applied to all business lines to solve complex business problems while improving the effectiveness and scalability of organizations. Machine learning will be helpful in predicting the results. Though it is difficult to use properly, but companies are prepared to invest in this time-consuming and costly process. This is because it has specific and important advantages over traditional analytical methods.

Machine learning brings many new ideas to the online marketplace, enabling them to quickly launch and maintain new business models and generate more revenue.

REFERENCES

Acquire. (2022). *Top 7 Futuristic Ecommerce Technology Trends to Watch*. Retrieved from: https://acquire.io/blog/ecommerce-technology-trends/

Bhagat, V. (2021). *The Role of Technology in Fostering E-commerce Business Growth*. TechTarget. Retrieved from: https://www.datasciencecentral.com/the-role-of-technology-in-fostering-e-commerce-business-growth/

Bigcommerce. (n.d.). *Artificial Intelligence in Ecommerce: How This Rapidly Evolving Tech Will Change the Online Storefront*. Retrieved from: https://www.bigcommerce.com/articles/ecommerce/ecommerce-ai/#benefits-of-using-artificial-intelligence-in-ecommerce-companies

Haponik, A. (2021). *The best Machine Learning Use Cases in E-commerce*. Addepto. Retrieved from: https://addepto.com/best-machine-learning-use-cases-ecommerce/#:~:text=Machine%20Learning%20in%20e%2Dcommerce%20can%20be%20very%20helpful%20in,detect%20new%20demands%20and%20trends

Imtiaz, M. A. (2018). *E-Commerce Business Aims and Objectives*. Retrieved from https://www.ukessays.com/essays/ecommerce/ecommerce-business-aims-objectives-7791.php?vref=1

IndustryWired. (2019). *How does technology impact on E-Commerce Industry?* IndustryWired. Retrieved from: https://industrywired.com/how-does-technology-impact-on-e-commerce-industry/

Koshal. (2011). *Difference Between Commerce and Business*. Retrieved from: https://www.difference-between.com/difference-between-commerce-and-vs-business/

Maday, J. (n.d.). *The history of e-commerce: A long and winding road. The future of Customer Engagement and Experience*. Retrieved from: https://www.the-future-of-commerce.com/2020/01/30/history-of-e-commerce/

Marr, B. (2016). A Short History of Machine Learning -- Every Manager Should Read. *Forbes*. Retrieved From: https://www.forbes.com/sites/bernardmarr/2016/02/19/a-short-history-of-machine-learning-every-manager-should-read/?sh=5d98c60815e7

Meiryani, Y. W. (2019). The Role of Information Technology in Ecommerce. *International Journal of Scientific & Technology Research, 8*(1). Retrieved from: https://www.ijstr.org/final-print/jan2019/The-Role-Of-Information-Technology-In-E-commerce.pdf

Multidev Technologies. (2015). *10 E-commerce Functions Every E-tailer Needs*. Retail Management Software Blog. Retrieved from: https://multidev.com/blog/10-e-commerce-functions-every-e-tailer-needs-2/

Netscribes. (2018). *5 Emerging technology trends in e-commerce*. Netscribes. Retrieved from: https://www.netscribes.com/ecommerce-technology-trends/#:~:text=In%20fact%2C%20technology%20plays%20an,capabilities%20for%20e%2Dcommerce%20success

Shaw, N. (n.d.). *Ecommerce Machine Learning: AI's Role in the Future of Online Shopping*. BigCommerce. Retrieved from: https://www.bigcommerce.com/blog/ecommerce-machine-learning/

Smart Insights. (2020). *5 ways to use Augmented Reality in your marketing strategy*. Retrieved from: https://www.smartinsights.com/digital-marketing-platforms/augmented-reality/5-ways-to-use-augmented-reality-in-your-marketing-strategy/

Thakur, M. (n.d.). *E-commerce vs Traditional commerce*. EDUCBA. Retrieved from: https://www.educba.com/e-commerce-vs-traditional-commerce/

Tutorials Point. (n.d.). *E-Commerce-Disadvantages*. Tutorials Point. Retrieved from: https://www.tutorialspoint.com/e_commerce/e_commerce_disadvantages.htm

Zande, V. J. (n.d.). *What is e-commerce? Definition, benefits, examples. The Future of Customer Engagement and Experience*. Retrieved from: https://www.the-future-of-commerce.com/2020/01/19/what-is-e-commerce-definition-examples/

Zobrist, T. (2019). *Five e-commerce Functions You Should Be Doing Daily*. Retrieved from: https://www.zobristinc.com/five-e-commerce-functions-you-should-be-doing-daily/

Chapter 2
The Digital Transformation of Rural Agricultural Business Management:
A Case Study of China

Poshan Yu
https://orcid.org/0000-0003-1069-3675
Soochow University, China & Australian Studies Centre, Shanghai University, China

Jiai Chen
Independent Researcher, China

Michael Sampat
Independent Researcher, Canada

Nyaribo Misuko
https://orcid.org/0000-0002-7890-2931
KCA University, Kenya

ABSTRACT

This chapter aims to study the development of futuristic e-commerce systems in rural China. This chapter will explore the current situation of the whole industrial chain in rural small and medium enterprises and their developing trends in B2C model. Why are rural agricultural small and medium-sized enterprises (SMEs) developing rapidly in China? What is the digital context for the development of rural SMEs in the agricultural sector? What digital transformations have rural SMEs experienced in terms of business models, especially in less developed areas, such as Tier 4 and Tier 5 areas, compared with international ones? Compared with the previous rural e-commerce, what are the advantages of optimizing the new system? This chapter will use CiteSpace to perform statistical and correlation analysis on Chinese agricultural e-commerce system, including the Web of Science (WOS) database and CSSCI database. Cases from China will be used for comparison. This chapter will provide suggestions for the development of futuristic e-commerce system in emerging economies.

DOI: 10.4018/978-1-6684-4969-1.ch002

Copyright © 2022, IGI Global. Copying or distributing in print or electronic forms without written permission of IGI Global is prohibited.

INTRODUCTION

China's e-commerce industry has enjoyed above-average growth in the last few years. In 2020, about 24.9 percent of the total retail sales in China were made online, up from 20.7 percent in 2019. The share of e-commerce retail has steadily grown over the past seven years. This chapter aims to study the development of futuristic e-commerce systems in rural China. This chapter will explore the current situation of the whole industrial chain in rural small and medium enterprises and their developing trends in the B2C model. Why are rural agricultural small and medium-sized enterprises (SMEs) developing rapidly in China? What is the digital context for the development of rural SMEs in the agricultural sector? What digital transformations have rural SMEs experienced in terms of business models, especially in less developed areas, such as Tier 4 and Tier 5 areas, compared with international ones? Compared with the previous rural e-commerce, what are the advantages of optimizing the new system? This chapter will use CiteSpace to perform statistical and correlation analysis on the Chinese agricultural e-commerce system, including the Web of Science (WOS) database and CSSCI database. Cases from China will be used for comparison. This chapter will provide suggestions for the development of futuristic e-commerce system in emerging economies.

THE CURRENT SITUATION OF CHINESE E-COMMERCE

The annual GDP exceeded the trillion yuan for the first time in 2020, reaching 1,015,986 billion yuan. Among them, the value added of the primary industry accounted for 7.7% of GDP; the value added of the secondary industry accounted for 37.8% of GDP; and the value added of the tertiary industry accounted for the most, at 54.5%. GDP continued to rise in all quarters, and economic growth continued to recover faster in the first quarter of 2020 due to the impact of the epidemic GDP was 2,065.4 billion yuan, down 6.8% year-on-year from the previous period, but in the fourth quarter of 2020 China's economy continued to grow to 296,298 billion yuan, up 6.5% year-on-year. The three major industries achieved steady growth with similar growth rates. In 2021, the value added of the primary industry in GDP was 7.3%, the value added of the secondary industry was 39.4%, and the value added of the tertiary industry was 53.3%. Combined with the statistical chart, it can be seen that the proportion of the three industries changed as the tertiary industry was rising year by year, the proportion of the secondary industry was relatively stable, and the proportion of the primary industry had a trend of shrinking year by year (Figure 1).

In 2020, about 24.9 percent of the total retail sales in China were made online, up from 20.7 percent in 2019. The share of e-commerce retail has steadily grown over the past seven years. E-commerce revenue forecast is expected to reach about 1,600 billion U.S. dollars on internet markets by segment in 2025 (Ministry Of Commerce Of The People's Republic Of China, 2020).

In 2020, Chinese overall e-commerce transactions exceeded 37.2 trillion yuan, increasing from around 34.8 trillion yuan the year before (Zheng, Zhang, & Song, 2020). Rural online retail sales reached 1.79 trillion yuan, an increase of 8.9% year-on-year.

On one hand, the number of rural Internet users is growing rapidly. As of December 2020, the number of rural Internet users in China was 309 million, accounting for 31.3% of the overall number of Internet users, up 54.71 million from March 2020 (Ministry Of Commerce Of The People's Republic Of China, 2020). According to the CNNIC, the number of online shoppers in China has surpassed the 700-million-mark in 2020, representing more than half of its population. An important target group'

Figure 1. Quarterly change in national GDP (billion yuan)
Data source: moa.gov.cn

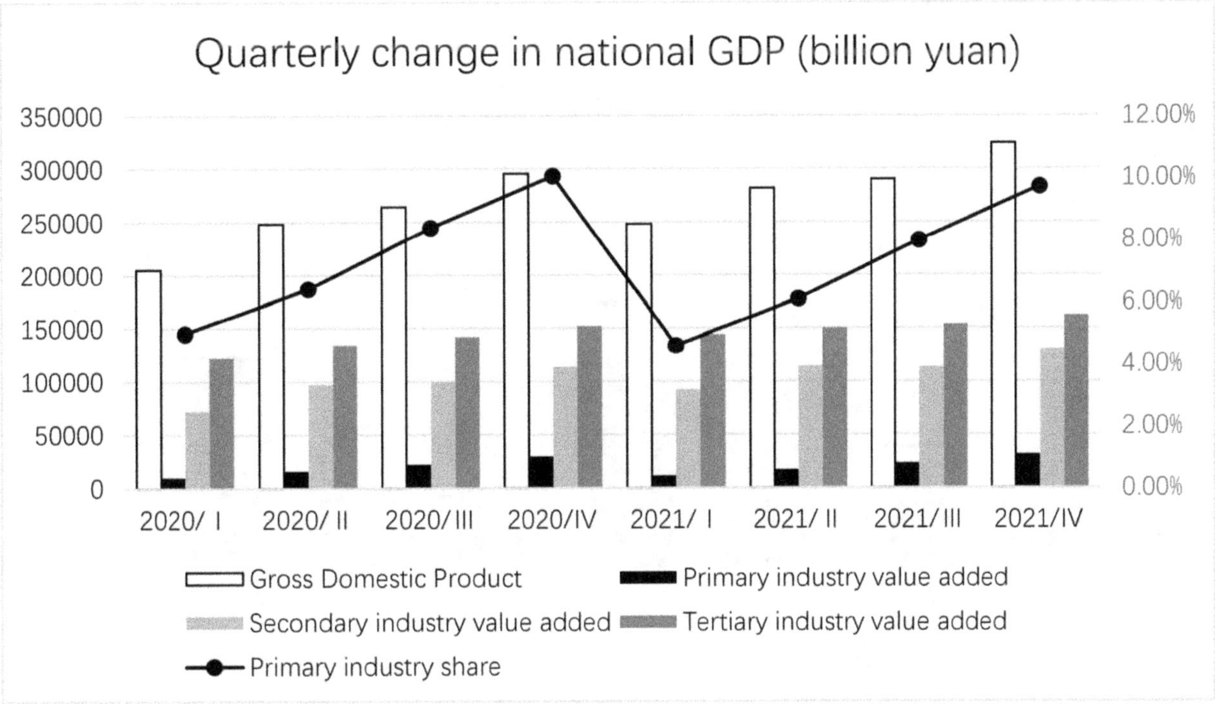

of China's booming e-commerce sector is the mobile user segment. As of March 2016, China ranked first in mobile commerce penetration (Nie, Ma, & Sousa-Poza, 2021). For many Chinese consumers, smartphones have begun to replace computers. To keep up with consumer demands, many of the major Chinese online shopping stores have developed their own mobile apps. The market volume of mobile e-commerce in China had reached around 5.1 trillion yuan in 2017, a percent surge from the previous year (Zheng et al., 2020). The number of mobile payment users in China from 2013 to 2020, as of December 2020, around 852.5 million people used mobile payment transactions in China, up from around 765 million users in March 2020.

Another factor rapidly utilized by the Chinese e-commerce industry is social media presence. Chinese consumers rely heavily on friends and peer groups for shopping information. Therefore, social media has gained a lot of relevance for e-commerce endeavors. As of the first quarter of 2020, the social commerce website Pinduoduo had more than 487 million monthly active users (McKinsey & Company, 2021).

On the other hand, innovation combined with digital transformation has been made to develop rural agriculture. In the historical process of China's social development, forty years before the reform and opening up, peasants did not have the right to choose their own jobs or sell their own products and were stuck to the land for their whole life. Moreover, the state only invested in the construction of cities and industries, and all rural construction, including the water conservancy and rural infrastructure construction during the People's Commune era, which was considered a great achievement, was funded by peasants with food and labor (Elijah et al, 2018). Nowadays, peasants are gradually becoming free if they can move between urban and rural areas. Today, the government invests in rural roads, water conservancy

Figure 2. Quarterly changes in per capita disposable income of rural residents (yuan)
Data source: moa.gov.cn

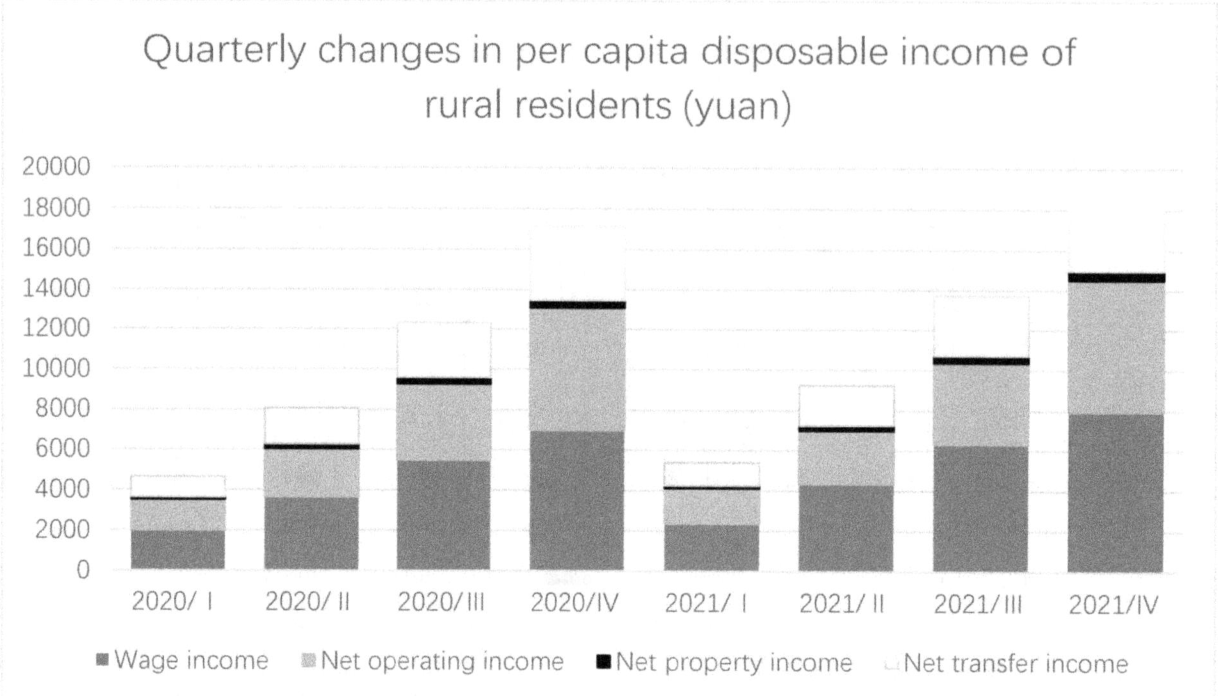

and most infrastructure construction, so the peasants no longer pay for most of it. In the meanwhile, with the encouragement of the policy mentioned below, the disposable income of rural residents rises.

The per capita disposable income of residents has been increasing year by year, and the growth rate of disposable income of rural residents is higher than that of urban residents. Chinese economy was greatly hit by the epidemic in 2020, but the disposable income of residents still maintained positive growth. in 2020, the national per capita disposable income of residents was 32,189 yuan, of which, the per capita disposable income of rural residents was 17,131 yuan. In terms of growth rate, although the overall disposable income of China's residents has been on a downward trend in recent years, the growth rate of disposable income of rural residents is significantly higher than the growth rate of disposable income of urban residents. Affected by the epidemic, the decline of disposable income of residents in 2020 is particularly obvious. 2020, the national per capita disposable income growth rate is 4.74%, and the growth rate of disposable income of rural residents is 6.93%. 2021, there is a rebound in disposable income of rural residents (Figure 2).

Forty years ago, agriculture relied heavily on human and cattle power, and nearly 800 million rural people, 82 percent of the country's population, needed to support more than 900 million people in agriculture (Fang et al., 2014). Now that farming and harvesting are mechanized in many remote mountainous areas of China, the labor intensity of agriculture has never been lower. With a significant decline in arable land, less than 600 million rural people, who account for just over 40% of the country, need to feed nearly 1.4 billion people by engaging in agriculture. From 1978 to 2017, China's total grain production grew from 305 million tons to 618 million tons. With a population increase of 44.4% and an annual

Figure 3. Visualization in terms of the paramount links relating to e-commerce terms
Source: Web of Science

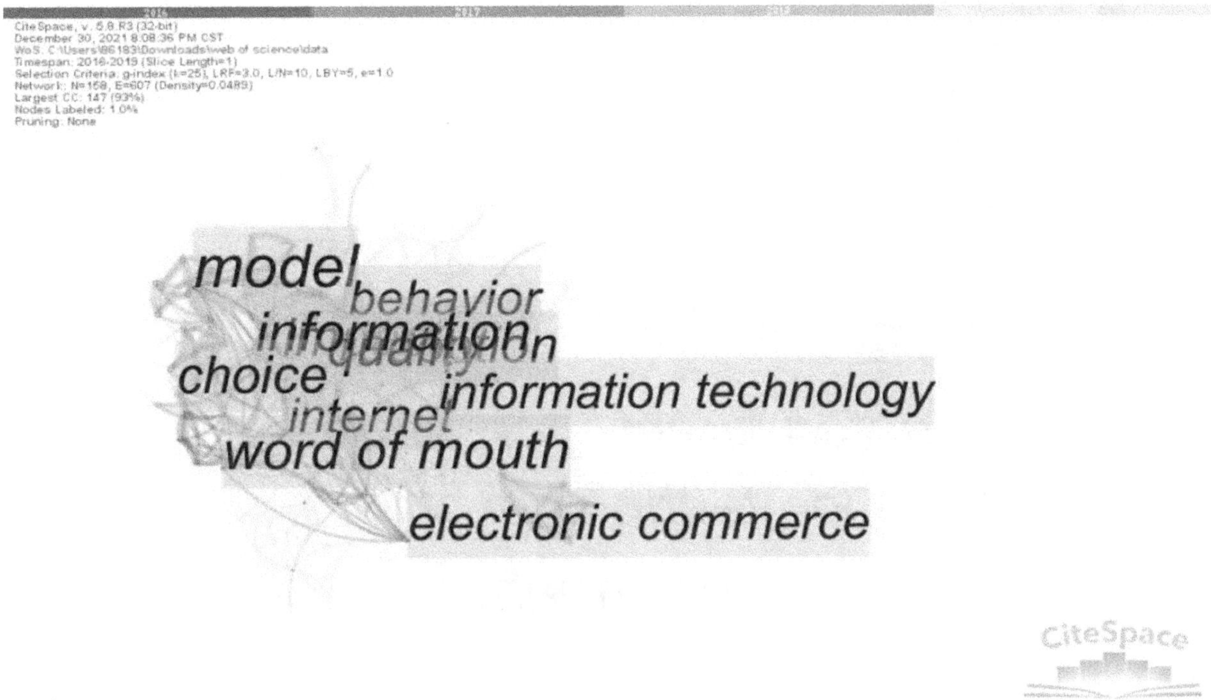

reduction of 3,000 square kilometers of arable land, grain production increased by 102.7% and the grain self-sufficiency rate reached 95%. This is the basic premise of China's industrialization and urbanization.

Using CiteSpace, we find that Chinese agricultural e-commerce is a hot button in Chinese e-commerce, related to information technology and innovation in small and medium enterprises. The combination of new businesses stimulates Chinese agriculture (Figure 3 - 6).

RURAL E-COMMERCE

According to data made public by the Food and Agriculture Organization of the United Nations (FAO), global food production was about 2.627 billion tons in 2017. Five countries produce more than 100 million tons of food. The U.S. accounts for 13% of the world's arable land and produces 500 million tons of food per year. India accounts for 11% of the world's arable land and produces 280 million tons of grain per year. Brazil accounts for 4% of the world's arable land and produces 240 million tons of grain per year. Russia accounts for 8% of the world's arable land and produces 130 million tons of grain per year. China, on the other hand, has about 7% of the world's arable land and produces 618 million tons of grain, or 23.5% of the world's total grain production (Zheng et al., 2020). Since July 1, 2007, China has been conducting the second national land survey, with the standard time point for data compilation being December 31, 2009. The survey was completed at the end of 2009, and on December 30, 2013, the Ministry of Land and Resources officially announced the survey results, showing that the current arable land in China reached 2.027 billion mu (Figure 7).

Figure 4. Visualization in terms of paramount links relating to small and medium enterprises terms
Source: Web of Science

China has four times the population of the United States but has far less total arable land and a high proportion of hilly, mountainous areas of arable land. Most areas are not suitable for large agricultural machinery and large-scale production is bound to lag far behind the United States. Nevertheless, China not only ranks first in the world in grain production, but also in meat production, fish production, cotton production, edible oil production, sheep production, and fruit and vegetable production. Compared with the United States, a recognized global agricultural powerhouse, China leads in the production of most agricultural products.

Although China has become the world's largest importer of agricultural products, and the volume of grain imports is the world's first, imports are mainly dominated by genetically modified soybeans used in the processing and production of edible oil and feed, which always have an absolute advantage in terms of staple foods. According to the data published by the General Administration of Customs of China, 13.062 million tons of grain were imported in 2017, of which soybean imports were as high as 95.53 million tons and corn imports were 2.83 million tons, both of which accounted for 75% of the total amount of imported grain; while rice imports accumulated 4.03 million tons and wheat imports accumulated 4.42 million tons, staple crops such as rice and wheat imports are very small and the self-sufficiency rate is above 95%. Therefore, imports are mainly to meet different levels of consumer demand, and the safety of rations is not a problem (Fang et al., 2014).

From the perspective of agricultural exports, the total amount of China's agricultural exports from 2015 to 2020 showed an up-and-down but overall upward trend. in 2020, affected by the epidemic, China's agricultural exports were $76.03 billion, down 3.23% year-on-year. in 2020, China's total agricultural imports were $170.8 billion, up 13.96% year-on-year. in 2021, China's agricultural imports and exports

Figure 5. Visualization in terms of the paramount links relating to e-commerce terms
Source: CSSCI

Figure 6. Visualization in terms of paramount links relating to small and medium enterprises terms
Source: CSSCI

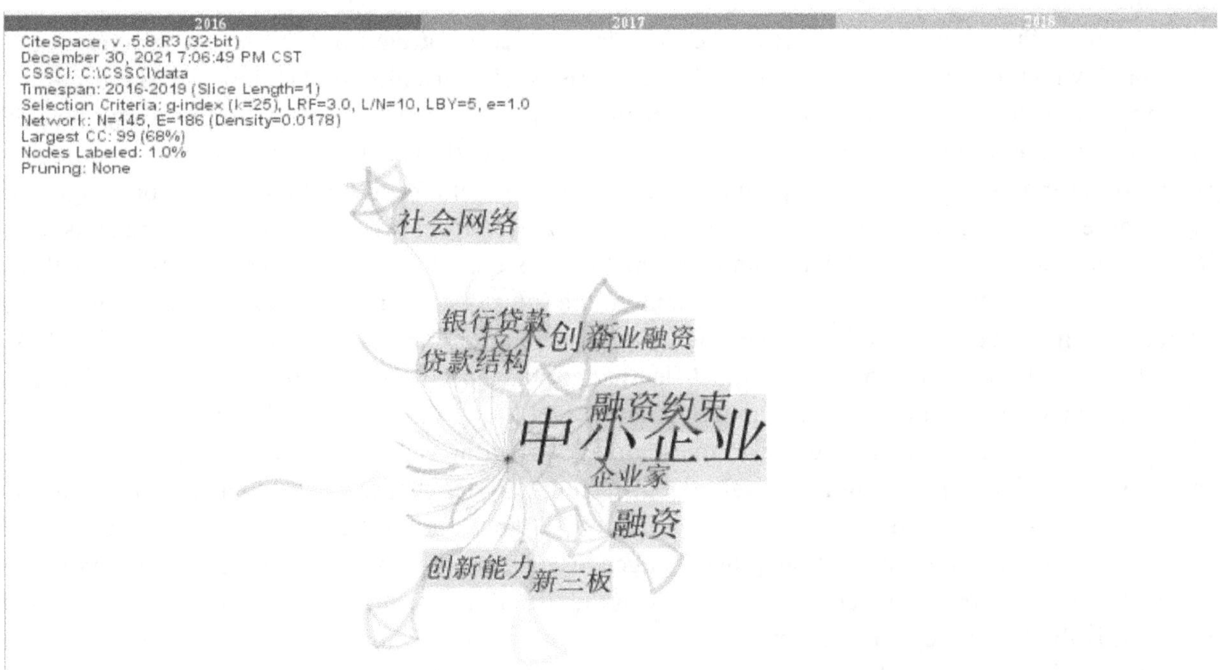

Figure 7. Annual changes in national agricultural land resources (thousands of hectares)
Data source: moa.gov.cn

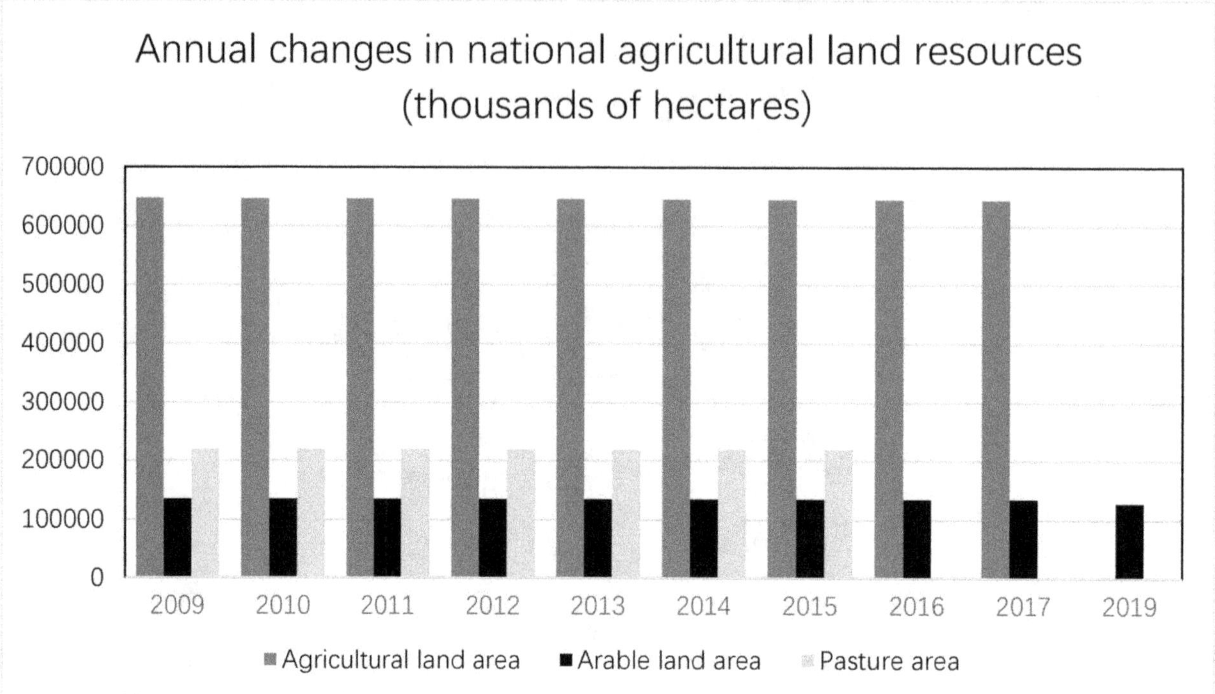

304.17 billion U.S. dollars, an increase of 23.2% year-on-year. Among them, exports of $84.35 billion, an increase of 10.9%; imports of $219.82 billion, an increase of 28.6%; trade deficit of $135.47 billion, an increase of 42.9% (Figure 8).

The United States has the unique resource endowment of concentrated arable land and sparsely populated land, which is suitable for equipping efficient large-scale agricultural machinery, plus agriculture has long completed the integration of capital concentration and high technology, which is always beyond the reach of small farmers in China's large-scale agriculture, with wheat, corn and soybean production accounting for about 40% of global production and up to 90% of agricultural products exported to foreign markets, making it the world's largest exporter of agricultural products. In addition to satisfying its population of 320 million, China can also satisfy the needs of 150 million people abroad with its agricultural products. Thus, it is very dependent on the international market and dominates the world agricultural market despite the frequent problems with surplus agricultural products (Zheng et al., 2020).

Different national conditions determine different national agricultural positioning. Because China is a large country with small farmers, a large population and a small land area with complex topography, it is impossible to implement large-scale mechanized agriculture like the United States, and it is not in line with the laws of agricultural development. Schultz argues that traditional small farmers are no less efficient than any entrepreneurs as "economic men", and that the key to transforming traditional agriculture is not a matter of scale, and that changes in scale are not a source of economic growth. The key is the introduction of modern factors, of which the use of new factors, depending on technological changes, is the key of keys. For example, France's famous wine has always adhered to the small scale of historical heritage, and there has been no large-scale operation. The basic condition of a country

Figure 8. Monthly changes in China's foreign trade in agricultural products (USD billion)
Data source: moa.gov.cn

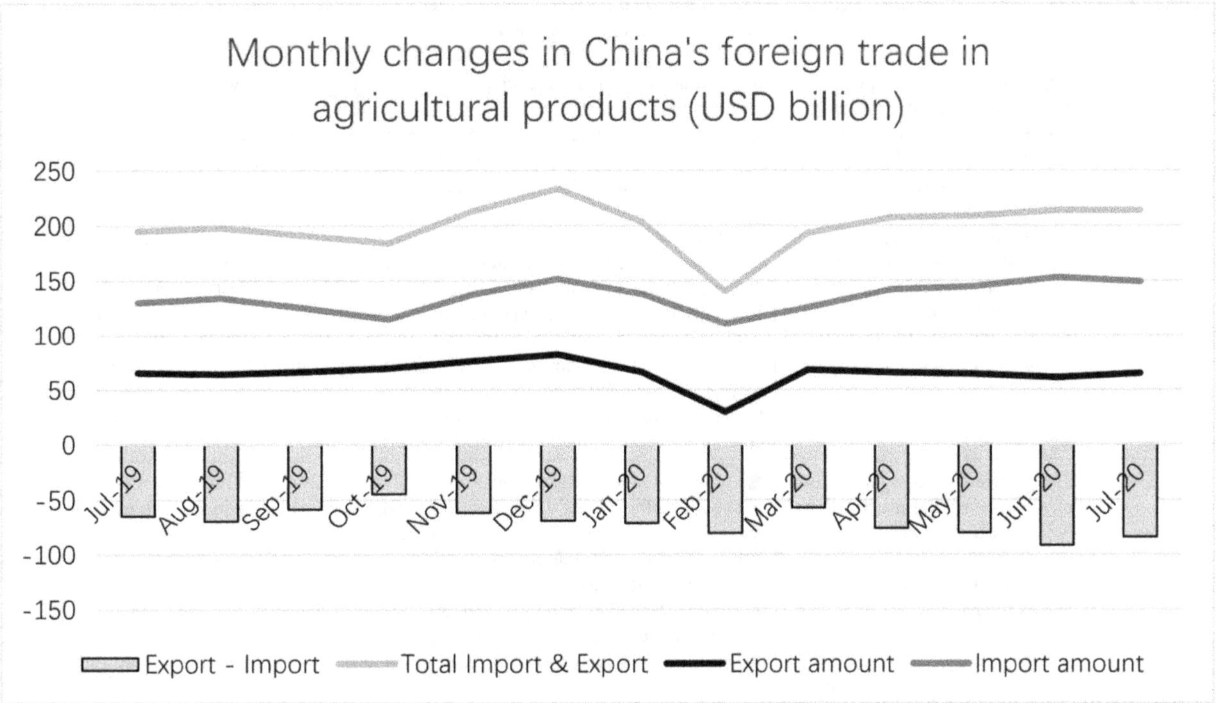

with many people and little land has determined the inevitable existence of smallholder agriculture for a considerable period. Compared with the resource endowment of the United States, even if China's urbanization comprehensively exceeds the level of the United States, it is by no means possible to develop into large-scale modern agriculture like the United States (Klerkx, Jakku, & Labarthe, 2019).

Against the backdrop of a near-complete harvest of all crops, FAO's forecast for world cereal production in 2021 remains unchanged this month at 2.799 billion tonnes, up 0.8% from 2020. This increase is almost entirely supported by increased maize production, which offsets a significant decline in world barley production. The forecast for world cereal consumption in 2021/22 was revised down slightly this month to 2.785 billion tons, but is still 0.9 percent above the 2020/21 level. FAO's 2022 end-of-season forecast for global cereal stocks is 856 million tons, an increase of 5.2 million tons from a year earlier and 2.8 percent from the beginning of the period. Worldwide cereal trade is expected to reach 473 million tons in 2021/22, up 3.7 million tons from last month's forecast, but 1.2 percent below the record level of 2020/21. FAO's forecast for global coarse grains trade in 2021/22 (July/June) is similarly revised upward by 2.4 million tonnes, contributed almost entirely by expectations of higher corn trade (FAO, 2022). Continued strong demand for corn from China and faster than expected shipments from Argentina in recent months set the main basis for a higher global corn trade volume of 1.7 million tons this month (Figure 9).

The fundamental difference between Chinese agriculture and that of developed countries is not a matter of competitiveness per se. Japan, which is also a small farmer in East Asia with China, has always adopted a heavy farming policy to tenaciously protect small farmers. Japan's urbanization rate is as high as 93%, the number of part-time farmers accounts for more than 80% of the total number of farmers,

Table 1. Some examples of International smart farming

Country	Current situation	Detail
U.S.	The U.S. has formed a perfect agricultural scientific research system, which can be divided into three major segments: education, scientific research and extension, with close integration of industry, academia and research, and high efficiency of scientific and technological transformation, and its contribution rate of agricultural science and technology reaches 70-80%.	● Agricultural company scientific research main body: enterprises are the main body of science and technology commercialization, and large leading agricultural companies invest funds in agricultural scientific research and technology transformation, such as DuPont and Monsanto. ● Agricultural incubator model: Science and technology incubators in the agricultural field are set up to carry out R&D incubation, startup and industrialization of smart agriculture technologies, such as the Great Lakes Agricultural Technology Business Incubator in the United States. ● Scientific Research Institute Scientific Research Main Body: Generally, government investment is the main focus, and market-oriented capital gradually enters and promotes technology marketization, such as the Weizmann Institute in Israel. In the U.S. agricultural research system, universities are the main body of basic research, and public and private research institutions are the main body of development research. ● Market-oriented fund model: There are mainly industrial funds and technology merger and acquisition funds for agricultural technology introduction, absorption and transformation, such as Israel Infiniti Group and Jerusalem Venture Capital Fund JVP, etc.
Israel	85% of Israel's citrus plantations have implemented integrated pest management, using natural organisms such as wasps or other insects to combat pests. Water utilization has reached over 95%. Israeli agricultural products already occupy 40% of the European market for fruits and vegetables and are the second largest supplier of flowers in Europe after the Netherlands.	● Advanced breeding techniques: Israel is constantly improving the disease resistance of seeds and the adaptability of crops through scientific techniques such as plant engineering, genetic engineering, hybridization and genetic modification. It also cultivates crop seeds that require less water and several new varieties that are resistant to disasters and diseases. ● Unique storage technology: To maintain the freshness of grain, Israel has designed and invented the barn. In addition, Israel's storage technology, the biology of grain storage pests, the application of phosphine technology, physical insecticide and other aspects of in-depth research. ● Soil research and development technology: The newly developed "soil" forms a substance called vermiculite at a temperature of 1,000 degrees, which is well ventilated and can retain moisture much more than its weight.
Japan	Japan has introduced drone technology, driverless technology and artificial intelligence in agricultural production to achieve 24H non-stop operation of unmanned autonomous farm vehicles.	● Drones: Companies are integrating other technologies with drone technology to give drones a broader range of uses. Some drones are equipped with mapping cameras or agricultural multispectral cameras to remotely observe farmland, understand crop growth, conduct pest and disease analysis, and provide data support for agricultural production decisions. ● The application of robotics and artificial intelligence technologies in Japanese agriculture is concentrated in the fields of intelligent identification such as soil and pest detection, tillage, sowing and harvesting. ● Agricultural Internet of Things technology, which integrates information technology and modern agricultural planting management, has become another key area of promotion for the development of smart agriculture in Japan.

and the modernization of half a century is still about 30 acres in size. Whether it is the ratio of people to land, or far higher prices compared to agricultural products abroad, Japan's agricultural products are no comparative advantage. Japan's agricultural prices are high, but are farmers' incomes high? Japan has a strong "agricultural association" that combines economic and social functions, which is not only responsible for organizing agricultural production, purchasing production and living materials, selling agricultural products and other economic activities, but also the distribution of various agricultural subsidies from the government, while representing the interests of farmers in all aspects and influencing the determination of agricultural market prices. It also represents the interests of farmers in all aspects, influencing the determination of market prices of agricultural products and the direction of national agricultural policies, and affecting the survival of Japanese family farms. Therefore, small farmers in Japan mainly use agricultural associations to integrate (combine) and coordinate the operation of agri-

Figure 9. Projected changes in world grain supply and demand (million tons)
Data source: moa.gov.cn

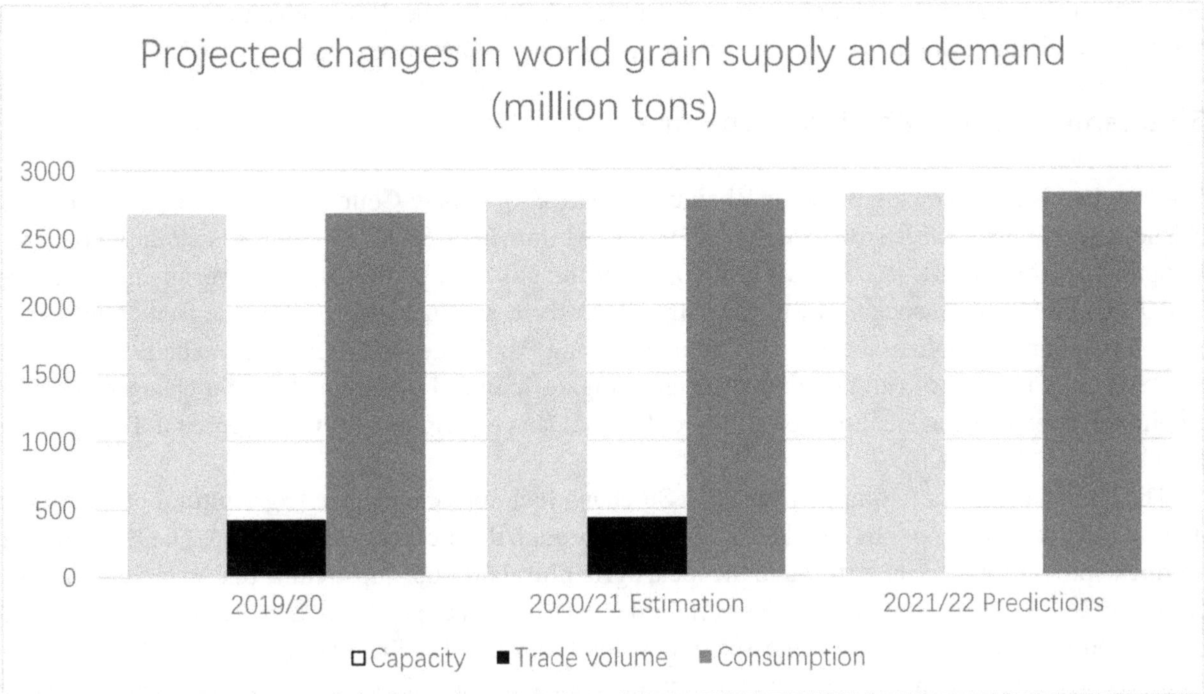

cultural links, and the basic model is "agricultural association + family farming. Despite the aging of the Japanese agricultural population and the small size of the agricultural industry, the government has provided comprehensive support and policy protection for agriculture, and there is a general consensus in society to buy domestic agricultural products at high prices and to resist foreign agricultural products, even at low prices (Hoyer et al, 2020). In Japan, the price of rice is sold at more than 100 RMB per pound, fruits are sold by the number of pieces, and most of the agricultural equipment is financially invested, especially the farmers are given orders first before production.

China is just the opposite. Previously, China's unique love affair with agricultural scale, and the company-plus-farmers agricultural industrialization leading enterprise agriculture, seems to have become a panacea to crack the scattered farmers and big market docking. But the result that emerged was the company lost money with government subsidies, made money with government tax exemptions, and the family-run farmers were excluded, and the interests of the agricultural family business were increasingly weakened. Therefore, to break this deadlock, the government introduced encouraging policies to support various new agricultural subjects, including family farms, agricultural cooperatives and agricultural enterprises (Li, Su, Zhang, & Mao, 2018). Various new subjects have their own strengths and complementary advantages. Family farms, with their moderate scale of operation, are an upgraded version of traditional farmers; cooperatives, as autonomous organizations of farmers, link pre-production, production and post-production, and develop as a group; and agricultural enterprises, with modern elements, talents, technology and capital advantages, are the backbone of agricultural products processing and circulation. The government is responsible for clearing obstacles, providing good services and stimulating their vitality and creativity. Many excellent cases of agricultural innovation have been generated.

Small and medium enterprises in the country, especially in less developed regions e.g. Tier 4 & 5, benefit from fitting into the e-commerce system and experiencing different kinds of digital transformations that are encouraged by the government. The foundation for the development of rural e-commerce has been continuously enhanced and several business models have been found (Li, 2022).

Suichang Model In Zhejiang Province

The first one is the Suichang model in Zhejiang province. Suichang County is located in the southwest of Zhejiang Province, with a total area of 2,539 square kilometers, 88.82% of which is mountainous, and a population of only 231,000. In March 2010, under the guidance of the county government, Suichang County Online Shop Association was formally established, and in January 2013, the first county-level special pavilion on Taobao, the Special China-Suichang Pavilion, was officially launched, announcing the "Suichang model" of rural e-commerce featuring agricultural products. The "Suichang Model" of e-commerce featuring agricultural products took initial shape (Ministry Of Commerce Of The People's Republic Of China, 2020).

The "Suichang Model" simply means that Suichang localities can realize "agricultural products into the city" and "consumer goods into the countryside" through the e-commerce platform. The "agricultural products into the city" - that is, through the local agricultural product "upstream" platform Sui.com, one end connects the supply source of agricultural products to rural cooperatives, and the other end connects to local online stores or micro-businesses to develop them into the local young people. The other end connects with local young people who have online shops or micro-businesses, and develops them into Sui.com's distribution members, helping them to sell their agricultural products to first- and second-tier cities (The State Council Information Office of the People's Republic of China, 2021). Consumer goods going to the countryside" - that is, through the local consumer goods "going to the countryside" platform catch street network, relying on small commercial stores in each village, in the store set aside a small piece of land of 8 to 10 square meters to build Service station, equipped with computer equipment for the service station, training shopkeepers to be part-time attendants, to help villagers in catching up with the street online shopping. At the same time, Catch Street Network establishes county-level operation centers and secondary distribution logistics from the county to rural areas, making e-commerce of agricultural products an effective way to promote the industrialization of agricultural products (Klerkx et al., 2019).

In 2012, the county's e-commerce transactions amounted to 150 million yuan, and in January 2013, the Suichang Pavilion on Taobao.com went online, and in 2014, the Catch Street project was launched to fully activate rural e-commerce. Suichang initially formed the "Suichang phenomenon" of county e-commerce featuring agricultural specialties, multi-category synergistic development and urban-rural interaction (China Communist Party News, 2016).

After the initial "Suichang Phenomenon", the pace of Suichang's exploration did not stop and was gradually upgraded to the "Suichang Model", which is driven by localized e-commerce integrated service providers to drive the ecological development of county e-commerce and promote local traditional industries, especially the agricultural products processing industry. The interaction of "integrated e-commerce service provider + online business + traditional industry" forms the county's economic development path in the information age (News, 2016).

Immediately after the launch of the Suichang "Catch Street" project, pushing open the prologue of rural e-commerce, the significance of Catch Street is to open the last kilometer of information technology in rural areas, so that rural people can enjoy the same online shopping convenience and quality of

Table 2. Four typical business models in rural e-commerce

	Suichang Model	Linan model	Qinghe Model	Tongyu model
	under government guidance			
Initiation	In January 2013, the first county-level special pavilion on Taobao, the Special China-Suichang Pavilion, was officially launched, announcing the "Suichang model" of rural e-commerce featuring agricultural products.	● Lin'an Cultural Tourism Bureau summarized and refined the village scenic resources survey, investigated the resources of 14 village scenic areas and established a village scenic operation investment project library. ● On May 5, 2017, Lin'an Cultural Tourism Bureau held the first meeting to attract operators for village scenic spots. ● The operator needs to submit the operating plan to the district cultural tourism bureau hired by the expert group to review and approve.	After the accidental success of a villager selling cashmere on Taobao in 2007, the online business community in Qinghe County increased rapidly, and the Qinghe County government also saw the opportunity to put forward the development strategy of "online and offline interaction, tangible market and intangible market complement each other".	● Company unites local cooperatives to form the cooperative association. ● Partners: villages, towns, and some deep processing enterprises with fixed bases. ● Cooperation with the Academy of Agricultural Sciences
Type	E-commerce featuring agricultural products	E-commerce featuring nuts	E-commerce featuring cashmere products	A direct supply model that sells Tongyu County's advantageous agricultural and sideline products
Main Measures	The "Suichang Model" means that Suichang localities can realize "agricultural products into the city" and "consumer goods into the countryside" through the e-commerce platform.		The government has set up an e-commerce service center to provide practitioners with skills training on Taobao introduction and online store enhancement. To design enough styles to attract consumers, the government also set up a cashmere products research and development center to provide sufficient styles for free (Chang & Meyerhoefer, 2021). The Qinghe Cashmere Quality Supervision Center came into being to protect the quality of products with national-level test results.	Comprehensive measures such as supply chain optimization have continuously improved the upward mode of agricultural products directly from the place of origin to help regional public brand building.
Development	In 2012, the county's e-commerce transactions amounted to 150 million yuan, and in January 2013, the Suichang Pavilion on Taobao.com went online, and in 2014, the Catch Street project was launched to fully activate rural e-commerce.	After several years, through the organization of the Chamber of Commerce, network publicity solicitation, field visits, business to attract business and other forms, the region's existing 14 village scenic spots signed operators, business to attract 51 enterprises, settled 53 projects, with a total investment of 520 million yuan.	The government has started to create a corresponding physical industry platform to carry out deeper incubation for enterprises.	Taobao launched a series of special zones for agricultural products, specially opened a "local fresh food" entrance for state-level poor counties and launched the "Foodie Help Farmer Channel". Jingdong opened the "National Fresh Products Green Channel". Pinduoduo Online "Fight against the epidemic, love and help farmers" special area.
Achievements	By the end of 2017, the county has established 229 village-level e-commerce service stations with more than 2,000 online stores, more than 200 online goods suppliers, more than 40 third-party service providers, and more than 6,000 people engaged in the rural e-commerce industry in the county, and Suichang's rural e-commerce public service platform has become a nationally renowned regional e-commerce service platform.	Lin'an actively carried out the linkage of urban and rural enterprises, including 7 agricultural product e-commerce demonstration villages, and the total sales of 38 e-commerce enterprises with more than 5 million yuan reached 565 million yuan; The formation of "two parks and multiple points" and other agricultural product bases.	In Qinghe, Hebei Province, e-commerce has become the most characteristic business group in Qinghe County and Qinghe has become the largest cashmere products network sales base in China. There are more than 20,000 Taobao Tmall stores in the county, with annual sales of 1.5 billion yuan, and cashmere yarn sales account for more than 70% of Taobao, making it a veritable Taobao county.	This little-known county began to enter the eyes of consumers nationwide. E-commerce plays an important role in fighting the epidemic and helping farmers with the encouragement of government.

life as the city (Nie et al., 2021). Urban people can eat rural agricultural products with confidence, to achieve urban and rural integration (Zheng et al., 2020).

By the end of 2017, the county has established 229 village-level e-commerce service stations with more than 2,000 online stores, more than 200 online goods suppliers, more than 40 third-party service providers, more than 6,000 people engaged in the rural e-commerce industry in the county, and Suichang's rural e-commerce public service platform has become a nationally renowned regional e-commerce service platform (Ministry Of Commerce Of The People's Republic Of China, 2020).

Linan Model In Zhejiang Province

The second is the Linan model in Zhejiang province. First, the establishment of an investment project library. Lin'an Cultural Tourism Bureau summarized and refined 16 items of village scenic resources survey, commissioned a third-party professional organization to investigate the resources of 14 village scenic areas, and established a village scenic operation investment project library (People.cn, 2020). The project library information is tailored to the needs of a rural tourism operation, and is relevant to the actual countryside, providing convenience for interested operators to quickly understand the "home base" and characteristics of villages (Ministry Of Commerce Of The People's Republic Of China, 2017).

Second, Attracting operators. On May 5, 2017, Lin'an Cultural Tourism Bureau held the first meeting to attract operators for village scenic spots, with the participation of more than 20 tourism and cultural and creative enterprises. In the past three years, through the organization of the Chamber of Commerce, network publicity solicitation, field visits, business to attract business and other forms, the region's existing 14 village scenic spots signed operators, business to attract 51 enterprises, settled 53 projects, with a total investment of 520 million yuan (People.cn, 2020). Third is the formation of the operating company. In the beginning, the operator and the village committee after the two sides reached cooperation intentions. The operator needs to submit the operating plan to the district cultural tourism bureau hired by the expert group to review and approve. After that, the village committee needs to be agreed upon by the villagers' assembly before signing the operation cooperation agreement with the operator (Meilatinova, 2021). The town government and the district cultural tourism bureau will act as witnesses to monitor the implementation of the agreement. The contracted operation time can be long or short, generally 10-30 years. After the contract, the operator and the village committee jointly set up the operating company. The village committee takes a stake in the right to use the village's collective visitor center, parking lot, cultural hall and other facilities, accounting for about 10%-20%. The operator takes a stake in the monetary capital with a registered capital of not less than 500,000 yuan, and the daily operating costs are borne by the operator. In the whole operation process, the government and village committees do not invest a penny. At last, the operator should set up a special operation team, with daily office space in the village and at least one staff member stationed in the village to carry out the work (Xinhua, 2021). If there is no substantial progress in the operation, the two sides can negotiate to cancel the agreement and the operator withdraws from the operation (Meilatinova, 2021).

Qinghe Model In Hebei Province

Third, Qinghe in Hebei province. In Qinghe, Hebei Province, e-commerce has become the most characteristic business group in Qinghe County and Qinghe has become the largest cashmere products network sales base in China. There are more than 20,000 Taobao Tmall stores in the county, with annual sales of 1.5 billion yuan, and cashmere yarn sales account for more than 70% of Taobao, making it a veritable Taobao county.

In the previous traditional industry era, the cashmere industry in Hebei Qinghe was nearly lost in the competition. After the accidental success of a villager selling cashmere on Taobao in 2007, the online business community in Qinghe County increased rapidly, and the Qinghe County government also saw the opportunity to put forward the development strategy of "online and offline interaction, tangible market and intangible market complement each other" (Fang et al., 2014). To take advantage of the situation, follow the trend, and constantly increase the guidance and support for e-commerce. In terms of infrastructure construction, the county has been stepping up efforts. At present, an e-commerce industry park, logistics industry gathering area and storage center, and a large number of e-commerce industry gathering service platforms are under construction, Qinghe is achieving the transformation from "Taobao village" to "Taobao County" to enhance (Texnet, 2020).

The government has set up an e-commerce service center to provide practitioners with skills training on Taobao introduction and online store enhancement, while actively docking with e-commerce platforms and carrying out a series of large-scale promotional activities to accumulate popularity and credibility online. To design enough styles to attract consumers, the government also set up a cashmere products research and development center to provide sufficient styles for free (Chang & Meyerhoefer, 2021). In the face of the market's cashmere products are difficult to distinguish between real and fake, the Qinghe Cashmere Quality Supervision Center came into being to protect the quality of products with national-level test results (Texnet, 2020).

With the gradual growth of e-commerce, the government's support is no longer limited to traditional training and docking with e-commerce platforms but have started to create a corresponding physical industry platform to carry out deeper incubation for enterprises. As an incubation base for e-commerce, Boundless Creator Coffee can provide one-stop services for e-commerce practitioners, including photography, graphic design and post-processing (Zheng et al., 2020). Inspired by the activities of Silicon Valley Garage Coffee Salon, the "Thursday Party" entrepreneurial sharing and experience exchange activities are organized to build a bridge for the exchange and collision of ideas. The services of "Qingyang Pioneer Space" include business and tax management, centralized office, project matching, technical practice guidance, business model coaching and financial support, providing space for business incubation. The cross-border e-commerce park focuses on the overseas market and sells Qinghe cashmere overseas with the help of the Alibaba platform. In the Qinhe case, government plays a fundamental role in e-commerce guidance, leading to a business model worth learning (Hebnews, 2014).

Tongyu Model In Jilin Province

Tongyu County, Jilin Province, is located in the western part of Songliao Plain, with flat terrain, high northwest and low southeast, and only 40 meters difference in elevation. The average altitude is 160m, and the soil is divided into seven types of soil, mainly black calcium soil, sandy soil and alkaline soil. The land in the western townships (fields) of Tongyu County is mostly lumpy, with good permeability, especially suitable for melon growth, not only high yield but also good quality, mostly yellow flesh, low sugar content, cool and palatable, a pure natural green drink (Ministry Of Commerce Of The People's Republic Of China, 2016). "The "Tongyu Model" is a direct supply model that sells Tongyu County's advantageous agricultural and sideline products with a unified brand for the whole country. This little-known county began to enter the eyes of consumers nationwide.

One, government endorsement is the key. Tongyu rural e-commerce is operated by a third-party company. The third-party operators want to quickly integrate into the local, and the government doing a good job of endorsement is the key (Dannenberg, Fuchs, Riedler, & Wiedemann, 2020). First, the local county party secretary and county governor highly agree with the direction of e-commerce and have seriously considered the many difficulties that may be encountered in landing the project (Ministry Of Commerce Of The People's Republic Of China, 2015). The county government takes rural e-commerce as a local "handful project" and provides policy support for e-commerce development. In the process of project operation, the secretary and the county governor participated in the design and planning.

Secondly, a strong collaborative body is formed. Young cadres from various departments are deployed to set up the "Tongyu County E-commerce Development Center" to coordinate and organize various resources with TP to "escort" the project to the ground. This is for the establishment of a special fund and the introduction of a series of policies to support the development of e-commerce (Hebi, 2015).

For a long time, the sales channels of Tongyu farmers have been narrow, lacking brand awareness, and have low product premium capacity. Therefore, branding is an important path to marketability. As a result, they established Tongyu agricultural products sub-packaging center for unified packaging. Establish a multi-layer quality inspection system and strengthen the construction of a product traceability system (Kamilaris, Kartakoullis, & Prenafeta-Boldu, 2017).

Tongyu model is based on the premise of "base support". Tongyu is located at 45°N latitude, in the world's most recognized "golden grain industry belt," and is famous as the "hometown of mixed grains and beans", "hometown of mung beans" and "hometown of sunflower". "Sunflower Township". Tongyu produced many single products in the mixed grains and beans and is the national "single champion." Based on this, Tongyu positioned itself as a weak alkaline granary at 45°N latitude and highly integrated the resources of its origin (Ministry Of Commerce Of The People's Republic Of China, 2016).

The partners of the "Tongyu model" include villages, towns, and some deep processing enterprises with fixed bases. Tongyu has a vast territory and each township has different characteristics, so the integration of heterogeneous products can enhance the competitiveness of the supply chain (Hoyer et al., 2020). Secondly, the company unites local cooperatives to form the "Three Thousand Harvest" cooperative association. The operator will influence the cooperatives through the cooperative association, and then the cooperatives will influence the farmers, to carry out the innovation of production methods (Li et al., 2018). Again, establish cooperation with the Academy of Agricultural Sciences. With the power of experts and research institutions, we can optimize varieties and categories, and inject scientific and technological power into the fields of seeds, planting and deep processing (Ministry Of Commerce Of The People's Republic Of China, 2015).

E-commerce plays an important role in fighting the epidemic and helping farmers with support from government. Under the influence of COVID-19, agricultural products in some areas have appeared poor due to problems in sales channels (Martinez-Dominguez & Mora-Rivera, 2020). Rural e-commerce has played an important role in solving the problem of unsold agricultural products (Kang & Eltahir, 2018). On the one hand, the e-commerce platform has opened a green channel and zone for agricultural products. Taobao launched a series of special zones for agricultural products, specially opened a "local fresh food" entrance for state-level poor counties and launched the "Foodie Help Farmer Channel". Jingdong opened the "National Fresh Products Green Channel". Pinduoduo Online "Fight against the epidemic, love and help farmers" special area (Li et al., 2018). On the other hand, the e-commerce platform explores the model of live broadcasting to help farmers (Wang, Wang, & Liu, 2016). Taobao helps agriculture-related merchants to open the Taobao live broadcast for free. Pinduoduo explores the e-commerce consumption poverty alleviation model of "city and county mayors as anchors and farmers sell more goods" (Wang & Coe, 2021). In 2020, in terms of driving farmers in poor areas to increase production and income, the network sales of 832 state-level poverty-stricken counties on Alibaba's platform reached 110.2 billion yuan, and 119 Taobao villages and 106 Taobao towns were born in 75 state-level poverty-stricken counties. The total transaction volume of Pinduoduo's agriculture-related commodities exceeded RMB270 billion (McKinsey & Company, 2021).

Comprehensive measures such as supply chain optimization have continuously improved the upward mode of agricultural products directly from the place of origin to help regional public brand building.

Meituan Preferentially launched the "Agricultural Fresh Direct Procurement" plan to accelerate the upward movement of high-quality agricultural products by increasing the intensity of direct procurement from the source to drive the development of cold chain logistics infrastructure for agricultural products and cultivate rural e-commerce leaders (Wang & Coe, 2021). The e-commerce platform has changed the consumption concept of sinking consumers through low-cost grouping and mini-program live broadcasting and lowered the threshold for attempting. Rural residents have access to the outside world through e-commerce, paying more attention to personalized, branded and diversified consumer experiences. The potential consumption from the rural market has been continuously released and the quality of consumption has been improved as well. Small-town youth with sufficient leisure time and strong purchasing power show the highest consumption potential in the sinking market. They have changed their conservative consumption concepts in the past, showing a willingness to upgrade consumption closer to urban youth (Martinez-Dominguez & Mora-Rivera, 2020).

BUSINESS MODEL WITH BIG DATA

In the data era, big data has mastered almost all the data information of enterprises and merchants, including consumer browsing records, purchase records, evaluation feedback, etc. and the transaction volume, transaction amount, inventory volume, credit evaluation, etc. of merchants on their platforms (Kamilaris et al., 2017).

The potential market size of smart agriculture in China reached 26.761 billion yuan in 2020. The combination of agriculture and big data refers to the application of the summary and analysis of big data to the agricultural industry, which has a guiding effect on all levels of the agricultural industry not only from production to sales but also from service to management (Kamilaris et al., 2017)

After these data resources are built and stored, with in-depth mining and analysis, they can guide enterprises and merchants to make business decisions. Big data brings new development opportunities for e-commerce, mainly in the following aspects. The first is information retrieval services. Second, high-quality information summary. Third, personalized and accurate product recommendations. Fourth, differentiated competition and detailed service areas. Fifth, optimize the allocation of resources (Loebbecke & Picot, 2015).

On one hand, big data, as a tool for enterprises to grasp market orientation, needs to be used to complete the analysis and processing of data with the help of agricultural quality traceability system (Klerkx et al., 2019). Due to the frequent food safety problems, food safety and quality traceability will remain at the forefront of the most important concerns of Chinese consumers, enterprises, and the state for some time to come.

The first step to ensure the quality and safety of food is to strengthen the supervision of "farm to table". With the addition of big data technology, a series of processes from "farm to table" is presented to consumers, allowing them to make a correct judgment on the safety performance of the selected food, and greatly deepening their understanding of the information of the selected pollution-free food. Based on the quality traceability system of agricultural products, the brand construction of special agricultural products shows the whole production process of these agricultural products with big data technology and gives them exclusive QR code ID cards to realize traceability of source, traceability of process, traceability of information and recall of products (Li et al., 2018). The traceability system will provide data-based product services from all aspects of pre-production, production and post-production, mak-

Table 3. Typical types of Smart Agriculture

Type	Technology	Result
Kaisheng Hofeng, rural revitalization solution provider	● Smart Glass Greenhouse: The company has built six smart glass greenhouse bases with a total area of over 2,000 mu. ● Agricultural Brain: The company empowers the upstream and serves the downstream through the R&D and promotion application of "digital technology + agricultural technology + operation process". In the seeds, agricultural materials, processing, logistics, sales and other aspects of the whole agricultural industry chain to solidify the traditional experience to form knowledge, knowledge written into operational procedures to guide modern agricultural production.	Dozens of varieties to achieve a balanced supply of annual, won the two international fast-food giants (KFC and McDonald's) in the domestic upstream raw material market of 60% of the market share, is the United States Yum Brands, General Mills, South Korea, New World and several other Fortune 500 companies in China business partners, products exported to Japan, South Korea and more than 20 countries and regions.
Huangjing Industrial Park, Walnut& pepper planting and breeding	Agricultural IOT perception layer, network transmission layer and application service layer. The main technologies are agricultural information collection technology, agricultural information transmission technology, agricultural information storage technology, agricultural information processing and agricultural information release and remote-control technology.	Through the reference of intelligent agricultural technology, a demonstration led to the development of Huangjing planting area of more than 10,000 mu, driving more than 500 farmers to plant yellow essence under the forest, and the average annual income of farmers increased by more than 20,000 yuan.
Guangdong Province 5G + AI intelligent pig farming	● Pig barn monitoring cameras and environmental sensors transmit video data of the pig barn environment to the management platform in real-time through a 5G network. ● Managers can remotely grasp the environmental indicators of pig farms, reducing human-pig contact and blocking the spread of epidemic diseases. The pig barn track inspection robot collects pig image information and performs AI video image analysis to intelligently measure pig weight and backfat data, providing a decision basis for pig reproduction optimization and precise feeding.	The accuracy rate of intelligent weight and fat measurement has now reached 97%. The new program has reduced feeding labor costs.
5G+AI unmanned agricultural machinery intelligent operation	● The 5G agricultural machinery unmanned operation system is deployed on top of the 5G cloud network fusion platform and docked with intelligent agricultural machinery equipment to realize the whole process of unmanned operation of agricultural machinery from the hangar and the farming road to the operation plot, covering all production aspects of rice cultivation tillage, planting, management and harvesting. ● In the hangar and road, location map modelling is firstly carried out, and application equipment based on RTK differential GNSS positioning technology, IMU data and UWB precision positioning technology is deployed to achieve centimeter-level positioning accuracy indoors and outdoors. ● It combines the core control system deployed in the edge cloud and the vision and radar terminals installed on the agricultural machines to intelligently sense the surrounding environment. ● AI deep learning algorithm is used to complete sign line recognition and obstacle detection when the farm machine is moving forward and reversing, to realize unmanned driving, parking, obstacle recognition and automatic obstacle avoidance of farm machines.	This technology has reduced the average labor cost of 1 person/ operation per farm machine and realized cost reduction and efficiency increase. By operating unmanned at night, the operation time of farm machinery is extended by one time on average.

ing QR code the only "identity authentication" in market circulation to build a protection mechanism and prevent counterfeit agricultural products from being mixed with pearls. Also, it helps improve the

Table 4. Typical types of Green Agriculture

Location	Type	Practice	Result
Fuyang City, Anhui Province	Rice industry	● Production chain: The construction of rice crop technology system. The development of technical specifications. The selection of the whole industry chain standardization base. ● Processing and circulation: Promotion of the front crushing operation of combine harvesters to reduce damage harvesting technology, brown rice micro slit enzyme inhibition and aroma enhancement, precise and flexible stratified milling technology, and rice "low-temperature storage" technology. ● Industrial chain: They have created a national modern agricultural industrial park with rice as the leading industry, and built a green production base with "underground pipeline + intelligent fertilizer distribution + precise irrigation" for the integration of water and fertilizer (methane) in paddy fields and developed new high-value products such as rice milk beverage and high protein powder of crushed rice.	In 2020, the industrial park will achieve a total output value of 5.2 billion yuan, with a three-industry structure ratio of 16.8:50.7:32.5.
Tongxiang City, Jiaxing City, Zhejiang Province	Pollution treatment	● Traceability: the city's 280 agricultural subjects to achieve subject traceability and process traceability, 189 fertilizer and medicine two system reform pilot subjects for red, yellow and green code dynamic management, strengthen the digital control of fertilizer and medicine. ● Reuse cycle: improve the "cooperative + enterprise" market-oriented collection, storage and transportation system. Use two-step fiber technology to produce organic fertilizer from raw materials such as vegetable tailings, waste fruit tree branches and livestock manure. ● End protection: Construction of nitrogen and phosphorus ecological interception ditch system and paddy field water retreat "zero direct discharge" project, and promotion of farmland water retreat management in the whole area. The city has set up 121 regular monitoring points of arable land quality and 6 long-term positioning monitoring points to enhance the environmental monitoring and early warning capability.	In 2020, it will reduce the unreasonable application of chemical fertilizers by 1267 tons and pesticides by 76.8 tons. The comprehensive utilization rate of straw reaches 97.19%. The total area of farmland to be treated is 12,000 mu, and the total nitrogen and total phosphorus will drop by more than 10% and 30% respectively.
Chongming District, Shanghai	Vegetable aquaculture, the meat industry	Develop a list of negative behaviors. Clear backward production capacity and non-standard production and operation behavior. Implement fine land management. Establish GIS agricultural geographic information supervision system to guide the land from "standardized and orderly" to "scale and efficiency" change. Gradually promote "two no" production from rice to vegetables, forestry and other areas of expansion, to encourage the exploration of "rice fish" "rice shrimp and turtle" and other three-dimensional breeding models. The implementation of rice straw mechanized return and off-field use, the realization of agricultural waste collection and transportation, and intelligent composting, near the use. Promote "machine for human", build a full mechanization base for vegetable cultivation, seeding and harvesting and a digital agriculture base for Cuiguan pear.	For two consecutive years in 2019-2020, the agricultural green development index was ranked among the top in the country, and the agricultural green development was at the leading level in the country.
Weichang Manchu-Mongol Autonomous County, Chengde City, Hebei Province	Pollution treatment	Every year, 11.7 tons of water-soluble fertilizer and 17,000 tons of organic fertilizer are distributed free of charge. The company has been vigorously promoting dry farming technologies such as standard film, degradable film and semi-full film mulching, and has established 19 old film recycling points and 2 used film processing plants. It implemented three major projects: "pilot full quantification of straw utilization", "straw baling direct-fired high-efficiency boiler" and "biomass cooking and heating stove installation".	The green prevention and control coverage rate reached more than 70%, the recycling rate of agricultural film reached more than 85%, and the comprehensive utilization rate of straw reached 100%.
Baofeng County, Pingdingshan City, Henan Province	Pollution treatment	The demonstration project of green development of rice production was completed in 5686 mu, and the demonstration area of green rice production, rice and oil crop rotation and rice and loach crop reached 10,500 mu throughout the year. Set up 329 monitoring points for pests and diseases, soil, meteorology, etc. Strictly carry out daily inspections of production bases, a total of 123 inspections of production entities. Promote solar-powered insecticidal lamps, sticky boards and other green prevention and control technologies.	The rate of large-scale livestock and poultry farms equipped with manure treatment facilities reached 100%. The quality of agricultural products met the standard rate of 100%.
Xinning County, Shaoyang City, Hunan Province	Navel Orange industry	● Monitoring and early warning: Establish and perfect the navel orange pest occurrence dynamic prediction observation and monitoring points. Establish a large real fly adult plumage monitoring point, and 3 woodlice monitoring points. ● Physical and chemical insect control: Apply plant-derived and microbial-derived preparations such as neem to control navel orange pests and diseases. Using the principle of color bias of navel orange pests, the use of lure yellow boards to control aphids, woodlice, whiteflies and other pests. ● Scientific use of pesticides: apply low toxicity and low residue pesticides, give preference to pesticides of biological origin, prohibit the application of highly toxic and high residue pesticides, and strictly apply pesticide filing system.	Demonstration and promotion of the application of the main pest control efficiency of navel oranges in the area from 80% to more than 90%, high-quality fruit rate from 75% to more than 85%, the average mu yield increase of more than 300 kg, the average mu increased income of more than 1,000 yuan.
Zhucheng City, Weifang City, Shandong Province	Pollution treatment	It focused on the treatment of livestock and poultry manure produced by large-scale farms, the construction of straw and manure mixed fermentation equipment in large-scale farms to produce organic fertilizer, and the development of a breeding cycle. Build small biogas projects in professional farming households, install anaerobic fermentation devices, and produce biogas fertilizer for surrounding farmland. Produce organic fertilizer through fermentation and produce organic fertilizer. Government timely deploys resources by building a livestock manure collection, storage and transportation information collection platform and arable land soil testing and formula fertilization platform.	The city's livestock and poultry manure resource utilization rate reached 93%, and straw comprehensive utilization rate of 96%. 630 large-scale field manure treatment facilities with a rate of 100%.
Taihe County, Ji'an City, Jiangxi Province	Meat industry	It built a traceability platform for agricultural product quality and safety and incorporated 100% of green food, organic agricultural products, geographical indication agricultural products production entities and new agricultural business entities into traceability management. Using big data, cloud computing, mobile Internet, the establishment of brand counters and special stores, etc., open up direct market access to green brand agricultural products.	In 2021, farmers in the county will increase their income by 1,215 yuan per capita from the operation of green brand agricultural products.
Wanrong County, Yuncheng City, Shanxi Province	Fruit industry	It Implemented the project of reflective film de-aluminumization technology application for apples and built 20,000 mu of organic fertilizer instead of a chemical fertilizer pilot demonstration base. Cooperate with Alibaba to develop "digital countryside", build a modern agricultural big data processing system, and build 6 smart orchards, 6 pest and disease early warning monitoring stations, 6 soil moisture monitoring stations, and 3 agricultural Internet of Things points.	In 2020, the county's soil testing and fertilization technology coverage rate of 95% or more.
Baofeng County, Pingdingshan City, Henan Province	Pollution treatment	Clearly define the directory of restricted and prohibited agricultural industries in the region. The first "100 mu and 1,000 head ecological party" is a combined cycle development model, with 100-200 mu of arable land as a unit, supporting the construction of a fertilization production line covering an area of 2-3 mu (including manure and water fermentation ponds and other facilities) to produce 1,000 pigs at a time, and a total of 2,000 pigs per year after two crops. The farming manure will be fermented and used on farmland after treatment. 22 monitoring points are set up for long-term monitoring of manure quality and soil physical and chemical indicators.	The planting cycle covered an area of nearly 200,000 mu, organic fertilizer application amounted to more than 15% per mu, and chemical fertilizer use was reduced by more than 10% per mu.

added value of agricultural products and enhances the competitiveness of agricultural products (Tian,

Vakharia, Tan, & Xu, 2018).

On the other hand, through the analysis of big data, the government can obtain information on consumers' needs for product selection in terms of quantity, quality requirements, choice of transportation methods, customer satisfaction and so on. After that, decisions can be made on which agricultural subjects or innovation plans are worthwhile investments. Through these data, the government can promptly help enterprises and other subjects adjust their business ideas and business direction, so does the planting and quality control of products to avoid market risks and find a more suitable development path for them. A one-stop anti-counterfeiting and quality control traceability system gives a unique two-dimensional code to a single product as an anti-counterfeiting ID card through professional machinery and equipment, realizing "one thing, one code" (Wang & Coe, 2021). It helps collect data and track the production, storage, distribution, logistics and transportation. For the government, information collection can be promoted and more precise analysis can be made. For enterprises, in market inspection, sales terminal and other aspects of the product, code traces the product through one thing, one code technology. Once the product has quality problems, it can be recalled quickly and precisely to reduce the loss of the enterprise (Nie et al., 2021).

How to improve the quality and efficiency of Chinese agricultural products? Brand is an important grip for agriculture to obtain market value and is the driving force and beacon of quality and efficiency. The key is how to make the brand agricultural products sell at good prices because the problem of high quality but high prices is prominent. Therefore, it is not possible to adopt a policy of low prices for agricultural products. As agriculture is an industry that combines natural reproduction and economic reproduction, the price of agricultural products is highly cyclical and seasonal. Overall, June each year is the period of growth of the National Agricultural Products Wholesale Price Index 200 in the coming February, and February to June each year is the period of decline of the National Agricultural Products Wholesale Price Index 200.

In 2021, the national wholesale price index of agricultural products is 122.12, compared with 122.19 in 2020, a decrease of 0.07; compared with 114.23 in 2019, an increase of 7.89. In the long term, the price of agricultural products in China maintains a trend of fluctuating growth (Figure 10).

Under the conditions of the market economy, the effective approach that the government of urban low-income groups needs to cope with is social security, not the social security responsibility of urban low-income groups and the national responsibility of food security at the expense of farmers' interests. A watermelon in China is less than twenty yuan apiece, in Japan three or four hundred yuan apiece, and the difference between the per capita income of Japanese farmers and other citizens is not large, while the income gap between urban and rural areas in China is too large.

Take Guizhou province as an example. In recent years, under the strong leadership and multiple initiatives promoted by the Guizhou Provincial Party Committee and the provincial government, Guizhou Province has experienced rapid development in vegetables, poultry, cattle and sheep and other special agricultural industries. The vegetable industry with organized, large-scale and standardized production is taking initial shape especially. However, there is a lack of production, display, sales and data analysis platforms for vegetables and other agricultural products. The statistics on the production of vegetables and other agricultural industries in Guizhou province can only be counted in a point-to-point manner without a scheduling platform, which was inefficient (Kamble, Gunasekaran, & Gawankar, 2020). Therefore, the vegetable group in Guizhou province has developed and built a big data platform for agricultural products in Guizhou, developed agricultural products wholesale stalls outside the province and built information interoperability sharing with agricultural products wholesale markets outside the

Figure 10. Monthly changes in the National Agricultural Wholesale Price 200 Index
Data source: moa.gov.cn

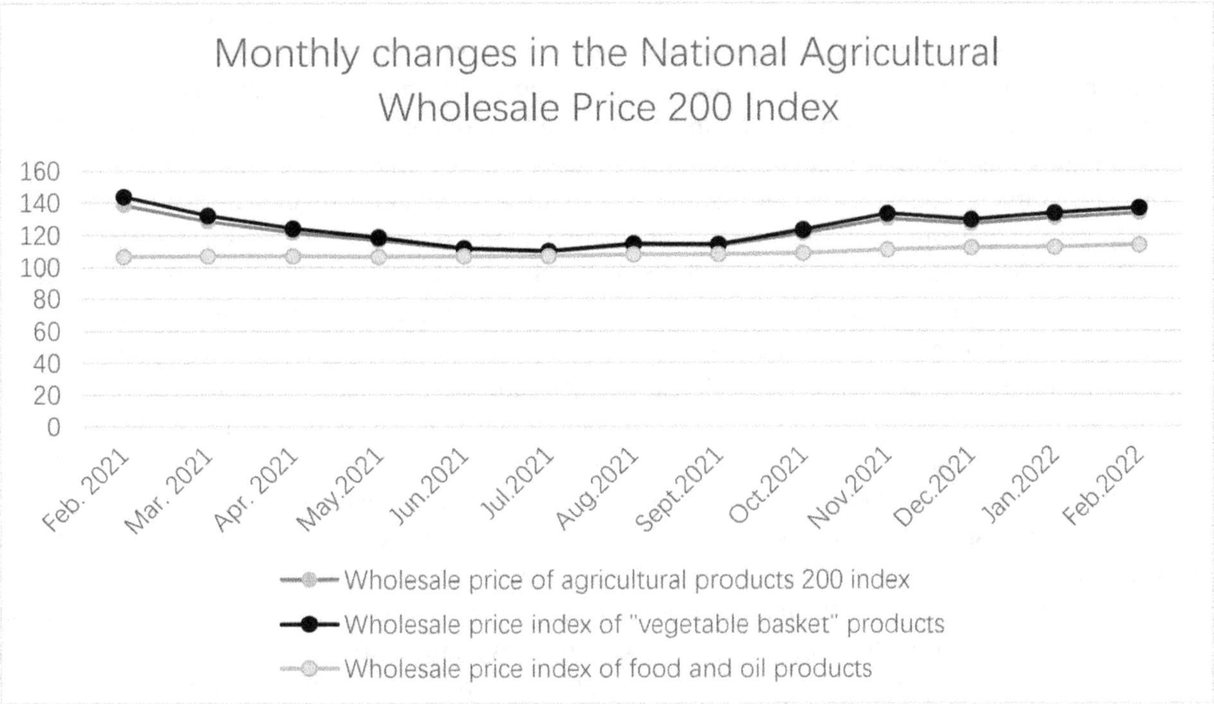

province. To guide the production of agricultural products in Guizhou and promote the export of Qian products to the mountains.

To bring Guizhou goods out of the mountains, the first thing to open up should be the time information channel. They think by grasping the market demand information all the time they can know what should be developed. However, among the 12 special agricultural products industries built in Guizhou, people are highly motivated to plant vegetables, with mature technology and wide coverage, which is a short and fast industry and has a very positive significance to help fight poverty and promote rural revitalization. They built up the information channel of vegetable supply and demand first and improved the construction of the channel of agricultural products out of the mountains in the province later.

It is understood that in 2020, the vegetable planting area in Guizhou Province reached 15 million mu, with an output of 28 million tons and an output value of 75 billion yuan (Ministry Of Commerce Of The People's Republic Of China, 2020). To turn Guizhou province into an important summer & autumn vegetable production base in the south, the Guizhou Vegetable Group has made every effort to promote the construction of the "Guizhou Agricultural Products Big Data Platform". This platform helps small and medium-sized enterprises to scientifically select planting varieties and connect information at both production and marketing ends (Li, 2022). At the same time, it helps them to efficiently and practically store and transport, reduce the vacancy rate of cold storage and logistics and transportation costs, and solve the financing problems of the agricultural industry chain. Moreover, it helps agricultural products circulation enterprises discover market opportunities, so that people and enterprises can see the development status of Guizhou's agricultural industry in one network (Li et al., 2018).

In the past, people and agricultural product producers in Guizhou were not very clear about what varieties to plant, who to sell to and where the market was, and they could only gamble on luck every year. After they set up the big data platform for agricultural products in Guizhou, they can know the production situation in Guizhou province, the demand situation of major markets in other provinces, and the price of products, to realize the production with purpose, difference and target (Tian et al., 2018). The platform collects Guizhou base planting information, cold storage information, cold chain logistics information, agricultural products trading information inside and outside Guizhou province, and national agricultural products price information in various ways to build Guizhou agricultural products base information network, cold chain logistics network and market trading network in multiple dimensions. Because of the platform, SMEs in Guizhou break through the production and marketing barriers, and build an agricultural products circulation ecosystem, forming a complete industrial supply chain (Wagner, Schramm-Klein, & Steinmann, 2020). At the same time, it collects market data, weather data and national production area data. Through analysis and judgment of the data, it issues early warnings for single products that may lag in sales and provides the basis for agricultural supply-side structure adjustment. Based on national price quotation data, it discovers opportunities for seasonal concentrated listing and bulk supply of bulk agricultural products in Guizhou, guiding business enterprises to expand the market of main sales area with high prices and large space with the provision of Guizhou agricultural products sales Market direction (Wang et al., 2016).

In different stages, rural SMEs in the agricultural sector experienced stepping up the digital context in transformation. To climb to a higher stage, the Chinese government should take part as resources can only be provided by the government, which is different from developed countries, leading by the market.

MARKETING MODELS

(1) Agricultural SMEs In Live Broadcast E-commerce

Since 2016 was called the "Chinese first year of live e-commerce", live broadcast e-commerce began to show a spurt of high-speed start, to 2019 has been called the golden age of live broadcast e-commerce, becoming a high-speed traffic train of e-commerce giants to guide user consumption, began to replace mobile e-commerce as the new windfall of online retail (Meilatinova, 2021). Avery agency statistics show that the market share of the domestic mobile live industry in 2016 was 12 billion yuan. And in 2018, according to media data, the domestic head e-commerce live streaming platform brought in more than 100 billion yuan, with a year-on-year growth rate of nearly 400% (Ministry Of Commerce Of The People's Republic Of China, 2020).

The accelerated development of the new model of live broadcast e-commerce has helped small and medium-sized enterprises. Foreign trade foundries and farmers achieve seamless docking of "production, sales and consumption", reduction in "information asymmetry" and compress the cost of intermediate channels, attracting more consumers to buy and further stimulating consumption potential (Wang et al., 2016). Live broadcast embodies a commercial innovation that provides consumers with a more realistic shopping experience by optimizing the display of online products and increasing the interaction of online consumption. Relying on platform traffic and the influence of KOL, fans accumulated on social platforms can be transformed into product consumers. Their random needs are transformed into real purchasing power (Kang & Eltahir, 2018). For consumers, anchors strictly screen trial products, which

Figure 11. Stages of Smart Agriculture
Data source: moa.gov.cn

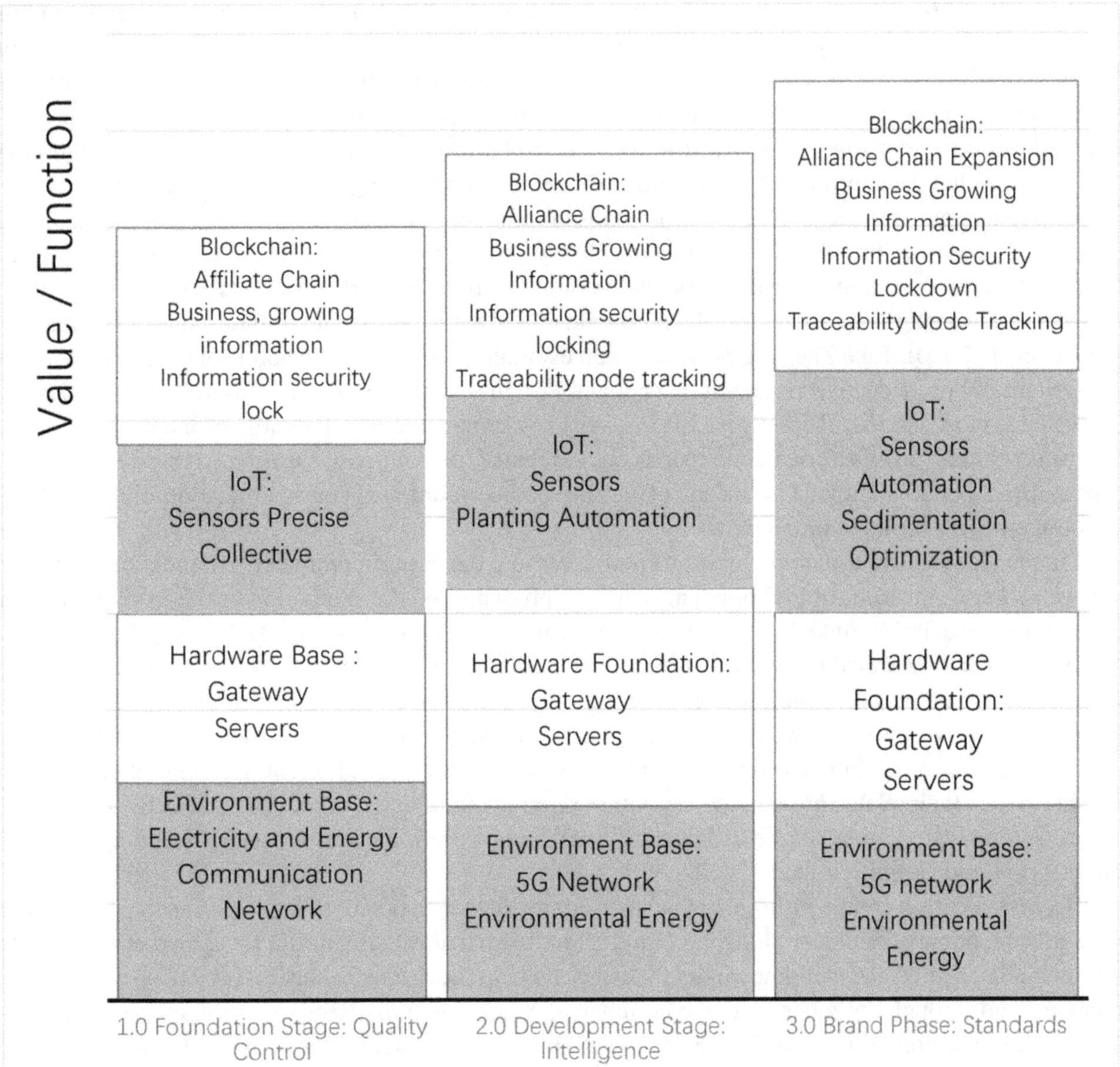

greatly reduces the cost of consumers' selection decisions. For the platform, the traditional e-commerce platform has greatly improved the user stickiness and use time because of the certain content attributes of the live broadcast injectors. The short video content platform accelerates the commercialization process because of live-streaming with goods, further enhancing the value of platform traffic. For brand owners, it is the start of transformation from traditional ones (Li et al., 2018).

2020 epidemic dealt a serious blow to the agricultural market and farmers. Affected by the environment, falling demand and other factors, a large number of vegetables and fruits lagged. Under the big wind of live-streaming with goods, many farmers began to try to use webcasting, short video and other forms to promote the sale of agricultural products to carry the banner of saving agricultural products (Fang et al., 2014).

Agricultural products e-commerce live broadcasts can be distributed on the cloud, a detonation of multiple live platforms, prying the public domain and private domain traffic pool, and multi-channel traffic acquisition. The use of live marketing interaction to accelerate the conversion of cash and improve user retention. Diversion channels limited to a single platform will be limited by the platform properties and recommendation mechanism. However, multi-platform exposure can promote multi-promotion activities, so that the exposure of the activities shows an exponential growth (Tian et al., 2018).

In recent years, more and more large agricultural products e-commerce live broadcast through live cloud distribution to broaden their marketing channels, covering news portals, vertical portals, local media, etc. Local agricultural products break the limit to a broader market, so that more and more high-quality agricultural products fly over the mountains, over the rivers, flying to thousands of households (Hoyer et al., 2020). Take Zhejiang province as an example. One of the core points of quality promotion of agricultural products live broadcast in Zhejiang Province is how to motivate users to form a fission. Nowadays, most successful cases give the answer as "e-commerce live + bundle of interests," through realistic rewards, such as price concessions, cash rebates, or points that can be exchanged for cash. These direct benefits output as a means of incentive, thus promoting the optimization of agricultural e-commerce live business promotion.

First is the effective use of the local promotion season, the "live e-commerce + bundle of interests". As we all know, the sales of traditional agricultural products and the promotion of the local promotion season are inextricably linked, which is a typical companion consumption (Dannenberg et al., 2020). Generally speaking, based on the daily promotion season, it can give full play to the utility value of "e-commerce live broadcast + interest bundle", form a comprehensive marketing promotion of agricultural products, and give you do not play its e-commerce live marketing advantages (Hsiang et al., 2017). Thus, operators can also combine the seasonal and seasonal differences of different agricultural products to further launch their related promotional activities, through affordable promotions, to effectively promote their "e-commerce live + bundle of interests" marketing system and the formation of an agricultural marketing trend (Kamilaris et al., 2017).

Second, focus on creating a brand image to promote the development of live e-commerce marketing. In market economy conditions, a strong brand effect is particularly important for a market to promote optimization, a good and well-known brand image can help the market to successfully open a side of the market. And through the mode of live e-commerce, Yuk enough to effectively promote the establishment and promotion of its brand image (Zheng et al., 2020). The agricultural market focus on the need to build its national brand image, based on the application of the live mode of e-commerce, fully expand the promotion, and effectively promote the development of its agricultural market of live marketing of e-commerce (Wang et al., 2016).

Third, the establishment of the "front store after the factory" model, to further play the advantages of live marketing of Zhejiang Province's electric business. Zhejiang Province currently has the location advantage of agricultural products planting and agricultural products production, and can fully establish the "front store and back factory" model, to further play the live marketing advantages of Zhejiang Province's e-commerce. The agricultural market should learn from the successful experience of other industries in Zhejiang Province, through the establishment of institutions in some regions, and take advantage of the trade window to take orders from many parties. They engage in the development of new products catering to the habits of foreign consumers and advanced technology, carrying out in-depth marketing of products and live e-commerce sales (Fu, Yang, & Han, 2021).

The marketing value of e-commerce is continuously improved under the joint promotion of users, platform attributes, data accumulation and technological development: 1) User side: online consumption habits are strengthened, consumer purchases are increased, and the marketing value of platform users is worth constantly being tapped; 2) E-commerce end: The e-commerce platform integrates media and consumption attributes. The content-based marketing model is constantly innovated to achieve the integration of product and effect for advertisers. 3) Technical end: Marketing-related data and technology continue to upgrade, laying a solid foundation for efficient service and precision marketing (Meilatinova, 2021).

The e-commerce marketing industry chain operates efficiently under the in-depth cooperation of advertiser agencies, marketing service providers, delivery platforms, e-commerce platforms and various media platforms (Zheng et al., 2020). Among them, e-commerce platforms play a central role in the operation process of the industrial chain. From the perspective of the horizontal industrial chain, e-commerce platforms have gradually begun to build or cooperate with external delivery platforms to invest in or deepen cooperation with marketing service providers. From the vertical perspective of the industrial chain, the resource synergy of e-commerce platforms and other media platforms has become deeper and broader, increasing the off-site traffic reach for brand owners and merchants (Wang & Coe, 2021). In e-commerce marketing, the modes of search advertising, display advertising, information flow advertising, live advertising and shopping guide marketing have helped brand owners and merchants achieve an increase in product exposure and sales in the form and diversified play of the e-commerce platform attributes and consumer consumption behavior trajectories, driving the rapid growth of the e-commerce marketing market with a compound annual growth rate of 41.9% in the past 5 years, and reaching a scale of 222.95 billion yuan in 2019 (Zhang et al, 2019).

(2) Agricultural SMEs In Community Model

What is a community in e-commerce? Community is not only a gathering of people but more importantly, there should be interaction and communication between people. Ordinary merchants sell products and have a group of loyal consumers. Merchants and consumers do not interact and are independent of each other. Consignment stores are different - consumers can not only come to consume, but also bring their own items for sale at any time and become the selling party (Nie et al., 2021). The store and the consumer need to intermingle and interact on common emotions, trust, products and benefits, at which point they become a community of interconnectedness. The community can experience a sense of participation because the members share the same values, mission and vision, so each member can experience a sense of participation.

Pioneering models have been born in the community operation of agricultural products: community farms, agricultural crowdfunding and so on (Kang & Eltahir, 2018). The operation model of community farms is similar to shared farms, where farmers produce healthy and high-quality food to the satisfaction of consumers, while consumers as "shareholders" can personally participate in the management and operation of the farm. Consumers also share the risks of production and farming, such as natural disasters for the farmers while enjoying the high-quality results achieving a win-win production and marketing (Tian et al., 2018). In this process, urban community residents can go to the farm to experience farming and the farm can also release production daily, distribution daily and summary to community residents through the modern mobile Internet platform, so that the production and operation of the farm can be planned promptly and activities can be carried out in an orderly manner according to the plan. As a result, community members can be quickly and accurately informed of the latest developments in farming and production.

Crowdfunding of agricultural products consists of consumers' crowdfunding money and farmers' decisions of producing according to orders (Fang et al., 2014). Then the agricultural products are delivered directly to consumers when the crops are ripe, which is a "field to tongue" model that is developing rapidly.

Some successful communities in China have also provided operational ideas for later companies. In the case of some edible oil companies, for example, the company's operations are divided into online and offline operations. Online, the company has opened a business school, private chef, oil tea recipes and other interactive sections around the community, which satisfies consumers while sharing information and precipitates consumption data, providing the basis for accurate product service. In terms of offline operation, it is mainly through the organization of some activities to strengthen the communication between community members (Martinez-Dominguez & Mora-Rivera, 2020). In addition to regularly organizing tea reading activities, food tasting, etc., but also organizing community members and local farmers to form a community of destiny, jointly responsible for planting and production links. Based on "emotion, trust, product and benefit" as the core of community marketing, may play a greater role in solving problems in the sales and enhancing the added value of agricultural products.

Take UNITAS Mellow Peanut Oil as an example, an SME in Henan province. After the preliminary market research, the company has developed a "UNITAS Mellow Peanut Oil 'Kitchen God Mom' Cooking Skills Sharing Contest" for mothers to show their talents. Let mothers have a platform to show their skills, and also make mothers more willing to participate and come forward, through such a show cooking competition (Li, 2022). After the creation of their own exclusive community, spreading through the community, the target is more accurate with a wider spread. Through the official WeChat account and micro-blog to release the news of the activity, the spread of fission can form a hot topic in the Puyang area in a short time, the birthplace of the company, with the participation of many self-media. As a result, the activity has heat and excitement and consumers are more willing to spread and share (Meilatinova, 2021). According to the activity of the participants, to create the exclusive community of UNITA mellow peanut oil, accurate dissemination. No matter what news, information and preferential activities, the community of consumers are loyal customers who are willing and happy to spread, expanding the dissemination of information and achieving accurate dissemination. Such means of publicity and publicity methods show the advantages of traditional channels do not have (Cheng, Lu, & Tsen, 2021).

In the future, the trend of Chinese e-commerce marketing will develop in the three directions of intelligence, globalization and content (Li, 2022). Intelligent: Pre-investment, mid-sale and post-marketing links are gradually intelligent to solve pain points for brand owners and merchants. Globalization: E-commerce platforms realize data integration and consumer global reach through advertising alliances, accelerating "planting grass" and "pulling grass". Contentlization: The e-commerce platform's self-built content ecology is soft enough to reach consumers and enhance the stickiness of the platform.

CONCLUSION

China's rural agriculture sector has enjoyed above-average growth in the last few years. Some sectors experienced transformation such as the fresh food e-commerce market to meet the demands and habits of the society. For rural e-commerce, regional advantages should be seized to find a suitable business model. On the other, some sectors chase new ways of selling to break through and have formed a typical business model from production to sales in the whole industrial chain. Chinese agriculture has reached a new stage towards smart agriculture and green agriculture with the usage of big data and other techniques. Compared with international cases, differences in developing new forms of agriculture can be found between China and other developed countries. In the business model, Chinese agriculture gain energy with the help of live broadcast e-commerce and the Community Model under the conditional of COVID-19. Future studies can continue to collect the data to fill in the developing methods in China.

ACKNOWLEDGMENT

The authors extend sincere gratitude to:

- Our colleagues from Soochow University, the Australian Studies Centre of Shanghai University and Krirk University as well as the independent research colleagues who provided insight and expertise that greatly assisted the research, although they may not agree with all of the interpretations/conclusions of this chapter.
- China Knowledge for supporting our research.
- The Editor and the International Editorial Advisory Board (IEAB) of this book who initially desk reviewed, arranged a rigorous double/triple blind review process and conducted a thorough, minute and critical final review before accepting the chapter for publication.

All anonymous reviewers who provided very constructive feedbacks for thorough revision, improvement, extension, and fine tuning of the chapter.

REFERENCES

Chang, H. H., & Meyerhoefer, C. D. (2021). COVID-19 and the Demand for Online Food Shopping Services: Empirical Evidence from TaiwanJEL Codes. *American Journal of Agricultural Economics, 103*(2), 448–465. doi:10.1111/ajae.12170

Cheng, C. Y., Lu, M. Y., & Tsen, H. P. (2021). Predicting Online Consumer Transaction from Big Data: Influential Factors and Strategic Planning. *Wireless Communications and Mobile Computing, 2021*, 1–9. Advance online publication. doi:10.1155/2021/8834713

Dannenberg, P., Fuchs, M., Riedler, T., & Wiedemann, C. (2020). Digital Transition by COVID-19 Pandemic? The German Food Online Retail. *Tijdschrift voor Economische en Sociale Geografie, 111*(3), 543–560. doi:10.1111/tesg.12453 PMID:32836487

Elijah, O., Rahman, T. A., Orikumhi, I., Leow, C. Y., & Hindia, M. N. (2018). An Overview of Internet of Things (IoT) and Data Analytics in Agriculture: Benefits and Challenges. *IEEE Internet of Things Journal, 5*(5), 3758–3773. doi:10.1109/JIOT.2018.2844296

Fang, Y. L., Qureshi, I., Sun, H. S., McCole, P., Ramsey, E., & Lim, K. H. (2014). Trust, satisfaction, and online repurchase intention: The moderating role of perceived effectiveness of e-commerce institutional mechanisms. *MIS Quarterly, 38*(2), 407. doi:10.25300/MISQ/2014/38.2.04

FAO. (2022). *FAO Cereal Supply and Demand Profile*. Retrieved from https://www.fao.org/worldfood-situation/csdb/zh/

Fu, Y., Yang, M., & Han, D. (2021). Interactive Marketing E-Commerce Recommendation System Driven by Big Data Technology. *Scientific Programming*, *2021*, 1–11. Advance online publication. doi:10.1155/2021/3873059

Hebi. (2015). *China's eight counties e-commerce model interpretation and inspiration two "Tongyu model"*. Retrieved from https://www.hebi.gov.cn/swj/741665/741688/1234529/index.html

Hebnews. (2014). *The "Qinghe model" has become one of the three typical Chinese e-commerce cluster development*. Retrieved from http://hebei.hebnews.cn/2014-10/22/content_4259183.htm

Hoyer, W. D., Kroschke, M., Schmitt, B., Kraume, K., & Shankar, V. (2020). Transforming the Customer Experience Through New Technologies. *Journal of Interactive Marketing*, *51*, 57–71. doi:10.1016/j.intmar.2020.04.001

Hsiang, S., Kopp, R., Jina, A., Rising, J., Delgado, M., Mohan, S., Rasmussen, D. J., Muir-Wood, R., Wilson, P., Oppenheimer, M., Larsen, K., & Houser, T. (2017). Estimating economic damage from climate change in the United States. *Science*, *356*(6345), 1362–1368. doi:10.1126cience.aal4369 PMID:28663496

Kamble, S. S., Gunasekaran, A., & Gawankar, S. A. (2020). Achieving sustainable performance in a data-driven agriculture supply chain: A review for research and applications. *International Journal of Production Economics*, *219*, 179–194. doi:10.1016/j.ijpe.2019.05.022

Kamilaris, A., Kartakoullis, A., & Prenafeta-Boldu, F. X. (2017). A review on the practice of big data analysis in agriculture. *Computers and Electronics in Agriculture*, *143*, 23–37. doi:10.1016/j.compag.2017.09.037

Kang, S., & Eltahir, E. A. B. (2018). North China Plain threatened by deadly heatwaves due to climate change and irrigation. *Nature Communications*, *9*(1), 2894. Advance online publication. doi:10.103841467-018-05252-y PMID:30065269

Klerkx, L., Jakku, E., & Labarthe, P. (2019). A review of social science on digital agriculture, smart farming and agriculture 4.0: New contributions and a future research agenda. *NJAS Wageningen Journal of Life Sciences*, *90-91*(1), 100315. doi:10.1016/j.njas.2019.100315

Li, K. (2022). SWOT analysis of e-commerce development of rural tourism farmers' professional cooperatives in the era of big data. *IET Communications*, *16*(5), 592–603. doi:10.1049/cmu2.12358

Li, L., Su, F., Zhang, W., & Mao, J. Y. (2018). Digital transformation by SME entrepreneurs: A capability perspective. *Information Systems Journal*, *28*(6), 1129–1157. doi:10.1111/isj.12153

Loebbecke, C., & Picot, A. (2015). Reflections on societal and business model transformation arising from digitization and big data analytics: A research agenda. *The Journal of Strategic Information Systems*, *24*(3), 149–157. doi:10.1016/j.jsis.2015.08.002

Martinez-Dominguez, M., & Mora-Rivera, J. (2020). Internet adoption and usage patterns in rural Mexico. *Technology in Society*, *60*, 101226. Advance online publication. doi:10.1016/j.techsoc.2019.101226

McKinsey & Company. (2021). *Why retail outperformers are pulling ahead.* Retrieved from https://www.mckinsey.com/industries/retail/our-insights/why-retail-outperformers-are-pulling-ahead

Meilatinova, N. (2021). Social commerce: Factors affecting customer repurchase and word-of-mouth intentions. *International Journal of Information Management, 57*, 102300. doi:10.1016/j.ijinfomgt.2020.102300

Ministry Of Commerce Of The People's Republic Of China. (2015). *Jilin Province on the promotion of e-commerce into rural areas in 2015 comprehensive demonstration project construction notice*. Retrieved from http://scjss.mofcom.gov.cn/article/jyjl/jyqc/201509/20150901117478.shtml

Ministry Of Commerce Of The People's Republic Of China. (2016). *The inspiration of "Tongyu model" to the development of e-commerce of agricultural products in China.* Retrieved from http://zys.mofcom.gov.cn/article/d/201605/20160501315059.shtml

Ministry Of Commerce Of The People's Republic Of China. (2017). *What changes are brought by "Internet+"*. Retrieved from http://trb.mofcom.gov.cn/article/zuixindt/201701/20170102495621.shtml

Ministry Of Commerce Of The People's Republic Of China. (2020a). *China E-Commerce Report (2020).* Retrieved from http://scjss.mofcom.gov.cn/article/jyjl/jdzswn/202001/20200102932689.shtml

Ministry Of Commerce Of The People's Republic Of China. (2020b). *Lishui City, Zhejiang Province, actively explore the "Internet + green water and green mountains" to be a pioneer pioneer in the development of rural electric business.* Retrieved from https://dzswgf.mofcom.gov.cn/news/5/2021/9/1631698018580.html

News, C. C. P. (2016). *Suichang Model Study - Service Driven County E-Commerce Development Model.* Retrieved from http://theory.people.com.cn/n1/2016/0804/c401815-28611279.html

Nie, P., Ma, W. L., & Sousa-Poza, A. (2021). The relationship between smartphone use and subjective well-being in rural China. *Electronic Commerce Research, 21*(4), 983–1009. doi:10.100710660-020-09397-1

People.cn. (2020). *Zhejiang Lin'an pecan processing new model to help farmers increase income.* Retrieved from http://zj.people.com.cn/n2/2020/1023/c186806-34368234.html

Texnet. (2020). *What is the "Qinghe Model"? Come to the 27th China - Qinghe International Cashmere and Wool Products Fair to find out!* Retrieved from http://info.texnet.com.cn/detail-825672.html

The State Council Information Office Of The People's Republic Of China. (2021). *Poverty Alleviation: China's Experience and Contribution.* Retrieved from http://www.scio.gov.cn/zfbps/ndhf/44691/Document/1701663/1701663.htm

Tian, L., Vakharia, A. J., Tan, Y., & Xu, Y. F. (2018). Marketplace, Reseller, or Hybrid: Strategic Analysis of an Emerging E-Commerce Model. *Production and Operations Management, 27*(8), 1595–1610. doi:10.1111/poms.12885

Wagner, G., Schramm-Klein, H., & Steinmann, S. (2020). Online retailing across e-channels and e-channel touchpoints: Empirical studies of consumer behavior in the multichannel e-commerce environment. *Journal of Business Research, 107*, 256–270. doi:10.1016/j.jbusres.2018.10.048

Wang, W. T., Wang, Y. S., & Liu, E. R. (2016). The stickiness intention of group-buying websites: The integration of the commitment-trust theory and e-commerce success model. *Information & Management*, *53*(5), 625–642. doi:10.1016/j.im.2016.01.006

Wang, Y., & Coe, N. M. (2021). Platform ecosystems and digital innovation in food retailing: Exploring the rise of Hema in China. *Geoforum*, *126*, 310–321. doi:10.1016/j.geoforum.2021.08.007

Xinhua. (2021). *"Lin'an Model" Promotes New Path of Rural Revitalization*. Retrieved from http://education.news.cn/2021-11/02/c_1211429647.htm

Zhang, B., Du, Z. J., Wang, B., & Wang, Z. H. (2019). Motivation and challenges for e-commerce in e-waste recycling under "Big data" context: A perspective from household willingness in China. *Technological Forecasting and Social Change*, *144*, 436–444. doi:10.1016/j.techfore.2018.03.001

Zheng, K., Zhang, Z. J., & Song, B. J. I. M. M. (2020). E-commerce logistics distribution mode in big-data context: A case analysis of JD. *COM*, *86*, 154–162. doi:10.1016/j.indmarman.2019.10.009

Chapter 3
Artificial Intelligence-Based Approaches for Product Recommendation in E-Commerce

Sumitra Samal
Shri Shankaracharya Institute of Professional Management and Technology, India

Kaveri Kar
Shri Shankaracharya Institute of Professional Management and Technology, India

Shraddha Taunk
Shri Shankaracharya Institute of Professional Management and Technology, India

J. P. Patra
https://orcid.org/0000-0003-2924-6090
Shri Shankaracharya Institute of Professional Management and Technology, India

ABSTRACT

Today's e-commerce is completely dependent on artificial intelligence. Whatever technology was used in the ancient days, there was a huge gap between a customer and a seller. From a seller's point of view, he wanted to sell the maximum product and a customer had to purchase the product whose price was lowest in the market but best in quality. In this situation, we need a system that can automatically recommend a suitable product to the customer so that we can buy his goods easily and at a low price. For this, artificial intelligence is the best method. Artificial intelligence recommendation system is a combination of machine learning algorithms that are used by developers to help users predict their choices and get related suggestions.Through this chapter, the authors show the different processes and uses of artificial intelligence that help the user for an accurate recommendation of a product such as search queries, past purchases, items placed in the shopping cart, viewing history, and the location of the customer or buyer.

DOI: 10.4018/978-1-6684-4969-1.ch003

Copyright © 2022, IGI Global. Copying or distributing in print or electronic forms without written permission of IGI Global is prohibited.

1. INTRODUCTION AND BACKGROUND OF E-COMMERCE

E-commerce, or digital trade, is the shopping for and promoting services or products through the net. For many people, E-Commerce (Galhotra, 2019) is something we take part in daily, like making an internet invoice charge or buying from an internet seller. Ecommerce can take less paperwork and contain some kind of transactions. The records of E-Commerce began over forty years in the past whilst the creation of early eras like Electronic Data Interchange (EDI) and teleshopping inside the Nineteen Seventies paved the manner for the present-day E-Commerce keep as we are aware of it today. E-Commerce is carefully intertwined with the records of the net. Online purchasing has become feasible whilst the net changed into opened to the general public in 1991. Amazon changed into one of the first e-commerce websites in the US to begin promoting merchandise online and lots of companies have observed since. In the early 1960s, due to the rapid development of electronic data interchange (EDI), the market of electronic commerce gradually touched new heights.EDI changed the conventional mailing and faxing of files via way of means permitting the virtual switch of information from one system to another. In today's time, if the economy of any country is to be evaluated, then what percentage of e-commerce is involved in the economy of that country, is also assessed. Nowadays, every person uses ATM, mobile banking, or any electronic payment platform to purchase any product, through which money transactions can be done easily. Due to this the market of e-commerce has become very big today. Being a seller, everyone wants that in the minimum time he can display as many products as possible in front of his client. Because in today's internet world, the customer of any one city can sit at his home and order his favorite goods from any other city or even from another country. Along with selling his goods to the customers, a seller has to keep in mind the likes or dislikes of his customer, such as price, discount offers, color, material, brand, warranty, guarantee, etc. It used to be very difficult to identify so many parameters at once and on that basis to provide our customer with what he needed. So AI came up with the solution to customers' demands, required purchasing items, and filtering that items according to customers' needs with this customer satisfaction can be fulfilled and required time can be saved (Zhang et al., 2021). This is where the entry of technology starts in the commercial market. Because technology was the only medium by which all these problems could be solved. In today's date e-commerce has become an integral part of the common man's life. Every product that he wants to buy can know about that product using any e-commerce application and can also compare with other companies' products using different parameters. According to a survey, in the years 2020 and 2021, more than 2 billion people have purchased their goods through e-commerce. So when so many people will make so many purchases then you can imagine how much data would be generated and only artificial intelligence (Song et al., 2019) and its algorithms will be able to collect all this data, analyze and present the right product to the customer. In this book chapter, we will talk about the various methods of Artificial Intelligence, its applications, use, and output.

Objective: The major objective of the chapter is to find out a platform for sellers of rural areas and enhance their financial condition.

Motivation: During the survey, we find out some major issues like the need of the market for products, the communication gap between customer and seller, identification of current needs of the market, etc. these issues motivated us to provide an e-commerce platform.

Contribution: through this chapter, we proposed an artificial intelligence-based way in existing E-Commerce systems to solve issues in product searching, content recommendation system, etc.

2. ARTIFICIAL INTELLIGENCE-BASED RECOMMENDER SYSTEMS

Different Artificial Intelligence strategies have been executed with recognizable and prescribed systems to meet the extending idea necessities of huge data information blasts. In this segment, we present six Artificial Intelligence techniques that have worked on the recommender systems are:

- Artificial Neural Network
- Collaborative Filtering
- Content-based Recommender System
- Swarm Intelligence
- Hybrid System
- Fuzzy Sets

2.1 Artificial Neural Network

Neural networks were first evolved during the 1950s to assist systems with acting like they are interconnected brain cells, similar to in a human mind. An artificial neural network organization is an endeavor to mimic the organization of neurons that make up the human mind. This is to enable the system to learn and settle on its own choices given information. We can define this Artificial Neural Network as a computational model (Abiodun et al., 2018) which depends on the design as well as the motivation behind natural neural organizations. The system of the counterfeit neural organization is human cerebrum processes data which contains a colossal measure of related handling units to work with exertion all the while towards movement data since they likewise produce critical results and it comprises of the accompanying 3 layers (input layer, output layer, and hidden layer) which are displayed in below Figure1.

Input Layer –It Comprises units (artificial neurons) that obtain inputs from the outside world, upon which the system will learn, recognize, or otherwise process.

Output Layer -The output layer receives the connections from hidden layers or the input layer. It comes before an output value in order to indicate the irregular prophecy of the reply.

Hidden Layer-This layer is present in between input and output layers. The objective of the hidden layer is that it converts the input into something that the output unit can use in some way.

2.1.1 Working Principle and System Architecture for Product Recommendation in E-Commerce

Information collection phase: As part of the first phase of product recommendation, we will try to determine whether the customer has searched the internet for the product before. What goods the customer has in his shopping cart, what price they are, and which filters are used by the customer to buy his goods or place an order. All these parameters will be stored in a product information database, which we will develop further in the form of the information collection part or Information collection phase. In the prediction task, a user profile or model is developed based on their attributes, their activities, and the content of the resources they visit. In order for a recommendation agent to function properly, the user profile/model must be carefully created. To make meaningful recommendations, the system has to know as much as possible about the user. Recommender systems use various types of input such as explicit feedback delivered by users about their attention to an item, and implicit feedback inferred

Figure 1. Artificial Neural Network (Mylavarapu, 2018)

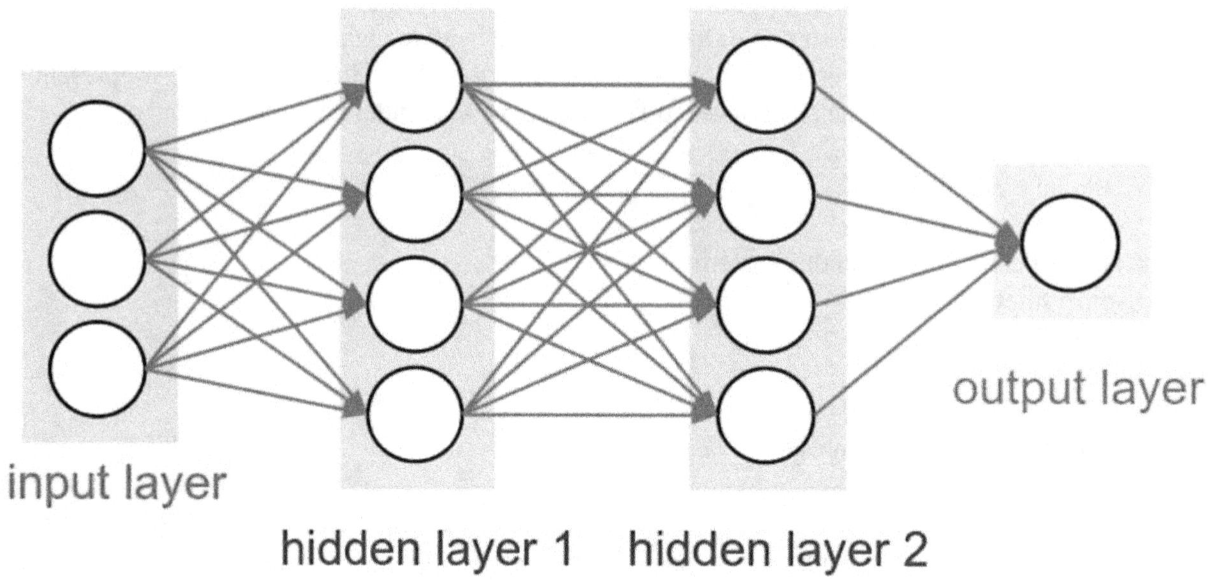

indirectly by observing user behavior, such as the most suitable, excellent explicit feedback. Feedback can also be obtained using both explicit and implicit means. A user profile is an assortment of individual data related to a particular user. The user profile is made up of information such as cognitive capacities, intellectual capabilities, learning styles, hobbies, preferences, and interactions with the system. The user profile is typically used to retrieve relevant data that is utilized to develop a user model. The success of any recommendation system (Xu & Sang, 2022) depends largely on its ability to represent user interests. To create relevant and accurate recommendations, appropriate models are required.

Learning phase: In this phase, we will use an information collection learning algorithm that will be useful to filter and exploit user characteristics based on the feedback collected during the different phases.

Prediction phase: It foresees the items that the user will prefer. It can be done using a dataset gathered during the data collection phase, either memory-based or model-based or by observing the system's behavior.

To select a product, the e-commerce platform will require the following process

- **Search Queries:** In this process, if the user has already searched for any product in the search engine, then through artificial intelligence, we get information that at some point in the future, the user will have the requirement of that product. Every time the user searches for any product, our recommendation system will analyze the user's previous search queries and will also remind the user about the product that he searched for in the past.
- **Past Purchases:** Through Past Purchase, our recommendation system analyzes the user's purchased item and displays other items used along with that item to the user. As an example, if a user has purchased pants, then our recommended system will analyze that that user may also need a belt. So next time whenever the user visits any e-commerce website automatically belt advertisement will appear in front of the user.

Figure 2. Phases of Production Recommendation

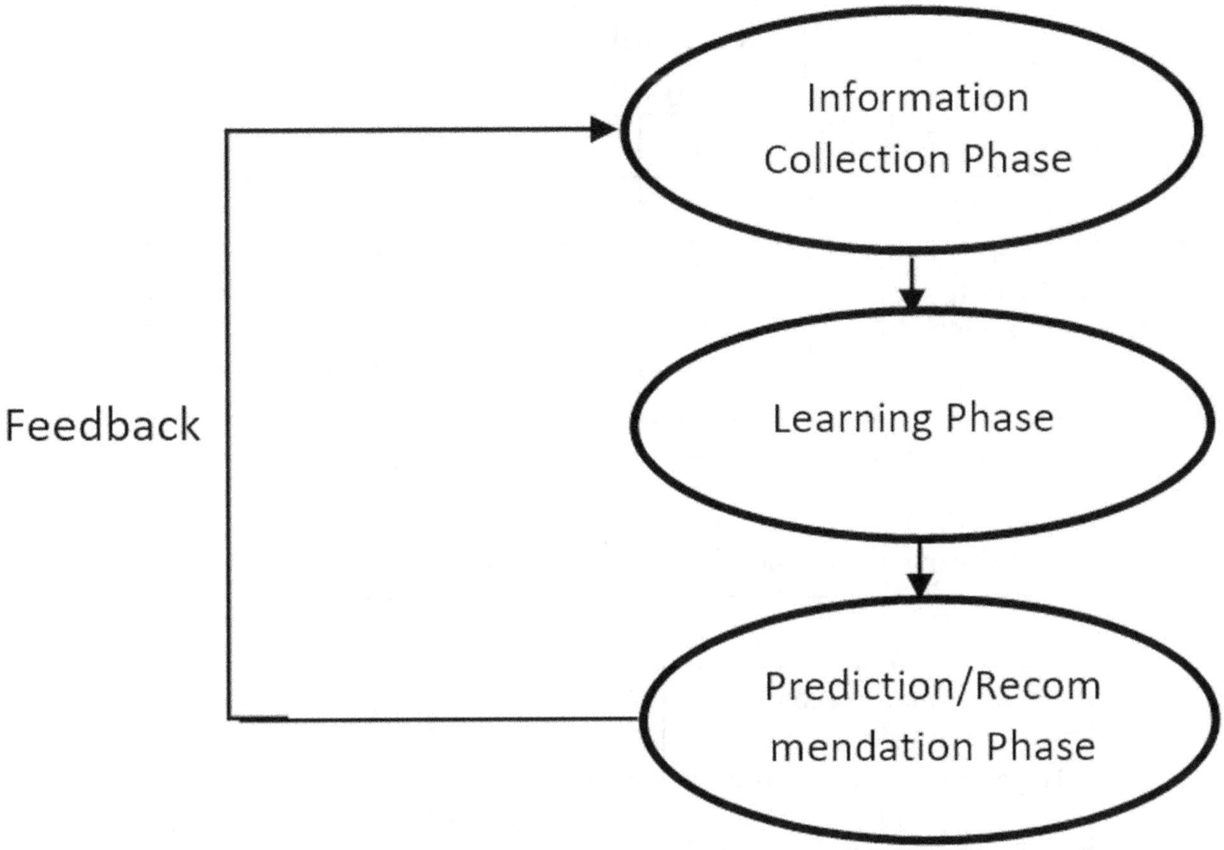

- **Items Placed in the Shopping Cart:** If a user has placed any product inside the shopping cart, our recommender system will analyze that the user required that item, but it may be due to price, quality, or unavailable of the product user could not purchase that item. Later on, if another company launches the same product in the market at a lower price or higher quality, then our recommended system will give information to the user about that product as well.
- **Viewing history:** In this phase, using the viewing history, we will find out what product the user has purchased in the past, keeping in mind that history, our recommendation system will display the new product.
- **Location:** This phase is also very important because, based on location, our recommendation system displays the product which can be easily delivered to the customer's location.

2.2 Collaborative Filtering

The collaborative filtering methodology (Murali et al., 2019), the most well-known of all product recommender systems, is based entirely on how other consumers and customers have previously rated a product they purchased. Collaborative filtering is a website-independent prediction method for content

Figure 3. Architecture of recommender systems

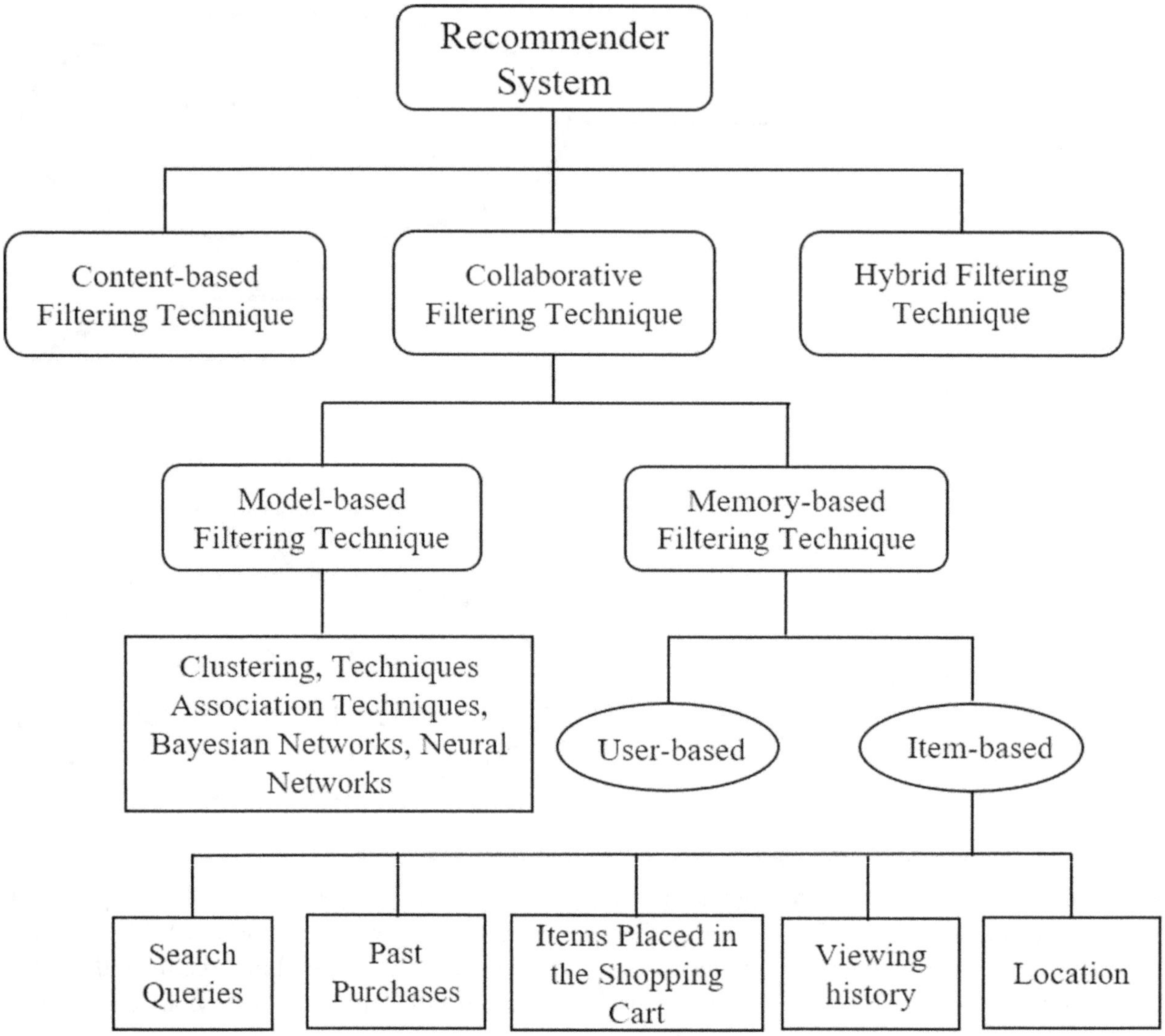

that cannot be easily and accurately represented via metadata, such as movies and music. The collaborative filtering method works by allowing users to create a database of item preferences.

We want to create a system that can propose products to consumers depending on their preferences. The first step is to look for users or objects that are comparable. The next stage is to estimate user ratings for things that have yet to be rated. As a result, we require responses to the following questions in order to construct an automatic recommendation system:

- How do you determine which customers or objects are similar to one another?
- How do you determine a user's score for an object based mostly on the scores of comparable users?
- How do you grade the accuracy of the rankings you calculate?

Figure 4. Working principle of Collaborative Filtering

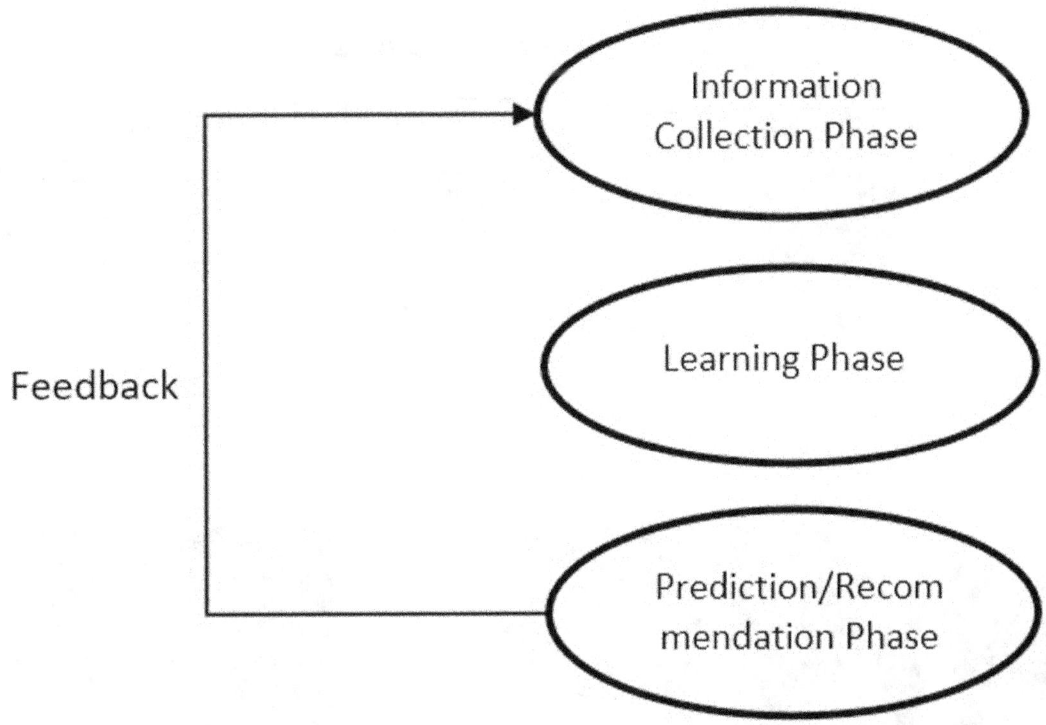

Collaborative filtering is a set of algorithms that includes a variety of approaches for locating comparable people or products, as well as several methods for calculating ratings based on the ratings of similar users. We must describe the type of collaborative filtering strategy based on the user's preferences.

The Collaborative filtering process uses two techniques one is a memory-based Technique and the second one is a model-based technique. Memory-based techniques use client rating recorded information to process the closeness between clients or things. The thought behind these strategies is to characterize a comparability measure between clients or things and see as the most like suggest inconspicuous things. Machine learning techniques are used in the model-based technique to predict users' evaluations of unrated items. Matrix factorization models, such as applying a Singular Value Decomposition to reconstruct the rating matrix, and Markov decision process-based models are two of the most prevalent types of model-based collaborative filtering techniques available. There are 2 fundamental kinds of memory-based cooperative separating calculations: User-Based and Item-Based.

User-Based: Here, we look for clients who have viewed similar content and use their preferences to suggest new things:

A disadvantage is that there will generally be a lot a greater number of clients than things, which prompts a lot greater client likeness lattices (this may be clear in the accompanying segment) prompting execution and memory issues on bigger datasets, which powers to depend on parallelization strategies or different methodologies by and large.

Figure 5. Example of user-based collaborative filtering
Source: *https://wallpapercave.com/bollywood-movie-poster-wallpapers*

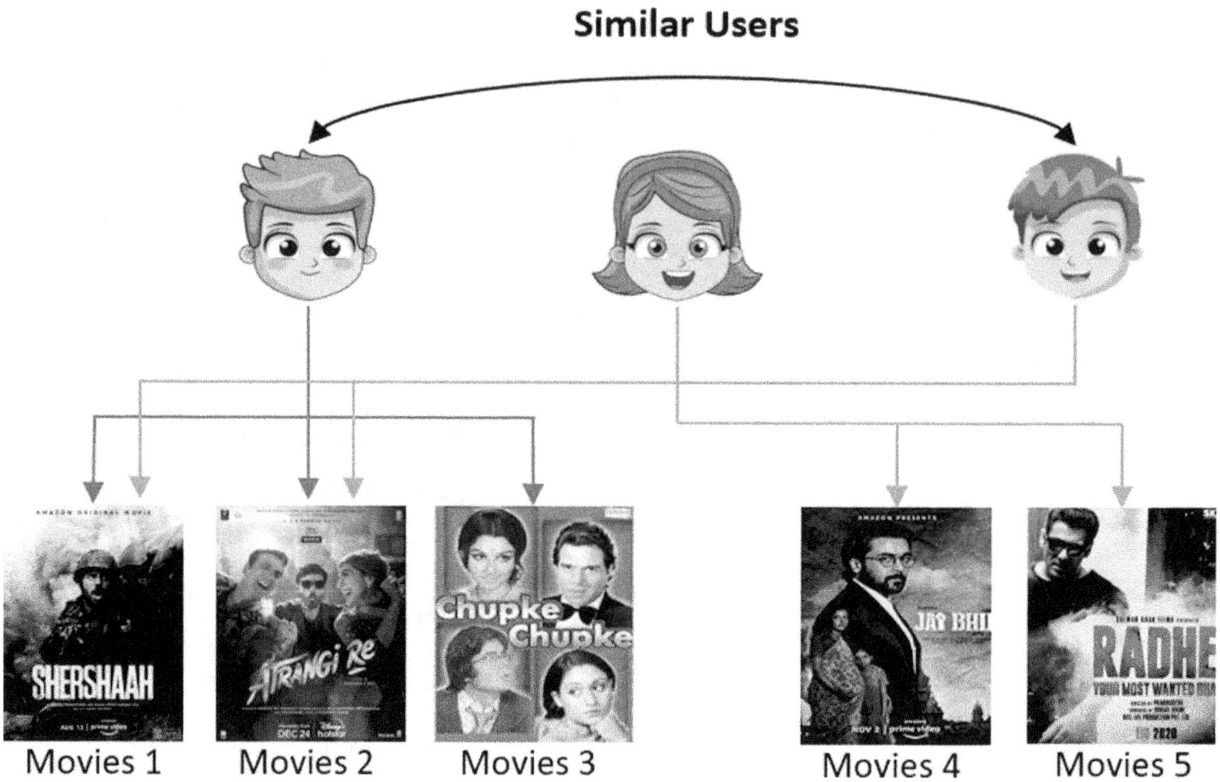

Item-Based: The concept is similar, but instead of starting with a specific movie (or group of movies), we look for related movies based on the tastes of other users.

Conflictingly to user-based techniques, thing similitude frameworks will generally be more modest, which will decrease the expense of tracking down neighbors in our closeness grid. A downside of item-based techniques is that there will in general be a lower variety in the proposals rather than user-based Collaborative filtering.

2.3 Content-Based Recommendation System

Content-based Recommendation systems are also commonly known as content-based filtering. They are widely used for recommendations as it uses the contents of item descriptions(Reina et al., 2021) to predict the utility of that item based on a user's profile. Research on information retrieval and information filtering has led to the development of this approach. In this context, "Content" refers to the contents of the attributes of things we like. For instance, a movie can be defined by its genre, director, writer, actors, and plot. You can obtain these properties directly from any structured data or from unstructured data. According to this method, items that have previously interested a particular user will be recommended based on their online information and interests. An item's description and the user's preferences are used

Figure 6. Example of Item-based collaborative filtering
Source:*https://wallpapercave.com/bollywood-movie-poster-wallpapers*

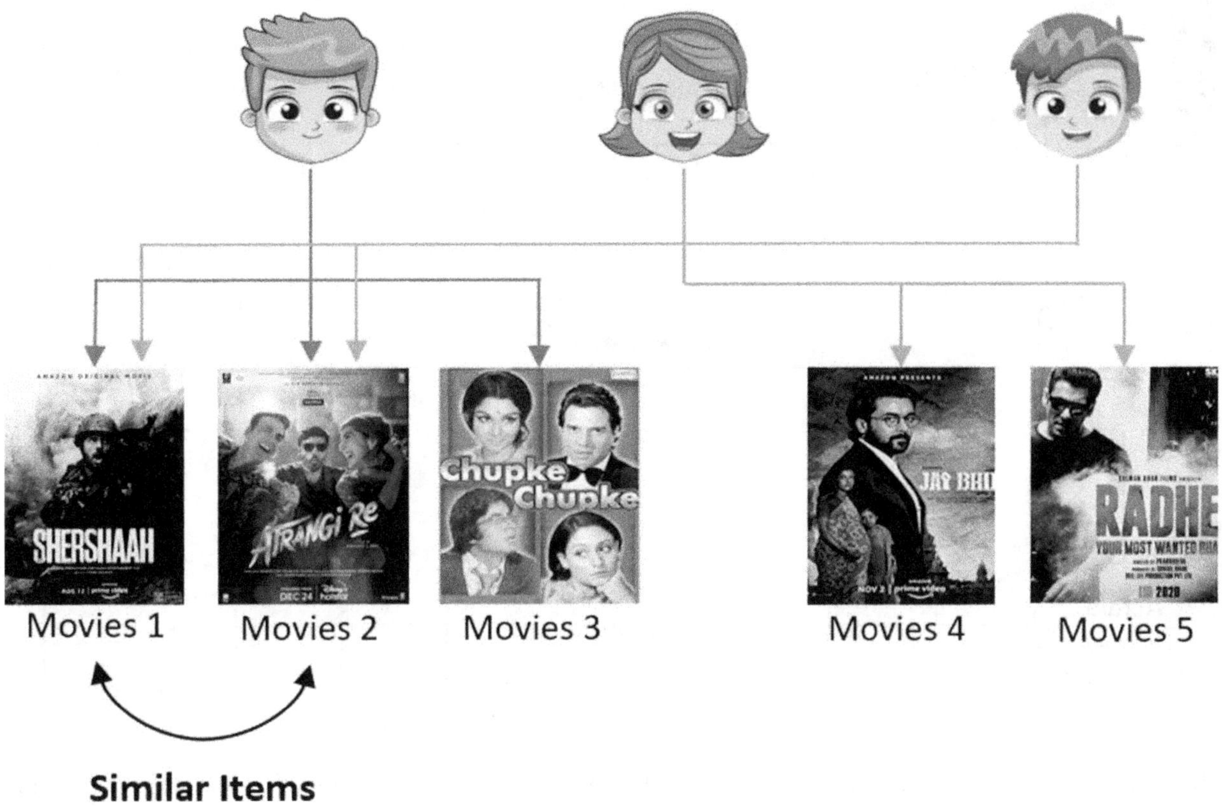

as the basis for content-based filtering. Websites, learning materials, books, movies, music, television programs, and e-services can be recommended effectively through content-based filtering techniques.

A content-based recommender treats recommendation as a classification problem for the user and develops a classifier for the user based on the items' characteristics(Cami et al., 2018). By using this approach, you can categorize products based on their keywords, learn what the customer likes, find similar products in the database, and then recommend similar products.

This type of recommender system heavily depends on user input. The items are described using keywords, and the user profile indicates what type of item this user likes. Google, for example, displays all the items that contain a set of keywords when a user searches for a phrase.

For creating a profile of a user, the system uses both his or her preferences and a history of interactions with the recommender system. The process of determining a user's profile can be viewed as a classic binary classification problem that has been extensively studied in the area of machine learning and data mining for which some established methods, including Naive Bayes, the nearest neighbor algorithms, and decision trees, have been applied. In order to create a recommendation list, a user's profile is compared to the item attributes. An item representation and a user profile are filtered and matched in a content-based recommender system utilizing the features acquired during the first and second stages. In the end, the recommendation has forwarded the items the user dislikes, and the items that do not seem to match

Figure 7. Content-based Recommendation System

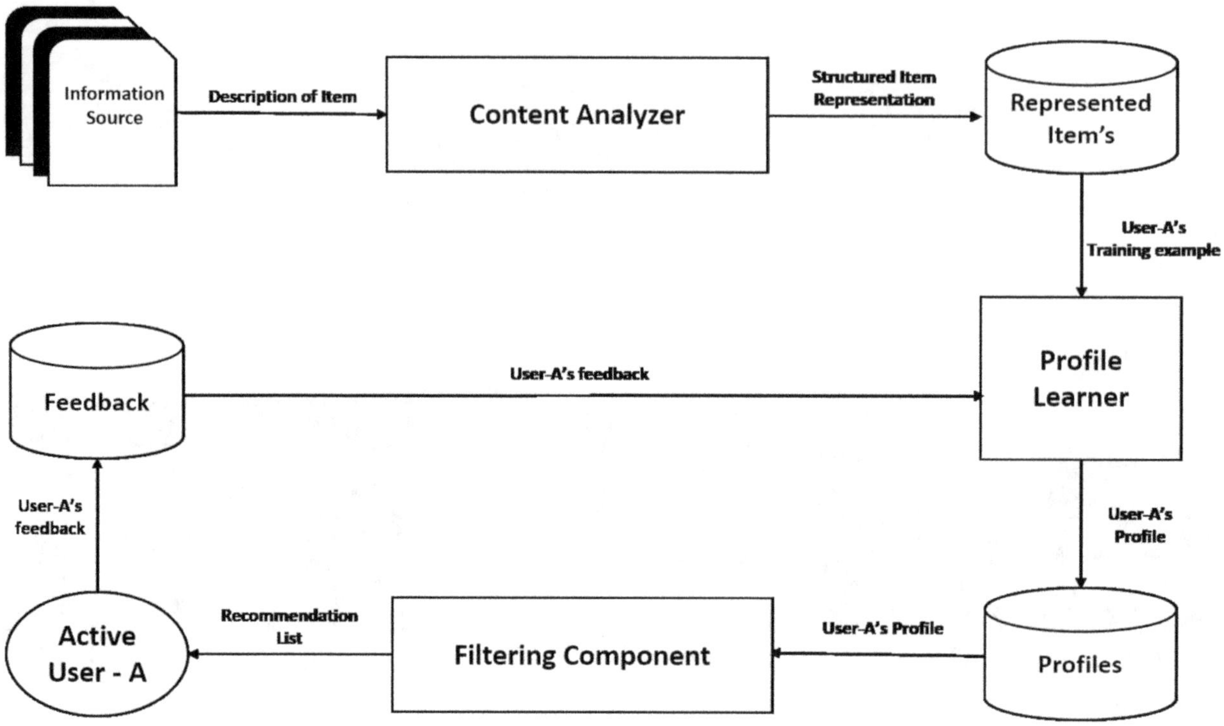

the user's taste are removed. To determine the relevance of a recommendation, the depiction of the item and the profile of the user have a clear bearing.

2.3.1 How Does It Work?

Users can provide data either explicitly or implicitly. By analyzing the data, one can create a user's profile (containing vectors that describe the preferences of the individual), which in the future can be used to suggest the user. Over time, as the user starts giving more feedback or taking more action, the accuracy of the recommendation increases. A utility matrix is used to describe how the user and item are related.

Taking a movie as an example, its actor, producer, director, release year, IMBD Rating or genre are the features of major importance. These will serve as a profile of an item and represent the essential features of that item. To measure the relationship between the items that the user likes and those that they dislike, we use the utility matrix of the data gathered from the user. Specifically, we assign a degree of preference to each user-item pair. After that, we define the user's relationship with the items by drawing a matrix of their preferences. By aggregating the profiles of these items, we can make the best estimate about which item users like.

As a result of not getting all the input from the user every time, there is a possibility that some columns might remain blank in the matrix, and the goal of this recommendation system is not to fill out the entire columns but to suggest the best possible product to the user which he/she will be interested in. According to this table, our recommender system won't suggest Movie 3 & 4 to User 2, since in

Table1. Movie Recommendation based on Content Filtering

	Movie – 1 (Shershaah)	Movie - 2 (Atrangi Re)	Movie – 3 (Chupke Chupke)	Movie – 4 (Jay Bhim)	Movie – 5 (Radhe)
User 1	3	2	1		
User 2	2	3			2
User 3	2	3	1	1	

Movie 3 both users 1 & 3 gave the same low rating, while in Movie 4 User 1 gave the same rating, so it is highly likely that our User 2 also won't like it. User 2 likes Movie 5 but is not liked by another user.

The content-based recommendation system works on two methods:

- Method 1 (The vector space method): Let's imagine you read and reviewed an Amitav Ghosh crime thriller book online. Additionally, you reviewed one more fictional book in the comedy genre compared to the crime thrillers and gave it a negative review. As a result of the information you provided, a rating system is made. On a scale of 0 to 9 the crime thriller and detective genres are rated 9, while other serious books fall between 9 and 0 and comedies are at the bottom. Based on this information you will most likely receive book recommendations from crime thriller genres since those are the highest-rated categories for you.

An individual's information is ranked according to a user vector created for this ranking system. Afterward, an item vector is created, in which books are ranked according to their genres. In order to recommend books, each book name is assigned a value based on a multiplication of the user and item vectors. The result is then used in the recommendation algorithm. By doing so, all the available books that have been searched by you are ranked and the top 5 or top 10 books are assigned according to this ranking.

- Method 2 (Classification method): Second, we have the classification method. A decision tree can be created to determine whether the user wants to read the book or not. Let's take The Alchemist as an example. Considering previously used user data, we look at the name of the author and it is not Amitav Ghosh, it is neither a crime thriller nor the kind of book you have ever reviewed. We conclude by not recommending this book to you as this is not based on its classifications.

2.3.2 Advantages and Limitations of Content-Based Recommender System

It is user-independent because it is based on item representation. The system does not suffer from the problem of sparse data. Recommending new items to users solves the problem of new items not starting. The result of the recommendation can be explained clearly and transparently which is a great advantage over other methods. However, content-based recommender systems have several limitations. In the absence of user profiles, the recommendation results are inaccurate. A content-based recommendation system always suggests similar items to users, which results in overspecialization. These kinds of recommendation lists tend to bore the end-users since most of the users these days want to discover new and trendy items rather than being limited to certain similar items to those they have already experienced. It

Figure 8. Content-based filtering for a book recommendation

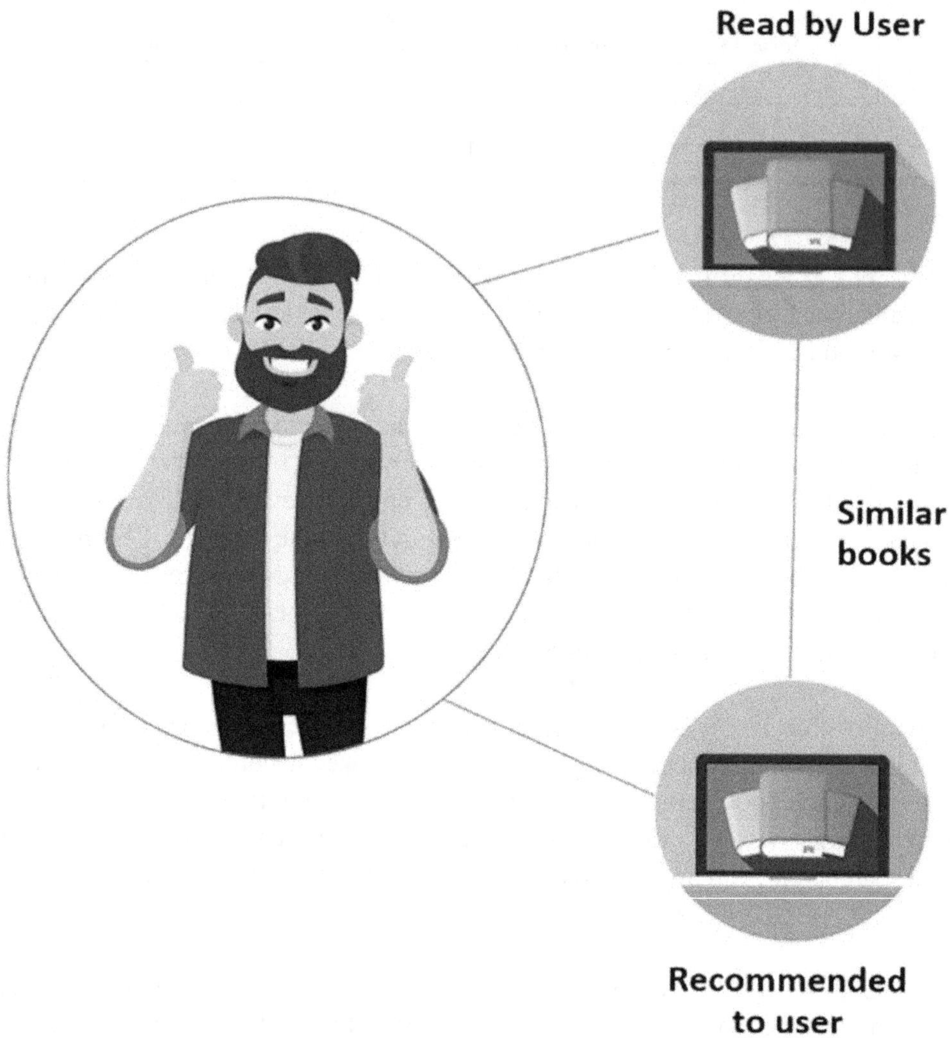

may not always be easy to represent items in the form needed by content-based recommender systems. Hence, this sort of system gives more appropriate results for recommending any articles or news instead of images or music.

2.4 Swarm Intelligence

Gerardo Beni and Jing Wang introduced the concept of Swarm Intelligence in 1989. A Swarm Intelligence system is an aggregation of distributed / self-organized, natural or artificial systems(Kaur & Kumar, 2020). It is inspired by natural systems, particularly biological systems. Using the knowledge of collective objects to solve a problem effectively is the essence of Swarm Intelligence. The word "swarm" represents a group of objects (humans, birds, etc.). As an example, if we are to give a problem description to a single individual and have him/her examine it and give a solution, then we would only

Figure 9. A Jar containing white and black balls

be considering the solution of that particular individual. However, the problem may be that the solution given by that individual may not be optimal or may not fit well for others. In order to avoid this, we give the problem to a certain number of people at once (a swarm) and ask them to come up with the most optimal solution possible. This will eventually help us to compute all their responses together to reach the most appropriate solution. Here, we are using the knowledge of the group at large to determine what the best solution or optimal solution for the problem is and that will be appropriate for all of them individually as well, so this is the idea behind swarm intelligence.

To demonstrate that collective knowledge of objects is superior to any individual knowledge, let's use an example. Think about a Jar that contains 250 white balls and 250 black balls. You need to predict how many white balls there are in the jar without touching it. Assume we take one response from a person and it predicts that we will find 150 white balls in the jar according to him/her. This result indicates that this estimation is not very bad since the error (difference) is only 100; however, we can optimize this even further to get a better result. What we'll do is instead of taking responses from just one person, we'll take responses from, say, ten people. Assuming that 'P' is a person, the following responses follow:

Once responses are collected from 10 different people, we can simply average their responses.

Table 2. Predictions collected according to fig. 9

Person	P1	P2	P3	P4	P5	P6	P7	P8	P9	P10
Count of White Ball	200	230	260	300	180	220	210	190	240	170

Average: (200 + 230 + 260 + 300 + 180 + 220 + 210 + 190 + 240 + 170) / 10

i.e. 220 (white balls in the jar)

We can now state that based on the collective predictions of 10 different people, 220 white balls are present in the jar. Here, the difference (error) is reduced from 100 to only 30 balls, compared with the previous error of 100 which was very close to the actual result of 250 white balls in the jar. Hence, we can say that swarm intelligence is founded upon the premise of using the collective knowledge of objects. Here, we have an optimal solution to a given problem based on a Swarm Intelligence approach. There is a wide range of applications of swarm intelligence such as weather forecasting, military-based applications, planetary mapping, data mining and cluster analysis, controlling nanobots using swarm intelligence to kill cancer tumors in the human body, make better financial decisions in business, etc.

To put it simply, we are using the network of brains to solve a particular problem. We can find many examples of swarm intelligence in nature, like ant colonies, swarms of bees, flocks of birds, hawks hunting, animal herding, bacterial growth, fish schooling, and microbial intelligence. The Swarm intelligence approach is unconvinced in its effectiveness. In many cases, they can find an optimal, or near-optimal solution, after determining appropriate parameters and evaluating convergence thoroughly - but they cannot guarantee it is an optimal solution of very high quality researched and extensively developed, despite this obvious drawback. As an alternative, one can calculate the quality of a solution by calçulating it for a special case that is able to do so. After this evaluation, all solutions that are at least as good as those of a special case are at least as confident. Nature-inspired metaheuristics are dominated by evolutionary algorithms (EA), particle swarm optimization (PSO), differential evolution (DE), ant colony optimization (ACO) and their variants.

2.5 Hybrid Recommendation Model

Hybrid RS merges two or more two RS methods with the logic to assure systems high-performance with the benefits of individually integrated methods. In common cases, as shown in Fig. 10, integrated collaborative filtering with other approaches to ignore the ramp-up problem and now we have a weighted hybrid model, based on a weighted average of all approaches, that can use to assess the outcomes of the recommended-item. Based on item-level sensitivity to hybridization, here system is modeled as a switching hybrid: the system uses only a few considerations to switch between the recommendation systems. The learner system uses a content-based and a collaborative hybrid approach, in which the content-based model is deployed first and then the collaborative model is used if it doesn't work.

Alternatively, this system is capable of incorporating similar information about items. Cascade hybrid RS involves with step by step procedure. The concept here involves generating user feedback initially, and then using a different approach to filter out recommendations from the candidate data set . When cascading, the system ignores secondary or lower priorities in its approach to properly categorizing products. This is because the second step in the cascade focuses only on products that need further classification. A cascade also includes criteria that allow for disturbances to occur during low-priority techniques, since the scores that come from high-priority recommenders can only be adjusted and irreversible.

Figure 10. Architecture of Hybrid Recommended system

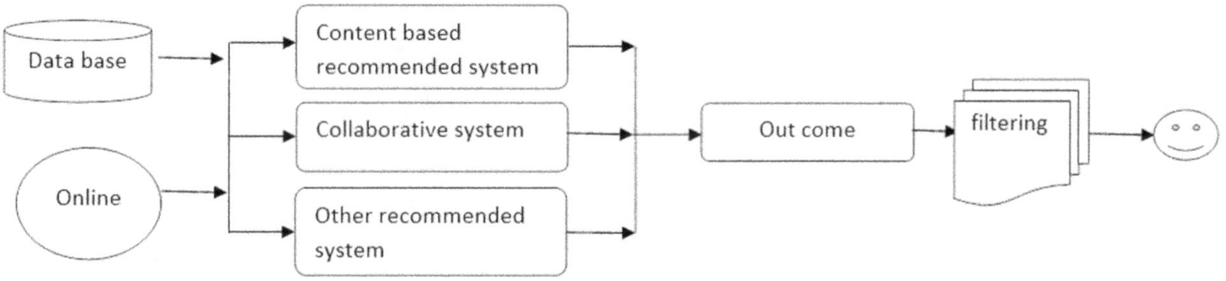

2.5.1 Implementation of Hybrid Recommended System

The flow of an implementation of hybrid RS is represented in Fig 11. It is used when a new user arrives at the system to check whether they are duplicate users. If they are matched with other user groups, then a hybrid recommendation system will recommend products compatible with the user group. Additionally, a hybrid RS system will suggest items based on a combined result of content-based and collaborative filtering, if the user is not related to any similar group.

Content-based and cooperative filtering, these styles face the issue when there isn't enough data to learn the relation between stoner and particulars. In similar cases, the third type of approach is used to make the recommendation systems named as Hybrid Recommendation System(Suresh et al., 2020). This approach overcomes the limitations of both content-based and collective filtering styles.

2.5.2 Hybrid Recommender System Advantages and Applications

Combining two or more recommendation systems into a hybrid RS improves the robustness and relevance of recommendations. This helps to overcome some of the deficiencies of independent recommendation systems. To increase the accuracy and effectiveness of the system, this hybrid RS is being developed. In order to do this, different systems can be margined on their individual benefits and the disadvantages of one system can be overcome in a different way.

Nevertheless, each RS takes time to execute, so there is a need for an online recommendation system that can quickly generate accurate recommendations with this approach number of products recommended Increases and the System is scalable with good performance. The hybrid approach helps to manage dynamic scenarios for the system and suggests a list of items instead of a single item.

The application part of this approach contains main fields. It has been observed that customer needs are ever-changing, despite the existence of different recommendation systems, and they can benefit from features such as keeping their data secure, browsing on desktop and mobile devices, and asking questions of personal assistants like Alexa and Google Assistant based on voice commands. The online scenario is expanding to many new segments, including matrimonial, medical consultancy, jobs, E-learning, etc. all with different requirements. Data mining can be used to continuously track user behavior and usage patterns, and artificial intelligence can be used to create a more customized recommendation system for each of these domains.

Figure 11. Hybrid Recommendation System

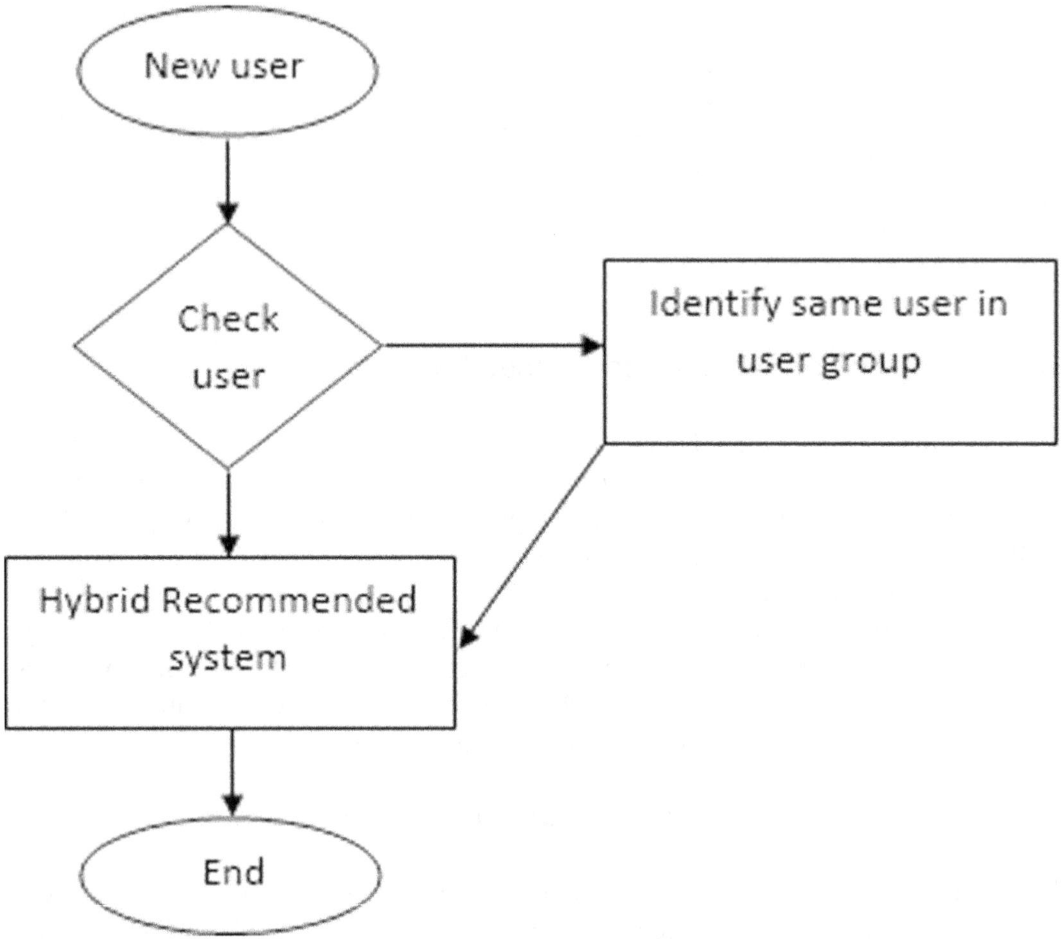

2.6 Fuzzy Set Approach

The term "online shopping" refers to the process of customers buying goods or services directly from sellers on the internet, without using any third-party intermediaries. It is a type of electronic commerce. The fuzzy logic approach is commonly used in machine control. The logic that is neither completely true nor completely false is fuzzy logic, which enables us to deal with ideas that cannot be expressed. Competing approaches such as neural networks and genetic algorithms are often as effective as FL, but FL has the advantage of addressing problems in a way that human operators can understand and use in controller design. This makes it easier for humans to interpret and find the outcome of their current tasks. Fuzzy shows as the interpretation of uncertain information in the fuzzy form . "Fuzzy logic" refers to the process of calculating data sets using the fuzzy method. This approach tries to show how E-satisfaction, E-loyalty & E-trust are based on organizational, technological, and customer aspects. Consumer satisfaction and trust are measured and analyzed in this approach to determine the effect on e-commerce loyalty. The background of fuzzy logic is based on online shopping and presents the related works (Yera & Martínez, 2017).The following advantages are presented in the fuzzy data algorithm:

- Software may readily implement and execute it,
- Business criteria may be included in the rules,
- Automate the e-commerce application with a decision-making procedure.

2.6.1 Benefits and Applications of Fuzzy Set Approach in e-Commerce

Advantages of the Fuzzy data set approach in various field is given below:

- Fuzzy logic describes the system symbolically and numerically. This has advantages over mathematical (numerical) or purely symbolic techniques, as the knowledge of the system is so widely available in such mixtures.
- Fuzzy logic evaluates the certainty or uncertainty of the membership of elements in a collection. The solution to some problems is based on the idea of rules defined by fuzzy logic in similar cases.
- These algorithms are not affected by configuration changes, incorrect or forgotten rules.
- In contrast to computer-accurate systems, the inference process is usually simple and saves computer power. This is especially interesting for real-time systems.
- Fuzzy techniques are often shorter than traditional approaches.

E-negotiation is a typical example of AI service systems (Yera & Martínez, 2017). Kowalczyk and Bui (2000) proposed a strategy for managing autonomous, multi-issue negotiations with fuzzy e-negotiation agents (FeNAs) when common knowledge and constraints are limited. Fuzzy constraint-based reasoning, combined with the principles of utility theory, is used by FeNAs to reach a consensus that maximizes an agent's utility at the highest level of fuzzy constraint satisfaction that is also accepted by the other agents. It is unreliable when information is defined as fuzzy constraints that describe an agent's satisfaction with potential solutions based on their priorities, constraints, and preferences. This fuzzy set approach can be applied to handle a range of problems involving e-negotiations with incomplete common knowledge and constraints.

3. CONCLUSION

The current recommender system has some limitations in terms of searching time, handling of a large amount of data and accuracy of recommendation. The hybrid recommendation system will help to reduce such issues. Even some better artificial intelligence-based recommendation systems may design in the future to match the accuracy and time complexity of the recommendation.

REFERENCES

Abiodun, O. I., Jantan, A., Omolara, A. E., Dada, K. V., Mohamed, N. A. E., & Arshad, H. (2018). State-of-the-art in artificial neural network applications: A survey. *Heliyon*, *4*(11), e00938. doi:10.1016/j.heliyon.2018.e00938

Cami, B. R., Hassanpour, H., & Mashayekhi, H. (2018). A content-based movie recommender system based on temporal user preferences. *Proceedings - 3rd Iranian Conference on Signal Processing and Intelligent Systems, ICSPIS 2017,* 121–125. https://doi.org/10.1109/ICSPIS.2017.8311601

Galhotra, B. (2019). Evolution of E-commerce in India: A Review and Its Future Scope. *Proceedings of the International Conference on Machine Learning, Big Data, Cloud and Parallel Computing: Trends, Prespectives and Prospects, COMITCon 2019,* 226–231. https://doi.org/10.1109/COMITCon.2019.8862252

Kaur, K., & Kumar, Y. (2020). Swarm Intelligence and its applications towards Various Computing: A Systematic Review. *Proceedings of International Conference on Intelligent Engineering and Management, ICIEM 2020,* 57–62. https://doi.org/10.1109/ICIEM48762.2020.9160177

Murali, M. V., Vishnu, T. G., & Victor, N. (2019). A Collaborative Filtering based Recommender System for Suggesting New Trends in Any Domain of Research. *2019 5th International Conference on Advanced Computing and Communication Systems, ICACCS 2019,* 550–553. https://doi.org/10.1109/ICACCS.2019.8728409

Mylavarapu, B. K. (2018). Collaborative Filtering and Artificial Neural Network Based Recommendation System for Advanced Applications. *Journal of Computer and Communications, 06*(12), 1–14. doi:10.4236/jcc.2018.612001

Reina, A., Ferrante, E., & Valentini, G. (2021). Collective decision-making in living and artificial systems [editorial]. *Swarm Intelligence, 15*(1), 1–6. doi:10.100711721-021-00195-5

Song, X., Yang, S., Huang, Z., & Huang, T. (2019). The Application of Artificial Intelligence in Electronic Commerce. *Journal of Physics: Conference Series, 1302*(3). Advance online publication. doi:10.1088/1742-6596/1302/3/032030

Suresh, A., Carmel, M. J., & Belinda, M. (2020). A Comprehensive Study of Hybrid Recommendation Systems for E-Commerce Applications Recommendation Systems for E-Commerce View project A Comprehensive Study of Hybrid Recommendation Systems for E-Commerce Applications. *International Journal of Advanced Science and Technology, 29*(3), 4089–4101.

Xu, L., & Sang, X. (2022). E-Commerce Online Shopping Platform Recommendation Model Based on Integrated Personalized Recommendation. *Scientific Programming, 2022*. Advance online publication. doi:10.1155/2022/4823828

Yera, R., & Martínez, L. (2017). Fuzzy tools in recommender systems: A survey. *International Journal of Computational Intelligence Systems, 10*(1), 776–803. doi:10.2991/ijcis.2017.10.1.52

Zhang, Q., Lu, J., & Jin, Y. (2021). Artificial intelligence in recommender systems. *Complex & Intelligent Systems, 7*(1), 439–457. doi:10.100740747-020-00212-w

Chapter 4
A Fuzzy-Based Intelligent Picking and Placing Warehouse Robot

Himanshu Bothra
School of Mechanical Engineering, Kalinga Institute of Industrial Technology (Deemed), Bhubaneswar, India

Shreyas Jha
School of Mechanical Engineering, Kalinga Institute of Industrial Technology (Deemed), Bhubaneswar, India

Kumar Kanishka Dey
School of Mechanical Engineering, Kalinga Institute of Industrial Technology (Deemed), Bhubaneswar, India

Anish Pandey
https://orcid.org/0000-0001-9089-3727
School of Mechanical Engineering, Kalinga Institute of Industrial Technology (Deemed), Bhubaneswar, India

Ashwani Kumar
School of Mechanical Engineering, Kalinga Institute of Industrial Technology (Deemed), Bhubaneswar, India

ABSTRACT

Autonomous robots that operate objects within a limited workspace have wide applications in the e-commerce industry, which helps in overcoming the lack of flexibility and improves operation efficiency by minimizing material delivery and handling time. In this work, a model has been developed for an intelligent picking warehouse robot that independently conducts pick and place operations on payloads of up to 2.2 kgs and have a maximum size in any dimension up to 20 cm. It consists of robotic system and various sub-systems, including mechanical design and analysis, perception pipeline, sensor fusion, control architecture, trajectory planning, and grasp synthesis. Performance evaluation of the model has

DOI: 10.4018/978-1-6684-4969-1.ch004

Copyright © 2022, IGI Global. Copying or distributing in print or electronic forms without written permission of IGI Global is prohibited.

been done using software simulation for picking systems in various tasks in warehouse settings. It autonomously identifies the pick-up locations, drop locations, and objects in its workspace using an on-board, RGB-D camera and other complimenting sensors to manipulate payloads using a triaxial gantry system.

INTRODUCTION

Achieving automation using robotics reduces operating costs, saves production time, and reduces error - all of which are important to any organization. With the increasing advancements in industrial automation and Industry 4.0, the need of the hour states the requirement of highly automated processes for more efficient and productive output. These days, markets require quick variations of operations indicating the machine's flexibility, alongside upgrades in efficiency, frameworks well-being, and individual safety. The industry need for warehouse robotics is growing rapidly with the growth of e-commerce. Pick and place operations in warehouses are the most labor-intensive activity in a warehouse. Industry reports estimate that warehouse picking constitutes up to 55% of operating costs. Our project attempted to solve this industrial problem by intelligently guiding the picking operations.

This project is a holistic and robust solution to the intelligent picking application in warehouse robotics. This robot has been developed by keeping three basic tenets - simple, scalable, and efficient. The system uses advanced computer vision algorithms with a fusion of sensors to map the entire workspace while simultaneously keeping track of an agent's location. It identifies the pick and drop areas in the workspace, plans, and then conducts picking and dropping operations. The presented work is a 2-finger modular gripper mounted upon a 3-DOF gantry system. We have proposed a multi-modal gripper concept in the future scope of the project to avail grasping action for a large variety of objects. The cost of the system is estimated to be INR 49,920/-. Using custom-designed parts that required precision machining would exponentially increase cost and execution time. Another constraint on the system design was regarding the availability of parts. We used off-the-shelf components instead of custom-designed parts that required precision machining, would shoot up costs and execution time, and would be difficult to procure in small quantities for a single system being developed. Thus, we designed using commonly available parts within our acceptable design region.

The major challenge intercepted for innovation was to make a capable robotic system with a large workspace, using readily available hardware at a fractional cost of similar systems while using software optimizations and sensor fusion to compensate for expensive specialized hardware.

Warehouse robotics is a field of robotics that sees a lot of products, and there are urgent requirements for them to be addressed. Like any hot robotics application, warehouse robotics has a considerable scope due to the sheer size and volumes. Multiple processes take place in warehouses, pick and place operations are one of them. Pick and place robots increase the speed and efficiency of the process and reduce error. Hence we have addressed this emerging problem statement to develop a product-based solution for our project and developed an intelligent pick and place robot to autonomously conduct pick and place operations in warehouses with speed and accuracy.

In (Bhandari, 2010; Brown et al., 2010; Speth et al. 2008) overall software improvements for intelligent picking systems in object detection and 6D pose estimation, semantic segmentation, trajectory optimization, and motion planning have been proposed. In (Bhatia et al. 2019; Geng et al., 2016; Moghaddam & Nof, 2016), complete end-to-end intelligent picking systems have been proposed. An optimal vision system that supports object contour detection using 2D data has been suggested here, which is inspired by the research works of (Vahid-Araghi & Golnaraghi, 2018). The operational workflow is motivated by (Beites et al., 2018), which aids in the reduction of cycle time for individual operations by avoiding the homing action of the robotic system. The researchers (Bolu & Korçak, 2021; Lee & Jeong, 2021; Sharma & Doriya, 2021) designed the different types of intelligent warehouse robots and implemented optimization algorithms (reinforcement learning) to reduce the path length between the start and the destination during navigation in the workspace.

The challenge was to develop an intelligent robotic system that would autonomously perform pick and place operations and identify the objects and its environments. The robot should be able to pick an object bearing a load of up to 2kgs and a limiting dimension of 20 cm on any edge. These constraints were based upon objective industrial warehouse standards.

The objectives for the project are: -

- Develop a holistic, robust, and stable solution for autonomous pick and place operations.
- The solution should be Simple, Scalable, and Efficient.
- Use of standard of the shelf components for fast procurement, simpler manufacturing, and low cost.
- Lower cost using a novel software approach
- Easy setup and installation.

Scalability and Deployment

We have strived to develop a holistic solution that efficiently meets the application's performance requirement and incorporated other non-functional yet critical requirements for this system to actually be used as part of the tremendous and massive scale logistics operations in warehouses' especially those of considerable size. Some of these are: -

- Meeting industrial safety requirements while working in close proximity to human resources.
- A simple and intuitive UI for operating and monitoring the system.
- Easy setup, installation, and maintenance.
- Cost favorable development as opposed to industrial rates.

The accurate scalability of the developed model is achieved after several experiments and trials. The received scalability data are:

- Payload capacity is 2 kgs, and the range of linear movement on the X-axis is 4.4 m, the Y-axis is 2.1 m, and the Z-axis is 1.6 m.
- The rotation of the gripper is 360 degrees about Z-axis, achieved through the hybrid stepper motor.
- The used workspace dimension is 9.9 cubic meters.
- Furthermore, the minimum distance between the pickup and drop area is 20 cm.

IMPLEMENTATION

This section will describe the detailed implementation of the robot through the following technicalities and simulation results, also presented in Figure 1.

- Hardware - Structure, Sensors, Actuators, MicroProcessors
- Software - Computer Vision and Control Algorithms
- Modeling, Simulation & Verifications performed:
- 3D modeling and structural analysis in Solidworks
- Finite Element Analysis with static load in ANSYS
- Simulation and Verification in MATLAB Simulink and CopelliaSim
- Control logic and Grasp planning in MATLAB Simscape
- Electrical and Electronic modeling and simulation in Proteus
- Computer Vision simulation and verification in MATLAB

Figure 1. Workflow of the system

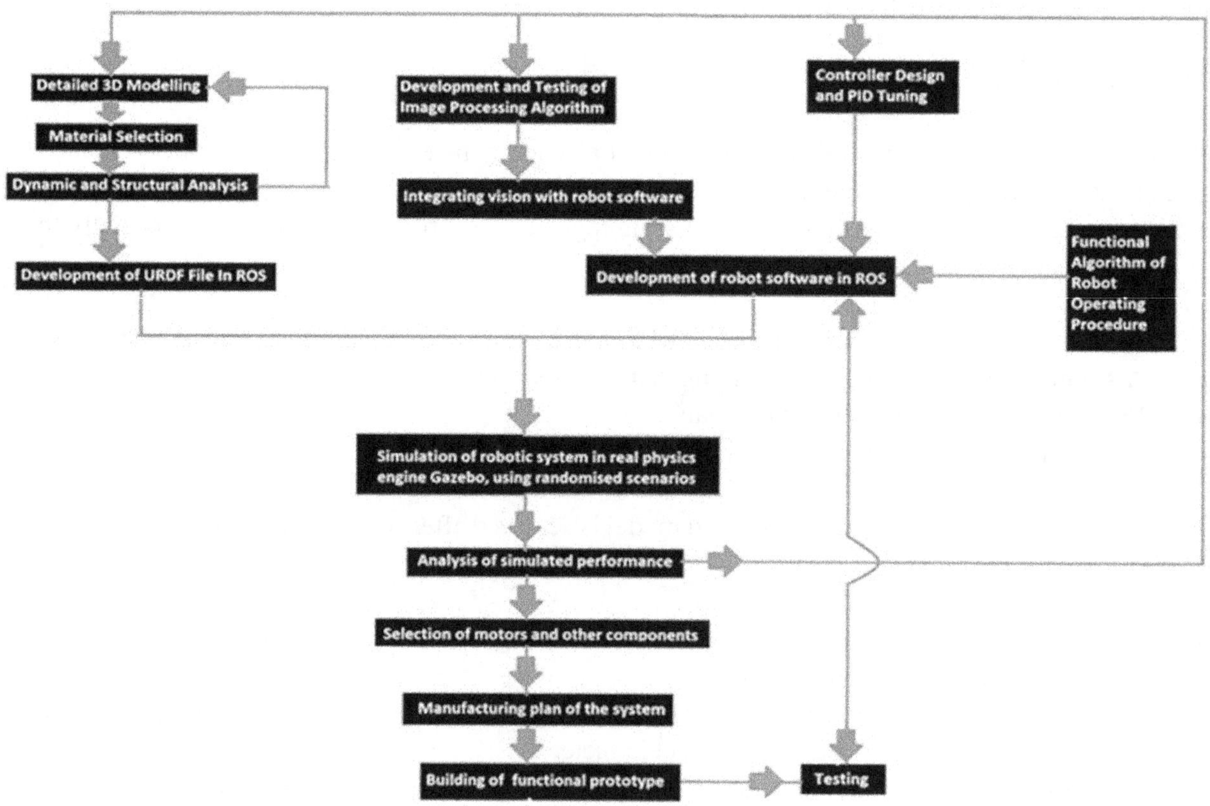

ROBOT SPECIFICATIONS

The study includes a gantry-style robot with a workspace of 14.78 cubic meters. The elevation view of the workspace is shown in Figure 2. It has four degrees of freedom. Electrically driven lead screw mechanisms facilitate the movement in cartesian space. The lead screws are of stainless steel SS304 grade, and most of the structural components are aluminum. Detailed specifications are presented in Table 1. This design is such that once there is a requirement and the procurement is completed, it would take 2-3 working days to assemble and set up the system. The controller used also has built-in connectivity options to be integrated into a virtual cloud and the software in place for managing the entire warehouse operations. We will also shed light on the types of real-time data it can currently reflect on the cloud to visualize the processes, additional possible metrics that it could provide if desired, and the predictive maintenance roadmap in place to plan and schedule downtime.

Table 1. Robot Specifications

Details	**Overall Dimension in meter**	--	
Length	4.5		
Breadth	2.2		
Height	1.8		
Robot Structure: Gantry	**Range of Movements in meter**	**Travel Speed* in cm/sec**	**Resolution in μm**
X	4.4	8.8	11.1
Y	2.1	11	11.1
Z (Vertical Reach)	1.6	4.44	7.4
*Based on the current selection of motors and drivers, under full load			
Rz (Gripper Rotation)	0-360°	600 RPM	0.9°
Total Workspace		14.78 cubic meters	
Degree of Freedom		4 (3 screw joints and 1 friction type external)	
Primary End-Effector		Two-finger gripper	
Estimated Weight (without payload)		95kgs	
Payload Capacity		Upto 2.2kgs	
Sensors		Linear position (x3), current sensor (x4), piezoelectric strange guage, limit switches (x6)	
Perception Hardware		Monocular camera, micro LIDER distance sensor	
Drives		Electric drive	
Power Supply		230V, 5A, 50Hz, 1-Phase Power Supply	

Figure 2. Elevation and Plane View of Workspace

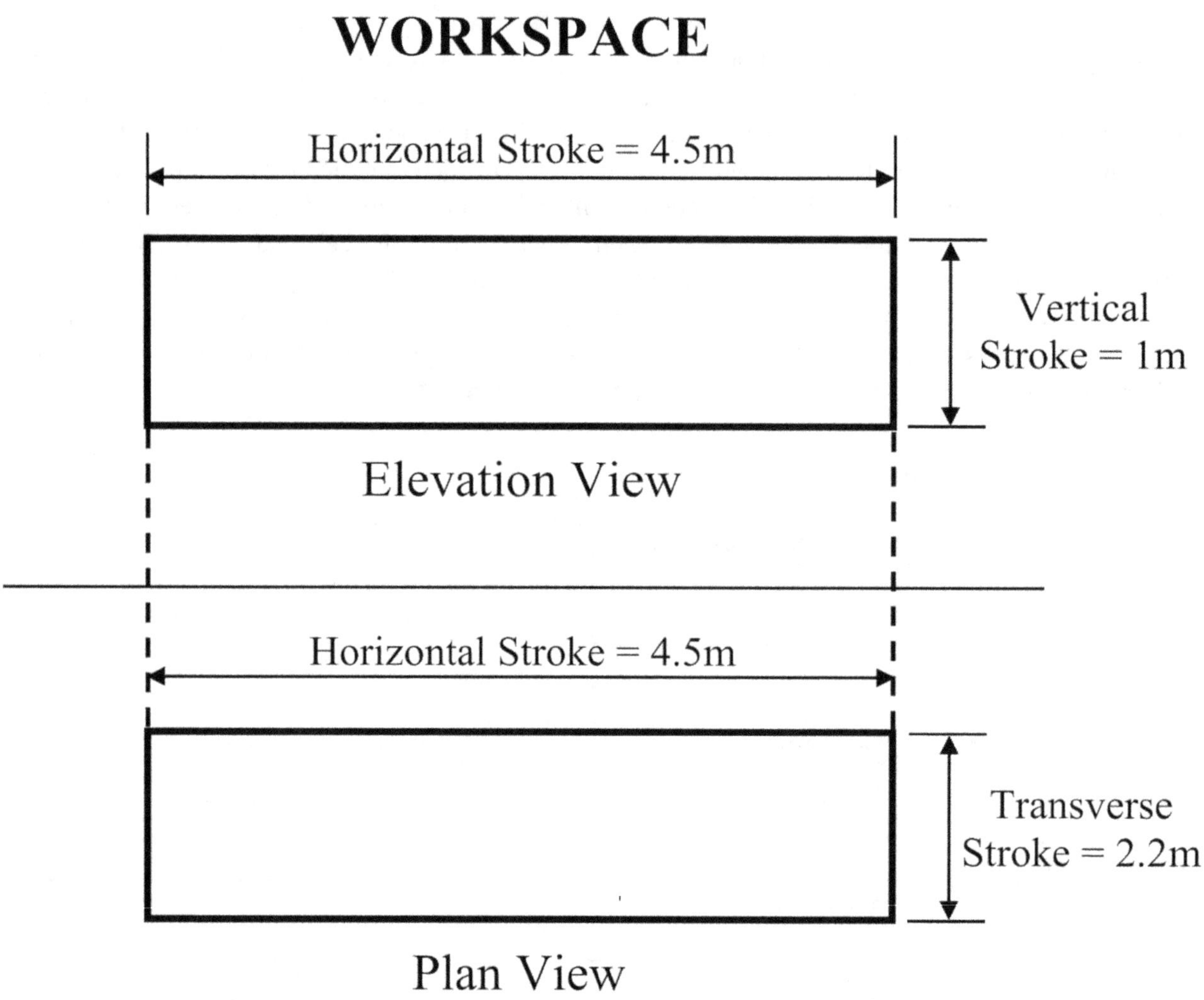

SYSTEM ARCHITECTURE

Figure 3 shows the general representation of the system architecture that presents how the various components fit in the picture together.

The basic system workflow consists of the following three sections -

1. Perception of the robot's environment is the primary task of the system. It responds to any change in its environment (dynamic environment). It also allows the robot to engage with a large variety of parts, making the operations more flexible.
2. Identifying the objects based on their 2D contour data and pose generation from our OpenCV algorithm will help us analyze the robot's functional workspace. Realizing the pickup and drop coordinates w.r.t. the current location of the gripper shall allow us to plan our trajectories accordingly.
3. The final step primarily consists of the actuation of the system. The manipulation module is primarily decomposed to execute in four steps:

Figure 3. System Architecture

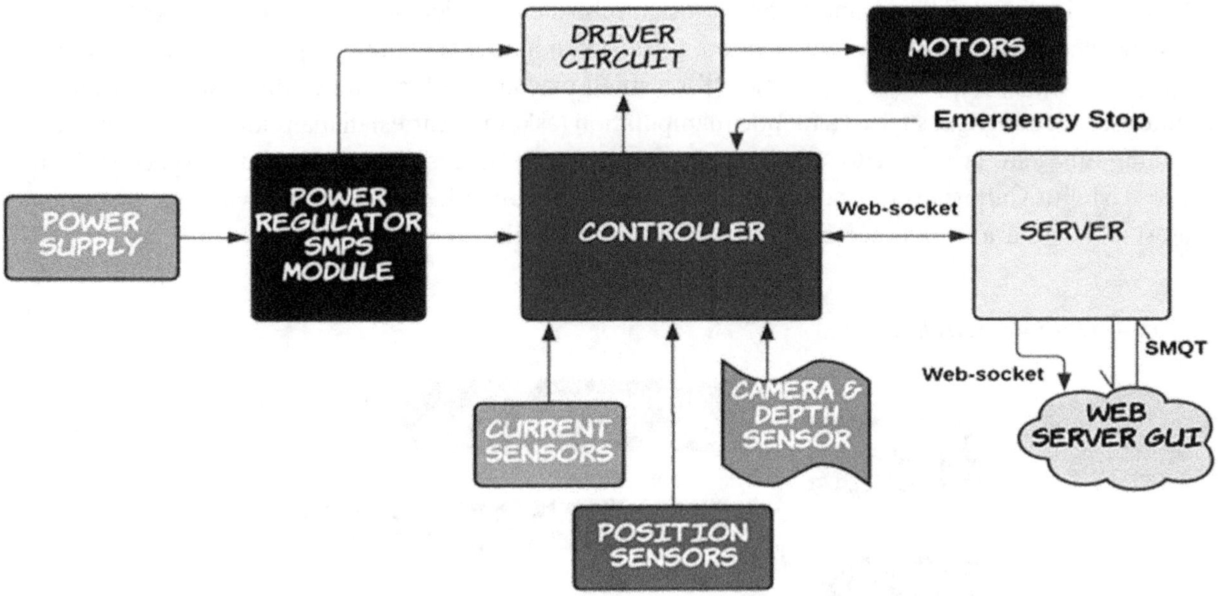

i. performing trajectory planning
ii. moving the physical robotic hand to approach to the object
iii. grasping (suctioning) the thing to move it to the requested position
iv. Releasing the object.

HARDWARE

To meet the design requirements, a systems engineering method has been used to evaluate options, which is using technical performance measures to execute trade-offs between options. The hardware architecture is shown in Figure 4, and details of the hardware are presented in Table 2.

Table 2. Choice of Hardware

Platform Feasibility Study				
Design Criteria	**Weightage**	**Industrial Robotic Arm**	**Mobile Manipulator**	**Gantry System**
Ease of Mechanical Development	3	2.5	2	4
Cost	5	2	1	4.5
Ease of Integration	1	3	2	4
Accuracy	3	5	4	3.5
Speed	2	3	2	5
Dexterity	2	4	4	2
Total (out of 80)		**49.5**	**37**	**63**

We have chosen a gantry system that allows for high structural and dynamic stability over serial robotic manipulators. The advantage of Cartesian robots over articulated manipulators is that they have the same shape irrespective of tool position. Cartesian manipulators are composed of three orthogonal linear actuators. If there is no requirement for a small mechanical footprint or the structure of the environment is not complex, such as a mobile manipulation task, then cartesian manipulators are well suited. Planning times are faster due to simpler inverse kinematics because the configuration space is the task space. Using a Cartesian manipulator with a wrist joint to work in a cartesian workspace eliminates almost all singularities in trajectory and reduces discontinuities.

Figure 4. Hardware Architecture

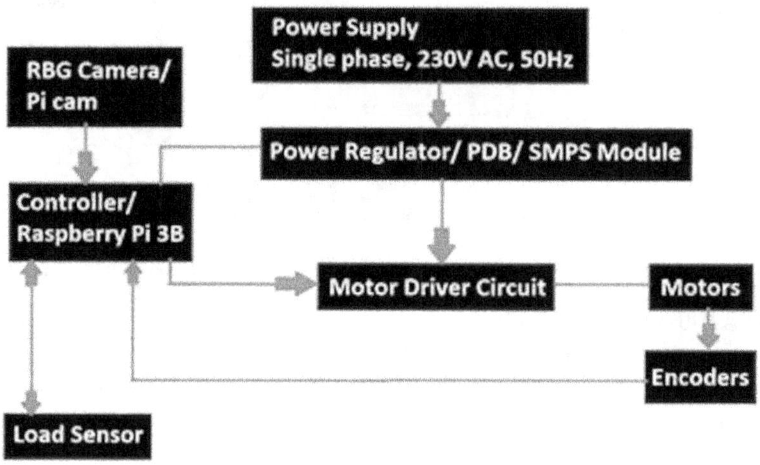

MECHANICAL SYSTEM DESIGN

The mechanical system design includes the gantry and gripper of the developed warehouse robot. The gantry provides stability to the robot when a robot moves in a large workspace to perform some action. The gripper is used to lift the objects even with smooth surfaces, which is the major concern when using a friction force gripper.

Gantry

A gantry system has been chosen for its high structural and dynamic stability while allowing a large workspace (14.78 cubic meters), as shown in Figures 5 to 7. The design facilitates rapid assembling and disassembling of the structure. Solidworks designed all the components first to allow work on the complex workspace, analyze robot, assembly, and avoid interference. Two types of motion analysis have been performed:

- Kinematic analysis is performed for parts and assembly motion under varying forces. The key results of interest were the assembly range of motion and evaluating part displacements, velocities, and accelerations.
- Dynamic motion analysis is performed to evaluate the forces generated by movement.

Finite element analysis and motion analysis have been performed to evaluate the mechanical performance of the robot. It helped by accurately determining the physical movements of the assembly under load. With the assembly motion and forces calculated, structural analysis of the components could be performed to ensure product performance.

Figure 5. Trimetric View of Gantry

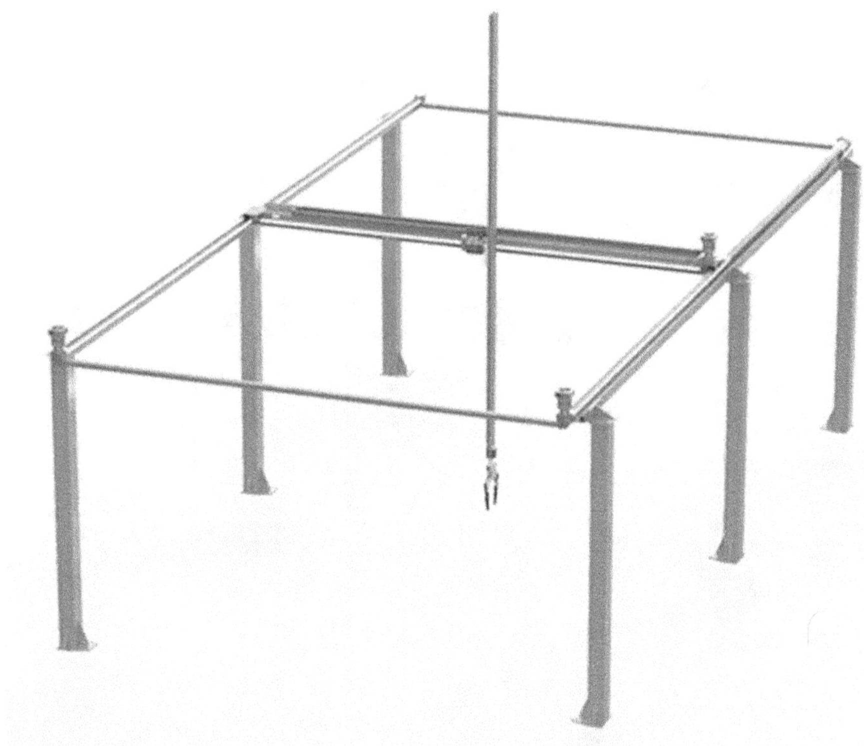

The mainframe consists of three orthogonal linear prismatic joints driven individually by lead screws to achieve the end-effector position in cartesian space. The leads are coupled to hybrid servo motors (with optical encoders and gear heads assembly) to provide accurate linear motion. A typical drive system consists of a current amplifier, a servo motor, a lead screw and coupling mechanism, a viscoelastic bearing, an anti-backlash nut, a guide rail, and a feedback sensor.

Backlash, a common problem in screw drive systems, is the relative axial clearance between a screw and nut without rotation of the screw or nut. We solved this using anti-backlash nuts and a closed-loop control structure. In the Z-axis, anti-backlash nuts have been used to prevent the rear-drive of the screw. To minimize vibrations, viscoelastic dampers are incorporated into one thrust bearing that supports a

Figure 6. Top View of Gantry

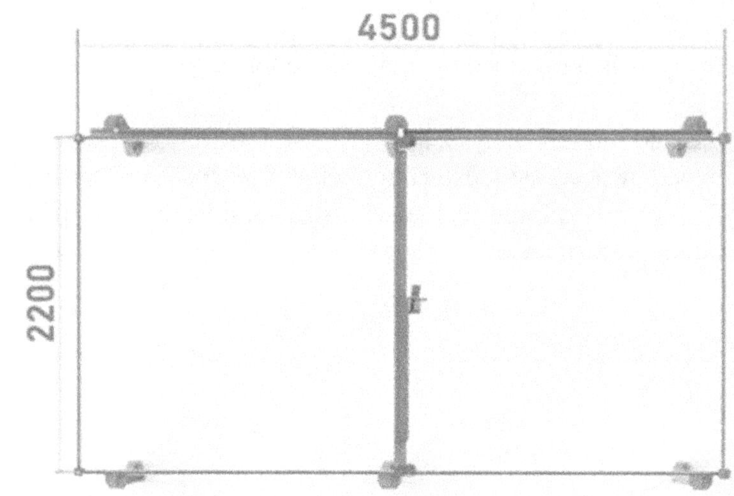

Figure 7. Side View of Gantry

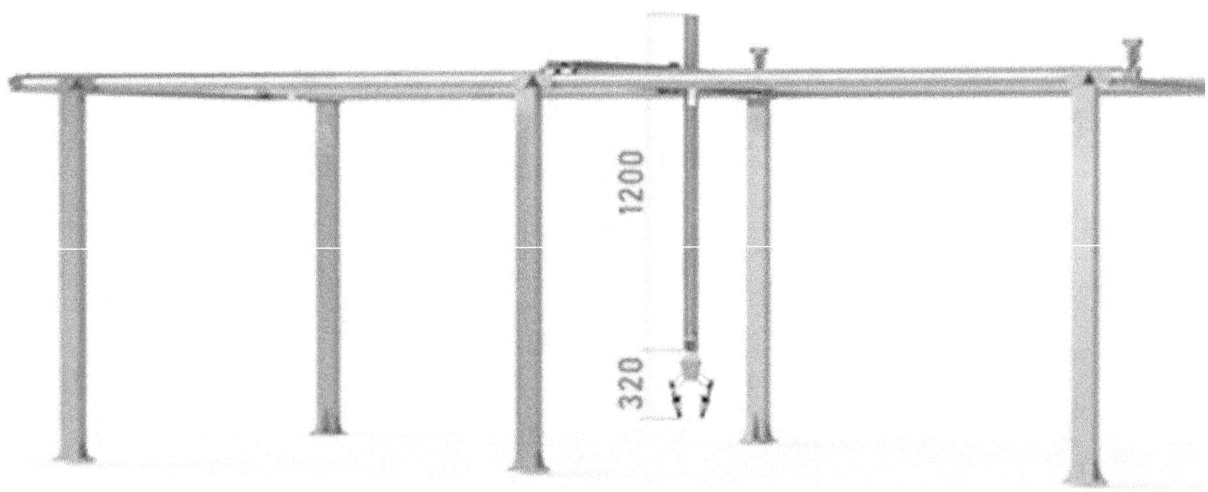

lead screw that provides high damping. Lead screw specification used given the application, load, and speed requirements - Diameter: 12mm, Lead angle: 4.44 or 3.37 degrees, Materials: SS304.

Gripper

The primary end-effector is a custom-designed parallel jaw friction gripper with a maximum stroke length of 220mm. Details are presented in Table 3. Using biomimicry, gecko-inspired surfaces, resist tangential forces by having lots of micro-scaled fibrillar stalks that adhere to a surface using powerful van der Waals forces have been used (Alizadehyazdi, Bonthron, & Spenko, 2020; Menon, Murphy, & Sitti,

Table 3. Gripper Specifications

Gripping Style	Gecko-inspired Friction gripper
Kinematics	Angular
Maximum capacity	5.2 kgs
Maximum stroke	220 mm
Weight	~ 350 g
Actuation	Hybrid NEMA 17 Stepper motor
Feedback Element	Piezoelectric strain gauge, current sensor
Programmable Aspect	Jaw stroke, Jaw speed, Gripping force

Figure 8. Gripper Motion

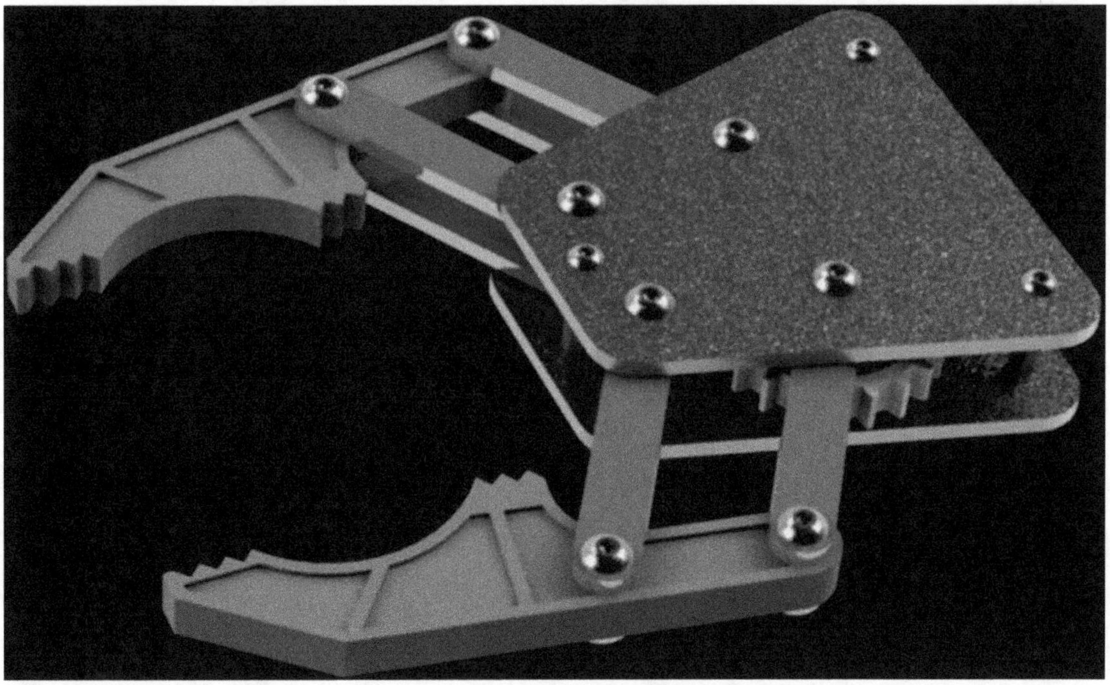

2004). This enables the gripper to lift objects even with smooth surfaces, which are the major concerns when using a friction force gripper, as shown in Figure 8 and Figure 9.

STRUCTURAL VALIDATION

To validate the design, the static structural simulations are performed in ANSYS. One of the most important things we needed to validate was that no buckling occurred in the lead screws, which would

Figure 9. Gripper Finger Opening Dimension

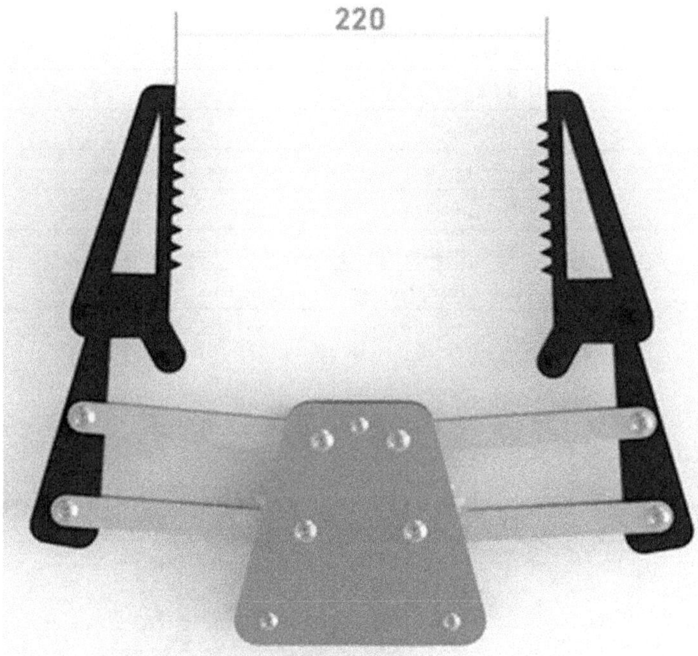

hamper the system's performance. We conducted a structural analysis of the system in ANSYS Student 2020 R1 to check for maximum deformation and maximum principal stress. The experiment was carried out using exact material properties on the CAD model of the lead screws and aluminum V-slot extract, the system's primary load-bearing component. We applied appropriate boundary conditions for each

Figure 10. Static Structural Simulation of V-slot extrusion for Y-axis in ANSYS

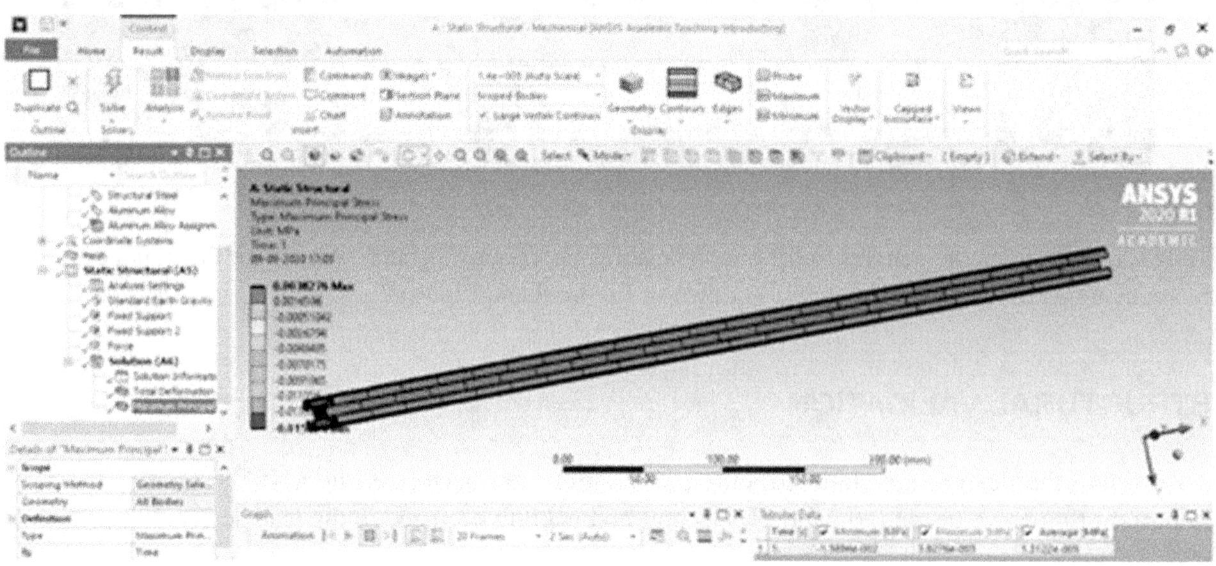

Figure 11. Structural Simulation of Y axis lead screw in ANSYS

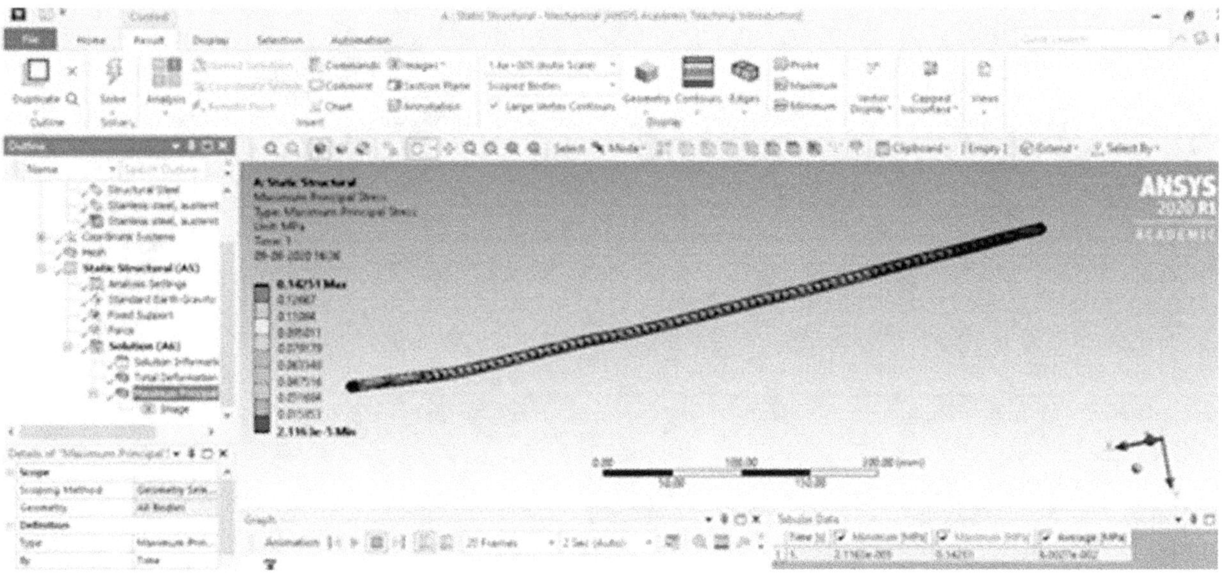

experiment and modeled the experiment using FEM in the static structural module. All results satisfy the design requirements. They do not deform the members significantly or lead to failure or plastic deformation. We also computed a FOS of 2.5 against the payload weight. The simulation output with the details of maximum deformation and maximum principal stress is induced in Figure 10 and Figure 11.

Similarly, simulation-based analyses were also conducted for X-axis lead screws, V-slot extrusions, and Z-axis lead screws.

MANUFACTURING PROCESS

The work requires the fabrication of frame and end effectors. The frame and end effectors of the robot are made up of Aluminum sheets because Aluminum sheets are lightweight and robust.

Frame

The manufacturing process of the frame is relatively simple but consists of a multitude of manufacturing processes. The V-Slot Aluminum Extrusion profile cut pieces were welded together using Metal Inert Gas (MIG) with 100 percent argon to manufacture the frame. The carriageway is fabricated by welding two pre-cut Aluminum plates together. Square steel hollow tube is welded with steel ribs, and Base plates on both ends are used as a multiway support structure. Aluminum guide rails are screwed over the frame after carefully mounting the guide block onto the Rail. The top plate of the carriageway is screwed to the guide block. Lead screws are aligned to end plates with viscoelastic dampers incorporated into the thrust bearings. Similar steps are repeated until the entire assembly of the base frame is complete.

Figure 12. Mechanical Drawing of Friction Type Angular Gripper

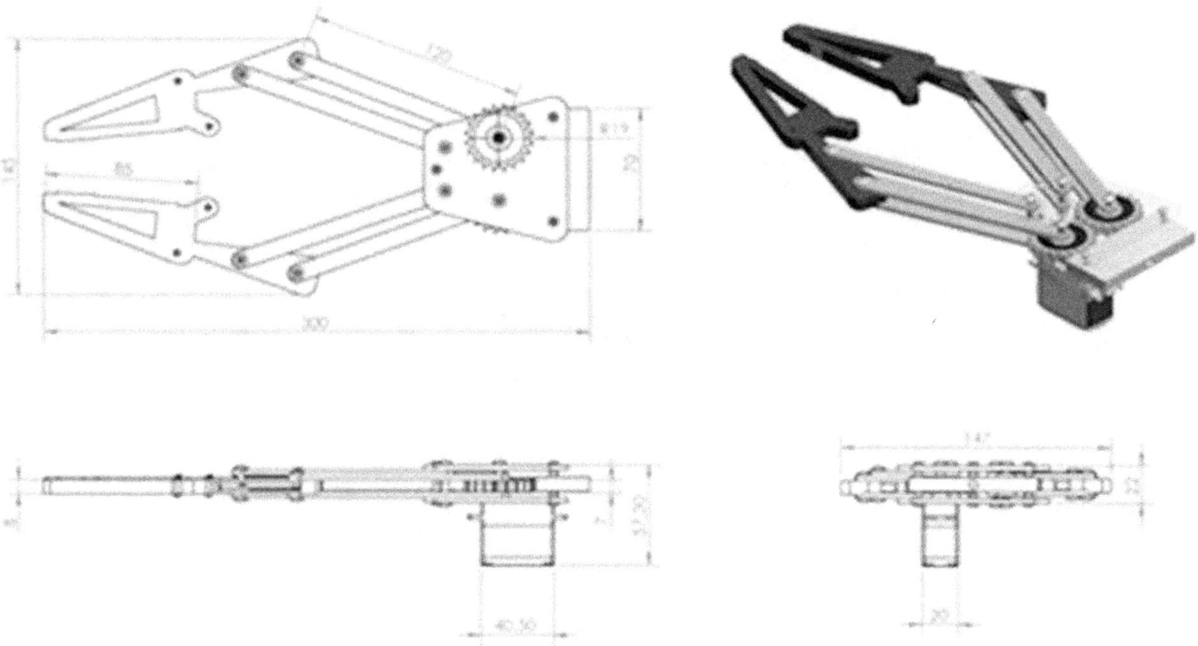

End Effectors

Aluminum sheets are cut as per the drawing to form the various sections of the gripper, as shown in Figure 12. Cast iron gear set is screwed into place on the base plate. These are used because they can bear high tensile pressure components and have self-lubricating properties. Aluminum strips are screwed onto the gear such that any rotational movement of the gear will cause the aluminum strip to move the gripping arm, reflecting the desired action. Gecko-inspired surface with micro-scaled fibrillar stalks is added to the gripping arms. This helps ensure that the gripper can pick the objects without them slipping.

ELECTRICAL COMPONENT SELECTION

The detailed specifications of the motor are presented in Table 4. All the electrical points are soldered to copper cable ends, and connections are secured with rubber shrink tubes. The electrical circuit diagram is presented in Figure 13. Motors with Encoder are mechanically screwed to the requisite positions and wiring connections made per drawing. Ultrasonics sensor and Strain gauge are attached to the gripper, and connections are made with the Raspberry Pi. Limit switches and Emergency stop buttons are installed to ensure the safety of others around during operations and emergencies. Appropriate current sensors are attached to monitor the performance of the system. Cable drag chains are placed throughout the wiring length to protect the wiring from interfering in operation.

Table 4. Motor Specifications

Max Gripper Load	**in kg**
Payload	2
G-force	--
Total	2
Components of 2 Finger Gripper	
Estimated Weight (Aluminium)	0.33
Rubber Padding (2mm)	--
Ultrasonic Sensor	--
Strain Guage	--
Added Weight Whilst Manufacturing	0.1
Gripper Actuation Motor	0.1
Total	0.53
Rz Max Load	
Max Gripper Load	2
Two Finger Gripper	0.53
Tolerance for Additional Gripper	0.5
Added Weight Whilst Manufacturing	0.1
Total	3.13
*Calculation for maximum load on Rz motor.	
Motor Requirements	Stepper Motor (torque output > 4kg-cm) Nema 17, 4.2 kg-cm stepper motor with 1.8 degree step angle or similar.

Perception Hardware

The perception hardware on the robot becomes very important as it allows the robot to understand its environments, variables, and position with respect to the environment. Raspberry Pi powers a mono RGB-D camera sensor and Micro ToF sensor for depth information. The perception hardware and software optimization make it computationally efficient while collecting sufficient data for processing and providing reliable results. Instead of getting a live video feed, which would be difficult to process on a real-time basis, we are capturing snapshots of the workspace from different locations and stitching all these images together to get a complete image of the robot's environment. This also eliminates the need for an ultra-wide-angle lens to capture the robot's workspace. This eliminates the complexities of correcting for distortions caused by the use of ultrawide lenses. This setup is compared to LIDAR, and the stereo camera setup is computationally more efficient while providing similar accuracy.

Figure 13. Electrical Circuit Diagram

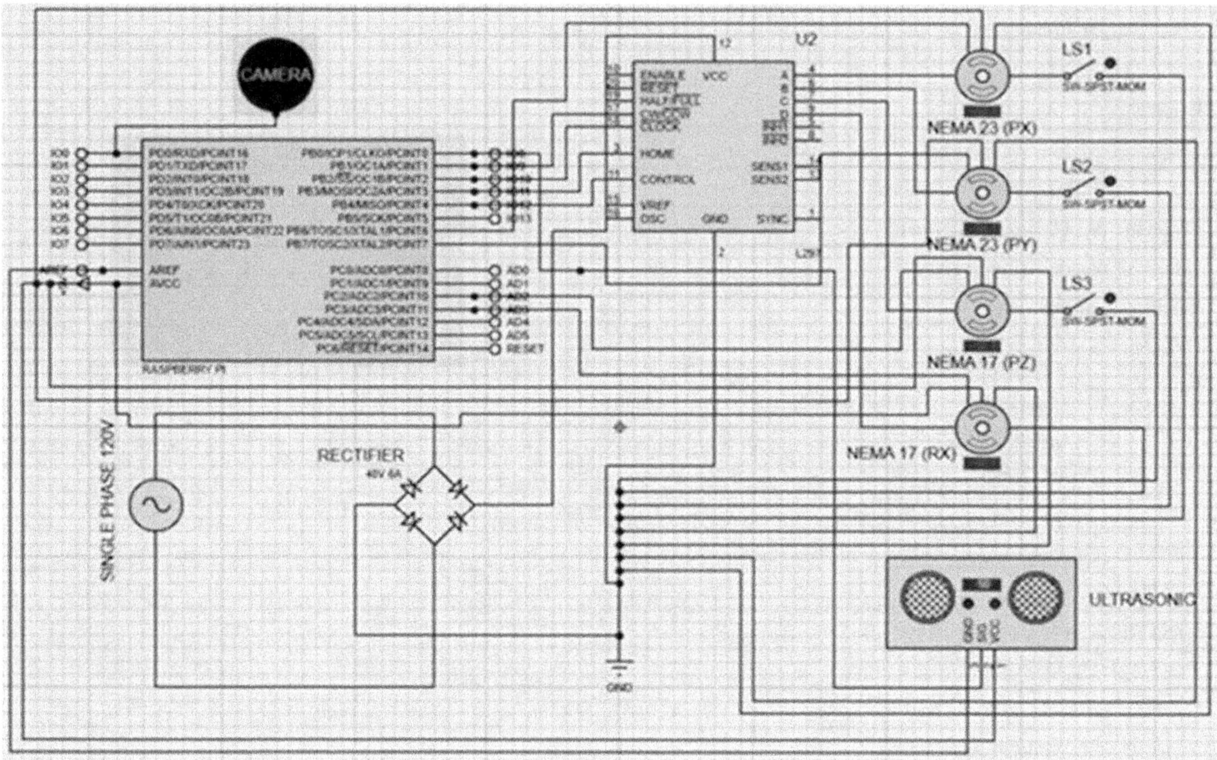

Perception Software

Perception software on the robot becomes very important as it allows the robot to have an understanding of its environment, its variables, and its position with respect to the environment. The perception software helps in eliminating the need for expensive specialized hardware.

Homing is done at the start of the operation, where the entire workspace is captured in small sections, and images are stitched to identify and pick and drop locations. The perception algorithm assists in perceiving the 2D pose data - centroid location (in the workspace), dimensions, and orientation. Using YOLO v2 and 6D pose estimation, object detection is performed through semantic segmentation using DBSCAN. When the end-effector is above the object's centroid, the depth information of the object is collected using a Micro ToF sensor for calculating the depth of dive for grasp. After a successful grasp is made (determined by inputs from the piezoelectric strain gauge and gripper motor current), the system moves the object to the drop location as per the trajectory plan. By incorporating parallel pick and place operation, the system avoids homing maneuver, which aids in saving time in each individual operation, thereby making the process less time-consuming (Beites et al., 2018). The perception algorithm was developed with OpenCV, DBSCAN, YOLO v2, mumpy, and matplotlib libraries, as shown in Figure 15. The algorithm was tested in real environments with test objects, achieving an accuracy of ± 0.8 cm in size and 0.5 deg for rotation, also presented in Figure 15. It is computationally efficient and has fast execution time, 0.262 sec, when compared to algorithms using LIDAR and stereo cameras while providing all required information for grasp planning algorithms to perform efficiently.

Figure 14. Computer Vision Flow Diagram

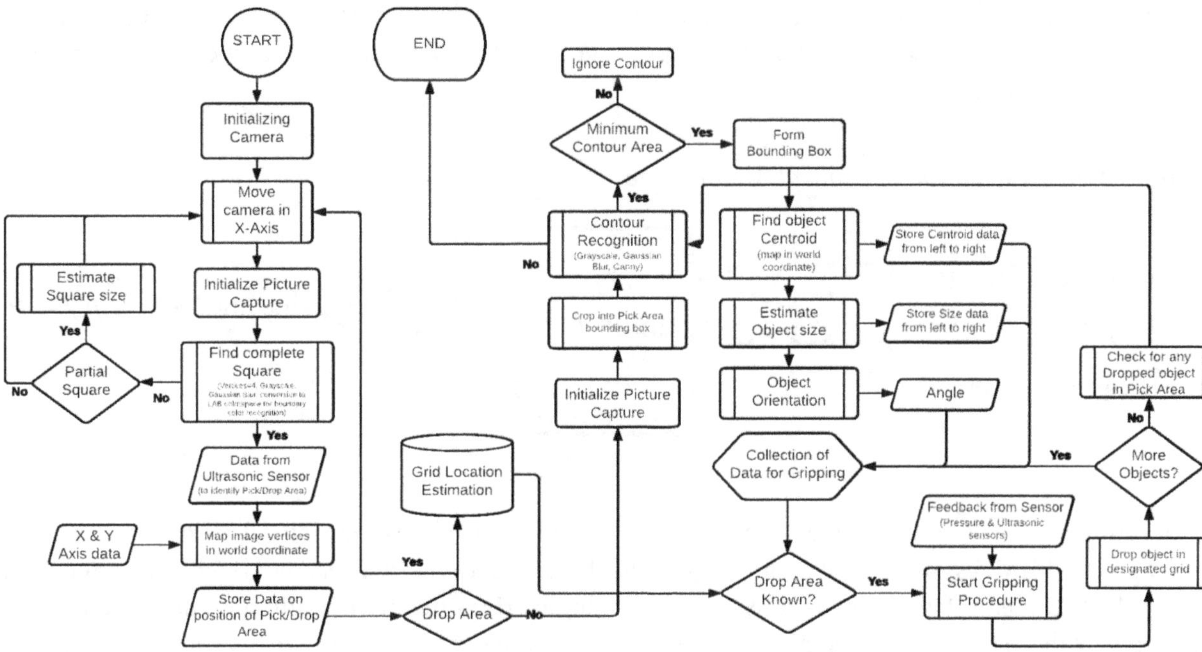

Figure 15. OpenCV Testing Results

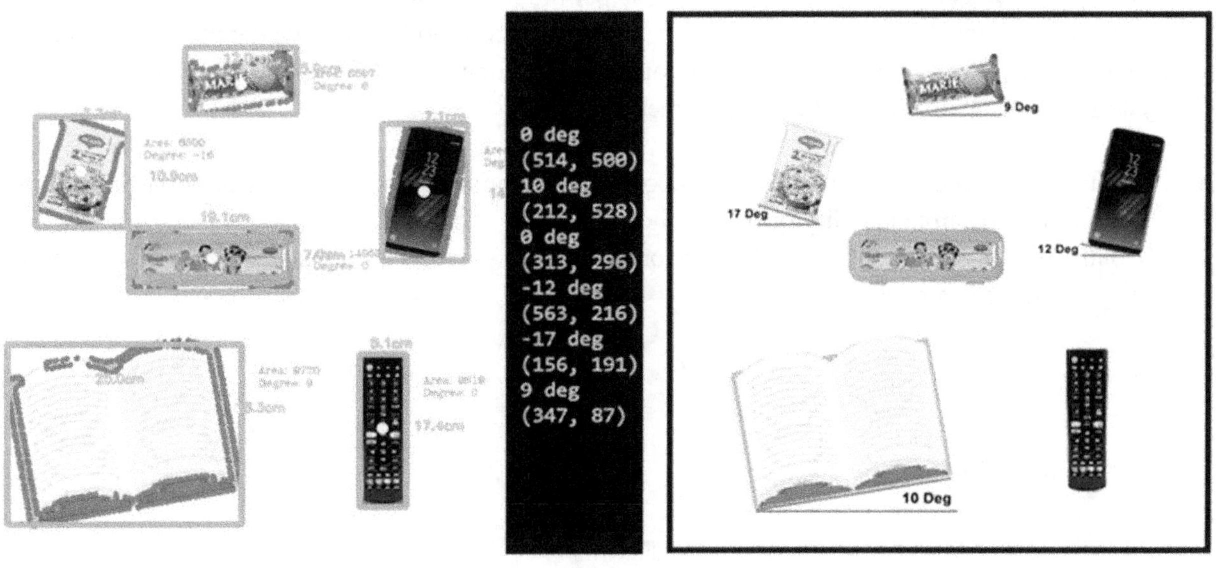

CONTROL ARCHITECTURE

The first and most critical step in the control design is the system modeling, which is presented in Figure 16. We modeled the dynamics of the system using Lagrange's equations. We used Stribeck's friction model to describe real friction. In the Stribeck friction model, the relationship between friction torque and sliding speed is expressed. The frictional force is a nonlinear phenomenon that is derived from the support bearing device of the motor, mechanical and electrical servo system. When the motor is running at high speed, the nonlinear friction of the system is negligible so that the servo unit can be regarded as a linear two-order system.

Figure 16. Representation of Control Architecture

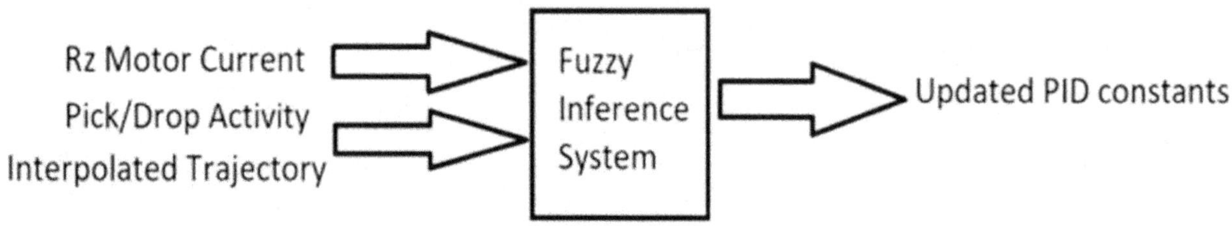

To automate and intellectualize the process of setting PWM signals for motor drivers, we developed a fuzzy logic MIMO system, as shown in Figure 17. Fuzzy supervisory is used to reduce the amount of tuning the PID controller with a fuzzy system. Fuzzy logic brings much flexibility into the system and is an excellent approach to solving nonlinear control problems. We came up with a fuzzy supervisory, which is a hybrid between the traditional PID controller and FLC that is designed to overcome the problem of tuning PID in nonlinear systems using FLC as an adaptive controller. This serves two essential aspects of 1) the system adjusting its dynamic response as per the fuzzy inference system, which fuzzifies PID constants based on the desired type of response. This is to accommodate for varying payloads, 2) in case we use different motors or other system components, our model-based design remains unaffected, and the system automatically adjusts to new parameters.

- Controller for movement to cartesian coordinate without payload (Emphasis on speed without comprising dynamic stability or overloading motors)
- Controller for movement to cartesian coordinate with payload (Emphasis on stability and minimizing g-force on payload).

Figure 17. Simulink Model for a Single Axis

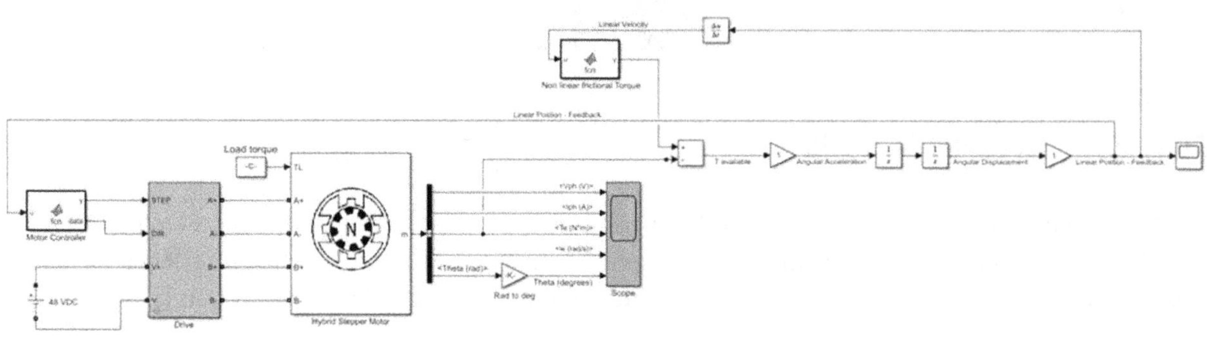

TRAJECTORY PLANNING

The trajectory plan of our system includes a comprehensive process workflow, as shown in Figure 18, which will minimize the distance traversed by the manipulator. We have aimed to limit the time and resources processed for this segment by implementing parallel pick and place operations. The mapping of the entire workspace prior to performing the pick and place operation helps develop an initial visual frame of reference for the robot, aiding in the location of every item in the batch. Sequencing the objects in order to be picked helps the robot save time - knowing which item to pick after dropping the current grasped object serves to avoid the homing action. The OpenCV algorithm assists in perceiving the 2D position data estimate of the object (Guo et al., 2017), thereby helping us to determine the physicality of the target object, i.e., its centroid location, dimensions, and so on. Upon realizing the number of objects to be picked (by mapping the entire functional workspace), we can progress with our plan. When the end-effector is right above the centroid of the target object, the RGB(D) camera is put into play to assess the 3D information of the object in order to determine the depth of dive for the manipulator. Once the height of the object has been determined, we conduct the grasp plan (which has been discussed in the next segment). After the process of grasping the item has been executed, the system realizes the coordinates of the drop location and advances towards the drop action. This has been done in order to opt for a more viable and modular grasping technique. In our solution, we have proposed a parallel pick and place operation methodology (Li, Huang, & Chetwynd, 2018), which will optimize our cycle time for analogous operations. This technique helps in reducing the cycle time of each individual operation, as simultaneous actions overlap in our trajectory plan, consequently shrinking the distance traversed by the manipulator. Trajectory generation builds real-time interpolation parameters. The interpolation device sends discrete position commands to each axis in the control system of each control period. We have assumed the target objects to be rigid and have basic geometric shapes.

Figure 18. Trajectory Plan Workflow

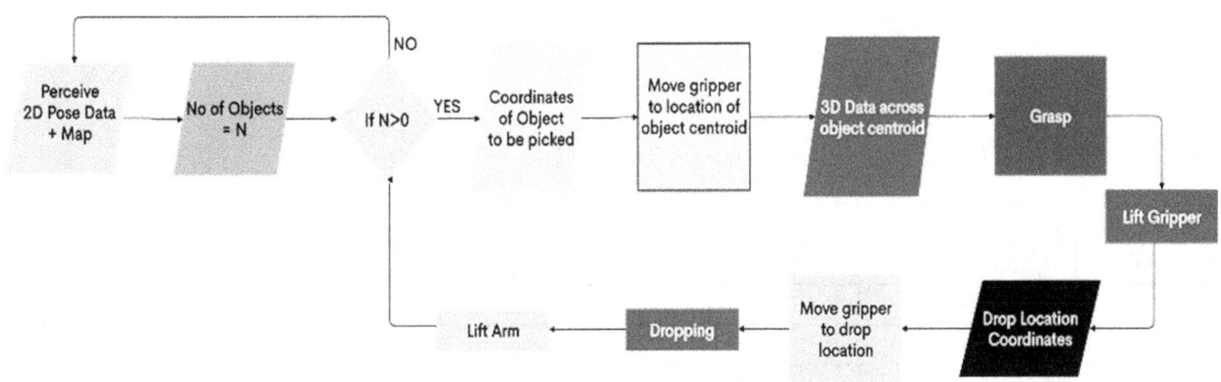

Planning and Inverse Kinematics

The destination location of the manipulator that is to be reached has been considered the object's absolute coordinates. The optimal trajectory planned in our Cartesian robotic system is in a straight line joining 2

Figure 19. Graphical Output of Trajectory Plan using Inverse Kinematics on MATLAB

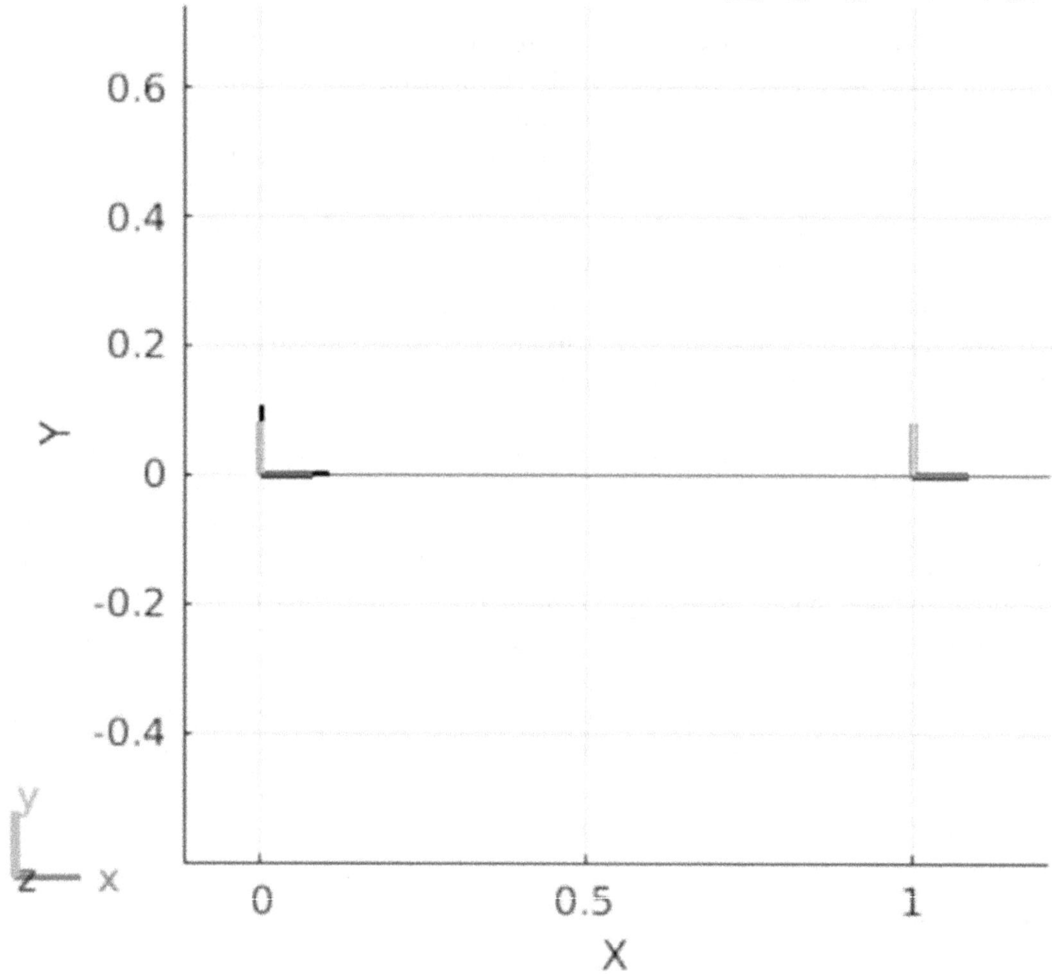

Table 5. Details of Robot's Rigid body Tree on MATLAB

Robot: (3 bodies)					
Idx	Body Name	Joint Name	Joint Type	Parent Name (Idx)	Children Name(s)
1	link1	joint1	prismatic	base(0)	link2(2)
2	link2	Joint2	prismatic	link1(1)	tool(3)
3	tool	fix1	fixed	Link2(2)	--

points in the Cartesian space. This type of trajectory is one such path that can be executed in minimum time, even if a velocity or acceleration constraint exists. Here, we presented the flow diagram of solving the Inverse Kinematics and the yielding plot obtained after simulating our trajectory algorithm for a given straight path on MATLAB, shown in Figure 19. Initially, the robot specifications have been defined, including the number of links, length of links, and the type of joints. The trajectory to be followed by the manipulator has also been established in the program. The details of the robot's rigid body tree are shown in Table 5. After that, the mathematical model of the path is solved using Inverse Kinematics.

Grasp Planning

We have opted for a very modular grasping technique, in which every part of the process has been fractionated into individual segments. The flow sequence is shown in Figure 20. They fundamentally constitute the Input of raw data from the sensors, Processing the information to make sense of the data to the controller, actuation of the manipulators based upon the processed information, and finally, the output being the successful grasping of the item. Our pick-and-drop algorithms are analogous, thereby making our solution simpler and more efficient.

2D pose data and the map of the workspace help determine the manipulator's centroid location. It also helps in establishing the dimensions of the object and its orientation, which will assist in ascertaining the gripper's spread of hand and alignment with respect to the object. The 3D data is observed using an RGB(D) camera, which serves the gripper's depth of dive. This 3D information is further used in placing operations as well.

Figure 20. Picking Operation Flow Diagram

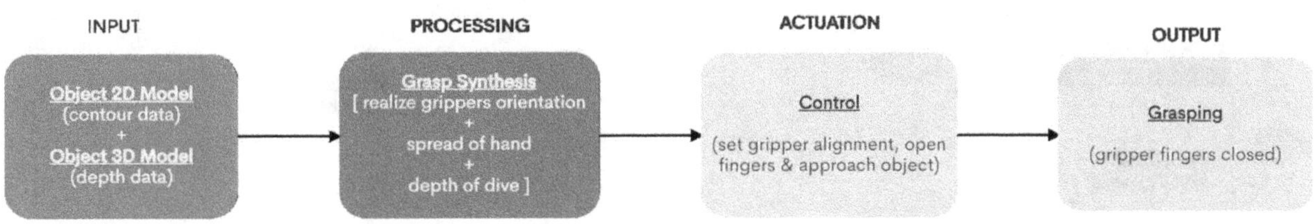

Integrated Software Architecture

The system architecture, inilazation and setuo for the system and working operation sequence have been explained with the help of Figure 21–Figure 23.

Figure 21. Integrated System Architecture

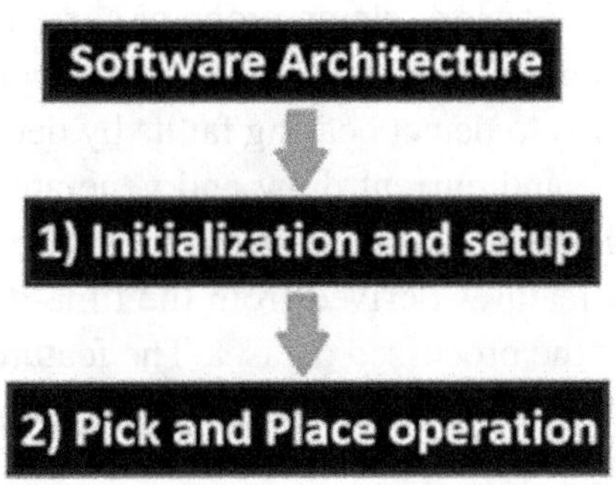

Figure 22. Initialization and setup

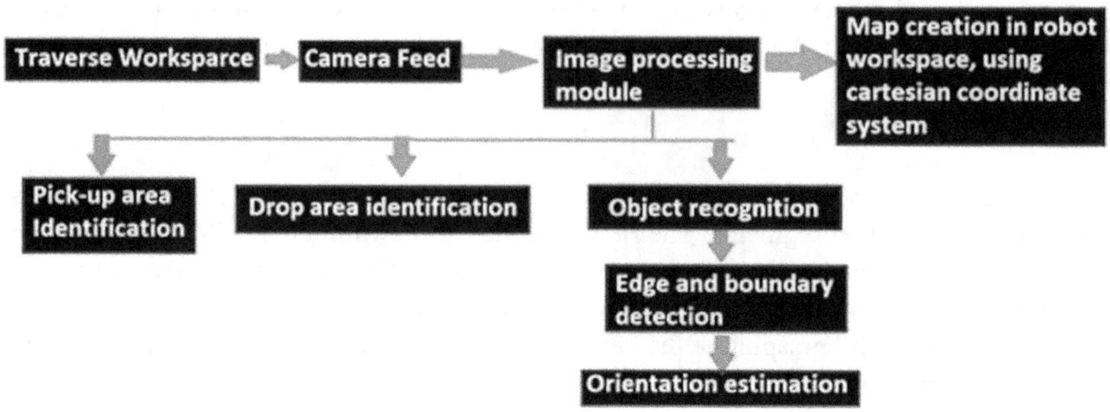

Figure 23. Pick and place operation sequence

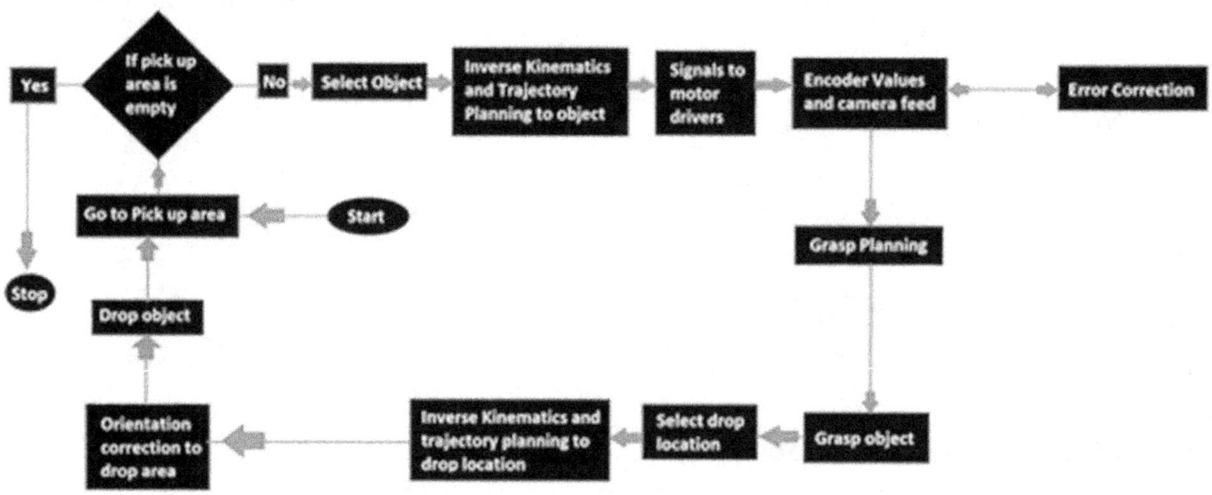

Predictive Maintenance

Motor Current Signature Analysis (MCSA) is used to diagnose problems in the used servo motors. Motor current is sensed by a current Sensor - clamp probe or current transformer with a resistive shunt across its output. The frequency range of interest in MCSA is typically 0-5 kHz. in accordance with the Nyquist theorem. MCSA is also used to detect bearing faults by detection of frequency components.

Data related to vibration, noise, and current draw and generated and stored using the various accelerometers and current sensors installed is visualized in the time domain. Based on the time-domain analysis, a collection of statistical features derived from the time-domain signal and spectral kurtosis is extracted. Noise is reduced from the processed dataset. The features from the dataset are ranked, and Principal Component Analysis is performed to normalize the features into the same scale. The data is further processed into the Exponential Degradation Models for Remaining Useful Life (RUL) estimation.

IMPACT ASSESSMENT

The work has been analyzed to evaluate its social and environmental effects. The assessment helps assess its acceptability in implementing the proposed method in the industrial environment.

Social Factors

The project applies to the logistics industry, which has a wide variety of industries. The individual stakeholders in each warehouse would be operations, maintenance, IT, safety, and finance. The project objectives are aligned to industry requirements in terms of autonomous functionality, safety, and maintenance.

Environmental and Sustainability Actors

There are no harmful environmental factors for the project. It is sustainable and modular by design. The system has induced minimum vibrations on the shop floor, and these can be further reduced by using viscoelastic bearings and a solid ground mount. Going forward, we would like to improve the system's power efficiency to contribute indirectly to environmental health by power savings.

RESULTS AND DISCUSSION

The product performance or the experimental results are presented in this section. We have completed the design, validation, and verification of each subsystem in the solution.

1. Mechanical design and structural validation
    a. Three-axis gantry system with electrical drives
    b. Custom designed gripper with gecko-inspired gripping surfaces
2. Electrical drive design and validation
    a. Motor and driver selection
    b. Sensors selection
3. Software
    a. Control architecture: Intelligent fuzzy supervisory controller for adaptive system response
    b. Computer Vision: Simulated CV test results give 0.8cm and 0.5 degrees accuracy.
        a. Inverse kinematics
        b. Path planning and optimization: Adapted a Parallel Pick and Place methodology for trajectory sequence optimization
        c. Trajectory planning
        d. Grasp planning
        e. Integrated software architecture
4. Manufacturing and Prototyping
    a. Vendor selection and BOM
    b. Manufacturing procedure
    c. Electrical Wiring Diagram
    d. Placement of components and usage of drag chain cable

   e. All components are sourced successfully locally, which also for fast development of robot hardware
5. License for commercialization
   a. Use of components with open BSD license
   b. No patents or IP infringements have been made
6. Complete solution
   a. Detailed design thinking for safety features and finished product
   b. Completely modular design. Software changes for gripper and other robot hardware.
   c. Safety features
   d. Connect ability and integration into the cloud systems
   e. Predictive maintenance

Innovations

A mono RGB-D camera sensor and a Micro ToF sensor for depth information are powered by Raspberry Pi. The perception hardware and software optimization make it computationally efficient while collecting sufficient data for processing and providing reliable results. Instead of getting a live video feed, which would be difficult to process on a real-time basis, we are capturing snapshots of the workspace from different locations and stitching [13] all these images together to get a complete image of the robot's environment. This also eliminates the need for an ultra-wide-angle lens to capture the robot's workspace. This eliminates the complexities of correcting for distortions caused by the use of ultrawide lenses. This setup is compared to LIDAR, and the stereo camera setup is computationally more efficient while providing similar accuracy.

Since the gripper position can be completely controlled in a cartesian frame and rotated about Z., a dual gripper holder can be accommodated in the design to have the same 4 DOF.

- We might incorporate a dual gripper configuration later when we get the detailed list of items to be picked.
- While this gripper is best suited for rigid objects, we have explored two more low costs and simple to assemble grippers:
    - Granular jamming effect gripper for objects with small dimensions (1cm to 5 cm) (components: balloon, funnel, coffee, syringe)
    - Suction grippers for flexible objects (components: vacuum/suction cup, motor-propeller combination, PVC pipe)

CONCLUSION

The robot can detect the pickup area, drop area, and objects using computer vision techniques supported by an onboard RGB camera. The robot can pick up an object of a maximum dimension area of 400 sq.cm from the pickup area by orienting the custom-designed gripper and drop it in an empty slot in the drop area autonomously. It can detect if an item is above 400 sq. cm and/or weighs more than its payload capacity and decide not to pick up the SKU/ throw an error. Real-time data about the number of items in the pickup area, number of items dropped, and estimated time to completion can be obtained from the robot. The robot is a 4 DOF gantry system, with linear actuation in 3 DOF and one rotation about the normal axis of the gripper. Electric drive systems power the robot. It is a servo-controlled robot that has a closed-loop control system. Payload capacity: Up to 2 kgs. Range of linear movement:X: 4.4 m, Y: 2.1 m, Z: 1.6 m. Rotation of gripper 360 degrees about Z-axis using a hybrid stepper motor. Total workspace 9.9 cubic metres.

LIMITATIONS

- The robot proposed is not mobile, hence has a limited workspace and cannot move its base once placed.
- The robot is designed to assume that the pickup and drop areas are within the robot's workspace. The problem statement specifies that the minimum distance between the pickup and drop area is 20cm. We have proposed a feasible solution when the pickup and drop locations are at most 50cm apart.

FUTURE SCOPE

We would like to improve the control behavior using onboard DAQ to tune model performance further. We would also like to combine the multiple grippers into a single multi-modal end-effector. We would like to leverage CornerNet and MediaPipe Objection for real-time 6D pose estimation for object detection. By improving software architecture, the system can also be used for vision-based inspection of its handling of packaged goods. Moreover, future work can include a comparative analysis between the implemented fuzzy method with other soft computing techniques.

REFERENCES

Alizadehyazdi, V., Bonthron, M., & Spenko, M. (2020). An Electrostatic/Gecko-Inspired Adhesives Soft Robotic Gripper. *IEEE Robotics and Automation Letters*, *5*(3), 4679–4686. doi:10.1109/LRA.2020.3003773

Beites, N., Dias, M., Mendes, M. J. G. C., Carreira, F., Campos, F., & Calado, J. M. F. (2018). A gantry robot automatic positioning system using computational vision. *1st Iberic Conference on Theoretical and Experimental Mechanics and Materials/11th National Congress on Experimental Mechanics*, 1031–1042.

Bhandari, V. B. (2010). Design of machine elements. Journal of the Franklin Institute, 256. doi:10.1016/0016-0032(53)90967-3

Bhatia, A., Johnson, A., & Mason, T. M. (2019). Direct Drive Hands: Force-Motion Transparency in Gripper Design. *Robotics Science and Systems: Online Proceedings*. Advance online publication. doi:10.15607/RSS.2019.XV.053

Bolu, A., & Korçak, Ö. (2021). Adaptive task planning for multi-robot smart warehouse. *IEEE Access: Practical Innovations, Open Solutions*, *9*, 27346–27358. doi:10.1109/ACCESS.2021.3058190

Brown, E., Rodenberg, N., Amend, J., Mozeika, A., Steltz, E., Zakin, M. R., Lipson, H., & Jaeger, H. M. (2010). Universal robotic gripper based on the jamming of granular material. *Proceedings of the National Academy of Sciences of the United States of America*, *107*(44), 18809–18814. doi:10.1073/pnas.1003250107

Geng, R. R., Mills, J. K., & Yao, Z. Y. (2016). Design and analysis of a novel 3-DOF spatial parallel microgripper driven by LUMs. *Robotics and Computer-integrated Manufacturing*, *42*, 147–155. doi:10.1016/j.rcim.2016.06.001

Guo, M., Gealy, D. V., Liang, J., Mahler, J., Goncalves, A., McKinley, S., . . . Goldberg, K. (2017). Design of parallel-jaw gripper tip surfaces for robust grasping. *Proceedings - IEEE International Conference on Robotics and Automation*, 2831–2838. 10.1109/ICRA.2017.7989330

Lee, H., & Jeong, J. (2021). Mobile robot path optimization technique based on reinforcement learning algorithm in warehouse environment. *Applied Sciences (Basel, Switzerland)*, *11*(3), 1209. doi:10.3390/app11031209

Li, Y., Huang, T., & Chetwynd, D. G. (2018). An approach for smooth trajectory planning of high-speed pick-and-place parallel robots using quintic B-splines. *Mechanism and Machine Theory*, *126*, 479–490. doi:10.1016/j.mechmachtheory.2018.04.026

Menon, C., Murphy, M., & Sitti, M. (2004). Gecko inspired surface climbing robots. *Proceedings - 2004 IEEE International Conference on Robotics and Biomimetics, IEEE ROBIO 2004*, 431–436. 10.1109/ROBIO.2004.1521817

Moghaddam, M., & Nof, S. Y. (2016). Parallelism of Pick-and-Place operations by multi-gripper robotic arms. *Robotics and Computer-integrated Manufacturing*, *42*, 135–146. doi:10.1016/j.rcim.2016.06.004

Sharma, K., & Doriya, R. (2021). Coordination of multi-robot path planning for warehouse application using smart approach for identifying destinations. *Intelligent Service Robotics*, *14*(2), 313–325. doi:10.100711370-021-00363-w

Speth, J., Morales, A., & Sanz, P. J. (2008). Vision-based grasp planning of 3D objects by extending 2D contour based algorithms. *2008 IEEE/RSJ International Conference on Intelligent Robots and Systems, IROS,* (3), 2240–2245. 10.1109/IROS.2008.4650632

Vahid-Araghi, O., & Golnaraghi, F. (2018). Friction-Induced Vibration in Lead Screw Drives. *Angewandte Chemie International Edition*, *6*(11), 951–952.

Chapter 5
Interpretive Structural Modelling of Critical Factors Influencing E-Commerce in India

Alisha Lakra
Kalinga Institute of Industrial Technology (Deemed), Bhubaneswar, India

Suchismita Satapathy
Kalinga Institute of Industrial Technology (Deemed), Bhubaneswar, India

Sushanta Tripathy
https://orcid.org/0000-0003-2470-4080
Kalinga Institute of Industrial Technology (Deemed), Bhubaneswar, India

Brajaballav Kar
https://orcid.org/0000-0002-2127-1147
Kalinga Institute of Industrial Technology (Deemed), Bhubaneswar, India

ABSTRACT

Digitization has made the channel of doing the business easier and timeless. With the fast-growing economy with e-commerce, it becomes a priority to study the parameters that influence e-commerce. In this paper, the authors have recognized nine factors: customer satisfaction, user interface, gender-related approach to e-commerce platform, company's association with customers, data breach, digital literacy, localization of internet content, digital infrastructure, and government policy. This chapter presents a keen study on the contributions of the factors on the e-commerce structure. Interpretive structure modelling technique has been used to provide a systematic judgement on the influence of provided parameters. MICMAC analysis has been carried out to classify the critical factors as per their dependence and driving powers. Results from the study have shown that customer satisfaction is the most dependent factor and the long-term goal to achieve for an e-commerce success. Government policy remains lowest in the strata and derives all the other parameters.

DOI: 10.4018/978-1-6684-4969-1.ch005

Copyright © 2022, IGI Global. Copying or distributing in print or electronic forms without written permission of IGI Global is prohibited.

INTRODUCTION

E-commerce can be simply defined as the channel of business through which the process of selling, buying and exchange of goods and services and transfer of money and data over any digital platform is done to complete a transaction. The advent of digitalization has changed our perception of doing business, from a long establishment of transactions through paper has transitioned to the digital mode of transactions, where the buying and selling of products are easier and timeless, making it more accessible.

There is no doubt in the scene where e-commerce has shown its growth from its first usage of online medium until now. In 1995 were there only around 16 millions users globally the number has increased to 4.9 billions worldwide, which roughly constitute the two-third of the global population (Johnson, 2022). The growth in internet users has seen the increase of global e-commerce sector. Concerning the type of transactions, e-commerce they can be roughly achieved through following ways:

- **Business to consumer**- common of all, it represents the process of transaction where a consumers purchases products directly through the business. For instance when a consumer buys a product from an online retailer.
- **Business to business-** it presents the process of transaction where a business is selling goods or services to another business. Here the buyer is not the end consumer but rather another business operator. This style of business takes place between wholesalers or retailers, where products under transaction are usually is raw material, unfinished produce or a part of component used for further assembly processes.
- **Consumer to consumer-** a direct transaction interaction where a consumer directly sells the product to another consumers. This type of transactions taking place can be seen on platforms like ebay, Etsy, OLX, etc.
- **Consumers to business-** a category of transaction where an individual sells his products or services to the business operators. This group essentially constitutes the photographers, free-lancers or consultants.

Nevertheless the sole stage of transaction in all forms is the digital platform. Comparing through the traditional method of transaction, the digital transaction of e-commerce is not only effortless but also provides a broader platform to do the business. It also reduces the transaction cost marginalizing to just the logistics costs, secures a better market share giving access to global markets with good business opportunity with an advantage of lower entry cost.

Various works have already shown the impact of digitalization in the business and it has always stood to be of gain. Where in developing countries the major concern lies in acquiring ways to connect the population through the internet, while in developed nations the concern is about the deployment of next generation technologies (E-commerce in developing countries, in press, 2013). Work has been done regarding the developed countries and lack of proper understanding of the impact is seen in under developed or developing countries. India is a growing economy and with rapidly increasing internet users the next step which lies ahead of us is to recognize the parameters that would affect the Indian e-commerce market and how it can be utilized by the organizations to benefit them.

The study of e-commerce in India has shown that, e-commerce has proven to be a major booster in the country's economy. In a report published by India Brand Equity Foundation in its Indian e-commerce Industry Analysis has estimated that e-commerce in India will grow to 99 billion by the year 2024, which is growing at a rate of 27% CAGR (Compound Annual Growth Rate) over the year of 2019-2024. Where major income share has been seen in the sectors of grocery and fashion and apparel. The induction of innovative models and ideas which has replaced the old structure has also been an additive factor to the economy. With a fast pacing business orientation there has always been a scope of disintegration, which comes as risks which adhere to the e-commerce. Cyber Security threat is pronounced as the major concern for failure in e-commerce business which primarily prevents consumers to depend on e-commerce. Recent massive data breach of Jubliant FoodWorks which handles the information data of Domino's India has been hit with a major blow of cyber attack. According to The Times of India, personal information of around 18 crore orders we made available online on the dark web (Hariharan, 2021). Immediate action taken by the company in securing the remaining data and prevention of escalation of leaked data only assured the customers on the business. E-commerce companies like BigBasket, and Aditya Birla Fashion and Retail were also hit by similar incidents. It was only the adaptive capability of the company to respond immediately to the tight situation gave them an upper hand in resolving the matter and also successfully maintained the trust of customers(Scholten & Schilder, 2015). Previous works have mentioned that Customer satisfaction is one of the priorities the organizations should look for while discussing the development of e-commerce. A consumers reliability is the reason why a business flourishes especially e-commerce, where transactions are made through mutual trust between the consumers and retailers or business operators. Since no physical contact is established between the consumers and business operators, it becomes essential for the business to establish trust, which is often achieved through good service and customer satisfaction. Recently Myntra an online e-tailer was in hitch when an NGO accused it of its logo being offensive. Without withering Myntra looked into the matters and immediate took steps to improvise their logo over their market, which not only gave it the slip from the accusation but also gained praise through public response for its swift action. Hence while doing e-commerce it is not only important to satisfy a customer but often how a company shows its resilience behaviour through different prospects improves the overall image of the business and improves trustworthiness among its consumers. It can roughly be explained as a tests of a business's flexibility, responsiveness, quality, productivity and accessibility(Rajesh, 2016). Other factor like government policy also plays an important role, even after two decade of internet introduction in India there wasn't much progress seen on the digital sector. But recent government policies and aid have been of great help. With the help of government's initiation to develop digital infrastructure in the country through fast tract process have not only attracted foreign investments but also encouraged institutes to develop domestically. Nykaa and Lenskart are such examples. Founded in 2012 and 2010 respectively are already in the unicorn club who mainly do business through online platform. All this was only possible because of speedy development of internet. Internet based commerce has always been proved to have an upper hand over the traditional method of business.

Many prior research study has focused on the parameters affecting the functioning of e-commerce but not much content is available in context to developing nations. In this paper we have tried to focus on one such affair that is the influence of e-commerce in India. The objective of this paper is to identify the parameters that has been influencing the e-commerce environment in India. Develop a correlation between the suggested parameters and determine the driving and dependence variables through those parameters.

With Indian e-commerce estimated to reach around US$200 Billion by the year 2026 it is a high time we must recognize the parameters which are influencing the e-commerce studying their long term and short term impacts and paraphrase our strategies for maximum benefit.

Through the study of prevalent data and information provide by previous writers, we have been able to identify some factors that are relevant to the Indian E-commerce. These factors identified were Government Policies, Digital Infrastructure, Data Breech, Digital Literacy, Localization of Internet Content, Company's inter-relation with customer, User Interface, Gender related Perception and Customer Satisfaction.

Our research gap suggested that:

1. There has been found no paper directly linking and developing the inter-relationship between the factors concluded.
2. The factors selected does not exhibit any impact as such in short term and long term scenario.

Hence after identifying the problem scenarios, the following situations has been put up:

RQ1: What is the inter-relationship between the factors put forward.
RQ2: Which factors among the suggested factors are to be considered as the short term focus and the long term focus which would be affecting the e-commerce in India.

To work on our objective, Interpretive Structural Modelling has been used to develop a relationship between the suggested parameters for e-commerce. The driving and dependence power has been derived through the use of MICMAC (Matriced' Impacts Croise's Multiplication Appliqué an un Classement) Analysis. The results from the ISM has been used as inputs for the MICMAC Analysis. Through further assessments the ISM Model gives a hierarchical idea of level of impact of parameters on the e-commerce society.

The paper is executed in a manner which follows the works of previous researchers operating on their findings related to e-commerce; following which the identification of parameters are done. Backing up the driving and dependence variables are recognized through the proposed ISM methodology. The results gives the understanding of the ISM framework. It concludes with the result discussion relating to practical implications and suggesting future scope.

LITERATURE REVIEW

Factors affecting e-commerce is a very broad term to work on. In this paper we have tried to simplify and categorize the long term and short term parameters that have undeniable effect on the e-commerce functionality. For a successful working of e-commerce it is very essential to maintain a consumer's trust and provide standardized satisfaction ((Tang & Zeng, 2021), (Malhotra et.al, 2017)). Immediate parameters affecting the ongoing trends in e-commerce are mainly the government policies (Chan & Palmeira, 2021) and the consumer's readiness to accept the change from their traditional method of transition to the digital platform. Through various studies we have concluded Table 1, which gives an overview of parameters that have been found to affect e-commerce while functioning in a system.

Chan & Palmeira (2021) mentioned that Government Policies are the core to any development in a particular region. It's impact is at odds because it changes with region and has underlying factors determining it. A developmental policies will bring forth the expansion of working environment of e-commerce, whose foundation is laid through development of digital infrastructure. With their installation the next challenge lies in the establishment of consumer's acquaintance to the digital advancements. The overall progress of the e-commerce lies on the nature of relationship of consumer with the organization. Giving prime priority to a consumer' satisfaction the company also has to keep in mind the it's presentation and keep at hand the approach to recover itself demanding situations.

Table 1. Parameters identification for e-commerce

Important Factors for Implementation	Description	Researcher
Government policies	Government ideology impacts the overall perception of the consumers. Government policies have helped introduce the digital the structure in a country which broadens consumer's scope of doing business.	Chan & Palmeria (2021), Wudie (2020)
Digital infrastructure	The use of electronic virtual tools has shown a positive result in developed countries by bringing in economic efficiency. The progress of establishments of digital infrastructure will only further develop the involvements of e-commerce.	Akhmetova et.al (2020), Chai et.al (2018)
Data breach	Data breach was seen to disrupt people's interest from digital platforms, this as a result has impacted the dependence of consumer on e-commerce. Trust is what needs to be accomplished by the business, which would help businesses continue their course of work through the consumers.	Chan & Palmeria (2021), Chun (2019)
Digital literacy	Development is seen in education sector through growth of digital literacy	Reddy et.al (2020)
Localization of internet content	Positive inter-dependency is seen between the cultural denomination and e-commerce acceptance. Language forms the mode of transaction between the business and consumers, and localization of internet content has shown better acceptance of e-commerce through the consumers.	Merhi (2021), Abbad (2018)
Company's inter-relation with customers	Improved relationship between the company and consumers have helped retained customers to the e-commerce resource. A company's agility to perform through various situations holds impression on the consumer.	Anand et.al (2018), Rajesh (2016)
User interface	User interface of a e-commerce impacts the customer's awareness and readiness to use the platform.	Pratama & Cahyadi (2020)
Gender related perception	A website's aesthetics and usefulness determines the gender related perception of that e-commerce site	Nissen & Krampe (2021)
Customer satisfaction	Direct relation has been seen between the customer satisfaction and e-commerce. With development of customer satisfaction e-commerce has only thickened. Customer's trust is the major driving force for the development of e-commerce.	Tang & Zeng (2021), Malhotra et.al (2017)

AFFECTING PARAMETERS

1. Government Policies

Government's policies lay the foundation for the development of practical usage of e-commerce in the country. The lack of standard resources and infrastructure in digitalization has kept the growth the e-commerce. This can be improved through Government's intervention of introducing various projects. The government's ideology has often impacted the business. There are conservationist and liberals in the political body who posses the power and ability to influence the consumers (Chan & Palmeira, 2021). Study has shown that how any political ideology has the capacity to aspire and mould systems in terms for the interest of a country where fractions like engagements, aid, support, freedom and security forms an integral part for the government while dealing with other competitors (Wudie, 2020). Seeking such competitiveness globally, India in recent years has introduced major policy changes which has targeted the commerce society in the country. Apart from challenging cross-border e-commerce, major changes in national level has been initiated. One of the major achievements came through in the payment structure in e-commerce industry when the mode of payment was made flexible from traditional cash payment to the digital platform of transaction. Under this initiative the government introduced the Pradhan Mantri Jan Dhan Yojna (Prime Minister's People's Wealth Scheme) whose sole purpose lies in the instigation of exclusive usage of digital payments and financial service through the consumers of all sections of the society, through this scheme Government of India has also introduced the Rupay(Rupee and Payment) system which is a payment service with an aim to established multi-lateral payment system .

2. Digital Infrastructure

India's digital payment took a leap with the Governments flagship programme of "Digital India" were its role lies to make country 'Faceless, Paperless, Cashless'. To promote a cashless society various forms of digital payments were made available like Banking Card, Internet Banking, Mobile Banking, Mobile Wallets, Mirco ATM, Pre-paid card, Point of Sale, USSD, AEPS and UPI. Among these the UPI(Unified Payment Interface) is game changer, developed under the initiative of Reserve Bank of India, India's central bank the National Payment Corporation of India(NPCI), UPI has provided the country with the key infrastructure to further improve the payment system in the country. It has the provision for inter-bank(person to person) and person to merchant (person to business) transaction. Apart form that, third party apps like GooglePay, PhonePay, Paytm, Amazon Pay, Samsung Pay, Whatsapp Pay and Mobiwiki are some of the examples that can also be integrated with the UPI for various transactions. This operation has been so successful that the National Payment Corporation of India's foreign arm, NPCI International Payments Ltd, has partnered with Liquid Group Pte. Ltd to facilitate cross-border UPI transactions in Asian countries. Singapore, Malaysia, Thailand, the Philippines, Vietnam, Cambodia, Hong Kong, Taiwan, South Korea, and Japan are among these countries (Liquid Group to power UPI or acceptance in 10 Asian Markets, 2021, in press). RuPay a domestic alternative for MasterCard and Visa has also been introduced for cheaper transaction. Study has shown that India is in the phase of rapid digitalization but with limited digital infrastructure (Bhaskar et.al, 2020, in press), country lacks the infrastructural capabilities to make most of its transactions cashless, key problems lying in failure of payment platforms and poor internet connectivity. It has been seen that digital customs has facilitated e-commerce on regards to single window system. Proper necessary amendment should be made to facilitate digital facility across country especially in the peripheral areas. Intervention of national government makes the processes fast paced ((Akhmetova, 2020), (Chai et.al, 2018)).

3. Data Breach

Data breach is a very serious issue why consumers don't want to be dependent on the digital medium for their transactions.When a transactions is made there is an exchange of data, where these are done commonly through mobile phones, tablets or computers, where it exposes itself to hitch like privacy and data breach. Irrespective of these situations, a business attempts to maintain a standard to provide certain level of security for their consumers in a way to provide a sense of reliability(Chun, 2019). Still though circumstances are unavoidable and data systems are breached which bares the personal information and data of the consumers. These cases are sometimes deflected and sometimes not, but what takes on consumers is the trust established between the company and the consumers.The situation challenges the business on how it handles the problem and how it shoulders the responsibility and it's strategy to deal consumers(Chan & Palmeira, 2021). In India there have recently been many cases of security breach, such as those of Domino's, where a security researcher revealed that credit card details of around 1 million customers of Domino's India were breached(2021), incident of Upstox(2021) were it was found that around 2.5 million records were compromised, similar incident of BigBasket were details of 20 million people were leaked(2020) and many others. Giving an easy access to a customer's personal information and data through the Dark Web. Given the complications, the Government and the company collectively had tried to disable any possible way of further circulating the information and trying to rebuild the trust of the customers. Hence it becomes extremely essential for a business to respond responsibly to such mishaps and protect the dignity of the consumers. Usually in these cases the company apologizes or even compensates for the loss of the consumer. Government also plays an important role wherein policy makers can take up the situation to formulate Bills which will protects a consumer's personal data and make a company responsible in case of any lapse.

4. Digital Literacy

Digital literacy is the major factor why the growth of e-commerce has been so prevalent. It is not just a domestic but a global challenge to educate the mass in fields of digital literacy. In India where considerable population lives in the rural region,it is very important that people get acquainted well with the internet for their digital upliftment (Reddy et.al, 2021). Hence importance lies in the development of digital literacy throughout the country. In India the two major components that has given the boost the digital exposure are easier access to digital equipment and availability of cheaper mobile network. With technological advancement and simpler government policies which has given tech companies easier access to Indian market, has only improved the market for better and tougher technological competition. This has given advantage to the consumer to provide themselves with product which is better, more advanced at a cheaper price tag. This has overall improved the digital environment in the country, where more competitions have give rise to more technological innovations leading organizations to develop more which all together gives an additional value in the country's economy.

5. Localization of Internet Content

India being a huge country with over 1.3 billion people with a varied set of culture and language, it becomes the chief priority for an e-commerce company to reach into larger portion of consumer. It was found that national culture does have affect on the adoption of e-commerce and it's usage, yet there is a lack of it's in-depth examination. Previous researchers have suggested that consumers are more attracted to the digital platform when the constrains of linguistic barrier is shortened or removed (Abbad, 2018). An introduction of multi-lingual interface on the platform will not only give customers better experience through their shopping but will also attract a larger crowd of consumer(Merhi, 2018). Such initiative will only show participation of consumers through a steady long term plan. Commencement of this procedure has already started as steps have been taken to introduce regional languages in the main stream e-commerce, popular languages like Hindi, Bangla, Tamil and Telegu has already been introduced in some e-commerce platforms like Amazon, Flipkart and Myntra and they have yielded a positive result. Future work can be done to include more languages and search parameters can be modified in a manner that they are able to identify the prospects of the consumers and deliver the conventional results.

6. Company's Interrelation with Customers

Owing to customer's interest company tries to maintain a good relationship with their customers. It is a common practice that company contact their customers on regular basis giving special attention festivals or any national events. Consumers are stocked with special discounts, cashback or gift voucher exhibiting captivating deals to keep them engaged(Anand et.at, 2018). In case of any predicaments how a company manages its reputation and deals with it's consumers builds a builds a company's integral bond with the consumers. These are some of the proven strategies which has helped keep the customers hooked to the business and the company and able to maintain an upright relationship with their consumers.

7. User Interface

A user interface leaves a first hand impression on a customer when he browses through the platform which will instigate the interest therein. To give an impressive impression on the customer the basic desire of a user interface is it needs to have arranged, clean and ease of use platform. In the virtual exchange of data it stages a standardized link between the customer and the company.When the customer becomes interested in the platform he will pay further attention to the usefulness of the application (Pratama & Cahyadi, 2020). So it is important that the platform maintains its agility to retain the customer to its business. It changes a person's perception and tries to build an anticipation within the consumers for the product or the service.

8. Gender Related Perception

Perception becomes an important aspect when a consumer is going through an e-commerce platform (Nissen & Krampe, 2021). Since the options are diverse, a less broader aspect, here in case considering the two gender shows that the category of men and women have different approach when it comes to the interpretation of e-commerce utilities. The main aspects that concerns the gender perception in an e-commerce is the website's aesthetics, usefulness, ease of use and purchase intention. The first thing that attracts a women's attention is the aesthetics of the platform which becomes an attracting element which helps maintain their engagement to the platform. Men, on the other side, are more attracted to the website's use and pragmatism (Putreve, 2003 & Sun et.al, 2010). Men and women perceive things differently as a result of biological cognitive activity or societal influencing (Pengnate & Sarathy, 2017), which influences their purchasing patterns to some extent.Men tend to make a purchase when they have an intention of purchase unlike women. Women on other hand give more priority to privacy and security when compared to men. Even though, irrespective of their gender a website's complexity is perceived differently depending on the consumer's cognitive ability to perceive the information presented to them which overall makes the difference in the purchase.

9. Customer Satisfaction

A business is successful when it is able to tend to the needs of the consumer and make them satisfied, hence it's top most priority. A customer's satisfaction is through the current purchase, will leave an imprint on the consumers which will assist them in returning back to the same business for their future purchases. It then eventually builds up an Eco-system where businesses are able to nurture their loyal consumers. This not only helps the business as the consumer is their frequent but also gives an advantage over their business competitors. Since in e-commerce there is only virtual interaction that exists between the consumer and the business, it becomes important for a business to retain a customer for it's business. Trust has been seen as the driving force to a customer's satisfaction (Anand et.al, 2018). Online trust can be defined as how a business presents its products to the consumers, the length of reliability of the information provided on the website and whether the company is able to deliver up to the standards of a customer's satisfaction (Malhotra et.al, 2017). Taking regular feedback is one of the examples for any company to update its information and statistics on the customer's behavior of their requirements and recommendations, which can be improved to give consumer a better experience of the business website.

Table 2. Focus of ISM by recent researchers

Authors	Objective
Suresh & Balajee(2021), Qu & Bao (2019)	Identification of factors responsible for developmental learning of an individual
Bathrinath et.al (2021), Bux et.al (2020)	Identification of significance of crucial parameters in manufacturing industry
Kumar et.al (2021), Rajput & Singh (2019)	Barrier identification in supply chain and industry 4.0
Jiang et.al (2022), Liu et.al (2021)	Evaluation of different parameters of it's affect on the cross border e-commerce

ISM METHODOLOGY

One of the Multi Criteria Decision Making (MCDM) Techniques is Interpretive Structural Modelling. It is a general-purpose analysis and decision-support tool that is used to evaluate the condition of an objective based on several parameters that affect it. ISM was described by John N Warfield (1793) as a methodology that may be utilised to address compounded issues, regardless of the content of the situation, as long as the characteristics that affect the context overall are properly identified. These identified parameters can be qualitative or quantitative in nature which gives ISM an all-inclusive advantage over other methods available to work flexibly. Thus ISM helps to interpret complex structures from different parameters and help users to build a structural model through expert's opinion.

In this paper nine parameters have been identified through background research work, which were found to have the influence over the functionality of e-commerce in a system.

The technique of ISM is carried out in following steps:

Step 1: Structural Self Interaction Matrix Formulation
Step 2: Fabrication of Reachability Matrix
Step 3: Development of Level Partition
Step 4: Acquiring classification of factors
Step 5: Generation of interpretive structure model

Table 3. List of the effecting parameters with their respective notations used

Parameters	Notations
Digital Infrastructure	DGI
Company's Inter-relation with Customers	CIC
Digital Literacy	DL
Customer Satisfaction	CS
Government Policies	GP
Localization of Internet Content	LIC
Gender Related Perception	GRP
Data Breach	DB
User Interface	UI

Step 1: Development of Circumstantial Relationship Between the Effecting Parameters

For the inspection of the parameters, a circumstantial relationship is developed between the affecting parameters. In which a relation is developed by judging the lead or dependent component of the parameter from their influence on other factors. For speculating this analysis, all the parameters are taken in x-axis(i) and also in the y-axis(j), where they are compared to relation of their influence to one other. The comparison is done using four letters V, A, X,and O where each letter represents a specific relation factor between the forthcoming adjacent factors.

The representation of relations is done the the following parametric values:

V: factor along i will lead factor along j
A: factor along j will lead factor along I
X: factor along i and j will lead each other

O: factors along i and j are unrelated

The allocation of these parametric values into the matrix will give the Self Structure Interaction Matrix (SSIM).

Table 4. Representation of Self Structure Interaction Model

Sl. No.	Factors	DGI	CIC	DL	CS	GP	LIC	GRP	DB	UI
1.	DGI		V	V	V	A	V	V	V	V
2.	CIC			A	V	A	A	A	A	A
3.	DL				V	A	X	V	O	V
4.	CS					A	A	A	A	A
5.	GP						V	V	V	V
6.	LIC							V	O	V
7.	GRP								A	O
8.	DB									V
9.	UI									

Step 2: Fabrication of Reachability Matrix

After the SSIM, the conversion of letters is done into their binary form which is called the reachability matrix. The diagonal is represented through the value of one. And following is representation the done to represent the other cells in the matrix:

a. If the (i,j) is recorded as V in the SSIM, then it is represented as 1 as of (i,j) position and 0 as in (j,i) in the reachability matrix
b. If the (i,j) is recorded as A in the SSIM, then it is represented as 0 as of (i,j) position and 1 as in (j,i) in the reachability matrix
c. If the (i,j) is recorded as X in the SSIM, then it is represented as 1 as of (i,j) position and 1 as in (j,i) in the reachability matrix
    e. If the (i,j) is recorded as O in the SSIM, then it is represented as 0 as of (i,j) position and 0 as in (j,i) in the reachability matrix

The sum of all the cells along the column of a row is value representation of the driving force for that parameter which is represented by that row. And the sum of cell along a row of a particular column gives the value representation of the dependency of that particular parameter in that column.

Step 3: Development of Level Partitioning

In this stage, a table with parameters that relate to their reachability set and antecedent set is created. Where a reachability set is a collection of parameters that reflect driving power along a row, and an antecedent set is a collection of parameters that represent dependency across a column.Following which,

Table 5. Reachability Matrix

Sl. No.	Factors	DGI	CIC	DL	CS	GP	LIC	GRP	DB	UI	Driving Power
1.	DGI	1	1	1	1	0	1	1	1	1	8
2.	CIC	0	1	0	1	0	0	0	0	0	2
3.	DL	0	1	1	1	0	1	1	0	1	6
4.	CS	0	0	0	1	0	0	0	0	0	1
5.	GP	1	1	1	1	1	1	1	1	1	9
6.	LIC	0	1	1	1	0	1	1	0	1	6
7.	GRP	0	1	0	1	0	0	1	0	0	3
8.	DB	0	1	0	1	0	0	1	1	1	5
9.	UI	0	1	0	1	0	0	0	0	1	3
Dependence Power		2	8	4	9	1	4	6	3	6	

an intersection set is written comparing the rechability set and the antecedent set, which is further evaluated to give the different levels of the hierarchy of the parameters. The factors which have the common reachability set and intersection set is labeled as level 1 in the factorial set of the parameters. Then the parameter is then separated and the processes is repeated with the remaining parameters comparing their reachability set and intersection set until all the parameters are labeled under different levels.

Table 6. Final result of Level partitioning after iterations of parameters

Factors	Reachability Set	Antecedent Set	Intersection Set	Level
1	1,2,3,4,6,7,8,9	1,5	1	V
2	2,4	1,2,3,5,6,7,8,9	2	II
3	2,3,4,6,7,9	1,3,5,6	3,6	IV
4	4	1,2,3,4,5,6,7,8,9	4	I
5	1,2,3,4,5,6,7,8,9	5	5	VI
6	2,3,4,6,7,9	1,3,5,6	3,6	IV
7	2,4,7	1,3,5,6,7,8	7	III
8	2,4,7,8,9	1,5,8	8	IV
9	2,4,9	1,3,5,6,8,9	9	III

Step 4: Segregation of Parameters

The parameters can be further classified into the following four quadrants as shown in the figure:

The 'Autonomous Variable' is represented by the first quadrant, which represents low dependent power and low driving power. The factors in this quadrant don't have much of an impact on the criterion's functionality. The second quadrant is the 'Dependence Variable' which showcases factors hav-

Figure 1. Clusters of parameters in various quadrants

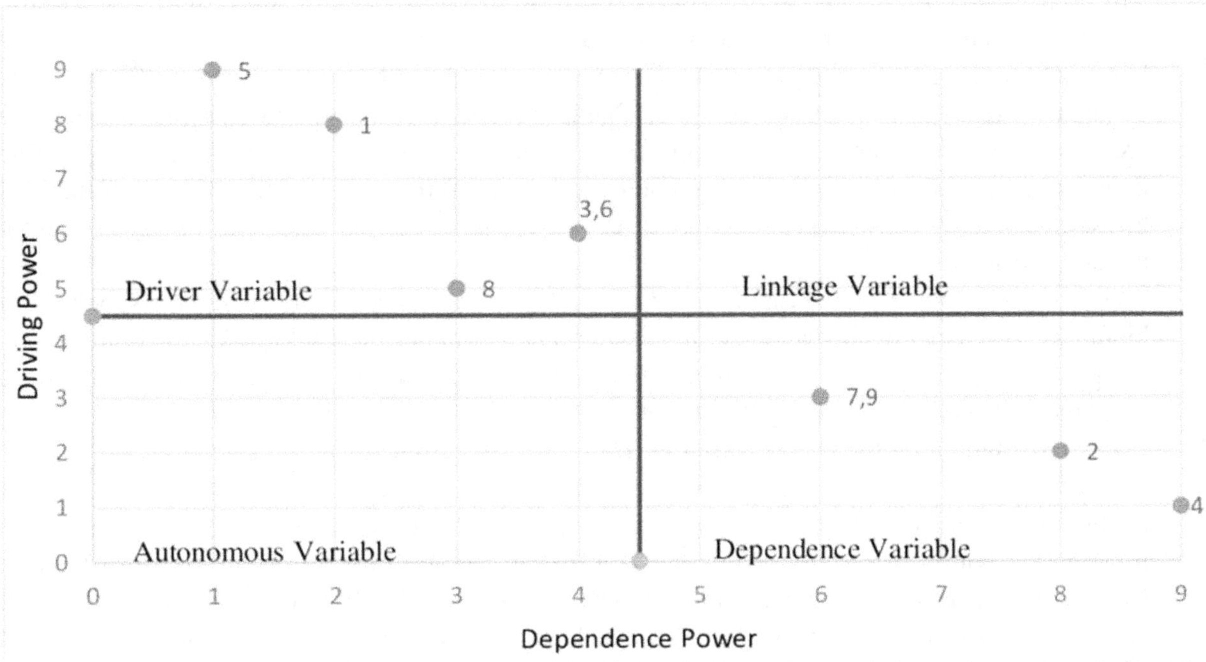

ing high dependence power and low driving power. These are those parameters which gives direct or immediate impact on the considered criteria. The third quadrant is the 'Linkage Variable' representing factors possessing high dependence power and high driving power. Factors clustered in this quadrant is very crucial as subtle change in the factors present in this quadrant impacts the whole of the hierarchy system of the parameters. The 'Driver Variable' in the fourth quadrant represents factors with moderate dependent power but strong driving power; the components in this quadrant comprise the criteria's short-term influencing parameters.

RESULTS AND DISCUSSION

The induction and development of e-commerce in developed nations has already shown it's potential in the constructive development and enhanced performance which has ultimately added to the economy of the country. Similar model can be applied in India for further growth and development. An analysis has been done and nine factors have been shortlisted which has been found to be categorically influential in the Indian market. The analysis of interaction between the parameters has been done through ISM methodology. The analysis has identified the hierarchy of parameters that can be taken into consideration while developing e-commerce in India.

Major findings from the study are:

1. There are no factors present under the Autonomous Variable, this cluster represent the parameters which are of less or no value to the criteria. They are the weak links in any system, and because they have no influence over other factors, they are largely isolated from it.
2. Four factors sum up the category of the Dependence Variable. These are Customer Satisfaction, Company's relation with the Consumers, Gender related Perception and User Interface.These are weak drivers that are heavily reliant on other variables. They are the long-term influencing parameters of the development of e-commerce in India, and they are visible at the top of the ISM hierarchy analogy. These dependent parameters are the most desired objectives of any system for better performance.
3. There are no factors under the Linkage Variables, they are the most unstable parameters in the ISM hierarchy. Any narrow change in the parameters present under the Linkage Factor immediately impacts other parameters instantly in the hierarchy of ISM analysis, this usually destabilizes the other parameters the influencing the context.
4. Five factors fall under the Driver Variable. These are Data Breach, Digital Literacy, Localization of Internet Content, Digital Infrastructure and Government Policies. These factors are present in the bottom tier in the hierarchy of the analysis. They are the parameters with least dependency and maximum driving force. Here the factors Data Breach, Digital Literacy, Localization of Internet Content, Digital Infrastructure and Government Policies give immediate impact on the e-commerce and are highly influential and will drive other factors. Proper implementation and execution of these factors will help the system to achieve its long term goals.

Interpretation of ISM methodology represents the following:

1. The contextual relationship established between the parameters exhibits its degree of dependency on each other. In addition to that the performance of e-commerce is correspondingly important for the growth of that e-commerce. Research has shown that a company's ability to adapt itself and display resilience will work on it's progressive development. ((Liu et.al, 2021)(Rajesh, 2016))
2. The MICMAC Analysis suggests factors like Government Policies, Digital Infrastructure, Digital Literacy, Localization of Internet Content and Data Breech represent the driving force for the e-commerce structure. Where much weight has been put on the role of Government Policies and Digital Infrastructure by the previous researchers for it's impact on the e-commerce environment. ((Chan & Palmeira, 2021), (Bhaskar et.al, 2020))
3. With the instigation of e-commerce, one major concern lies in the management of data of consumers who are relying on the service. Systems like Block Chain Technology and Big Data Analytics have attracted e-commerce company giving them a superiority over their competitors. These tools have been found to from the basic fundamentals that act as an important enabler for the adoption of e-commerce.(Behl et.al, 2019)

Figure 2. ISM Model for parameters affecting e-commerce in India

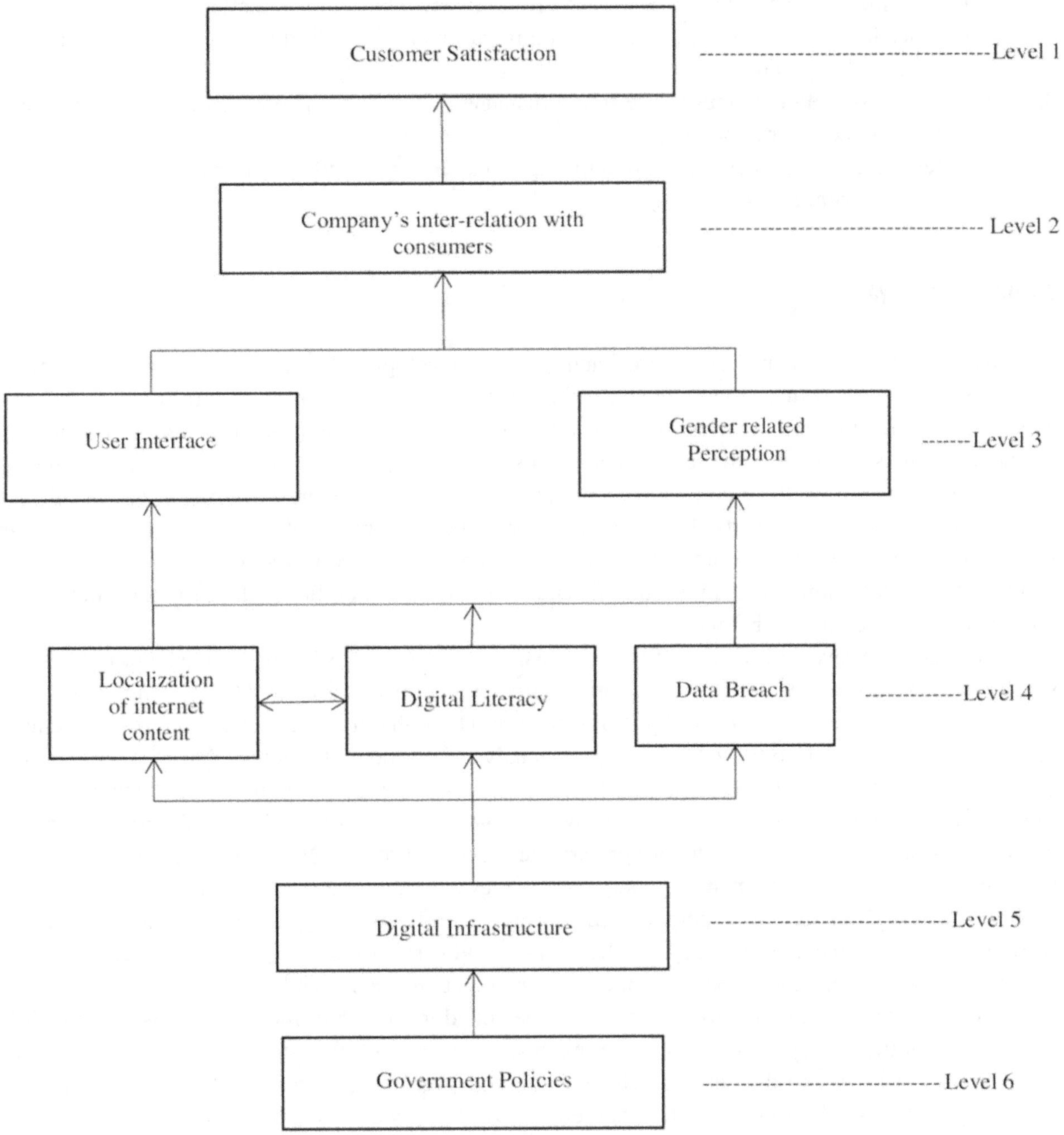

MANAGERIAL IMPLICATIONS

This paper projects to analyze the parameters affecting the e-commerce so as to helps forecast and implement a stable foundation for a rising e-commerce. Some of the improvements that can be concluded from this paper can be:

1. Importance should be given to the development of relationship between the e-commerce company and government must be established to develop progressive environment for the e-commerce system.
2. It suggests the managements the possible identification of future shortcomings from activities that could affect other parameters.
3. It gives supportive guidelines to the future managers to make decisions that overall gives a successful e-commerce environment
4. It contemplates critical parameters that managers can interpret and must be positive in controlling the impact of parameters.

CONCLUSION

Although e-commerce has proven its proficiency in the development of economic structure of many countries, it is essential that proper understanding of the working of e-commerce in India needs to be emphasized. Unlike other countries India has a multi-cultural heritage structure which has its impact on the consumers and thereon the e-commerce ecosystem in the country. The need to understand the effect of this structure on the e-commerce is highly essential. It affects the consumer's state of mind to adapt to the new systems. Efforts should be made for proper integration of the e-commerce ecosystem with the consumer's lifestyle. A definite study with the prospects of consumer of how they are affected by the e-commerce, their expectations and demands and their adaptability to the system of transaction through e-commerce should be made.

In this paper we have described an ISM model whose primary inputs has been taken through expert's suggestion which states the urgency of action required by parameters affecting the e-commerce system in India. Here we have primarily identified nine factors. Through our previously put questions, we have been able to justification to those. The suggested analysis has shown the inter-relation among the parameters. The featured ISM model categorizes which factors are long term goals and which need short time attention. The MICMAC analysis has shown the nature of each of the factors, describing them as autonomous, dependent, linkage and driver variables. The proposed ISM Model features a systematic guideline for the Indian e-commerce industry on how they can categorize and prioritize their parameters for better working system. This paper views the overall general parameters that could possibly affect the working of e-commerce in the country. Further work on industry specific e-commerce can be conducted for better understanding and association of e-commerce to that specif industry.

For extended work more inclusive factors can be added to the table. Indian consumers are mainly seen to rely on the concept of touch and buy method. A framework that suggest development of trust between the customer and the business. Since an e-commerce lacks such type of physical interaction from the consumers, it becomes essential for them to develop trust between them. This trust is developed only when the e-commerce company is able to reach the standards of the consumers and satisfy their requirements. With the onset of Covid-19 pandemic, when the consumers had more restricted contact, the channel of e-commerce proved to be most helpful. The online shopping of groceries, medicines and apparel became more prominent. The touch and buy concept concern the online payment. Consumers here have the affinity of first see the product and then pay. They intend to pay to the standards of the product. Another issue is with that of online payment system. Owing to the security and data breach company should be transparent while dealing these matters with the consumers. Multiple payment channels provided by the e-commerce companies has only strengthen their hold on the e-commerce in India.

Heeding to such situations the Government of India has actively promoted online method of payment through various campaigns and schemes. The introduction of UPI payment system was a game changer in the country, where consumers get the freedom of platform for their online transaction with a single identity username. It's favourable outcome has only been displayed through the extensive use of the UPI payment system throughout the country. Which has henceforth proved that the Government's intervention of the development of digital infrastructure will only enhance the growth of e-commerce. Utilities like voice search commands can also be incorporated for ease of use for the consumers. Factors like sustainability should be worked on as it attracts customer. Consistent training and skills should be developed among the working professionals as they help integrate more customers into the business. These can be some of the additional factors that can be added to the table for more intensive study.

REFERENCES

Abbad, M. (2018). Limitations and Usage of E-commerce in Developing Countries. *12th International Conference on Business, Social Sciences, Humanities and Education (BSSHE-18)*, 13-14. 10.17758/ERPUB.ED0318117

Akhmetova, Z., Baimukhanbetova, E., Belgozhakyzy, M., Alibaeva, A., & Tulebaeva, N. (2020). The development of e-commerce in modern conditions. *The 1st International Conference on Business Technology for Sustainable Environment System*, 159. 10.1051/e3sconf/202015904028

Anand, K. J., Niraj, R., Park, C. H., & Agarwal, M. K. (2018). The effect of relationship and transactional characteristics on customer retention in emerging online markets. *Journal of Business Research*, *92*, 25–35. doi:10.1016/j.jbusres.2018.07.007

Bathrinath, S., Koshy, A. R., Bhalaji, K. A. R., & Koppiahraj, K. (2021). Identification of the critical activity in heat treatment process using TISM. *Materials Today: Proceedings*, *39*(1), 60-65. doi:10.1016/j.matpr.2020.06.157

Behl, A., Dutta, P., Lessmann, S., Dwivedi, Y. K., & Kar, S. (2019). A Conceptual framework for the adoption of Big Data Analytics by e-commerce startups: A case-based approach. *Information Systems and e-Business Management*, *17*(2-4), 285–318. doi:10.100710257-019-00452-5

Bhaskar, C., Ajay, B., & Ravi, S. C. (2020). Which economies showed the most digital progress in 2020? *Harvard Business Review*. Retrieved from https://hbr.org/2020/12/which-economies-showed-the-most-digital-progress-in-2020

Bux, H., Zhang, Z., & Ahmad, N. (2020). Promoting sustainability through corporate social responsibility implementation in the manufacturing industry: An empirical analysis of barriers using the ISM-MICMAC approach. *Corporate Social Responsibility and Environmental Management*, *27*(4), 1729–1748. doi:10.1002/csr.1920

Chai, Y., Duan, Y., Ma, S., & Wang, J. (2018). New Digital Infrastructure, Cross-Border E-commerce and Global Vision of Creating Electronic World Trade Platform. *Global Trade and Customs Journal*, *13*(4), 157–167.

Chan, E. Y., & Palmeira, M. (2021). Political ideology moderates consumer response to brand crisis apologies for data breach. *Computers in Human Behaviour, 121*. doi:10.1016/j.chb.2021.106801

Chun, S. H. (2019). E-Commerce Liability and Security Breaches in Mobile Payment for e-Business Sustainability. *Sustainability*, *11*(3), 715. doi:10.3390u11030715

F-commerce in developing countries. Opportunities and challenges for small and medium sized enterprises. (2013). *World Trade Organization.* Retrieved from https://www.wto.org/english/res_e/booksp_e/ecom_brochure_e.pdf

Hariharan, S. (2021). User info linked to 18 crore's Domino's order leaked. *The Times of India.* Retrieved from https://timesofindia.indiatimes.com/business/india-business/user-info-linked-to-18-crore-dominos-orders-leaked/articleshow/82898118.cms

Jiang, H., Lin, Y., Luo, X., & Shao, T. (2022). Understanding the Selection of Cross-Border Import E-Commerce Platforms Through the DANP and TOPSIS Techniques: A Multi-Study Analysis. *Journal of Global Information Technology Management*, *25*(1), 26–53. doi:10.1080/1097198X.2021.2022397

Johnson, J. (2022). *Internet usage worldwide- statistics and facts*. Retrieved from https://www.statista.com/topics/1145/internet-usage-worldwide/#topicHeader__wrapper

Kumar, S., Raut, D. R., Nayal, K., Kraus, S., Yadav, S. V., & Narkhede, E. B. (2021). To identify industry 4.0 and circular economy adoption barriers in the agriculture supply chain by using ISM-ANP. *Journal of Cleaner Production, 293*. doi:10.1016/j.jclepro.2021.126023

Liquid Group to power UPI or acceptance in 10 Asian Markets. (2021). *National Payment Corporation of India*. Retrieved from https://www.npci.org.in/PDF/npci/press-releases/2021/NPCI-International-Press-Release-LIQUID-GROUP-TO-POWER-UPI-QR-ACCEPTANCE-IN-10-ASIAN-MARKETS.pdf

Liu, X., Dou, Z., & Yang, W. (2021). Research on Influencing Factors of Cross Border E-Commerce Supply Chain Resilience Based on Integrated Fuzzy DEMATEL-ISM. *IEEE Access: Practical Innovations, Open Solutions*, *9*, 36140–36153. doi:10.1109/ACCESS.2021.3059867

Malhotra, N., Sahadev, S., & Purani, K. (2017). Psychological contract violation and customer intention to reuse online retailers: Exploring mediating and moderating mechanisms. *Journal of Business Research*, *75*(6), 17–28. doi:10.1016/j.jbusres.2017.01.013

Merhi, M. I. (2021). Multi-Country Analysis of E-commerce Adoption: The Impact of National Culture and Economic Development. *Pacific Asia Journal of the Association for Information Systems, 13*(3). https://aisel.aisnet.org/pajais/vol13/iss3/4

Nissen, A., & Krampe, C. (2021). Why he buys it and she doesn't - exploring self-reported and neural gender differences in the perception of e-commerce website. *Computers in Human Behavior*, *121*, 106809. doi:10.1016/j.chb.2021.106809

Pengnate, S. F., & Sarathy, R. (2017). An experimental investigation of the influence of website emotional design features on trust in unfamiliar online vendors. *Computers in Human Behavior*, *67*, 49–60. doi:10.1016/j.chb.2016.10.018

Pratama, T., & Cahyadi, A. T. (2020). Effects of User Interface and User Experience on application sale. *IOP Conference Series Material Science and Engineering*, 879(1). 10.1088/1757-899X/879/1/012133

Putreve, S. (2003). Exploring the origins and information processing differences between men and women: Implications for advertisers. *Academy of Marketing Science Review*, *10*, 1–16.

Qu, Y., & Bao, X. (2019). Identification and Analysis of Influencing Factors of College Students' Degree of Learning Effort based in ISM. *Advances in Social Science, Education and Humanities Research,* Volume 340. *International Conference on Education Innovation and Economic Management*. 10.2991/iceiem-19.2019.43

Rajesh, R. (2016). Forecasting Supply chain resilience performance using gray prediction. *Electronic Commerce Research and Applications*, *20*, 42–58. doi:10.1016/j.elerap.2016.09.006

Rajput, S., & Singh, S. P. (2019). Identifying Industry 4.0 IOT enablers by integrated PCA-ISM-DEMATEL approach. *Management Decision*, *57*(8), 1784–1817. doi:10.1108/MD-04-2018-0378

Reddy, P., Chaudhary, K., Sharma, B., & Chand, D. (2021). Contextualized game-based intervention for digital literacy for the Pacific Islands. *Education and Information Technologies*, *26*(5), pp5535–pp5562. doi:10.100710639-021-10534-y PMID:33935574

Reddy, P., Sharma, B., & Chaudhary, K. (2020). Measuring the digital competency of freshmen at a higher education institute. *Pacific Asia Conference on Information Systems Proceedings, 6*. https://aisel.aisnet.org/pacis2020/6

Scholten, K., & Schilder, S. (2015). The role of collaboration in supply chain resilience. *Supply Chain Management*, *20*(4), 471–484. doi:10.1108/SCM-11-2014-0386

Sun, Y., Lim, K. H., Jiang, C., Peng, J. Z., & Chen, X. (2010). Do males and females think in the same way? An empirical investigation on the gender differences in web advertising evaluation. *Computers in Human Behavior*, *26*(6), 1614–1624. doi:10.1016/j.chb.2010.06.009

Suresh, M., & Balajee, T. B. K. (2021). Modelling of factors influencing on the informal learning among school teachers: An ISM- MICMAC approach. *Materials Today: Proceedings*. doi:10.1016/j.matpr.2020.11.547

Tang, G., & Zeng, H. (2021). Evaluation of Tourism E-Commerce User Satisfaction. *Journal of Organizational and End User Computing*, *33*(5), 25–41. Advance online publication. doi:10.4018/JOEUC.20210901.oa2

Warfield, J. N. (1973a). Binary matrices in system modeling. *IEEE Transactions on Systems, Man, and Cybernetics*, *SMC-3*(5), 441–449. doi:10.1109/TSMC.1973.4309270

Wudie, A. A. (2020). Analysis of Speeches by the Former President of the US, Barack Hussein Obama, Regarding the Middle East and Northern Africa. *International Journal of Translation, Interpretation, and Applied Linguistics*, *2*(1), 20–32. Advance online publication. doi:10.4018/IJTIAL.2020010102

Chapter 6
A Collaborative Cloud Model of Auto Scaling With Load Balancing for Effective E-Commerce

Saurabh Bilgaiyan
Kalinga Institute of Industrial Technology (Deemed), Bhubaneswar, India

Bhabani Shankar Prasad Mishra
Kalinga Institute of Industrial Technology (Deemed), Bhubaneswar, India

Rashid Ansari
Kalinga Institute of Industrial Technology (Deemed), Bhubaneswar, India

Santwana Sagnika
Kalinga Institute of Industrial Technology (Deemed), Bhubaneswar, India

ABSTRACT

Cloud computing focuses on the collaboration of distributed resource services over the network. This chapter focuses on the problem of unequal distribution of traffic load across a different number of subnets of a VPC (virtual private cloud) in a cloud computing environment. It also highlights the idea of collaborating auto scaling and load balancing to achieve an equal distribution of load across the servers. This chapter demonstrates the efficiency of our techniques through detailed process. The load balancer behaves as a single point of contact for the traffic. The benefit of this combined technique can easily be implemented in an e-commerce system (i.e., during sales/certain events, there is a huge spike in traffic at once, which may result in the crashing of the server). Here, load balancer and auto scalability can work in combination for smooth user experience. Finally, this chapter concludes that the collaboration of load balancer along with auto scaling will increase the performance of the instances.

I. INTRODUCTION

DOI: 10.4018/978-1-6684-4969-1.ch006

Copyright © 2022, IGI Global. Copying or distributing in print or electronic forms without written permission of IGI Global is prohibited.

According to the U.S. National Institute of Standards and Technology (NIST): ''Cloud computing can be defined as a computing paradigm which enables efficient, convenient and on-demand access to a shared pool of configurable computing resources. These resources can be quickly scale in or scale down as per the requirement" (Bilgaiyan et al., 2014). In other words, Cloud computing can be referred as the access, configuration and manipulation of physical and software resources at a remote location. Through cloud computing software and hardware resources can be accessed and configured through any location on a pay per use on demand basis. It provides features such as scalability, connectivity, availability, reliability, pay-as-you-go, management of a large amount of data, high computing power, and elasticity to transform IT from a product based to service based. Many Business or Enterprises are hosting their applications on the cloud because of it's fast advancing technology. However, the large scale use of the cloud models creates a dependency issue for both service and providers. These issues are essential to cloud because of several types of faults may occur in the cloud environment leading to failures and performance degradation (Bilgaiyan et al., 2014; Kumari & Kaur, 2018). Cloud computing infrastructure includes the servers, storage devices, network facilities, security along with backup and recovery services to users. These hardware components are located at various places around the globe known as data centers which are well guarded with a goal to prevent data leaks. Apart from these all the other hardware and software component that helps in making cloud computing possible such as the virtualization software, are called as cloud computing infrastructure. The virtualization software offers virtualized resources to the users so that they can create their any number of virtual machines as per demand (Kumari & Kaur, 2018). The deployment models are based on the objective and platform in which the task is being performed. It takes in consideration the budget of the organization, resources and power. The most commonly used deployment models in cloud environments are public, private, community and hybrid cloud. The public cloud allows public access to the cloud systems and services offered by a cloud provider. The private cloud offers resources and services that can be accessed only within the organization. The community model is used wherever there is an inter dependency between several organizations and communities with common interest. The hybrid cloud is a collaboration of both public cloud and private cloud. Here, critical events are achieved using the private cloud services and non-critical events are implemented by using the public cloud (Ali et al., 2018; Kumari & Kaur, 2018).

Cloud computing has played an important role in e-commerce for its smooth operation, growth and has become popular in a small span of time because of its efficiency.As everyone has limitation of resources in their business. Scaling up or down the business when required is not possible, which increases the overall cost . By using cloud computing technology now we don't have to invest large amount in purchasing resources and store a huge space for our data.We can easily boost or reduce the space according to the customer's demand. It facilitate storage,computing and many more services on pay-per-use, which decrease the over all cost of operation.

It also make analyzing easy using different tools, so that decision can be made more accurately."Targeting the premium customer",Every business has some customers are ready to invest for better user experience and visits the website regularly, By monitoring the visits on the various products,you can guess the taste of your customers,you can make suggest more related products at same place. you can predict the sells of particular products and make sure these kinds of products are still in stock.Resulting, positive growth of your business.(Rana et al., 2014). AWS was launched by Amazon.com in 2006. It was built from within to handle the online retail operations of amazon.com. AWS introduced a cloud computing model based on the idea of pay-as-you-go and was one of the very first company to do so. It provides it users with many services like compute, storage, networking, database, big data analytic and IOT to name a few. (Khan et al., 2011). This research is based on integrating various features of AWS and will be discussed in the further sections.

This chapter has been organized by following section

Figure 1. Cloud Service Architecture

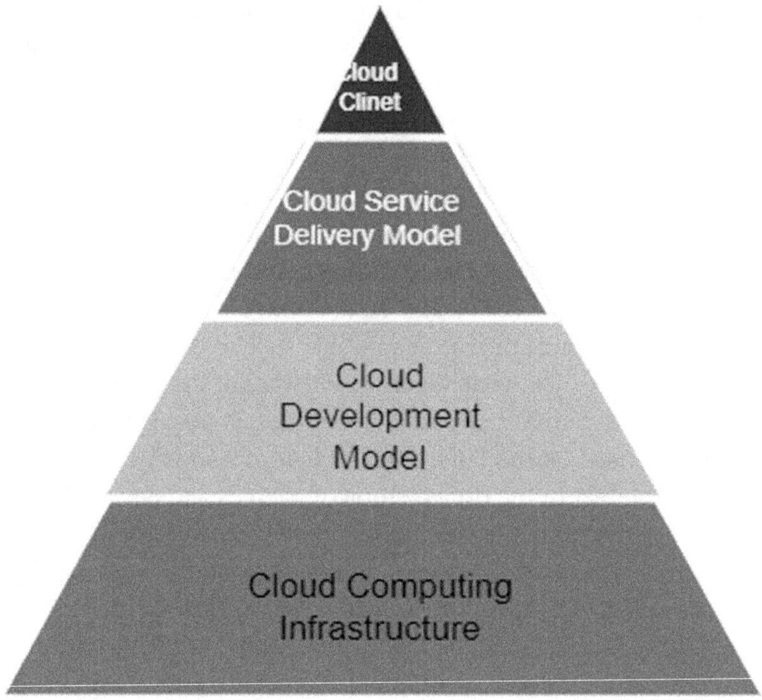

Basic Concepts: This section describe the basic and core cloud services like Auto scaling,Load balancer etc.

Related Work: This section include the other work related to auto scaling and load balancing or on different topics like fault tolerance etc.

Proposed Work: This section describe the main focus of work,i.e. advantage of collaboration of load balancing and auto scaling.

Result and Analysis: This Showcase the result and analytical part of the research.

Conclusion: As, name its include the brief conclusion of the overall work of the paper.

II. BASIC CONCEPTS

A. Amazon Web Services

AWS launched by Amazon.com, provides its users with world class technology that gives them access to virtualized resources accessible by all and across any corner of the world. With the help of AWS, client no longer have to spend money and time on procuring infrastructure to either deploy their applications or develop one. AWS provides them with all services that are necessary and the users only pay on the basis of the consumption of those services. AWS is spread across the availability zones in different regions of the world (Amazon, n.d.). An availability zone is a location that holds many data centers. AWS is implemented through these data centers. When an AWS user creates instances, it is hosted in these availability zones. The performance is maximized because data is duplicated on not just one AZ but across multiple AZs, so that in the event of failure or data center crash, the user's data is still safe and secure. This increases the reliability of the infrastructure and makes it resilient to failure. As per 2017, AWS offers more than 90 services ranging from computing, storage, networking, big data, analytics, IOT, database to tools for developers. AWS can be accessed through HTTP, using RESR architecture and SOAP protocol.

B. Load Balancing

The Load balancing is a feature of AWS. It is a process that automatically distributes the incoming application traffic load across multiple computing resources, IP addresses and containers. It handles the dynamically changing workload of the incoming traffic in a single or across multiple Availability Zones(Citrix, n.d.). Elastic Load Balancing comprises of three types of load balancer: classic load balancer, network load balancer and application load balancer. The benefit of using a service like load balancing is that it dynamically allocates local workload evenly across all system nodes. The absence of load balancer can cause the customer to wait long to get/process the data that are actually needed in real-time. Different companies use different load balancer along with multiple load balancing algorithms. The most commonly used algorithm is the round robin algorithm. Load balancing is a less expensive and easy to implement technique. They have the ability to handle sudden incoming traffic received from any given time. The main objective of using a load balancer is to prevent any sudden mishap, so that even if one node fails the load can be shifted to other nodes (Amazon, 2006a).

C. Auto Scaling

The Auto Scaling feature of AWS is a term used to measure the number of active servers and scales them automatically based on the work load on each server. It monitors applications and network traffic to adjust the capacity of the instances so as to maintain a steady and predictable performance at a very inexpensive price. The auto scaling feature is easy to set up. Auto Scaling provides good fault tolerance because it can detect an unhealthy instance from a healthy instance and terminate them. Amazon auto scaling can be configured to be used in several working zones. So, if an availability zone becomes faulty the auto scaling launches instances in another availability zone to provide fault tolerance (Amazon, 2006a).

D. Virtual Private Cloud (VPC)

Amazon Virtual Private Cloud (Amazon VPC) helps users to create their own virtual network by separating a portion of the AWS Cloud so that the users can launch their resources identified by them. They have absolute control over the network environment ranging from selecting their own IP address range, creation of subnets and configuration of routing tables. Both IPv4 and IPv6 are allowed for a safe and convenient access to resources and applications (Amazon, 2006b).

Figure 2. Load Balancing in Cloud

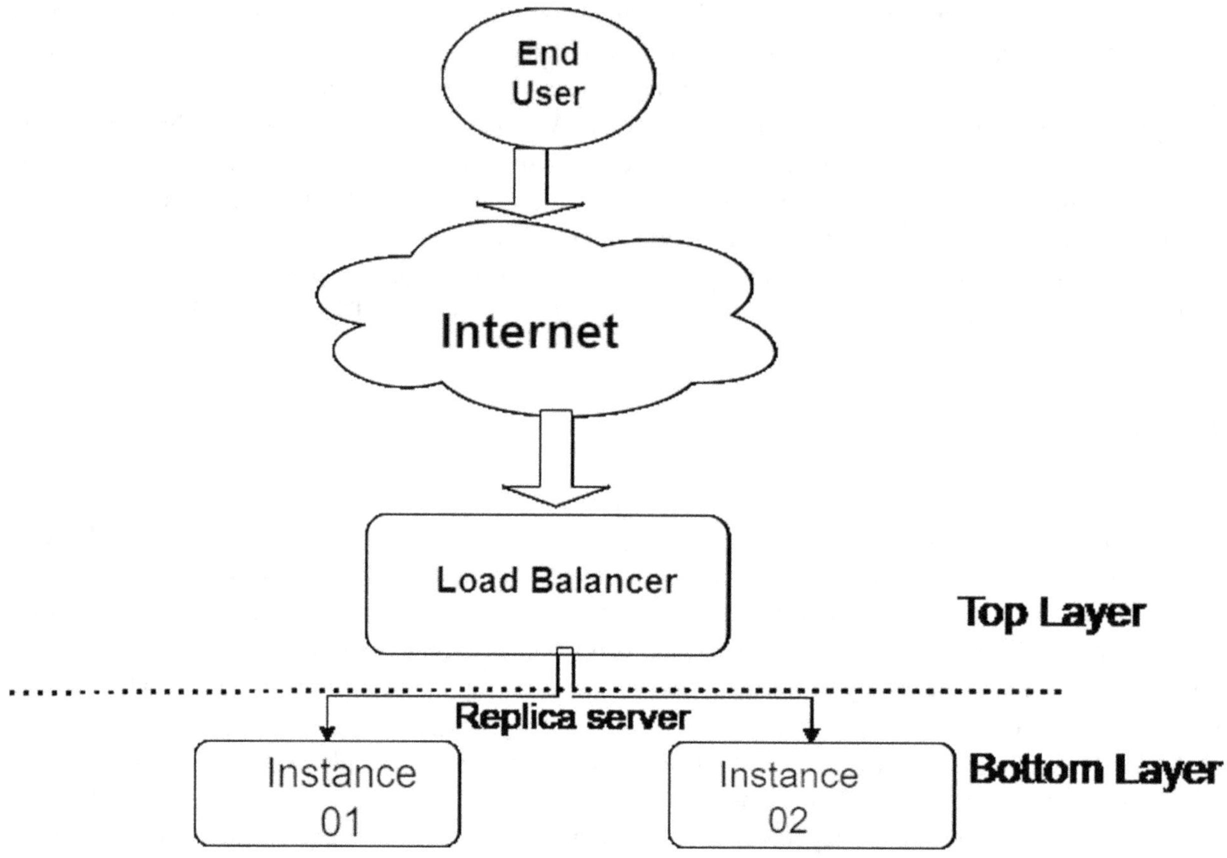

Auto Scaling in Cloud

E. Elastic IP

An Elastic IP is a combination of static and public IP address which is useful for dynamic cloud computing. An Elastic IP helps the user to advertise his/her AWS instance within the AWS infrastructure. The benefit of having an elastic IP is that it never changes, hence it becomes easy to advertise our content to the public internet. This helps the DNS queries to ease the content loading process(Amazon, 2006c). Also, in case of any failure within the AWS infrastructure, the Elastic IP can to immediately remapped to another instance within the VPC (AWS, n.d.).

II. RELATED WORK

Research work regarding the collaboration of AWS features has not yet been done extensively. However, few research papers do shed light on the usage of autoscaling and load balancing in network traffic management and have been discussed in this paper. Jing Liua et al. in his works has proposed a paper on Task fault-tolerance in dynamic system consisting of multiple components. The paper focuses on the problem

Figure 3. Auto Scaling in Cloud

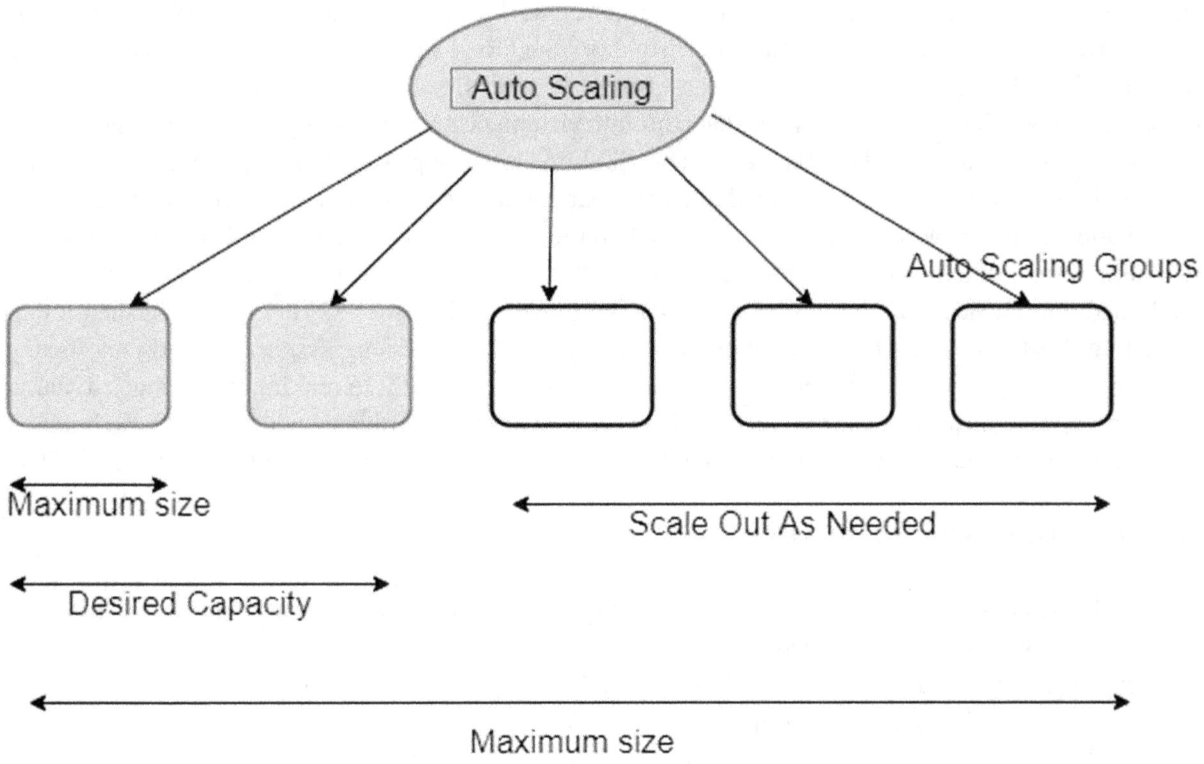

Figure 4. Virtual Private Cloud

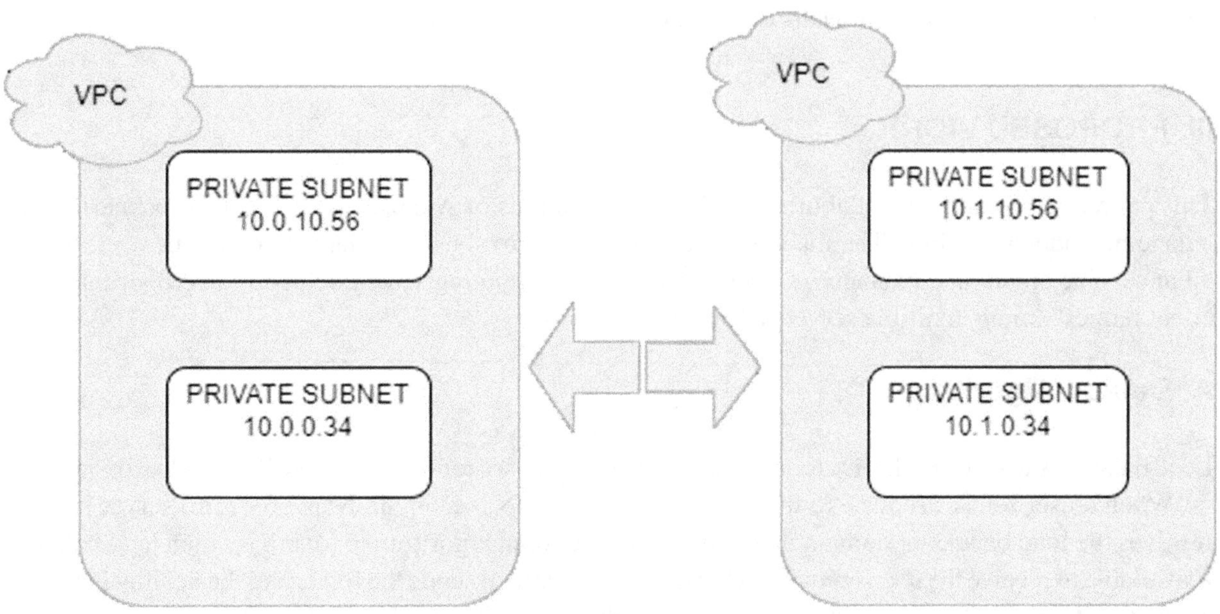

that within a constant time frame maximum number of permanent failures of a task in a system can be supported (Lu et al., 2019). Keith Lewis et al. proposed his work on Virtual Private Cloud Security. The paper covers all the aspects and features of virtual private cloud security along with its advantages (Zia & Tian, 2013). HefeiJia et al. has proposed a work on Secure allocation of Instances in cloud. The paper deals with how to handle the security threats through virtualization technology feature of cloud(Lu et al., 2019). Lorido-Botran et al. Has also given contributions regarding Auto Scaling in cloud.In his paper, auto-scaling procedure has been devided into three parts: reactive approaches, proactive approaches, and mixed approaches. Reactive approaches is based on the changing of current load. Proactive approaches use future prediction by analyzing the current load. Mixed approaches is the combination of both above explained approaches(Botran & Alonso, 2014). Mazzucco and Dumas (2011) also published a paper regarding this topic. Their focus is not on creating a perfect auto scaling system, instead they focus on maximizing the profits by an admission control mechanism to adapt it to making the changes dynamic . Cloud computing also uses its services for file sharing over cloud . Both scheduling and load balancing need to be performed in an organized manner for file sharing (Mukhopadhyay & Mukhopadhyay, 2016).

A. Cloud Uses in E-commerce

As cloud allows e-commerce to lease the computing power, storing facility and many more, as a result the growth of business is not still(Sun, 2012).

You don't need to have fancy office or office at all to run your business on cloud,which reduces the overall cost of starting a business(Vinoth et al., 2022).

Cloud brings stability to your e-commerce, as it had load balancing and auto scaling feature which manage sudden spikes in traffic (Vinoth et al., 2022).

For young Entrepreneurship, E-commence can be the easiest approach to attract client globally and get a chance to stand along with bigger organization (Singh et al., 2021).

During transmission there is high risk of chance that data can be modified,accessed or even destroyed, Cloud facilitate numbers of firewalls to protect the users data (Parast et al., 2022).

III. PROPOSED WORK

This paper is a research on collaboration of multiple features of Amazon Web Services, primarily load balancing and auto scaling. The main focus of this work is to showcase the advantages of working this alliance. The cloud load balancer is a service in cloud computing which helps in the redistribution of client request among multiple servers (Priya et al., 2019).

A. Default Algorithm

Load balancers work on multiple algorithms however, AWS uses round robin algorithm for load balancing.

When a user sends a request to the load balancer, the DNS (Domain Name System) server initially resolves the load balancing domain name. It uses round robin algorithm to identify which load balancer is available to receive the user's request. This load balancer then sends the request to the healthy instances present in its zone. The load balancer uses round robin algorithm to identify healthy instances from unhealthy instances for TCP connections and least outstanding algorithm for HTTP/HTTPS connections.

Table. 1 Comparative analysis of existing work

Authors	Proposed methodology	Finding	Advantage	limitation
Lu, Y.,Lin, C.,Lai et al	investigating service development and service request scheduling for composite cloud service in dynamic cloud environment .	The simulation studies has shown that the proposed scheme can outperform other existing relevant methods significantly in terms of average service response time.	The proposed method has a advantage in terms of improved execution performance of composite cloud services in dynamic cloud environments	Other parameters can also be included
Botran, L., Alonso, M., Lozano	classification of the technologies for automating application scaling.	It has been observed that the proposed methods is able to identify the required number of resources to meet the requirement of service level agreement.	The Rules defined in the proposed method can be be applied to easily automate the process of auto-scaling of a particular application. These rules can specially accurate for applications with regular and predictable patterns.	In the situation of bursty and heavy workloads, the client should consider a more advanced and powerful auto-scaling system
chunling Sun	Analysing the current actuality of the application for enterprise E-commerce,	Cloud computing has been observed as a next generation revolutionary computing model that may significantly change the working aspects of the business model. It has also been observed that combination of e-commerce and cloud computing may have greater impact over the enterprises.	As a emerging technology, cloud computing is offering greater mobility and collaborative opportunities to the bossiness.	e-commerce is access through internet, so a good reliable internet is must crucial part,as everything Is depend on it,
Zong-pu, Tian, Xino	using encrypted file systems technology to encrypt the file	This Proposed method has achieved the security of storage resource by using eCryptfs file system non-interactively. It has also provided the solution to the main security problems in private cloud.	The proposed method has offered an encryption of private cloud file storage server and shown a security private cloud scheme based on eCryptfs	typically recommend you limit your filenames to ~140 characters
Raja Mukhopadhyay	an algorithm ASCII XORING which aims to encrypt data stored in the virtual machine and its transfer over the network	The proposed method has presented an advanced model for the cloud. The model has shown that it can protect the integrity and confidentiality of users's data is the main area of concentration.	The protecting the integrity and confidentiality of data.	The proposed model has not considered whether it might have any significant change in performance or not.

However, with advancement, now AWS uses round robin routing algorithm for TCP and least outstanding request for HTTP/HTTPS in Classic Load Balancers. Round robin algorithm is used in Application Load Balancers and Flow Hash Algorithm in Network Load Balancer(Sontakke et al., 2015). Traffic management has been used in cloud for load balancing and quality of service but Latency still is a chal-

Figure 5. Revenue by Cloud (Almarabeh & Majdalawi, 2019)

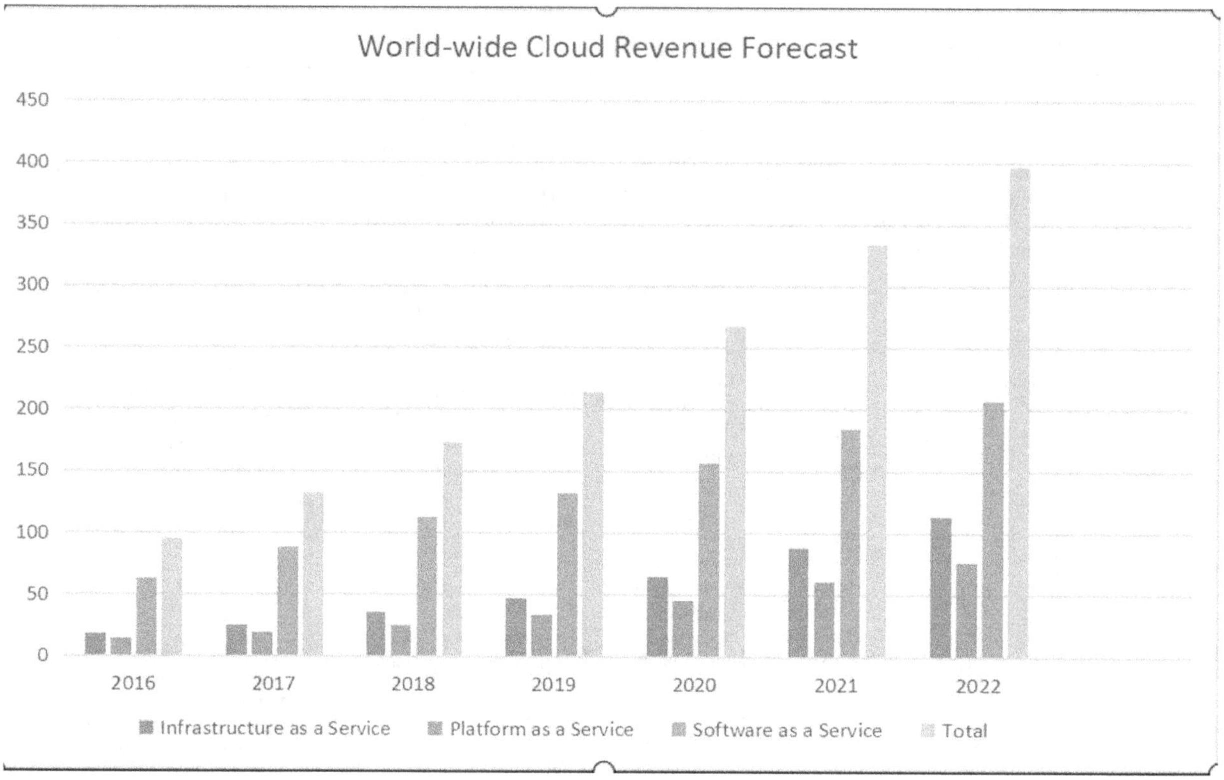

lenge for resource allocation . The main focus of the work is the collaboration of resource scheduling with load balancing algorithm(Almarabeh & Majdalawi, 2019).

B. Problem Formulation

Analogue of the standard formula for the sum of the geometric progression is defined as -

N(t)=m(m^{t})-1/m-1 ------------- (1)

where, m = number of transcriptions and t = time.

The total number of person N(t) who will receive the round robin letter is given as follows -

$$N(t) = \sum_{i=0}^{t-1} \Delta i = \sum_{i=0}^{t-1} m(m+1)^i) + 1 = (m+1)^t \quad (2)$$

where, m = number of transcriptions and t = time (Xcellhost, 2009).

Figure 6. Benefits of Cloud

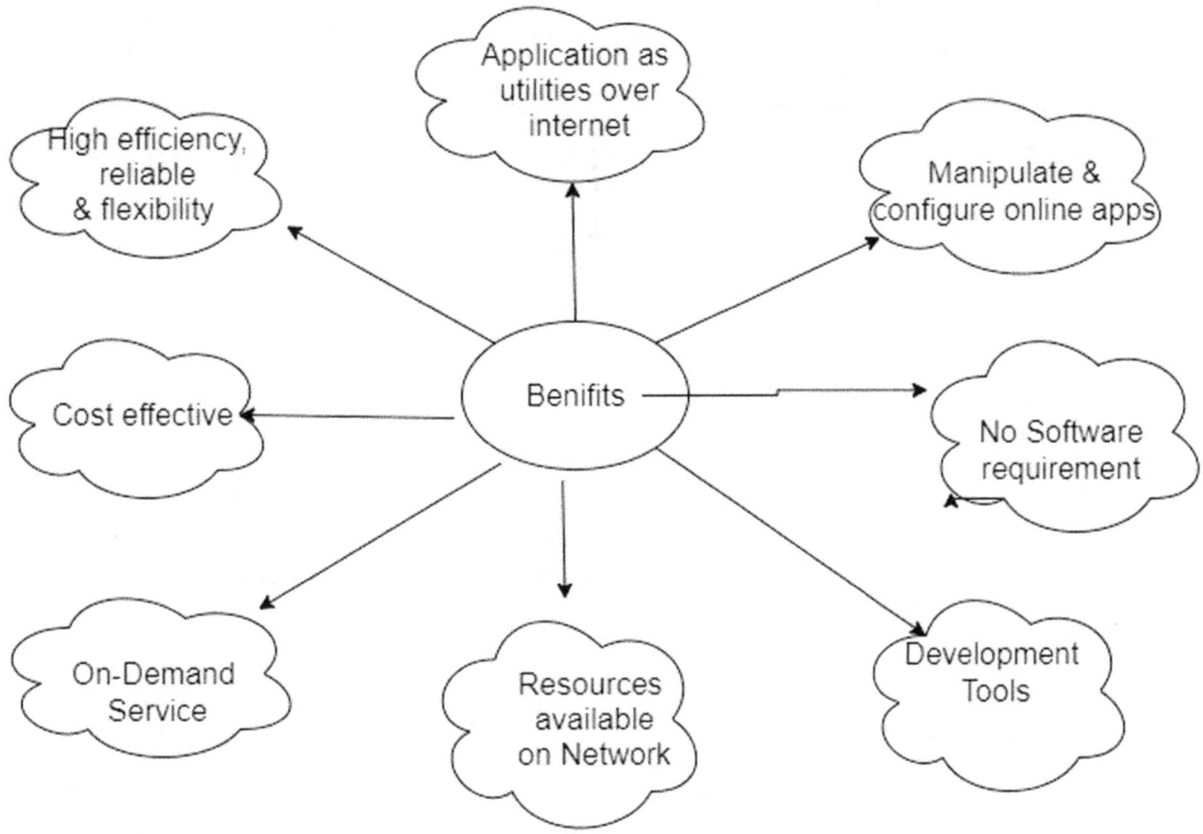

C. Auto Scaling Mechanism

Auto scaling is a service of cloud computing that helps create a system that automatically add and remove EC2 instances in response to changing load. The adding or removal of the instances depends on the traffic on the server (Winthrop, 1966). After the successful implementation of the collaboration, the advantages of this research were recorded and are presented in the further section.

D. Methodology

The flowchart in "Fig.5" explains the working methodology of proposed work. Load Balancing: The load balancer acts as a single point of contact for all the incoming load. The load balancer prevents the increase of load on any one VM by redistributing the traffic equally across the instances.

Auto Scaling: The function of an auto scaling group is to add or terminate instances, based on the incoming traffic. Hence it is important to ensure that the load is equally distributed across all instances.

In this paper, research has been done to collaborate load balancing with auto scaling so the load balancing service with the help of auto scaling can automatically route incoming web traffic across dynamically changing number of instances such that there is no increase of load on any one particular

Figure 7. Flowchart for Proposed Work

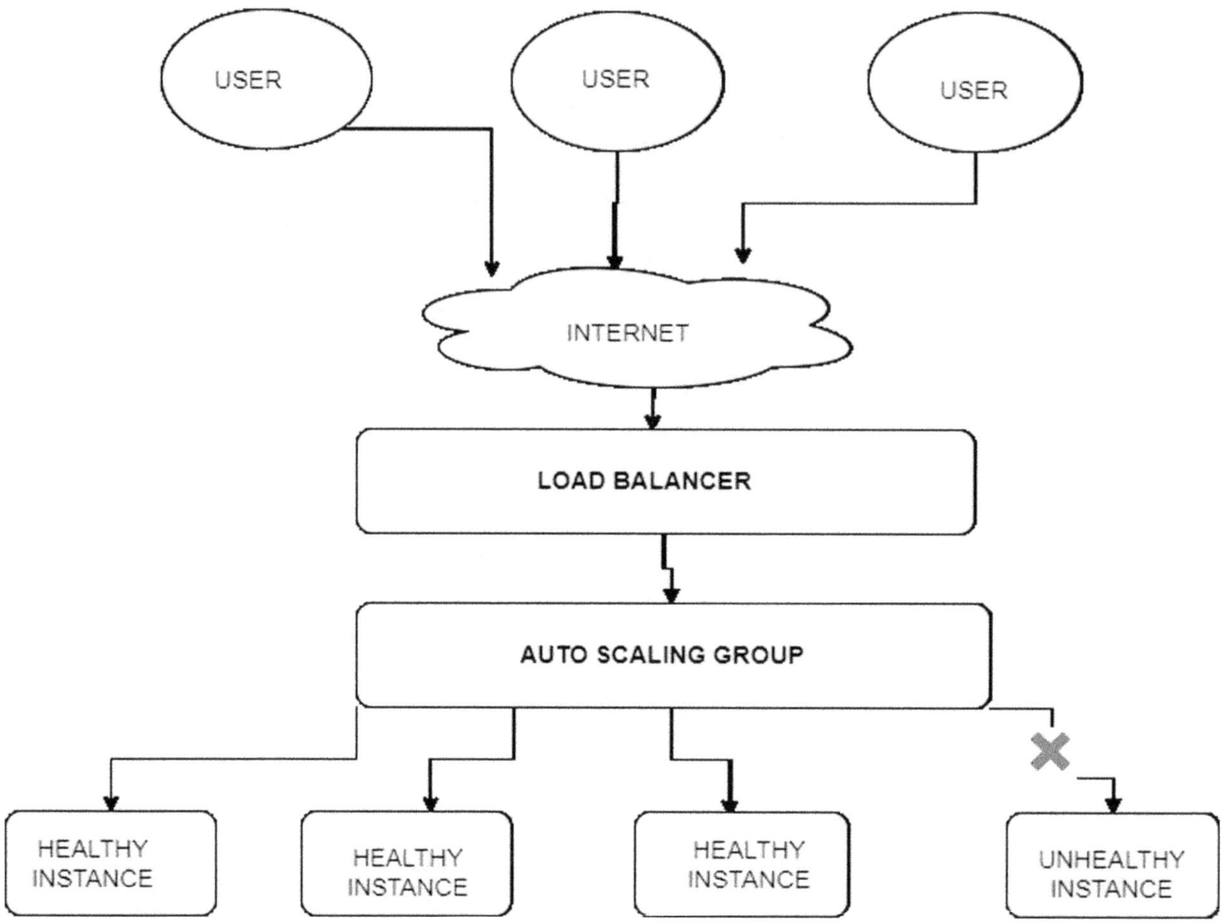

server. This is important because even though Auto Scaling is present its usage is limited and depends on company's budget. The Elastic Load Balancer accepts incoming requests and routing them to healthy instances. An existing instance failing its health checks and be taken out of service. The load balancer uses health check to determine the instances that are unhealthy so the load is only forwarded to healthy instances. Once all available instances are listed with the load balancer, they enter a state where they can be added. The instances then pass a heath check so that they can now enter a in-service state. Once a listed and healthy instance enter an in-service state, the auto scaling group can now easily scale up and add more healthy instances or terminate or replace unhealthy instances. In case of a load balancer even if one listed instance doesn't fail the health check, then the load balancer enters the in-service state. However, if none of the listed instances pass the health check, then the load balancer cannot enter the in-service state.

Figure 8. Server Performance on Load Balancing

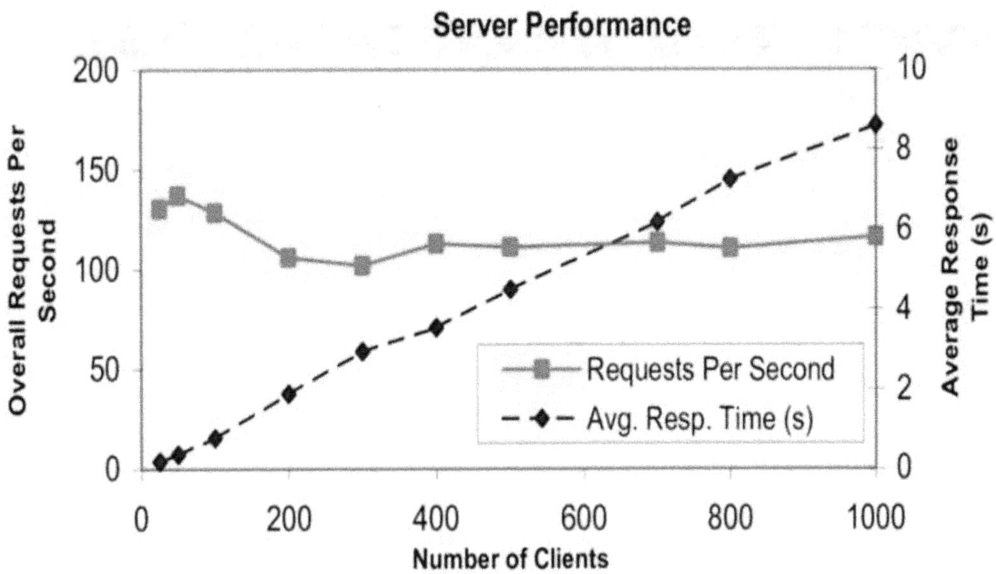

IV. RESULT AND ANALYSIS

Firstly, a Virtual Private Network is created which provides a secure access to our server. It is done using the Networking and Security Services in AWS. An instance is created in which HTTP service is set permanently on and an image is created for that instance. Now, auto scaling feature is implemented and during that process the load balancer is incorporated from which the traffic will be received. After that the policies are decided. Here, to check the working of the collaboration of auto scaling with load balancing, load is increased manually using LINUX command prompt. This results in 2 more instances being created with equal load distribution among them. The load among each of the instances can be checked using the commands executed on the prompt. Similarly, to decrease the load we use the command prompt. Graph in "Fig. 7" shows that the traffic is being equally divided among the instances that are being created.

The "Fig. 8" displays how this collaboration results in enhancement of virtual .

V. CONCLUSION

In conclusion, cloud computing is fast advancing technology has potential to have a great impact on the e-commerce, education and other sectors also. Cloud computing offers scalability, elasticity, high availability and many more features. However, the scope of lot of research which is still required in this area as the concern related to security and privacy are not been answered by the experts and remains open.

This survey paper has discussed cloud computing concepts, its components, service model, and deployment models. This research focused on the collaboration of auto scaling with load balancing. This collaboration is quite instrumental because it led to enhanced performance by 30% compared to

Figure 9. Collaboration results in enhancement of virtual machines based on traffic load machines based on traffic load and how once the load goes down the virtual machines terminate on their own.

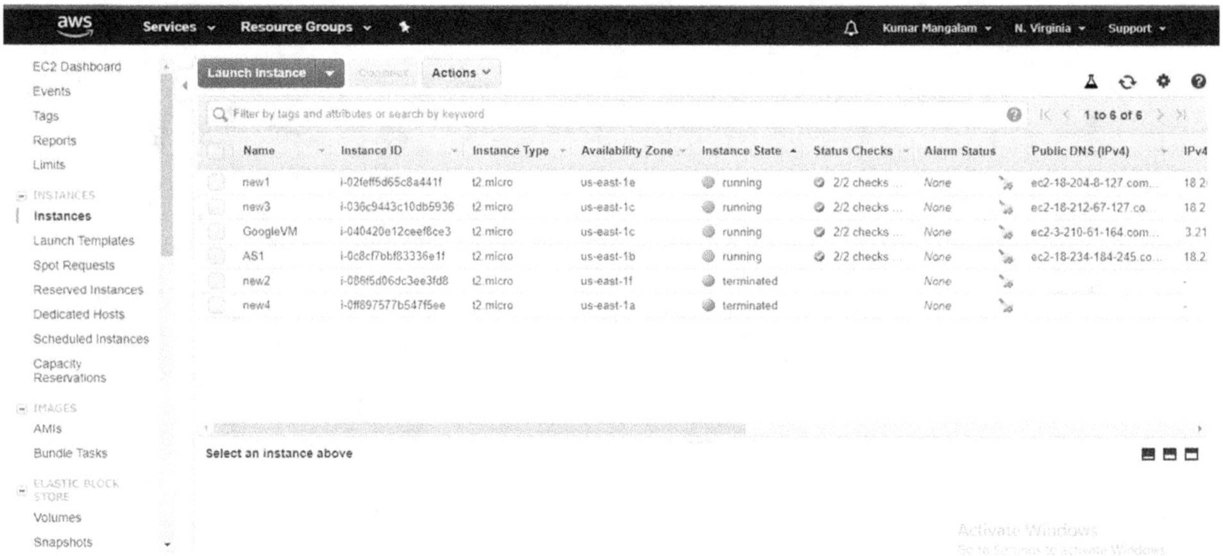

Figure 10. Increase in the performance of the instances

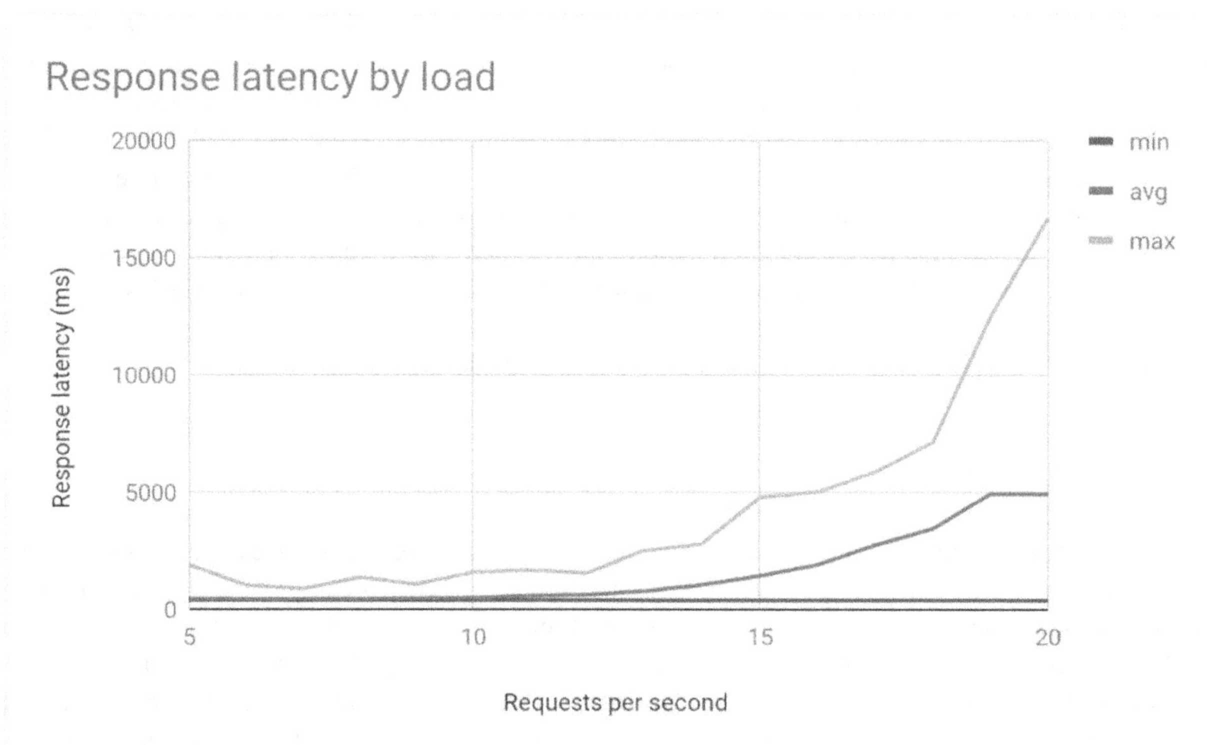

the individual services. While Amazon web services (AWS) provides many services, this collaboration not only combines auto scaling with loading balancing but also executes it in a virtual private cloud to have full control over the network.

REFERENCES

Ali, K., Mazen, A., & Hassanein, E. (2018). A Proposed Hybrid Model for Adopting Cloud Computing in E-government by Department of Information Systems. *Future Computing and Informatics Journal, 3*(2), 286-295.

Almarabeh, T., & Majdalawi, Y. K. (2019). Cloud Computing of E-commerce. *Modern Applied Science, 13*(1), 27–35. doi:10.5539/mas.v13n1p27

Amazon. (2006a). *What is ec2*. http://aws. amazon/ec2

Amazon. (2006b). *What is VPC*. http://aws. amazon/vpc

Amazon. (2006c). *Features of vpc*. http://aws.amazon/vpc-eips

Amazon. (n.d.). https://docs.aws.amazon.com/whitepapers/latest/aws-overview/introduction.html?pg=gs&sec=syj&refid=14a4002d-4936-4343-8211-b5a150ca592b

AWS. (n.d.). *Elastic IP addresses*. https://docs.aws.amazon.com/AWSEC2/latest/UserGuide/elastic-ip-addresses-eip.html

Bilgaiyan, S., Sagnika, S., & Das, M. (2014, February). Workflow scheduling in cloud computing environment using cat swarm optimization. In *2014 IEEE International Advance Computing Conference (IACC)* (pp. 680-685). IEEE. 10.1109/IAdCC.2014.6779406

Botran, L., & Alonso, M. (2014). Lozano: A Review of Auto Scaling Techniques for Elastic Applications in Cloud Environment. *Journal of Grid Computing, 12*(4), 559-592.

Citrix. (n.d.). https://www.citrix.com/en-in/solutions/app-delivery-and-security/load-balancing/what-is-load-balancing.html#:~:text=Load%20balancing%20is%20a%20core,responsiveness%20and%20prevent%20server%20overload

Khan, N., Noraziah, A., Deris, M., & Ismail, E. (2011). CLOUD COMPUTING:Comparison of Various Features. In *Published in DEIS* (pp. 1–11). Springer.

Kumari, P., & Kaur, P. (2018). A Survey of Fault Tolerance in Cloud Computing by Department of Computer Science & Information Technology. *Journal of King Saud University - Computer and Information Sciences, 5*(2), 1-18.

Lu, Y., Lin, C., Lai, K., Tsai, M., Wu, Y., Chang, H., & Huang, K. (2019). Service Deployment and Scheduling for Improving Performance of Composite Cloud Services. *Computers and Electrical Engineering, 74*(1), 616-634.

Mukhopadhyay, R., & Mukhopadhyay, I. (2016). Data encryption in virtual machine transfer over cloud network. In *IEEE 7th Annual Information Technology, Electronics and Mobile Communication Conference (IEMCON)*. IEEE. 10.1109/IEMCON.2016.7746078

Parast, F. K., Sindhav, C., Nikam, S., Yekta, H. I., Kent, K. B., & Hakak, S. (2022). Cloud computing security: A survey of service-based models. *Computers & Security*, *114*, 102580. doi:10.1016/j.cose.2021.102580

Priya, Sathiya, C., & Kannan, K. (2019). *Resource Scheduling Algorithm with Load Balancing for Cloud Service Provisioning*. Elsevier.

Rana, M., Bilgaiyan, S., & Kar, U. (2014, July). A study on load balancing in cloud computing environment using evolutionary and swarm based algorithms. In *2014 international conference on control, instrumentation, communication and computational technologies (ICCICCT)* (pp. 245-250). IEEE.

Singh, S., Chaudhary, S., Sharma, V., Gupta, A., & Vatsa, M. (2021, October). Cloud Computing and E-Commerce Based Entrepreneurship. In *2021 2nd International Conference on Smart Electronics and Communication (ICOSEC)* (pp. 1468-1474). IEEE.

Sontakke, V., Patil, P., Waghamare, S., Kulkarni, S., Saravanapriya, M., & Patil, N. (2015). *Survey on Dynamic Resource Allocation Strategy for Cloud Computing*. Elsevier.

Sun, C. (2012). Research of E-Commerce based on cloud computing. In *Advances in Computer Science and Information Engineering* (pp. 15–20). Springer. doi:10.1007/978-3-642-30223-7_3

Vinoth, S., Vemula, H. L., Haralayya, B., Mamgain, P., Hasan, M. F., & Naved, M. (2022). Application of cloud computing in banking and e-commerce and related security threats. *Materials Today: Proceedings*, *51*, 2172–2175. doi:10.1016/j.matpr.2021.11.121

Winthrop, H. (1966). *The Mathematics of the Round-Robin*. Elsevier.

Xcellhost. (2009). *Load balancing algorithms*. https://cloud/load-balancing-different-types-load-balancing-algorithms-cloud-computing

Zia, Z., & Tian, X. (2013). A novel security private cloud solution. In *6th International Conference on Information Management, Innovation Management and Industrial Engineering*. IEEE.

Chapter 7
Analytical Review on Techniques and Challenges in Sentiment Analysis

Santwana Sagnika
Kalinga Institute of Industrial Technology (Deemed), Bhubaneswar, India

Nilanjana Das
Kalinga Institute of Industrial Technology (Deemed), Bhubaneswar, India

Swastika Pandey
Kalinga Institute of Industrial Technology (Deemed), Bhubaneswar, India

Saurabh Bilgaiyan
Kalinga Institute of Industrial Technology (Deemed), Bhubaneswar, India

ABSTRACT

Opinion mining and sentiment analysis help in extracting valuable information from the huge user data generated in the form of opinions and reviews from the customers and comments. Such a huge increase in data available on the electronic or social media has also increased interest in this field. Sentiment analysis helps in extraction of opinions of others (writer or speaker) from a given source (text) using different methods and techniques like NLP, text mining, and linguistic computation and classifying them into positive, negative, and neutral opinions. Decision making for both consumers as well as the seller becomes much easier with such type of classification. This chapter consists of survey report on different elements of sentiment analysis, its applications, and challenges involved. The chapter studies and compares some of the techniques used to evaluate the item's reputation using sentiment analysis. A number of tools and features for sentiment analysis are also included in this chapter that can later help to perform better sentiment analysis of data.

DOI: 10.4018/978-1-6684-4969-1.ch007

Copyright © 2022, IGI Global. Copying or distributing in print or electronic forms without written permission of IGI Global is prohibited.

1. INTRODUCTION

Today's information-based society, which is also sometimes referred to as the digital age, is driven by the rapidly growing informational data. Modern life is dependent on many web applications including social media websites with an insatiable desire to share information. A majority of the informal subjective content which is most probably expected to rapidly increase in the near future is generated by the younger generation who account for most of the online users. Users are constantly invited to share their experiences, opinions, reviews about a product or service and comment on virtually anything with all the other users. Meaningful information extracted from the web based data can be used to study and add more value for multiple application domains. Scientific survey could be employed on these informative texts from a social and political perspective (O'Connor et al, 2010, Sagnika et al, 2020).

Rich feedback obtained from research analysis can help to smartly lead business for companies and product owners (Gamon et al, 2005, Tang et al, 2009). On the other hand, customers can make a smart choice by learning about the positive and negative features of a product or service. Unstructured data (opinionated text) is majorly produced as data which is processed in sentiment analysis and then labelled into different categories, namely positive and negative. One among the tasks of sentiment analysis is to identify whether the provided data is objective data, expressing purely fact, or subjective data, mentioning writer's opinions (Maas et al, 2011). E-commerce forums benefit a lot from automated analysis of sentiments based on user-generated reviews.

The sentiment analysis task can be broken down into 5 different steps in order to analyze the data, which are as follows:

- **Data compilation:** The first and foremost task of sentiment analysis is to collect and compile the data generated by the user which can be from social network, blogs, reviews, forums. The collected data is generally unstructured, which is communicated in various ways by using different languages, slangs, meaning, context, vocabularies, etc. Processing such amount manually is almost impossible. This can be made a bit easier by taking help of text analytics and natural language processing for extraction and classification.
- **Text preparation:** This is the second step of sentiment analysis in which the extracted data is cleaned before analysis. The text which is irrelevant from the required information or non- textual content is identified and hence eliminated.
- **Sentiment detection**: In this step the extracted informative data collected from various reviews and opinions are examined. This data is then filtered where subjective information such as opinions, views and beliefs are kept whereas objective information such as facts, factual information is drained out.
- **Polarity classification**: In this step the extracted subjective statements are then characterised into positive, negative, neutral; liking, disliking; good, bad. This is marked by considering various parameters used differently by different techniques.
- **Output Presentation**: The aim of sentiment analysis is to extract meaningful information from unstructured data. After sentiment analysis, the result of the analysis is then displayed in user readable format which can be represented by graphs like line graphs, pie chart and bar charts. The time can be assessed and graphically represented by constructing sentiment timeline for a given value (averages, percentage and frequency) over time.

In past few years, many enhancements, methods and techniques have been suggested for various problems faced during sentiment analysis in different tasks at different levels. Sentimental analysis undergoes various challenges, some of which are categorized and outlined as follows.

- **Implicit Sentiment** – Some sentences do not have a specific word which represents the sentiment indeed the strong sentiment is inbuilt in the sentence.
  Ex. *One has to work harder in order to become a person like him.*
- **Domain Dependency Sentiment** – The domain influences the vocabulary and the structure, which expresses both the subjectivity and the polarity. Differing polarity is denoted by many words in different domains, as shown.
  Ex. *The play was motivated from a British novel.*
  I was motivated from the article.
- **Pragmatics** – There should be recognition of the user's elements of communication.
  Ex. *It was great to see you after such a long duration.*
  It rained and nullified my current mood.
- **Negation Handling-** It is sometimes difficult to handle a negation in a sentence. A negative word (like, not) followed by overturning the polarity of any word is a method.
  Ex. *I did not like the meal served.* But this method cannot be successful in some situations like – Not only was the served meal delicious, the service provided by the staff was also amazing.
- **Subjectivity Detection** - It is important to discriminate between the sentences which are either neutral in meaning or rich in sentiment.
  Ex. *I love to eat cookies. I hate "cookies in the computer".*
- **World Knowledge** – Sometimes to recognize the sentiment one should have the whereabouts and the knowledge of the entity present in the statement.
  Ex. *She is as benign as a witch.* Therefore, a person has to know about "witch" so that he can understand the correct sentiment in the sentence.
- **Entity identification-** It is necessary to identify and distinguish which sentiment is used for which entity when a particular sentence contains multiple entities.
  Ex. *Sunita is better than Anita.* In this example, a negative sentiment is for Anita and a positive sentiment is for Sunita.
- **Let Down Expectations** - It may happen that sometimes the writer disapproves what he showcases as the content's positive context initially.
  Ex. *A fun read book which is full of motivating and inspiring virtues for college students/adolescents but all in vain due to dearth of imagination and creativity.*

In this chapter, the authors try to provide a comprehensive and detailed understanding of sentiment analysis and its usefulness from the perspective of e-commerce, since business and e-commerce are the fields most benefited by sentiment analysis. The reader shall get a proper idea of the concepts, techniques, approaches, and subtasks in this field. Most popular tools are also discussed, along with challenges and directions for future research. Major machine learning and deep learning methods applied in this area are described, compared and analyzed. Overall, this chapter serves as fundamental literature for a thorough understanding of sentiment analysis and its components.

This chapter gives a comprehensive overview of concepts and research on sentiment classification for the introductory researcher, particularly features, tasks, tools, approaches, to sentiment analysis, classification of existing solutions, analytical comparison of common algorithms, challenges and future scope of work. The rest of the chapter consists of these topics in the same order.

2. FEATURES FOR SENTIMENT ANALYSIS

A feature in the context of machine learning and pattern recognition can be explained as a discrete measurable property of an event to be measured. Feature engineering becomes a fundamental job while conducting sentiment analysis which involves creating a feature vector with the help of a piece of text. Kaushik and Mishra (Kaushik and Mishra, 2014) list some general features suitable for the sentiment analysis processes.

A. **Term presence and term frequency -** Term frequency is studied to be one of the important text classification tasks. In simple words term frequency can be explained as quantitative measurement of a term in a piece of text. The terms involve unigram or n-gram and the number of times they occur is their frequency. But soon it was realized that term presence holds higher significance than term frequency in sentiment analysis because sometimes polarity of whole sentence gets reversed by the presence of a single term. According to Pang et al. (Pang et al, 2002) for movie review sentiment analysis, unigrams lead to more desirable results than bi-grams. On the other hand, according to Dave et al. (Dave et al, 2003) for product review polarity classification, tri-grams and bi-grams give superior results. Kamal (Kamal, 2013) used a mathematical formula to calculate Term Frequency - Inverse Document Frequency (TF-IDF) which measures how many times a particular unigram occurs in a review document with respect to its number of occurrences in the whole corpus which contains many review documents. TF-IDF remains one of the most popular methods for text analysis, because it not just considers frequency but is also able to attach significance to specific words.

B. **Term position -** Sometimes position of a term in a sentence can also contribute towards text classification, like the terms which appear at one segment of text or sentence contains more weight than the term appearing in a different segment of the text. For example, a term which is a negation can alter the meaning of an entire sentence if it is present at the beginning of the sentence. Commonly more weightage is given to the first and last few sentences of the text than the terms which occur around the middle. Kamal also used the position as one of the features to calculate whether an unigram is subjective or objective. He used an approach in which the position attribute would set to -1, 0, 1 depending on the position of the unigram whether it occurred in the beginning, middle or at the end of the sentence.

C. **N-gram features -** N-grams are texts which are widely applied in text mining and natural language processing tasks for recognizing the context. Within a given window, N-grams are basically a group of co-occurring words. In N-gram, if N=1, it is mentioned as unigrams which are actually single words present in a particular sentence. Similarly if N=2, this is known as bigrams and when N=3 this is addressed as trigrams, and so on. However, studies show that it is not clear which will perform better, whether it is the N-grams of lower order or the N-grams of higher order.

D. **Subsequence kernels –** Sentence or word level modes are generally used in sentiment analysis. Bickel et al. (Bickel et al, 2007) used a technique for implicit capturing of the feature space with the help of a subsequence kernel. The word subsequence kernel of order n, is the weighted sum of all word sequences of length n that is occurring in both strings that are being used for comparison. The mathematical representation is

$$K_n(s,t) = \sum_{u \in £^*} \sum_{i:s[i]=u} \sum_{j:t[j]=u} \lambda^{(i[n]-i[1]+1)+(j[n]-j[1]+1)} \quad (1)$$

Where; i[n] – i[1] + 1 is the total length of the span of s constituting the subsequence *u*'s particular occurrence, λ is a kernel parameter similar to gap penalty, i is a vector of length n consisting of the indices of string s corresponding to the subsequence *u*.

E. **Adjectives only -** Very frequently, adjectives are extensively used to communicate clearly or to give more specific meaning. This feature is also widely used in sentiment analysis. Humans widely use adjectives to denote their sentiments and higher performance is achieved in sentiment analysis techniques that consider adjectives.

F. **Adjective – Adverb Combination -** Adverbs individually do not have polarity, but can help in determining the polarity of sentence when combined with an adjective. Benamara's (Benamara et al, 2007) classification shows how adverbs can modify the sentiment of sentences.
   1. Strongly intensifying adverbs: *immensely, exceedingly*
   2. Adverbs of doubt: *probably, maybe*
   3. Weakly intensifying adverbs: *slightly, barely*
   4. Adverbs of affirmation: *totally, certainly*
   5. Negation and minimizers: *never*

Two different types of AACs were actually defined by the work, namely, Unary AAC, containing one adverb and one adjective, and binary AAC, containing multiple adjectives and adverbs.

G. **POS -** This is another feature popularly used for sentiment analysis. POS tags like adjective, noun, adverb, verb, etc. can be used to denote a unigram's tag and then depending on all the tags of unigrams in a sentence, it can be decided whether the sentence is subjective or objective. Among the tags, adjective is the best indicator of subjectivity according to many researchers. Another such indicator is a modifier, generally an adverb whose presence can greatly measure the subjectivity of a sentence. In POS tagging, labels are used to represent terms' positions in a grammatical context. Each term is attached to a label. So, with the help of POS tags, it is possible to recognize various adverbs and adjectives used as sentiment indicators (Turney, 2002). Based on all the tags of a sentence, it is then finally decided whether the sentence is a subjective sentence or an objective sentence.

H. **Opinion phrases -** For extraction of positive or negative sentiment, opinion word/phrase is used. The semantic orientation of an opinion word/phrase can be determined by statistical-based or lexicon based approaches. To identify the polarity of the sentiment of an extracted adjective, WordNet was used by Hu and Liu (Hu and Liu, 2004). Naive Bayes (NB) and Support Vector Machines (SVM) are most frequently used machine learning algorithms. For sentiment analysis on movie reviews, Support Vector Machines are commonly used [Pang et al, 2002, Efron et al, 2003], while

Naïve Bayes are used for web discourse (Pang et al, 2002, Pang and Lee, 2004). As compared to NB, SVM has shown better performance. Another technique based on link metrics and features is Link analysis technique. Co-citation was used by Efron (Efron et al, 2004) for website opinions whereas message-send/reply was used by Agarwal et al., (Agarwal et al, 2003) for classification of sentiments in USENET newsgroups.

Based on the summation of all positive and negative polarities of sentiment, to classify message sentiment generally Score-based methods are used. Phrase pattern matching was used by Fei et al., (Fei et al, 2004), Nasukawa and Yi (Nasukawa and Yi, 2003), which checks the text for manually created phrase tags which are polarized (negative or positive). +1 and -1 are respectively assigned to positive and negative phrases. Messages having positive sum value are classified as positive sentiments whereas those having negative sum value are considered to be negative sentiments.

I. **Negation -** The feature negation can be very helpful in predicting the subjectivity of a sentence. The presence of negation can reverse the polarity of a sentiment, hence making it important feature to be taken into consideration (Abbasi et al, 2008).

3. SENTIMENT ANALYSIS TASKS

Sentiment analysis consists of many tasks which can be further divided in sub tasks. In the existing literature, various types of categorizations are suggested for these tasks (Liu, 2012, Ravi and Ravi, 2015). Aydogan (Aydogan and Akcayol, 2016) classified sentiment analysis tasks into four categories which are- subjectivity categorization, sentiment classification, review worth measurement, and opinion spam detection. Figure 1 shows these steps.

Subjectivity classification generally deals with deciding whether a sentence used by a technique expresses emotions, opinions, assessments or beliefs. Subjectivity classification is a demanding task to handle, but improvements have given a positive influence on the study of sentiment analysis (Chenlo and Losada, 2014, Li and Li, 2013).

Sentiment classification deals with finding the orientation of sentiment in provided text. It deals in the areas of cross lingual sentiment analysis, multi lingual sentiment analysis, cross domain sentiment analysis, polarity determination and vagueness resolution.

The **review usefulness measurement** deals with the investigation of useful and not-so-useful reviews. Machine learning algorithms have been used to assess the review's quality (Chen and Tseng, 2011, Ghose and Ipeirotis, 2010, Lee and Choeh, 2014).

Over the years, **opinion spam detection** has become an important topic of research. Opinion spam detection basically deals with the authentication of genuine reviews and reviewer, i.e. it detects whether the reviews are posted by real buyers with honest intentions (Ott et al, 2013, Costa et al, 2014, Lin et al, 2014). It has the ability to detect whether the buyer who writes the review has genuinely purchased the product or service. The geographical locations of the reviewers assist in detecting fake buyers or group spammers.

Some common parameters which are used in existing research in sentiment analysis are discussed as follows.

Figure 1. Sentiment Analysis Tasks

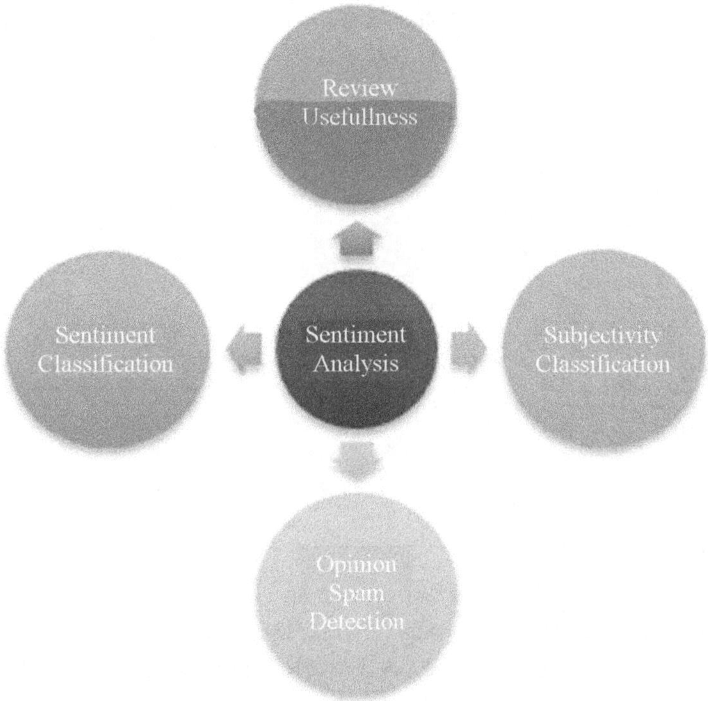

Ø Sentiment Analysis Features

- Semantic features – Appraisal groups, Positive and Negative tags, semantic orientation.
- Syntactic features - Phrase patterns, Words/ POS tag n-grams.
- Stylistic features –Lexical and structure measures of style.
- Link based features – send/reply patterns, web links, document citations.

Ø Sentiment Classification Methods

- Machine Learning Techniques – Support Vector Machine, Maximum Entropy, Naive Bayes.
- Similarity score Techniques – Lexicon, sentiment score counts, Sentiment pattern etc.
- Link Analysis Techniques - Message send/reply patterns, citation analysis.

Ø Sentiment Analysis of Data Set Domains

- News articles –Web pages and online articles.
- Reviews - product, music and movie reviews.
- Web discourse – Social Website (Facebook, twitter, YouTube).

Ø Precision, Accuracy and Recall

The formula of accuracy, precision and recall are as follows (Li and Wu, 2010).

$$Precision(P) = \frac{tp}{tp + fp} \quad (2)$$

Table 1. Confusion matrix

	Machine (Yes)	Machine (No)
Human (Yes)	*tp*	*fn*
Human (No)	*fp*	*tn*

$$Recall\left(R\right)=\frac{tp}{tp+fn} \tag{3}$$

$$Accuracy\left(A\right)=\frac{tp+tn}{tp+tn+fp+fn} \tag{4}$$

Ø Data Source and Data Size

Data source refers to the place (e.g. web pages, websites, journals, movie reviews, product reviews, customer feedback) from where data sets have been taken. Data size can be explained as the number of words/sentence/terms/expression/review/feedback taken as an input to the technique used for sentiment analysis.

4. TOOLS FOR SENTIMENT ANALYSIS

Some major sentiment analysis tools have been mentioned which are widely used in diverse techniques.

A. Emoticons

Nowadays, emoticons have become the simplest way to express emotions in text messages, making it the easiest way to detect polarity of a message by taking into consideration the emoticon used in the message. These emoticons graphically attempt to represent facial expressions like happy, sad, confused faces, although there is a wide range of non facial expressions too. The popularity that emoticons received in the past few years have given them place in English Oxford Dictionary (e.g., <3 represents the heart symbol). There are sets of such emoticons as listed in Figure 2, which can be referenced to extract sentence's polarity, broadly categorized into positive, negative and neutral polarity.

B. LIWC

LIWC (Linguistic Inquiry and Word Count) (Tausczik and Pennebaker, 2010) is a commercial software which analyses text and evaluates its structural, emotional and cognitive components. The evaluation is done using dictionaries containing words and the categories they are classified into. LIWC software also provides users' choice of customization, in the sense that instead of using the standard dictionary

Figure 2. Polarity of common emoticons

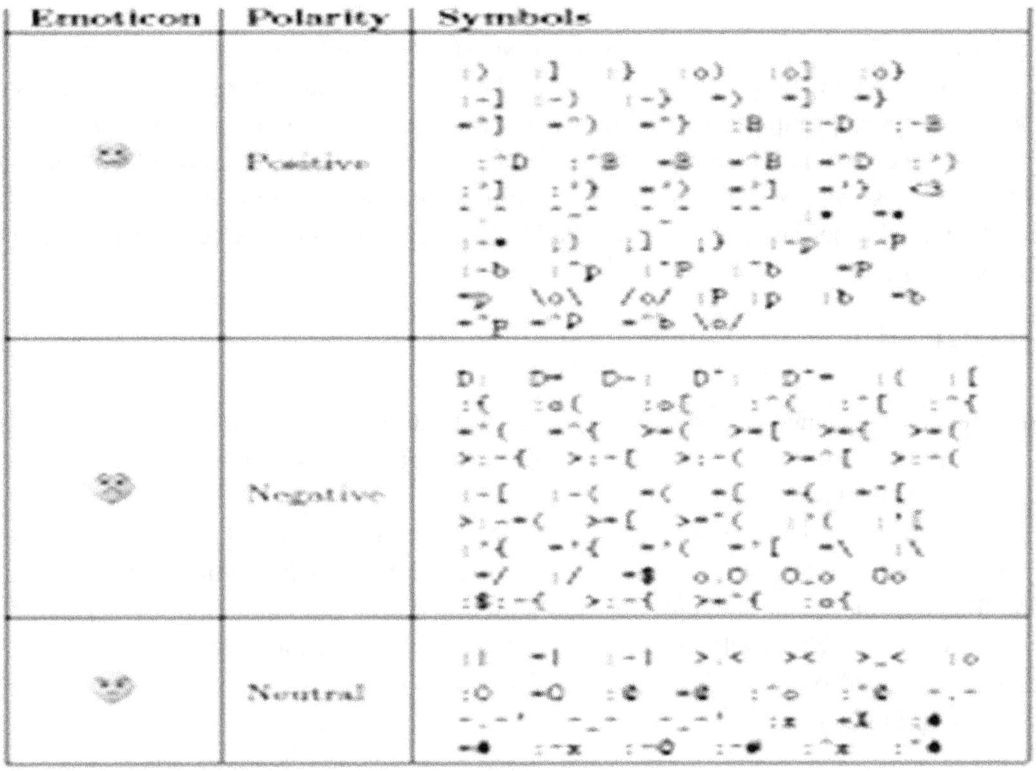

they can include customized dictionaries. LIWC provides other sets of sentiment analysis in addition to conventional methods for detecting positive and negative polarity. For example, the word "accept" can be categorized into following categories- positive emotion, affective, positive feeling, assent and cognitive process.

C. SentiStrength

Applications which need adaptive polarity or content driven identification models are best suited for machine learning based models. The set of words present in the LIWC dictionary decides the core classification of the work in (Tausczik and Pennebaker, 2010) and now the authors have added some new features in the online social network context .The new features include a set of words which acts as a booster to enhance ("very") or weaken ("somewhat") the sentiments, negative and positive words, use of repeated punctuation marks (e.g., "Great!!!!!") and a list of emoticons.

For testing, the author has used opinionated text from six different Web 2.0 sources which are Runners World Forum, Digg, BBC Forum, Twitter, MySpace and YouTube Comments and released a tool called SentiStrength (Thelwall, 2014). In context to online social networks, SentiStrength produces best results by implementing state-of-the-art machine learning methods.

D. SentiWord Net

SentiWordNet (Liu, 2012) is a tool based on WordNet (Miller, 1995), which is an English lexicon dictionary. This tool is widely used in opinion mining. This lexical dictionary creates synonym sets called synsets which contains groups of verbs, nouns, adjectives and other grammatical classes. In order to identify the sentiment of the given text as positive, negative or neutral, SentiWordNet with synset associated three scores from WordNet dictionary. Semi supervised machine learning is used to obtain the value of scores in the range of 0 to 1, and add up to 1, along with the labelled lexicon dictionary SentiWordNet was evaluated with.

E. SenticNet

SenticNet uses natural language text at semantic level to derive polarity of common sense concepts. SenticNet (Cambria et al, 2010) is an approach of sentiment analysis which scrutinizes semantic web techniques and artificial intelligence.

The polarity for around 14,000 concepts has been created using natural language processing techniques. For example, in the sentence "Tired, it's Saturday night", firstly SenticNet identify the concept which are "Boring" and "Saturday night" for the sentence. Then each concept is awarded with polarity score by the SenticNet. The resulting sentiment score is average of the individual polarity scores. To measure the polarity of opinion of patients SenticNet was tested and assessed as a tool by National Health Service in England.

F. SASA

SASA (SailAil Sentiment Analyzer) (Wang et al, 2012) is a machine learning-based tool. The Amazon Mechanical Turk evaluated it where tweets were labelled as positive, neutral, negative or undefined by the turkers. SASA was also used to evaluate 17,000 labelled tweets on the 2012 U.S. Elections. SASA is an open source tool.

G. Happiness Index

Happiness Index (Dodds and Danforth, 2010) can be explained as a scale of sentiment that employs the famous Affective Norms for English Words (ANEW) (Bradley and Lang, 1999). Happiness index can be calculated with the help of ANEW terms which score the text between score 1 to 9, denoting the quantity of happiness present in the text. ANWE is a compilation of 1,034 words generally associated with dominance, arousal and affective aspects of valence.

H. Panas-t

The PANAS-t (Gonçalves et al, 2013) is a psychometric scale used to detect fluctuations in mood of Twitter users (Gonçalves et al, 2013). The method is inherited from well known method of psychology also known as Positive Affect Negative Affect Scale (PANAS) (Watson et al, 1998). PANAS-t is works on sets of words correlated to basically eleven moods which are surprise, joviality, serenity, terror, assurance, sadness, shyness, attentiveness, guilt, fatigue and unfriendliness. This method tracks the increase or decrease of sentiment over time. Based upon the entire data, PANAS-t utilizes normative values of sentiments to associate each text to a specific sentiment.

I. EWGA

EWGA uses Entropy Weighted Genetic Algorithm. By using wrapper-model, the tool efficiently selects features for sentiment classification.

J. AFINN

It mostly focuses on languages used in microblogging platforms. It is a list of English words rated in the range of -5(negative) and +5(positive) for valence.

K. NRC

In NRC Hashtag Sentiment Lexicon, the lexicon is divided into three files, namely pairs-pmilexicon.txt, unigrams-pmilexicon.txt and bigrams-pmilexicon.txt. Along with positive and negative sentiment these lexicon also consist of frequently used English nouns, adjectives, adverbs and verbs that are annotated by eight emotions (fear, joy, anger, sadness, trust, disgust, anticipation and surprise).

L. Sentiment 140

Previously known as Twitter Sentiment, Sentiment140 extracts positive and negative opinions for a topic, product or brand on Twitter. Machine learning algorithms are used to build classifiers used in Sentiment140. This tool has the quality to classify individual tweets rather than the conventional tools showing aggregated numbers which makes it tricky to evaluate the accuracy of the classifier.

M. FRN

Feature Relation Network (FRN) considers two syntactic n-gram relations which are subsumption and parallel relations (Abbasi, 2003).

5. APPROACHES TO SENTIMENT ANALYSIS

The existing research on sentiment analysis can be categorized on different basis, like text view, technique applied, level of analysis detail, rating level, etc. Considering a methodology viewpoint, the popular approaches are machine learning, lexicon-based, rule-based and statistical methods. Fig. 3 presents a clear idea of the classification of sentiment analysis. Some of them are explained below:-

- **Machine learning method** utilizes different learning algorithms to find out sentiments by training the classification model using a known dataset.

- **Lexicon-based method** includes calculation of polarity of sentiment for reviews using the semantic orientation of sentences or words. Semantic orientation refers to the estimate of subjectivity and opinion in the text.
- **Rule-based method** searches for opinion terms in the text and then categorizes them based on the number of negative or positive words. It refers to the various rules for categorization such as booster words, idioms, negation words, emoticons, dictionary polarity, etc.
- **Statistical models** represent individual reviews as a mixture of inherent ratings of aspects. It takes into consideration that the aspects and their ratings can be denoted by multinomial distributions and attempts to cluster sentiments into ratings and head terms into aspects.

Due to fully automatic implementation and the ability of machine learning based approach to deal with large collections of web data, it is more practical than any other opinion mining approach. Machine Learning-Based approaches can be categorized into three main categories which are supervised learning, unsupervised learning and semi-supervised learning approaches (Liu et al, 2013).

In traditional topical classification learning, the supervised learning technique is a well-tested and successful solution. It has been researched and accepted for opinion mining with satisfactory results (Liu et al, 2013). In this approach, labelled training data is used to train a classifier on the basis of a feature set. The first to perform sentiment analysis on movie reviews written online were Pang et.al (Pang et al, 2002). Some of the important supervised classification algorithms include: Discriminative classifier called **Support Vector Machine (SVM)** which is based on training data, does not make any prior assumptions and directly measures P(Y|X); a generative classifier called **Naïve Bayes**, which based on training data measures prior probabilities of P(X|Y) and P(Y). The posterior probability of P(Y|X) is generated by it based on prior probabilities; **K- Nearest Neighbour (KNN)** is the lazy learning algorithm K for which classification model does not require prior construction. SVM and Naïve Bayes are considered to be the most widely used and efficient algorithms of supervised learning for both topical and opinion classification. Supervised learning has certain limitations amongst which the biggest one is that, it is sensitive to the quality and quantity of training data. It may also fail if the training data is insufficient or biased. For supervised leaning based approaches the challenges arise during opinion detection at the sub-document level as there is less information available to the classifier.

In situations like text classification, it becomes generally difficult to create already-labelled documents for training, as creating them needs a lot of human effort, whereas it is comparatively easier to gather unlabeled documents. So to overcome these difficulties, **unsupervised learning** is used. To extract inherent topics from text documents, traditional techniques such as LDA and pLSA are used. Topics are considered to be a feature, and then each feature is distributed over terms. Many research studies have been made for unsupervised learning as it is less dependent on the topic or domain and provides better performance (Nizam and Akin, 2014, Martín-Valdivia et al, 2013, Ghorbel and Jacot, 2011). The limitation of the unsupervised learning approach is that because functional objectives of topic models don't always associate well with the human judgement, hence it often produces incoherent topics. Such a learning approach often needs a large amount of data to be trained appropriately. Besides all these limitations, unsupervised learning still provides ways to acquire information about data not having any annotations.

Semi-supervised learning derives inspiration from either supervised or unsupervised learning approaches by learning from a combination of labelled and unlabelled data. SSL gets motivated by the fact that in real world applications there is lack of sufficient labelled data, and unlabeled data do not hold much information about the necessary classes. But unlabeled data contains details about joint allocation over features of classification (Liu, 2012). Hence if little amount of data is present in the target domain, then semi-supervised learning methods provide better results as compared to supervised and unsupervised learning methods. Based on a survey (Prakash and Nithya, 2014), the most frequently used semi-supervised learning algorithms include: co-training, multi-view training, self-training, graph-based methods and generative training.

- **Document level** – Here the whole document is considered as a basic unit of information (talking about a topic) where opinion is expressed as a negative or positive sentiment. At this level, it is possible to categorize the overall user sentiment into a positive or negative opinion. For example for a given product or service, it is possible to identify whether the overall views or opinions expressed is negative or positive opinion. Document level classification approach with the help of supervised learning methods is used to classify movie reviews (Pang et al, 2002).
- **Sentence level** – Here each sentence is classified with respect to sentiment conveyed in it. If the sentence is found out to be subjective, then it is classified into either a positive or a negative sentiment.
- **Aspect level** – The sentiment is classified according to the aspects of the entities. Different opinions for different aspects can be given for the same entity. Here the focus is directly on the opinion itself rather than looking at the construction of the language (sentences, paragraphs, phrases, clauses, etc). It is based on the notion that a sentence generally consists of a target (opinion) and a sentiment (positive or negative).
- **Statistical models-** In this type of model there is a mix of hidden aspects and ratings for each review. An assumption is taken that the representation of aspects and their ratings can be done by multinomial distributions and attempts to perform clustering of sentiments into ratings, as well as head terms into aspects.

6. STUDY OF EXISTING SOLUTIONS

Sentiment analysis is a classification problem and can be solved considering it as either a binary classification task (i.e., positive and negative) or a multi-class classification task (i.e., positive, negative, neutral, extremely positive, extremely negative, etc.). Most of the existing approaches solve this problem using a binary approach. Some work has also been done on multi-class methods, though they give lower performances.

Some solutions that represent the categories mentioned in the previous section are discussed in table 2.

From an analysis of the data in Table 2, it was observed that the most common classifier models in literature were found to be naive bayes and SVM. Modern methods include CNN and LSTM based models, based on which a lot of research is ongoing. On the other hand, a majority of research has been done on English datasets. Among other languages, there is a good amount of work available in Chinese. There is also the existence of a wide range of lexical resources and corpus of text which can be used for reference in sentiment analysis. A good number of datasets are also available, including data obtained from Twitter, Amazon, IMDb, Yelp, TripAdvisor, etc. The limitations show that there is still large scope for future work and research in this field, which can aid various businesses and other applications.

Figure 3. Classification of Sentiment Analysis

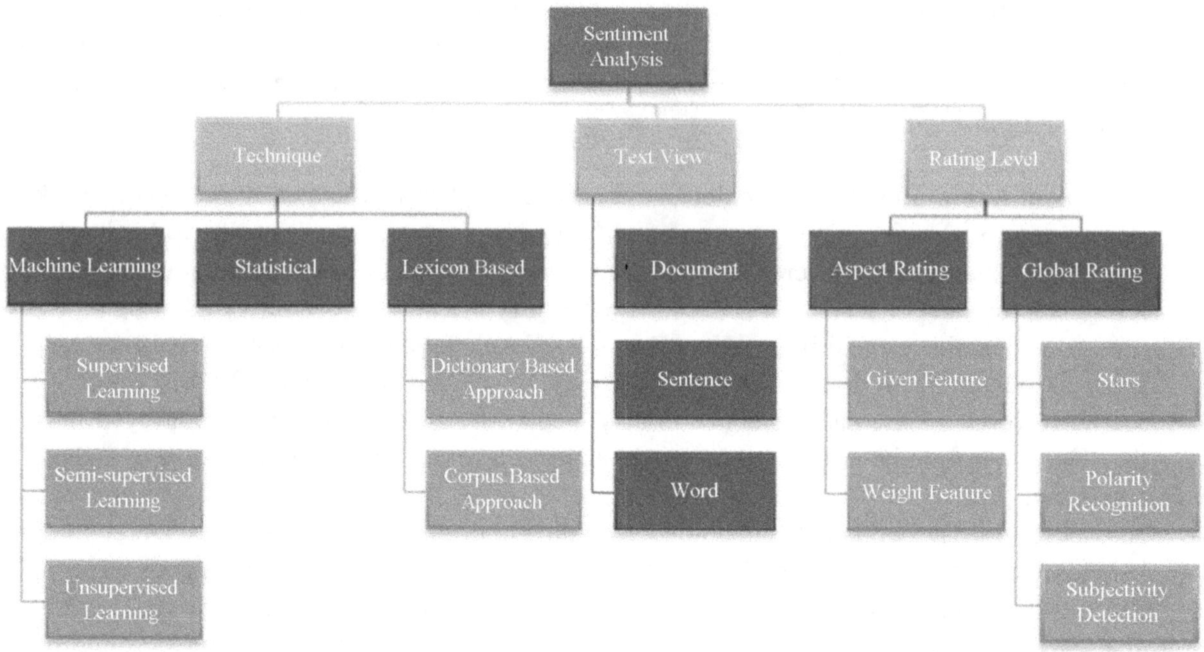

Table 3 mentions some common applications of sentiment analysis in various fields. As observed from the collected literature, e-commerce is field which has maximum usage of sentiment analysis. Both businesses and consumers benefit from sentiment analysis of reviews and opinions that aid decision-making. In addition to that, fields like finance, politics, public policy, etc. also are benefited by performing sentiment analysis on various user-generated documents, articles, blogs, etc.

6. ANALYTICAL COMPARISON OF COMMOMLY USED ALGORITHMS

Some of the commonly used algorithms in machine learning are Naive Bayes, Support Vector Machines, K-Nearest Neighbours, Random Forest. For a better understanding we have compared two algorithms Naive Bayes and Support Vector Machine, which are the most commonly applied and best performing algorithms on sentiment analysis as observed. We have calculated the accuracy, kappa coefficient and average standard deviation for training algorithm for each train - test split ranging from 0.05 – 0.50 with an interval of 0.05. We have then plotted three bar graphs, accuracy vs train – test split shown in fig.4, kappa vs train – test split shown in fig.5 and standard deviation vs average accuracy shown in fig.6. We found out that more the standard deviation, lesser the accuracy and vice-versa.

We have tabulated the observations of the algorithms Support Vector Machine and Naive Bayes. For calculating the standard deviation we used the stdev() in Python. For the standard deviation we have calculated the average accuracy. In Naive Bayes theorem, Posterior Probability, P (C | ti) can be calculated using prior probability, P (C) with likelihood, P (ti | C) and P (ti) [93]. SVM is one of the most commonly used supervised machine learning algorithms which uses an optimal hyperplane as decision boundary to separate two classes (Mungra et al, 2020). A kernel function is used to define the boundaries and a

Table 2. Comparative Study of Previous Works

Authors	Techniques and methods	Efficiency	Objective	Data Size	Language	Data Source	Limitations
Byrd et al.	Maximum Entropy, Naive Bayes, and a Dynamic Language Model classifier	Accuracy - 70%	Twitter Data Mining For Influenza Detection and Surveillance	1,848,130 tweets	English	Twitter Streaming API with location filters	Limited geographical areas are considered
Dai et al.	Weighted word embeddings	Best Accuracy –78.5%	Weighted word embeddings for sentiment classification in Big Data	9,000 tweets	English	Super Bowl 50 Tweets, Wikepedia, Presidential Election Tweets, Airline Services Tweets	Below state-of-art accuracy, can be improved by adding features
Abdelwahab et al.	Naïve Bayes and SVM classifier, decision fusion technique	Best Accuracy - Ensemble 1- 76.47% Ensemble 2- 75.45%	Analyzing the effect of Size of Training Set on Naïve Bayes and SVM, for Sentiment Analysis on Twitter data	5,051 tweets	English	SEMEVAL 2014 competition	False positives and high running time of SVM.
Williams and Mahmoud	Naive Bayes and Support vector Machines	Precision - NB - 0.81 & 0.77 SVM - 0.78 & 0.70 Recall - NB -0.81 & 0.77 SVM -0.78 & 0.70	Analyzing, Classifying, and Interpreting Emotions in Software Users' Tweets	360, 873 tweets	English	Twitter Search API	Accuracy improvement possible, limited to unigrams.
Xuan et al.	Lexical extraction, MEM classification	Accuracy - 92.1%	Linguistic Features for Subjectivity classification	Movie Review data, 5000 subjective and 5,000 objective	English	Pang and Lee	Feature extraction requires precision and varies based on content.
Levow et al.	ATAROS corpus	Accuracy 71-81%	Recognizing stance strength and polarity in unprompted speech		English	23 dyads, by 26 female and 20 male speakers.	Can subsume multiple dialog acts with potentially different stance-taking behaviours.
Chatterji et al.	CRF based statistical sequence leveling technique, statistical bag of-word technique (based on SVM)	Accuracy -70.08%	Hybrid Approach for Identification Sentiments around Aspects	6400 manually annotated sentences	English	Tweet word cluster by Owoputi et al.	Accuracy improvement is possible, limited to specific domain.
Zang et al.	Text corpus and link network, generative model TopicBlock	Precision - 72.36% Recall – 47.87% Mod – 0.32	TopicBlock: Mining of User Interests in Text and Links' Analysis in Social Networking	Email, author collaborations and research papers and author data	English	Citeseer dataset	Temporal information is not considered.
Lerttripinyo et al.	ACRoSS (ACcom odation Recommendation Summarization System), FNMF (feature-based weighted non-negative matrix factorization) method	Precision- 61%.	Recommendation System of Accommodation from User Reviews based on Feature-based Weighted Non-negative Matrix Factorization	10 accommodation, 100 or more reviews each	English	booking.com, agoda.com, tripadvisor. com	Data retrieval can be enhanced, review quality can be improved.
Zou et al.	Probabilistic generative model for real-time event credibility prediction, online streaming prediction algorithm, semi-supervised ranking model	Performance accuracy- 82.3%, Online Streaming Prediction accuracy- 78.3%	Mining of Streaming Tweets for Real-Time Event Credibility Prediction	29,345 tweets	English	facebook.com, twitter.com, and snopes. com	Dataset size dependent for good performance.
Syaifudin at al.	Rule based method, Hidden Markov Model based or Fachri's study	Accuracy of 88.618%, Precision-99.013% Recall- 79.936%.	Using Rule-based Method for Identification of Quotation from Indonesian Online News	299 news or 3,506 sentences	Indonesian	http://kompas. com, http:// tribun news. com, http:// tempo.co	NER system can be improved for better performance of method.
Shaheen et al.	WordNet, ConceptNet, Emotion Recognition Rule (ERR), K-Nearest Neighbors (KNN) classifier, Point Mutual Information (PMI)	F-Score - 84%.	Emotion Recognition from Text Based on Automatically Generated Rules	570 sentences training dataset, 18,00 sentences from 2,488,982 tweets		blog posts from Aman, 2007	The method is dependent on large size of training dataset.
Wenping Zhang et al.	Energy Cascading Model (ECM), Network-Based Predictive Model	Accuracy - 67.7%	Dynamic Business Network Analysis to predict Correlated Stock Price Movement	292,880 stock records	English	Yahoo Finance API	Performance of ANN is not up to potential.
Yu-Sheng Chen et al.	Latent Dirichlet Allocation (LDA), interactive visualization	Highest precision- 81.16% with 43.07% recall	LDA-based Sentiment Visualization Technique for Hotel Reviews	10,000 reviews about Thailand hotels with 41,971 sentences	English		Accuracy of extracting sentiment pairs can be improved.
Hanifah et al.	SVM, Binary weighting method, rule-based approach	Binary weighting method accuracy rate-83%. Rule-based approach gave results 98% -100% for extraction	Information Extraction from Twitter for Smart Cities	800 tweets with #lalinbdg and #sikonbdg	Indonesian	Twitter API	Information extraction accuracy is less.

continued on following page

Table 2. Continued

Authors	Techniques and methods	Efficiency	Objective	Data Size	Language	Data Source	Limitations
Bhargava et al.	SentiWordNet, Google Translate API	Highest precision for Tamil with precision- 0.564 and recall 0.517	Sentiment Analysis for Mixed Script Indic Sentences	792 utterances	Bengali, Gujarati, Hindi, Kannada, Malayalam, Marathi, Tamil, Telugu	FIRE 2015	Basic classification models are applied; better models can give better results.
Duwairi et al.	Crowdsourcing, Naïve Bayes, k-nearest classifier (k-NN), Support Vector Machines (SVM)	Maximum accuracy NB- 76.78% SVM- 71.68% k-NN- 59.99%	Sentiment Analysis in Arabic Tweets	350,000 tweets	Arabizi and Arabic dialects	Twitter's Search API	Limited dictionary is available that limits the performance.
Ahsan et al.	Tweet segmentation algorithm[88],convolutional neural network (CNN), linear Support Vector Machine (SVM)	Accuracy -73.06%	Towards Using Visual Attributes to Infer Image Sentiment Of Social Events	856 social event concept, 10,500 images		Google News articles, Microsoft Bing	Errors in differentiating polarized and neutral statements.
Nasrin et al.	Lexicon – based analysis, Naive Bayes	Page is fraud if the fraud percentage is greater than 40%	A proposition using sentiment analysis to detect whether a facebook business page is a fraud or not	Posts from Facebook business pages	English	Facebook business pages	Theoretical approach that needs implementation.
Ramanathan and Meyyapan	ConceptNet, Opinion extraction, Sentistrength, SentiWordNet, Opinion lexicon, Alchemy API tool, Naive Bayes	Domain Specific Ontology Method – 72.77, Entity Specific Opinion Extraction Method – 75.44, Combined Lexicon Base Method – 79.43, Conceptual Semantic Sentiment Analysis Method – 85.54	Sentiment Analysis of people's feedback on Oman Tourism by Twitter text mining	4,432 tweets from Twitter dataset	English	Twitter dataset	Limited dataset leads to limited accuracy.
Ghosh	Web scraping, PageRank, ROUGE	Efficiency is 78.2%	Hotel review summarization based on sentiment analysis	Hotel reviews from the website https://www.tripadvisor.in/	English	TripAdvisor	Multiple summaries can improve accuracy.
Sisodia et al.	Bag of words, TF-IDF, Bigrams, Naive Bayes, C4.5, SVM, Bagging, AdaBoost, Random forest classifier, Weka tool	Accuracies found out for different machine learning algorithms for different feature extraction methods	Comparing the performance of different machine learning algorithms used for sentiment analysis of movie reviews	25,000 reviews from Kaggle, 1000 bollywood reviews from 2013-2016	English	Kaggle	Includes only machine learning models for comparison.
Dhara Mungra et al.	Bag of words, Information Gain, Logistic regression, SVM, ANN, Decision trees, Random Forest, MV	Accuracies are obtained for different algorithms on 3 datasets	To show the superiority of majority voting ensemble model	IMDB dataset, Amazon dataset, Yelp dataset	English	IMDB, Amazon, Yelp	Inclusion of more models can give better conclusions.

linear kernel is used for binary classification. Some of the applications of SVM are facial expression recognition, text classification, gene analysis and many more (Sisodia et al, 2020).

7. CHALLENGES

Sentiment Analysis helps in analysing and solving problems in the field of text analytics. However, there are some challenges in sentiment analysis like slangs, handling negations, polysemy which creates problems as compared to conventional text based analytical techniques. Some such issues are listed as follows (Ghag and Shah, 2013, Sagnika et al, 2020).

A. Handling Negation

The polarity of an adjective is taken to be opposite if a negation term appears close to an adjective. For example, "the display is clear", should be categorized as a positive review and "the display is not clear", should be categorized as a negative review. By such type of categorization the polarity is reversed by

Table 3. SENTIMENT ANALYSIS APPLICATIONS

Business Domain	E-commerce and online marketing
	Reputation of product or brand
	Recommendation in the choice of products
	Evaluate guest likes and dislikes for your property and your competitor's properties
	Component of other technology
	Business for Brand Brisking
	Inform and make operational improvements or capital expenditures
	Online advertisement: Blogger centric contextual advertisement Dissatisfaction centric online advertisement
Politics	Knowing about politician's position
	Applications to provide voting advise
	Plotting new propagation strategy
	Expected poll results
Finance	Shares evolution
	Price of commodity
	Financial risk individuation
Public actions	Legal matter "blawgs"
	Policy or government regulation proposals
	Applications as a Sub-Component Technology Detecting hostile, warmed dialect in sends, spam identification, connection touchy data discovery and so forth.
	Intelligent transportation system
	Monitoring of real world events

Figure 4. Accuracy vs Train – Test Split for SVM and NB

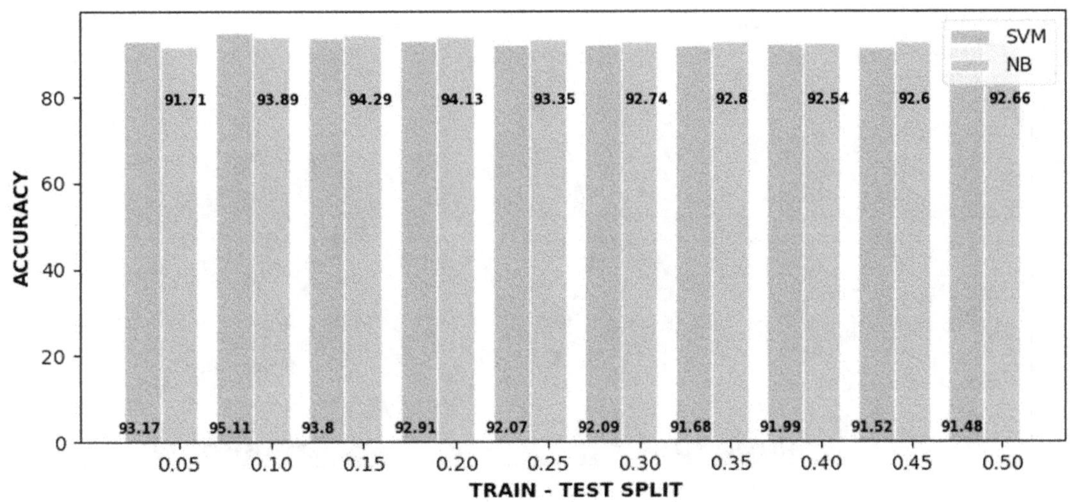

placing 'not' with the occurring adjective. But such type of categorization generally fails in sentences, such as "I don't mean that the display is not clear". Here it is difficult to categorize the sentence, as it will be probably categorized as negative, whereas it has to be categorized as positive, in case of two distinct class labels, or neutral, in case of three class labels. Mathematical formulae can be applied to such problems i.e. Polarity = - (Polarity of adjective). But such type of a model will again fail in some cases such as, "No wonder the food is good".

Figure 5. Kappa vs Train – Test Split for SVM and NB

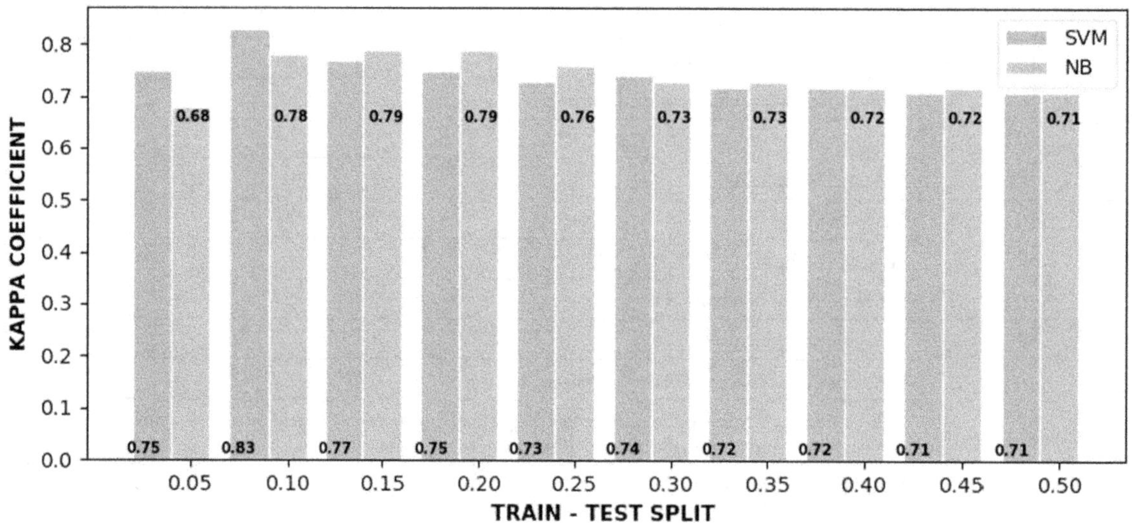

Figure 6. Standard Deviation vs Average Accuracy for SVM and NM

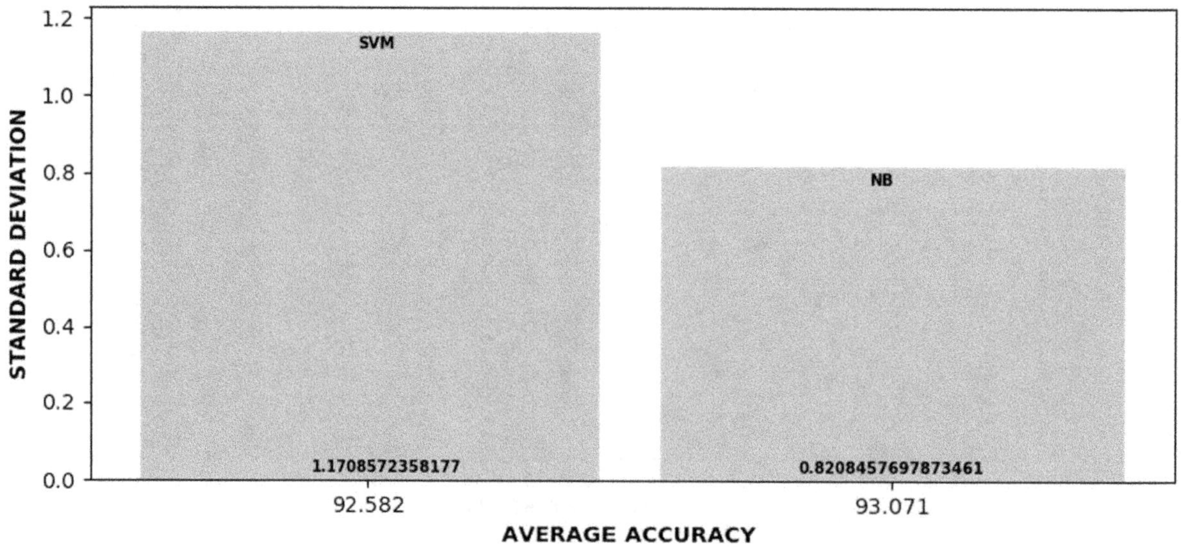

Table 4. Observations for SVM

Train – Test Split	Accuracy	Precision	Recall	Kappa Coefficient	Standard Deviation
0.05	93.17	1- Star:- 0.84	0.75	0.75	1.1708572358177
		5- Star:- 0.95	0.97		
0.10	95.11	1- Star:- 0.91	0.82	0.83	
		5- Star:- 0.96	0.98		
0.15	93.80	1- Star:- 0.87	0.75	0.77	
		5- Star:- 0.95	0.98		
0.20	92.91	1- Star:- 0.86	0.73	0.75	
		5- Star:- 0.94	0.97		
0.25	92.07	1- Star:- 0.79	0.76	0.73	
		5- Star:- 0.95	0.96		
0.30	92.90	1- Star:- 0.80	0.77	0.74	
		5- Star:- 0.95	0.96		
0.35	91.68	1- Star:- 0.79	0.75	0.72	
		5- Star:- 0.94	0.96		
0.40	91.99	1- Star:- 0.78	0.76	0.72	
		5- Star:- 0.95	0.96		
0.45	91.52	1- Star:- 0.77	0.75	0.71	
		5- Star:- 0.94	0.95		
0.50	91.48	1- Star:- 0.76	0.76	0.71	
		5- Star:- 0.95	0.95		

B. Handling Polysemy

Polysemy can be explained as an aspect of semantic ambiguity where one word is associated with two or more distinct meanings. For example adjective ‘good’ can be associated with different meanings in different sentences like

- pleasurable, enjoyable, or satisfying
- suitable for an intended purpose.
- generally valid and acceptable.
- emphatically full or complete.

It is quite a challenging task to find out the Polysemy, or correct words considering the context.

C. Mapping Slangs

Slangs are used during online texting where short forms of the original words or phrases are used. Ex-gn is slang for goodnight and ni8 for night. Nowadays these are often used in day today life texting but are not defined in traditional dictionaries. Such types of wrong words are mostly filtered out of the tools

Table 5. Observation for Naive Bayes

Train – Test Split	Accuracy	Precision	Recall	Kappa Coefficient	Standard Deviation
0.05	91.71	1- Star:- 0.85	0.64	0.68	0.8208457697873461
		5- Star:- 0.93	0.98		
0.10	93.89	1- Star:- 0.90	0.75	0.78	
		5- Star:- 0.95	0.98		
0.15	94.29	1- Star:- 0.90	0.75	0.79	
		5- Star:- 0.95	0.98		
0.20	94.13	1- Star:- 0.93	0.74	0.79	
		5- Star:- 0.94	0.99		
0.25	93.35	1- Star:- 0.90	0.71	0.76	
		5- Star:- 0.94	0.98		
0.30	92.74	1- Star:- 0.92	0.67	0.73	
		5- Star:- 0.93	0.99		
0.35	92.80	1- Star:- 0.92	0.67	0.73	
		5- Star:- 0.93	0.99		
0.40	92.54	1- Star:- 0.89	0.66	0.72	
		5- Star:- 0.93	0.98		
0.45	92.60	1- Star:- 0.91	0.66	0.72	
		5- Star:- 0.93	0.99		
0.50	92.66	1- Star:- 0.93	0.63	0.71	
		5- Star:- 0.93	0.99		

since they are not available in the existing language lexicons, which can lead to loss of data. Hence, by mapping slangs to the original words or by adding opinionated slangs to the lexicons, the result of the lexicon analysis can be improved.

D. Domain Generalisation

The sentiment analysis tools for better results carries out the process of analysis by targeting a particular domain. But certain word or sentence which is negative in a domain can be positive in some other domain, making it challenging task for a generalised sentiment analyser.

E. Opinion Object Identification

In sentiment analysis, the opening sentence or in the initial sections of the documents, generally the object is mentioned towards which the opinion is expressed. In further documents the object with opinionated information is cited with pronouns like “it”, “that” and “this”.

F. Maintaining Opinion Time

Opinions for a product or service are dynamic and changing within fractions of time nowadays. Some traditional sentiment analyser analyses, calculates and stores the opinion for a product which is reflected in the query result. But these opinions towards products do not remain the same over a period of time.

G. Language Generalisation

These days technology has made it possible for interaction of people from any part of the world, hence creating large amount of opinions which can be expressed in many languages. Although there are few sentiment analysers which categorize reviews of Chinese and Vietnam languages, but almost all of them are developed to aim at English language. Multi language opinion miners can be a great help for sentiment analysis.

H. Feature Matrix Construction

People can directly give their opinions about the product or they can review a product which can include opinions towards various features of the product. In such scenarios it is an aggregation of opinion, rather than a single opinion towards the product. Sometimes reviewers comment on features which are not present in the predefined list of opinions which is to be considered for calculations. Dynamic feature matrix can solve the problem by taking dynamic opinions also into consideration.

I. Hidden Sentiments Identification

Other than classification problems in sentiment analysis, identifying hidden sentiment like excitement, anger, sadness is also a tedious task.

J. Lexicon Updating/Down-Dating

The lexicons, also referred as dictionary, should be updated with more new and frequently used words and restrain the words which are not in use anymore. The accuracy of the lexicon generally determines the performance of the sentiment analyser. Smaller lexicon will give faster results whereas larger lexicon will give better or accurate results. Hence, lexicon should be optimized according to the requirement of the hour.

K. Sarcasm Detection

The presence of sarcasm in any language is hard to detect for a machine. Sarcastic statements have different obvious and implied meanings, which can lead to misclassification of the sentiment. Hence, effective methods to identify sarcasm are necessary, and are still open to research.

8 CONCLUSION AND FUTURE WORK

This is a survey paper which presents an overall coverage of sentiment analysis. The literature survey explains different features and their selection methods in sentiment analysis, sentiment analysis tasks, the work done in recent publications which had been done in the field of classification and analysis of existing solutions. The following observations and conclusions have been drawn from the study, which show the way to future work in this area.

- It is observed that over few years many new methods have been evolved which serve high estimation capability. Many of the analysis problems still employ Naive Bayes (NB) and Support Vector Machines (SVM), which remain the most popular machine learning models for sentiment analysis.
- Many deep learning models have been successfully applied, but with the evolution of faster and hybrid models, sentiment analysis can benefit from the use of newer and advanced deep learning methods.
- A number of quality studies have been made on different languages; still English and Chinese remain the most studied language among the others. In terms of linguistic complexity, languages like Arabic, Malayalam & Tamil are complex, but are experimented by the researchers successfully. There is a lot of scope for development of sentiment analysis models in all other languages.
- All the algorithms and methodology presented in this paper use many interesting measures, including accuracy, precision and recall values. On comparing the results of survey research work, in future more new interestingness measures can be employed to improve the accuracy of the systems.
- The challenges discussed, such as negation, sarcasm detection, slangs, polysemy, and other language related aspects have scope available for further research and development. Individual languages also require specialized methods for handling the unique inherent factors present that influence the sentiment.
- For making the system portable for any type of product, implicit aspect types can be conducted. Future systems may contain more dynamic and comprehensive models that can mine the inner interests of users in various social networks, using expanded dictionary with resolved memory issues.

REFERENCES

Abbasi, A. (2003). Intelligent feature selection for opinion classification. *Technology (Elmsford, N.Y.)*, *54*(14), 1269–1277.

Abbasi, A., Chen, H., & Salem, A. (2008). Sentiment analysis in multiple languages: Feature selection for opinion classification in web forums. *ACM Transactions on Information Systems*, *26*(3), 1–34.

Abdelwahab, O., Bahgat, M., Lowrance, C. J., & Elmaghraby, A. (2015, December). Effect of training set size on SVM and Naive Bayes for Twitter sentiment analysis. In 2015 IEEE international symposium on signal processing and information technology (ISSPIT) (pp. 46-51). IEEE.

Agrawal, R., Rajagopalan, S., Srikant, R., & Xu, Y. (2003, May). Mining newsgroups using networks arising from social behavior. In *Proceedings of the 12th international conference on World Wide Web* (pp. 529-535). Academic Press.

Ahsan, U., De Choudhury, M., & Essa, I. (2017, May). Towards using visual attributes to infer image sentiment of social events. In *2017 International Joint Conference on Neural Networks (IJCNN)* (pp. 1372-1379). IEEE.

Aman, S., & Szpakowicz, S. (2007, September). Identifying expressions of emotion in text. In *International Conference on Text, Speech and Dialogue* (pp. 196-205). Springer.

Amazon. (n.d.). *Amazon mechanical turk*. https://www.mturk.com/

Aydoğan, E., & Akcayol, M. A. (2016, August). A comprehensive survey for sentiment analysis tasks using machine learning techniques. In *2016 International Symposium on INnovations in Intelligent SysTems and Applications (INISTA)* (pp. 1-7). IEEE.

Benamara, F., Cesarano, C., Picariello, A., Recupero, D. R., & Subrahmanian, V. S. (2007). Sentiment analysis: Adjectives and adverbs are better than adjectives alone. *ICWSM*, *7*, 203–206.

Bhargava, R., & Sharma, Y. (2017, January). MSATS: Multilingual sentiment analysis via text summarization. In *2017 7th International Conference on Cloud Computing, Data Science & Engineering-Confluence* (pp. 71-76). IEEE.

Bhargava, R., Sharma, Y., & Sharma, S. (2016, September). Sentiment analysis for mixed script indic sentences. In *2016 International conference on advances in computing, communications and informatics (ICACCI)* (pp. 524-529). IEEE.

Bickel, S., Brückner, M., & Scheffer, T. (2007, June). Discriminative learning for differing training and test distributions. In *Proceedings of the 24th international conference on Machine learning* (pp. 81-88). Academic Press.

Bradley, M. M., & Lang, P. J. (1999). *Affective norms for English words (ANEW): Instruction manual and affective ratings* (Vol. 30). Technical report C-1, the center for research in psychophysiology, University of Florida.

Byrd, K., Mansurov, A., & Baysal, O. (2016, May). Mining twitter data for influenza detection and surveillance. In *Proceedings of the International Workshop on Software Engineering in Healthcare Systems* (pp. 43-49). Academic Press.

Cambria, E., Hussain, A., Havasi, C., Eckl, C., & Munro, J. (2010). Towards crowd validation of the UK national health service. *WebSci10*, 1-5.

Cambria, E., Speer, R., Havasi, C., & Hussain, A. (2010, November). Senticnet: A publicly available semantic resource for opinion mining. 2010 AAAI fall symposium series.

Chatterji, S., Rahul, R. K., & Arora, A. (2015, July). A hybrid approach for identifying sentiments around aspects. In *2015 IEEE 2nd International Conference on Recent Trends in Information Systems (ReTIS)* (pp. 33-37). IEEE.

Chen, C. C., & Tseng, Y. D. (2011). Quality evaluation of product reviews using an information quality framework. *Decision Support Systems*, *50*(4), 755–768.

Chen, Y. S., Chen, L. H., & Takama, Y. (2015, November). Proposal of lda-based sentiment visualization of hotel reviews. In *2015 IEEE International Conference on Data Mining Workshop (ICDMW)* (pp. 687-693). IEEE.

Chenlo, J. M., & Losada, D. E. (2014). An empirical study of sentence features for subjectivity and polarity classification. *Information Sciences*, *280*, 275–288.

Costa, H., Merschmann, L. H., Barth, F., & Benevenuto, F. (2014). Pollution, bad-mouthing, and local marketing: The underground of location-based social networks. *Information Sciences*, *279*, 123–137.

Dai, X., & Prout, R. (2016, August). Unlocking Super Bowl insights: Weighted word embeddings for Twitter sentiment classification. In *Proceedings of the 3rd Multidisciplinary International Social Networks Conference on Social Informatics 2016, Data Science 2016* (pp. 1-6). Academic Press.

Dave, K., Lawrence, S., & Pennock, D. M. (2003, May). Mining the peanut gallery: Opinion extraction and semantic classification of product reviews. In *Proceedings of the 12th international conference on World Wide Web* (pp. 519-528). Academic Press.

Dodds, P. S., & Danforth, C. M. (2010). Measuring the happiness of large-scale written expression: Songs, blogs, and presidents. *Journal of Happiness Studies*, *11*(4), 441–456.

Duwairi, R. M., Marji, R., Sha'ban, N., & Rushaidat, S. (2014, April). Sentiment analysis in Arabic tweets. In *2014 5th international conference on information and communication systems (ICICS)* (pp. 1-6). IEEE.

Efron, M., Marchionini, G., & Zhiang, J. (2003, October). Implications of the recursive representation problem for automatic concept identification in on-line governmental information. *Proceedings of the ASIST SIG-CR Workshop*.

Fachri, M. (2014). *Named entity recognition for Indonesian text using hidden Markov model*. Universitas Gadjah Mada.

Fei, Z., Liu, J., & Wu, G. (2004, September). Sentiment classification using phrase patterns. In *The Fourth International Conference onComputer and Information Technology, 2004. CIT'04.* (pp. 1147-1152). IEEE.

Freeman, V., Chan, J., Levow, G. A., Wright, R., Ostendorf, M., & Zayats, V. (2014). Manipulating stance and involvement using collaborative tasks: An exploratory comparison. *Fifteenth Annual Conference of the International Speech Communication Association*.

Gamon, M., Aue, A., Corston-Oliver, S., & Ringger, E. (2005, September). Pulse: Mining customer opinions from free text. In International symposium on intelligent data analysis (pp. 121-132). Springer.

Ghag, K., & Shah, K. (2013, January). Comparative analysis of the techniques for sentiment analysis. In *2013 International Conference on Advances in Technology and Engineering (ICATE)* (pp. 1-7). IEEE.

Ghorbel, H., & Jacot, D. (2011). Sentiment analysis of French movie reviews. In *Advances in Distributed Agent-Based Retrieval Tools* (pp. 97–108). Springer.

Ghose, A., & Ipeirotis, P. G. (2010). Estimating the helpfulness and economic impact of product reviews: Mining text and reviewer characteristics. *IEEE Transactions on Knowledge and Data Engineering*, *23*(10), 1498–1512.

Ghosh, D. (2020). A Sentiment-Based Hotel Review Summarization. In *Emerging Technology in Modelling and Graphics* (pp. 39–44). Springer.

Gonçalves, P., Araújo, M., Benevenuto, F., & Cha, M. (2013, October). Comparing and combining sentiment analysis methods. In *Proceedings of the first ACM conference on Online social networks* (pp. 27-38). ACM.

Gonçalves, P., Benevenuto, F., & Cha, M. (2013). *Panas-t: A pychometric scale for measuring sentiments on twitter.* arXiv preprint arXiv:1308.1857.

Hanifah, R., Supangkat, S. H., & Purwarianti, A. (2014, September). Twitter information extraction for smart city. In *2014 International Conference on ICT For Smart Society (ICISS)* (pp. 295-299). IEEE.

Hu, M., & Liu, B. (2004, August). Mining and summarizing customer reviews. In *Proceedings of the tenth ACM SIGKDD international conference on Knowledge discovery and data mining* (pp. 168-177). ACM.

Kamal, A. (2013). *Subjectivity classification using machine learning techniques for mining feature-opinion pairs from web opinion sources.* arXiv preprint arXiv:1312.6962.

Kaushik, C., & Mishra, A. (2014). Comparative analysis of sentiment analysis techniques. *ITSI Trans Electric Electron Eng (ITSI-TEEE), 2*(1).

Kulis, B., Saenko, K., & Darrell, T. (2011, June). What you saw is not what you get: Domain adaptation using asymmetric kernel transforms. In *CVPR 2011* (pp. 1785–1792). IEEE.

Lee, S., & Choeh, J. Y. (2014). Predicting the helpfulness of online reviews using multilayer perceptron neural networks. *Expert Systems with Applications*, *41*(6), 3041–3046.

Lerttripinyo, T., Jatukannyaprateep, P., Prompoon, N., & Pattanothai, C. (2015, July). Accommodation recommendation system from user reviews based on feature-based weighted non-negative matrix factorization method. In *2015 12th International Joint Conference on Computer Science and Software Engineering (JCSSE)* (pp. 108-113). IEEE.

Levow, G. A., Freeman, V., Hrynkevich, A., Ostendorf, M., Wright, R., Chan, J., . . . Tran, T. (2014, December). Recognition of stance strength and polarity in spontaneous speech. In 2014 IEEE Spoken Language Technology Workshop (SLT) (pp. 236-241). IEEE.

Li, N., & Wu, D. D. (2010). Using text mining and sentiment analysis for online forums hotspot detection and forecast. *Decision Support Systems*, *48*(2), 354–368.

Li, Y. M., & Li, T. Y. (2013). Deriving market intelligence from microblogs. *Decision Support Systems*, *55*(1), 206–217.

Lin, Y., Zhu, T., Wu, H., Zhang, J., Wang, X., & Zhou, A. (2014, August). Towards online anti-opinion spam: Spotting fake reviews from the review sequence. In 2014 IEEE/ACM international conference on advances in social networks analysis and mining (ASONAM 2014) (pp. 261-264). IEEE.

List of text emoticons: The ultimate resource. (n.d.). www.cool-smileys.com/text-emoticons

Liu, B. (2012). Sentiment analysis and opinion mining. *Synthesis Lectures on Human Language Technologies, 5*(1), 1-167.

Liu, Z., Dong, X., Guan, Y., & Yang, J. (2013, October). Reserved self-training: A semi-supervised sentiment classification method for chinese microblogs. In *Proceedings of the Sixth International Joint Conference on Natural Language Processing* (pp. 455-462). Academic Press.

Maas, A., Daly, R. E., Pham, P. T., Huang, D., Ng, A. Y., & Potts, C. (2011, June). Learning word vectors for sentiment analysis. In *Proceedings of the 49th annual meeting of the association for computational linguistics: Human language technologies* (pp. 142-150). Academic Press.

Martín-Valdivia, M. T., Martínez-Cámara, E., Perea-Ortega, J. M., & Ureña-López, L. A. (2013). Sentiment polarity detection in Spanish reviews combining supervised and unsupervised approaches. *Expert Systems with Applications, 40*(10), 3934–3942.

Miller, G. A. (1995). WordNet: A lexical database for English. *Communications of the ACM, 38*(11), 39–41.

MSN messenger emoticons. (n.d.). http://messenger.msn.com/resource/emoticons.aspx

Mungra, D., Agrawal, A., & Thakkar, A. (2020). A voting-based sentiment classification model. In *Intelligent Communication, Control and Devices* (pp. 551–558). Springer.

Nasrin, S., Ghosh, P., Chowdhury, S. M., Abujar, S., & Hossain, S. A. (2020). Fraud detection of Facebook business page based on sentiment analysis. In *Proceedings of International Joint Conference on Computational Intelligence* (pp. 279-287). Springer.

Nasukawa, T., & Yi, J. (2003, October). Sentiment analysis: Capturing favorability using natural language processing. In *Proceedings of the 2nd international conference on Knowledge capture* (pp. 70-77). Academic Press.

Nizam, H., & Akın, S. S. (2014). Sosyal medyada makine öğrenmesi ile duygu analizinde dengeli ve dengesiz veri setlerinin performanslarının karşılaştırılması. *XIX. Türkiye'de İnternet Konferansı, 1*(6).

O'Connor, B., Balasubramanyan, R., Routledge, B. R., & Smith, N. A. (2010, May). From tweets to polls: Linking text sentiment to public opinion time series. *Fourth international AAAI conference on weblogs and social media.*

OMG! Oxford English Dictionary grows a heart: Graphic symbol for love (and that exclamation) are added as words. (n.d.). tinyurl.com/klv36p

Ott, M., Cardie, C., & Hancock, J. T. (2013, June). Negative deceptive opinion spam. In *Proceedings of the 2013 conference of the North American chapter of the Association for Computational Linguistics: Human language technologies* (pp. 497-501). Academic Press.

Owoputi, O., O'Connor, B., Dyer, C., Gimpel, K., Schneider, N., & Smith, N. A. (2013, June). Improved part-of-speech tagging for online conversational text with word clusters. In *Proceedings of the 2013 conference of the North American chapter of the association for computational linguistics: human language technologies* (pp. 380-390). Academic Press.

Pang, B., & Lee, L. (2004). *A sentimental education: Sentiment analysis using subjectivity summarization based on minimum cuts.* arXiv preprint cs/0409058.

Pang, B., Lee, L., & Vaithyanathan, S. (2002). *Thumbs up? Sentiment classification using machine learning techniques.* arXiv preprint cs/0205070.

Prakash, V. J., & Nithya, D. L. (2014). *A survey on semi-supervised learning techniques.* arXiv preprint arXiv:1402.4645.

Ramanathan, V., & Meyyappan, T. (2019, January). Twitter text mining for sentiment analysis on people's feedback about oman tourism. In *2019 4th MEC International Conference on Big Data and Smart City (ICBDSC)* (pp. 1-5). IEEE.

Ravi, K., & Ravi, V. (2015). A survey on opinion mining and sentiment analysis: Tasks, approaches and applications. *Knowledge-Based Systems*, *89*, 14–46.

Saenko, K., Kulis, B., Fritz, M., & Darrell, T. (2010, September). Adapting visual category models to new domains. In *European conference on computer vision* (pp. 213-226). Springer.

Sagnika, S., Mishra, B. S. P., & Meher, S. K. (2020). Improved method of word embedding for efficient analysis of human sentiments. *Multimedia Tools and Applications*, *79*(43), 32389–32413.

Sagnika, S., Pattanaik, A., Mishra, B. S. P., & Meher, S. K. (2020). A Review on Multi-Lingual Sentiment Analysis by Machine Learning Methods. *Journal of Engineering Science & Technology Review*, *13*(2).

Sequiera, R., Choudhury, M., Gupta, P., Rosso, P., Kumar, S., Banerjee, S., . . . Chakma, K. (2015, December). Overview of FIRE-2015 Shared Task on Mixed Script Information Retrieval. In FIRE workshops (Vol. 1587, pp. 19-25). Academic Press.

Shaheen, S., El-Hajj, W., Hajj, H., & Elbassuoni, S. (2014, December). Emotion recognition from text based on automatically generated rules. In *2014 IEEE International Conference on Data Mining Workshop* (pp. 383-392). IEEE.

Singh, S. K., Paul, S., & Kumar, D. (2014). Sentiment analysis approaches on different data set domain: Survey. *International Journal of Database Theory and Application*, *7*(5), 39–50.

Sisodia, D. S., Bhandari, S., Reddy, N. K., & Pujahari, A. (2020). A comparative performance study of machine learning algorithms for sentiment analysis of movie viewers using open reviews. In *Performance Management of Integrated Systems and its Applications in Software Engineering* (pp. 107–117). Springer.

Sisodia, D. S., Bhandari, S., Reddy, N. K., & Pujahari, A. (2020). A comparative performance study of machine learning algorithms for sentiment analysis of movie viewers using open reviews. In *Performance Management of Integrated Systems and its Applications in Software Engineering* (pp. 107–117). Springer.

Syaifudin, Y., & Nurwidyantoro, A. (2016, July). Quotations identification from Indonesian online news using rule-based method. In *2016 International Seminar on Intelligent Technology and Its Applications (ISITIA)* (pp. 187-194). IEEE.

Tang, H., Tan, S., & Cheng, X. (2009). A survey on sentiment detection of reviews. *Expert Systems with Applications*, *36*(7), 10760–10773. doi:10.1016/j.eswa.2009.02.063

Tausczik, Y. R., & Pennebaker, J. W. (2010). The psychological meaning of words: LIWC and computerized text analysis methods. *Journal of Language and Social Psychology*, *29*(1), 24–54.

Thelwall, M. (2014). Heart and soul: Sentiment strength detection in the social web with sentistrength, 2017. *Cyberemotions: Collective emotions in cyberspace*.

Turney, P. D. (2002). *Thumbs up or thumbs down? Semantic orientation applied to unsupervised classification of reviews.* arXiv preprint cs/0212032.

Wang, H., Can, D., Kazemzadeh, A., Bar, F., & Narayanan, S. (2012, July). A system for real-time twitter sentiment analysis of 2012 us presidential election cycle. In *Proceedings of the ACL 2012 system demonstrations* (pp. 115-120). Academic Press.

Watson, D., Clark, L. A., & Tellegen, A. (1988). Development and validation of brief measures of positive and negative affect: The PANAS scales. *Journal of Personality and Social Psychology*, *54*(6), 1063.

Williams, G., & Mahmoud, A. (2017, May). Analyzing, classifying, and interpreting emotions in software users' tweets. In *2017 IEEE/ACM 2nd International Workshop on Emotion Awareness in Software Engineering (SEmotion)* (pp. 2-7). IEEE.

Xuan, H. N. T., & Le, A. C. (2012, November). *Linguistic features for subjectivity classification. In 2012 international conference on asian language processing*. IEEE.

Yahoo messenger emoticons. (n.d.). http://messenger.yahoo.com/features/emoticons

Zang, W., Zhou, C., Wang, X., & Guo, L. (2014, December). Topic Block: Mining User Inner Interests for Text and Link Analysis in Social Networks. In *2014 15th International Conference on Parallel and Distributed Computing, Applications and Technologies* (pp. 159-165). IEEE.

Zhang, W., Li, C., Ye, Y., Li, W., & Ngai, E. W. (2015). Dynamic business network analysis for correlated stock price movement prediction. *IEEE Intelligent Systems*, *30*(2), 26–33.

Zou, J., Fekri, F., & McLaughlin, S. W. (2015, August). Mining streaming tweets for real-time event credibility prediction in twitter. In *Proceedings of the 2015 IEEE/ACM International Conference on Advances in Social Networks Analysis and Mining 2015* (pp. 1586-1589). IEEE.

Chapter 8
Consumer Sentiments About Online Shopping in the Indian Scenario During COVID-19:
A SWOT, ISM, and AHP Approach

Sohini Rudra
Kalinga Institute of Industrial Technology (Deemed), Bhubaneswar, India

Sushanta Tripathy
https://orcid.org/0000-0003-2470-4080
Kalinga Institute of Industrial Technology (Deemed), Bhubaneswar, India

Deepak Singhal
Kalinga Institute of Industrial Technology (Deemed), Bhubaneswar, India

ABSTRACT

To abate the rapid spread of corona virus, most countries restricted social life. The primary purpose of this study is to look into the elements that influence online consumer sentiments regarding shopping during a pandemic. This research focuses on the study of different factors' significance and priority using strength, weakness, opportunity, threat (SWOT) analysis; interpretive structural modelling (ISM); and analytical hierarchy process (AHP) after extracting the different crucial factors using critical review of previous literature and expert opinions. The ISM methodology has helped to present a structural relationship among the key factors and helped to derive the short-term goals and long-term goals. Finally, the AHP model has ranked the existing three popular websites of India comparing their effectiveness using the factors such as product quality, customer satisfaction, low perceived risk, and social media. This chapter will be a strong vaccine for the Indian online shopping consumer sentiments during and post-pandemic scenario.

DOI: 10.4018/978-1-6684-4969-1.ch008

Copyright © 2022, IGI Global. Copying or distributing in print or electronic forms without written permission of IGI Global is prohibited.

1. INTRODUCTION

In the last two decades, the internet has proven to be a successful platform for marketing goods and services since it has removed all the barriers of distance. The internet also helps in the business field to obtain data and analyzing the information for the creation of better and effective products. The basic use of the internet in business is selling products. From the last decade, the marketing landscape has already started changing but before this, companies and their customers had no relation with respect to each other's respective worlds (Jaffe, 2010). Social media and web technologies expedite consumers to interact and communicate. Companies are using many social media sites (like Facebook, Instagram, and Twitter) or well-developed websites to promote information regarding their brands. Aside from issues like rising disposable income, a lack of free time, or comfort, online marketing is becoming more important due to factors like increased reach, reduced planning time, lower costs, flexible payment models (online billing, payment options, and booking options), improved targeting, better technologies, and a decrease in sales points.

Covid-19 has severely altered the lifestyle of people. Increased hand washing, usage of masks, hand sanitizers, and household cleaning products indicates the inclination of people towards maintaining hygiene (Vishal, May 2020). Aside from that, the continued spread of covid-19 not only posed a concern to the food supply chain, but it also prompted consumers to consider food security.Due to this consumers started stockpiling the essential products specifically agricultural products (Wang, An, Gao, KIprop, Geng, 2020). Above mentioned factors eventually influenced customer's online shopping behaviour. With government help in logistic management, consumers are more reliant on fresh food e-commerce platforms than retail channels. (Hao, Wang, Zhou, 2020).

Now, this covid-19 outbreak as the first and second waves has created unprecedented challenges for sellers of all levels around the world. The entire world is now in the clutch of the coronavirus. Due to a long time lockdown, street-side businesses were completely shut down most of their owner transferred their business into the online platform. The Covid-19 pandemic has caused an unanticipated health and economic crisis, causing consumers' lifestyles, preferences, and habits to change.Though many businesses have faced a huge loss during this lockdown period, some sectors of the economy- like E-commerce have been profited due to stay-at-home orders and social distancing (Halan, 2020). Covid-19 has also completely changed the way the world thinks, by converting personal hygiene and social distancing as the person's priority. This pandemic is expected to be the inflection point for the graph of development of the e-commerce industries in India.

In this Covid-19 situation, to avoid direct contact with people (to maintain social distance) most of the customers are preferring online shopping. Work from home in India before and after the first wave of covid-19 has created a positive shift in the trend of online shopping. A huge percentage of Indian consumers were either in containment zones or had restricted alternatives for completing critical purchases at the end of lockdown 1.0. This encouraged consumers to try new channels, products, and brands, resulting in shifts in consumer buying behaviours and purchasing paths. (Amazon, 2020)

Customers are relying on Amazon far more than usual in this pandemic circumstance, according to Amazon, one of the biggest E-commerce players in the country as well as the world. Store closures and empty shelves forced the customers to move toward online shopping. Amazon became the saviour for the essential products like hand sanitizer, mask, household products and groceries. Amazon set sales records in the second quarter of 2020 because to a surge in online orders (Annie,2020). To avoid a corona virus outbreak inside Amazon's warehouse, they implemented over 150 measures to prevent virus transmission, ranging from better sanitation to social distancing measures to disguising requirements. One of the greatest grocery players of India Big Basket, during Covid-19, declared that they are experiencing unprecedented demand so they have restricted access to their website only to existed customers. (Halan, 2020)

An efficient supply chain is one that speeds up e-commerce procedures to satisfy the demands and expectations of customers (Chavan et al., 2022). Materials acquisition, manufacture, and timely distribution of essential items to clients are all part of managing supply chains in e-commerce (Worakamol et al., 2022) .Most mitigation techniques offered previous to COVID-19, such as redundancy and flexibility, are still being examined as feasible solutions to reduce supply chain disruptions as a result of COVID-19, but there are greater pressures for digitization and supply-based localisation (Diego et al., 2022; Pujawan & Bah, 2022). Due to the complete lockdown over a long period and implication of work from home, it is no wonder that various e-commerce sites have been visited by the customer rapidly and that also affected the customer's online shopping behavior. It has been discovered that 66% of Indian urban active users conduct online research prior to purchasing things, whether offline or online. (Amazon, 2020). So in this Covid-19 situation as well as the post-covid-19 situation existing online shopping websites should focus on some factors which will help them to reach the point of customer satisfaction and will eventually help them to influence consumer sentiments towards repurchasing behavior.

To justify the motivation, the authors intend to execute:

- A SWOT analysis, which has been done to find out the various factors related to the existing e-commerce websites, which will help these online shopping websites to explore new opportunities of improvement.
- Identify the factors which can influence consumer sentiments towards purchasing behavior during this covid-19 situation and will also impact the Indian consumer's repurchasing behavior by satisfying their needs, using the Interpretive Structural Modelling method.
- The authors also plan to use the Analytical Hierarchy Process to prioritise websites based on the above-mentioned variables and validate the ISM output.

To accomplish these objectives the authors have used two MCDM techniques (Multiple Criteria Decision Making): that is ISM method and AHP method.

ISM method (Interpretive Structural Modelling)- This method has been used by the authors to identify various critical factors influencing customer's online shopping behaviors and how these factors can help to build customer satisfaction which will influence the repurchasing behavior. This method has also helped the authors to classify the critical factors into driving and dependent factors which are going to help the existing e-commerce websites to understand the customer's intention more prominently.

AHP method (Analytical Hierarchy Process)- The detected attributes and selected websites of India were ranked using this multiple criterion decision-making technique.A comparison matrix has been formed based on the features of those websites. The features and the websites have been ranked as per the input of expert opinions.

The paper has been framed as follows.The second portion represents the work of several previous authors, with a focus on major conclusions. Similarly, section 3 shows other methodologies such as SWOT (strengths, weaknesses, opportunities, and threats), Interpretive Structural Modelling (ISM), and Analytical Hierarchy (AHP). Section 4 exhibits the findings of the above methods and discusses them.

Figure 1. Framework of the study towards consumer's behavior towards online shopping during Covid-19

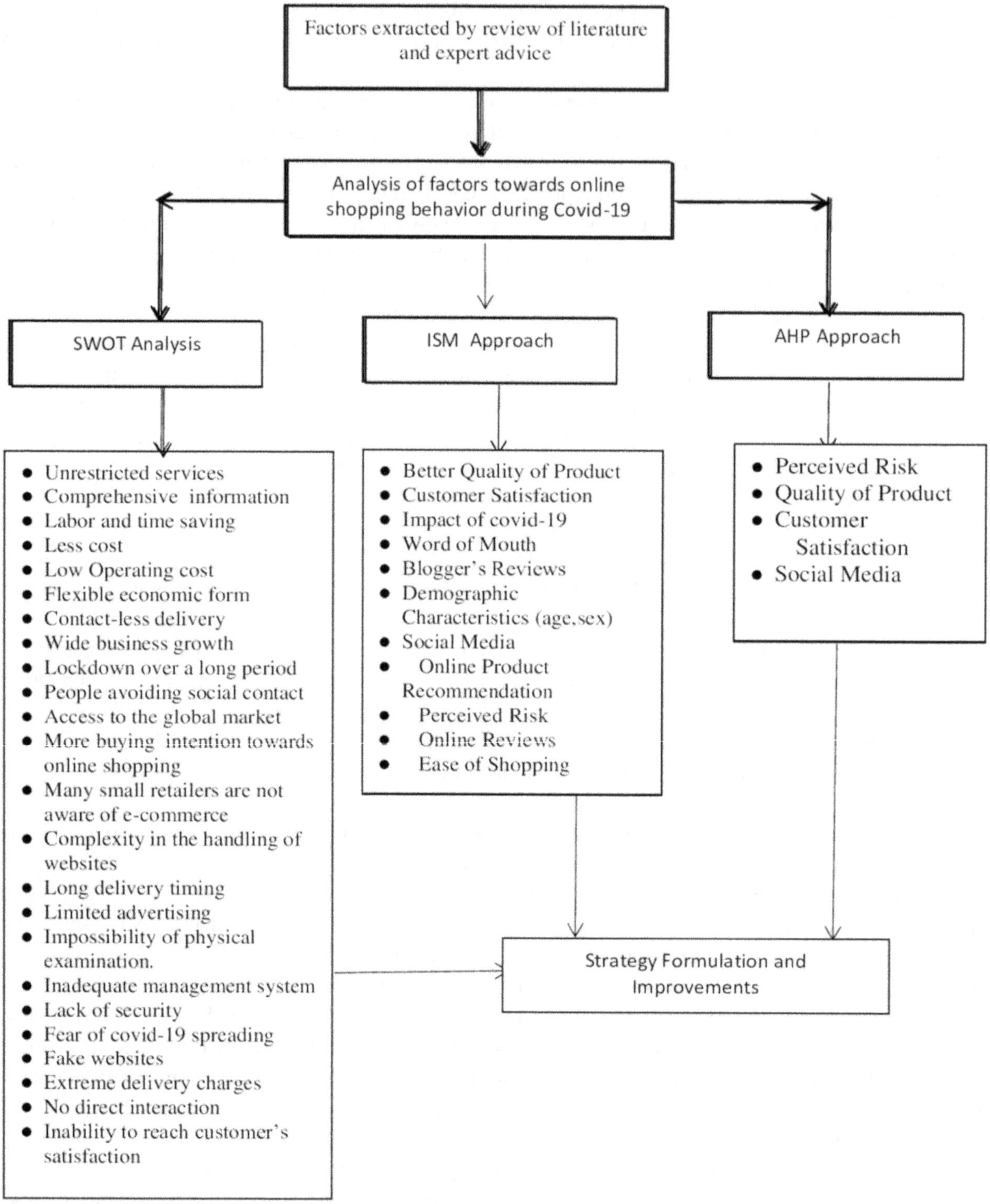

The practical implications of the proposed methodology are discussed in Section 5. Section 6 of the study finishes with limitations and future scopes. The framework of the paper has been illustrated in Figure 1.

2. LITERATURE REVIEW

In the past few years authors have found out various reasons which directly or indirectly affect customer's online shopping behavior:

In Table:I Literature Review, the authors have mentioned, key focus and findings of some specific research paper on customers' online shopping behaviour. Authors have also identified and marked bold the significant key factors mentioned by various authors in different papers on customer online purchase intention.In various literature (Table 1) the authors have identified how past shopping experience and security risk directly affects customer's online shopping behavior. Also, various literature shows that online shopping behavior can be dependent on the generation means the age of the consumer also it can be stated (reviewing various opinions) that online shopping behavior may vary based upon the gender of the consumer.

Various literature of the past few years have mentioned the above factors but in this pandemic situation, the most specific thing that triggers customer's online shopping behavior is safety which includes contact-less delivery, safe packaging, sanitation. So nowadays consumers are agreeing to pay more just to secure these safety issues. The author has also mentioned in this paper, how this pandemic and complete lockdown over a long period has positively affected consumer's online shopping behavior.

3. SOLUTION METHODOLOGY

In this current covid-19 situation, the economy of a developing country depends upon its business strategies. Nowadays, online marketing, notably E-commerce, has emerged as the most effective tool for increasing trading volume. SWOT analysis is a strategic planning technique that can be used to aid in the early phases of decision-making and as an evaluation tool. In the table: 2 SWOT analysis on the present condition of existing online shopping websites has been executed. Extraction of factors and sub factors is not enough for decision making. The authors needed to establish a managerial guideline ranking. There are several methods available to rank these factors under Multi Criteria Decision Making Technique. For the intended ranking, the authors chose the Interpretive Structural Modelling technique and the Analytical Hierarchy process.

3.1 Data Collection

For the SWOT analysis, authors have identified the opportunities and threats related to online shopping with respect to external environment. On the contrary, the writers looked into the strengths and weaknesses of present resources and activities that could enable future opportunities or threats be avoided.

A comprehensive literature review has been executed to discover the factors affecting consumer's online shopping behavior. The authors used terms like "factors determining consumer's online shopping behaviour," "consumer's repurchasing behaviour," "customer satisfaction," and "the impact of covid-19 in e-commerce" to search scholarly databases like Scopus, Web of Science, and Google Scholar. A list of

Table I. Literature Review

Authors and year	Key focus	Findings
1. Zhuo and Xiaoting, 2010	● The factors affecting customer's online shopping behavior.	● The increase of the level of **buyer's trust** increases the customer's buying intention. ● **The quality** of online shopping information is helpful to increase customer's buying intention.
2. Chang and Wang, 2010	● Customers who believe their value to be high have a stronger correlation between satisfaction and loyalty than customers who perceive their value to be low.	● Customers who perceive a high level of value are more likely to be satisfied and loyal than customers who perceive a low level of value.
3. Khare and Rakesh, 2011	● Indian student's intention to purchase through online shopping.	● In online purchasing, utilitarian shopping values and websites play a significant influence. ● The ease of use of website features, product prices, information, and payment method flexibility are all critical.
4. Dange and Kumar, 2012	● Consumer intention, motive, and characteristics ● Framework for online Consumer behavior	● Online security, privacy, trust, and trustworthiness affect consumer buying behavior.
5. Sinha and Kim,2012	● Indian consumers' attitude towards online shopping ● Investigation of Indian consumers' risk perceptions about online shopping.	● Males' perceived risk is crucial, while female convenience risk is more relevant. ● For females, attitude is the significant factor whereas, in the case of a male, innovativeness is one of the important factors. ● Females will consider risks if the method is simple and easy to use, however males will conduct multiple risk assessments before engaging in online buying.
6. Ruoh-Nan Yan, Karen H. Hyllegard and LaVon F. Blaesi, 2012	● Effects of brand name and message explicitness on consumer purchase behavior.	● Consumers having, low product knowledge have a favorable attitude towards brand names and advertisements. ● Marketers should use more direct messages to market friendly products.
7. Hsu, Lin, and Chiang,2013	● To see if the blog reader's faith in the blogger has anything to do with the perceived utility of the blogger's advice. ● The influence of a blog reader's impression on his or her online purchase behaviour.	● Consumers always rely on online product recommendations before making a final purchasing decision. The perceived value of a blogger's trust and recommendations has a big impact on blog readers.
8. Chandra and Sinha, 2013	● Factors affecting online shopping behavior, A study regarding Bhilai Durg	● Women who purchase online were more likely to have higher incomes compared to those who are regarded as non-purchaser. ● To add value to the online shopping experience, trust is everything ● Experienced buyers are more intended towards online shopping than inexperienced buyers.
9. G.pateli et al. 2013	● Experience has a moderate effect on the link between some antecedents and satisfaction. ● The link between customer happiness and the likelihood of making a purchase.	● The relationship between performance and satisfaction, as well as client buy intent, is heavily influenced by the experience.
10. Prashant Raman,2014	● Factors that affect female shoppers' attitude towers online shopping.	● Ease in shopping is the first factor for the female consumer. ● The risk of online transactions acts as a barrier in the case of online shopping. ● Traditional shopping and reliability issues also resist female consumers from buying.
11. Thakur and Srivastava, 2015	● Various techniques to influencing online commerce adoption intention, both directly and indirectly, while minimising consumer perceived risk.	● Word of mouth can affect the online shopping behavior of a consumer strongly. ● Online shops should create some targeted advertising efforts for the more inventive customer category. ● Perceived risk is a key inhibitor of internet shopping.
12. Nittala, 2015	● Factors influencing urban customers' online shopping behaviour in Andhra Pradesh, India. ● Both researchers and online businesses can benefit from electronic marketing.	● In a developing country, internet purchasing behaviour is influenced by the online shopper's positive attitude, product risk, financial risk, perceived risk, and pricing.
13. Akar and Nasir, 2015	● The factors influencing consumer's online purchase behavior.	● Social media plays an important role in the case of online buying ● Payment type, service value, feedback, product variability, guarantee, increases online buying intention.
14. Kidane and Sharma, 2016	● Factors affecting consumer's purchasing decisions through e-commerce in different cultures and societies.	● Return policy, trust, warranty, cashback, cash on delivery are factors that affect consumers' buying intention strongly.
15. Sarkar and Khare,2017	● Personality traits such as value consciousness and coupon liability have an impact on online shopping attitudes.	● Consumers in emerging markets are more value-conscious, thus bundling products with discounts or price reductions may help to increase customer purchasing intent. ● The complex coupon redemption process affects consumer's online shopping behavior badly.
16. Ariffin et al., 2018	● The relationship between consumer perceived risk and consumer's online purchase behavior	● Consumer financial risk, product risk, security risk, time risk, social risk, and psychological risk have all been linked to online purchase intent. ● Security risk is the main trigger of consumer's online purchase behavior. ● In the instance of customer purchasing intent, the societal risk was found to be insignificant.

factors, directly or indirectly affecting consumer's online shopping behavior has been found out. Based on this data ISM methodology has been forwarded.

In case of the AHP model, authors have chosen three of the most competitive websites as the decision alternatives and these websites have been compared based on the result obtained from ISM table. In this paper, apart from the identification of various factors affecting consumers' online shopping behavior authors have also the motive to prioritize the existing e-commerce websites based on the product availability during this pandemic and also depending on the influencing factor determined through the above ISM model.

There are more than thirty online shopping websites are available in India (Amazon, Nykaa, Myntra, Pepperfry), different websites are popular for different categories of products. To shortlist websites among these available options, authors need to focus on the type of products that have a severe demand during this pandemic situation as well as the post-pandemic situation. The effect of the corona virus is different for different kinds of products (Andrienko, 2020). Authors referred to various research papers, news updates, and expert opinions to conclude which type of product has the maximum demand during this pandemic in the case of online shopping. Some of the researchers have identified food, grocery, sanitary products were most frequently purchased online products during this pandemic (Statista, May 2020). According to McKinsey & Company's market study, the entire world experienced a dramatic swing in March 2020, with products such as toilet paper, beans, and cleaning supplies doubling in sales while cosmetics, appliances, and gadgets were generally avoided. Based on this information authors have eliminated all the websites which do not offer the above-mentioned, high-demand product categories. So, the authors shortlisted Amazon, Flipkart, and Snapdeal, these three online shopping websites, offer all the product categories which have a high demand during this pandemic situation.

The inclusion and exclusion criteria of the study are as follows. The study has included the expert's opinion based on different areas, working experience and research experience. But it has not considered the location, gender and qualification of the experts. In this paper apart from the rigorous research result, authors have also incorporated the expert opinions. Thirteen number of experts have been consulted for this study during a marketing conclave (October, 2020) at KSOM, KIIT Deemed University, Bhubaneswar which consist with five academicians and eight online customer care personnel. Five academicians having more than 15 years of research experience in customer behavior, e-commerce, and purchasing behavior and eight customer care support personnel having more than 10 years of service were also been asked to collect their views and experiences in this particular field.

3.2 SWOT Analysis

The purpose of SWOT Analysis is to analyze, gather and evaluate information regarding the customer inclination towards the online shopping during this covid-19 situation. Various blogger's reviews, newspapers, research papers and finally expert's view have been referred to accomplish the analysis.

Still now in India infrastructure of E-commerce is not well developed as evident from Table 2. Many small retailers of the town side in India are not aware of E-commerce or the concept of online marketing, which has affected their business growth during this lockdown. Insufficient advertisements, inadequate management systems are the most noticeable weaknesses of online marketing in India.

Table 2. SWOT Analysis

Strength	Weakness
● Unrestricted services ● Comprehensive information ● Labor and time saving ● Less cost ● Low Operating cost ● Flexible economic form ● Contact-less delivery	● Many small retailers are not aware of e-commerce ● Complexity in the handling of websites ● Long delivery timing ● Limited advertising ● Impossibility of physical examination. ● Inadequate management system
Opportunities	**Threats**
● Wide business growth ● Lockdown over a long period ● People avoiding social contact ● Access to the global market ● More buying intention towards online shopping	● Lack of security ● Fear of covid-19 spreading ● Fake websites ● Extreme delivery charges ● No direct interaction ● Inability to reach customer's satisfaction

3.3 Interpretive Structural Modelling(ISM)

The authors of this work followed a step-by-step procedure to achieve their goals. First, based on a comprehensive literature review and expert comments, the essential aspects that can influence customer satisfaction during this covid-19 circumstance have been determined (5 academicians, 10 customer care support). The ISM model was then created to determine the relationship between those variables.**ISM** model was proposed by Warfield in 1973. ISM helps to transform the poor articulated, unclear mental model of systems into a clear, visible, well defined models (Sushil,2012).

From the Literature Review section (Table: 1) and also considering the expert opinions authors have found out how customer satisfaction is dependent upon the better quality of product and in a less perceived risk. Through word of mouth, social media, blogger's reviews played a very significant role in the time of covid-19. So authors have identified that there are various factors that directly and indirectly affect consumer's online shopping behavior in this covid-19 situation as well as the repurchasing intention, the presence of a large number of factors and interactions between these factors generates difficulty in categorization so ISM model has been implemented to articulate the clear model.

3.3.1 Significance of ISM Approach

- According to Raut, Narkhede, and Gardas, 2017 ISM method helps to convey complex systems more simply, it helps to provide elucidation of the fixed object.
- Ism models are structured based on the relation between the critical factors which helps to identify the significance of the digraph model which has been generated based on those relations. ISM also helps to identify the sequence and supervision of the complexity caused by the relationships among various factors. (Wnkhade, Kundu, 2020)

All these significances influenced authors to apply the ISM technique to find out the complex relationship among the various factors which affect consumer's online shopping behavior and also how consumer's repurchasing behavior can be determined by these factors.

Table 3. Structural Self Interaction Matrix (SSIM)

Sl	Critical Success factors	Notations	1	2	3	4	5	6	7	8	9	10	11
1	Better Quality of Product	BQP		V	A	V	A	A	A	V	A	V	A
2	Customer Satisfaction	CS			A	A	A	A	A	A	A	A	A
3	Impact of covid-19	I-COVID				V	V	V	V	V	V	V	V
4	Word of Mouth	WOM					A	A	A	X	A	X	A
5	Blogger's Reviews	BR						V	X	V	V	V	V
6	Demographic Characteristics (age,sex)	DC							A	V	O	V	O
7	Social Media	SM								V	V	V	V
8	Online Product Recommendation	OPR									A	X	A
9	Perceived Risk	PR										V	O
10	Online Reviews	OR											A
11	Ease of Shopping	ES											

ISM modeling follows series of steps which includes:

- Key factors determination through critical review of literature and expert guidance.
- Structural Self Interaction Matrix(SSIM) formation.
- Development of Partition level table using Reachability Matrix
- MICMAC Analysis
- Development of ISM model

3.3.2 Structural Self Interaction Matrix (SSIM)

The authors have taken a total of 11 factors based on that the ISM model has been developed. Assume x and y are any two of those factors; For defining the relationship between numerous essential aspects for the consumer's online buying behaviour, four symbols have been used to denote the direction of the link between the parameters x and y.

(1)V: if parameter x will influence to parameter y.

(2) A:if parameter y will influence to parameter x.
(3) X: if parameters x and y will influence to each other.
(4) O: if parameters x and y having no relationship between them.

The SSIM is produced in Table 3 based on contextual correlations.

Based on the external research and expert opinions the authors have developed the Table: 3. In this table Blogger's reviews (BR) will lead to positive or negative Word of Mouth (WOM), so in the SSIM table WOM and BR got A but BR and WOM got V. Also word of mouth (WOM) and online reviews (OR) will lead to each other so WOM and OR will be X in SSIM. Perceived risk (PR) and ease of shopping (ES) are not at all related so in SSIM matrix (PR, ES) got O.

Table 4. Reachability Matrix

Sl	Critical Success factors	Notations	1	2	3	4	5	6	7	8	9	10	11	Driving power
1	Better Quality of Product	BQP	1	1	0	1	0	0	0	0	0	1	0	5
2	Customer Satisfaction	CS	0	1	0	0	0	0	0	1	0	0	0	1
3	Impact of covid-19	I-COVID	1	1	1	1	1	1	1	0	1	1	1	11
4	Word of Mouth	WOM	0	1	0	1	0	0	0	1	0	1	0	4
5	Blogger's Reviews	BR	1	1	0	1	1	1	1	1	1	1	1	10
6	Demographic Characteristics(age, sex etc.)	DC	1	1	0	1	0	1	0	1	0	1	0	6
7	Social Media	SM	1	1	0	1	1	1	1	1	1	1	1	10
8	Online Product Recommendation	OPR	0	1	0	1	0	0	0	1	0	1	0	4
9	Perceived Risk	PR	1	1	0	1	0	0	0	1	1	1	0	6
10	Online Reviews	OR	0	1	0	1	0	0	0	1	0	1	0	4
11	Ease of Shopping	ES	1	1	0	1	0	0	0	1	0	1	1	6
	Dependence		7	11	1	10	3	4	3	10	4	10	4	

3.3.3 Reachability Matrix

The SSIM table is used to build the reachability matrix. To build a reachability matrix, the SSIM symbols V, A, X, or O are replaced by 1s or 0s. The following guidelines are adhered to: (a) If SSIM's (i,j) position is V, the reachability matrix's (i,j) position becomes 1 and the (j,i) position becomes 0. (b) If the SSIM's (i,j) position is A, the reachability matrix's (i,j) position becomes 0 and the (j,i) position becomes 1.Similarly,If SSIM's (i,j) position is X, the reachability matrix's (i,j) position becomes 1 and the (j,i) position also becomes 1. (d) If the SSIM's (i,j) position is O, the reachability matrix's (i,j) position becomes 0 and the (j,i) position becomes 0. Table 4 shows the reachability matrix obtained from SSIM.

3.3.4 Level Partitions

The set has been derived for each factor from the final reachability matrix reachability set and antecedent. The component itself, as well as additional elements that can be influenced by it, make up the reachability set. The antecedent set, on the other hand, consists of the component itself as well as any other elements that may impact it. Factor 1(Better Quality of Product) may influence Factor2 (customer satisfaction), Factor 4 (Word of Mouth), Factor 8(online product recommendation), Factor 10 (online reviews) so they are under the Reachability matrix. Whereas Factor 1's antecedent set consists of the impact of covid 19, blogger's reviews, demographic characteristics, social media, and perceived risk. For each factor, the intersection of these two sets is calculated, and the level of each factor is determined (the intersection of Reachability and antecedent set in case of Factor 1 is factor 1 and the level has been determined as 3). The top level of the ISM model should be the specific factor that will not lead to any other factors in the ISM hierarchy. When the top-level factor has been determined, it will not be evaluated again, and the same method will be followed to determine the next-level variables. This approach will be repeated until each factor's level is determined.

Table 5. Level Partitions

	Reachability set	Antecedent set	Intersection Set	Level
Factor 1	1,2,4,8,10	1,3,5,6,7,9,11	1	3
Factor 2	2	1,2,3,4,5,6,7,8,9,10,1	2	1
Factor 3	1,2,3,4,5,6,7,8,9,10,11	3	3	6
Factor 4	2,4,8,10	1,3,4,5,6,7,8,9,10,11	4,8,10	2
Factor 5	1,2,4,5,6,7,8,9,10,11	3,5,7	5,7	5
Factor 6	1,2,4,6,8,10	3,5,6,7	6	4
Factor 7	1,2,4,5,6,7,8,9,10,11	3,5,7	5,7	5
Factor 8	2,4,8,10	1,3,4,5,6,7,8,9,10,11	4,8,10	2
Factor 9	1,2,4,8,9,10	3,5,7,9	9	4
Factor 10	2,4,8,10	1,3,4,5,6,7,8,9,10,11	4,8,10	2
Factor 11	1,2,4,8,10,11	3,5,7,11	11	4

3.3.5 MICMAC Analysis

Duperrin and Godet created MICMAC (Cross impact matrix multiplication applied to classification) in 1973. It consists of four clusters. The MICMAC analysis helps to classify all the critical factors based on driving power and dependence.It is shown in figure-2.

The previously determined and described success factors are divided into four groups:

Ø **Autonomous factors** are those that have little or no driving power and are not reliant on others.
Ø Factors with little driving power but high dependency are referred to as **dependent factors.** (word-of-mouth, product suggestion online)
Ø Factors with a high driving power and a high dependence on each other are known as **linkage factors.**
Ø Factors with high driving power but low reliance are referred to be driving factors (impact of covid-19, blogger's reviews)

Table 4 shows the driving strength and reliance of each of these components.

The goal of this study is to establish a structured relationship between the different essential aspects that influence consumers' online shopping and repurchasing behaviour. This research has helped to identify the driving and dependence factors through the MICMAC analysis.

3.4 Proposed Analytical Hierarchy Process (AHP)

Thomas. L. Saaty invented the Analytical Hierarchy Process (AHP) in the 1970s. It's a way for ranking numerous choice factors using numbers. As per the objective of this paper, authors have used this AHP technique to rank the existing websites based on their ability to influence customer's online shopping behavior as well as repurchasing behavior, especially during this Covid-19. Now in this AHP technique comparisons are done based on the standard preference table proposed by Saaty (Table 6).

Figure 2. MICMAC Analysis

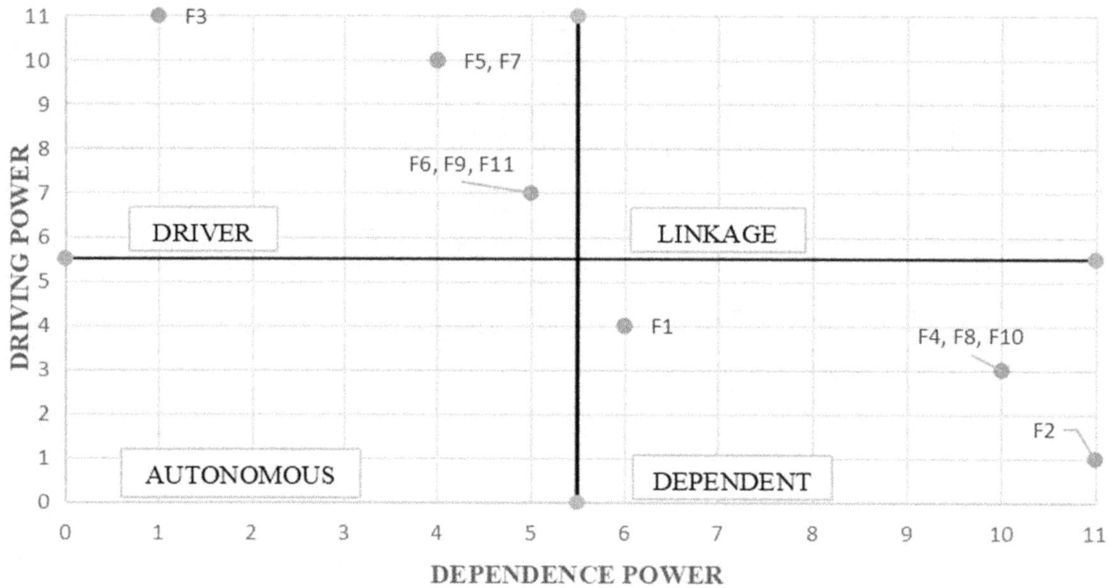

Table 6. Saaty's pairwise comparison scale

Saaty's pairwise comparison scale	Preference Level
1	Equally Preferred
3	Moderately Preferred
5	Strongly Preferred
7	Very Strongly Preferred
9	Extremely Preferred
2,4,6,8	Intermediate preference value

Now based on this standard preference table various criteria have been compared based on various literature reviews and expert opinions. This AHP technique consists of various steps (Figure 3). The several criterion have been selected based on literature, expert opinion, and the result of ISM model. The priority of each criterion was then computed in terms of its contribution to selecting the best among the alternatives, and a comparison matrix was created. Then the normalized pairwise matrix has been formed. Finally the consistency pairwise comparison matrix has been determined.

Figure 3. Framework of AHP model

Step 1: A pairwise comparison matrix m*m (where m=no of criteria here m=4) has been formed according to the Saaty's table mentioned in Table 7.

Table 7. Pairwise Comparison Matrix

Comparison	Perceived Risk	Quality of Product	Customer Satisfaction	Social Media
Perceived Risk	1	2	5	1/3
Quality of Product	1/2	1	1/2	1/7
Customer Satisfaction	1/5	2	1	1/6
Social Media	3	7	6	1

Step 2: Data normalisation is a procedure in which data attributes in a data model are grouped in tables to improve data management cohesion and efficiency. The most popular definition in statistics and its applications is the process of converting values measured on different scales to a similar scale, usually before aggregating or average them. Table 8 shows how the pairwise comparison matrix was normalised using the following equation:

$$M_{ij} = x_{ij} / \sum_{i=1}^{m} xij \quad (1)$$

Table 8. Normalization Matrix

Comparison	Perceived Risk	Quality of Product	Customer Satisfaction	Social Media	Row Sum	Priority
Perceived Risk	0.21	0.16	0.4	0.20	0.97	0.243
Quality of Product	0.106	0.083	0.04	0.087	0.316	0.079
Customer Satisfaction	0.043	0.16	0.08	0.103	0.386	0.0965
Social Media	0.64	0.58	0.48	0.61	2.31	0.5775

Where i= 1, 2, 3….m and j=1, 2, 3…..m
In eq(1) a_{ij} is the ith row and j^{th} column call in Table:1

Figure 4. Pairwise comparison matrices

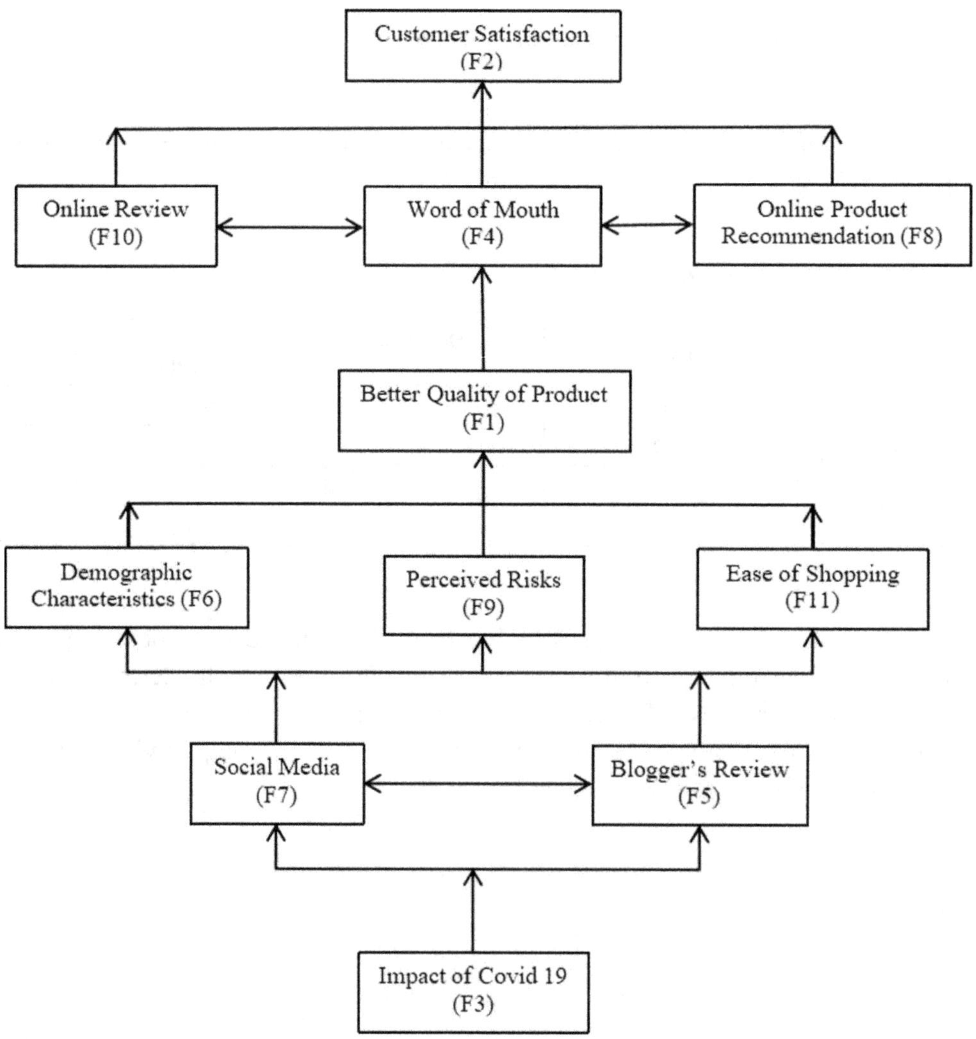

Step 3: The earlier steps have been repeated for alternative suppliers for each criterion as shown in table 9.
Step 4: Normalization of the pairwise matrices has been done (Figures 5 and 6).

Figure 5. Normalization of pairwise matrix

Perceived Risk

	Website A	Website B	Website C	Row sum	Priority
Website A	0.111	0.12	0.095	0.325	0.109
Website B	0.567	0.613	0.631	0.81	0.604
Website C	0.322	0.267	0.274	0.863	0.288

Customer Satisfaction

	Website A	Website B	Website C	Row sum	Priority
Website A	0.198	0.179	0.146	0.794	0.264
Website B	0.754	0.682	0.485	1.921	0.64
Website C	0.047	0.139	0.1	0.285	0.095

Figure 6. Normalization of pairwise matrix

Quality of Product

	Website A	Website B	Website C	Row sum	Priority
Website A	0.599	0.544	0.629	1.772	0.591
Website B	0.162	0.147	0.119	0.428	0.143
Website C	0.24	0.309	0.251	0.799	0.267

Social Media

	Website A	Website B	Website C	Row sum	Priority
Website A	0.186	0.161	0.386	0.733	0.244
Website B	0.745	0.644	0.471	1.86	0.62
Website C	0.069	0.195	0.143	0.407	0.135

Step 4: Calculation for ranking the websites:

Finally the multiplication of criteria wise websites priority matrix with criteria priority matrix has resulted the priority of selected website.

Table 9. Ranking the websites

	Perceived Risk	Quality of Product	Customer Satisfaction	Social Media				
Website A	0.109	0.591	0.264	0.244	×	0.243 0.079 0.0965 0.5775	=	0.2374 0.578 0.5021
Website B	0.604	0.143	0.640	0.620				
Website C	0.288	0.267	0.095	0.136				

At the objective of this paper, the authors also intended to prioritize some of the present websites of India, based on the above-identified factors with the help of the Analytical Hierarchy Process. Now from the current existing websites, authors have taken Amazon, Flipkart, Snapdeal as these three websites are more reliable and more viewed websites (Singh, 2016). The authors have found in some literature that based on customer satisfaction Amazon is more preferred than Flipkart (Francis and Habeeb, 2016). Some consumers prefer Amazon for a cheap price, security, product variability, and better product quality (Bharadwaj, 2019). In case of Flipkart, consumers often suggest that the packing might have been better, products are not been cared properly (Sudhakar &Syed,2016). Amazon is leading in every aspect of the survey among amazon, Flipkart, snapdeal, myntra, jabong, w.r.t. price-quality, etc (Chalotra, Midha, 2017). Despite of being an international enterprise Amazon has not failed to understand Indian customer's sentiment. Though Flipkart and Snapdeal are giving intense competition Amazon (Chalotra & Midha, 2017). Satish Meena, a senior forecast analyst at Forrester, stated that shipping costs, shipment times, product review ratings, low price guarantees, and merchant return policies are the most appealing factors to customers., and Amazon is rated higher for all these cases in India (Rebecca, 2021).

4.RESULT AND DISCUSSION

The results of three analysis such as SWOT, ISM and AHP to determine the significance of different factors affecting consumer sentiments towards online purchase have been discussed below.

4.1 SWOT Analysis

From the SWOT analysis (Table 2) we get to know, the unhindered services of various online shopping sites, availability of needed commodities at less price, comprehensive information about products, increase consumers' buying intention, and the contact-less delivery act as the strength of online marketing during this covid-19 situation, whereas in case of the retailers, online marketing saves labor need, time and operating cost which helps to make the business profitable. The strengths and weaknesses of online marketing are frequently internally related. To grab the future opportunities (specified in SWOT analysis), the retailers should focus on the weaknesses of online marketing, as the weakness itself acts as a potential threat to business. Addressing the strengths and shortcomings of online shopping and improving the situation through consumer, merchant, and market macro-control efforts would encourage a harmonious development of online shopping (Milong, 2011).

4.2 ISM Methodology

The goal of this study is to establish a structured relationship between the different essential aspects that influence consumers' online shopping and repurchasing behaviour. This research has helped to identify the driving and dependence factors through the MICMAC analysis. The elements are divided into six tiers in the ISM-based approach (Figure 4). The Impact of Covid-19, F3 is the lowest level VI in the hierarchy, and it can be considered the most powerful motivator for motivating clients to buy online. Now, level V includes social media and blogger reviews, as well as F7 and F5, which have considerable driving power in the hierarchy and impact each other. In level IV there are Demographic characteristics (F6), perceived risk (F9), ease of shopping (F11). Level II consists of Online reviews(F10), word of mouth(F4), online recommendations (F8), all these factors are also interdependent, achieving all these goals will help to reach level 1, customer satisfaction (F2). From the MICMAC analysis, it has been noticed that there is no autonomous factor that means there is no factor that is the weak driver and weak dependent. F3, F5, F6, F7, F9, F11 are driving factors that indicate that these factors influence customer's online shopping behavior the most. F1, F2, F4, F8, f10 are dependent factors, they are mostly dependent on the rest of the factors. There are no linking factors with a high driving power and a high degree of dependence.

Figure 7. Interpretive Structural Model

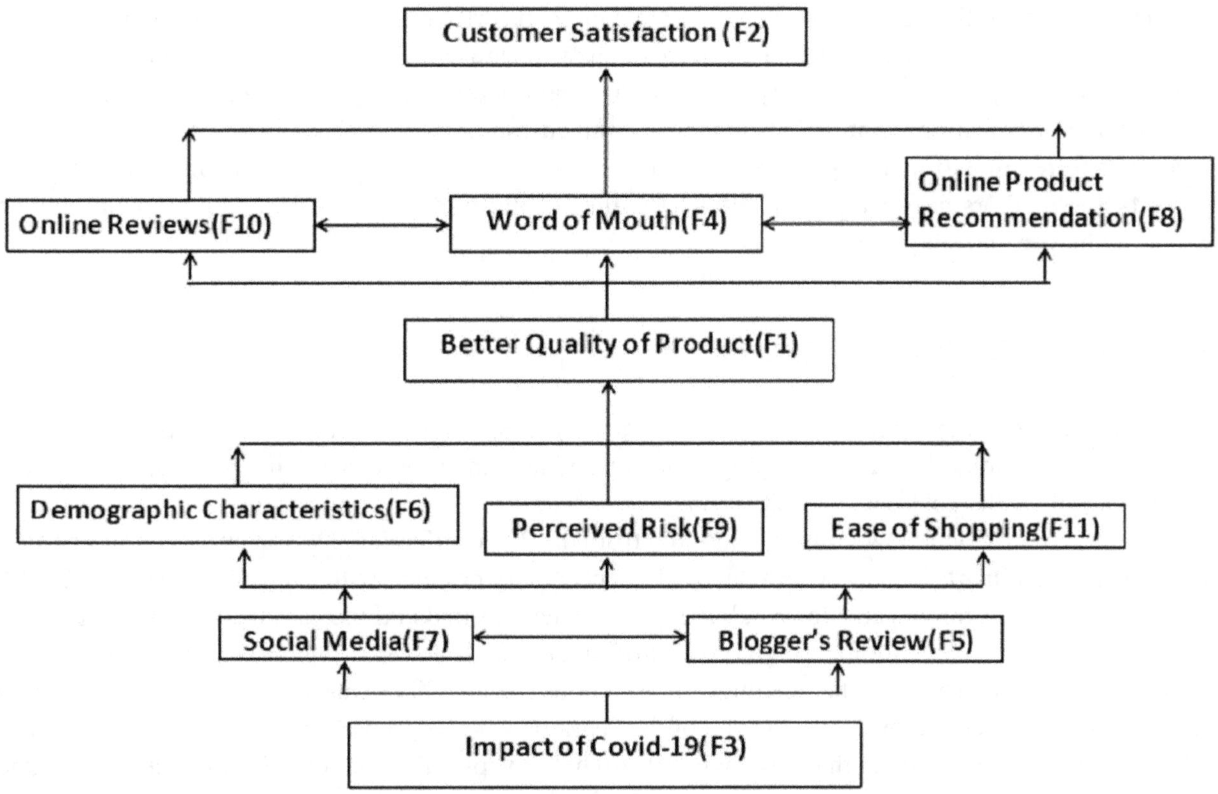

4.3 AHP Methodology

As per the objective of this paper the authors intended to rank the existing websites based on their ability to influence consumer's online purchasing behavior as well as repurchasing intention using the AHP technique. Now from the various literature and expert opinions, It has been identified that Perceived Risk, Quality of Product, Customer satisfaction, and positive social media reviews or recommendation play a crucial role in the case of online purchasing behavior. At first, the author has put random names to the existing websites as Website A, Website B, and Website C these three websites have been compared according to Saaty's reference table based on the previous four criteria. The authors have followed expert opinions to prepare the pairwise comparison matrix of the four criteria. Applying this AHP technique authors have identified the priority matrix based on which it can be stated that Website B has the highest influence on customer's online shopping behavior as well as repurchasing behavior after Website B, Website C comes. Now from the current existing websites, authors have taken Amazon, Flipkart,

Snapdeal as these three websites are more reliable and more viewed websites (Chanchani, 2016). The authors have found in some literature that based on customer satisfaction Amazon is more preferred than Flipkart (Francis and Habeeb, 2016). Some consumers prefer Amazon for a cheap price, security, product variability, and better product quality (Bharadwaj, 2019) Flipkart is also preferred by the customers due to its easy return and refund policy (Dubey, 2020). Various studies prove that the shopping experience provided by Amazon is greater than Flipkart and snapdeal (Moorthy, 2019). Amazon is leading in every aspect of the survey among amazon, Flipkart, snapdeal, myntra, jabong, w.r.t. price-quality (Chalotra, Midha, 2017). So following the obtained AHP technique priority matrix and based on expert opinions, various literature we can conclude that Amazon is the first choice to the customers for online shopping due to its security system, good quality of the product, product variability which helps Amazon to reach the customer satisfaction point and also influence the customer to repurchase. After Amazon, Flipkart is also preferred due to its low price, easy return policy, product variability, etc, so after analyzing all these factors authors have stated that Flipkart is the second preferred website after Amazon, among Flipkart amazon and snapdeal.

5. PRACTICAL IMPLICATION:

The study accredits how perceived risk, product quality, positive word of mouth, customer satisfaction can influence customer's online shopping behavior and also the repurchasing intention during this covid-19 as well as the post-covid-19 situation.

Despite the strict lockdown imposed in India from the 24th of March, 2020 various e-commerce sites like Amazon, Walmart, Flipkart were able to deliver necessary products to their customers (Halan, 2020).

Presently the customers are slowly adjusting to the new normal and they are trying to shift from the "Survival mode". People are focused more on affordable goods and shifting away from pricey names, according to researchers, and the amount of transactions on sites like Amazon, Flipkart, and Snapdeal has reverted to pre-covid levels. By the end of the year, the value of transactions should have increased. The experts are also expecting that this covid-19 will help to uplift the market of E-commerce by around $85 billion by 2024 (Abrar, 2020). During the pandemic, several websites are offering various incentives to entice buyers to repurchase, such as Walmart's fashion outlet Myntra's End Reason Sale, which allowed 400 offline stores and 60 reputable brands go live with their inventory. (Abrar, 2020). Amazon conducted India's Prime day sale on 7th August due to that almost 209 sellers gained a profit of crore rupees (Halan, 2020).

6. CONCLUSION:

The authors intended to find out the specific factors that play a crucial role in the consumer's online shopping behavior. Emphasizing these factors can help various e-commerce sites to achieve the most customer attraction. In this pandemic situation cleanliness, social distancing, proper packaging are the most important criterion to maintain reputation and attract consumers for the e-commerce websites, but the authors have found out various other factors from numerous literature of past few years and consulted many experts. The authors classified those factors into driving factors, dependent factors, connection factors, and autonomous factors using the ISM technique (Interpretive Structural Modelling) which have helped to identify the short term and long term goals for the online shopping sites to achieve customer satisfaction in this pandemic as well as the post-pandemic situation. Positive Word of Mouth, effective social media reviews can be treated as short term goals to increase consumer's repurchasing behavior and better product quality, assurance of customer's security will be treated as long term goals all these things will increase shopping site's reputation and also the no of customers. Another objective of this paper was to give rank to the existing websites of India comparing their effectiveness in the factors determined through the ISM method by the authors, using AHP (Analytical Hierarchy Process). The authors have taken Amazon, Flipkart, and snapdeal, these three most popular websites of India to compare. By this methodology and analyzing some current literature about these e-commerce websites the author has given 1st rank to Amazon based on its product quality, customer satisfaction, low perceived risk. Flipkart has been ranked 2nd and Snapdeal 3rd.

REFERENCES

Akar, E., & Nasir, V.A. (2015). A review of literature on consumers' online purchase intentions. *Journal of Customer Behaviour, 14*(3), 215-233. https://doi.org/ 14441 363 630837 doi:10.1362/147539215X

Amazon. (2020 December 18). Impact of COVID-19 on shopping behavior in India. *Amazonadvertising*. Retrieved from https://advertising.amazon.com/ blog/covid-19-impact-on-shopping-behavior-in-india

Andrienko, O. (2020). *Ecommerce & consumer trends during coronavirus*. SEMrush Blog, Erişimadresi. https://www.semrush.com/blog/ecommerce-covid-19/

Bharadwaj, S. (2019). The War between Flipkart and Amazon India: A Study on Customer Perception. *International Journal of Research in Humanities, Arts and Literature*, *7*(5), 391–402.

Chalotra & Midha. (2017). Investigation of Amazon, Flipkart, Snapdeal, Jabong & Myntra: A Comparative Study. *Asia Pacific Journal of Research in Business Management*, *4*(9), 57–65.

Chandra & Sinha. (2013). Factors Affecting The Online Shopping Behaviour: A Study With Reference to Bhilai Durg. *International Journal of Advanced Research in Management and Social Sciences*, *2*(5).

Chavan, P., Neb, K., Shakya, R., & Ambekar, S. (2022). Role of Analytics in E-Commerce Supply Chain Management. In Changing face of e-commerce in Asia (pp. 187-203). Academic Press.

Davis, S., & Toney, L. (2020 July 29), How Coronavirus (COVID-19) Is Impacting Ecommerce. *ROI Revolution*. Retrieved from https://www.roirevolution.com/blog/2020/08/ coronavirus-and-ecommerce/

Deepak, H. (2020 March 25). Impact of COVID-19 on online shopping in India. *Economic Times*. Retrieved from https://retail.economictimes.indiatimes.com/re-tales/ mpact-of-covid-19-on-online-shopping-in-india/4115

Francis, S. K., & Syed, H. (2016). A Comparative study between Flipkart and Amazon India. *International Journal of Research in Regional Studies, Law, Social Sciences, Journalism and Management Practices*, *1*(8), 3–11.

García-Tadeo, Peram, Kumar, Vives, Sharma, & Manoharan. (2022). Comparing the impact of Internet of Things and cloud computing on organisational behavior: A survey. *Materials Today: Proceedings, 51*(8). https://doi.org/ doi:10.1016/j.matpr.2021.11.399

Gardas, B., Raut, R. D., & Narkhede, B. E. (2017). A state-of the-art survey of interpretive structural modelling methodologies and applications. *International Journal of Business Excellence, 11*(4), 505. doi:10.1504/IJBEX.2017.082576

Hao, N., Wang, H. H., & Zhou, Q. (2020). The impact of online grocery shopping on stockpile behavior in Covid-19. *China Agricultural Economic Review, 12*(3), 459–470. doi:10.1108/CAER-04-2020-0064

Herald, D. (2020 July 14). *Impact of COVID-19 on E-Commerce Business*. Retrieved from https://www.deccanherald.com/ brandspot/pr-spot/ impact-of- covid -19-on-e-commerce-business-861185.html

Hsin Chang, H., & Wang, H. W. (2011). The moderating effect of customer perceived value on online shopping behaviour. *Online Information Review, 35*(3), 333–359. doi:10.1108/ 14684521111151414

Hsu, C., Chuan-Chuan Lin, J., & Chiang, H. (2013). The effects of blogger recommendations on customers' online shopping intentions. *Internet Research, 23*(1), 69–88. doi:10.1108/10662241311295782

Jaffe, J. (2010). *Flip the funnel: how to use existing customers to gain new ones*. Wiley.Book.

Kamalul Ariffin, S., Mohan, T., & Goh, Y.-N. (2018). Influence of consumers' perceived risk on consumers' online purchase intention. *Journal of Research in Interactive Marketing, 12*(3), 309–327. doi:10.1108/JRIM-11-2017-0100

Khare, A., & Rakesh, S. (2011). Antecedents of Online Shopping Behavior in India: An Examination. *Journal of Internet Commerce, 10*(4), 227–244. doi:10.1080/ 15332861. 2011.622691

Krishna, V. (2020 May 21). Almost 50 pc Indians are stockpiling essentials, shopping online during COVID-19: Mintel. *Mintel's Consumer Tracker.* Retrieved from https:// yourstory.com/2020/05/mintel-consumer-tracker-indians-stockpiling-essentials-coronavirus/amp

Kumar & Dange. (2012). A Study of Factors Affecting Online Buying Behavior: A Conceptual Model. SSRN. https://dx.doi.org/ doi:10.2139/ssrn.2285350

Madhav, C. (2016, April 28), Amazon pips Snapdeal to become India's 2nd largest online marketplace after Flipkart. *The Economic Times.* Retrieved from https://m.economictimes. com/industry/services/retail/amazon-pips-snapdeal-to-become-indias-2nd-largest-online-marketplace-after-flipkart/articleshow/52017176.cms

Madhav, C. (2017 January 20), Growth comes at a price for Flipkart, Amazon & Snapdeal. *The Economic Times.* Retrieved from https://economictimes.indiatimes.com /small- biz/startups/growth-comes-at-a-price-for-flipkart-amazon-snapdeal /articleshow /56674800.cms

Menezes, R. (2021 March 22). *Amazon beats Snapdeal on the ecommerce leaderboard, but is it the leader yet?* Retrieved from https:// indianonlineseller. com/ 2016/04/amazon-beats-snapdeal-on-the-ecommerce-leaderboard-but-is-it-the-leader-yet

Milong, L. (2011). The Analysis of Strengths and Weaknesses of Online-Shopping. In M. Dai (Ed.), *Innovative Computing and Information. ICCIC 2011. Communications in Computer and Information Science* (Vol. 231). Springer. doi:10.1007/ 978- 3-642 -23993-9_66

Nittala, R. (2015). Factors Influencing Online Shopping Behavior of Urban Consumers in India. *International Journal of Online Marketing*, *5*(1), 38–50. doi:10.4018/ IJOM.2015010103

Palmer, A. (2020September 29). How Amazon managed the coronavirus crisis and came out stronger. *CNBC Tech.* Retrieved from https://www.cnbc.com/2020/09/29/ how-amazon- managed-the-coronavirus-crisis-and-came-out-stronger.html

Pappas, Pateli, Giannakos, & Chrissikopoulos. (2014). Moderating effects of online shopping experience on customer satisfaction and repurchase intentions. *International Journal of Retail & Distribution Management*, *42*(3), 187–204. doi:10.1108/IJRDM-03-2012-0034

Peerzada, A. (2020 June 27). Covid-19 may lift India's e-commerce market to around $85 billion by 2024. *Business Standard.* Retrieved from https://www.business-standard.com/ article/economy-policy/ despite-pandemic-india-s-e-commerce-expected-to-grow-three-fold-by-2028-120062402043_1.html

Pujawan, I. N., & Bah, A. U. (2022, January). Supply chains under COVID-19 disruptions: Literature review and research agenda. In *Supply Chain Forum International Journal*, *23*(1), 81–95.

Raman, P. (2014). Factors influencing women consumers' buying behavior towards online shopping in India. *Contemporary Management Research*, *8*(2), 23–56.

Sarkar, S., & Khare, A. (2017). Moderating effect of price perception on factors affecting attitude towards online shopping. *J Market Anal*, *5*, 68–80. doi:10.1057/ s41270-017 -0018-2

Sharma, A. (2011). Take-off of online marketing: Casting the next generation strategies. *Business Strategy Series*, *12*(4), 202–208. doi:10.1108/ 17515631111155160

Shelly, S. (2016, October 6). Snapdeal slips against its two main rivals, Flipkart & Amazon. Can it get its mojo back? *The Economic Times*. Retrieved from https://economictimes. indiatimes. com/small-biz/ startups/snapdeal-slips-against-its-two-main-rivals-flipkart-amazon-can-it-get-its-mojo-back/articleshow/54705032.cms

Sinha & Kim. (2012). Factor Affecting Indian Consumer's Online Buying Behavior. *Innovative Marketing*, *8*(2), 2012.

Statista. (2020). *Frequently purchased online food products during the coronavirus (COVID-19) pandemic in India as of May 2020, by gender*. https://www.statista.com/statistics /1128411/india-coronavirus-frequent-online-products/

Sushil. (2012). Interpreting the Interpretive Structural Model. *Global Journal of Flexible Systems Management*, *13*, 87-106. https://doi.org/ doi:10.1007/s40171-012-0008-3

Thakur, R., & Srivastava, M. (2015). A study on the impact of consumer risk perception and innovativeness on online shopping in India. *International Journal of Retail & Distribution Management*, *43*(2), 148–166. doi:10.1108/IJRDM-06-2013-0128

Wang, E., An, N., Gao, Z., Kiprop, E., & Geng, X. (2020). Consumer food stockpiling behavior and willingness to pay for food reserves in COVID-19. *Food Security*, *N0*(12), 739–747. doi:10.100712571-020-01092-1

Wankhade, N., & Kundu, G. K. (2020). Interpretive Structural Modelling (ISM) Methodology and its application in Supply Chain Research. *International Journal of Innovative Technology and Exploring Engineering, 9*(4), 1101-1109. https://doi.org/ doi:10.35940/ijitee.D1607.029420

Wisetsri, W., Syam, E., Alanya-Beltran, J., Ramchandra Kulkarni, G., Vardhan Reddy, R. K., & Firdos Alam Sheikh, M. (2022). Assessing and comparing the role of information and communication technology (ICT) and supply chain management (SCM) and its impact on contribution of e-commerce. *Materials Today: Proceedings*. https://doi.org/ doi:10.1016/j.matpr.2021.12.429

Yan, R. N., Hyllegard, K. H., & Blaesi, L. F. (2012). Marketing eco-fashion: The influence of brand name and message explicitness. Journal of Marketing Communications, 18(2), 151-168. https://doi.org/ doi:10.1080 /13527266.2010.490420

Zhuo, D., & Xiaoting, Z. (2010). An Empirical Study on Factors which Affect Consumers' Online Shopping Behavior. *2010 International Conference on E-Business and E-Government*, 2200-2203. doi: 10.1109/ICEE.2010.556

Chapter 9
COVID-19 Test Report and Vaccine Certificate Verification Through Blockchain and E-Commerce

Puja Banerjee
Kalinga Institute of Industrial Technology (Deemed), Bhubaneswar, India

Saurabh Bilgaiyan
Kalinga Institute of Industrial Technology (Deemed), Bhubaneswar, India

Adarsh Tikmani
Kalinga Institute of Industrial Technology (Deemed), Bhubaneswar, India

ABSTRACT

COVID-19 was first reported in December 2019 and has spread since then. Different vaccines are under development and digital technologies are used for contact tracing, vaccine monitoring, screening of infection, etc. But the healthcare providers are dealing with many challenges, such as cases of fake documents (i.e., test reports and vaccine certificates). Blockchain can help mitigate the challenges with its features, such as data transparency, accuracy, and decentralization. Even in general day purpose, the verification of the documents is required for booking of airline ticket, hotel room, etc. E-commerce deals with online selling and buying of products, which together with blockchain can fulfill the requirement. This chapter proposes a framework for verification of COVID-19 test reports and vaccine certificates with the help of blockchain technology and e-commerce. The aim of the proposed framework is to validate the details online so that the proper treatment and medication can be provided to the patient. IPFS is used to store the data.

DOI: 10.4018/978-1-6684-4969-1.ch009

Copyright © 2022, IGI Global. Copying or distributing in print or electronic forms without written permission of IGI Global is prohibited.

INTRODUCTION

In March 2021, WHO published a report on a falsified vaccine that was circulated in Mexico, affecting health systems and possessing a high risk to public health globally. Since the vaccine provided to the patient is falsified, thus the certificate provided for the same is not verified to be real or fake ("Using Medical Product Alert," 2021). From the time of the emergence of Covid-19 (Novel Coronavirus), not only global health but the global economy was also got affected. Falsification of test reports, medicines, vaccines, vaccine certificates, etc. has been reported on a large scale. To combat these kinds of contexts, the healthcare sector is adopting different technologies, such as Artificial Intelligence (AI), Blockchain, Internet of Things (IoT), etc. Among such technologies, blockchain and e-commerce can be used together to provide security and privacy and verify the products ("Using 5 blockchain healthcare use cases in digital health," n.d.). E-Commerce is used in different fields for selling and buying services and products online. Together with blockchain, which has unique characteristics (such as decentralization, transparency, immutability, etc.), E-commerce services can be more secure and safe ("Using Healthcare E-Commerce Global Market Report," 2021).

This chapter focuses on the negative impacts of Covid-19, which led to black marketing of test reports, vaccines, vaccine certificates, etc. The author emphasizes the importance of e-commerce in the healthcare sector, by proposing a framework to verify the documents so that the black marketing could be reduced. For enhancement of the working of the framework, the concept of blockchain is implemented together with e-commerce.

This chapter is arranged in four sections. Section 1 discusses how blockchain and e-commerce together can help to validate the vaccine certificates and test reports of Covid-19. This section also gives the background review on Covid-19, blockchain, and e-commerce and the motivation to write this chapter. Section 2 provides some work of other authors related to Covid-19, blockchain, and e-commerce. Section 3 describes the design overview, workflow, and performance analysis of the proposed system. Section 4 mentions the conclusion summarizing the motive and concept of the proposed system.

Background

The following subsections provide a background review on Covid-19, blockchain, and e-commerce. It gives a statistical analysis of the effects of Covid-19 and the vaccine distribution. Also, some pictorial representation to show the features of blockchain and elements of e-commerce.

Covid-19

In December 2019, the first case of Covid-19 was reported in Wuhan City, China. Since then, it has spread worldwide affecting people of all ages. Also known as Novel Coronavirus, it is a respiratory illness and causes some effects of breathlessness, cough, fever, etc.

Some symptoms of Covid-19:

- Common:
  - Cough,
  - Fever,
  - Sore throat,

  - Smell or Taste lost,
  - Tiredness,
  - Headache,
  - Body pains and aches,
  - Irritated or red eyes.
- Serious:
  - Chest pain,
  - Breathlessness,
  - Confusion,
  - Pale Lips or Skin,
  - Sleepiness.

The people were getting affected with this virus through mere physical contact, like hand-shaking, group meetings, etc. Thus, to control the situation, strict orders, such as lockdown, quarantine, etc were implemented and the vaccination development was focused on reducing the effect of this virus. Also, many digital technologies were developed for contract tracing, screening of infection, vaccine monitoring, etc. Though many efforts have been put down, a lot has to be done as the virus is emerging with new variants every few months (Using Coronavirus disease, n.d.; Coronavirus, 2022).

Figure 1 shows the Covid-19 statistics based on cases and deaths per million people. Figure 2 shows the statistics on Covid-19 vaccine doses with people getting at least one dose, or fully vaccinated or vaccine boosters, per 100 people.

Blockchain

Blockchain is a distributed system that has unique characteristics, such as accuracy, immutability, transparency, etc. It is a digital ledger that provides security and safety while data transactions in a Peer-to-Peer network. Blockchain technology was introduced as an underlying concept of Bitcoin, in the year 2008, by an unidentified person "Satoshi Nakamoto". A block contains two parts: head and body. The body contains the data or transaction, while the head contains the hash of the previous and present block, Merkle tree root, and timestamp. Each time a transaction occurs, a new block gets created and added to the chain after validation, using some mathematical calculation on the previous block hash. For this mathematical calculation, a random and unique number is used called NONCE, which also gets stored in the head part of the block. The very first block of the chain (known as Genesis) is marked as Block 0 and acts as an ancestor to other blocks since it does not have any previous block and its hash is used to create the first block of the chain (Satoshi, 2008). Figure 3. picturizes the blockchain and its most common features.

The features of blockchain that makes it useful and trustworthy:

- Security – The data entered into the network is highly secured.
- Privacy – The data is maintained and stored privately.
- Accuracy – The data manifested is correct and pure.
- Immutability – The data cannot be altered or deleted from the network.
- Authenticity – The data presented is original and genuine.
- Transparency – Provides clarity to the data in the network.

Figure 1. Covid-19 Statistics on Covid-19 Cases and Deaths

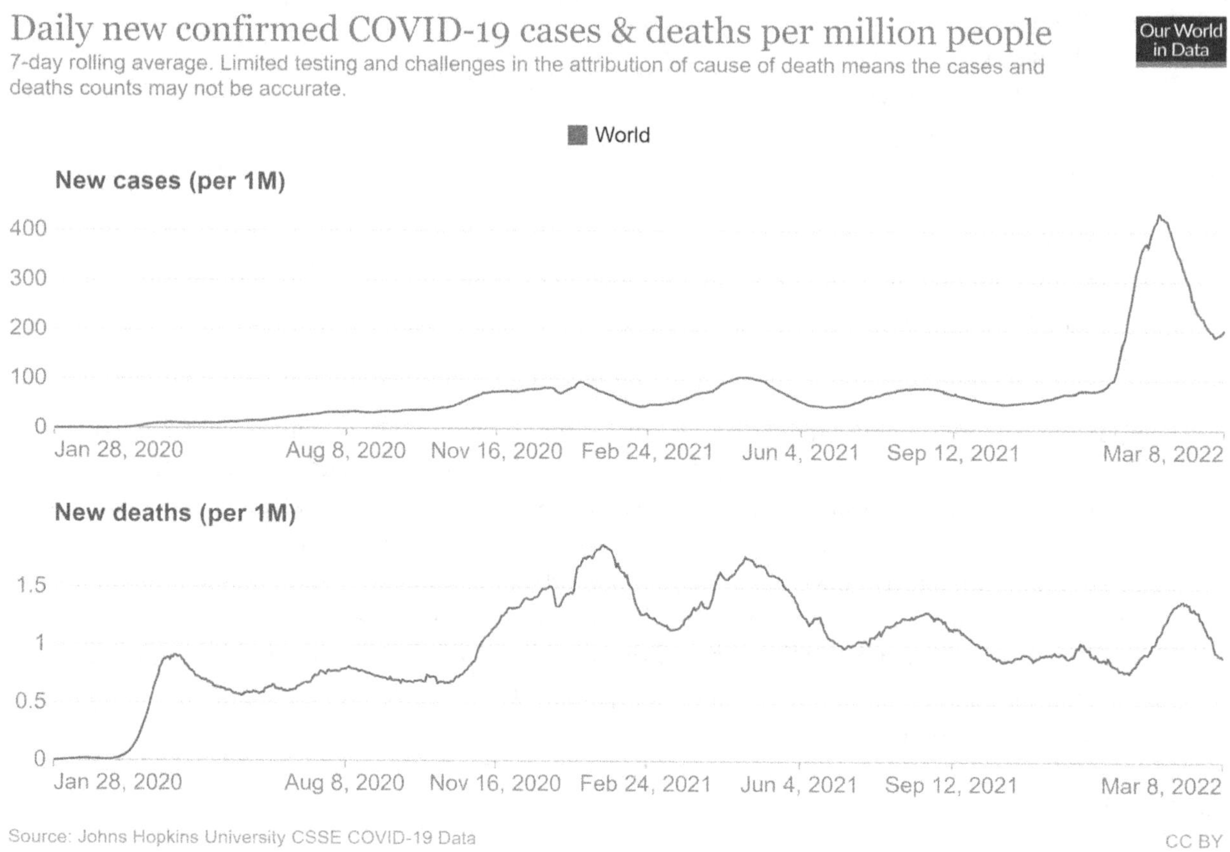

- Decentralization – The network is not controlled by any single person or organization. The control is provided to every node in the network.
- Distributed Ledger – A shared database among the network to store and use data.
- Traceability – The transaction done in the network can be tracked or detected.

The use of the technology evolved through generations:

- Blockchain 1.0 (the first generation) was the underlying concept of Bitcoin.
- Blockchain 2.0 (the second generation), then came into highlight with the Smart Contract concept.
- Blockchain 3.0 (the third generation) focuses on the growth of non-financial applications (Ibrar et al., 2021).

E-Commerce

E-Commerce refers to the selling and buying of products and services using electronic communication and digital information processing technology. The transactions can occur between or among organizations, or between organizations and individuals. The concept of e-commerce was first put up by Michael

Figure 2. Covid-19 Statistics on Covid-19 Vaccine Doses

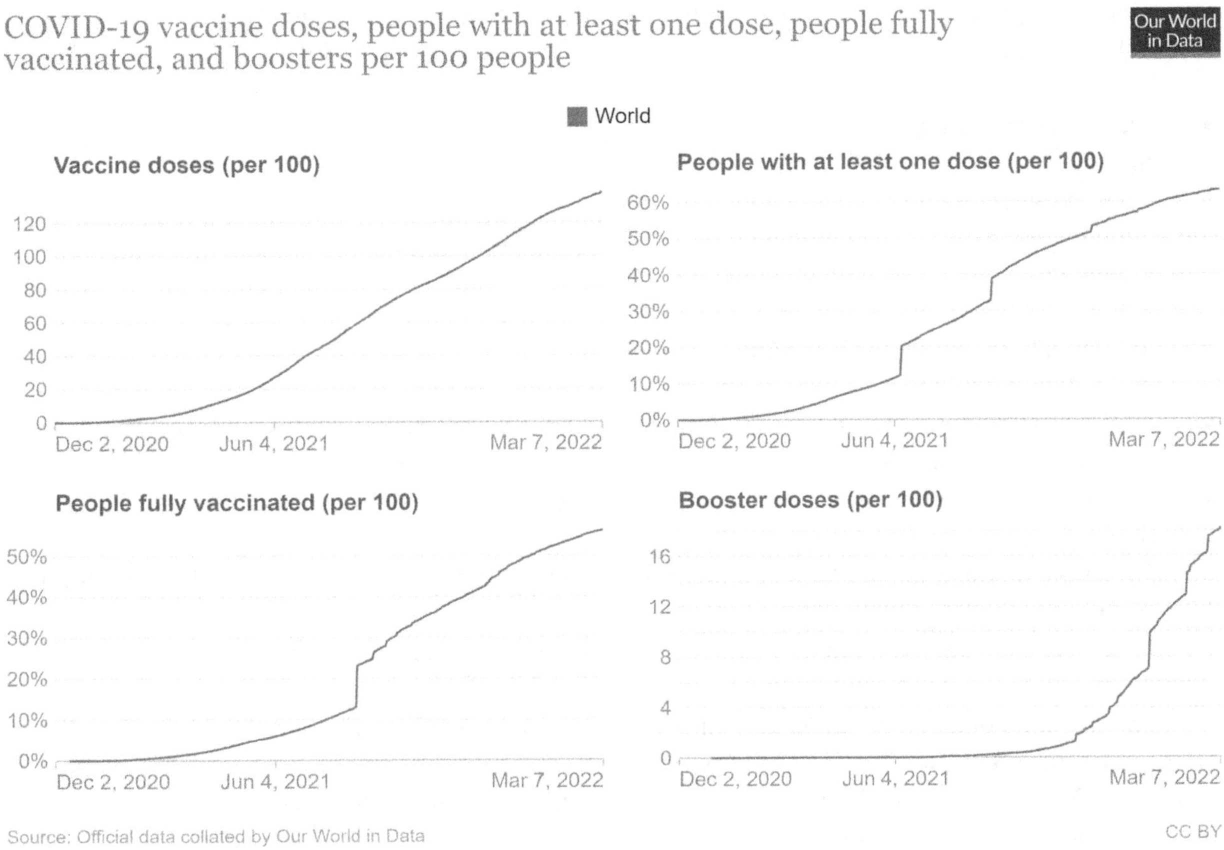

Figure 3. Blockchain and its features

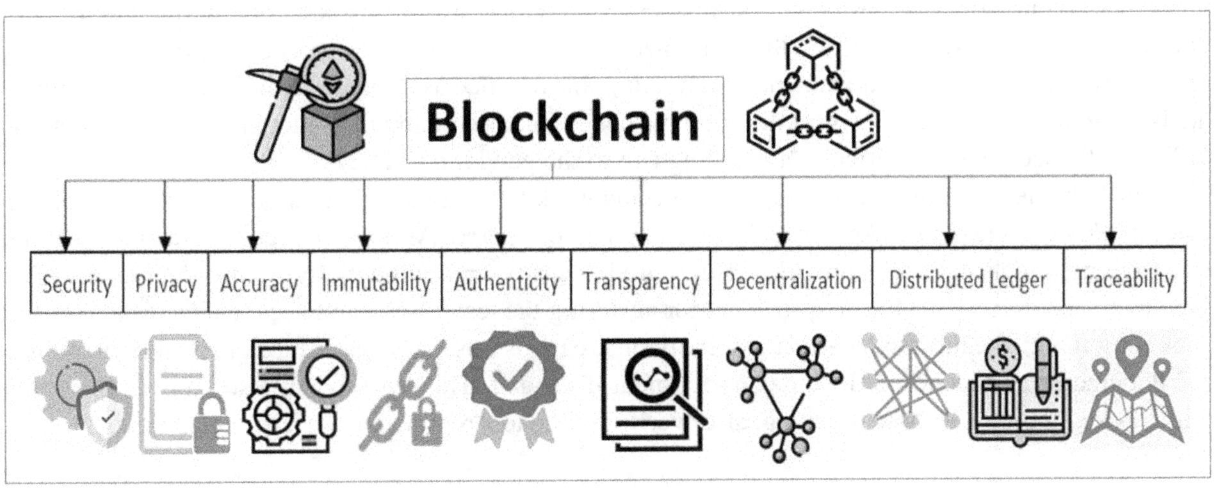

Aldrich, in the year 1979. In 1982, Boston Computer Exchange launched as the first e-commerce company. The concept then evolved and has become a daily life part of the global public.

The features that make E-Commerce feasible are:

- Ease of Networking,
- Speed,
- Cost Saving,
- No boundaries,
- User-friendly.

There are different types of E-Commerce, namely:

- Business-to-Business (B2B) – A transaction of goods and services between two or more businesses or organizations.
- Business-to-Customer (B2C) – A transaction of goods and services from businesses or organizations to their customers.
- Customer-to-Business (C2B) – A transaction of goods and services from individuals to different businesses or organizations.
- Customer-to-Customer (C2C) – A transaction of goods and services between individuals.

Some examples of famous e-commerce sites in the market are Amazon, Flipkart, Netmeds, Pharmeasy, Shopify, Carrd, eBay, etc. ("Using What is Ecommerce, n.d.; 9 Characteristics of Well-Designed E-Commerce Websites," 2021). Figure 4. shows some components of e-commerce to point out the design of an e-commerce site and its uses of it.

Motivation

In March 2021, The Indian Express published an article on fake test reports and vaccine certificates of Covid-19 and its effects. These fake test reports and vaccine certificates are used by people to travel overseas for their needs, neglecting the lockdown and quarantine rules or procedures. People are using the dark web for selling fake documents and treating this practice as a source of income. The individuals are buying these fake documents for different purposes, but are risking lives globally ("Using How fake COVID-19 vaccination certificates are adding fire to the pandemic," 2021).

In this chapter, the authors are proposing a framework to verify the Test reports and vaccine certificates of Covid-19 using blockchain technology and e-commerce. As e-commerce will deal with online transactions, blockchain will provide the required security and authenticity of the documents. This system can be used by healthcare providers for verifying the test reports and vaccine certificates before providing the medication to a patient. An individual can also use this system for online verification of the documents and request a doctor's appointment if needed. This system can also be used for online flight ticket booking, or hotel booking, after verifying the test reports and vaccine certificates.

Figure 4. E-Commerce Components

RELATED WORK

Ajay et al., in the year 2001, discussed the new concept of involving e-commerce in the healthcare domain. The paper describes the challenges faced by the healthcare sector in its traditional way, such as case studies, information flow, communication, etc. The involvement of e-commerce helps in defying the challenges, making the healthcare sector more effective and efficient. Also, there are the description of some technologies, such as pattern recognition, expert systems, artificial intelligence, etc. to support the study. In the year 2010, A.H.M. et al., described business models and methods to support electronic health (e-health) applications. The paper thoroughly discusses the methods, perspectives, and benefits of business models in e-health, supporting the study with some examples. The perspectives followed are Customer, Finances, Infrastructure, and Value Proposition. The paper also discusses the complications and challenges faced while applying business models to e-health, for its innovation. Xingxiong et al., in the year 2018, presented a system built using blockchain technology for e-commerce, energy, and finance. The system is built for trust, trade, and payment securely and creatively. The architecture, method, components, platform, and technical solution of the system are discussed thoroughly. Also, it describes the application of the system using some scenarios from a business perspective. In the year 2019, Justice et al., proposed a blockchain solution for updating vaccination status and test results of Covid-19 and preserving its privacy, using Smart Contracts. A framework for the same has been provided describing the architecture and work of the system. The paper is supported by a discussion of algorithms, implementation cost, and performance analysis of the proposed system. In the year 2020, Hemant et al. acknowledge the role of blockchain technology in the e-commerce industry. The authors mentioned the challenges faced by accustomed e-commerce and the opportunities that blockchain is providing to overcome those challenges. The paper presents some e-commerce applications in which blockchain technology has been used such as Supply chain, Payment, Ethical Practices, etc. Vinay et al., in the year 2020, detailed a study on the contribution of evolving technologies in managing the impact of Covid-19. The technologies discussed in this paper are Blockchain, Artificial Intelligence (AI), Drones, Internet-of-Technology (IoT), and Fifth Generation (5G) of Wireless Communication Technology. A thorough analysis of symptoms, stages, diagnosis, treatment, and prevention of Covid-19 and the areas in which these evolving technologies can impact have been discussed. In the year 2021, Horst et al. suggested a few high-level questions to identify the influence of blockchain technology on e-commerce. These questions are research-based and have been discussed to motivate the researchers for investigating further in this section. The categories covered under this study are mainly focused on issues related to technological, organizational, legal, consumer, and quality. Wei et al., in the year 2021, provide a literature review on COVID-19 related blockchain applications in healthcare. The main applications discussed are contact tracing, pandemic control, immunity monitoring, etc. The paper also focuses on non-COVID-19 related blockchain applications in healthcare, such as EMRs, supply chain management, m-Health, etc. Charts are designed to show the distribution of articles about both COVID-19 and non-COVID-19 related blockchain applications. In the year 2021, Nida et al. proposed a contact tracing system using blockchain technology for pandemics. The paper discusses the working of the proposed system and how it enhances the challenges faced by existing contact tracing apps, such as data transparency, medical privacy issues, etc. The paper thoroughly discusses the system architecture, workflow, and usage scenario of the proposed framework. Also, the performance of the proposed system has been simulated and challenges are discussed. Abid et al., in the year 2021, highlight the fourteen notable implementations of blockchain technology in healthcare. The paper also discussed the need, unified workflow, benefits, enablers, and capabilities of blockchain in healthcare. In the year 2021, Stefan et al., suggests a theory, in the context of e-commerce, to help Small and Medium-Sized Enterprises (SMEs) to emerge from markets, in the crisis period of the Covid-19 pandemic. This paper helps to select business partners, who will co-operate in the right manner for innovation and development of SMEs in this critical situation. Also, to support the paper, some SMEs from Herzegovina and Bosnia were interviewed in March-April 2020, and data were collected to compare the traditional and new ways of conducting business. Malgorzata Wiścicka-Fernando, in the year 2021, focuses on online shopping using mobile technologies in the Covid-19 pandemic. A survey was held in April 2020 on Polish customers to collect data online through mobile and Hypothesis Tests were performed to conclude the result. Two categories were defined to perform the Hypothesis Tests: (i) Average number of transactions based on online shopping done per month before and during the Covid-19, and (ii) Average number of transactions based on online shopping per month and responded age group during the Covid-19.

The papers discussed are summarized in Table 1.

PROPOSED FRAMEWORK

The proposed framework is a blockchain-based e-commerce system, designed to verify the Covid-19 test reports and vaccine certificates of individuals. This system can be used by healthcare providers before

Table 1. Discussion of papers, based on author, idea, and technology used

S. No.	Year	Author	Idea	Analysis	Technology Used	Related To
1	2001	Ajay et al.	Involvement of new concept of e-commerce in healthcare.	Describes the challenges faced by the healthcare sector in its traditional way.	Some scenarios explain the working system of traditional healthcare.	E-Commerce, Healthcare
				The involvement of e-commerce helps in defying the challenges, making the healthcare sector more effective and efficient.	A thorough description of e-commerce, its types, and some newly evolved technologies.	
2	2010	A.H.M. et al.	Innovation of e-health using business models.	Discusses the methods, perspectives, and benefits of business models in e-health.	Some examples to point out the strength and weaknesses of the models.	E-Commerce, Healthcare
3	2018	Xingxiong et al.	A blockchain system for e-commerce, energy, and finance.	The motive is to build a trust system, trade system, and payment system securely and creatively for energy, finance, and e-commerce.	A thorough discussion of system architecture, method, components, platform, and technical solution.	E-Commerce, Blockchain
					Business perspective scenarios to support the application.	
4	2019	Justice et al.	A blockchain solution for updating vaccination status and test results of Covid-19 and preserving its privacy.	System design, workflow, algorithms used, implementation cost and performance analysis have been discussed thoroughly.	Implementation is done on the Ethereum platform.	Blockchain, Covid-19, Healthcare
					Smart Contract to verify the transactions.	
					IPFS is used for data storage.	
5	2020	Hemant et al.	Usage of blockchain in the e-commerce industry.	Discusses the challenges faced by accustomed e-commerce and the opportunities blockchain provides to overcome those challenges.	Examples of real-life scenarios to support the theory.	E-Commerce, Blockchain
6	2020	Vinay et al.	Management of Covid-19 situation using evolving technologies.	Describes thoroughly the symptoms, stages, diagnosis, treatment, and prevention of Covid-19 and the impact of the evolving technologies.	Statistical chart and table to show the effects and symptoms of Covid-19.	Blockchain, Covid-19, Healthcare
				The technologies discussed are AI, Blockchain, Drones, IoT, and 5G.	Pictorial representation of the evolving technologies.	
7	2021	Horst et al.	The influence of blockchain technology on e-commerce.	The aim is to motivate the researchers for investigating further how the blockchain influences e-commerce.	High-level (19, in count) research questions based on a few defined categories.	E-Commerce, Blockchain
8	2021	Wei et al.	Blockchain applications related to both Covid-19 and non-Covid-19.	Covid-19 related blockchain applications are contact tracing, pandemic control, immunity monitoring, etc.	Pictorial representation of the healthcare ecosystem.	Blockchain, Covid-19, Healthcare
				Non-Covid-19 related blockchain applications are EMRs, supply chain management, m-Health, etc.	Chart designed to show the distribution of articles.	
9	2021	Nida et al.	A contact tracing system using blockchain technology.	Discusses the working of the proposed system and how it enhances the challenges faced by the existing contact tracing app.	Implementation is done on the Ethereum platform.	Blockchain, Covid-19, Healthcare
					The working of the system is explained through some algorithms.	
					IPFS is used for data storage.	
10	2021	Abid et al.	Usage of blockchain in healthcare.	Discussed the need, unified workflow, benefits, enablers, and capabilities of blockchain in healthcare.	Examples of fourteen notable implementations of blockchain in the healthcare industry,	Blockchain, Healthcare
11	2021	Stefan et al.,	A theory to help SMEs to emerge in the Covid-19 period.	Helps to select business partners for innovation and development of SMEs in this pandemic situation.	Data were collected through interviews to compare the traditional and new ways of conducting business.	E-Commerce, Covid-19
12	2021	Malgorzata Wiścicka-Fernando	A study on online shopping using mobile in Covid-19 pandemic.	To analyze the effect by calculating the average number of transactions done, based on online shopping during Covid-19.	For analysis, data were collected and Hypothesis Tests were performed, categorized on age group and comparison before and during Covid-19.	E-Commerce, Covid-19

providing the medication to a patient, or by an individual before making a request for a doctor appointment, or booking an online flight ticket or hotel room. The following subsections discuss the system design, workflow, and performance analysis.

System Design Overview

In this proposed framework, the user is required to fill up the online registration form before selecting the document (Covid-19 test reports or Covid-19 vaccine certificates) that the individual wants to verify. There can be two different types of users: Healthcare providers, or An Individual. If the user is a health provider, the user will fill out the online registration form for the Covid-19 patient and verify the documents, before providing the required treatment and medication. If the user is an individual and observes some symptoms or positive test reports of Covid-19, even are fully vaccinated, the user can fill up the online form and verify the documents before booking an online appointment with a doctor. If the ledger validates the details of the test reports or vaccine certificates, then the documents are real and the chances of recovery of the patient are high. But if denied, the documents given will be considered to be counterfeit. Also, this system can be used for online booking of flight tickets or hotel rooms, as validation of the documents will reduce the chances of a pandemic situation. Figure 5. gives an overview of the system design.

Figure 5. System Design Overview

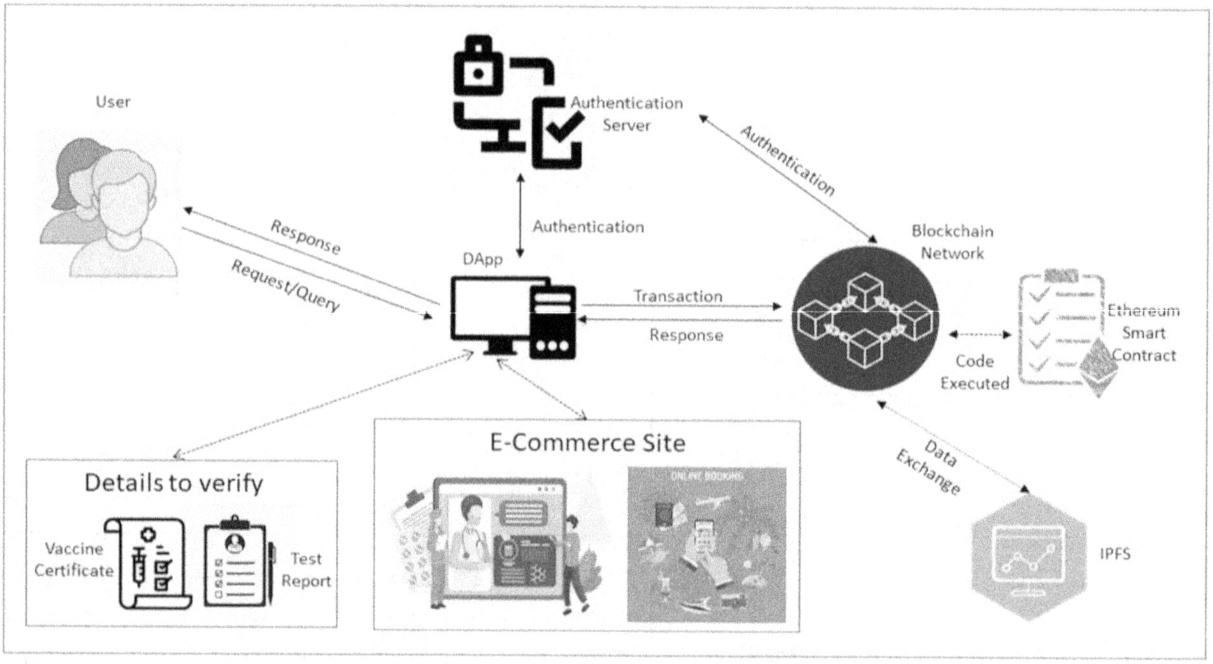

System Workflow

The following subsections discuss some pseudo-codes that are followed and the technology used to explain the workflow of the proposed framework.

Pseudo-Codes Followed

This section discusses the samples of pseudo-codes that are followed to write the smart contract for the development of the proposed framework.

Pseudo Code Sample 1: Smart Contract for Registration of User

Pseudocode sample 1 defines the steps for the registration of an individual. A function to take individual details as input and store it in IPFS.

```
function registration (variables…)
        send individual's data to IPFS
                IPFS stores the individual's data in distributed ledger
                        Assigns hash to the data stored
                                Sends the hash to blockchain
end function
```

Pseudo Code Sample 2: Smart Contract to Check Covid-19 Test Report

Pseudocode sample 2 defines the step to verify the Covid-19 test report. If patient_reg_num (prn) matches with the record stored in IPFS, then the individual or hospital_admin (hadmin) will receive the patient_data (pdata) and can verify the test report.

```
function verifyTestReport (variables...)
        if (msg.sender = individual or hadmin) then
                if (prn) == true then
                        retrieve pdata from specified prn
                        return (pdata) to individual or hadmin
                else Abort session
                end if
        else Abort session
        end if
end function
```

Pseudo Code Sample 3: Smart Contract to Verify Covid-19 Vaccine Certificate

Pseudocode sample 3 defines the step to verify the Covid-19 Vaccine Certificate. If the beneficiary_ref_id (benrid) matches the record in IPFS, then the individual or hospital_admin (hadmin) will receive a message "real certificate" and will get the certificate_details. But if benrid does not match any such entry, then the individual or hadmin will receive a message "no record found", and the vaccine certificate shown will be considered artificial.

```
function verifyVaccineCerificate (variables...)
        if (msg.sender = individual or hadmin) then
                if(benrid) == true then
                        return (message: real certificate) to individual or
hadmin
                        return (certificate_details) to individual or hadmin
                else
                        return (message: no record found) to individual or
hadmin
                end if
        else Abort session
        end if
end function
```

Technology Used

For the development of an e-commerce site, HTML (HyperText Mark-up Language) is used to create the web pages and JS (JavaScript) is used to validate those pages. A page for user registration is created, which after successful registration will direct the user to select the particular document (Covid-19 test report or Covid-19 vaccine certificate) that needs to be verified.

To work with the blockchain technology, the Ethereum framework will be used, since, it is open-source software and helps in building smart contracts. Smart contracts are the programs written and executed to act as an agreement to process the transaction submitted by the user. The data will be stored in IPFS (InterPlanetary File System), and shared through it, due to its cryptographic hash feature. Also, it helps to enhance the scalability issue of blockchain.

System Performance Analysis

This section discusses the performance of the system analyzed based on the amount of energy used in different functions. When the Smart Contracts are compiled and deployed on the blockchain platform, which is Ethereum in this project, it generates some value, such as transaction hash, gas used, gam limit, execution cost, etc.

Table 2. shows the energy used in different functions.

When a transaction is done, a block generates, that gets added to the chain, extending the blockchain network. Some base information of the block generated in the execution of the functions, written for deploying and debugging the project:

- transaction hash :
  - 0xb2b5e7ec5418f03d20b3d3690607f0b447c0439a5024eba4cd522d509afa1f30 (for Registration function)
  - 0xb01889576f6de31eb2e13bfe3a957473b115afcec1d7e7e4b5a5c5adf146f325 (for VerifyTestReport function)

Table 2. Function name and energy used

S.No.	Function Name	Gas Limit	Transaction Cost	Gas Cost	Gas Estimates
1	Registration	3000000	572202 gas	31 Wei	481518
2	verifyTestReport	3000000	112729 gas	31 Wei	55705
3	verifyVaccineCertificate	3000000	112729 gas	31 Wei	55705

    - 0x5dfc08514ae66a6e01a113825fadb4bcd4f9f23bf0222958accd1de3db82799d (for VerifyVaccineCertificate function)
- "block.chainid": "0xd05"
- "block.gaslimit": 160000000
- "block.basefee": "1 Wei (0x01)"
- "block.number":
    - 0 (for Registration function)
    - 1 (for VerifyTestReport function)
    - 2 (for VerifyVaccineCertificate function)
- "msg.sender" or "tx.origin" or from: "0x5B38Da6a701c568545dCfcB03FcB875f56beddC4"
- to:
    - Registration.(constructor)
    - VerifyTestReport.(constructor)
    - VerifyVaccineCertificate.(constructor)
- "msg.sig": "0x60806040"
- gas 80000000 gas
- "block.difficulty":
    - "69762765929000" (for Registration function)
    - "70762765929000" (for VerifyTestReport function)
    - "71762765929000" (for VerifyVaccineCertificate function)
- "block.timestamp":
    - 1647777672 (for Registration function)
    - 1647778056 (for VerifyTestReport function)
    - 1647778284 (for VerifyVaccineCertificate function)

CONCLUSION

Since the first case was reported in December 2019, the Novel Coronavirus (or Covid-19) spread rapidly affecting the daily life routine of the global public. The people faced situations like quarantine and lock-down, which were implemented to reduce the effects of the Coronavirus by maintaining social distance. Though medicines, vaccines, digital technologies, etc were in development for identifying the symptoms and mitigating the effect of the coronavirus, it also affected the global public economically. Thus, many cases of using the dark web for the generation of fake test reports, vaccines, and vaccine certificates were in news. Many kinds of research and frameworks are under development to prevent the production of counterfeit objects or verify the reports and certificates. This chapter uses the concept of e-commerce and blockchain technology together to build a system that verifies the test reports and vaccine certificates of Covid-19. E-Commerce deals with the selling and buying of products and services. Blockchain is a distributed ledger in a decentralized network, which provides the required privacy, security, and safety to the transaction of data. The authors explained the system architecture, workflow (using some pseudo-codes), and performance has also been analyzed. This is a new concept for verifying the test reports and vaccine certificates of Covid-19, which will help to maintain the rules and regulations imposed by the government to deal with the pandemic situation. An individual, or the healthcare provider (for the patient) will do the registration process, before verifying the documents (i.e., test results or vaccine certificates of Covid-19). An individual, if faces any symptoms of Covid-19, even after being fully vaccinated and the test reports show positive, can use this system to make an online doctor appointment. Also, an idea of using this system for online booking of flight tickets, or hotel rooms has been proposed. The process is the user will first register themselves, and then verify their documents before doing the online payment for the appointment with the doctor, or booking of flight tickets, or hotel room. It will help in the proper medication and treatment of Covid-19 patients.

Since the proposed system is a new approach, there are many chances of modification or extension of the system in various other domains. Also, this proposal will help future researchers in extending, updating, and developing the system, for global advantage.

REFERENCES

5 blockchain healthcare use cases in digital health. (n.d.). https://stlpartners.com/articles/digital-health/5-blockchain-healthcare-use-cases/

9 Characteristics of Well-Designed E-Commerce Websites. (n.d.). https://www.vandelaydesign.com/well-designed-ecommerce-websites/

Aggarwal, A., & Travers, S. (2001). E-Commerce in Healthcare: Changing the Traditional Landscape. Springer.

Bari, N., Qamar, U., & Khalid, A. (2021). *Efficient Contact Tracing for pandemics using blockchain.* Science Direct. doi:10.1016/j.imu.2021.100742

Bulsara & Vaghela. (2020). Blockchain Technology for E-commerce Industry. *IJAST, 29*(5), 3793-3798.

Chamola, V., Hassija, V., Gupta, V., & Guizani, M. (2020). *A Comprehensive Review of the COVID-19 Pandemic and the Role of IoT, Drones, AI, Blockchain, and 5G in Managing Its Impact* (Vol. 8). IEEE.

Coronavirus, COVID-19. (n.d.). https://my.clevelandclinic.org/health/diseases/21214-coronavirus-covid-19

Coronavirus disease (COVID-19). (n.d.). https://www.who.int/health-topics/coronavirus#tab=tab_1

Haleem, A., Javaid, M., Singh, R. P., Suman, R., & Rab, S. (2021). *Blockchain technology applications in healthcare: An overview*. Science Direct.

Healthcare E-Commerce Global Market Report 2021. (2021). https://www.prnewswire.com/news-releases/healthcare-e-commerce-global-market-report-2021-301451529.html

How fake COVID-19 vaccination certificates are adding fire to the pandemic. (n.d.). https://indianexpress.com/article/technology/tech-news-technology/how-fake-covid-19-vaccination-certificates-are-adding-fire-to-the-pandemic-7241485/

Limberg, A. H. M. V., & Gemert-Pijnen, J. V. (2010). Towards innovative business modeling for sustainable eHealth applications. In *2010 Second International Conference on eHealth, Telemedicine, and Social Medicine*. IEEE.

Markovic, S., Koporcic, N., Arslanagic-Kalajdzic, M., Kadic-Maglajlic, S., Bagherzadeh, M., & Islam, N. (2021). *Business-to-business open innovation: COVID-19 lessons for small and medium-sized enterprises from emerging markets*. Science Direct.

Medical Product Alert N°2/2021: Falsified COVID-19 Vaccine BNT162b2. (2021). https://www.who.int/news/item/26-03-2021-medical-product-alert-n-2-2021-falsified-covid-19-vaccine-bnt162b2

Nakamoto, S. (2008). *Bitcoin: A Peer-to-peer Electronic Cash System*. www.bitcoin.org

Ng, W. Y., Tan, T.-E., Movva, P. V. H., Fang, A. H. S., Yeo, K.-K., Ho, D., Foo, F. S. S., Xiao, Z., Sun, K., Wong, T. Y., Sia, A. T.-H., & Ting, D. S. W. (2021). Blockchain applications in health care for COVID-19 and beyond: A systematic review. *The Lancet. Digital Health*, *3*(12), e819–e829. doi:10.1016/S2589-7500(21)00210-7 PMID:34654686

Odoom, J., Soglo, R. S., Danso, S. A., & Xiaofang, H. (2019). A Privacy-preserving Covid-19 Updatable Test Result and Vaccination Provenance based on Blockchain and Smart contract. In *2019 International Conference on Mechatronics, Remote Sensing, Information Systems and Industrial Information Technologies (ICMRSISIIT)*. IEEE.

Treiblmaier, H., & Sillaber, C. (2021). *The impact of blockchain on e-commerce: A framework for salient research topics*. Science Direct.

What is Ecommerce? (n.d.). https://ecommerceguide.com/guides/what-is-ecommerce/

Wiścicka-Fernando, M. (2021). The use of mobile technologies in online shopping during the Covid-19 pandemic - an empirical study. In *25th International Conference on Knowledge-Based and Intelligent Information & Engineering Systems*. Science Direct.

Yaqoob, I., Salah, K., Jayaraman, R., & Al-Hammadi, Y. (2021). Blockchain for healthcare data management: opportunities, challenges, and future recommendations. Springer.

Zhu, X., & Wang, D. (2019). Research on Blockchain Application for E-Commerce, Finance and Energy. In *ESMA 2018 IOP Conf. Series: Earth and Environmental Science*. IOP Publishing.

Chapter 10
Product Return in Online Purchase and Demography: E-Commerce Scenario in India

Brajaballav Kar
https://orcid.org/0000-0002-2127-1147
Kalinga Institute of Industrial Technology (Deemed), Bhubaneswar, India

Satyaballav Kar
GIET University, Rayagada, India

Sushanta Tripathy
https://orcid.org/0000-0003-2470-4080
Kalinga Institute of Industrial Technology (Deemed), Bhubaneswar, India

ABSTRACT

The rapid growth in online purchases and product return pose challenges to the supply chain. The demography influences purchases. After an extensive literature review, the authors examine if the product return in online purchases depends on demographic factors and product categories. This online survey-based research analyzed the 619 responses and identifies that age, gender, profession, search intensity have a significant relationship with the return frequency. After using statistical analysis, findings suggest that the family income, payment method, purchase frequency, monthly spending do not have a significant influence on return frequency. Similarly, analysis indicated age, gender, profession, and search intensity to be significant. Textile and household goods showed a significant relationship with return frequency from the different categories. This research emphasizes the role of demography factors; however, online purchase and return is a complex process involving the role of product, retailer, website, and delivery.

1. INTRODUCTION

By 2025, 900 million are expected to become internet users in India; the gross merchandise value is

DOI: 10.4018/978-1-6684-4969-1.ch010

Copyright © 2022, IGI Global. Copying or distributing in print or electronic forms without written permission of IGI Global is prohibited.

expected to be 20 billion USD (*Indian E-commerce Industry Analysis*, 2021). Another report quoted by Forbes estimates the value to be 120 USD by the same year (Rozario, 2021). The Indian e-commerce industry growth is estimated to be at a 23% compounded annual growth rate (CAGR) (*Retail Industry in India*, 2021). The retail e-commerce sector gives 8 percent of the total employment and contributes 10 percent to the total gross domestic product of India. According to Invest India report, a government agency to promote investment, almost 50 percent of the smartphones, and 20 percent of all apparel sales in India are through e-commerce. One hundred percent of pin codes in India have registered e-commerce transactions. The average selling price (ASP) in tier-2 and smaller towns is marginally less compared to tier-1 or metro cities. Electronics and apparel constitute nearly 70 percent of the total e-commerce transaction market value. Ed-tech, hyperlocal, and food-tech are newer categories within e-commerce showing significant growth (*Retail Industry in India*, 2021).

Government of India programs like Digital India, make in India, startup India, skill India, and the national retail policy are going to increase internet usage further (*E-commerce in India: Industry Overview, Market Size & Growth*, 2021). Foreign direct investment and investment by private players have increased substantially to further the cause of e-commerce growth in India. Retail companies have also put in efforts to increase sales. The online reviews available on the website (Ullal et al., 2021), and 'deal of the day' (Nigam et al., 2020) have influenced sales.

Customer demography plays an important role in retail e-commerce. Thirty-four (maximum) percent of internet users in India are in the age range of 20 to 29 years and twenty percent are in the age range of 30 to 39 years (Keelery, 2021). Usually, online buyers are more affluent compared to offline buyers (Rajaretnam & N. Sheth, 2017). Age and education along with service quality dimensions have been found to influence the use of e-government services (Sharma, 2015). Even the internet addition is associated with gender (Nitin Anand et al., 2018). The period of pandemic introduced some growth opportunities in e-Pharmacies, grocery, social commerce, vernacular version of the e-commerce, hyperlocal and fast delivery, and festive sales (Kakaria, 2021).

The retail e-commerce sector has its challenges. Many Indian customers are first-time buyers and demonstrate higher consumer remorse and return products (Khurana, 2013). Cash on delivery, payment gateway failure rate, internet penetration, non-standardized postal address, and smartphone usage are some of the challenges (Khurana, 2013).In an emerging market like India, the major focus remains on extending the market and ensuring growth. Therefore, product return in the e-commerce scenario gets scant attention. A significant observation is that compared to the other seventeen countries where it operates, the product returns for Amazon are more in India, at around 30 percent of the total sales thus, indicating a product as well as country-specific context (Variyar, 2018).

Product return is a part of consumer behavior and returns management is a part of order fulfillment (Nguyen et al., 2018). A product return is a lost sale that reduces cash, profits, and margins. Returns involve logistics, additional inspection, re-stocking, damage to the product, markdowns, and stock-out expenses. Ironically, the product returns have increased with the improvement of overall quality (Lee, 2015). The working capital requirement increases to manage returns. The point of return is described as a 'moment of truth' for customer service. The intention to purchase and actually order a product is the antecedent of the return decision. Thus, the intensity of the product return decision has to be more than the intensity of the decision to retain the product to result in a return. Antecedents of the return decision include factors up to purchase and subsequent post-purchase experience. A substantial mismatch between expectation and perceived or realized benefits is likely to trigger a return. Expectedly, individual and contextual factors shape the customer's purchase and post-purchase experience.

Customer's decision to return triggers activities related to return logistics. Product returns penalize associated supply chain agents differently. E-commerce aggregators bear a penalty if the return is due to dissatisfaction. Courier companies bear a penalty if the return is due to damage in transit. Given the higher number of factors, and their interactions involved in the design and operations of an efficient forward as well as reverse supply chain becomes challenging (Salema et al., 2010). The reverse logistics supply chain has a higher level of uncertainty compared to forward logistics (Barker & Zabinsky, 2008). However, the impact of the specific factors related to a country and context on returns is not adequately investigated. It is known that the returns are influenced by exchange policies (S. S. Kar & Sahoo, 2009). While the style and design influence apparel purchase (Kumar & Kanchan, 2019), the return in apparel cases was because of imperfect size, improper fabric quality, and issues related to color (Misra & Arivazhagan, 2017). An estimate indicated that INR 87 million was spent on handling return logistics costs only for the fashion products category in India (Bansal, 2018). The cost incurred in reverse logistics is also substantially higher than forward logistics (Ganguly, 2016). Thus, understanding the factors influencing product returns becomes important.

The need to study product return behavior assumes significance considering its impact on the profitability of the organization, reverse supply chain demands, and the huge variations in product returns observed in different markets. Further, the need to understand the individual product return behavior has been emphasized in extant research (Petersen & Kumar, 2009). Also, the importance of studying the overall product return behavior is called upon by different studies (Seo et al., 2016). Researchers have also indicated that product return is an 'evolving phenomenon' impacts consumer behaviors and thus, merits further investigation (Saarijärvi et al., 2017).

Emerging practices related to online purchases and returns are likely to influence the levels of return as well. For example, buy online and return in store (BORIS), renting rather than buying, home-try programs, and offering curated choices to customers are expected to influence returns (B. Kar et al., 2022). Additional factors include the return policy, dynamic pricing, website design, inventory visibility, fraudulent intentions, information-seeking behavior, post-purchase dissonance, and customers' sensitivity and sense of empowerment to return (B. Kar et al., 2022).

This study assumes significance since Amazon experiences the highest level (30% of sales) of product return in India, compared to any other market where it operates. Secondly, based on the purposive literature review, the demography factors are more plausible independent variables influencing product returns and thus merits investigation. We also considered a few other factors associated with the purchase process, as discussed in the instrument section. We considered the following specific research objectives (a) To identify if the demography factors (age, gender, profession, annual family income, personal expenditure per month (INR), buy for, payment method, purchase frequency per month, spending per month for online purchases (INR), search intensity) have any significant relationship with return frequency, (b) To identify if product categories have a significant association with product return frequency, (c) To find if these factors in combination predict the return frequency.

The introduction section discusses the importance and the growth of e-commerce in India; the growth in the concomitant possibility of product return in an online purchase scenario and the need for research in this area. The literature review section identifies the return characteristics of consumers and their relationship with demographic characteristics. In section 3, the methodology applicable to this research has been discussed. The rationale for an online survey-based methodology, descriptive statistics, chi-square, and the multinomial logistics regression techniques have been discussed. The results and discussion section notes and deliberates different outcomes of the study. Section 5 identifies different managerial implications from this study. Finally, section 6 concludes with the future scope and limitations of the study.

2. LITERATURE REVIEW

Purchase is the antecedent to purchase return. Demography as an independent factor is related to the consumption of products and services. In this section, we limit our discussion to demographic variables and their relationship with product returns. Purchase over the internet significantly depends on the demographic variables which can be used to profiling and segmenting customers (Akhter, 2003). Demographic segmentation of customers is an established practice to understand differences in purchase intention. Education, income, and gender influence purchase attitudes as well as intention (Wang et al., 2019). The influence of demographic variables on purchase intention is related to product categories as well. In the case of online purchase of health food demographic variables did not show any significant effect (Hasanov & Khalid, 2015) but in the case of luxury brands the age, gender, income, education, and the perceived social status influenced purchase intention (Park et al., 2021). Online shopping intention for clothing, jewelry, or accessories involves demography factors among others (Young Kim & Kim, 2004). Some characteristics depend on demography which subsequently influences consumption behavior. For example, the risk perception or tech-savviness has been associated with age, particularly for generation Y (Nawi et al., 2019). Mobile commerce decisions also are predictable based on age, and social class among other factors (Bigne et al., 2005). Online users' age influence the perceived ease of purchasing and gender influence perceived usefulness (Law & Ng, 2016). Socio-demographic factors also influence e-grocery shopping (Dominici et al., 2021).

Extending the logic, product return as a part of consumption behavior can also be influenced by demography. Younger customers are expected to return more than older customers (Zhou et al., 2018). Age also was found to influence average product return frequency (Makkonen et al., 2021). Another study did not report any relationship between age and product return (Huang, 2015). The relationship of age with product return is equivocal.

Gender has a relationship with average product return frequency (Makkonen et al., 2021). A study found males to have higher levels of product dissatisfaction and emotional dissonance than females but males did not cause higher rates of product returns (Powers & Jack, 2015). The significant relationship between cognitive dissonance and product return was only for females, product dissonance was more for females (Huang, 2015). and Gender and Females consider return labels significantly more important (Ulbrich et al., 2010). Product return reasons were found to be affected by only gender and average product return frequency (Makkonen et al., 2021)

Some identified factors leading to purchase return can be linked to the demography. The intention to return products depends on price perception (Jiang & Rosenbloom, 2005). The average online shopping frequency and payment method preference affect average product return frequency (Makkonen et al., 2021).

While there are many research findings and an intuitive understanding that the purchase decisions have a significant relationship with demography, it is less intuitive for product return decisions. Particularly, if the purchase is through online mode. A customer undertakes various steps starting from information search, comparing reviews, getting the influencer opinion, comparing prices, placing an order, paying for the product, receive, and experience the product before arriving at the return decision. One or more factors can influence the return. A return decision can be triggered due to a mismatch of expectation and actual at any particular stage or combination of stages.

Researchers have categorized returners as heavy, medium, light, and occasional, based on their buying experience, perceived risk, and return frequency. Each category has differences in their initial shopping motivations, group-specific reasons, and spending patterns. Thus, the returners are not an amorphous category (Foscht et al., 2013). Various demographic groups were found to have significant differences in their return behavior (Nikhila Anand, 2021). Like demand sensitivity, the customers are likely to have return sensitivity (Li et al., 2013). Few others have proposed that the customers are likely to have return sensitivity similar to the demand sensitivity, (Li et al., 2013). Purchase of products online and returns in emerging markets have been argued to be a research need, seeking nuanced understanding (B. Kar et al., 2022).

3. METHODOLOGY

An online survey-based methodology was considered appropriate for this study. A list of mail ids was prepared through personal contacts and the google form questionnaire was sent to those mail ids requesting a response. Further, they were requested to send the questionnaire to their contacts. It was also shared on different social media platforms. A total of 619 responses could be collected. The responses were anonymous.

The instrument included demography information (age, gender, profession, approximate annual family income, personal average monthly expense). Since the product can have a different user than the buyer, we included a question 'buy for (self, family, others). The usual mode of payment included cash on delivery (COD), credit card, net Banking, E-wallet/ UPI, and debit card. We included a question on the frequency of purchases per month. The spending per month on online purchases and the usual frequency of return for such purchases were included in the questionnaire.

Descriptive statistics were used to understand the distribution of the responses. The chi-square test was used to understand the relationship between various non-parametric factors, and return frequency classified as 'rarely', 'few times', and 'often'. Since, the outcome variable was categorical, multinomial logistics regression was considered suitable for the analysis. The return frequency category was taken as the dependent variable and multinomial logistics regression was run to understand the return frequency as the function of demographic characteristics. The return frequency category 'rarely' was used as the reference group for the regression.

4. RESULTS

Male constituted 60.9 percent of the sample. Most of the individuals (83.5 percent) indicated searching in detail while purchasing the product, the rest indicated their search effort as 'as required." The purchase frequency response per month indicated that 38.9 percent purchase 0 to 1 times, 43.3 percent buy 2-3 times, 9.2 percent buy 4-5 times, and 8.6 percent of the respondents buy more than 5 times within a month. The detailed frequency distribution of age, profession, payment mode and spending per month on online purchases is given in table 1. Table 2 has the distribution information of family income, personal expenditure per month, and return frequency.

Table 1. Age, Profession, Payment mode, spending

Age N (%)	~25	26-36	37-47	48-58	59 & more
	405 (65.4%)	114 (18.4%)	43 (6.9%)	49 (7.9%)	8 (1.3%)
Profession N (%)	Student	Working Pvt.	Working Govt.	Not Working	Business
	387 (62.5%)	150 (24.2%)	48 (7.8%)	28 (4.5%)	6 (1.0%)
Payment Mode N (%)	COD	Credit Card	Net Banking	E-Wallet/ UPI	Debit Card
	244 (39.4%)	39 (6.3%)	110 (17.8%)	90 (14.5%)	136 (22.0%)
Spending Per Month for online purchase N (%)	0-500	500-1000	1000-2500	2500-5000	>5000
	90 (14.5%)	189 (30.5%)	201 (32.5%)	100 (16.2%)	39 (6.3%)

Table 1 indicates that 39.4 percent (maximum) of the purchases are on cash in delivery mode, while the use of credit cards for online purchases is only 6.3 percent. The sample includes 62.4 percent young population (up to 25 years of age).

Table 2 indicates that the individuals primarily purchase online for themselves (66.2 percent. Maximum (72 percent) indicate that they return products only a few times.

Table 3 presents the chi-square test results of various demography variables and search intensity with return frequency.

Table 3 indicates that age, gender, profession, and search intensity are significantly related to return frequency (p<.01). The personal expenditure per month (p=.071), and buy for (p=.053) were significant at p<.1 level. The annual family income and spending per month on online purchases did not indicate a significant relationship with return frequency.

Table 4 presents the relationship of return frequency with different categories of items purchased online.

'Textile/ Dresses' and 'Household Goods' indicate a significant (p<.01) relationship with return frequency. The fashion jewelry category shows a significant relationship at p<.1. Prior research also indicates that the cost and types in the apparel product category were associated with product returns (Kincade et al., 1998) and in general, the higher average price and variety at a subcategory level tend to increase the return probability (Samorani et al., 2019).

To understand the aggregate impact of various demographic variables consisting of nominal and ordinal variables, the multinomial logistics regression was conducted (table 5, 6, and 7). The dependent

Table 2. Family income, personal expenditure, return frequency

Annual Family Income In (00,000 INR) N (%)	0-5L	6-10	>10
	198 (32.0%)	194 (31.3%)	227 (36.7%)
Personal Expenditure (Month) N (%)	0-5000	5001-10000	>10000
	251 (40.5%)	167 (27.0%)	201 (32.5%)
Primarily Buy For N (%)	Self	Family	Others
	410 (66.2%)	163 (26.3%)	46 (7.4%)
Return Frequency N (%)	Rarely	Few Times	Often
	87 (14.1%)	446 (72.1%)	86 (13.9%)

Table 3. Relationship between the demography and return frequency

	Category	Rarely	Few Times	Often	Total	Chi-Square
Age	~25	46 (7.4)	299 (48.3)	60 (9.7)	405 (65.4)	χ^2= 26.268, df= 8, p= .001
	26-36	16 (2.6)	85 (13.7)	13 (2.1)	114 (18.4)	
	37-47	6 (1)	31 (5)	6 (1)	43 (6.9)	
	48-58	16 (2.6)	29 (4.7)	4 (0.6)	49 (7.9)	
	> = 59	3 (0.5)	2 (0.3)	3 (0.5)	8 (1.3)	
	Total	87 (14.1)	446 (72.1)	86 (13.9)	619 (100)	
Gender	M	61 (9.9)	255 (41.2)	61 (9.9)	377 (60.9)	χ^2= 9.335, df = 2, p= .009
	F	26 (4.2)	191 (30.9)	25 (4)	242 (39.1)	
	Total	87 (14.1)	446 (72.1)	86 (13.9)	619 (100)	
Profession	Student	41 (6.6)	299 (48.3)	47 (7.6)	387 (62.5)	χ^2= 31.020, df = 8, p= .000
	Working Pvt	21 (3.4)	105 (17)	24 (3.9)	150 (24.2)	
	Working Govt.	17 (2.7)	23 (3.7)	8 (1.3)	48 (7.8)	
	Not Working	6 (1)	16 (2.6)	6 (1)	28 (4.5)	
	Business	2 (0.3)	3 (0.5)	1 (0.2)	6 (1)	
	Total	87 (14.1)	446 (72.1)	86 (13.9)	619 (100)	
Annual Family Income (INR in 100, 000)	0-5	26 (4.2)	135 (21.8)	37 (6)	198 (32)	χ^2= 6.359, df = 4, p= .174
	5-10	31 (5)	142 (22.9)	21 (3.4)	194 (31.3)	
	>10	30 (4.8)	169 (27.3)	28 (4.5)	227 (36.7)	
	Total	87 (14.1)	446 (72.1)	86 (13.9)	619 (100)	
Personal Expenditure per month (INR)	0-5000	27 (4.4)	196 (31.7)	28 (4.5)	251 (40.5)	χ^2= 8.628, df = 4, p= .071
	5001-10000	24 (3.9)	116 (18.7)	27 (4.4)	167 (27)	
	>10000	36 (5.8)	134 (21.6)	31 (5)	201 (32.5)	
	Total	87 (14.1)	446 (72.1)	86 (13.9)	619 (100)	
Buy For	Self	49 (7.9)	305 (49.3)	56 (9)	410 (66.2)	χ^2= 9.328, df = 4, p= .053
	Family	30 (4.8)	114 (18.4)	19 (3.1)	163 (26.3)	
	Others	8 (1.3)	27 (4.4)	11 (1.8)	46 (7.4)	
	Total	87 (14.1)	446 (72.1)	86 (13.9)	619 (100)	
Pay Through	COD	27 (4.4)	184 (29.7)	33 (5.3)	244 (39.4)	χ^2= 11.299, df = 8, p= .185
	Credit Card	7 (1.1)	29 (4.7)	3 (0.5)	39 (6.3)	
	Net Banking	21 (3.4)	69 (11.1)	20 (3.2)	110 (17.8)	
	E-Wallet/ UPI	10 (1.6)	71 (11.5)	9 (1.5)	90 (14.5)	
	Debit Card	22 (3.6)	93 (15)	21 (3.4)	136 (22)	
	Total	87 (14.1)	446 (72.1)	86 (13.9)	619 (100)	
Purchase Frequency per Month	0-1	42 (6.8)	165 (26.7)	34 (5.5)	241 (38.9)	χ^2= 10.197, df = 6, p= .117
	2-3	35 (5.7)	195 (31.5)	38 (6.1)	268 (43.3)	
	4-5	9 (1.5)	40 (6.5)	8 (1.3)	57 (9.2)	
	>5	1 (0.2)	46 (7.4)	6 (1)	53 (8.6)	
	Total	87 (14.1)	446 (72.1)	86 (13.9)	619 (100)	
Spending Per Month for online purchases (INR)	0-500	17 (2.7)	57 (9.2)	16 (2.6)	90 (14.5)	χ^2= 8.799, df = 8, p= .360
	500-1000	24 (3.9)	139 (22.5)	26 (4.2)	189 (30.5)	
	1000-2500	30 (4.8)	142 (22.9)	29 (4.7)	201 (32.5)	
	2500-5000	13 (2.1)	79 (12.8)	8 (1.3)	100 (16.2)	
	>5000	3 (0.5)	29 (4.7)	7 (1.1)	39 (6.3)	
	Total	87 (14.1)	446 (72.1)	86 (13.9)	619 (100)	
Search Intensity	As Required	18 (2.9)	60 (9.7)	24 (3.9)	102 (16.5)	χ^2= 12.249, df = 2, p= .002
	Detailed	69 (11.1)	386 (62.4)	62 (10)	517 (83.5)	
	Total	87 (14.1)	446 (72.1)	86 (13.9)	619 (100)	

Note: Number in bracket indicates percentage from the total, df= degrees of freedom, p= probability

variable was the frequency of return (rarely, few times, and often) whereas, independent variables were age, gender, profession, annual family income, personal expense per month, buy for, pay through, pur-

Table 4. Product Category and return frequency

		Return Frequency				
		Rarely	**Few Times**	**Often**	**Total**	**Chi-Square**
Books	No	48 (7.8%)	240 (38.8%)	51 (8.2%)	339 (54.8%)	χ^2= .884, df= 2, p= .643
	Yes	39 (6.3%)	206 (33.3%)	35 (5.7%)	280 (45.2%)	
	Total	87 (14.1%)	446 (72.1%)	86 (13.9%)	619 (100.0%)	
Electronics Items/ accessories	No	28 (4.5%)	112 (18.1%)	25 (4.0%)	165 (26.7%)	χ^2= 2.160, df= 2, p= .340
	Yes	59 (9.5%)	334 (54.0%)	61 (9.9%)	454 (73.3%)	
	Total	87 (14.1%)	446 (72.1%)	86 (13.9%)	619 (100.0%)	
Textiles / Dresses	No	45 (7.3%)	126 (20.4%)	36 (5.8%)	207 (33.4%)	χ^2= 21.202, df= 2, p= .000
	Yes	42 (6.8%)	320 (51.7%)	50 (8.1%)	412 (66.6%)	
	Total	87 (14.1%)	446 (72.1%)	86 (13.9%)	619 (100.0%)	
Toys	No	77 (12.4%)	401 (64.8%)	77 (12.4%)	555 (89.7%)	χ^2=.157, df= 2, p= .925
	Yes	10 (1.6%)	45 (7.3%)	9 (1.5%)	64 (10.3%)	
	Total	87 (14.1%)	446 (72.1%)	86 (13.9%)	619 (100.0%)	
Fashion Jewelry	No	75 (12.1%)	342 (55.3%)	71 (11.5%)	488 (78.8%)	χ^2= 4.788, df= 2, p= .091
	Yes	12 (1.9%)	104 (16.8%)	15 (2.4%)	131 (21.0%)	
	Total	87 (14.1%)	446 (72.1%)	86 (13.9%)	619 (100.0%)	
Sports or health products	No	64 (10.3%)	315 (50.9%)	59 (9.5%)	438 (70.8%)	χ^2= .527, df= 2, p= .768
	Yes	23 (3.7%)	131 (21.2%)	27 (4.4%)	181 (29.2%)	
	Total	87 (14.1%)	446 (72.1%)	86 (13.9%)	619 (100.0%)	
Automobile accessories	No	79 (12.8%)	382 (61.7%)	76 (12.3%)	537 (86.8%)	χ^2= 1.911, df= 2, p= .385
	Yes	8 (1.3%)	64 (10.3%)	10 (1.6%)	82 (13.2%)	
	Total	87 (14.1%)	446 (72.1%)	86 (13.9%)	619 (100.0%)	
Household Goods	No	63 (10.2%)	229 (37.0%)	56 (9.0%)	348 (56.2%)	χ^2= 16.341, df= 2, p= .000
	Yes	24 (3.9%)	217 (35.1%)	30 (4.8%)	271 (43.8%)	
	Total	87 (14.1%)	446 (72.1%)	86 (13.9%)	619 (100.0%)	

chase frequency per month, spend per month for online purchases, and search intensity. The multinomial regression was run with the last category as the reference category (Details in the appendix table 7).

Table 5 indicates that the final model is significant. The goodness of fit also confirms the model fit statistics.

Table 6 indicates that age, gender, profession, and search intensity significantly predict the product return frequency. The product return frequency 'rarely return' is taken as the base for comparison with 'few times' and 'often.'

The following can be observed from the parameter estimate values (Table 7). (a) Comparing the return frequency 'few times' to 'rarely,' given other variables are held constant, the multinomial logit for other age groups is higher compared to the age group 59 or more. Compared to females, males are less likely to return (multinomial logit -0.337). The persons working in government or public sector organizations are less likely to return compared to businesspersons. An interesting observation is that compared

Table 5. Multinomial Logistics Regression Model Fit

Model Fitting Information	Model Fitting Criteria: -2 Log Likelihood Intercept Only= 934.346 Final= 825.044, Likelihood Ratio Tests (χ^2 =109.302, df=54, p=.000
Goodness-of-fit	Pearson χ^2 = 1100.267, df= 1052, p=.147 Deviance χ^2 = 794.449, df= 1052, p= 1.000
Pseudo R-Square	Cox and Snell= .162, Nagelkerke= .204, McFadden .112

to people with more than INR 10,00,000 per annum income, individuals with less family income are likely to return less frequently. A similar observation could be made for the amount spent per month on online expenses. However, if the per month individual expenses are less, individuals are more likely to return 'few times' compared to 'rarely.' Finally, if the search intensity is 'detailed' then the likelihood of returning is less (multinomial logit -0.307) when comparing return frequency 'few times' to 'rarely'

When comparing returning frequency 'rarely' to 'often' in the multinomial logit regression model almost all the age groups indicate a higher likelihood compared to the age group of 59 years or more. Males are more likely than females to return products often. Compared to businesspersons, students are less likely to return products when return frequency 'often' is compared to 'rarely'. Interestingly, in this scenario lower family income group is more likely to return products whereas the middle-income group is less likely to return product 'often.' When the per-month expense is considered, the lower-income groups are less likely to return products 'often.' Compared to the debit card users, the credit card and e-wallet users are less likely but users using the payment method of cash on delivery or net banking are more likely to return products often. The buyers are less likely to return 'often' if their purchase frequency is less (-ve multinomial logit value). Similar behavior is observed if the online spending per month is lower the product return likelihood reduces. Lastly, if the search intensity is detailed, then the possibility of return is higher when we compare the return frequency 'often' compared to the return frequency 'rarely'

Table 6. Likelihood Ratio Tests

Effect	Model Fitting Criteria	Likelihood Ratio Tests		
	-2 Log Likelihood of Reduced Model	Chi-Square	df	Sig.
Intercept	825.044[a]	.000	0	.
Age	845.124	20.080	8	.010
Gender	832.308	7.264	2	.026
Profession	842.510	17.465	8	.026
Annual Family Income	830.980	5.936	4	.204
Per Month Expense	828.657	3.613	4	.461
Buy For	827.347	2.303	4	.680
Pay Through	833.583	8.538	8	.383
Purchase Frequency Month	837.426	12.381	6	.054
Online Spend Per Month	832.912	7.868	8	.446
Search Intensity	831.499	6.455	2	.040

When the return frequency 'often' and 'few times' are compared against the return frequency of 'rarely' following interesting observations are made from the multinomial logit model. In the case of 'few times' to 'rarely' comparison, males are less likely to return a product but when 'often' to 'rarely' are compared males are more likely to return products. A similar observation is made in the case of students vis-a-vis business persons in 'few times' to 'often' compared with 'rarely' as the basis. The likelihood associated with the lowest annual family income group undergoes a change in behavior from 'few times (-ve)' to 'often (+ve)' when compared to the return frequency of 'rarely.' Similarly a reversal of behavior is observed in the case of expenses per month as well as 'buy for' variables from +ve multinomial logit value to the –ve, in the situation of return frequency 'few times' to 'often.' Compared to the payment method of debit card, the multinomial logit value changes from –ve to +ve in case of the payment method of net banking whereas the behavior is opposite when the payment method of e-wallet is considered. A detailed search for product information reduces the product return in the scenario of 'few times' to 'rarely.' However, the behavior is different when the scenario 'often' to 'rarely' is considered. Such reversal of behavior is indicative of other possible intervening variables.

5. DISCUSSION

This study reports demographic characteristics such as age, gender, and profession influence returns, item categories influence return frequency. Around 72 percent of the respondents classify themselves as returning 'few times' and 14 percent classify themselves as returning 'often'. It is important to note that such a distribution of return frequency is related to the level of return e-commerce companies actually face in India. A different level of frequency distribution can change the actual level of return in the Indian context. Younger persons are significantly more likely to return the product purchased online. There can be various possible explanations for such behavior. Technology savviness, information seeking, an inclination to experimentation, social influence, trust in a channel, and other factors related to individual personality explain young consumer's behavior. More females classify them as returning a few times but, more males classify them as returning often than females. Textile and household item categories have a significant relationship with return frequency than other categories. Item categories and the number of choices within the categories have been identified to be a factor in the product return. This study indicates those who do a 'detailed search' are less likely to return 'often.' Such a factor possibly can indicate an optimizing behavior of customers. Cash on delivery is the preferred mode of payment for online transactions in India. However, the payment methods did not show any significant relationship with the frequency of product return.

Both Chi-Square and Multinomial logistics regression indicate similar results and indicate consistency of findings in this study. This research contributes to establishing the influence of demographic characteristics on return frequency in the case of online purchases.

6. MANAGERIAL IMPLICATIONS

Customer demography influences the return behavior in the case of online purchases. Thus, the demography variables can be used as an input to design return policies of e-commerce organizations. Design of individual return policies may be cumbersome but, designing return policies based on demographic

Table 7. Parameter Estimates of Multinomial Regression

Return Frequency [a]	B	Std. Error	Wald	df	Sig.	Exp (B)	95% Confidence Interval for Exp(B)	
							Lower Bound	Upper Bound
Few Times								
Intercept	1.465	1.788	0.672	1	0.412			
[Age= up to 25]	2.344	1.327	3.119	1	0.077	10.426	0.773	140.572
[Age= 26-36]	2.825	1.309	4.656	1	0.031	16.853	1.296	219.219
[Age= 37-47]	3.461	1.363	6.445	1	0.011	31.846	2.201	460.741
[Age= 48-58]	2.499	1.301	3.686	1	0.055	12.165	0.949	155.921
[Age= 59 and more]	0[b]			0				
[Gender= Male]	-0.337	0.293	1.327	1	0.249	0.714	0.402	1.267
[Gender= Female]	0[b]			0				
[Profession= Student]	1.589	1.088	2.132	1	0.144	4.901	0.580	41.374
[Profession= Work Pvt.]	1.157	1.054	1.205	1	0.272	3.181	0.403	25.125
[Profession= Work Govt.]	-0.141	1.082	0.017	1	0.897	0.869	0.104	7.242
[Profession= Not Working]	0.470	1.169	0.162	1	0.687	1.601	0.162	15.812
[Profession= Business]	0[b]			0				
[Annual Family Income= 0-5L]	-0.334	0.347	0.925	1	0.336	0.716	0.363	1.414
[Annual Family Income= 6-10L]	-0.473	0.327	2.083	1	0.149	0.623	0.328	1.184
[Annual Family Income = More than 10L]	0[b]			0				
[Per Month Expense= 0-5K]	0.448	0.379	1.396	1	0.237	1.566	0.744	3.294
[Per Month Expense =5-10K]	0.033	0.353	0.009	1	0.925	1.034	0.518	2.063
[Per Month Expense = >10K]	0[b]			0				
[Buy For= Self]	0.160	0.506	0.100	1	0.751	1.174	0.436	3.161
[Buy For= Family]	0.007	0.525	0.000	1	0.990	1.007	0.360	2.815
[Buy For= Others]	0[b]			0				
[Pay Through= COD]	0.460	0.339	1.835	1	0.176	1.583	0.814	3.079
[Pay Through= Credit Card]	-0.205	0.554	0.137	1	0.711	0.814	0.275	2.414
[Pay Through= Net Banking]	-0.221	0.382	0.335	1	0.563	0.802	0.380	1.694
[Pay Through= E-Wallet]	0.288	0.440	0.430	1	0.512	1.334	0.564	3.158
[Pay Through= Debit Card]	0[b]			0				
[Purchase Frequency Month=0-1]	-2.823	1.175	5.769	1	0.016	0.059	0.006	0.595
[Purchase Frequency Month =2-3]	-2.429	1.165	4.345	1	0.037	0.088	0.009	0.865
[Purchase Frequency Month =4-5]	-2.616	1.195	4.794	1	0.029	0.073	0.007	0.760
[Purchase Frequency Month = '>5']	0[b]			0				
[Spend Per Month=0-500]	-1.283	0.854	2.260	1	0.133	0.277	0.052	1.477
[Spend Per Month =500-1000]	-0.877	0.815	1.159	1	0.282	0.416	0.084	2.054
[Spend Per Month =1000-2500]	-1.068	0.786	1.845	1	0.174	0.344	0.074	1.605
[Spend Per Month =2500-5000]	-0.650	0.802	0.656	1	0.418	0.522	0.108	2.516
[Spend Per Month = More than 5000]	0[b]			0				
[Search Intensity= detailed]	-0.307	0.334	0.844	1	0.358	0.736	0.383	1.416
[Search Intensity=As required]	0[b]			0				
Often								
Intercept	1.558	1.970	0.625	1	0.429			
[Age= up to 25]	1.742	1.274	1.870	1	0.171	5.707	0.470	69.276
[Age= 26-36]	1.242	1.254	0.981	1	0.322	3.461	0.297	40.399
[Age= 37-47]	1.569	1.355	1.341	1	0.247	4.804	0.337	68.421
[Age= 48-58]	-0.007	1.307	0.000	1	0.996	0.993	0.077	12.878
[Age= 59 and more]	0[b]			0				
[Gender= Male]	0.406	0.378	1.155	1	0.282	1.502	0.716	3.151
[Gender= Female]	0[b]			0				
[Profession= Student]	-0.139	1.402	0.010	1	0.921	0.871	0.056	13.591
[Profession= Work Pvt.]	0.251	1.373	0.033	1	0.855	1.285	0.087	18.941
[Profession= Work Govt.]	-0.323	1.412	0.052	1	0.819	0.724	0.045	11.533
[Profession= Not Working]	0.305	1.496	0.042	1	0.838	1.357	0.072	25.485
[Profession= Business]	0[b]			0				
[Annual Family Income= 0-5L]	0.156	0.426	0.134	1	0.714	1.169	0.507	2.696
[Annual Family Income= 6-10L]	-0.528	0.432	1.490	1	0.222	0.590	0.253	1.376
[Annual Family Income = More than 10L]	0[b]			0				
[Per Month Expense= 0-5K]	-0.069	0.487	0.020	1	0.888	0.934	0.359	2.425
[Per Month Expense =5-10K]	-0.060	0.443	0.019	1	0.891	0.941	0.395	2.241
[Per Month Expense = >10K]	0[b]			0				
[Buy For= Self]	-0.438	0.592	0.546	1	0.460	0.645	0.202	2.061
[Buy For= Family]	-0.698	0.632	1.217	1	0.270	0.498	0.144	1.719

contintinued on following page

Table 7. Continued

Return Frequency [a]	B	Std. Error	Wald	df	Sig.	Exp (B)	95% Confidence Interval for Exp(B)	
							Lower Bound	Upper Bound
[Buy For= Others]	0[b]			0				
[Pay Through= COD]	0.221	0.428	0.266	1	0.606	1.247	0.539	2.885
[Pay Through= Credit Card]	-0.891	0.819	1.184	1	0.277	0.410	0.082	2.042
[Pay Through= Net Banking]	0.020	0.477	0.002	1	0.966	1.021	0.400	2.602
[Pay Through= E-Wallet]	-0.349	0.580	0.362	1	0.547	0.705	0.226	2.199
[Pay Through= Debit Card]	0[b]			0				
[Purchase Frequency Month=0-1]	-2.232	1.255	3.162	1	0.075	0.107	0.009	1.256
[Purchase Frequency Month =2-3]	-1.722	1.241	1.927	1	0.165	0.179	0.016	2.033
[Purchase Frequency Month =4-5]	-1.849	1.280	2.085	1	0.149	0.157	0.013	1.936
[Purchase Frequency Month = '>5']	0[b]			0				
[Spend Per Month=0-500]	-0.706	0.974	0.525	1	0.469	0.494	0.073	3.332
[Spend Per Month =500-1000]	-0.750	0.918	0.668	1	0.414	0.473	0.078	2.854
[Spend Per Month =1000-2500]	-0.955	0.884	1.167	1	0.280	0.385	0.068	2.177
[Spend Per Month =2500-5000]	-1.276	0.944	1.825	1	0.177	0.279	0.044	1.777
[Spend Per Month = More than 5000]	0[b]			0				
[Search Intensity= detailed]	0.476	0.392	1.473	1	0.225	1.609	0.746	3.469
[Search Intensity=As required]	0[b]			0				

a. The reference category is: Rarely.
b. This parameter is set to zero because it is redundant.

factors will help organisation to have a manageable number of return policies. The return policies can focus on maximising the repurchase intention by having flexible return policies or rigid policies to minimise returns. However, driving optimality can take demographic characteristics as an input. Since the information search behavior influences the return frequency, organisations need to provide extensive information at various stages of customer information seeking.

Demography also helps in the positioning strategies of companies (Chatterjee, 2013). Thus, companies can consider marketing communication strategies consistent with demography and associated return behavior.

6. CONCLUSION

This study was conducted in a market where an established e-commerce company experiences the largest level of product returns compared to any other market. Assuming a standardized operation practice, the customer behavior is one of the plausible reasons for such a large-scale product return in the case of online purchases. Few interesting observations could be made from this study. Cash on delivery is the predominant payment method, followed by debit cards, net banking, and e-wallets, and the credit card is the least used method of payment in online purchases. Only 14 percent of the respondents classify themselves as heavy returners. A cross-country comparison can help to identify if such distribution is peculiar to India. The total return can be a function of identified weights multiplied by the return frequency distribution (Total Return= $\sum$RFi*wi, where RFi is the return frequency distribution of category i, and w is the corresponding weight). This could classify different fractions contributed by different returners' categories. Young individuals (less than equal to 25 years of age) constitute the highest among all returners' types and constitute more than 50% of people who return products often. The significant relationship of the search intensity with return frequency indicates the influence of factors other than demographic factors on product return. The industry report also indicates about fifty percent of the returns as fraudulent and the rate of return is different for different categories of products (*Consumer Returns in the Retail Industry*, 2018). There have been efforts to capture a comprehensive online post-purchase customer experience (OPPCE) scale that influences customer satisfaction identified dimensions as experiences with order fulfillment, ease of return, and responsiveness of customers which are most important (Pham & Ahammad, 2017). Such research directions indicate a return as a broader and more complex phenomenon than only being dependent on demographic factors. Research also has indicated that the guilt and post-purchase regrets triggers return decision, indicating a cognitive-affective interplay (Nikhila Anand, 2021).

Data is collected during the COVID-19 period, with supply chain issues and disruptions which could have impacted the response. Limitations associated with internet-based survey research are inherent in this research as well. The mode of data collection through an internet-based questionnaire implied that the respondents are internet savvy, and can understand questions in the English language, at the same time, this method introduced an unintended bias against the other group. However, it is to be noted that e-commerce sites are predominantly in the English language. E-commerce vendors have started using different vernacular languages for their sites. The responses to the questionnaire could also be influenced by recency-effect. The categorical scale used for return frequency was subjective in nature and can be quantified in future studies. Variations in scales and geographies in future studies are likely to bring significant insights to understanding of the return behavior.

An episodic capture of the actual return event is likely to offer deeper insights into the behavioral aspects which could not be gathered through a survey response. A comparative study of e-commerce company-specific returns are likely to identify if the influence of demographic characteristics is stable across companies. However, this study will be a strong guideline for online market leaders to formulate a sound policy of product return, consistent with consumer characteristics.

REFERENCES

Akhter, S. H. (2003). Digital divide and purchase intention: Why demographic psychology matters. *Journal of Economic Psychology*, *24*(3), 321–327. doi:10.1016/S0167-4870(02)00171-X

Anand, N. (2021). Effects of Demography on Opportunistic Product Return Behaviors in E-Commerce. *Honors Undergraduate Theses 924*. https://stars.library.ucf.edu/honorstheses/924

Anand, N., Jain, P. A., Prabhu, S., Thomas, C., Bhat, A., Prathyusha, P. V., Bhat, S. U., Young, K., & Cherian, A. V. (2018). Internet Use Patterns, Internet Addiction, and Psychological Distress Among Engineering University Students: A Study from India. *Indian Journal of Psychological Medicine*, *40*(5), 458–467. doi:10.4103/IJPSYM.IJPSYM_135_18 PMID:30275622

Bansal, V. (2018). *Product Returns: Fashion e-comm firms like Flipkart, Myntra uncover fake product returns, Technology News, ETtech*. https://tech.economictimes.indiatimes.com/news/internet/fashion-e-comm-firms-like-flipkart-myntra-uncover-fake-product-returns/62533671

Barker, T. J., & Zabinsky, Z. B. (2008). Reverse logistics network design: A conceptual framework for decision making. *International Journal of Sustainable Engineering*, *1*(4), 250–260. doi:10.1080/19397030802591196

Bigne, E., Ruiz, C., & Sanz, S. (2005). The Impact of Internet User Shopping Patterns and Demographics on Consumer Mobile Buying Behaviour. *Journal of Electronic Commerce Research*, *6*(3), 193–209. www.amena.es

Chatterjee, S. (2013). A Study of Demographic Variables Affecting Consumer Buying Behaviour with Reference to Synthetic Detergents. *Indian Journal of Marketing*, *43*(5), 58–63. doi:10.17010/ijom/2013/v43/i5/36387

Consumer Returns in the Retail Industry. (2018). https://appriss.com/retail/wp-content/uploads/sites/4/2018/12/AR3018_2018-Customer-Returns-in-the-Retail-Industry_Digital.pdf

Dominici, A., Boncinelli, F., Gerini, F., & Marone, E. (2021). Determinants of online food purchasing: The impact of socio-demographic and situational factors. *Journal of Retailing and Consumer Services*, *60*, 102473. doi:10.1016/j.jretconser.2021.102473

E-commerce in India: Industry Overview, Market Size & Growth. (2021, December 17). *IBEF*. https://www.ibef.org/industry/ecommerce.aspx

Foscht, T., Ernstreiter, K., Maloles, C. III, Sinha, I., & Swoboda, B. (2013). Retaining or returning?: Some insights for a better understanding of return behaviour. *International Journal of Retail & Distribution Management*, *41*(2), 113–134. doi:10.1108/09590551311304310

Ganguly, P. (2016). *E-commerce: E-commerce players in India bring down product returns this festive season, Technology News, ETtech*. https://tech.economictimes.indiatimes.com/news/internet/e-commerce-players-in-india-bring-down-product-returns-this-festive-season/55553507

Hasanov, J., & Khalid, H. (2015). The Impact of Website Quality on Online Purchase Intention of Organic Food in Malaysia: A WebQual Model Approach. *Procedia Computer Science*, *72*, 382–389. doi:10.1016/j.procs.2015.12.153

Huang, L. (2015). *The impact of gender, age, price and cognitive dissonance on the e-commerce apparel product returns*. University of Groningen. Faculty of Economics and Business. https://feb.studenttheses.ub.rug.nl/14622/1/Thesis_s2659883.pdf

Indian E-commerce Industry Analysis. (2021). https://www.ibef.org/industry/ecommerce-presentation

Jiang, P., & Rosenbloom, B. (2005). Customer intention to return online: Price perception, attribute-level performance, and satisfaction unfolding over time. *European Journal of Marketing*, *39*(1–2), 150–174. doi:10.1108/03090560510572061

Kakaria, T. C. (2021, December 31). An overview of E-commerce in 2021: Growth, hits, and misses. *Times of India*. https://timesofindia.indiatimes.com/blogs/voices/an-overview-of-e-commerce-in-2021-growth-hits-and-misses/

Kar, B., Tripathy, A., & Pathak, M. D. (2022). What Causes Product Returns in Online Purchases? A Review and Research Agenda. *Prabandhan: Indian Journal of Management*, *15*(4), 46–62. doi:10.17010/pijom/2022/v15i4/162837

Kar, S. S., & Sahoo, S. K. (2009). Organised Retailing in India: Issues and Challenges. *Indian Journal of Marketing*, *39*(11), 10–14.

Keelery, S. (2021). *India - internet users by age group 2020*. https://www.statista.com/statistics/751005/india-share-of-internet-users-by-age-group/

Khurana, A. (2013, December 23). *8 Challenges for ecommerce in India*. Pitneybowes. https://www.pitneybowes.com/us/blog/8-challenges-ecommerce-india.html

Kincade, D. H., Giddings, V. L., & Chen-Yu, H. J. (1998). Impact of product-specific variables on consumers' post-consumption behaviour for apparel products: USA. *Journal of Consumer Studies & Home Economics*, *22*(2), 81–90. doi:10.1111/j.1470-6431.1998.tb00718.x

Kumar, P., & Kanchan. (2019). Purchasing Criteria for Apparels among Indian Consumers. *Indian Journal of Marketing*, *49*(1), 48–60. doi:10.17010/ijom/2019/v49/i1/140606

Law, M., & Ng, M. (2016). *Age and gender differences: Understanding mature online users with the online purchase intention model*. doi:10.1080/21639159.2016.1174540

Lee, D. H. (2015). An Alternative Explanation of Consumer Product Returns from the Postpurchase Dissonance and Ecological Marketing Perspectives. *Psychology and Marketing*, *32*(1), 49–64. doi:10.1002/mar.20757

Li, Y., Xu, L., & Li, D. (2013). Examining relationships between the return policy, product quality, and pricing strategy in online direct selling. *International Journal of Production Economics*, *144*(2), 451–460. doi:10.1016/j.ijpe.2013.03.013

Makkonen, M., Frank, L., & Kemppainen, T. (2021). The Effects of Consumer Demographics and Payment Method Preference on Product Return Frequency and Reasons in Online Shopping. In A. Pucihar, M. Kljajic Borstnar, R. Bons, H. Cripps, A. Sheombar, & D. Vidmar (Eds.), *Digital Support from Crisis to Progressive Change* (pp. 567–580). University of Maribor. doi:10.18690/978-961-286-385-9.2

Misra, S., & Arivazhagan, D. (2017). Application of Design Thinking Techniques in Marketing of Fashion Apparel E - Commerce. *Indian Journal of Marketing*, *47*(8), 18–30. doi:10.17010/ijom/2017/v47/i8/117430

Nawi, N. C., Mamun, A. Al, Hamsani, N. H. B., & Muhayiddin, M. N. (2019). Effect of Consumer Demographics and Risk Factors on Online Purchase Behaviour in Malaysia. *Societies, 9*(1), 10. doi:10.3390/soc9010010

Nguyen, D. H., de Leeuw, S., & Dullaert, W. E. H. (2018). Consumer Behaviour and Order Fulfilment in Online Retailing: A Systematic Review. *International Journal of Management Reviews*, *20*(2), 255–276. doi:10.1111/ijmr.12129

Nigam, A., Dewani, P. P., & Behl, A. (2020). Exploring Deal of the Day: An e-commerce strategy. *Benchmarking*, *27*(10), 2807–2830. doi:10.1108/BIJ-03-2020-0129

Park, J., Hyun, H., & Thavisay, T. (2021). A study of antecedents and outcomes of social media WOM towards luxury brand purchase intention. *Journal of Retailing and Consumer Services*, *58*, 102272. doi:10.1016/j.jretconser.2020.102272

Petersen, J. A., & Kumar, V. (2009). Are Product Returns a Necessary Evil? Antecedents and Consequences. *Journal of Marketing*, *73*(3), 35–51. doi:10.1509/jmkg.73.3.035

Pham, T. S. H., & Ahammad, M. F. (2017). Antecedents and consequences of online customer satisfaction: A holistic process perspective. *Technological Forecasting and Social Change*, *124*, 332–342. doi:10.1016/j.techfore.2017.04.003

Powers, T. L., & Jack, E. P. (2015). Understanding the causes of retail product returns. *International Journal of Retail & Distribution Management*, *43*(12), 1182–1202. doi:10.1108/IJRDM-02-2014-0023

Rajaretnam, J., & Sheth, N. J. (2017). *A Multi-Stage Model of Adoption of Online Buying in India*. doi :10.1080/08911762.2017.1369609

Retail Industry in India. (2021). https://www.investindia.gov.in/sector/retail-e-commerce

Rozario, K. (2021, July 13). E-Commerce In India Set To Reach $120 Billion In 2025, Says Report. *Forbes*. https://www.forbes.com/sites/kevinrozario/2021/07/13/e-commerce-in-india-set-to-reach-120-billion-in-2025-says-report/?sh=48af2f446119

Saarijärvi, H., Sutinen, U.-M., & Harris, L. C. (2017). Uncovering consumers' returning behaviour: A study of fashion e-commerce. *International Review of Retail, Distribution and Consumer Research*, *27*(3), 284–299. doi:10.1080/09593969.2017.1314863

Salema, M. I. G., Barbosa-Povoa, A. P., & Novais, A. Q. (2010). Simultaneous design and planning of supply chains with reverse flows: A generic modelling framework. *European Journal of Operational Research*, *203*(2), 336–349. doi:10.1016/j.ejor.2009.08.002

Samorani, M., Alptekinoglu, A., & Messinger, P. R. (2019). Product return episodes in retailing. *Service Science*, *11*(4), 263–278. doi:10.1287erv.2019.0250

Seo, J. Y., Yoon, S., & Vangelova, M. (2016). Shopping plans, buying motivations, and return policies: Impacts on product returns and purchase likelihoods. *Marketing Letters*, *27*(4), 645–659. doi:10.100711002-015-9381-y

Sharma, S. K. (2015). Adoption of e-government services: The role of service quality dimensions and demographic variables. *Transforming Government: People, Process and Policy*, *9*(2), 207–222. doi:10.1108/TG-10-2014-0046/FULL/PDF

Ulbrich, F., Christensen, T., & Stankus, L. (2010). Gender-specific on-line shopping preferences. *Electronic Commerce Research*, *11*(2), 181–199. doi:10.1007/s10660-010-9073-x

Ullal, M. S., Spulbar, C., Hawaldar, I. T., Popescu, V., & Birau, R. (2021). *The impact of online reviews on e-commerce sales in India: A case study*. doi:10.1080/1331677X.2020.1865179

Variyar, M. (2018). *Amazon India: Amazon gets more product returns in India than any other markets, Technology News, ETtech*. https://tech.economictimes.indiatimes.com/news/internet/amazon-gets-more-product-returns-in-india-than-any-other-markets/66946547

Wang, L., Wong, P. P. W., & Narayanan, E. A. (2019). *The demographic impact of consumer green purchase intention toward Green Hotel Selection in China*. doi:10.1177/1467358419848129

Young Kim, E., & Kim, Y. (2004). Predicting online purchase intentions for clothing products. *European Journal of Marketing*, *38*(7), 883–897. doi:10.1108/03090560410539302

Zhou, W., Hinz, O., & Benlian, A. (2018). The impact of the package opening process on product returns. *Business Research*, *11*(2), 279–308. doi:10.100740685-017-0055-x

Chapter 11
E-Healthcare System for Disease Detection Based on Medical Image Classification Using CNN

Himansu Das
https://orcid.org/0000-0002-3995-2768
Kalinga Institute of Industrial Technology (Deemed), Bhubaneswar, India

Mahendra Kumar Gourisaria
https://orcid.org/0000-0002-1785-8586
Kalinga Institute of Industrial Technology (Deemed), Bhubaneswar, India

Badal Kumar Sah
Kalinga Institute of Industrial Technology (Deemed), Bhubaneswar, India

Saurabh Bilgaiyan
Kalinga Institute of Industrial Technology (Deemed), Bhubaneswar, India

J Chandrakanta Badajena
College of Engineering and Technology, Bhubaneswar, India

Radha Mohan Pattanayak
Godavari Institute of Engineering and Technology (Autonomous), India

ABSTRACT

With the advancement of the internet, the e-commerce sector has seen a tremendous opportunity in the field for e-healthcare, which has resulted in decrement of labor cost, faster insurance claims, and much more. Machine learning has paved various regimes, which the future of medical treatment and teaching could be based upon. Thereafter, with the advent of these methods, the timeline of extracting and segregating patients started to become a more straightforward process. The sorting process could be primarily based on symptoms, medical reports, and medical test results. Had this been based on human interpretation, it may render itself limited due to subjectivity, complexity, and factors of human error. Thus, herein, the method of convolution neural network (CNN)-based algorithm is applied on x-ray data sets to determine brain tumor and coronavirus in patients. The authors also try to provide a short snapshot of what the future could be for the medical industry with the incorporation of deep learning to access and cure various diseases.

DOI: 10.4018/978-1-6684-4969-1.ch011

Copyright © 2022, IGI Global. Copying or distributing in print or electronic forms without written permission of IGI Global is prohibited.

INTRODUCTION

E-healthcare uses a huge range of digital technologies in the context of providing an effective result in the patient's health. The best example could be the internet, it enables e-health users to get in touch with health care professionals by mail to get accessibility to medical records and get an overall insight into their health. This process helps in quick and paperless response by a doctor to their patients and helps to cure the disease at the initial stage (Das et al., 2020).

Machine learning (Rout et al., 2020) in the simplest terms can be defined as the science of making machines function without overt programming of each step. Considering the previous decade, we have initiated the era of self-driving cars, speech & handwriting recognition software, and an immensely amended understanding of the human genome. It has slowly started to become an integral part of various prospects of the society, finding its use in fields of finance (Rout et al., 2020; Pattanayak et al., 2021; Pattanayak et al., 2020), self-driving cars, voice search and voice-activated assistants (Ayush et al., 2019), and healthcare (Sahoo et al., 2019; Das et al., 2020; Dey et al., 2018; Das et al.,2020; Chakraborty et al., 2020, March). Thereafter, we consider deep learning (Kumar et al., 2020, July; Sahoo et al., 2020) which is a subset of machine learning and allows for the formation of intelligence that mimics that of a human brain by analysis of data sets and creating patterns out of them for the process of decision making. The protocol on which deep learning works is by training algorithms using a large amount of data and allowing the setup to learn through future data sets. When it comes to our area of primary focus, deep learning in healthcare (Shen et al., 2017), the efforts and innovation being infused in the medical industry are allowing for the improvement of tools for computer-aided detection of diseases. Modern medicine has started to be heavily relying on the synthesis and analysis of information and data from various resources such as medical imaging, structured laboratory data, unstructured narrative data, and certain observational data. This opens certain virtues for the segment of machine learning and deep learning to participate in the process of clinical decision-making. The use of electronic health records has enhanced the integration at a rapid pace and has made medical image analysis an active field of advancement for deep learning for classification (Rout et al., 2020; Das et al., 2015; Panigrahi et al., 2020).

The adoption of deep learning in our field of observation, brain tumors, and novel coronavirus, is vital for the magnified cure process. Brain tumors, which are the aftermath of atypical growths and frenzied cell division in the brain can be of two forms: malignant or benign. The timely detection of such tumors can lead to the prospect of improved life quality and expectancy. In addendum, the early detection of novel coronavirus (which has created a widespread pandemic across the globe) could avoid the transmissibility and thus prove to be vital in controlling the effects on the individual as well.

For the effective study, we have considered medical imaging, primarily X-Rays to determine the presence of both these diseases in patients. The reason for the adoption of X-rays is bifold. Primarily as it is cost-effective and thus can be advocated to be an easily accessible choice to the lower income group of the society. And secondly, it is easily available across all demographics of society.

It is also considered here that the detection of these diseases through the process of X-ray imaging requires exactitude from professional radiologists which can be considered a unique and exclusive resource for some regions of the world. It can also be a falter to human error. Thus, the introduction of deep learning would allow for accurate detection. The implementation of these imaging systems with deep learning algorithms is also to fast-track the detection process and move to the cure segment.

Here, deep learning adopts an algorithm known as Convolutional Neural Network (CNN) which functions on the principle of assigning the machine to learn weightage and biases [18] towards the input data under various aspects and apply the same to predict and differentiate future understudy cases. It is named rightly as a neural network as it inhibits the pattern of neurons in the human brain. It can effectively obtain the three-dimensional and sequential dependencies of an image via the usage of applicable filters. The structural design makes a better customizing to the image dataset due to the decrease in the number of constrictions implicated and the reusability of weights. In other words, the network can be trained to understand the intricacy of the image well. We have used a total of 9 layers comprising 7 convolution layers and one each of a fully connected layer and a sigmoid layer. We have taken the deep learning approach to identify the existence of novel coronavirus and a brain tumor in patients through the analysis of X-ray imaging. CNN-based methods have proved to increase the performance of image classifications through data augmentation and analysis.

The introduction of Deep Learning has also made a significant impact in the e-healthcare sector. Patients can have an overall insight into their health just by providing minimal to extreme data on one's medical history. It has also caught the eye of e-commerce giants intending to cure patients at the initial phase or emerging phase of diseases. This may not only result in cost-effective treatment and increase the overall life expectancy of humans but also ensure better treatment across all demographics of the society (Lundervold et al., 2019).

RELATED WORK

Such research has always been enhanced in the facilitation of medical treatments by enabling speed and precision. The introduction of a deep learning model in Medical imaging and its analysis is a well-discussed vista. These models are always designed along the lines of medical imaging and its resonance in identifying the cause behind certain diseases and their respective cures. Many books, educational reports, and research studies have taken place describing the use of deep learning in medical imaging, disease detection, and analysis of cures. The reverse prospect of medical imaging as a prime area of focus when analyzing deep learning has been ascertained.

Alexander Lundervold et al., 2019, in their research on "an overview of deep learning in medical imaging focusing on MRI" found the reliance of deep neural networks on complicated and inter-connected graded data for training.

Adding to it, Muhammad Imran Razak et al., 2018, in their study on "deep learning for medical image processing", achieved the result of deep learning being a central authority towards the automation of daily life activities. They also discussed the unlimited opportunities deep learning could advance in medical prospects if the healthcare data is efficiently delivered to it.

Likewise, Samir Yadav and Shivajirao Jadhav., 2019, in their analysis of "deep convolutional neural network-based medical image categorization for disease analysis" found the importance of medical image classification on small data sets. Their paper also studied the applications of CNN for the evaluation of the performance of these models.

When it came down to disease-specific analysis. Zahra Sobhaninia et al., 2018, in their paper on "brain tumor segmentation using deep learning by type-specific sorting of images" found a new approach for CNN to automate the segmentation of the most common types of brain tumors, primarily glioma meningioma, and pituitary. They stated that this technique could be a useful tool for segmenting brain tumors in medical resonance images.

In similar research on “Brain Tumor Detection Using Deep Neural Network and Machine Learning Algorithm”, Mosoumeh Siar and Mohammad Tesnehlab., 2019, presented a new method of feature extraction algorithms and CNN to detect tumors in the brain images. They also stated that the level of accuracy in such detection would further add to the evaluation and analysis metric for the physicians, during the diagnosis process.

Ahmad Sarhan., 2020 in “Detection and Classification of Brain Tumor in MRI Images Using Wavelet Transform and Convolutional Neural Network”, developed and presented an approach to the categorization of Brain cancer using deep neural networks. He proposed that the system would process the total brain image with wavelet decomposition and would thus not require any segmentation of the input images.

In rather recent studies on “COVID-19 Deep Learning Prediction Model Using Publicly Available Radiologist-Adjudicated Chest X-Ray Images as Training Data: Preliminary Findings” Mohd Zulfaezal Che Azmin et al., 2020, focused the strength of the study to be the use of decided labels which have robust medical associations with COVID-19 cases and used jointly restricted and publicly available data for the training, validation, and testing. Although, they suggested that when deep learning models are being applied for medical issues on newer diseases like COVID-19, precautionary measures are to be taken while interpretations.

Similarly, Ali Narin et al., 2020 in the study on “Automatic Detection of Coronavirus Disease (COVID-19) Using X-ray Images and Deep Convolutional Neural Networks”, proposed a deep transfer learning-based work using Chest X-ray images for different outcomes such as normal, COVID-19, and mostly found pneumonia patients to predict COVID-19 patients automatically.

Likewise, Sohaib Asif and Yi Wenhui., 2020, in their research on “Detection of COVID-19 Using X-ray Images with Deep CNN and ML via automation” focused on the development of such models to prevent the widespread of the disease whilst early detection. It is to be noted, that their proposed classification model for the detection of COVID achieved more than 96% accuracy.

Linda Wang et al., 2020, in their report on “COVID-Net: a tailored deep convolutional neural network design for detection of COVID-19 cases from chest X-ray images”, created a deep CNN design in-order to detect COVID-19 cases from CXR images which is an open-source project/research and available to the general public for an insight knowledge.

METHODOLOGY

Deep learning(DL) is a subset of Machine Learning which is built upon the hierarchical level of neural networks. The neural networks work like a human brain, with neurons connected to form a network. CNN is a very popular DL method for image classification which takes different classes of an image as an input and learns various perspectives of those images to classify between them. The preprocessing of a CNN algorithm is very much less than a classifier algorithm because of the densely connected neurons. CNN includes various layers which comprise an input layer, output layer, convolutional layers, pooling layers, normalization layers, and fully connected layers, different CNNs have a different number of layers, sizes, and images that are chosen experimentally based on trial and error.

In our study, we have proposed a model with 9 layers which comprises different layers and compared our model with other pre-trained models like VGG-16 and ResNet which use the approach of transfer learning.

Figure 1. Images in Row1 and Row2 show 3 sample images of Covid-19 cases and Normal cases

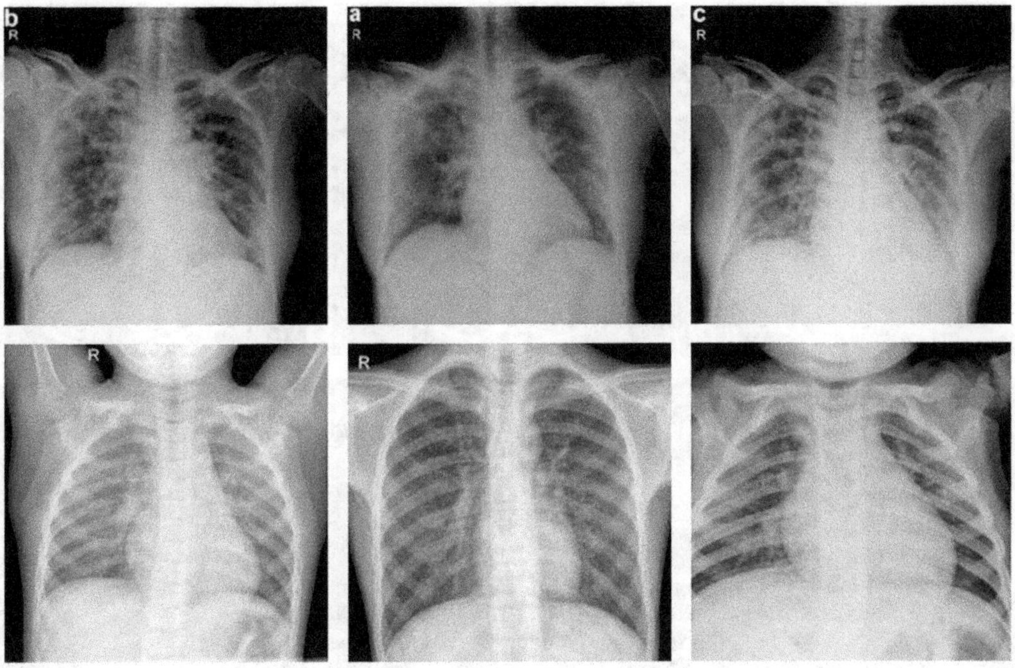

Comparision of Covid and Normal Images

Datasets

In covid detection a total of 1,692 images have been used, comprising of covid-chest-xray (https://github.com/ieee8023/covid-chestxray-dataset) dataset which includes 351 covid images and we have used Chest-Xray-Images(Pneumonia) (Kermany er al., 2018) as a normal image which comprises 1341 images. The visualization of X-ray Images of both the classes is shown in Fig 1

In our second case i.e. Brain tumor detection, we have used a dataset provided by Kaggle with a total of 253 images which comprises 155 positive class images and 98 negative class images. The visualization of X-ray Images of both the classes is shown in **Fig 2**.

Further classification of total images in 3 different classes for both cases is shown in Table 1.

Proposed CNN Methodologies

Our proposed CNN architecture includes various operations which are as follows:

Convolutional Operation

In mathematical terms, convolution is derived from two different functions, after integration which expresses how shapes can be modified, this can be expressed as:

Figure 2. Images in Row1 and Row2 show 3 sample images of Brain Tumor cases and Normal cases

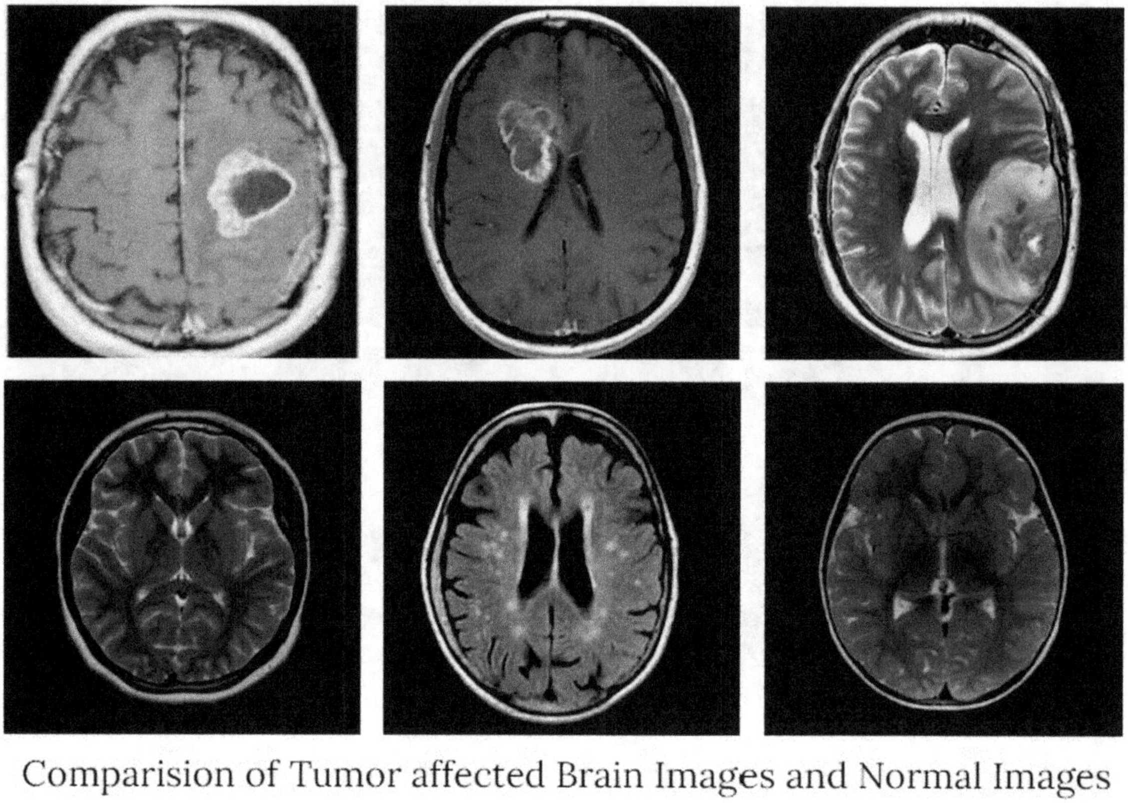

$$(f*g)\cdot\int_{-\infty}^{\infty} f(\tau)g(t-\tau)d\tau \qquad (1)$$

Our model has a total of 9 layers which comprises a total of 7 convolution layers and uses a kernel size of (3×3). Kernels are matrices that slide through the whole image along the width and the height.

Activation Function

Activation functions are attached to each end of a neuron and used to get an output of a neural network that ranges from -1 to 1(depending upon the function). Activation functions are classified into Linear and Non-Linear Activation Functions and these functions are further classified into Sigmoid, Tanh, ReLU, etc. In our study, we have used the ReLU function as it is one of the most widely used activation

Table 1. Classification of Images

CASE	Training Image	Validation Image	Testing Image
Covid Detection	1083	270	339
Brain Tumor	193	50	10

Figure 3. Convolution Operation

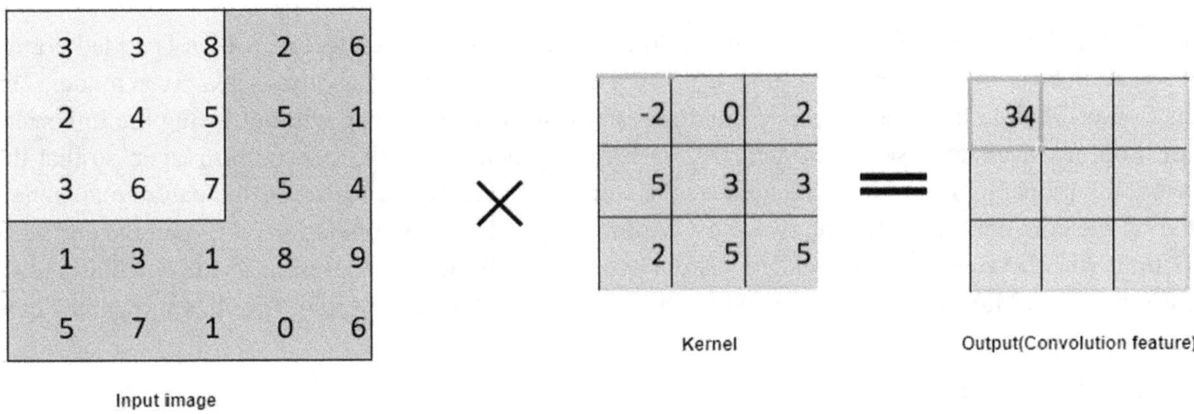

functions having many advantages, one of its major advantages is that it does not activate all neurons at a time. As you can see in **Fig 4.** ReLU Operation converts negative values to zero, thus making it more computationally efficient.

Figure 4. Representation of RELU

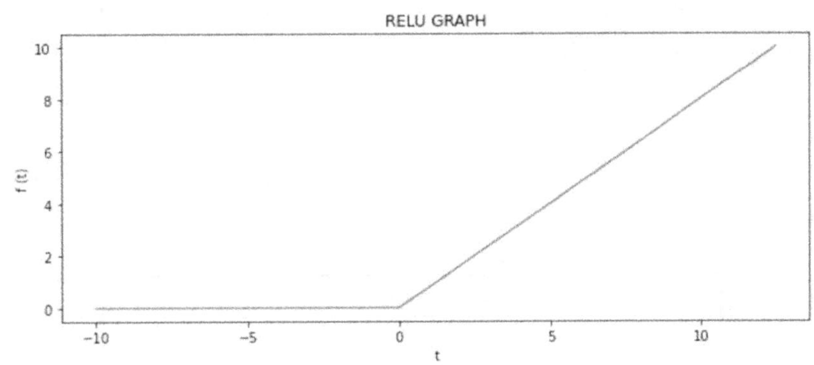

Equational representation of ReLU function is shown in (2), here if t is less than or equal to 0 then*f*(*t*) zero, i.e the neurons are not activated, and *f*(*t*) is 1 if t is greater than zero, thus we can say that ReLU is half rectified.

$$f(t) = \max(0, t)$$
$$f^{\prime}(t) = \frac{\partial f(t)}{\partial t} = \begin{cases} 0, if\ t \leq 0 \\ 1, if\ t > 0 \end{cases} \qquad (2)$$

Pooling

The pooling layer of a CNN is one of the building blocks of CNN architecture which is added after a convolution layer to order layers within a CNN that might be repeated many times in a given model. The function of Pooling layers is to reduce the dimensions of the feature map without losing the important part. Pooling layers are used to summarize the feature generated by the convolution layer, so that the forthcoming operations are implemented on the summarized feature, instead of the feature map generated by the convolution layer. The two most commonly used pooling operations are Average and Max Pooling, where Average pooling calculates the average of all the pixels present in the patch as shown in **Fig 5.**, while Max Pooling only considers the maximum value present in the pool as shown in **Fig 6**.

Figure 5. Average Pooling

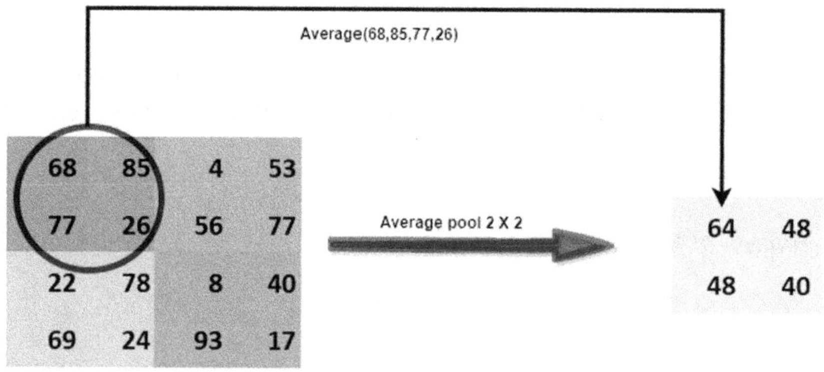

Figure 6. Max Pooling

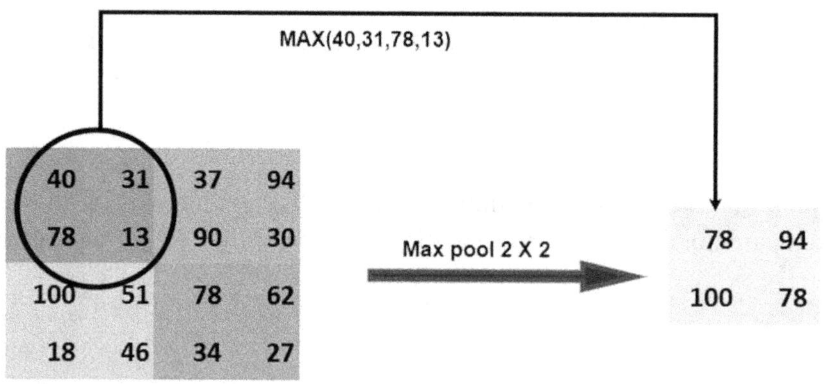

Optimization Algorithms

Optimization algorithms are used to alter the attributes of neural networks(i.e. weights and learning rate) to reduce loss. In our study we have used two different optimizers in both cases, for covid detection, we have used Adam Optimizer, whereas for Brain Tumor Detection we have used RmsProp optimizer. The purpose behind using Adam optimizer is that we don't want to move fast, instead, we want to move slow for a careful search, so is the purpose of RmsProp also, but the basic difference between them is that Adam uses a smooth version of gradient descent as shown in Eq 3.,

$$g = \frac{1}{m} \nabla_{\theta} \sum_{i} L(f(x^{(i)};\theta), y^{(i)})$$

$$m = \beta 1_{\mathrm{m}} + (1 - \beta 1)_{\mathrm{g}}$$

$$\mathrm{s} = \beta 2\mathrm{s} + (1 - \beta 2)\ _{\mathrm{g}}\mathrm{Tg}$$

$$\theta = \theta - \varepsilon_k \times m \,/\, \sqrt{s + eps} \tag{3}$$

Whereas Rmsprop uses raw stochastic gradient as shown in Eq 4.

$$g = \frac{1}{m} \nabla_{\theta} \sum_{i} L(f(x^{(i)};\theta), y^{(i)})$$

$$s = decay\_rate \times s + (1 - decay\_rate) g^T g$$

$$\theta = \theta - \varepsilon_k \times m \,/\, \sqrt{s + eps} \tag{4}$$

Loss Function

The loss function evaluates how well our model fits our dataset, if the prediction is good, the loss function will return a lower value else a higher value, depending on how good the algorithm is tuned. There are 3 different kinds of the loss function, i.e. Binary classification loss function, Regression Loss function, and Multi-class classification loss function. In our study, we have used the Binary classification loss function, and in which we have used Binary Cross entropy as we are training a binary classifier

$$H_p(q) = -\frac{1}{N} \sum_{i=1}^{N} y_i . \log(p(y_i)) + (1 - y_i) . \log(1 - p(y_i)) \tag{5}$$

Fully Connected Layer

Fully connected layers are one of the most essential components of a CNN in which each node of one layer is connected to each node of the second layer as shown in **Fig7.** so that it is successful in the clas-

Figure 7. Fully connected layer

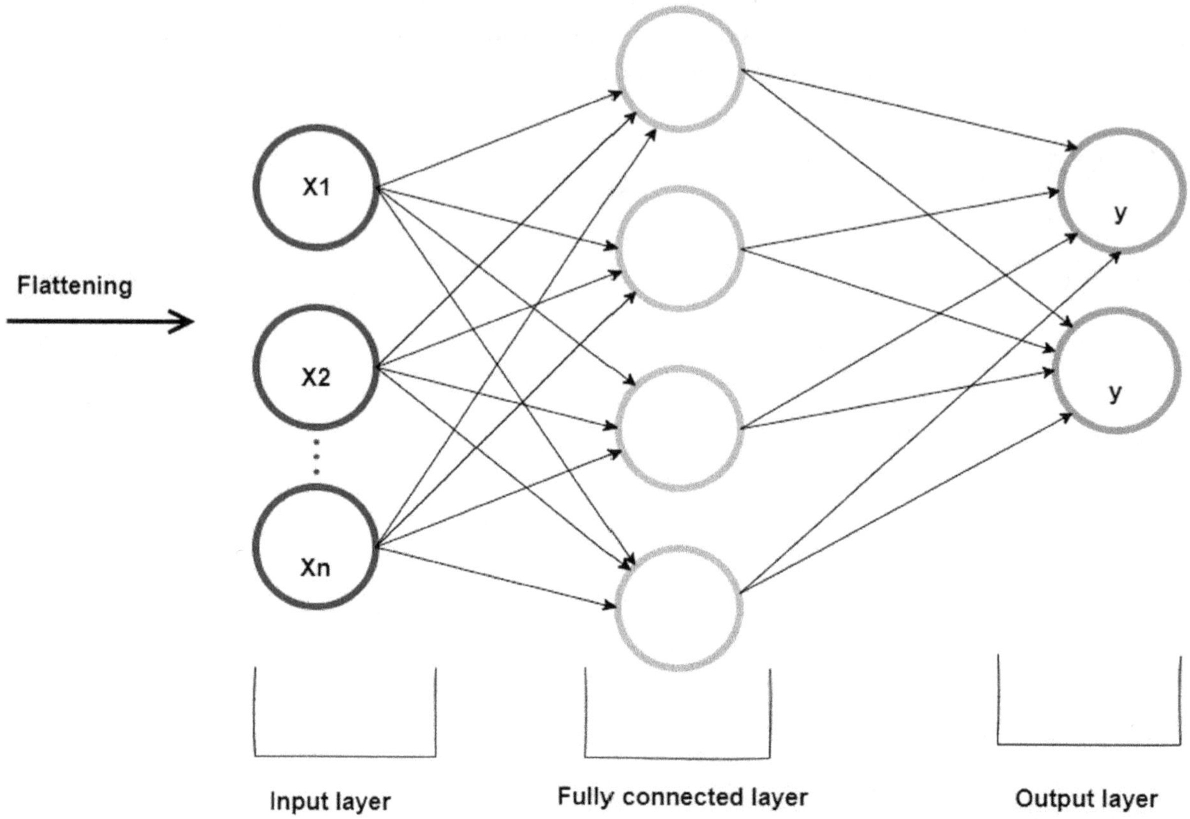

sification of images. The input to a fully connected layer is the output of either the pooling layer or a convolution layer which is further flattened into a single vector that represents the probability of a certain feature belonging to a label.

For designing a new CNN architecture, the above components are combined in a way that the model can reveal its maximum efficiency against the dataset. Various factors should be taken care of while designing a CNN architecture among which two major factors are firstly try to understand the problem to be solved and the requirements that are to be met, secondly try to optimize your model to the best computational and memory efficiency. Our model is built keeping in mind both factors, and further compared in the result analysis section with some famous models. Our proposed architecture in this study has a total of 10 layers which comprises 7 convolution layers, 2 fully connected layers, and 1 sigmoid classifier, the detailed structure of our proposed architecture is shown in **Fig 8.**

RESULT ANALYSIS

The result analysis section includes the following components:

Figure 8. Proposed CNN architecture

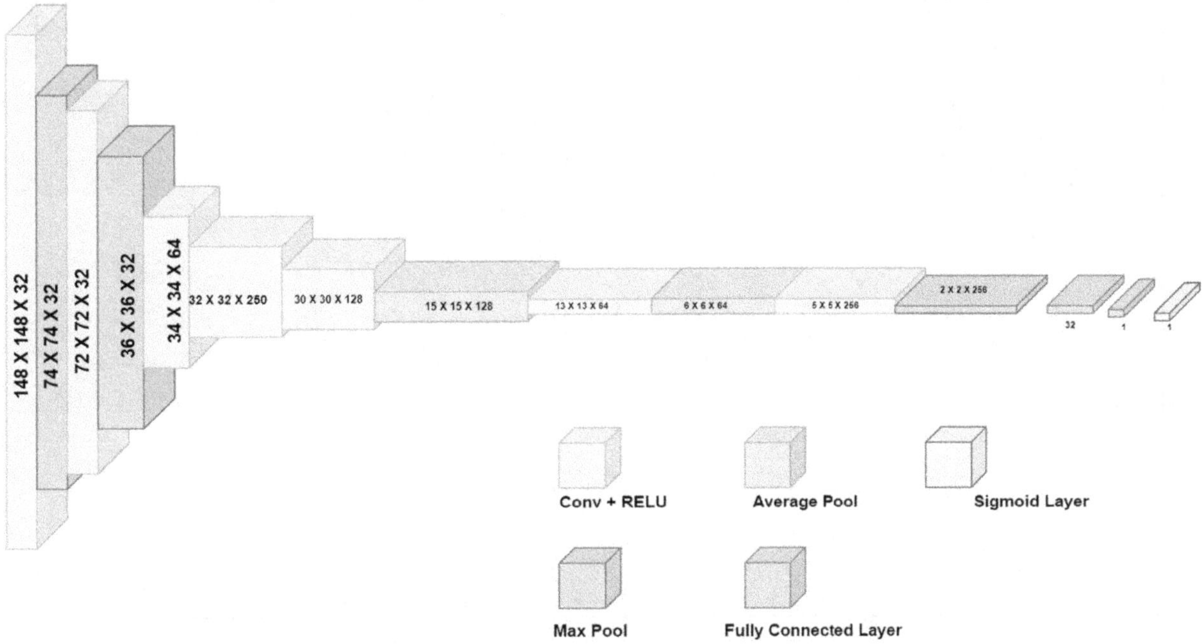

System Configuration

The system configuration used in our study is provided by Kaggle and is free for access. For training our CNN model, we have used the default learning rate of the model with several epochs as 120 for both different cases. For result analysis purposes we have trained three other models to show a better analysis in comparison to that of our model, we have trained VGG-16, Resnet-50, and Inception-V3 model.

Experimental Results and Analysis on the Covid Dataset

Fig 9 shows the training and validation accuracy comparison of all our four models on the covid data-set, i.e. VGG-16, Resnet-50, Inception-V3, and our model. The training accuracy achieved by VGG-16 is 98.22%, training accuracy achieved by Resnet-50 is 94.00%, training accuracy achieved by Inception-V3 is 98% while the training accuracy achieved by our model is 99.63% which performs the best among all these four models.

Figure 10 shows the training and validation comparison of loss for all our four models on the covid data-set, i.e. VGG-16, Resnet-50, Inception-V3, and our model. The training loss achieved by VGG-16 is 0.0434, the training loss achieved by Resnet-50 is 0.1485, the training loss achieved by Inception-V3 is 0.0041 while the training loss achieved by our model is 0.0072.

For a better analysis of accuracy and loss over the covid data-set, the data is presented in tabulated form as shown in Table 2 and Table 3.

Figure 9. Training and validation accuracy of VGG-16, Resnet-50, Inception-V3, and Proposed model

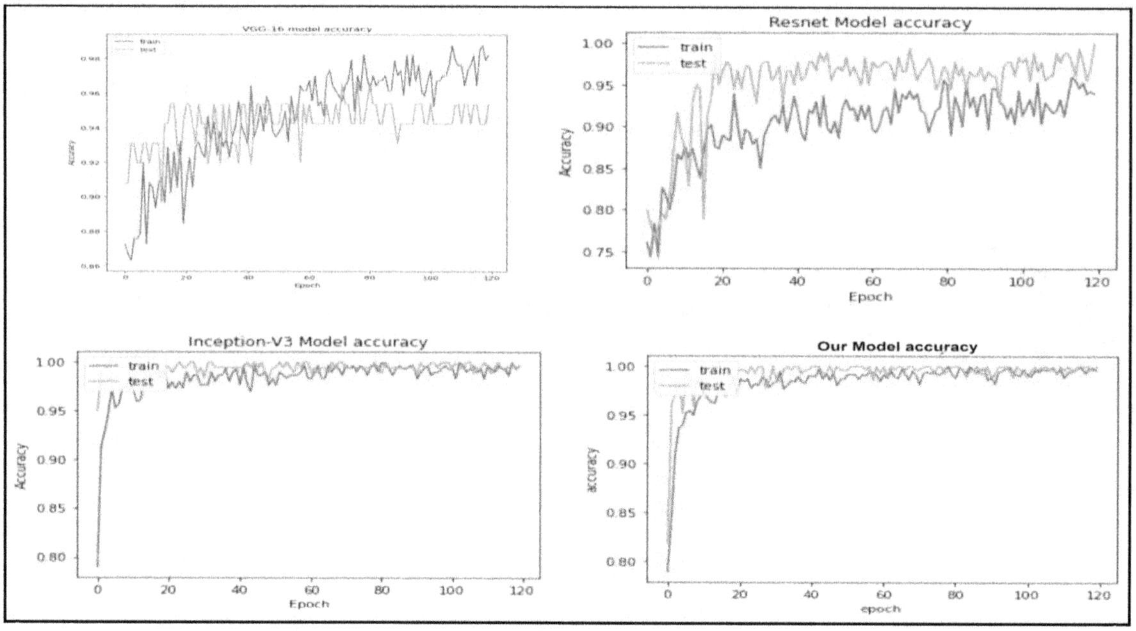

Figure 10. Training and validation loss of VGG-16, Resnet-50, Inception-V3, and Proposed model

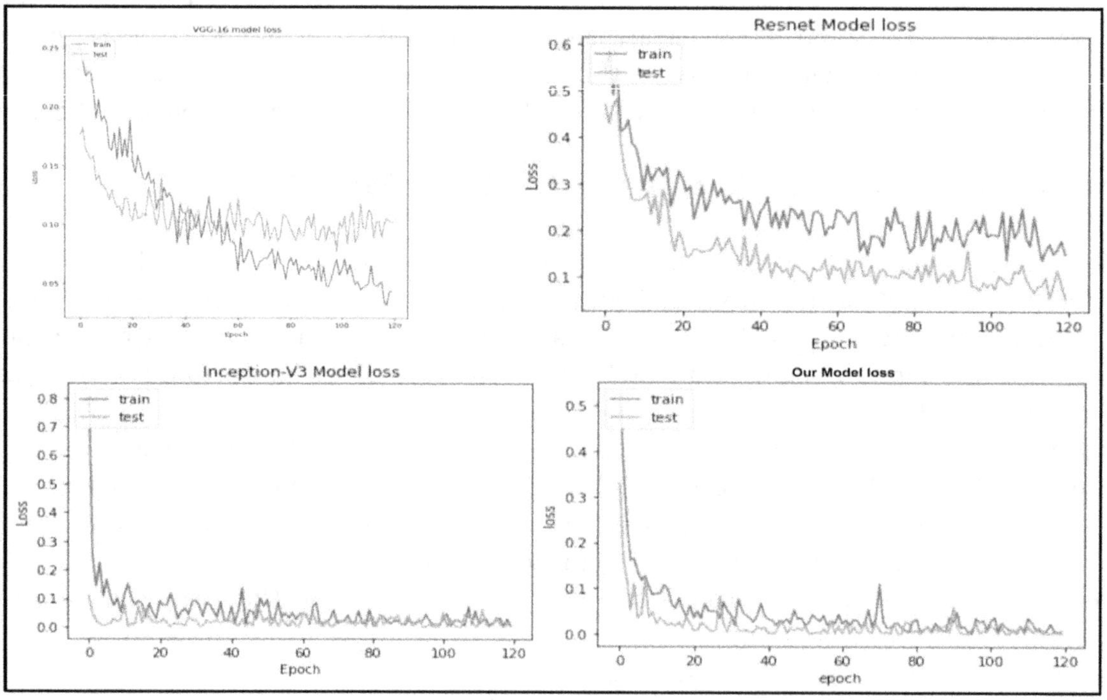

Table 2. Accuracy comparison of different methods

Models	Training Accuracy(in %)	Validation Accuracy(in %)
VGG16	98.22	95.40
Resnet-50	94.00	97.22
Inception-V3	98.00	98.44
Proposed Model	99.63	99.60

Table 3. Loss comparison of different methods

Models	Training Loss	Validation Loss
VGG16	0.0434	0.9540
Resnet-50	0.1485	0.0544
Inception-V3	0.0041	0.0167
Proposed Model	0.0072	7.2330 e-4

Experimental Results and Analysis of Tumor Data-Set

Fig 11 shows the training and validation comparison of the accuracy of all our four models on brain tumor data-set, i.e. VGG-16, Resnet-50, Inception-V3, and our model. The training accuracy achieved by VGG-16 is 97.24%, training accuracy achieved by Resnet-50 is 94.32%, training accuracy achieved by Inception-V3 is 89.93% while the training accuracy achieved by our model is 98.43% which performs the best among all these four models.

Fig 12 shows the training and validation comparison of loss for all of our four models on the Tumor data-set, i.e. VGG-16, Resnet-50, Inception-V3, and our model. The training loss achieved by VGG-16 is 0.3027, the training loss achieved by Resnet-50 is 0.6273, the training loss achieved by Inception-V3 is 0.2225 while the training loss achieved by our model is 0.0572.

For a better analysis of accuracy and loss over the Tumor data-set, the data is presented in tabulated form as shown in Table 4 and Table 5.

CONCLUSION

E-healthcare system has made a wide range of possibilities for convenience for both patients and doctors. The involvement of Machine Learning (to be precise, Deep Learning) has worked as a 'cherry on the cake' for tracing disease with much more accuracy and in almost all demographic societies because of cost-effectiveness. In this paper, we have examined three of the pre-trained models, i.e. VGG-16, Resnet-50, and Inception-V3, and compared the results with our proposed model. In this study, we have tuned all the different perspectives like kernel size, pooling layer, convolutional layer, and more importantly the optimization technique to achieve the best of our proposed model. Our proposed model eliminates the majority of the problems that exist in our pre-trained models as experimentally shown

Figure 11. Training and validation Accuracy of VGG-16, Resnet-50, Inception-V3, and Proposed model

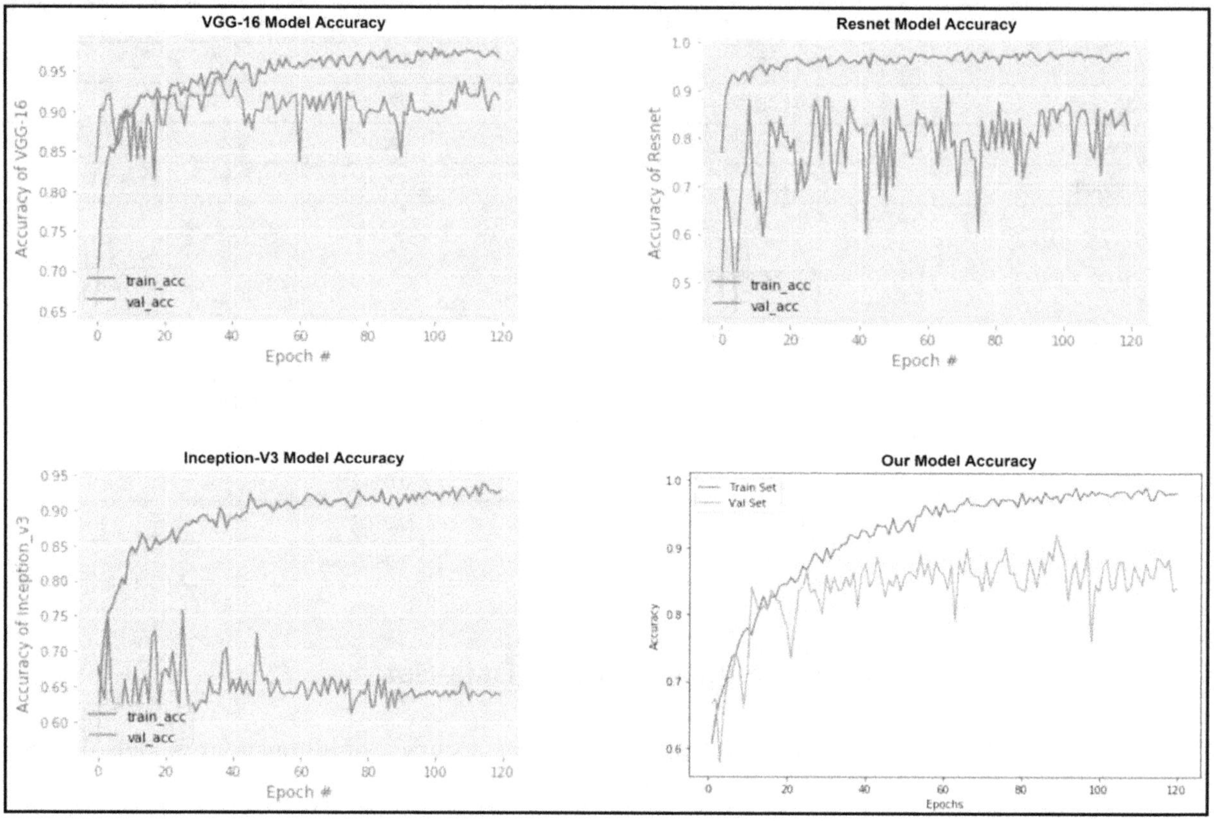

with both the Covid data-set and Brain tumor data-set. The reason that our model is better than already existing models is because of the use of kernels of size 3×3 and the use of both the average pooling as well as max-pooling layers. The use of large kernel sizes and a single pooling function results in decaying the performance of the model.

In the last few years, DL study has gained a middle ground to the automation of our daily lives and brought improved advances compared to traditional machine learning techniques. After seeing the amazing performance of DL, many researchers believe that in the next 15 years, DL applications for learning will make a personal impact and most of the daily machine operations will be automated. However, the entry of DL in health education especially in the medical field is as slow as compared to other real-world problems because of the unlikeliness of training images. In the future, if large datasets with better likeliness are present then this model can be of great use in the medical field to detect various diseases like Covid-19, Brain tumors, etc. This model can be furthermore extended and improvised to build and use in e-healthcare devices and eventually can create an impact in the field of Bio-medical and e-health learning.

Figure 12. Training and validation loss of VGG-16, Resnet-50, Inception-V3, and Proposed model

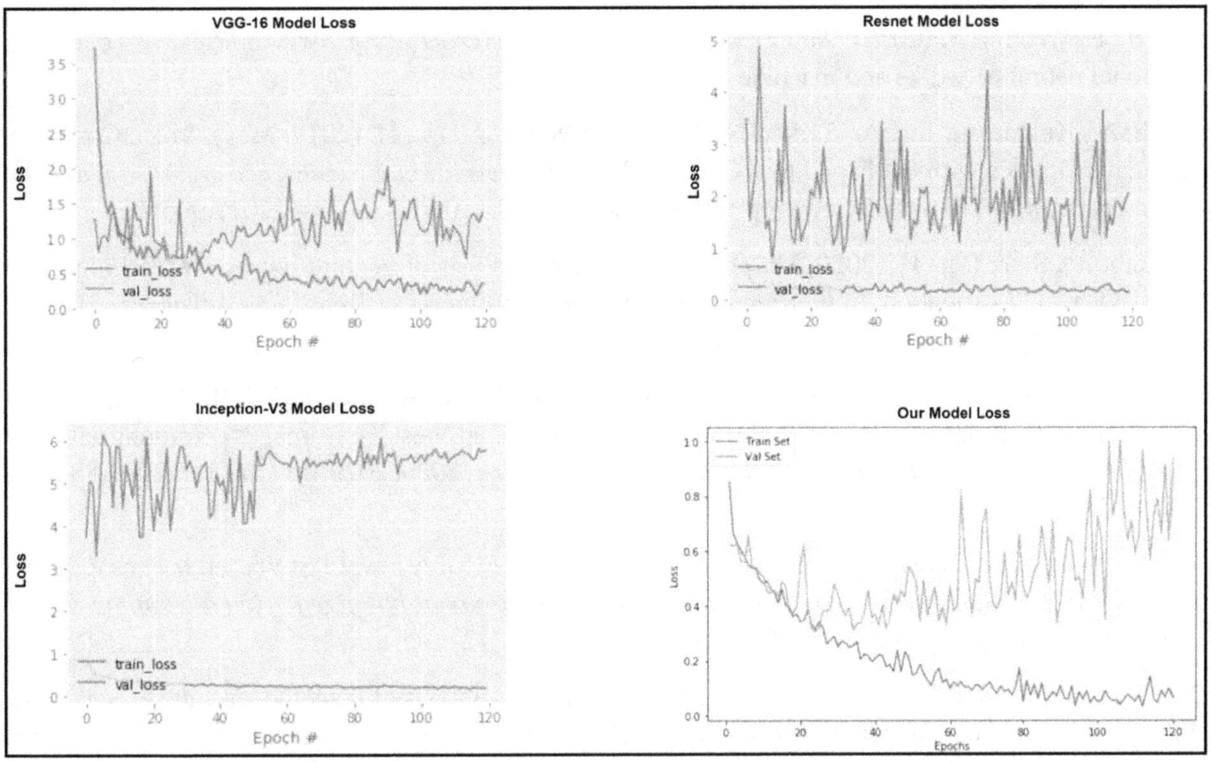

Table 4. Accuracy comparison of different methods

Models	Training Accuracy(in %)	Validation Accuracy(in %)
VGG16	97.24	91.58
Resnet-50	94.32	81.94
Inception-V3	89.93	63.86
Proposed Model	98.43	84.11

Table 5. Loss comparison of different methods

Models	Training Loss	Validation Loss
VGG16	0.3027	0.9158
Resnet-50	0.6273	2.0415
Inception-V3	0.2225	5.7651
Proposed Model	0.0572	0.9362

REFERENCES

Asif, S., & Wenhui, Y. (2020). Automatic detection of COVID-19 using X-ray images with deep convolutional neural networks and machine learning. medRxiv.

Ayush, A., Kumar, A., Jha, A., Sarkar, N., Moharana, S. C., & Das, H. (2019, May). Voice Controlled Automatic Dustbin with Garbage Level Sensing. In *2019 International Conference on Intelligent Computing and Control Systems (ICCS)* (pp. 450-453). IEEE. 10.1109/ICCS45141.2019.9065323

Chakraborty, S., & Das, H. (2020, March). Performance Analysis of Feature Extraction Techniques for Medical Data Classification. In *International Conference on Emerging Trends and Advances in Electrical Engineering and Renewable Energy* (pp. 387-401). Springer.

Che Azemin, M. Z., Hassan, R., Mohd Tamrin, M. I., & Md Ali, M. A. (2020). COVID-19 deep learning prediction model using publicly available radiologist-adjudicated chest X-ray images as training data: Preliminary findings. *International Journal of Biomedical Imaging, 2020*, 2020. doi:10.1155/2020/8828855 PMID:32849861

Das, H., Jena, A. K., Nayak, J., Naik, B., & Behera, H. S. (2015). A novel PSO-based backpropagation learning-MLP (PSO-BP-MLP) for classification. In *Computational intelligence in data mining-volume 2* (pp. 461–471). Springer. doi:10.1007/978-81-322-2208-8_42

Das, H., Naik, B., & Behera, H. S. (2020). An experimental analysis of machine learning classification algorithms on biomedical data. In *Proceedings of the 2nd International Conference on Communication, Devices, and Computing* (pp. 525-539). Springer. 10.1007/978-981-15-0829-5_51

Das, H., Naik, B., & Behera, H. S. (2020). Medical disease analysis using neuro-fuzzy with feature extraction model for classification. *Informatics in Medicine Unlocked, 18*, 100288. doi:10.1016/j.imu.2019.100288

Das, H., Naik, B., Behera, H. S., Jaiswal, S., Mahato, P., & Rout, M. (2020). Biomedical data analysis using the neuro-fuzzy model with post-feature reduction. *Journal of King Saud University-Computer and Information Sciences*.

Dey, N., Ashour, A. S., Kalia, H., Goswami, R. T., & Das, H. (Eds.). (2018). *Histopathological image analysis in medical decision making*. IGI Global.

Kermany, D., Zhang, K., & Goldbaum, M. (2018). Labeled Optical Coherence Tomography (OCT) and Chest X-Ray Images for Classification. Mendeley Data, *2*. doi:10.17632/rscbjbr9sj.2

Kumar, A., Razi, R., Singh, A., & Das, H. (2020, July). Res-VGG: A Novel Model for Plant Disease Detection by Fusing VGG16 and ResNet Models. In *International Conference on Machine Learning, Image Processing, Network Security and Data Sciences* (pp. 383-400). Springer. 10.1007/978-981-15-6318-8_32

Lundervold, A. S., & Lundervold, A. (2019). An overview of deep learning in medical imaging focusing on MRI. *Zeitschrift für Medizinische Physik, 29*(2), 102–127. doi:10.1016/j.zemedi.2018.11.002 PMID:30553609

Narin, A., Kaya, C., & Pamuk, Z. (2020). *Automatic detection of coronavirus disease (covid-19) using x-ray images and deep convolutional neural networks.* arXiv preprint arXiv:2003.10849.

Panigrahi, K. P., Das, H., Sahoo, A. K., & Moharana, S. C. (2020). Maize leaf disease detection and classification using machine learning algorithms. In Progress in Computing, Analytics, and Networking (pp. 659-669). Springer. doi:10.1007/978-981-15-2414-1_66

Panigrahi, K. P., Sahoo, A. K., & Das, H. (2020, June). A CNN Approach for Corn Leaves Disease Detection to support Digital Agricultural System. In *2020 4th International Conference on Trends in Electronics and Informatics (ICOEI)* (pp. 678-683). IEEE. 10.1109/ICOEI48184.2020.9142871

Pattanayak, R. M., Behera, H. S., & Panigrahi, S. (2021). A novel probabilistic intuitionistic fuzzy set-based model for high order fuzzy time series forecasting. *Engineering Applications of Artificial Intelligence*, *99*, 104136. doi:10.1016/j.engappai.2020.104136

Pattanayak, R. M., Panigrahi, S., & Behera, H. S. (2020). High-order fuzzy time series forecasting by using membership values along with Data and Support Vector Machine. *Arabian Journal for Science and Engineering*, *45*(12), 10311–10325. doi:10.100713369-020-04721-1

Razzak, M. I., Naz, S., & Zaib, A. (2018). Deep learning for medical image processing: Overview, challenges and the future. *Classification in BioApps*, 323-350.

Rout, J. K., Rout, M., & Das, H. (Eds.). (2020). *Machine Learning for Intelligent Decision Science.* Springer Singapore. doi:10.1007/978-981-15-3689-2

Rout, M., Jena, A. K., Rout, J. K., & Das, H. (2020). Teaching-learning optimization-based cascaded low-complexity neural network model for exchange rates forecasting. In *Smart Intelligent Computing and Applications* (pp. 635–645). Springer. doi:10.1007/978-981-13-9282-5_60

Sahoo, A. K., Mallik, S., Pradhan, C., Mishra, B. S. P., Barik, R. K., & Das, H. (2019). Intelligence-based health recommendation system using big data analytics. In *Big data analytics for intelligent healthcare management* (pp. 227–246). Academic Press. doi:10.1016/B978-0-12-818146-1.00009-X

Sahoo, A. K., Pradhan, C., & Das, H. (2020). Performance evaluation of different machine learning methods and deep-learning-based convolutional neural networks for health decision making. In *Nature-inspired computing for data science* (pp. 201–212). Springer. doi:10.1007/978-3-030-33820-6_8

Sarhan, A. M. (2020). Detection and Classification of Brain Tumor in MRI Images Using Wavelet Transform and Convolutional Neural Network. *Journal of Advances in Medicine and Medical Research*, 15–26. doi:10.9734/jammr/2020/v32i1230539

Shen, D., Wu, G., & Suk, H. I. (2017). Deep learning in medical image analysis. *Annual Review of Biomedical Engineering*, *19*(1), 221–248. doi:10.1146/annurev-bioeng-071516-044442 PMID:28301734

Siar, M., & Teshnehlab, M. (2019, October). Brain Tumor Detection Using Deep Neural Network and Machine Learning Algorithm. In *2019 9th International Conference on Computer and Knowledge Engineering (ICCKE)* (pp. 363-368). IEEE. 10.1109/ICCKE48569.2019.8964846

Sobhaninia, Z., Rezaei, S., Noroozi, A., Ahmadi, M., Zarrabi, H., Karimi, N., . . . Samavi, S. (2018). *Brain tumor segmentation using deep learning by type-specific sorting of images.* arXiv preprint arXiv:1809.07786.

Wang, L., Lin, Z. Q., & Wong, A. (2020). Covid-net: A tailored deep convolutional neural network design for detection of covid-19 cases from chest x-ray images. *Scientific Reports*, *10*(1), 1–12. doi:10.103841598-020-76550-z PMID:33177550

Yadav, S. S., & Jadhav, S. M. (2019). Deep convolutional neural network-based medical image classification for disease diagnosis. *Journal of Big Data*, *6*(1), 1–18. doi:10.118640537-019-0276-2

Chapter 12
Consumer-Centric E-Commerce Systems

Selva Nidhyananthan
https://orcid.org/0000-0001-9131-8409
Mepco Schlenk Engineering College, India

Mageshwar Subramanian
Mepco Schlenk Engineering College, India

D. Suganya
VSVN Polytechnic College, India

ABSTRACT

This chapter focuses on meeting the challenges such as security, reliability, and performance of e-commerce and user interface design advancement using new business strategies and state-of-the-art technical solutions. Security for user data and payment data are addressed with secured data communication and block chain technology, respectively. The shortcomings of popular e-commerce platforms are discussed by taking Amazon as an example. Online scenario now and in the future is analyzed with an envisioned case study. Bright opportunities for transformation in business models, aggregator, user interface, and vendor/customer recommendations are investigated utilizing deep learning technologies. The solutions provided and strategies explained in this chapter will help e-commerce at least for the next 10 years to have flawless and swift progress.

INTRODUCTION

A common man/woman as a customer now-a-days wish to buy the needed goods such as groceries, fabrics, food items, home appliances, fancy items, vehicles, vehicle spare parts, electronic gadgets, books, stationary, fruits, beverages, confectioneries, medicines, play items etc., and wish to avail services such as payment for insurance, Systematic Investment Plan, education fee, electricity bill, water bill, mobile & DTH recharge, rent payment, broadband/landline bill, donation, metro recharge, QR tickets, FASTAG,

DOI: 10.4018/978-1-6684-4969-1.ch012

Copyright © 2022, IGI Global. Copying or distributing in print or electronic forms without written permission of IGI Global is prohibited.

loan EMI, municipal tax, wallet recharge, clubs and associations etc., using e-commerce with the help of internet. A customer is an end user of good or services. Customer can be an individual or a company who purchases goods or services and they will never sell what they bought to others. Customers are so important for the existence of the business, in specific, loyal customers are the sole reason for the success of the business.

We are now in the information era; taking the advantage of internet has become quite common among people of all financial and educational categories. Earlier people used to go to shop for purchasing and physically go to the entity to avail the services. But now after the proliferation of usages for internet, payment gateways and e-commerce User Interface platforms people now prefer ONLINE mode than offline mode. Earlier elders in the family used to purchase goods but now even children and aged grand parents used to order items online. This has widen the customer base and varieties of items and services for business. Earlier purchases will be at its maximum during festival seasons, but now purchase is uniformly distributed throughout the year across the globe. Branded goods dominated the market once, but because of the power of technology the one who is dominating the market is the customer. Customers are well informed through media and other digital sources, they have more options to buy now. It has jolted up the market, allowing the best competitors to come out as the new leaders of the market and make use of the technology enabled business. Companies/individuals having a vision to broad base its customer base need to grasp the digital business technologies to meet the growing requirements of the evolving consumer. With dramatically increasing usage of smart phones, consuming goods and availing services trend continues to grow intense.

The chapter categorically covers 1. Aggregator (App interface between buyer and seller), 2.Advanced Payment Systems and 3. Role of Deep Learning in e-commerce along with Case Analysis. Beside these Studies on Amazon, the products which are not covered by Amazon, Opportunities for new products and services through e-commerce and seamless secured data communication are integral part of the chapter.

LITERATURE REVIEW

Myriad of analytic, research and review literatures deal with various aspects of e-commerce such as e-Technology, planning e-business, starting an e-business, barriers in adopting e-business, reason for failures, the patronage of the Internet all over the world, evolution in banking technologies, information systems management, approach of managers, deep learning approaches and security aspects in e-business. Some of the said aspects are reviewed in following literature review.

A framework of theoretical analysis (Alawneh.A, 2007) that helps the scholars to think about the concept of value creation and value addition in the new digital economy coveys the importance of value system in business leveraging e-Technology ((Alawneh.A, 2009). To create value to the commodity or service first of all we need to start a business. The article on 'How to start a e-business (Amit. B, 2007 & Daft, 1982)' give a clear cue on the difficulties being faced by large companies and Internet and Web technologies (Misic, 2006) can remake the business world in better way. At the same time the barriers in adopting e-business (Aranda.M, 2005), especially in construction industry is reviewed to give awareness to those who are willing to start e-business. He says slow adoption rate of e-business in construction industry does not reflect the maturity of the technology but is due to adoption barriers peculiar to the nature of construction. Accordingly for any e-business there will be certain barriers based on the nature of business undertaken. The patronage of the Internet all over the world is monumental and has remained on the increase from inception. Study over Nigerian territory (Ayo, 2006 & Chiemeke, 2006) indicate how long the country has to travel to expand the usage of internet to enhance the e-business more and more. Banking industry is a backbone of Indian financial system and it is afflicted by many challenging forces. One such force is revolution of information technology (Amar.K, 2009). Electronick banking in Finland (Karjaluoto, 2002) briefs customer beliefs and reactions to a new delivery channel. This study focuses on developing a theoretical model with a practical justification within the field of electronic banking. The purpose of this study was to determine those factors that influence the formation of consumer attitude toward electronic banking. Another important aspect of this study was to develop more insights into how attitude toward technology in general impacts on consumer behavior in an IT-environment. However, this electronic banking literature lacks empirical evidence about how a person's attitude affects their choice of financial service delivery channel. Banking sector has undergone tremendous changes to facilitate payment transactions in e-business using G-pay, Phone pay, paytm, with NEFT or UPI transfer. The text book on E-Business & Commerce (Strategic Thinking & Practice (Brahm.c, 2009) facilitates the readers of the book to be prepared to create real plans for their own organizations by way of emphasizing an analytical and critical approach (Earl.M, 2000, David W, 2001 & David, 2017) to understand the strategic decision-making. Security aspects in e-business are greatly dealt (Eben.O, 2003) to safe guard the money and data of customers and businessmen. An e-business information systems management strategy (Hackbarth, 2000) was built to approach the e-business in a system based approach and theoretical approach (Mendo, 2005).

The Book on 'How to succeed in e-business' (Kalakota, 1999), provides the Complete Project Lifecycle for Decision-support Applications. This book addresses aspects like how traditional managers approach business with CRM, ERP, and SCM technologies, how managers have to use modern technology and to understand the terminology and take action--to grasp the opportunities or defend against the invading virtual competitors. Most manufacturers prefer to sell their products on E-commerce websites because of low maintenance and high returns. The first part of the research work (Kali Pradeep, 2020) explains the role of data science to identify potential customers, items recommendations and fraud detections. Different stages of building E-commerce websites and the role of proper handling of data is then highlighted. The second part of the work is about the use of deep learning approaches (Yann, 2015) like Recurrent neural networks in analyzing textual information is presented. The reasons behind the failure of the India's first e-commerce company (Vaitheeswaran, 2017) Indiaplaza was briefed as set of inexplicable events. He also openly explained his extraordinary trials and tribulations while dealing with business failure and the impossible pressures that can threaten entrepreneurs in India (Joseph P.T, 2012). This literature is the strong alarm for those who start start-up or e-commerce business. To address, needs of organizations, merchants, commerce to cut costs and to improve quality/services/speed of delivery; more commonly associated with buying and selling of information, products and services via computer networks today (Sridhar, 2017) e-commerce draws on technologies such as mobile commerce, electronic funds transfer, supply chain management, Internet marketing and online transaction processing.

Aggregator

Aggregator is a website or program that assembles related things of content and portrays them or connects to them. An e-Commerce aggregator is a interface between multiple companies on one side and consumers on other side. An e-Commerce aggregator is a website or mobile application that handle multiple offers from competing companies and sells them to consumers through internet. Using e-commerce aggregator, customers get the benefit of comparing the features, prices, appearance and performance of the item selected, so that they will get the satisfaction of buying the best at the relatively less price. Support should be sought from Deep learning technology to enhance the features of aggregator. This chapter explains how it can be done in an effective way. Figure 1 depicts the outline of proposed model of Technology enabled and Customer oriented e-commerce system.

Figure 1. Model of Technology enabled and Customer oriented e-commerce system

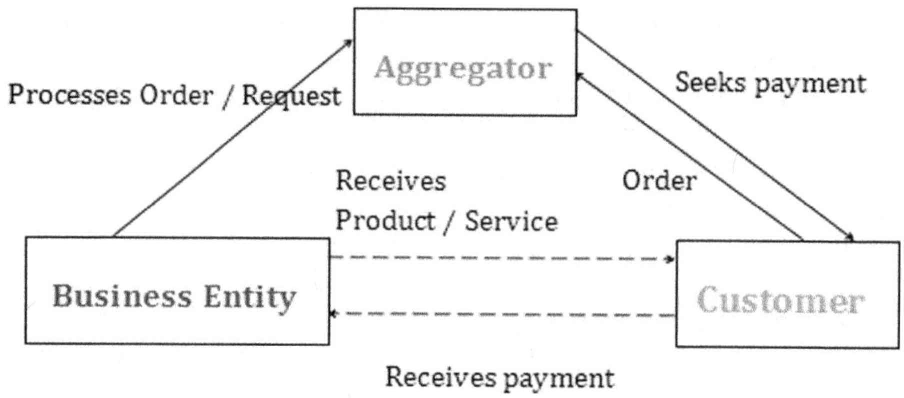

Payment System

After Amazon entered into e-commerce there was a boom in e-commerce business, millions of business started through e-commerce. But until the year 2008, the payment for items ordered through e-commerce was made by cheque or Demand drafts worldwide. During 2008, Paypal introduced payments for e-commerce through credit cards. This made the payment process simpler for the customers. In the year 2014, the total share of e-commerce in total industrial growth was 3.5%. Now in aggregator, payments are made through UPI payment, Internet banking, Debit card etc., in no matter of time.

Aggregators such as Amazon may do away with third party payment apps like Google Pay or PhonePe. Instead they may have the payment mode embedded into the Amazon application itself. This will eliminate the commission paid to the payment gateways, speed up the transactions and give better service to the buyers.

Emerging Paradigms in Digital Payments

Digital payment, also called as cashless payment is the fastest emerging technology in financial Services.

Today's digital payments is the culmination of centuries of evolution in payment system. It started with the barter trade. It evolved into various stages such as Commodities, metals, paper currency and Plastic money i.e. Credit and Debit cards, and finally into Online payments.

Credit cards and Debit cards can be called as the earliest forms of digital payments as it requires digital authentication and online transfer of money and confirmation of payments.

However, true digital payments require that the user does not carry any physical forms of cash or cards. Thus credit and debit cards cannot be called as true digital payments. But they laid the foundation for digital payments. Different protocols developed for plastic money have found their way into digital payments. These protocols have helped to speed up the development of the various forms of digital payments, including contact less payments, cashless payments etc.

India started developing the different payments system through the NPCIL. Today, NPCIL has a number of Digital Payment solutions which has helped India to reach the front-lines of Digital Payments.

The extant protocols for digital payments can be summarized as follows:

Mobile App Based Payment Systems

One of the most widely used payments systems in India. Here, the app is downloaded into a mobile phone. The app is linked to the users' bank account. This enables the users to make payments as well as receive payments. Multiple bank account can be linked to the app and this permits the users to transfer money from one of his account to another account as well as payments to outside parties. The authentication is done by PIN which is normally a a 4 digit numeric code.

Google Pay, Paytm, PhonePe and Bharat Pe are some of the type examples. These apps are available on both Google Pay and iOS platforms. Though, the interface may differ, their kernels are identical and share common protocols.

The primary drawback with these payments apps are that they require the user to possess both a smartphone as well as internet connections.

A. **Internet free Mobile apps**: Another one of the promising technology is the internet free and smartphone free apps which work through NFS technology and UPPI codes sent from feature phone. This technology is developed specifically for the feature phone users.
B. **Audio QR based authentication and transactions**:

Audio QR is a variation of the familiar QR platform. It is based on transmission of ultrasound not normally audible to human ears. The payer is enabled to transfer funds from his hand held device normally a smartphone.The authentication is also done through such Audio QR codes generated from the device .

C. **Charge Cards**: though not an emerging technology but an existing technology, it is a very popular digital payment in some countries such Australia and Japan.Basically they operate like Wallets, with the value stored in Credit cards sized cards. The cards are used by swiping them on machines to authenticate the payment. Money can be transferred into such through an online mode through normal Online banking protocols.
D. **On Device Wallets**: this is a promising a payment system for small payment up to a few hundred rupees. One such option is the so called UPI-Lite app which permits the user to top up his On Device Wallet. Once the wallet is topped up, it can be used to make payment to other devices to other devices which are similarly UPI Lite enabled.

The primary advantage is it can operate without internet connections. For the banking systems it offers the advantage of reducing the load on the core banking infrastructure of the member Bank.

The UPI Lite is planned to initially offer only debit transactions. Credit transactions will be offered in the future. The maximum amount that can be stored will be restricted to Rs.2000 at any given time to avoid money loss in case of loss of device. The limit may be enhanced in the future.

Blockchain Technology

Blockchain is a decentralized system. Blockchain technology in e-commerce is proposed in this article to secure the online payments for goods and services. A blockchain for an aggregator is basically an electronic ledger of transactions that is duplicated and distributed across the entire network of computers on the blockchain network of that aggregator. Since the same payment data is available in multiple numbers across the network, hacking data in all the storage places of network or breaking the chain is difficult. Hence it is impossible to change, hack, or cheat the system. This article explains the concept behind this security mechanism in more detail.

Blockchain Backbone

Blockchain literally means 'chain of blocks. Each block in the chain of blocks contain digital records of any transactions with time-stamp on the computers distributed in the network of computers. Each block has its cryptographic hash, like a unique key. Every block contains its hash and the previous block's hash, along with data, which connects the blockchain. Since each computer in the chain of computers in adopted with unique high end crypto system it is very hard for the hackers to break the system and to steal the information from the blocks. Whenever a new payment is done, a new block is added to the blockchain. Each transaction needs to be validated by all the network computers through common consensus. Blockchain accomplices secure and low cost international payment processing services through the use of encrypted distributed ledgers which provide trusted online verification of transactions without the need for third parties such as correspondent banks and clearinghouses. Blockchain technology was initially used to support the cryptocurrency but is now being used for various transaction applications.

Third party intermediaries are involved with the present day payments system. To make a payment, one has to pass through several bodies such as the payment gateway, international exchange, debtor and creditor. But having third party in transactions have many shortcomings. Foremost we need to pay fort heir service, next unnecessarily it delays the transaction.With blockchain payment systems, we can have simple payment, maintain the authenticity of the transactions without the need for middle men,finally save the transaction data securely. Details of payments that take place via a blockchain network are highly secure. Since every block contains its hash and the hash of the previous block, they are time wise linked. Hence, no one can tamper with the records on the blockchain, as any change would be visible in the entire network. Since, with blockchain, one can Transfer funds across international boundary, eliminate the intermediaries in the payment process, ensure safety of data, small enterprises and even individuals have now initiated export business of traditional items such as neem tree tiny sticks for bruising the teeth, ground nuts for and ground nut candy for healthy eating, spinach for body health.

Blockchain tools designed for individuals, businesses, or financial institutions will have a few differing features depending on the use case. Across all uses, blockchain payment solutions allow customers to quickly and securely make transactions on a blockchain. Companies choose to use blockchain payment solutions for a number of reasons. Some tools enable the creation of smart contracts, or protocols used to facilitate, verify, and enforce transactions. These contracts are well documented and provide a higher level of traceability. These forms of payment are also quicker than traditional tools since they do not require a financial institution and transactions can be completed across country borders with ease. Some of the less complex and customizable blockchain payment products offer a product similar to payment gateways. The only difference here is the documentation and traceability provided by the blockchain and the simplified international payment process.

Blockchain Payment System Functionality

The blockchain payments system is not complicated at the same time it is effective. Let us understand step by step process done in blockchain in cross border payment transaction. Suppose you reside in India and pay Rs.5,00,000 to a friend living in Singapore. Both of your banks are linked to say INDSGR blockchain network, and here's how the payment would take place:

Stage 1: You will send a payment request from Rs. 5,00,000 from your bank say State Bank of India SBI to your friend's bank say Bank of Singapore BOS.
Stage 2: BOS bank in Singapore will receive a transaction request of Rs. 5,00,000.
Stage 3: BOS bank will approve the request after confirming with your friend in Singapore.
Stage 4: After SBI bank receives the transaction approval, Rs. 5,00,000 will be deducted from your account.
Stage 5: 5,00,000 rupees will move to SBI's pool account, and it will move to INDSGR.
Stage 6: The nodes in INDSGR nodes are updated with new hashes to ensure data safety.
Stage 7: The money will then be credited to your friend's SGR bank account in of Singapore.

Now that you understand the working of blockchain payment systems let us look at how one can address the challenges of blockchain in payments.

STUDIES ON AMAZON

This section of the chapter provides a detailed study on the business model of Amazon and what are the products they do not deal among crore of items they are retailing through e-commerce. This article is going to see the the goods one aggregator is not merchandising as the opportunity for a new business or startup with different set of customer base. All the kinds of data in varities of custoomer bases of number of aggregators or e-commerce business entities are the reliable feed for the Deep learning architectures for designing new age e-commerce systems.

NEW PRODUCTS AND SERVICES

The e Commerce scenario is currently dominated by products based aggregators such as Amazon and Flipkart. While they offer a wide range of products in an online mode, the next wave of e Commerce may be driven by online offering of services. Transport service providers Ola and Uber and fintech companies such as Policy Bazaar.com and Paisa Bazaar.com are already driving the growth in financial services. Future products may include Online offering of legal, accounting, educational and even engineering services.

We may witness aggregators in services such as plumbing, electricals, painting, cleaning and minor repairs. There may be aggregators devoted exclusively to medical or legal services. We can even expect aggregators in such services as astrology, palmistry etc. There may emerge aggregators in education which will enable individual educators to offer their services online.

The possibility is truly limitless. Consumer is the driving force behind all the changes in business world. Customers want the online buying to happen as quick as possible with less time consumption and spend more time on other productive or official activates. Almost one out of four online purchases are now made on smartphones and by the end of 2022 it will be three out of four. Since placing orders through smartphone apps is easy and since the smart phone is available with the individual all the time except during sleep people find it easy to place orders and tend to place orders for new products and services. The real credit of this goes to recommending systems. This article suggests the readers to refer the recommendation trends if needed.

Data Security

Data in this chapter context mean customer feedback data, banking data, customer behavior data, product and services data, after sales service data and many more customer centric data. All data need to be secured from unintended and unlawful usages by the business organization the customer is associated with or any other organization or any individual or groups or by the anonymous autonomous system itself.

Modern world has evolved from hot cash payments to building cashless payments.The world is undergoing the digital evolution, the payments industry has adopted many ingenious technologies to simplify payment procedures. For example, the secure and ultra fast UPI (Universal Payment Interface) payment system idea is conceived and implemented only in India in the world and it continues to be the most fastest and secure digital payment system in the world. UPI system powers multiple bank accounts into a single mobile application. By incorporating blockchain technology in UPI payment system, enterprises can run their business processes while maintaining high security and transparency through decentralized ledger system.

Secured Data Communication

With best technologies available in their mobile phone at hand, consumers expect seamless e-commerce experiences online. The current scenario of e-commerce is expected to change massively by 2022, by then, the coalition of the Internet of Things and deep learning inspired by neural networks will automate smart refrigerators and home inventories to perform shopping process through e-commerce on their own. Future seamless payment methods will be simply voice assisted or thought assisted. .

EVERYTHING WILL BE ONLINE IN NEAR FUTURE

In the near future, shopping would be fully integrated into current life moments using Internet of Things. By the middle of February 2022, every petrol pump, retail shop, saloon, petty shop etc., in even rural India is equipped with QR scanning based online payment mechanism. Thump print This brings comfort to both customer and vendor. Using various social network sites or online shopping portals or virtual shopping wallets, new business models and products will evolve and occupy the market place.

ONLINE business or shopping is found to be advantages because it offers many benefits to the customers, some of them are customer convenience, more variety, better prices, more control, easy price comparison, easy features comparison for the same product of different brands, no crowds, now car parking requirement, no costly mall with air condition requirements, access to used or damaged inventory, availing products and services 24x7, booking gifts in advance and delivering them on the specific day and different modes of payment such as through UPI, NEFT, credit/debit cards or cash on delivery.

But ONLINE business has its own short comings as well. To list a few, Shipping Problems and Delays, Risk of Fraud, Less Contact With customer Community, Spending Too Much Time Online, Returns Can Be Complicated, Customer Doesn't Know Exactly What customer is Getting, Unfriendly, Scammy, or Complicated Websites and no sales assistance physically.

Comparing weaknesses the positives are more in ONLINE business. These weaknesses will also become obsolete by technological progress. Now-a-days every one is having access to Internet at very less price. Hence in the near future every buy & sell and transaction will be ONLINE.

CASE ANALYSIS

This section of the chapter provides a detailed case study on a new age start-up.

his section of the Book chapter analyses the secret behind the success of few Indian startups and the impact of customer centrist approach in their business. The sample startups taken are:

1. Myntra
2. Ola Cabs
    1. FreshMenu
    2. 1mg and
    3. Unacademy

All the five example startups are taken from different sectors of product and services. Some of these startups are by male entrepreneur and some others are by females.

1. **Myntra**: This startup was established by Mukesh Bansal & Co. and successfully running their fashion wear and accessories business. Myntra is an Indian Fashion e-commerce company, which sells men and women garments, accessories, shoes and many more products related to fashion. The company first had its official website through which they ran the business. In the year 2015 the then CEO of the company closed the website and started running their business only through mobile App but immediately they witnessed 16^ drop in their business. After few years now the business is running parallel in both the platforms and the business has grown. Here the lesson is that all people will not switchover to the trending technology from the traditional technology. This was learned by Myntra from their customers and succeeded in business.
2. **Ola Cabs**: Ola is the India's most popular brand as for as booking the vehicle for travel is concerned. Bhavish Aggarwal is an Indian entrepreneur and co-founder of Ola Cabs, India's most popular Cab Aggregator and Ridesharing company. OlaCabs is more specifically into providing Taxi services and conquered in rural and urban India. It is more popularly known as Ola. Aggarwal started as an online cab aggregator in Mumbai. Seeing the success of Ola, it is known to be one of the fastest-growing businesses in India. The other few examples in this transportation sectors are Fast track taxi and redbus.

3. **FreshMenu** Rashmi Daga, the founder & CEO of Fresh Menu, once worked as sales head at Ola cabs. Also she has worked as sales head for education, jewelry, IT, medical industries. Having gained knowledge about business and about customer likes and dislikes she started Bangalore-based an online food delivery service that aims to deliver freshly prepared food at customer home or office desk. Fresh Menu is dedicated to offer tasty and healthy food packages to its customers. The Fresh Menu's online food delivery service provides a range of meal packages for lunch and dinner that includes both international and our own cultural food items in a fresh manner. Fresh Menu has facilitated customers to order online and enjoy tasty and healthy foods through their mobile application.
4. **1mg**1mg is the first and biggest online pharmacy that was founded in 2013 by Prashant Tandon & Co. The company started with the goal of making it easier for Indians to get their medicines online. In 2013, the company launched its first website along with a mobile app for iOS devices; both are still available today. There are a number of key factors that have contributed to the success of India's most trusted online pharmacy, namely: A focus on customer satisfaction, A wide selection of products and brands, Fast and reliable delivery and Affordable price. One of the main reasons why customers trust online pharmacies like 1mg is because they put a focus on customer satisfaction.
5. **Unacademy** In just five years, Unacademy has become India's leading online education platform. With over 10 million registered users, the company is offering affordable and quality education to everyone. Unacademy is an online learning platform that offers free and paid courses in a wide range of subjects, from school level to competitive exams. It also offers UPSC preparation, job skills, entrepreneurship, and more.Knowing the need of customers, unacademy is offering its services and attaining good heights.

All the examples cited above as case analysis are e-commerce businesses. They all have succeeded because of one main reason, they have thoroughly studied the customers and their needs and providing goods and services online in a fairly simplest and economic way.

Role of Deep Learning

This section elaborates the role of Deep learning techniques and architectures in innovative e-commerce.

Machine learning is creating a learning attribute to machines, Artificial intelligence is imitating the human brain to some extent, modeling it and exporting the model to the machine to make it think like human and Deep learning is the finest subset of machine learning, it abstracts the data of any kind in a meaningful way and helps to arrive at a decision or action. Deep learning architectures have multi-layered artificial neural network to perform stages of data abstraction and to carry out a range of tasks. Deep learning differs from its superset machine learning systems in that it is capable of learning on its own and improving the performance as it analyses large data sets. The basic requirement of Deep learning architectures is that it should be fed with huge amount of data in terms of millions to avoid the conflict of ending in local minima or resulting in under fitting. Figure 2. Shows the Block diagram of Deep learning Architecture.

Deep learning technology in business world brings new hopes and innovation in e-commerce, e-linking, and customer support. Deep learning algorithms use artificial neural networks to learn a certain task just like what biological neural networks do in human brain. The enthusiasm in knowing about deep learning

Figure 2. Block diagram of Deep learning Architecture

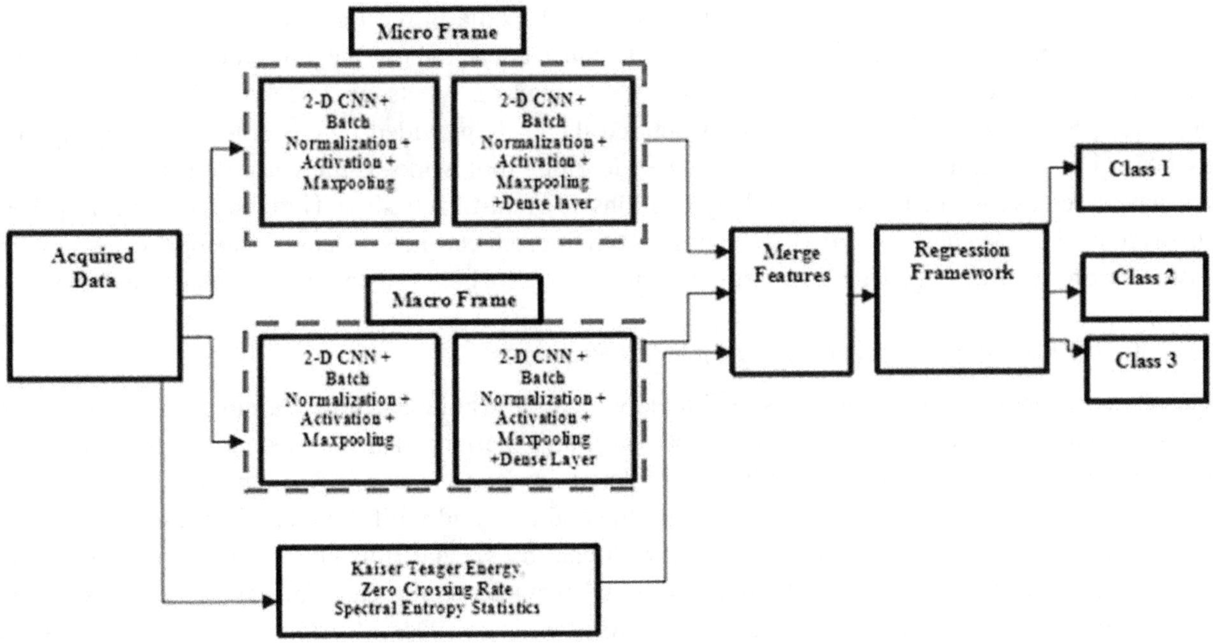

and using it in varieties of applications in different domains has significantly increased over the past few years. With many companies especially startups implementing this technology for good, deep learning is so popular now. Understanding deep learning architecture functions layer wise is difficult because the underlying concepts are advanced mathematics. Neural networks are trained by exposing it to many example data, and discovering the commonalities among them to arrive at course level to detail level of abstraction of what rare exposed to it. Deep learning can be implemented into many aspects of modern day business towards automation and customer satisfaction. Deep Learning helps to decode complex unstructured data and derive consumer insights that are crucial for creating successful business. Deep Learning if implemented with right objective, this technology will transform customer centric business processes to larger extent.

Evolution in Customer Product

Deep learning and other smart solutions are even renovating children's toys. Conventional Talking Tom toy repeats whatever the child or the speaker in front speaks in the voice of tom. The doll where remarkable changes invoked with the help of deep learning is Hello Barbie doll. This doll listens, records, interacts with ToyTalk servers.in cloud and then responds to the child. This conversation is analyzed by a system equipped with deep learning, selecting an appropriate response from 8,000 recorded possibilities based on the characteristics and history of the child who is conversing with the doll. The concept and constituent of the talking dolls are now completely changed as adaptive and useful with the incorporation of Deep learning technique.

Let us see how Deep Learning is transforming sales and marketing good and services:

Achieving and Analyzing Customer Feed Back

Now-a-days voice of the customer is available in social media in the form of text, image, video and scores in an unstructured way. Customers express their feedback about the good they purchased or the services they availed in social Medias like Tweeter, Instagram, Whatsapp, Facebook, YouTube, Forum etc., Deep learning gets insights from unstructured data sets provided by customers or company and assists in business enhancement. Simply the deep learning tool works as the voice of a customer. Deep learning assesses customer feedback and expectations on a real-time basis and individuals and enterprises involved in business can get information to upgrade their products and services. Based on these premium insights from deep leaning, Brands can articulate themselves for better customer centric sales and services.

Robots in Enhancing Deep Learning Enabled Business

One form of robot is chat bot which is facilitated with abilities like listening, summarizing, getting apt response and giving voice response to customers as if an experienced and skilled human being is doing towards customers. Chat bots take the benefit of data mining, deep learning, and natural language processing, thus creating new ways to interact with the end user and willful buyer of goods and services. People can have personalized communication with chat bots. Chat Bots help business to have timely conversations with needy and give them product and service recommendations and guidelines. In the near future most of the business entities in the world will have Deep learning enabled Chat Bots as receptionists in the place of real human receptionists.

Data Analytics With Deep Learning

Home automation, Industrial automation, healthcare automation, educational service automation are gaining momentum and creating profitable avenues for organizations and individuals across the world. In all these fields, analyzing the unstructured data obtained through Internet of Things products with data analytics is helped by Deep learning. It helps to capture data from the machines through sensors in different scenarios and monitor them in an easy and cost-effective way as for as Industrial automation is concerned. Through these analytics, deep learning can help to reinforce the interactions between machines and users better and based on the data, the business performance can be enhanced from time to time in all the sectors mentioned above.

Predictive Analysis on Customer Behavior

Based on the learnt historical behavior of customers and common public deep learning architectures perform better predictive analysis and help business entities develop crystal clear ideas of customer preferences. Deep Learning plays a highly significant role in the data analysis process. Despite whether it's a small organization or big organization or individual business man, entrepreneurs will have the chance to perform successful data analytic with deep learning.

CONCLUSION

To be in business and catch up with the needs of tomorrow's consumers, individuals /companies need to build their e-commerce and popularizing strategy, and asses their level of technology with current online strategy. Technology enablers such as Deep learning, Artificial neural networks, web/app management systems, quicker and safer payments can be leveraged and optimized to achieve a best-in-class business.

REFERENCES

Alawneh, A., & Hattab, E. (2007). E-Business Value Creation: An Exploratory Study. *Proceedings of the Seventh International Conference on Electronic Business*, 181-188.

Alawneh, A., & Hattab, E. (2009). Importance of value system in business leveraging e-Technology. *International Arab Journal of e-Technology, 1*(2), 1-8.

Amit, B., & Steve, M. (2007). How to Plan E-Business Initiatives in Established Companies. *MIT Slogan Management Review, 49*(1), 11-22.

Aranda-M, G., & Stewart, P. (2005). *Barriers to E-Business Adoption in construction international literature review*. https://www.researchgate.net/publication/27476067_Barriers_to_ebusiness_adoption_inconstruction_international_literature_review

Ayo, C. K. (2006). The Prospects of e-Commerce Implementation in Nigeria. *Journal of Internet Banking and Commerce, 11*(3), 68–75.

Brahm, C. (2009). *E-Business and Commerce Strategic Thinking and Practice*. Houghton Mifflin.

Chiemeke, S. C., Evwiekpaefe, A., & Chete, F. (2006). The Adoption of Internet Banking in Nigeria: An Empirical Investigation. *Journal of Internet Banking and Commerce, 11*(3), 33–49.

Daft, R. L. (1982). Bureaucratic versus Nonbureaucratic Structure and the Process of Innovation and Change. In S. B. Bacharach (Ed.), *Research in the Sociology of Organizations* (pp. 129–166). JAI Press Inc.

David, W. (2001). *E-Commerce Strategy, Technologies and Applications*. McGraw Hill.

Earl, M. (2000). Evolving the E-Business. *Business Strategy Review*, 33–38.

Eben, O. (2003). *A Systematic Approach to E-Business Security*. University of New Brunswick, Canada, Faculty of Administration. http://ausweb.scu.edu.au/aw03/papers/otuteye/paper.html

Hackbarth, G., & Kettinger, W. J. (2000). *Building an E-Business Strategy: Information Systems Management*. Taylor and Francis. Doi:10.1201/1078/43192.17.3.20000601/31243.10

Joseph, P. T. (2012). E-Commerce: An Indian Perspective (4th ed.). Eastern Economy Edition, PHI India.

Kalakota, R., & Robinson, M. (1999). E-Business: Roadmap for success. Addison-Wesley.

Karjaluoto, H., & Mattila, M. (2002). Electronic Banking in Finland: Consumer Beliefs and Reactions to a New Delivery Channel. *Journal of Financial Services Marketing, 6*(4), 346–361.

LeCun, Y., Bengio, Y., & Hinton, G. (2015). Deep learning. *Nature, 521*. Advance online publication. doi:10.1038/nature14539

Mendo, F., & Fitzgerald, G. (2005). Theoretical Approaches to Study SMEs E-Business Progression. *CIT. Journal of Computing and Information Technology*, *13*(02), 123–136.

Misic, V., & Zhao, J. (2006). E-Business Reference Models. In *Reference Modeling for Business Systems Analysis*. doi:10.4018/9781599040547

Pradeep, K. (2020). Data Science and Deep Learning Applications in the e-Commerce Industry: A Survey. *Indian Journal of Computer Science and Engineering*, *11*(5). Advance online publication. doi:10.21817/indjcse/2020/v11i5/201105135

Rahmath, S., Hema, D., & Abdullah, K. (2011). In emerging economy: Indian consumer's perspective. International Arab Journal of e-Technology, *2*(1), 56–64.

Seshadri, S. (2017). E-Commerce Technology Made Easy. *IJITR, 5*, 6183-6198. https://www.researchgate.net/publication/317278278_E-Commerce_Technology_Made_Easy

Seshadri, S. (2017). *An Introduction To E-Commerce Technology*. https://www.researchgate.net/publication/317277929_An_Introduction_To_E-Commerce_Technology

Sohani. (2009). *Technology and Banking Sector*. ICFAI University Press.

Vaitheeswaran. (2017). *Failing to Succeed: The Story of India's First E-Commerce Company.* Rupa Publications.

Whiteley. (2017). *E-Commerce: Strategy, Technologies and Applications.* McGraw Hill Education.

Chapter 13
Framework for Blockchain-Based Smart Healthcare Systems

Bhanumathi Velusamy
https://orcid.org/0000-0001-5661-347X
Department of Electronics and Communication Engineering, Anna University, India & Regional Campus Coimbatore, India

Vishnuvarthan Rajagopal
https://orcid.org/0000-0002-3236-3389
Department of Electronics and Communication Engineering, Anna University, India & Regional Campus Coimbatore, India

ABSTRACT

Healthcare is one of the basic human needs and an important aspect of connected living. With the advancement of technologies, it is gradually transitioning away from traditional hospital-centric care towards a more virtual and distributed care. Health 4.0 is new buzz word in the healthcare systems. It is artificial intelligence (AI)-based intelligent devices enabled through the internet of medical things (IoMT). It is made up of medical sensors, cloud, edge and fog-computing, and wireless communication technology. The data collected from the patients are sensitive as it is crucial for diagnosis and to make critical decisions. Hence, the cyber criminals invest significant amounts of effort, time, and resources to exploit these data. So, in order to improve the security of the system, a framework for a blockchain-based smart healthcare system is proposed. In addition to it, the prelude on the Health 4.0 components and the current research challenges, benefits, and applications are discussed. Finally, the use case along with the applications of blockchain in the healthcare sector are discussed.

INTRODUCTION TO HEALTH 4.0

One of the most basic human needs is healthcare (Li & Carayon, 2021). The basic enabling technologies include wireless sensor network and processing algorithms to generate a meaningful information from the data collected through the sensors. But, it faces a number of challenges, including high costs for

DOI: 10.4018/978-1-6684-4969-1.ch013

Copyright © 2022, IGI Global. Copying or distributing in print or electronic forms without written permission of IGI Global is prohibited.

Figure 1. Components of Health 4.0

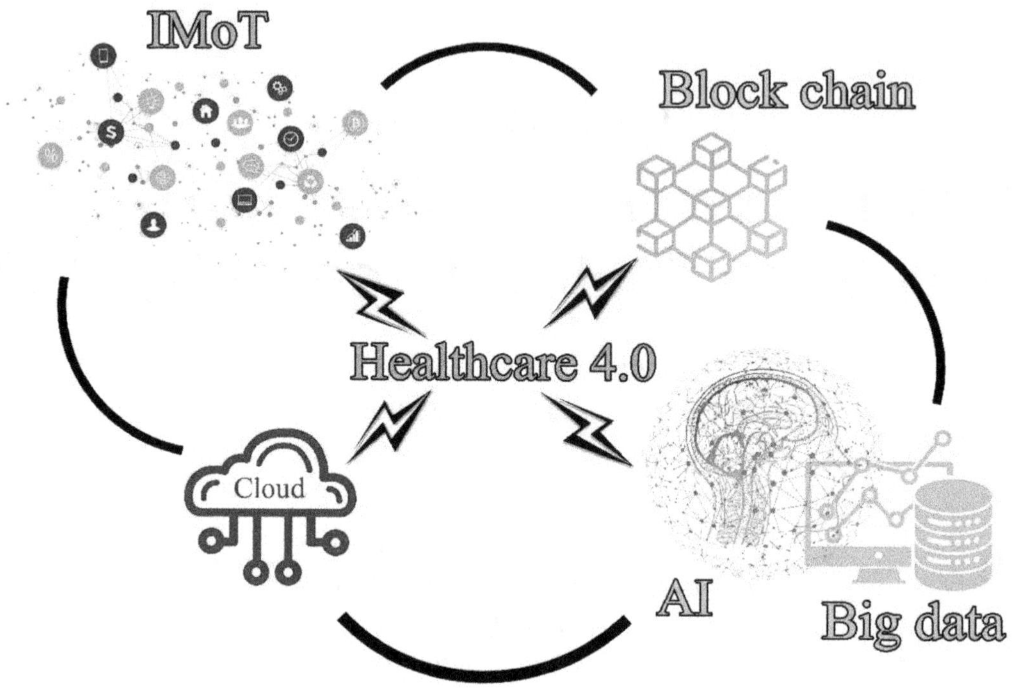

professionals, healthcare services, and equipment; a lack of skilled professionals; the need for collaboration between healthcare providers and supporting industries; and fierce competition among healthcare providers. These problems are forcing healthcare practitioners to think about incorporating and implementing new healthcare models based on cutting-edge information and communication technologies (Tortorella, et al., 2021). As the Industry 4.0 era ushers in smart and autonomous industrial processes with benefits such as improved operation, lower costs, and higher quality, Health 4.0 takes on the principles of Industry 4.0 to address these concerns.

Health 4.0 offers a new and exciting vision for the healthcare industry (Yang, et al., 2020). The principles of health 4.0 is adapted from Industry 4.0 principles. It is a new buzz word in the healthcare systems which is an Artificial Intelligence (AI) based intelligent devices enabled through the Internet of Medical Things (IoMT). It transforms the healthcare business model by improving interactions among patients, stakeholders, infrastructure, and the value chain (Tortorella, et al., 2021). Health 4.0 integrate the latest technologies such as IoMT, AI, machine learning, cloud-, edge-, fog-computing, big data analytic and blockchain (Haleem, Javaid, Singh, & Suman, 2022). These technologies are referred to as components, and they are depicted in Figure 1. The main objectives of Health 4.0 are:

1. Provide high-quality healthcare services and
2. Improved efficiency and effectiveness while keeping expenses and resource usage under control.

The major elements of Health 4.0 are: smartness and interconnection (Chanchaichujit, Tan, & Eaimkhong, 2019). Smartness refers to the use of AI tools for improving treatment, diagnosis and individualized patient-care management system. Interconnection refers to integrating all the healthcare aspects to create an effective information network. Some of the elements that are interconnected in Health 4.0 are: interaction between patients and caregivers, interaction within the professional care team, equipment and devices, insurance, billing and costs.

Design of Health 4.0

Design is crucial in the development of smart healthcare systems and the delivery of healthcare with greater effectiveness and efficiency. Understanding and influencing the patient experience for the best potential outcome is an important role of design in advancing smart healthcare systems (Sisodia & Jindal, 2021). Hence, Health 4.0 is designed based on six design principles:

- *Interoperability*, the ability to connect various medical systems and devices;
- *Virtualization*, the ability to make virtual/digital duplicates of various medical devices, systems, and processes;
- *Decentralization*, the ability of health-care systems to control over themselves by making appropriate decisions;
- *Real-time capability*, the ability to gather and analyze health data in order to take appropriate action;
- *Service Oriented,* the ability to develop software services for medical devices and systems interactions;
- *Modularity,* the ability to update individual modules, to meet new requirements and to reuse available modules to build new health/medical systems.

Challenges

Device connectivity, information management, interoperability, security, and privacy are the major problems that Health 4.0 encounters (Lopes, Marrone, Pereira, & Dias, 2019). And since, a large number of IoMT devices are used to identify and diagnose diseases, several concerns such as hardware faults, battery drain, and communication challenges arises.

- The complexity and black box aspect of machine learning models slows down stakeholders' and customers' understanding and adoption of the technology.
- The government is slower to respond and can't keep up with the rapid growth of new ideas and products in a growing category that has attracted billions of dollars from investors who are looking to back the next big unicorn.
- Clinical executives are frequently tasked with determining how well a new technology based on artificial intelligence will affect patient care, but they may lack the necessary knowledge or a wealth of research and literature to do a comparative comparison.
- A startup faces unique obstacles in attempting to establish synergy among a broad mix of highly educated and skilled employees with varying degrees of clinical and data science skills.
- When it comes to user autonomy, there are numerous obstacles, including data security, privacy, and potential bias.

Figure 2. Applications of Health 4.0

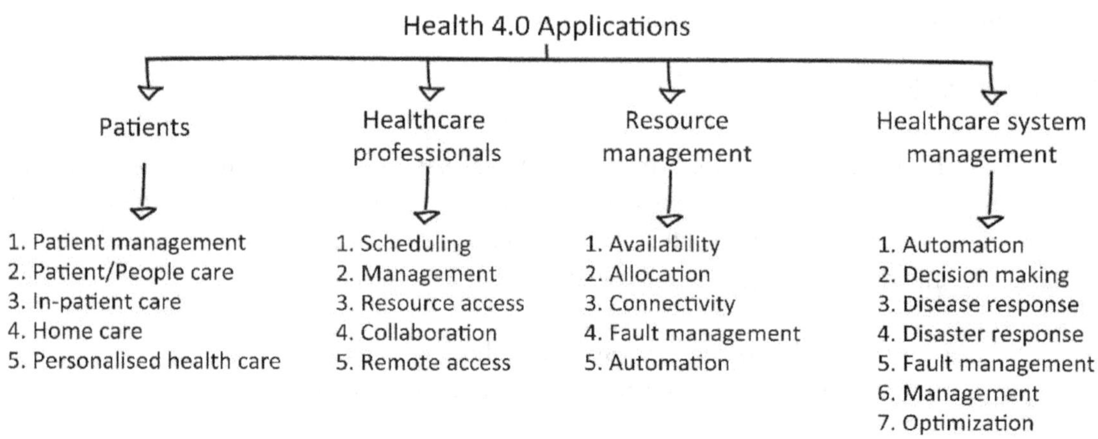

- Machine learning need high quality data to train itself. But acquiring the patients data is a tough process as it is limited due to the privacy and protection concerns and industry reluctance to share them.

Applications of Health 4.0

Health 4.0 has numerous capabilities and a diverse set of resources. Its applications take all the advantages of the technologies, software, equipment and the tools to provide reliable, robust and high-quality services (Paul, et al., 2021). Based on (Jameela, Nader, & Eman, 2020), the applications are grouped into four categories: patients, healthcare professionals, healthcare system management, and resource management and are elaborated in the Figure 2.

The research areas focused in this chapter include: state of the art regarding IoMT and medical sensors for smart health care, cloud- and edge-based smart health care and security and privacy of the IoMT.

Motivation of the Chapter

In this section, we discuss possible types of attack (Mahajan, et al., 2022) that target health data and the reasons that emphasis need for blockchain.

- The system can be entirely crippled by denial of service. This attack primarily targets servers and high-performance systems (Ferrag, Shu, Djallel, & Choo, 2021). Such unauthorized access could be limited by blockchain.
- Man-in-the-middle attack: The primary goal of this attacker is to steal personal information. An eavesdropper could gain personal information by hacking the system Wi-Fi because health records are connected to IoT devices. Blockchain helps in protecting data by using cryptographic methods and so improves security. (Rasool, Ahmad, Rafique, Qayyum, & Qadir, 2022).
- The Sybil attack entails the creation of many malicious nodes on IoT devices in order to slow the system (Avila, Sanmartin, Jabba, & Gomez, 2022). For digital payments, the existing cryptocur-

rency payment technology, QR code, is commonly employed. As a result, one user can generate multiple unauthorized QR codes to get access to the system. Blockchain is capable of ensuring integrity of the data and system.

- Phishing: QR codes are currently utilized to link to websites. Phishing attempts, such as the theft of credit card and personal health information, are now conceivable as a result. Blockchain can be used to prevent this (Mahajan, et al., 2022).

Objectives

The objectives of this chapter are:

- To provide the prelude on the impact of the health 4.0 on the advancement of e-healthcare systems and to understand the components constituting Health 4.0, current research challenges, benefits and applications of health 4.0
- To understand the need for block chain in healthcare system and to introduce a framework, working, use cases and applications of blockchain-based smart healthcare system

Major Contribution

The major contributions of this chapter are summarized below:

- To identify the problems that the modern healthcare system faces and to discuss the components in detail with their advantage and challenges in the given environment, to review the framework of AI in healthcare, risks and challenges, application of incorporating AI in healthcare system
- To discuss IoMT architecture, various medical sensors on the market, and also wearable and implantable sensors that aid in patient monitoring system, and the need for edge computing and big data in the healthcare system
- To identify the need for security and privacy of healthcare data and to demonstrate a new blockchain framework with its potential use cases and applications of blockchain-enabled e-healthcare scenarios.

ARTIFICIAL INTELLIGENCE IN HEALTHCARE SYSTEMS

The advancement of healthcare systems is immense with the application of AI. AI in healthcare refers to the application of machine learning (ML) algorithms and other cognitive technologies in medical contexts (S.Young, 2022). AI can assist clinicians in making more accurate diagnosis and treatment plans with the use of patient data and other information. It also helps to make healthcare more predictive and proactive by analyzing huge data and providing better preventive care ideas for patients. It can, for example, predict and track the spread of infectious diseases like corona viruses by evaluating data from government, healthcare, and other sources. The application of AI to healthcare data can literally be a matter of life and death.

One of the biggest challenge in healthcare is to capturing data in a meaningful format so that it can be analyzed (Kaur, Garg, & Gupta, 2021). Also, data by itself is incapable of producing insight. As a

Figure 3. Framework for AI-based healthcare solution

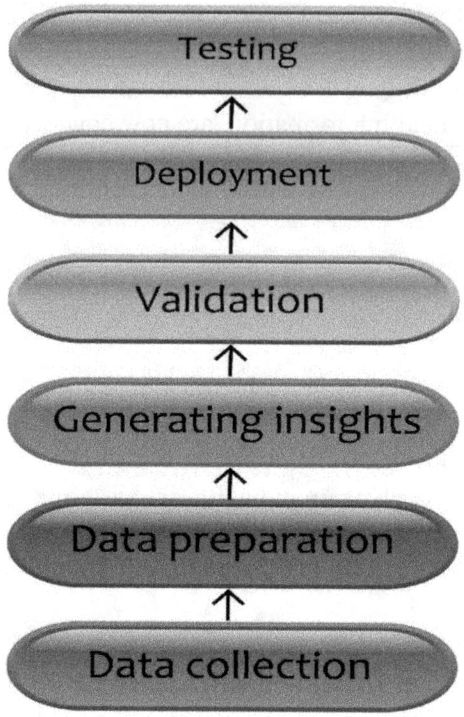

result, AI techniques are used to find patterns in data, and healthcare professionals are required to form and validate insights (S.Young, 2022). The next major challenge is, regardless of the fact that various AI-based healthcare technologies have been developed, acceptance of AI remains limited. This could be owing to insufficient or incorrect evaluation, as well as a lack of internationally recognized AI evaluation standards.

Framework of AI-Based Healthcare System

A generic framework is provided below in Figure 3 to make development and deployment of AI-based healthcare solution easier (Huffman, 2018).

- ***Data collection:*** To get the most out of AI, it has to be able to obtain a large amount of patient data. Deep learning algorithms, for example, require a large dataset to train on and deliver meaningful results. This is a major challenge in healthcare, as the necessary data is frequently unavailable.
- ***Data preparation:*** It is a critical step since healthcare data is often very noisy, and the quality of AI is solely dependent on the quality of data that is fed into it (Diaz, et al., 2021). As a result, data must be cleansed before being fed into a model or algorithm. This is frequently the most time-consuming process, and it absorbs the majority of a data scientist's work.
- ***Insight generation***: There are lots of distinct analytical methods to generate insights, and the impact on the outcome depends on choice of method the data scientist chooses. Hence, data scientists must understand the details of each method and how to configure them. That's why a close

collaboration is required between people who know data science and people who know the clinical area (Mehta, Pandit, & Shukla, 2019). Finally, the outcome must be assessed by the clinical expert to confirm if it is accurate and reliable.

- ***Validation:*** Often, the model or algorithm may discover a pattern in the data that is either useless or misleading (Hond, et al., 2022). Hence the data must be validated by the healthcare personals and it is better to conceive of AI-enabled solutions as an enhancement rather than a replacement for human capabilities.
- ***Deployment & Testing***: Every system cannot be connected to an AI-enabled solution. It must be designed in a particular workflow involving both IT and clinical experts. Also, the models must be tested after they have been implemented to ensure their reliability (Paul, et al., 2021). In addition to that, AI must ensure six principles when it is implemented in healthcare, they are: protecting human autonomy; promoting human wellbeing and safety, ensuring explain ability, intelligibility and transparency, ensuring inclusiveness and equity, promoting AI that is responsive and sustainable, fostering responsibility and accountability.

Advantages of AI in Health

- Keeping well: AI can help people stay healthy by encouraging good behavior in individuals through the use of technology apps.
- Early detection: AI aids in the more accurate detection of diseases such as cancer, even in the early stages (Haleem, Javaid, Singh, & Suman, 2022).
- Diagnosis: AI can review and store information from case studies of treatment and response, symptoms, and medical journals. It can help with disease diagnosis at a rate that is exponentially faster than a human (Haleem, Javaid, Singh, & Suman, 2022).
- Decision making: AI's pattern recognition and predictive analysis aid in making timely healthcare decisions and actions, as well as task prioritization (Lu & Liao, 2022).
- Cost minimization: With the use of AI, the performance of the health system can be enhanced while expenses are minimized (López Seguí, et al., 2020).
- Chatbots: Through interactive communication, AI chatbots could assist in stigmatizing pathological patients such as (HIV/AIDS, psychiatric disorders) for prompt access and follow-up services (Parviainen & Rantala, 2022).
- Prediction: AI could able to predict the spread of diseases or vulnerabilities within specific groups or communities (Chanchaichujit, Tan, & Eaimkhong, 2019).
- AI can help in terms of mother and child health, such as pregnancy monitoring, child malnutrition, and so on (Dansharif, Iyawa, Owoseni, & Iyawa, 2021).

Risks and Challenges

- It takes a lot of high-quality data to train an AI-based health system, which is itself a huge difficulty in healthcare systems.
- Data bias - AI that has been trained on the data of one country cannot be used for another country. The data could large differ between communities due to climatic, food practice and topographical changes (Aceto, Persico, & Pescape, 2020).

- Individual and population-based data collection, usage, storage, and sharing raise important questions about consent, ownership, and access (Imran, Mahmood, Morshed, & Sellis, 2021).
- AI necessitates a significant financial investment and expense and is hence out of reach for many organizations (Chanchaichujit, Tan, & Eaimkhong, 2019).

Applications

AI can play an important role in unprecedented situation such as covid-19 (Adadi, Lahmer, & Nasiri, 2021) by diagnosing the virus, identifying the disease hotspots, patient care, disease management, predicting future outbreaks etc. Deep mind, a Google project, blends machine learning and neuroscience to create neural networks that imitate the human brain. Some of the latest applications which are under research based on AI health is listed in the Table 1.

Table 1. Applications of AI-Health

Ref.	Application	Technologies	Medical sensor	Remarks
(X. Yuan, 2022)	Heart disease prediction model	Machine learning, Fuzzy logic & gradient boosting prediction tree	Electrocardiogram	Predicts binary and multiple classification heart disease simultaneously
(Sethuraman, Kompally, Mohanty, & Choppali, 2021)	MyWear: A smart garment	Deep neural network	Electrocardiogram (ECG), Electromyography	Wearable garment measures heart rate and depicts the force exerted by the muscles. Uses DNN to predict the abnormality from the collected data.
(Nandy, Adhikari, Chakraborty, Alkhayyat, & Kumar, 2022)	Brain signal classification	Neural networks	Electroencephalography (EEG)	Categorizes the brain signal and determines the correct response for the patients who are unable to talk, hear or both.
(Prathaban, Balasubramanian, & Kalpana, 2021)	Headband for Real-time epileptic seizure forecasting	Convolutional neural network, Phase Transition Predictor	Seizure Predictor Tag (SPT)	Predicts the patients seizure state before an hour.
(Hong, et al., 2022)	Multi-posture recognition system	Artificial intelligence, cloud	Force sensitive resistors, Baroceptor, Inertial sensor	Predicts the posture of the patients
(Sharma, et al., 2021)	Remote patient monitoring system	Machine learning, cloud	ECG, Photoplethysmography, temperature, accelerometer	Early detection of Covid-19 using bio-wearable sensor system

INTERNET OF MEDICAL THINGS

Internet of Things used to monitor the medical signals is termed as IoMT or Healthcare IoT. The IoMT can be defined as the system of inter-related medical computing devices which has the ability to transfer data across the network without any human interventions. It integrates a bundle of technology such as medical sensors, middleware systems, cloud computing and end-user applications (Ahmed, Albuquerque,

Wei, & Wang, 2021). IoMT is paired with smart phones to track and servile the patients and prevent them from chronic illness. IoMT is capable of providing more accurate diagnosis, causing fewer errors, and lowers the healthcare expenses. Some of the applications of IoMT are: medical bot, patient monitoring system, smart health bond, smart hospital, etc.

IoMT Architecture

Implementation of IoMT in any application involves four major components: medical sensors, communication technology, internet and data storage, processing and monitoring (Ahmed, Albuquerque, Wei, & Wang, 2021). The layers constituting IoMT architecture are: sensing, network, data processing and application layer (Mukhopadhyay, et al., 2021) and the architecture of IoMT is presented in Figure 4.

- ***Sensing layer:*** Sensing layer is also known as perception layer. This is the physical layer where the sensors, actuators and other connected devices gather data from the patients. Sensors accepts, processes and sends the data over the network. Some of the commonly used medical sensors are temperature, blood pressure, ECG and pulse & oxygen sensors. The data measured through this layer are sent to data processing layer via the network layer.

- ***Network layer:*** Since the sensors have very limited processing capability, data must be transported to some processing units for analyzing and to derive information from them. In order to send data from sensing layer to data processing layer, network layer is used. The most commonly used network technologies are LPWAN (Low-Power Wide Area Network), Bluetooth, ZigBee, Wi-Fi and RFID. The biggest challenge with network layer is that, radio is the major energy consumer in a sensor node (Vishnuvarthan, Sakthivel, Bhanumathi, & Muralitharan, 2019). So, efficient routing protocol must be used in order to prolong the network lifetime of the sensors.
- ***Data processing layer:*** In healthcare systems, the data processing layer is like head of the system where all the important process and decisions are taken. The most commonly used technology in data processing layer is cloud-computing. In cloud, most complex algorithms are run to clean, process and analyze the collected data from the patients which is not possible to run at sensing layer. In recent years, edge- and fog- computing are used to improve the efficiency of the healthcare system (Aceto, Persico, & Pescape, 2020). The detailed explanation about cloud- and edge-computing is presented later in the chapter.
- ***Application layer:*** This is the top layer of IoMT architecture. The primary goal of application layer is to provide an interface between the application and the end-user (Donta, Srirama, Amgoth, & Annavarapu, 2021). When the number of application increases, the need for modify or new protocols increases. Some of the most commonly used application protocols are Hypertext Transfer protocol, constrained application protocol, Data Distribution Service etc. As it is difficult to modify or create a new protocol, machine learning methods can be employed to make these protocols dynamic and intelligent. The major benefits of using application protocol in IoMT are exchange data between devices, energy efficiency, latency and throughput.

Figure 4. IoMT Architecture

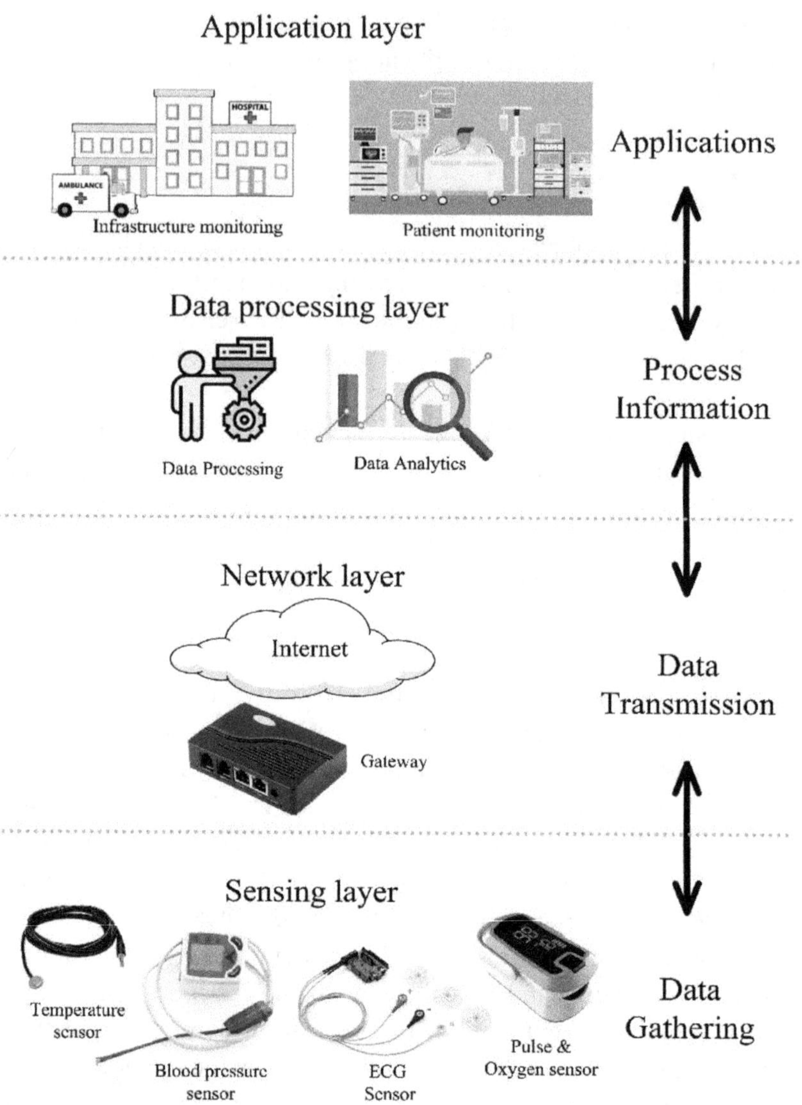

Medical Sensors

Medical sensors play a critical role in the safe operation of many medical devices across a wide range of applications (Jain, et al., 2021). Some of the devices where sensors may be deployed are: ventilators, oxygen concentrators, dialysis and anesthesia delivery machines. The majorly used medical signals are temperature, heart rate, blood pressure, electrocardiograms (ECG), electroglottographs (EGG), electromyograms (EMG), etc. The basic requirements of these medical signals are accuracy, stability, configurability, long term supply and support. And to measure these signals, sensors such as airflow, oxygen, pressure, temperature, humidity and magnetic are used (Ilie, 2021). The devices and the sensors used in the devices are listed in Table 2. In Table 2, P is pressure sensor, O_2 is oxygen sensor, T is temperature sensor and F is force sensor. The data generated by the sensors assist in the diagnosis,

Table 2. Application of some common sensors in medical devices

Device	Airflow	P	O2	T	Humidity	Magnetic	Thermistor	Barcode	Switches	F
Anesthesia delivery machine (Ionescu, 2019)	Ö	Ö	Ö	Ö	Ö	Ö	×	×	×	×
Ventilators (T.Anitha & G.Gopu, 2021)	Ö	Ö	Ö	Ö	Ö	Ö	×	×	×	×
Oxygen concentrator (Lopez, Garcia, & Aponte, 2019)	Ö	Ö	Ö	Ö	Ö	Ö	×	×	×	×
Infusion pumps (Cardiovascular Pharmacology in Noncardiac Surgery, 2019)	×	×	×	×	×	Ö	×	Ö	Ö	Ö
Dialysis machine (Yao, et al., 2021)	×	Ö	×	×	×	Ö	Ö	Ö	×	×
Hospital hardware (Li J., 2021)	×	×	×	Ö	Ö	Ö	Ö	Ö	Ö	×

monitoring, prevention, and treatment of a disease or injury (Dwivedi, Mehrotra, & Chandra, 2022). In addition to that, sensors are also used to measure the external parameters especially in the intensive care units, lab equipment, hospital wards, dental practices, and in-home care products. Medical devices used for cleaning, calibration of equipment, and examination of specimens can also incorporate the sensors.

Sensors can either be wearable or implantable technology (Koydemir & Ozcan, 2018). Both the technologies assist in the advancement of healthcare by offering real-time advice for better health management and tracking. Because of developments in packaging and manufacturing technologies, various microelectronic and micromechanical sensors, such as accelerometers, gyroscopes, and image sensors, may now be integrated in a small area on a rigid or flexible substrate with high sensitivity at a cheap cost. Table 3 provides a comprehensive review about both the technologies.

CLOUD- AND FOG/EDGE-COMPUTING IN HEALTHCARE SYSTEMS

Cloud computing is the brain of the Health 4.0 system (Aceto, Persico, & Pescape, 2020). Cloud computing in healthcare refers to the use of remote servers to store, manage and access healthcare data over the internet. It provides healthcare professionals and organizations an advantage by giving them access to a network of remote servers for secure storage of patient's data. As a result, it saves a lot of money on the physical infrastructure needed for data storage and security (Hartmann, Hashmi, & Imran, 2019). And since the records are available electronically, doctors can easily share information and give better treatment to their patients.

Health 4.0 uses large number of IoMT sensors to collect data from the patients and make intelligent decisions from them. Aggregating these data together and drawing insights from them needs huge computational power. But putting these huge computation power to all the sensors becomes more expensive.

Table 3. Wearable and implantable sensors for biomedical applications

	Wearable	Implanted
Body parts	Head, torso, arm, leg and foot	Ingestible pills(Stomach), Pacemaker (Under the upper chests' skin)
Devices	Smart watches, arm/head bands, glasses, ear phone, earring, shirt	Pacemakers, cardioverter defibrillators, deep-brain simulator
Materials used for fabrication	Smart textiles and stretchable electronics	Biocompatible
Power	Battery	Battery
Parameters	Activity levels, blood oxygen saturation level, blood pressure body temperature, calories burned, Heart rate, sleep patterns, step monitoring, respiration rate.	Blood pressure, heart rate, pH, and temperature
Treat diseases & control movements	Cannot treat disease or control movements of the body	Can treat irregular heartbeats and controls movement of Parkinson's disease patients through electrical signals in brain.
Challenges	Misalignment between user and device causes erroneous data, fabrication materials should be washable and dry-able and should not break when bend/fold	Requires surgical placement, less patient comfort & needs bio-compatible materials
Advantage	Light-weight wearable device, easy replacement of batteries/sensors, patients wearing comfort	Miniaturized device, high precision, good lifetime through energy harvesting and MEMS
Disadvantage	High security and privacy risks, personal calibration required, less durable and less reliable	Requires surgery to replace the sensors if there is hardware glitch/ requires battery replacement, wireless telemetry, costly devices.

Instead, passing all the data and doing all the analysis at the cloud reduces huge investments (Li, et al., 2019).

Need for edge-computing: With the exponential increase of IoT devices each year, computing at data centers or cloud will be a huge challenge. Network reliability, latency and bandwidth congestion pose huge risks especially in data collection in health sector. Rather sending the data to the cloud, the data processing could take place locally. Edge computing allows the user to store, process and analyze the data locally. The data from the sensors are collected in the edge computing framework in the neighborhood, assembles the information and are sent to the Cloud at the regular intervals (Zhang, Sun, Jin, Lin, & Liu, 2021). The local frameworks can be a patient's mobile device or a server at hospital.

As most of the data are processed locally, edge computing increases the efficiency of the system, reduces the latency of the computation, improves the speed of data transmission; reduces the cost; improve patients experience and provides greater privacy and security. The huge workload for medical practitioners are reduced by reducing the need for collecting and managing the patients' data. Edge computing is more secure than cloud computing because the data does not transmit data (Ray, Dash, & De, 2019). Also, it paves the way for people to have access to advanced healthcare systems in even the most remote locations and to be more aware of their own health status.

Edge-computing has greater practical impact in healthcare industry (Amin & Hossain, 2021), to say few,

- allows continuous monitoring of diabetics and congestive heart-failure patients (Subramanian & Thampy, 2021)

Figure 5. General edge architecture of Healthcare system

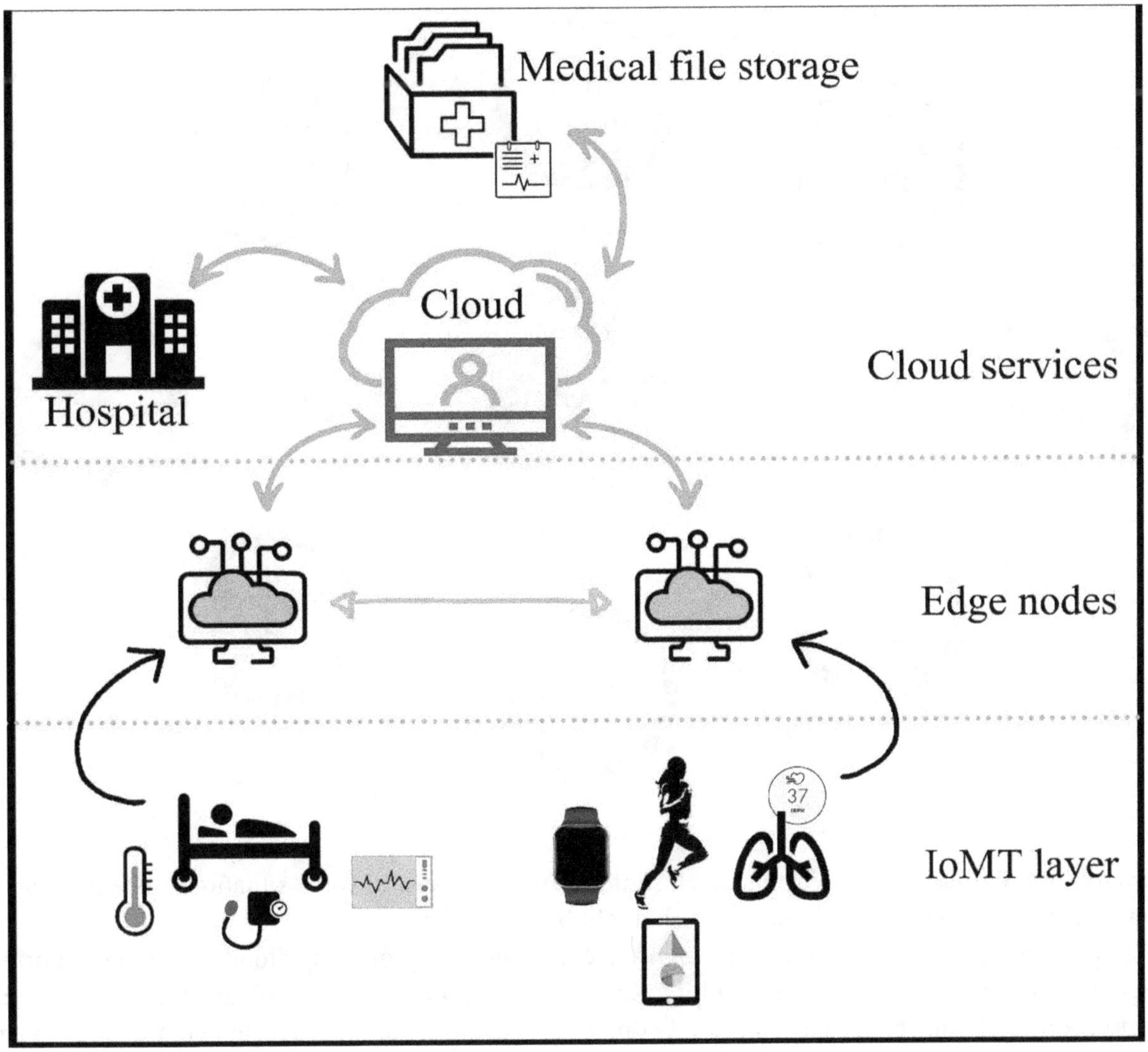

- applications at intensive care unit that need quick analysis of data and faster execution of commands are easy and faster to execute as there is no need to upload data to the cloud
- transmission of crucial data from ambulance to hospital so that the emergency department can equip them with the knowledge to save a life
- less prone to system failure as it is not controlled by central system like cloud
- Cost of implementation is lower because it does not require storage or data transmission infrastructure as cloud.

Edge computing has its own set of challenges and some of which are listed here. The need for a wide spread of 5G networks, as well as interoperability and security of medical devices, is a major impediment towards using edge computing. Edge computing is unable to store lots of data, and data transfer speeds

Figure 6. Data source for Healthcare big data

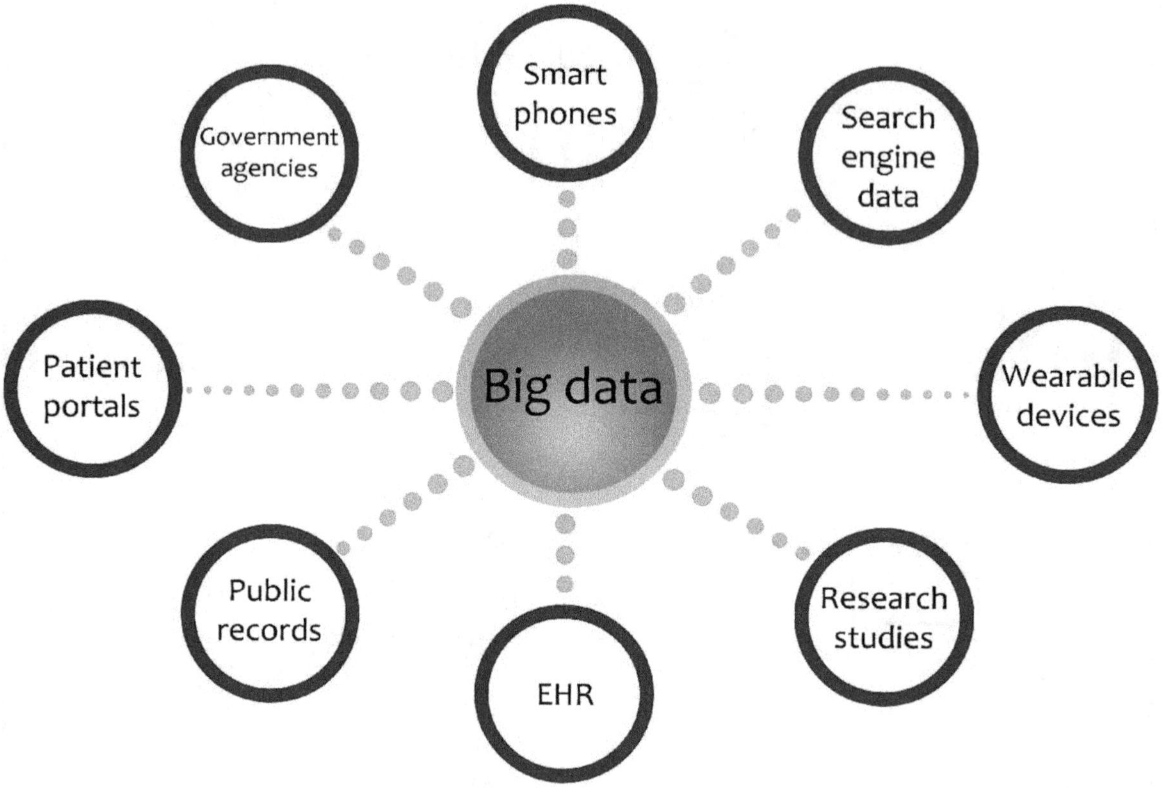

may suffer as 5G use grows (Hartmann, Hashmi, & Imran, 2019). In some situations, patients may be required to wear a number of sensors, which might be uncomfortable.

Importance of Cloud-computing: Though there is no necessity of using cloud-computing, it brings substantial benefits like cost and scalability. So, in recent years, many technological giants have been working on combining both edge- and cloud-computing to bring a new data management strategy (Yang, Liang, & Ji, 2021). By bringing both the technology together, the amount of data transmitted and the storage requirement gets reduced massively. Moreover, it brings great control over data and boosts privacy and security. The general edge architecture for healthcare system is given in Figure 5.

Since edge computing sends all sensor data to the cloud, the data can be vast, irrelevant, and unnecessary. With the inclusion of fog-computing layer between edge- and cloud-computing, the system to decide what data is relevant and delete the unnecessary data (Verma & Sood, 2018). This can cut a lot of traffic, make data transmission faster, and reduce latency. In addition, the volume of space required for data storage in the cloud is also reduced. Despite these benefits, fog computing has numerous drawbacks, including the fact that it costs money for infrastructure, time for computations, and knowledge to acquire the optimum solution from the infrastructure (Kumari, Tanwar, Tyagi, & Kumar, 2018). Moreover, not all system requires fog computing as it just acts as a mediator between edge- and cloud-computing for data-filtering process. In a nutshell, fog-computing cannot replace edge-computing, yet in many cases, edge-computing can exist without fog-computing (Omoniwa, Hussain, Javed, Bouk, & Malik, 2019).

BIG DATA IN HEALTHCARE

Big data is another important technology in Health 4.0 and is defined as data with greater diversity, coming in higher volumes and with greater velocity (Omoniwa, Hussain, Javed, Bouk, & Malik, 2019). In healthcare, the medical sensors generate a huge volume of data and processing the data is possible only using big data because traditional processing techniques cannot handle such vast data. Data sources for healthcare big data include electronics health records (EHR), patient portals, smart phones, research studies, and wearable devices. The corresponding figure is represented in Figure 6. Biomedical research on public health also generates a significant amount of big data, which, when correctly handled and processed, can provide useful information to health care providers, patients, researchers and administrators. With better access and availability of data, big data offers faster and more accurate diagnoses. Sensitive information is collected, stored, and used as part of healthcare services. As a result, they require trustworthy operations and policies, as well as adequate data for auditing and ensuring compliance.

Working of Big data: Big data involves three key actions and are - integrate, manage and analyze (Imran, Mahmood, Morshed, & Sellis, 2021). (1) Big data gathers data from a wide range of sources, processes, and standardizes it so that it can be used for business analysis. (2) Obviously, the data must be stored, thus storage is required. Cloud computing has grown in popularity in recent years because of its lower investment cost and scalability. (3) The last step is to analyze the data that has been stored. Various machine learning and artificial intelligence techniques can be used to explore the data and make new discoveries in order to analyze it.

Advantages of Healthcare Big Data

- Reducing costs: The investment in staffing allocation can be reduced with big data. The forecasting study also saves money by reducing the frequency of readmissions to emergency clinics (Rehman, Naz, & Razzak, 2021).
- Advancement in healthcare system: As big data is developing day by day, it will be a huge help in advancing research and technology, as well as improving the healthcare industry (Imran, Mahmood, Morshed, & Sellis, 2021).
- Health tracking: IoT and big data analytics are supporting a lot in tracking the user's health record (Mehta, Pandit, & Shukla, 2019). It not only aids in the tracking of a patient's sleep, exercise, distance walked, or heart rate, but also in the tracking of other data such as blood pressure, pulse oximeters, glucose monitors, etc.
- Assisting high risk patients: The best data for understanding the patterns of numerous patients will be available once all medical records are digitized. It's an effective technique to keep track of high-risk patients and give them with personalized care.
- Preventing human errors: There are numerous possibilities for a professional to administer the incorrect medication. This can be harmful to the patient, even it can result in death. Big data can be used to analyze client information and the prescribed prescription, which can help to reduce errors (Jameela, Nader, & Eman, 2020). This tool can assist doctors who attend a large number of patients in a single day.
- Treating difficult disease: Patients on various treatment programs can have their data analyzed for trends and patterns to see which ones have the best success rates. This is important in the fight against AIDS, cancer, and multiple sclerosis (Haleem, Javaid, Singh, & Suman, 2022).

Challenges With Healthcare Big Data

- *Data Storage and scalability:* The primary challenge of big data is data storage. Storage on an on-site server has a number of advantages, including security, accessibility, and minimum uptime. However, the initial investment and storage scalability are major concerns. Although cloud-based infrastructure is a preferable alternative in terms of initial investment and scalability, cloud providers also faces issues such as security and policy compliance. In recent years, some firms have chosen a hybrid approach to address these challenges, where the data is stored on both on-site computers and in the cloud (Hussien, Yasin, Udzir, Ninggal, & Salman, 2021).
- *Data Cleaning and standardization:* To ensure correctness, accuracy, and relevance, data collected in the real world must be cleaned. Also, because the data is received from a variety of sources, it must be transformed to a standardized format before being analyzed to extract useful information. Cleaning and standardization can be done manually or with the help of machine learning algorithms (Ridzuan & Zainon, 2019). In either case, this approach takes a significant amount of time from data scientists.
- *Data Visualization:* Visualization is essential for real-time monitoring, analysis of insights, periodic business dashboards, and operational dashboards. However, the difficulty is that it necessitates the use of special tools and expertise (Peral, Gallego, Gil, Tanniru, & Khambekar, 2020).
- *Data sharing:* One of the primary pain areas is sharing healthcare data between different businesses due to a lack of standardization. Furthermore, such sensitive data necessitates robust privacy protections (Mahajan, et al., 2022).
- *Data Security:* Healthcare big data is vulnerable to cyber-attacks and fraudulent activities due to the large amount of sensitive data involved. As a result, a tool for fraud detection and prevention is necessary (Yaqoob, Salah, & Jayaraman, 2021). For data audit and compliance, contracts, agreements, and laws must be established across organizations.
- *Lack of big data skills:* In healthcare, big data is truly 'big' and diversified. Collecting, cleaning, processing, managing, and analyzing such huge volumes of data is a challenging task. A lack of big data skill set will make the task difficult (Chanchaichujit, Tan, & Eaimkhong, 2019). But with big data and big data analytics in healthcare, you can easily overcome these difficulties.

Applications

- *Electronic health records* (Imran, Mahmood, Morshed, & Sellis, 2021): Electronic Health Records (EHR) are digital documents that contain all of a patient's medical information and current state. This is a very effective way of treatment and some private hospitals have adopted EHR systems. Changes to the records are possible, which implies that if a doctor makes a modification, it will be reflected everywhere. Also, these records will inform the patient when it is time to have a test or see a doctor.
- *Reduce fraud and enhance security*: Personal information can be taken and exploited for a variety of illicit actions. As a result, these data are vulnerable due to their high black-market value. Analytics delivers firewall and antivirus security to prevent data theft. This can detect any suspicious behavior in the database, preventing black hat hackers from gaining access to anyone's personal information (Aceto, Persico, & Pescape, 2020).

- *Real time alerting*: Another advantage is that patients can wear smart devices that communicate data to doctors in real time. Even in the event of an emergency, the doctor will be contacted, and patients can be saved by prompt treatment (Haleem, Javaid, Singh, & Suman, 2022).
- *Informed strategic planning*: It is possible to organize the data gathered from various patients and this will assist the relevant authorities in identifying the areas where healthcare services are most required. In this approach, healthcare services can be expanded in places where they are most needed.
- *Patient predictions for improved staffing*: Data from previous records could be utilized to forecast how many patients would arrive in the next hour or day. This allows for the planning and employment of employees, lowering labor costs significantly (Paul, et al., 2021).

BLOCK CHAIN IN HEALTHCARE

Healthcare services necessitate the collection, storage, and use of sensitive data and classified information on a regular basis. Further, healthcare systems extend to include multiple organizations across the value chain and hence creating contracts, agreements and policies, as well as enough data to audit and ensure compliance (Singh, Firmin, & Chadhar, 2022). Blockchain is one efficient technology which provides these services. It allows to store the non-modifiable records and used for verification and security. In addition, it can provide mechanisms to ensure data sharing is fair and patients' privacy is protected.

Blockchain is a mechanism that allows to keep a single, secure, and immutable record of all user transactions without the involvement of third-party intermediaries (Casino, Dasaklis, & Patsakis, 2019). All that is required to conduct transactions is a wallet, and blockchain is one such wallet that allows users to spend cryptocurrencies such as BTC, ETH, and others. Cryptographic methods (public and private keys) are required to protect these wallets, and it also allows users to monitor and control their transactions.

Working: When a user creates a transaction on the blockchain, a block is created at first to represent that transaction. The desired transaction is broadcast through a peer-to-peer network, which is made up of computers known as nodes, which subsequently validate it. A validated transaction can include cryptocurrency, records, or contracts. Following the confirmation of a transaction, it is combined with other blocks to generate a new data block for the ledger. Each new transaction creates a safe block, which is encrypted and linked to the others using cryptographic principles. When a new block is created, it is added to the current Blockchain network, ensuring its immutability and security.

Framework for Block Chain

The block chain healthcare framework (Quasim & Algarni, 2020) is shown in Figure 7. The body is fitted with a multitude of sensors, and the data is collected in the sink. The sink then encrypts the data and sends it to the LPWAN gateway, which then sends it to the blockchain network for medical data addition. Healthcare data comes from a variety of sources, including doctor's offices, pharmacies, medical imaging systems, prescriptions, and insurance firms. A local acquisition node stores this data in an LPWAN gateway. The data is transmitted over the gateway by the peer nodes in this network, and the data is processed by the blockchain nodes. The following section details the components of the proposed system.

Figure 7. Blockchain framework for healthcare

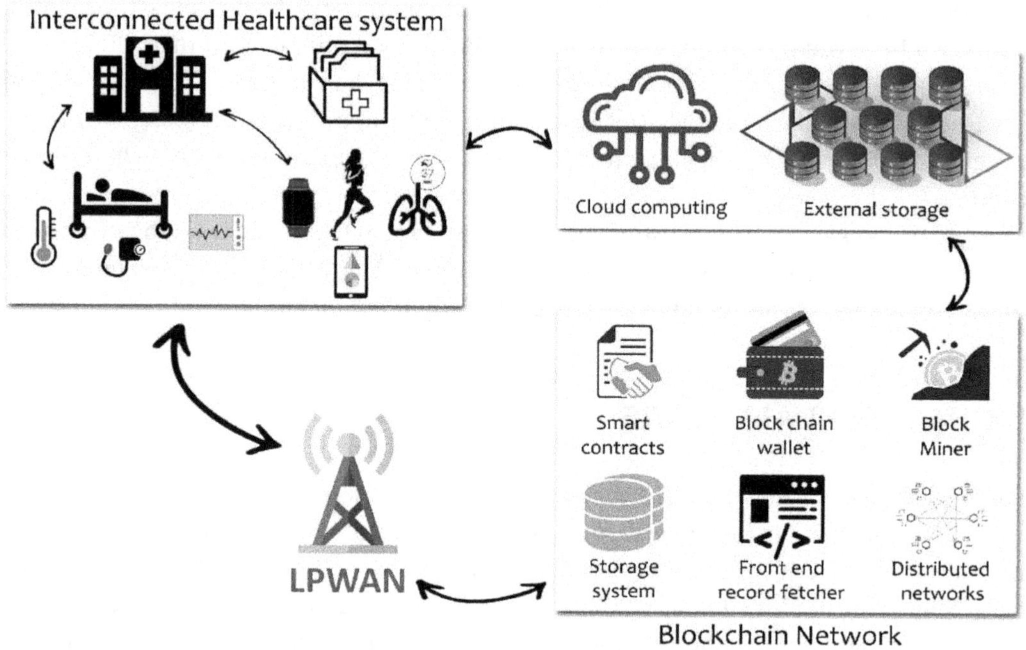

- *LPWAN:* It's a powerful computer that serves as both a gateway and a full node in a network. The key task is to transfer data to the network and to assess the performance of the IoT system without relying on others (Chaudhari & Borkar, 2020).
- *End devices*: End devices are sensor nodes that are used to monitor the patient or the environment. The capabilities of sensors cannot accommodate blockchain functionalities (Krishnan, Rajagopal, & Rathinasamy, 2018). As shown in Figure 7, the IoT / LPWAN gateway collects data and sends it to a blockchain network. By this type of implementation, storage or processing infrastructure is not required for this form of communication between an IoT-based healthcare system and a blockchain node.
- *Cloud computing and External Storage:* Cloud computing will be an essential part of the system for medical professionals, pharmacists, and patients to access the data once the records are linked to blockchain. Cloud computing reduces implementation cost, increases security and scalability of the system. Cloud computing technologies such as virtualization, cryptography, and web services are vulnerable due to insecure implementation. As a result, a key management system must be integrated into the cloud architecture.
- *Blockchain network:* The blockchain network is made up of number of elements. They are storage system, smart contracts, blockchain wallet, block miner, front-end record fetcher, and distributed networks.
    - *Smart contracts* are computer programs that execute when certain criteria are met. They are stored in blockchain and are used to automate the execution of the contract so that all participants can be immediately certain of the outcome, without the need for any intermediaries or time waste.

    - A *blockchain wallet* is a type of digital wallet that lets users store and manage cryptocurrencies like Bitcoin, Ether and other digital currencies. It allows users to send and receive cryptocurrencies, as well as change them back into their local currency.
    - *Distributed networks*: The same data is saved across distributed networks, ensuring that all partners have access to the same data. This ensures the network's reliability and security.
    - *Storage system*: Blockchain storage is a method of storing data in a decentralized network that makes use of idle hard disc space from people all around the world. The decentralized architecture is a viable alternative to centralized cloud storage and can address many of the issues that plague centralized systems.
    - *Block miner*: It is a block chain mining software that allows computers (nodes) to securely connect with one another. It aids in cryptocurrency mining.
    - *Front-end record fetcher*: A blockchain is a distributed database that can be accessed by a network of computers. As a result, the frontend is quite important. It's in charge of marshalling and unmarshaling data from smart contracts, as well as managing interactions with the wallet (hardware or software) and, of course, the user experience.

Use Cases

- *Store individual patients information:* Individual patient information, such as physiological information, diagnosis, treatments, and prescriptions, is fed into the system by the healthcare provider. This information is stored in the on-site server or in cloud. Healthcare providers will examine the recorded data and question its accuracy, which they will verify by comparing it to the actual information kept on the Blockchain system.
- *Analyzing the effect of particular treatment:* Through validated access to patient data, researchers can efficiently examine any procedure on a substantial portion of the patient population (Jan, et al., 2021). This yields important outcomes that improve the way these patients are managed. In addition to that, pharmaceutical firms will collect data in real-time using the Blockchain infrastructure to give a wide range of precisely customized prescription drugs or services to patients. The job of pharmacists is also made easier by blockchain since pharmacies have the access to the data. As a result, patients can be given clear instructions on how to take their prescription. The current state of the patients can be updated for clinicians using wearable data collected in real-time, and they can be alerted to any emergency.
- *Clinical Trial:* Blockchain Technology is utilized in clinical studies to overcome issues like misleading results and data disintegration that don't meet the study's goals and objectives (Yaqoob, 2021).
- *Identification of false content: the* motivation for block chain technology is that it is user-friendly and provide patients with secure real-time access to their health and insurance records (Mamta, Li, Leung, Psannis, & Yamaguchi, 2021). For the first time, technology made it possible for the general public to observe a clinical trial unfold in real time. It provides better clarity and allow for the detection of false content.
- *Improves safety:* by addressing pharmaceutical validity and drug tracking issues, as well as enabling secure interoperability, blockchain increases overall patient safety. It is the only way to replace the present supply chain management system and prevent counterfeit medication manufacturers from bringing their products to market in a more secure manner, regardless of the medi-

cal facilities and organizations involved. With interoperability of block chain, doctors can examine complete medical information more easily which enable them to identify their diagnosis and build a better and more precise operation.

Blockchain Healthcare Companies

Some of the healthcare companies which uses blockchain technology for various purpose (Daley, 2021) are listed below:

- ***MedPiper*** is a platform for healthcare professionals to find jobs. The platform makes use of blockchain technology to allow educators and employers to verify profile credentials and link those verified profiles to employment criteria. It assigns doctors to duty vacancies based on their profile, geography, and availability.
- ***EMRChain*** provides AI and blockchain-based Electronic Medical Record (EMR) management software. Some of the features of the software are storing patient's medical information and allowing permission-based access, sending data from the EMR system, analyzing patient data, and making recommendations to doctors and patients.
- ***NanoHealthCare*** *Token* is a blockchain based health management platform which creates an AI-based value chain for preventive care. It is capable of storing health records, data sharing and security, and billing and claims.
- ***Medicalchain***: Patients' information can be requested by hospitals, doctors, and laboratories, keeping the patient's identity protected from prying eyes. Furthermore, Medicalchain's blockchain secures the integrity of health records while also establishing a single point of truth.
- ***Robomed*** blends AI and blockchain to provide a single point of care for patients. The company uses chatbots, wearable diagnostic gadgets, and telemedicine sessions, to collect patient data and share it with the patient's medical team.

CONCLUSION

According to the definition of Health 4.0, a strategic idea for the health domain evolved from the Industry 4.0 concept. It is thought to include the recent technological developments that have changed the way health is managed and delivered. In this chapter various components constituting Heath 4.0 is reviewed with their advantages, challenges and applications. As a result of incorporating the most recent breakthroughs in these technologies, the medical system will be able to increase service efficiency, lower costs, and democratize health care. While Blockchain enables the storage of cryptographic records, which also needs AI. So, we have also presented a new block-chain based framework for smart-health to improve the security and privacy of the system. With blockchain, patients can gain ownership of their personal medical information, and any changes to the records will be checked retrospectively to identify exactly how they have changed over time and who made them. It also allows patients' data to be shared across numerous providers without fear of security or privacy breaches and grants researchers to communicate massive volumes of data on every aspect of a patient's life.

REFERENCES

Aceto, G., Persico, V., & Pescape, A. (2020). Industry 4.0 and Health: Internet of Things, Big Data, and Cloud Computing for Healthcare 4.0. *Journal of Industrial Information Integration*, *18*, 100129. doi:10.1016/j.jii.2020.100129

Adadi, A., Lahmer, M., & Nasiri, S. (2021). Artificial Intelligence and COVID-19: A Systematic umbrella review and roads ahead. *Journal of King Saud University - Computer and Information Sciences*.

Ahmed, S. H., Albuquerque, V. H., Wei, W., & Wang, W. (2021). Guest Editorial AI and 5G Empowered Internet of Medical Things. *IEEE Journal of Biomedical and Health Informatics*, *25*(10), 3688–3690. doi:10.1109/JBHI.2021.3108337

Allen, P. J., Nissan, A., Picon, A. I., Kemeny, N., Dudrick, P., Ben-Porat, L., Espat, J., Stojadinovic, A., Cohen, A. M., Fong, Y., & Paty, P. B. (2005). Technical complications and durability of hepatic artery infusion pumps for unresectable colorectal liver metastases: An institutional experience of 544 consecutive cases. *Journal of the American College of Surgeons*, *201*(1), 57–65. doi:10.1016/j.jamcollsurg.2005.03.019 PMID:15978444

Amin, S. U., & Hossain, M. S. (2021). Edge Intelligence and Internet of Things in Healthcare: A Survey. *IEEE Access: Practical Innovations, Open Solutions*, *9*, 45–59. doi:10.1109/ACCESS.2020.3045115

Anitha, T., & Gopu, G. (2021). Controlled mechanical ventilation for enhanced measurement in pressure and flow sensors. *Measurement: Sensors*, *16*, 100054.

Avila, K., Sanmartin, P., Jabba, D., & Gomez, J. (2022). An analytical Survey of Attack Scenario Parameters on the Techniques of Attack Mitigation in WSN. *Wireless Personal Communications*, *122*(4), 3687–3718. doi:10.100711277-021-09107-6

Cardiovascular Pharmacology in Noncardiac Surgery. (2019). In L. P. Nguyen, & N. S. Gerstein, Essentials of Cardiac Anesthesia for Noncardiac Surgery (pp. 247-288). Elsevier.

Casino, F., Dasaklis, T. K., & Patsakis, C. (2019). A systematic literature review of blockchain-based applications: Current status, classification and open issues. *Telematics and Informatics*, *36*, 55–81. doi:10.1016/j.tele.2018.11.006

Chanchaichujit, J., Tan, A. M., & Eaimkhong, S. (2019). An Introduction to Healthcare 4.0. In *Healthcare 4.0*. Palgrave Pivot. doi:10.1007/978-981-13-8114-0_1

Chaudhari, B., & Borkar, S. (2020). Design considerations and network architectures for low-power wide-area networks. In *LPWAN Technologies for IoT and M2M Applications* (pp. 15–35). Academic Press. doi:10.1016/B978-0-12-818880-4.00002-8

Daley, S. (2021, July 30). *How Using Blockchain in Healthcare Is Reviving the Industry's Capabilities*. Retrieved from BuiltIn: https://builtin.com/blockchain/blockchain-healthcare-applications-companies

Dansharif, A. R., Iyawa, G. E., Owoseni, A., & Iyawa, R. (2021). mHealth for Self-Management in Pregnancy: Perceptions of Women in Low-Resource Settings. *Procedia Computer Science*, *181*, 738–745. doi:10.1016/j.procs.2021.01.226

Diaz, O., Kushibar, K., Osuala, R., Linardos, A., Garrucho, L., Igual, L., Radeva, P., Prior, F., Gkontra, P., & Lekadir, K. (2021). Data preparation for artificial intelligence in medical imaging: A comprehensive guide to open-access platforms and tools. *Physica Medica, 83*, 25–37. doi:10.1016/j.ejmp.2021.02.007 PMID:33684723

Donta, P. K., Srirama, S. N., Amgoth, T., & Annavarapu, C. S. (2021). *Survey on recent advances in IoT application layer protocols and machine learning scope for research directions*. Digital Communications and Networks. doi:10.1016/j.dcan.2021.10.004

Dwivedi, R., Mehrotra, D., & Chandra, S. (2022). Potential of Internet of Medical Things (IoMT) applications in building a smart healthcare system: A systematic review. *Journal of Oral Biology and Craniofacial Research, 12*(2), 302–318. doi:10.1016/j.jobcr.2021.11.010 PMID:34926140

Ferrag, M., Shu, L., Djallel, H., & Choo, K.-K. (2021). Deep Learning-Based Intrusion Detection for Distributed Denial of Service Attack in Agriculture 4.0. *Electronics (Basel), 10*(11), 1257. doi:10.3390/electronics10111257

Haleem, A., Javaid, M., Singh, R. P., & Suman, R. (2022). Medical 4.0 technologies for healthcare: Features, capabilities, and applications. *Internet of Things and Cyber-Physical Systems, 2*, 12–30. doi:10.1016/j.iotcps.2022.04.001

Hartmann, M., Hashmi, U. S., & Imran, A. (2019). Edge computing in smart health care systems: Review, challenges, and research directions. *Transactions on Emerging Telecommunications Technologies*.

Hond, A. A., Leeuwenberg, A. M., Hooft, L., Kant, I. M., Nijman, S. W., Os, H. J., ... Chavannes, N. H. (2022). Guidelines and quality criteria for artificial intelligence-based prediction models in healthcare: A scoping review. *npj. Digital Medicine, 5*(2). PMID:35013569

Hong, Z., Hong, M., Wang, N., Ma, Y., Zhou, X., & Wang, W. (2022). A wearable-based posture recognition system with AI-assisted approach for healthcare IoT. *Future Generation Computer Systems, 127*, 286–296. doi:10.1016/j.future.2021.08.030

Huffman, J. (2018, July 09). *AI in healthcare: a six-step framework for getting the most out of your data*. Retrieved from https://www.philips.com/a-w/about/news/archive/blogs/innovation-matters/20180709-ai-in-healthcare-a-six-step-framework-for-getting-the-most-out-of-your-data.html

Hussien, H. M., Yasin, S. M., Udzir, N. I., Ninggal, M. I., & Salman, S. (2021). Blockchain technology in the healthcare industry: Trends and opportunities. *Journal of Industrial Information Integration, 22*, 100217. doi:10.1016/j.jii.2021.100217

Ilie, A. (2021). *Sensing Better Health: Complete Guide to Medical Sensors - Benefits and Applications*. Retrieved from Honeywell: https://sps.honeywell.com/us/en/support/blog/siot/complete-guide-to-medical-sensors-benefits-and-applications

Imran, S., Mahmood, T., Morshed, A., & Sellis, T. (2021). Big data analytics in healthcare – A systematic literature review and roadmap for practical implementation. *IEEE/CAA Journal of Automatica Sinica, 8*(1), 1-22.

Ionescu, C. M. (2019). Computer-assisted Drug Delivery for General Anesthesia: Completing the Puzzle: Plenary Talk. *2019 IEEE 17th World Symposium on Applied Machine Intelligence and Informatics (SAMI)*, 13-16.

Jain, S., Nehra, M., Kumar, R., Dilbaghi, N., Hu, T., Kumar, S., Kaushik, A., & Li, C.-Z. (2021). Internet of medical things (IoMT)-integrated biosensors for point-of-care testing of infectious diseases. *Biosensors & Bioelectronics*, *179*, 113074. doi:10.1016/j.bios.2021.113074 PMID:33596516

Jameela, A.-J., Nader, M., & Eman, A. (2020). Health 4.0: On the Way to Realizing the Healthcare of the Future. *IEEE Access: Practical Innovations, Open Solutions*, *8*, 211189–211210. doi:10.1109/ACCESS.2020.3038858 PMID:34976565

Jan, M. A., Cai, J., Gao, X.-C., Khan, F., Mastorakis, S., Usman, M., Alazab, M., & Watters, P. (2021). Security and blockchain convergence with Internet of Multimedia Things: Current trends, research challenges and future directions. *Journal of Network and Computer Applications*, *175*, 102918. doi:10.1016/j.jnca.2020.102918 PMID:34690484

Kaur, A., Garg, R., & Gupta, P. (2021). Challenges facing AI and Big data for Resource-poor Healthcare System. *2021 Second International Conference on Electronics and Sustainable Communication Systems (ICESC)*, 1426-1433. 10.1109/ICESC51422.2021.9532955

Koydemir, H. C., & Ozcan, A. (2018). Wearable and Implantable Sensors for Biomedical Applications. *Annual Review of Analytical Chemistry (Palo Alto, Calif.)*, *11*(1), 127–146. doi:10.1146/annurev-anchem-061417-125956 PMID:29490190

Krishnan, M., Rajagopal, V., & Rathinasamy, S. (2018). Performance evaluation of sensor deployment using optimization techniques and scheduling approach for K-coverage in WSNs. *Wireless Networks*, *24*(3), 683–693. doi:10.100711276-016-1361-5

Kumari, A., Tanwar, S., Tyagi, S., & Kumar, N. (2018). Fog computing for Healthcare 4.0 environment: Opportunities and challenges. *Computers & Electrical Engineering*, *72*, 1–13. doi:10.1016/j.compeleceng.2018.08.015

Li, J. (2021). Artifcial intelligence hospital hardware system and clinical observation of molecular heparin sodium in hemodialysis patients. *Microprocessors and Microsystems*, *81*, 103690. doi:10.1016/j.micpro.2020.103690

Li, J., & Carayon, P. (2021). *Health Care 4.0: A Vision for Smart and Connected Health Care*. Academic Press.

Li, W., Liu, B. M., Liu, D., Ping, L. R., Wang, P., Luo, S., & Ni, W. (2019). Unified Fine-Grained Access Control for Personal Health Records in Cloud Computing. *IEEE Journal of Biomedical and Health Informatics*, *23*(3), 1278–1289. doi:10.1109/JBHI.2018.2850304 PMID:29994490

Lopes, J. M., Marrone, P., Pereira, S. L., & Dias, E. M. (2019). Health 4.0: Challenges for an Orderly and Inclusive Innovation. *IEEE Technology and Society Magazine*, *38*(3), 17–19. doi:10.1109/MTS.2019.2930265

Lopez, L. J., Garcia, A. R., & Aponte, G. P. (2019). Internet of things in healthcare monitoring to enhance acquisition performance of respiratory disorder sensors. *International Journal of Distributed Sensor Networks, 15*(5).

López Seguí, F., Franch Parella, J., Gironès García, X., Mendioroz Peña, J., García Cuyàs, F., Adroher Mas, C., García-Altés, A., & Vidal-Alaball, J. (2020). A Cost-Minimization Analysis of a Medical Record-based, Store and Forward and Provider-to-provider Telemedicine Compared to Usual Care in Catalonia: More Agile and Efficient, Especially for Users. *International Journal of Environmental Research and Public Health, 17*(6), 2008. doi:10.3390/ijerph17062008 PMID:32197434

Lu, K., & Liao, H. (2022). A survey of group decision making methods in Healthcare Industry 4.0: Bibliometrics, applications, and directions. *Applied Intelligence*. Advance online publication. doi:10.100710489-021-02909-y PMID:35002080

Mahajan, H. B., Rashid, A. S., Junnarkar, A. A., Uke, N., Deshpande, S. D., Futane, P. R., Alkhayyat, A., & Alhayani, B. (2022). Integration of Healthcare 4.0 and blockchain into secure cloud-based electronic health records systems. *Applied Nanoscience*. Advance online publication. doi:10.100713204-021-02164-0 PMID:35136707

Mamta, B. B., Li, K. -C., Leung, V. C., Psannis, K. E., & Yamaguchi, S. (2021). Blockchain-Assisted Secure Fine-Grained Searchable Encryption for a Cloud-Based Healthcare Cyber-Physical System. *IEEE/CAA Journal of Automatica Sinica, 8*(12), 1877-1890.

Mehta, N., Pandit, A., & Shukla, S. (2019). Transforming healthcare with big data analytics and artificial intelligence: A systematic mapping study. *Journal of Biomedical Informatics, 100*, 103311. doi:10.1016/j.jbi.2019.103311 PMID:31629922

Mukhopadhyay, S. C., Tyagi, S. K., Suryadevara, N. K., Piuri, V., Scotti, F., & Zeadally, S. (2021). Artificial Intelligence-Based Sensors for Next Generation IoT Applications: A Review. *IEEE Sensors Journal, 21*(22), 24920–24932. doi:10.1109/JSEN.2021.3055618

Nandy, S., Adhikari, M., Chakraborty, S., Alkhayyat, A., & Kumar, N. (2022). IBoNN: Intelligent Agent-based Internet of Medical Things framework for detecting brain response from Electroencephalography signal using Bag-of-Neural Network. *Future Generation Computer Systems, 130*, 241–252. doi:10.1016/j.future.2021.12.019

Omoniwa, B., Hussain, R., Javed, M. A., Bouk, S. H., & Malik, S. A. (2019). Fog/Edge Computing-Based IoT (FECIoT): Architecture, Applications, and Research Issues. *IEEE Internet of Things Journal, 6*(3), 4118–4149. doi:10.1109/JIOT.2018.2875544

Parviainen, J., & Rantala, J. (2022). Chatbot breakthrough in the 2020s? An ethical reflection on the trend of automated consultations in health care. *Medicine, Health Care, and Philosophy, 25*(1), 61–71. doi:10.100711019-021-10049-w PMID:34480711

Paul, S., Riffat, M., Yasir, A., Mahim, M., Sharnali, B., Naheen, I., Rahman, A., & Kulkarni, A. (2021). Industry 4.0 Applications for Medical/Healthcare Services. *Journal of Sensor and Actuator Networks, 10*(3), 43. doi:10.3390/jsan10030043

Peral, J., Gallego, E., Gil, D., Tanniru, M., & Khambekar, P. (2020). Using Visualization to Build Transparency in a Healthcare Blockchain Application. *Sustainability*, *12*(17), 6768. doi:10.3390u12176768

Prathaban, B. P., Balasubramanian, R., & Kalpana, R. (2021). A Wearable ForeSeiz Headband for Forecasting Real-Time Epileptic Seizures. *IEEE Sensors Journal*, *21*(23), 26892–26901. doi:10.1109/JSEN.2021.3120307

Quasim, M. T., & Algarni, F. (2020). A Blockchain based Secured Healthcare Framework. *2020 International Conference on Computational Performance Evaluation (ComPE)*, 386-391. 10.1109/ComPE49325.2020.9200024

Rasool, R. U., Ahmad, H. F., Rafique, W., Qayyum, A., & Qadir, J. (2022). Security and privacy of internet of medical things: A contemporary review in the age of surveillance, botnets, and adversarial ML. *Journal of Network and Computer Applications*, *201*, 103332. doi:10.1016/j.jnca.2022.103332

Ray, P. P., Dash, D., & De, D. (2019). Edge computing for Internet of Things: A survey, e-healthcare case study and future direction. *Journal of Network and Computer Applications*, *140*, 1–22. doi:10.1016/j.jnca.2019.05.005

Rehman, A., Naz, S., & Razzak, I. (2021). Leveraging big data analytics in healthcare enhancement: Trends, challenges and opportunities. *Multimedia Systems*. Advance online publication. doi:10.100700530-020-00736-8

Ridzuan, F., & Zainon, W. M. (2019). A Review on Data Cleansing Methods for Big Data. *Procedia Computer Science*, *161*, 731–738. doi:10.1016/j.procs.2019.11.177

Sethuraman, S. C., Kompally, P., Mohanty, S. P., & Choppali, U. (2021). MyWear: A Novel Smart Garment for Automatic Continuous Vital Monitoring. *IEEE Transactions on Consumer Electronics*, *67*(3), 214–222. doi:10.1109/TCE.2021.3085888

Sharma, N., Mangla, M., Mohanty, S. N., Gupta, D., Tiwari, P., Shorfuzzaman, M., & Rawashdeh, M. (2021). A smart ontology-based IoT framework for remote patient monitoring. *Biomedical Signal Processing and Control*, *68*, 102717. doi:10.1016/j.bspc.2021.102717

Singh, S., Firmin, S., & Chadhar, M. (2022). An interpretive study of stakeholders' privacy issues in blockchain: A healthcare context. *Australasian Computer Science Week*, *2022*, 235–238. doi:10.1145/3511616.3513122

Sisodia, A., & Jindal, R. (2021). A meta-analysis of industry 4.0 design principles applied in the health sector. *Engineering Applications of Artificial Intelligence*, *104*, 104377. doi:10.1016/j.engappai.2021.104377

Subramanian, G., & Thampy, A. S. (2021). Implementation of Blockchain Consortium to Prioritize Diabetes Patients' Healthcare in Pandemic Situations. *IEEE Access: Practical Innovations, Open Solutions*, *9*, 162459–162475. doi:10.1109/ACCESS.2021.3132302

Tortorella, G. L., Saurin, T. A., Fogliatto, F. S., Rosa, V. M., Tonetto, L. M., & Magrabi, F. (2021). Impacts of Healthcare 4.0 digital technologies on the resilience of hospitals. *Technological Forecasting and Social Change*, *166*, 120666. doi:10.1016/j.techfore.2021.120666

Verma, P., & Sood, S. K. (2018). Fog Assisted-IoT Enabled Patient Health Monitoring in Smart Homes. *IEEE Internet of Things Journal*, *5*(3), 1789–1796. doi:10.1109/JIOT.2018.2803201

Vishnuvarthan, R., Sakthivel, R., Bhanumathi, V., & Muralitharan, K. (2019). Energy-efficient data collection in strip-based wireless sensor networks with optimal speed mobile data collectors. *Computer Networks*, *156*, 33–40. doi:10.1016/j.comnet.2019.03.019

Yang, G., Pang, Z., Jamal Deen, M., Dong, M., Zhang, Y.-T., Lovell, N., & Rahmani, A. M. (2020, September). Homecare Robotic Systems for Healthcare 4.0: Visions and Enabling Technologies. *IEEE Journal of Biomedical and Health Informatics*, *24*(9), 2535–2549. doi:10.1109/JBHI.2020.2990529 PMID:32340971

Yang, Z., Liang, B., & Ji, W. (2021). An Intelligent End–Edge–Cloud Architecture for Visual IoT-Assisted Healthcare Systems. *IEEE Internet of Things Journal*, *8*(23), 16779–16786. doi:10.1109/JIOT.2021.3052778

Yao, L., Zhang, H., Zhang, M., Chen, X., Zhang, J., Huang, J., & Zhang, L. (2021). Application of artificial intelligence in renal disease. *Clinical eHealth, 4*, 54-61.

Yaqoob, I., Salah, K., Jayaraman, R., & Al-Hammadi, Y. (2021). Blockchain for healthcare data management: Opportunities, challenges, and future recommendations. *Neural Computing & Applications*. Advance online publication. doi:10.100700521-020-05519-w

Young, S. (2022). AI in healthcare startups and special challenges. *Intelligence-Based Medicine*, *6*, 100050. doi:10.1016/j.ibmed.2022.100050

Yuan, X., Chen, J., Zhang, K., Wu, Y., & Yang, T. (2022). A Stable AI-Based Binary and Multiple Class Heart Disease Prediction Model for IoMT. *IEEE Transactions on Industrial Informatics*, *18*(3), 2032–2040. doi:10.1109/TII.2021.3098306

Zhang, Y., Sun, Y., Jin, R., Lin, K., & Liu, W. (2021). High-Performance Isolation Computing Technology for Smart IoT Healthcare in Cloud Environments. *IEEE Internet of Things Journal*, *8*(23), 16872–16879. doi:10.1109/JIOT.2021.3051742

Chapter 14
Fractional Order PID Controller for Tracking Control of SCARA Robot

Sreejita Samadder
School of Automation, Banasthali Vidyapith, India

Samriddhi Dave
School of Automation, Banasthali Vidyapith, India

Vijay Mohan
Department of Mechatronics, Manipal Institute of Technology, India & Manipal Academy of Higher Education, India

Bharat Bhushan Sharma
Department of Electronics & Communication Engineering, JSS Academy of Technical Education, Noida, India

ABSTRACT

E-commerce packaging has unique needs, and new robot technology is meeting those needs. These needs include handling mixed pallet loads, workforce problems, and a range of secondary packaging types. This chapter presents the trajectory tracking control of an industrial SCARA robot in a realistic simulated environment with the help of fractional order PID (FOPID) and PID controller. FOPID controller has two extra degrees of freedom, thereby providing added flexibility to the design over the PID scheme. The optimum parameters of these controllers are obtained using the genetic algorithm (GA) by minimizing a weighted sum of absolute errors as an objective. Further, a comparative study of the controllers is performed for set-point tracking and model parameter uncertainty based on settling time, rise time, overshoot, and integral absolute error (IAE). The results have proved that FOPID outperforms its integer-order counterpart under a variety of operating conditions.

DOI: 10.4018/978-1-6684-4969-1.ch014

Copyright © 2022, IGI Global. Copying or distributing in print or electronic forms without written permission of IGI Global is prohibited.

INTRODUCTION

Advanced information technology and artificial intelligence have enabled automation-based companies to bring about seismic shifts in the way that they handle day-to-day operations during the past few decades. Smart manufacturing and smart factories are at the vanguard of a new industrial revolution, which is currently in progress. The development of new developing technologies, such as industrial robots built to function in hazardous situations, is underway in order to address the needs of consumers in the future smart industrial sector. By utilising these technologies, manufacturers can achieve more flexible manufacturing while also decreasing human requirements and accelerating the development process. Industrial robots can be configured to perform a variety of tasks. Robots are able to optimise output and increase productivity in smart industrial environments because of their agility and flexibility.

A more flexible control strategy and a more calculative grasp over manipulators were required by the expansion of the automation sector, which were met by current control strategies and intelligent algorithms (Chhabra et al., 2020; Mohan et al., 2019). With recent technological advancements and the introduction of computers, businesses are shifting toward automation. Automation is the process of completing a task with more accuracy and precision by employing computer software or robotics. Warehouse automation is essential in this day and age, as delays in delivery enrage clients in the e-commerce industry. Automation has made its way into this industry and is transforming the way businesses manage their fulfilment processes. Currently, robots are working in collaboration with people, and in certain cases, they are functioning independently. The logistics trends in e-commerce are changing at a breakneck speed. Companies are increasingly seeking for alternative methods of ensuring timely delivery to clients in order to drive commercial success. The current trend in logistics operations is therefore toward automation rather than human labour as companies attempt to keep up with demand from the rapidly rising e-commerce market. Amazon has emerged as the modernizer among the key competitors in the e-commerce market, having embraced robotic technologies in its fulfilment centres. Amazon was a pioneer in the use of robots in fulfilment facilities, and it continues to be so today. Amazon began using 1,300 robots in 2011 and has since increased this number. Amazon was enthusiastic about the prospect of employing robots in its warehouse. Amazon's warehouses currently have 15,000 robots scattered across ten different locations.

One can easily envision robots taking over for people in numerous areas when it comes to performing simple repetitive activities. In five years, a robot will be less expensive than a full-time human employee, including perks and compensation. The entire concept of automation is around ensuring that customers are satisfied. While robots and automation may limit employment possibilities and may result in inaccuracies in delivery, they will be critical in improving the efficiency of the supply chain as well as the overall economy. Automation is the ideal solution for the dynamic and complicated difficulties that manufacturers, contract logistics providers, and distributors are faced with every day. Industry automation enables them to manufacture more things with higher quality and precision in a shorter period of time. Automation also lowers labour costs (Chen et al., 2021; Zheng et al., 2018).

Consider the following scenario, assume you have a low-budget pancake business. As a result, he may have two or three co-workers who will assist him in making pancakes according to the instructions. However, as the firm expands and the number of clients increases rapidly, the manufacturing process must be accelerated and greater output with the exactly the same product quality as previously. If the number of employees increases, it is probable that one of the co-workers may add too many ingredients or will make another mistake that will lower the quality of that batch of pancakes. If the error is repeated repeatedly, the business will suffer a significant financial loss. To tackle the problem of business losses, one must hire an engineering firm that will automate the manufacturing process. The automatic machinery will make the manufacturing process considerably faster, easier, and more accurate while preserving product quality. With the use of such automatic machines, the firm will be more profitable and will require less staff. This is the underlying reason for industrial automation. Many industries, such as steel manufacturing, textiles, oil and refining, and so on, are now fully automated. There are numerous jobs that require human intervention that cannot be completed by automated machinery or robots (Alcácer & Cruz-Machado, 2019). A writer's job, like that of a journalist or many others, cannot be mechanised. Some vocations require humans as a basic requirement. Furthermore, some jobs cannot be automated since the initial cost of automation is large, making automation for such jobs neither practical nor lucrative. As a result, there are some restrictions to work automation (Parmar et al., 2021).

Intelligent control is the study of control systems that seek to imitate key aspects of human intelligence. Unpredictability, adaptability, and huge data processing are a few examples. In the modern era of intelligent control, everything that isn't conventional control tends to be included. It is difficult to define intelligent control because there is no universal definition of human intellect or intelligent behaviour, and because there has been a centuries-long debate over what constitutes intelligence.

As a result, intelligent control is multidisciplinary in character, including and expanding on theories and methods from a wide range of fields. Mathematics and biological systems are used in the design of this system. Intelligent control systems are employed in a variety of industries, including robotics and automation, communications, manufacturing, and traffic control, to name a few. Fuzzy control and genetic algorithms, planning systems and expert systems are all linked with one another, as is the use of neural networks. To represent knowledge, computer science and artificial intelligence have developed a toolset that includes semantic networks, frames, reasoning techniques, and computer languages such as prelude, amongst other things. Intelligent controllers are capable of adapting and learning on the basis of existing adaptive control principles and machine learning technologies. It is made possible by sensors, actuators, computing, and communication networks to create the hardware required for intelligent control systems to be developed. Nowadays robots play an important role in almost every element of human existence, including the demands of the industrial sector. Procedures used in modern industrial manufacturing are both precise and quick to execute. Human operations are necessary for a range of robotic system tasks, including setup, programming, troubleshooting, maintenance, and error management. Human operations are also required for robot maintenance. As a result of human operators entering robotic work zones, potentially hazardous situations arise. Human perception, decision-making, and action plans must all be examined in order to prevent mishaps caused by robots from occurring. System designers and technology managers are required to take into consideration the restrictions of the operator's perceptual process when designing and laying out robotic systems. The ultimate goal of improving the efficiency and quality of high-tech work environments is to save human lives in the short and long term. To ensure the safe operation of industrial robots, it is vital to develop comprehensive safety training programmes for employees. Robotics and Artificial Intelligence (AI) are two of the most important topics in research and development (R & D) that have resulted in substantial advances in Computer Science and electronics. Autonomous Systems are self-governing systems that do not require the involvement of a human.

An important technology in modern manufacturing has been the development of industrial automation. Industrial iterative upgrading has been promoted and technology, efficiency, and quality of industrial output have all improved as a result of industrial process automation control. Meanwhile, the degree of industrial production safety has improved significantly. Cloud computing, IoT, and AI are all being developed and deployed to enable industrial automation and move toward an intelligent path toward industry 4.0 (Javaid et al., 2021). Manufacturing has a big impact on economic and social progress. For many years, the term "industry 4.0" has been used to refer to research institutes and universities. Despite the fact that the concept has been discussed for many years in academic circles, the term "Industry 4.0" has only just been coined and is already widely accepted in both academic and industry circles. Industrial machine suits and intelligent products are evolving, and the impact of this transformation on potential customers is being studied by industry. As a result, organisations must first understand the fundamentals of Industry 4.0 in order to prepare for the imminent shift from machine-dominated to digital manufacturing. To make a successful transition, they must thoroughly examine their current problems and relative potentials in regard to the Industry 4.0 needs.

A considerable impact on social life is predicted by experts for the Fourth Industrial Revolution (Industry 4.0) and related improvements. As noted previously, some social transformation is expected. All of these technologies are projected to become increasingly common in the manufacturing business in the near future. Most of the community's attention is expected to be on wearable internet apps, big data analysis and implementations, and other related applications. For the manufacturing society to meet customer expectations and sustain a competitive advantage, this societal disruption is unavoidable.

Industrial process automation can benefit from information analysis of manufacturing processes, which can aid in the control of factory automation systems. Currently, industrial process control is hampered by a lack of adequate information control. The disparity between industrial output and employment, as well as the increasing use of mechanical automation in manufacturing, are becoming increasingly obvious as the economy and society progress rapidly. Reduced production and employment are necessary to achieve industrial process control automation's goal of eliminating human error. Intelligent technology support and cooperation together with promotion of automation development are both essential if we are to raise our control automation level. Automation of data collection on the operation of industrial equipment is made possible thanks to the use of an intelligent control system. Functioning and processing enable the application of intelligent control over the operation of equipment and the output of industrial processes. Information technology is utilised to improve industrial production processes' control systems, make their intelligent control functions easier to implement, and collect production data more efficiently than ever before.

Intelligent control technology has been shown effective in industrial process automation development and research. The use of intelligent control technology enables the efficient transmission and sharing of production data. Controlling and optimising production in real-time is made possible by monitoring industrial equipment in real-time. Innovative control systems have helped modern industry become more efficient. However, the production value is reduced due to technological limits. Industry 4.0 and the change of scalable intelligence rely heavily on industrial robots. Using robot control technology, it is possible to accomplish intelligent control of robots in the workplace, which includes directing their movement location and the amount of time they take to complete a task. In addition to its ease of use in the software's menu structure, it is also simple to develop. A lot of progress has been achieved recently (Jondhale et al., 2022; Oztemel & Gursev, 2020).

Background

For study, research, and industrial application, a number of robotic manipulators are available. Selective Compliance Articulated Robotic Arm (SCARA) is one of the most efficient manipulators available, boasting distinct and competitive industrial requirements. SCARA is a sort of industrial robot that works in the manufacturing industry. In pick-and-place or assembly processes where great speed and accuracy are required, the SCARA robot is the most widely utilised robot (Legnani & Faglia, 1992). In general, a SCARA robot can operate at a greater pace and with customizable specifications than other types of robots available.

The Yamanashi University laboratory of Professor Hiroshi Makino created the first SCARA robot in 1978. SCARA's four-axis design was unique at the time. Its simplicity was genius; with less movement, it could accomplish more, at a high rate of speed and precision. SCARA robots were first used on commercial assembly lines in 1981 and continue to provide the highest price/performance ratio for high-speed assembly. The Japanese flexible assembly method, based on the SCARA robot, sparked a global boom in small electronics manufacturing, resulting in the creation of devices that fueled the economy and forever altered the globe (Makino, 2014). During the Fourth Industrial Revolution, a tendency toward more flexible manufacturing and higher productivity was created. With the advent of computers and other electronic devices, the majority of industrial processes are now automated and may be controlled remotely. In the industrial and material handling industries, automation of operations with robotic arms that have improved dependability, accuracy, and repeatability has had a significant impact on the industry. High-speed mass production has resulted as a result of this development. Manufacturing and material handling procedures that made use of robotic arms were more productive and required less human intervention as a result. When compared to traditional gantry and delta mechanisms, robotic arms have a lower degree of freedom. For a variety of jobs in the business, a wide variety of robotic arms are employed. The SCARA robot is fairly common to observe on an assembly line in any industry because of its versatility.

It is most commonly used for pick and place labour, but it may be utilised for a variety of other tasks as well. A SCARA robot arm is an abbreviation for Selective Compliance Articulated Robotic Arm. SCARA robots are well-known for their positional accuracy and process repeatability, among other characteristics. SCARA robots are more flexible in the horizontal plane and have strong robustness for movement in the vertical direction compared to other robots. As a result, it is an excellent machine for performing pick and place work of any kind. A wide variety of commercial SCARA robots are available on the market in a variety of configurations and sizes, as well as variable operating linear speeds, among other characteristics. The recent advancement has resulted in the employment of SCARA robots in manufacturing processes such as 3D printing, CNC milling, drilling, and laser cutting, among others. SCARA is one of the most powerful industrial robots available. This sort of robot was developed to increase the speed and reproducibility of pick and place operations from one site to another, as well as to speed up and enhance assembly procedures. SCARAs are utilised in a variety of industries, including automotive, electronic, food processing, pharmaceutical, and others, where manufacturers must feed bulk components of varying sizes (Padhy, 1992).

The SCARA robot is a versatile machine that can execute a variety of activities depending on the application. The SCARA robot is more efficient at packaging and transporting jobs. The SCARA robot is also used for 3D printing and has advantages over typical 3D printing devices like the cartesian 3D printer and the Delta 3D printer. The SCARA robot is capable of performing the various production operations, including laser cutting, drilling, milling, and engraving, with ease. Recent work on the development of the SCARA robot has mostly centred on enhancing performance and increasing positioning and end-effector trajectory control precision. This is accomplished via the various innovative control systems. Thus, it can be stated that the SCARA robot is the optimal configuration for industrial technologies and has also been shown capable of use in the medical field as a surgical robotic arm. Using a nonlinear autoregressive exogenous input neural network model, the authors modelled the dynamic behaviour of the SCARA robot. The authors have proposed and validated the model using real-time experimental data. The projected data confirmed the location and dynamic behaviour of the actual system. Considered dynamic characteristics included contact, flexibility, backlash, and friction. Bayesian regression accurately calculated the dynamics of the SCARA robot. The dynamic simulation of the four-arm SCARA mechanism, which was employed for 3D printing, was carried out by the authors. The advantages of the SCARA mechanism over the gantry and parallel systems used by 3D printers are outlined by the authors in their paper. The research presents the results of an inverse kinematic analysis and a dynamic analysis of the SCARA mechanism, both performed using software. There is particular emphasis in this study on the effect of 3D printing factors on the dynamic behaviour of the end effector as well as the positioning of its mechanism. A cost-effective SCARA 4-DOF robotic manipulator designed for pick-and-place operations. The robot's end-effector can support around 2 kg of payload. The author has employed such methodologies as concept generation, parameter optimization, production, simulation of the theoretical model, and validation. The mathematical model of an electromechanical system was simulated numerically in MATLAB, and electronic control was implemented by programming a PLC board. The work concluded the reduction in SCARA robot fabrication costs.

The work documented the usage of a SCARA manipulator for picking to generate automatic, higher-quality plucking of tea leaves. The author introduced a controller-based neural adaptive compensator to quickly and precisely position the end effector. In MATLAB/Simulink, the mathematical model was numerically simulated. The theoretical model was validated by experimental evidence. The authors found that the given controller enabled the end-effector to accurately follow the intended trajectory with a tiny RMS error. The authors have described the design of a cost-effective SCARA robot for industrial applications, including the SCARA robot's design approach and simulation. The authors have compared various industrial SCARA robots based on their joint configuration, motor connection method, and various joint stiffness and functioning metrics. The authors have developed a MATLAB model to replicate the trajectory of the SCARA robot's end-effector. Utilizing the PID controller, the tolerances were closely constrained. It was determined that rotational acceleration is greatest when the SCARA manipulator's linkages are collinear.

The mathematical modelling of SCARA robot friction. Pneumatic semi-rotary drive is regarded to be the SCARA robot's input. The friction was modelled mathematically using mass flowrate curves. The authors assert that pneumatic control in SCARA manipulators has received relatively little attention in the past since the positioning accuracy is insufficient. The authors conclude that the reported work is applicable to the development of a nonlinear controller for a pneumatically-driven SCARA robot. In their research, the writers validated the theoretical system using simulation and experimentation. Unlike other robots, SCARA kinematics allows this robot to modify movement in the horizontal plane while maintaining great vertical rigidity. The SCARA arm's mechanics are normally highly robust and can sustain unexpected force and collisions without difficulty. It takes little maintenance and is simple to implement. SCARA robots are extremely reliable and have a high rate of speed and accuracy. One of the most significant benefits is its compact design (Visioli & Legnani, 2002). The PID controller, which has been in use for more than 50 years, is widely employed in the control of industrial processes in the fabrication, electromechanical, pharmaceutical, thermoelectric, illumination industries, electrolytic, and many other fields. PID control is by far the most often used control method because its control structure is basic, it is straightforward to operate and alter, and it has certain robustness qualities. PID control is also the least expensive control method. Great efforts have been made in recent years to develop and distribute it as a significant and reliable technical project and tool for industrial process control as part of a big and reliable technical project and instrument.

The quality of parameter setting has an impact on not only the quality of control, but also the stability and resilience of the control system as a result of the parameter setting. As a result of the complexity, diversity, variability, and uncertainty inherent in modern industrial processes, it is conceivable to see a shift in the parameters of models and a change in the model structure. Three-mode or PID control is one of the most powerful but also one of the most complicated forms of operation. This mode combines the advantages of proportional, integral, and derivative control systems. Industrial robot manipulators commonly use proportional-integral-derivative (PID) control, which is a type of feedback control. It is because of this that closed-loop systems suffer from poor transient performance and even loss of stability when the integrator in the PID controller is overloaded. A large number of robot manipulators employ proportional-derivative (PD) control in conjunction with gravity and friction compensations, necessitating the use of gravity and friction models in order to operate properly.

METHODOLOGY

SCARA has maintained its hold over industry as it offers controlled tracking with PID, optimization of the articulated robot for maximum weight loss, harmonic drive transmissions and a lot many other advantages. SCARA robots exhibit highly nonlinear behavior and complex uncertain dynamic response which makes it difficult to model and control. Because of its simplicity, ease of use, and global availability, the proportional integral derivative (PID) controller is the most extensively used controller in industry. As a result of intelligent control, the field of industrial control engineering has undergone a sea change. In recent years, significant progress has been made in the field of intelligent compensation for PD/PID regulation. Several researchers have tried to enhance its capability for controlling complex system such as SCARA. Introduction of fractional calculus, fuzzy logic and artificial intelligence are methods utilized to design efficient PID control strategies (Chhabra et al., 2016, 2019; Mohan et al., 2017). Applied hybrid additions improve efficiency at cost of increased parameters which has driven the curiosity of many enthusiasts across the globe to explore fields like heuristic algorithms. Advanced multi-objective evolutionary algorithms are utilized for tuning the controller to obtain finest accuracy and best possible control (Panjwani et al., 2019; Panjwani et al., 2021b). Notable work has been carried out to control different manipulators with hybrid artificial intelligent control techniques to bring efficient results.

The following work presents the utilization of MATLAB, Simulink environment for the construction and control of SCARA manipulator. The PID and FOPID controllers are in charge of controlling variables such as trajectory tracking, precision, and other external parameters that affect the manipulator's performance. The attribute of a PID controller of using a control loop feedback mechanism to control process variables makes it the most correct and stable controller. It is the most used dynamic control technique. FOPID controller is also implemented for better comparison results and self-tuning accessibility as it raises the flexibility and results in enhanced degrees of freedom. Several methods for tuning the controllers have been accustomed for standardization to date and the functioning of the PID and FOPID controller work satisfactorily considering the minimal input information provided for the design. Different tuning procedures develop enormous variations in the outcomes. Genetic Algorithm has served a big role in the simulation of the work presented in this paper. It is possible to create a genetic algorithm using the ideas of Charles Darwin's theory of natural selection as a search heuristic. The fundamental features of genetic algorithms are chromosome representation, fitness selection, and biologically inspired operators, among other things. Inversion is a technique that is commonly utilised in GA implementations. Typically, the chromosomes are represented as a string of binary numbers. Chromosomes include two potential alleles (variant forms of genes) for each locus (particular site on chromosome) - zero and one - for each gene. To generate offspring using the crossover operator, a random locus is selected, and it modifies the sequences across chromosomes to produce offspring. The process of mutation is characterised by the random flipping of some bits of chromosomes on the basis of probability. The value of modulation very much relies on the compatibility of the tuning methods with the plant behaviour and the implementation goals.

The block diagram given in figure 1 gives the insight about the methodology used in this work.

Figure 1. Block Diagram for the FOPID tracking control of SCARA

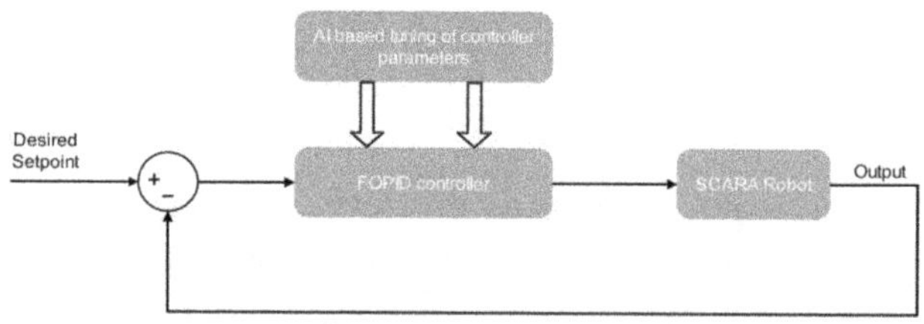

The values of superior parameters of the controllers (FOPID and PID) are obtained using the predominating heuristic calibration routine. The outcome for both controllers is compared for better results and inferences are considered.

Dynamics of SCARA Robot

Selective Compliance Articulated/Assembly robot arm is one of the fastest robots working in the industry. SCARA robot is designed to mimic the movement of human hand and increase efficiency and reduce fatigue. It is a two-link arm that is capable of performing assembly activities such as inserting a round pin into a round hole without being stuck in place. Due to its compact size and perfection for repeatability, SCARA robot is gaining high demand in the automation industry. Two independent motors are used to provide motion to links individually and controls the position of the robot in X and Y axis. The final location of the end effector at link-2 is dependent on joint-1 angle, length of link-1 and link-2. The mechanical structure of SCARA robot is shown in figure 2 and dynamics of SCARA robot is described below (Kumar & Sharma, 2018).

$$\begin{bmatrix} \tau_1 \\ \tau_2 \end{bmatrix} = \begin{bmatrix} S_1 + S_2 C_\theta & S_3 + \frac{1}{2} S_2 C_\theta \\ S_3 + \frac{1}{2} S_2 C_\theta & S_3 \end{bmatrix} \begin{bmatrix} \ddot{\theta}_1 \\ \ddot{\theta}_2 \end{bmatrix} + \begin{bmatrix} (S_4 - S_2 S_\theta \dot{\theta}_2)\dot{\theta}_2 & -\frac{1}{2} S_2 S_\theta \dot{\theta}_2 \\ \frac{1}{2} S_2 S_\theta \dot{\theta}_1 + S_5 \dot{\theta}_2 & 0 \end{bmatrix} \tag{1}$$

Where S_1, S_2, S_3, S_4, S_5 are the payload masses and their values are S_1=5.0, S_2=0.9, S_3=0.3, S_4=3.0 and S_5=0.6. Also, here $S_{\theta=}\sin\theta 2$ $_{a}$nd $C\theta=_{co}s\theta 2$.

Figure 2. Model of SCARA robot

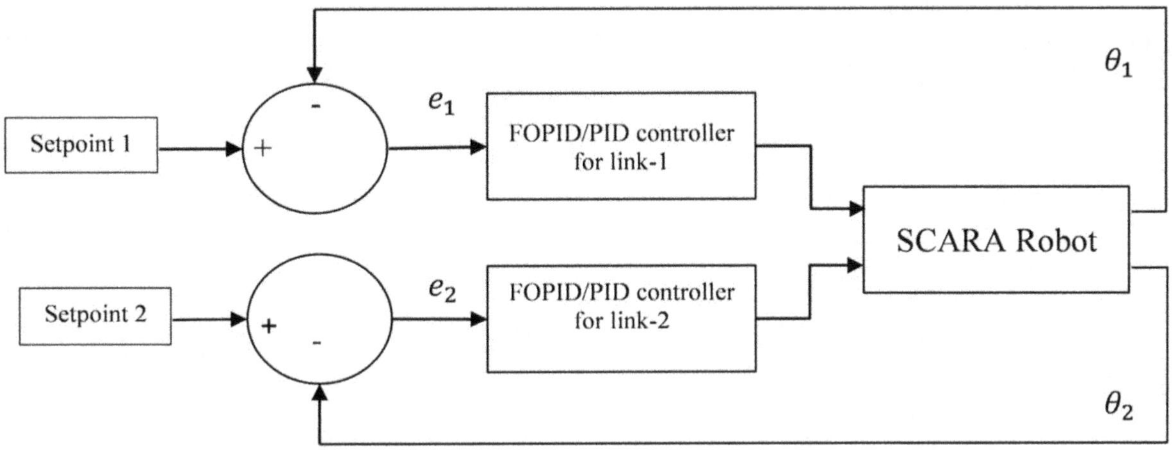

Controller Design

The FOPID controller serves the purpose of controlling the joint angles of the SCARA manipulator. In recent times, as the difficulty level is increasing in the field of robotics, the classical PID controller has been unable to provide proper outcomes. Thus, the fractional order PID controller was introduced by merging fractional calculus with classical PID control structure. A FOPID controller has two additional parameters over PID controller, thus five variables need to be tuned. The variables are gains KP, KI, KD and the order of integration (α) and differentiation (β). The transfer function of FOPID Controller is given as

$$C(s)=\frac{U(s)}{E(s)}=K_P+\frac{K_I}{s^{\alpha}}+K_D s^{\beta} \quad (2)$$

To obtain the transfer function of PID from a FOPID controller, the values of α and β are consider as 1. Thus, transfer function of PID Controller can be given as

$$C(s)=\frac{U(s)}{E(s)}=K_P+\frac{K_I}{s}+K_D s \quad (3)$$

where, $C(s)$ and $E(s)$ denotes the transfer function of the controller and error of the system respectively. Controller output is represented by $U(s)$, whereas s signifies the complex frequency. The control structure of FOPID/PID for SCARA robot is depicted in fig.3. Numerical simulation of a fractional order operator may not be a simple task due to absence of exact analytical analysis. To overcome this hurdle approximations are used to solve the fractional order differ-integral operators. Oustaloup approximation is one of the best approximation methods for finding the appropriate results. Based on an approximation of the fractional order system behaviour in the frequency domain, this strategy is being used in this work (Oustaloup et al., 2000). The approximation for a fractional order operator $G_t(s)=s^{\gamma}$ is

$$G_t(s)=\prod_{i=1}^{N}\frac{S+\omega_i^{'}}{S+\omega_i} \tag{4}$$

$$\omega_i^{'}=\omega_b\omega_u^{\frac{2i-1-\gamma}{N}} \tag{5}$$

$$\omega_i=\omega_b\omega_u^{\frac{2i-1+\gamma}{N}} \tag{6}$$

$$K=\omega_h^{\gamma} \tag{7}$$

$$\omega_u=\sqrt{\frac{\omega_h}{\omega_b}} \tag{8}$$

The approximation is considered valid in the frequency range of [ωb ωh]. The gain K is adjusted so that the approximation has unit gain at 1 rad/sec. The order of approximation N is chosen beforehand. High order of N results in logarithmic spacing of poles between the range of -ωh and -ωb and the approximation shows the best result in the interior of the band rather than the boundary.

Genetic Algorithm

For the purpose of tuning the parameters of controllers, we have used genetic algorithms in this study. It is a stochastic algorithm based on the theory of probability and is used in genetic algorithms (Sharma et al., 2018). In order to find information in a vast amount of data, it is necessary to use search engines (Banshwar et al., 2018). This algorithm is based on the process of natural selection, in which the best fit individuals are selected for reproduction in order to produce offspring of the next generation of individuals (Panjwani et al., 2021a; Sharma et al., 2021). The algorithm works on string structures and is based on the rule that the fittest structure would be selected at every generation based on some definite criterion. The algorithm is run for 50 generations with population size of 20. Using a flowchart, such as that illustrated in figure 4, the appropriate operation of the genetic algorithm is demonstrated and the fitness function considered is given as

Figure 3. FOPID/PID control structure for SCARA robot

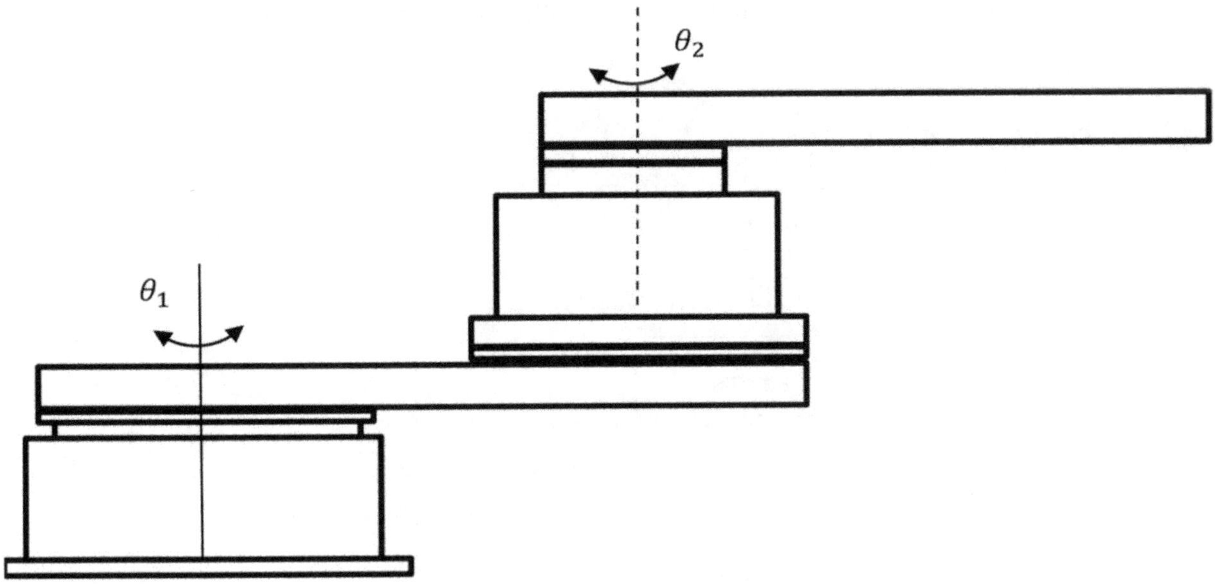

$$J = 0.5 \times \int |e_1| dt + 0.5 \times \int |e_2| dt \tag{9}$$

RESULTS

The performance of standard PID and fractional-order PID controllers for tracking control of the SCARA robot is compared in this section. There is a specialised controller for each link in the closed-loop system being evaluated for simulation of the manipulator, according to the system's design. The optimum controller parameters are sought in the range depicted in Table 1 by searching through the data.

Sampling time is chosen as 0.001 sec with controlling torques $\tau1$ and $\tau2$ between range [-10, 10] Nm. A single objective function is considered for the task with maximum generation set to 50. Table 2 lists the GA parameters used for configuring the PID and FOPID controllers. Fitness functions are used to guide simulation towards optimal solutions. Figure 5 shows the fitness function curve vs generation. It can be interpreted that FOPID drives the system towards the final value faster than PID. The value of fitness function at 50th generation is 0.617 for FOPID and 0.626 for PID.

Set Point Tracking

Manipulator links must follow a required path/trajectory to perform the tasks it has been allotted, such as pick and place, welding, painting, assembly, etc. The optimum parameters of the controllers for link-1 and link-2 are recorded in Table 3. The performance of PID and FOPID controller is compared in terms of IAE, settling time, rise time and overshoot, and their values are given in Table 4. The IAE values for link-1 and link-2 are 1.007 and 0.2481 for PID controller, 0.9993 and 0.2372 in the case of FOPID controller. Figures 6, 7, 8, and 9 depict the setpoint tracking of links, errors, and control effort. From the results it is clear that FOPID outperform the PID controller for setpoint tracking.

Figure 4. Flowchart of Genetic Algorithm

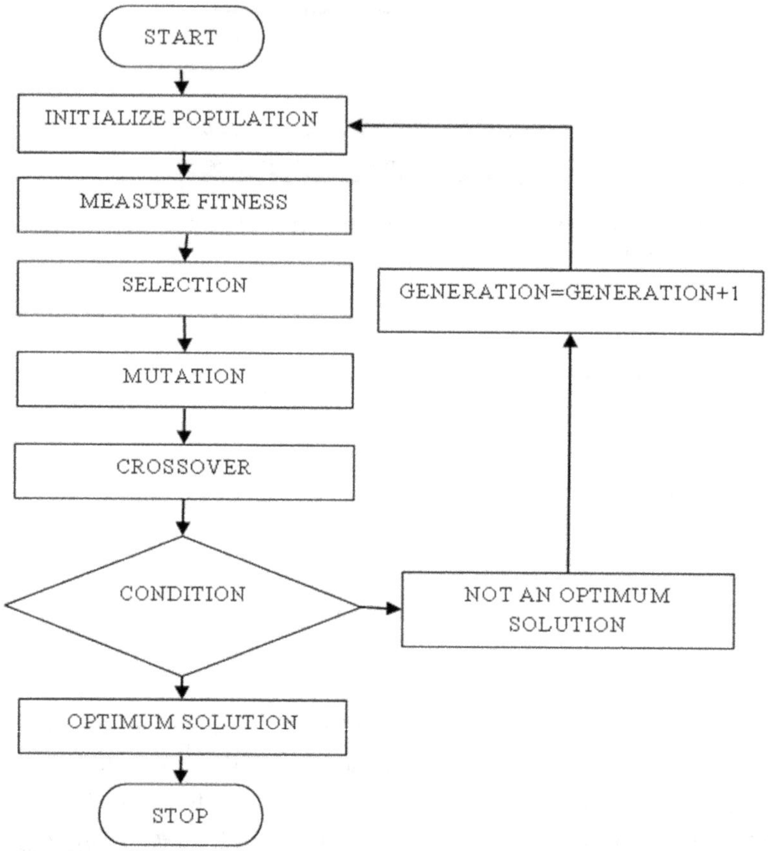

Table 1. Search space for controller parameters

Controller parameters	FOPID link-1	PID link-1	Controller parameters	FOPID link-2	PID link-2
K_{P_1}	[0, 50]	[0, 50]	K_{P_2}	[0, 50]	[0, 50]
K_{I_1}	[0, 10]	[0, 10]	K_{I_2}	[0, 10]	[0, 10]
K_{D_1}	[0, 50]	[0, 50]	K_{D_2}	[0, 50]	[0, 50]
$\alpha 1$	[0, 0.999]	-	$\alpha 2$	[0, 0.999]	-
$\beta 1$	[0, 0.999]	-	$\beta 2$	[0, 0.999]	-

Table 2. Search space for controller parameters

Parameter	Method and value used in GA for FOPID and PID
Number of objective functions	1
Number of design variables	10, 6
Population sizes	20
Maximum Generation	50
Selection function	Stochastic uniform
Mutation method	Constraint dependent
Crossover method	Constraint dependent
Sampling time	0.001 sec

Figure 5. Fitness function vs generation plot of PID and FOPID.

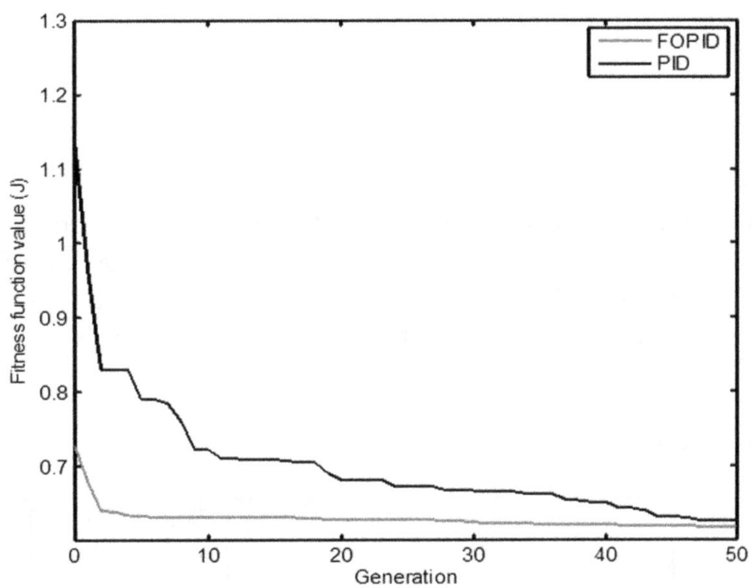

Uncertainty Analysis

Model uncertainty is incorporated in the system and measured with respect to IAE values. The controllers are designed to measure uncertainty and quantitative comparison is made on basis of IAE values. The controlling torques $\tau\mathbf{1}$ and $\tau\mathbf{2}$ between range [-10,10] Nm. From the Table 5, it can be observed that IAE (Integral Absolute Error) values for both link1 and link2 when controlled by FOPID controller are smaller as compared to PID controller output for link1 and link2. Hence, the manipulator is robust considering the parameter unreliability and has superior disturbance rejection performance.

Figure 6. Positioning of link 1

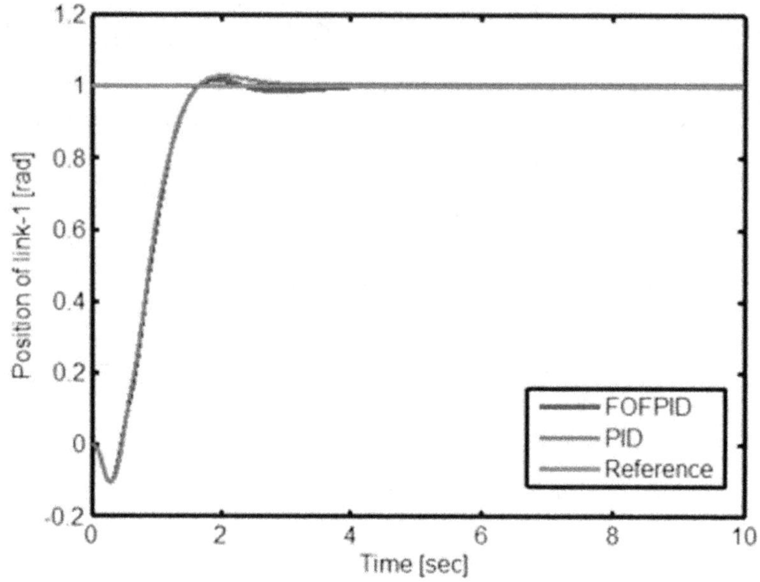

DISCUSSION

The study describes a nonlinear robotic manipulator with two degrees of freedom (DOF). The controller in use is of fractional order, which allows for greater flexibility and degrees of freedom due to the increased number of possible combinations. In addition, a conventional PID controller is employed to control the manipulator in order to do a comparative study. Various factors, such as the uncertainty pa-

Figure 7. Positioning of link 2

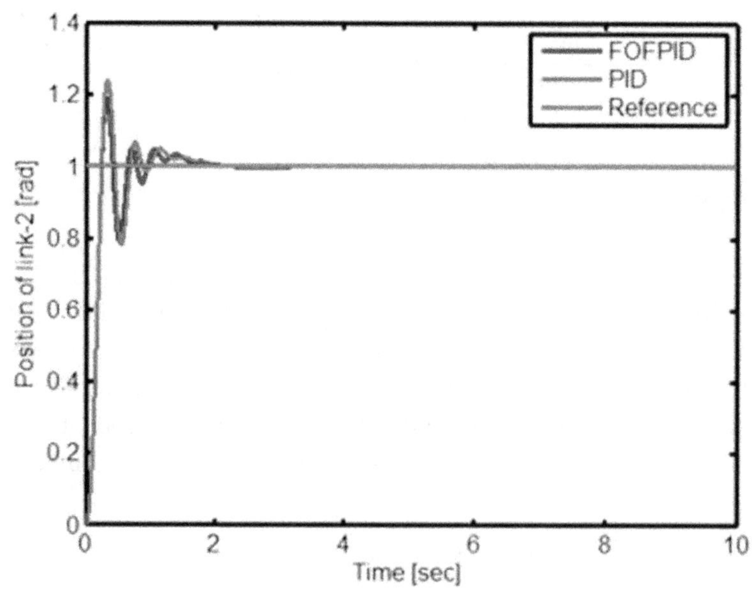

Figure 8. Tracking error

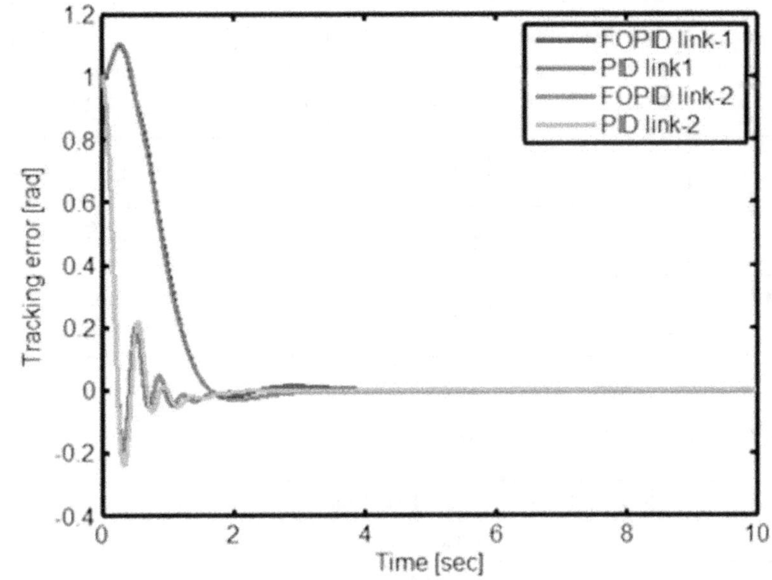

rameter, trajectory tracking, and disturbances, are tolerated by the system. The controller's responsibility is to address the issues that have arisen as a result of the procedure. If we look at the FOPID controller in comparison to the standard PID controller, we can see that the results obtained from simulation of the 2-DOF manipulator with the help of the FOPID controller reveal that it is more capable of dealing with a wide range of challenges.

Figure 9. Control effort

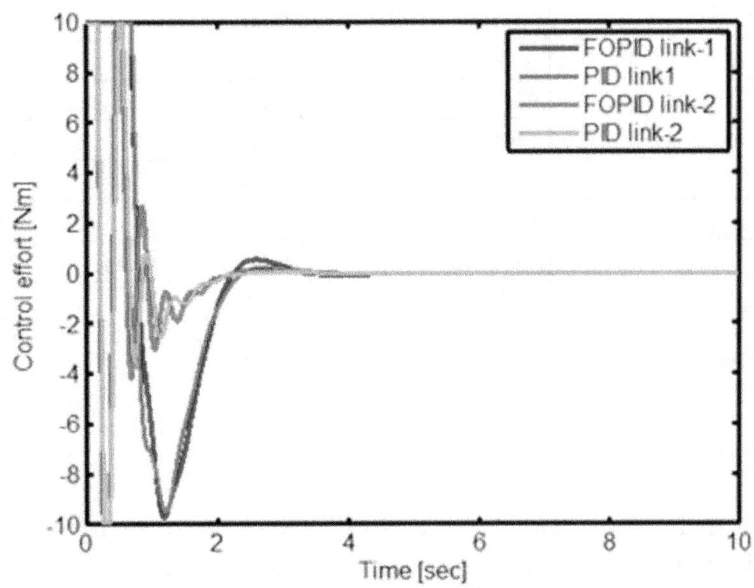

Table 3. Optimum controller parameters

Controller parameters	FOPID link-1	PID link-1	Controller Parameters	FOPID link-2	PID link-2
K_{P_1}	23.688	49.994	K_{P_2}	43.829	49.651
K_{I_1}	6.351	0.193	K_{I_2}	3.28	0.108
K_{D_1}	21.31	25.168	K_{D_2}	4.671	0.941
$\alpha 1$	0.143	1	$\alpha 2$	0.152	1
$\beta 1$	0.844	1	$\beta 2$	0.549	1

Table 4. Performance comparison of controllers

Controllers	Settling Time	Rise Time	Overshoot (%)	IAE
FOPID link-1	1.563	0.8073	1.87	0.9993
PID link-1	2.2245	0.8096	2.87	1.007
FOPID link-2	1.5484	0.1513	18.99	0.2372
PID link-2	1.6221	0.151	23.8	0.2481

Table 5. Uncertainty percentage of link 1 and link 2

Percentage uncertainty	IAE of FOPID link-1	IAE of PID link-1	IAE of FOPID link-2	IAE of PID link-2
-10	0.943	0.951	0.221	0.230
-8	0.953	0.962	0.224	0.234
-6	0.964	0.973	0.227	0.237
-4	0.975	0.984	0.231	0.241
-2	0.987	0.995	0.234	0.244
0	0.999	1.006	0.237	0.248
2	1.011	1.017	0.240	0.251
4	1.023	1.029	0.243	0.255
6	1.035	1.040	0.246	0.258
8	1.048	1.051	0.249	0.262
10	1.060	1.063	0.252	0.265

CONCLUSION

In this work, FOPID and PID controllers are suggested for precise control of the SCARA manipulator. The main objective of this work is to control the optimum parameters using both PID and FOPID controllers separately and illustrate a comparison between the two. In FOPID additional performance parameters, order of derivative (β), and order of integral (α) needs to be optimized along with Kp (proportional), Ki (integral), and Kd (derivative) constants. Hence, FOPID requires more parameters to be optimized which increases the chances of a finer termination outcome. In terms of robustness, tracking efficiency, disturbance rejection, and other characteristics, the FOPID controller outperforms and produces better outcomes than the typical PID controller. The superiority of the FOPID controller is established. The multi-purpose optimization technique (GA) helps in achieving the finest fitness curve with better optimal values. The FOPID controller outperforms the PID controller in terms of error-free outcomes, despite the fact that the former controller makes use of a greater number of variables..

REFERENCES

Alcácer, V., & Cruz-Machado, V. (2019). Scanning the industry 4.0: A literature review on technologies for manufacturing systems. *Engineering Science and Technology, An International Journal, 22*(3), 899-919.

Banshwar, A., Sharma, N. K., Sharma, B. B., Sood, Y. R., & Shrivastava, R. (2018). Mixed GA-OPF based optimal procurement of energy and operating reserve in deregulated environment. *Journal of Intelligent & Fuzzy Systems, 35*(5), 4963–4969. doi:10.3233/JIFS-169780

Chen, M., Sinha, A., Hu, K., & Shah, M. I. (2021). Impact of technological innovation on energy efficiency in industry 4.0 era: Moderation of shadow economy in sustainable development. *Technological Forecasting and Social Change, 164*, 120521. doi:10.1016/j.techfore.2020.120521

Chhabra, H., Mohan, V., Rani, A., & Singh, V. (2016). Multi objective PSO tuned fractional order PID control of robotic manipulator. The international symposium on intelligent systems technologies and applications. In *Advances in Signal Processing and Communication* (pp. 345–352). Springer.

Chhabra, H., Mohan, V., Rani, A., & Singh, V. (2020). Robust nonlinear fractional order fuzzy PD plus fuzzy I controller applied to robotic manipulator. *Neural Computing & Applications, 32*(7), 2055–2079. doi:10.100700521-019-04074-3

Javaid, M., Haleem, A., Singh, R. P., & Suman, R. (2021). Substantial capabilities of robotics in enhancing industry 4.0 implementation. *Cognitive Robotics, 1*, 58–75. doi:10.1016/j.cogr.2021.06.001

Jondhale, S. R., Mohan, V., Sharma, B. B., Lloret, J., & Athawale, S. V. (2022). Support Vector Regression for Mobile Target Localization in Indoor Environments. *Sensors (Basel), 22*(1), 358. doi:10.339022010358 PMID:35009896

Kumar, A., & Sharma, R. (2018). Linguistic Lyapunov reinforcement learning control for robotic manipulators. *Neurocomputing, 272*, 84–95. doi:10.1016/j.neucom.2017.06.064

Legnani, G., & Faglia, R. (1992). Harmonic drive transmissions: The effects of their elasticity, clearance and irregularity on the dynamic behaviour of an actual SCARA robot. *Robotica, 10*(4), 369–375. doi:10.1017/S0263574700008201

Makino, H. (2014). Development of the SCARA. *Journal of Robotics and Mechatronics, 26*(1), 5–8. doi:10.20965/jrm.2014.p0005

Mohan, V., Chhabra, H., Rani, A., & Singh, V. (2019). An expert 2DOF fractional order fuzzy PID controller for nonlinear systems. *Neural Computing & Applications*, *31*(8), 4253–4270. doi:10.100700521-017-3330-z

Mohan, V., Rani, A., & Singh, V. (2017). Robust adaptive fuzzy controller applied to double inverted pendulum. *Journal of Intelligent & Fuzzy Systems*, *32*(5), 3669–3687. doi:10.3233/JIFS-169301

Oustaloup, A., Levron, F., Mathieu, B., & Nanot, F. M. (2000). Frequency-band complex noninteger differentiator: Characterization and synthesis. *IEEE Transactions on Circuits and Systems. I, Fundamental Theory and Applications*, *47*(1), 25–39. doi:10.1109/81.817385

Oztemel, E., & Gursev, S. (2020). Literature review of Industry 4.0 and related technologies. *Journal of Intelligent Manufacturing*, *31*(1), 127–182. doi:10.100710845-018-1433-8

Padhy, S. K. (1992). On the dynamics of SCARA robot. *Robotics and Autonomous Systems*, *10*(1), 71–78. doi:10.1016/0921-8890(92)90016-R

Panjwani, B., Mohan, V., Rani, A., & Singh, V. (2019). Optimal drug scheduling for cancer chemotherapy using two degree of freedom fractional order PID scheme. *Journal of Intelligent & Fuzzy Systems*, *36*(3), 2273–2284. doi:10.3233/JIFS-169938

Panjwani, B., Singh, V., Rani, A., & Mohan, V. (2021a). Optimizing Drug Schedule for Cell-Cycle Specific Cancer Chemotherapy. In Soft Computing: Theories and Applications (pp. 71-81). Springer. doi:10.1007/978-981-16-1696-9_7

Panjwani, B., Singh, V., Rani, A., & Mohan, V. (2021b). Optimum multi-drug regime for compartment model of tumour: Cell-cycle-specific dynamics in the presence of resistance. *Journal of Pharmacokinetics and Pharmacodynamics*, *48*(4), 543–562. doi:10.100710928-021-09749-w PMID:33751365

Parmar, H., Khan, T., Tucci, F., Umer, R., & Carlone, P. (2021). Advanced robotics and additive manufacturing of composites: Towards a new era in Industry 4.0. *Materials and Manufacturing Processes*, 1–35.

Sharma, B. B., Banshwar, A., Pathak, M., Sharma, N. K., & Joshi, A. (2021). Microcontroller-based PID Temperature Controller Using Genetic Algorithms. In *Advances in Renewable Energy and Sustainable Environment* (pp. 277–283). Springer. doi:10.1007/978-981-15-5313-4_26

Sharma, N. K., Banshwar, A., Sharma, B. B., Sood, Y. R., & Shrivastava, R. (2018). Mixed GA-OPF based prioritized optimal location and rating of wind power generation in deregulated electricity market. *Journal of Intelligent & Fuzzy Systems*, *35*(5), 5071–5075. doi:10.3233/JIFS-169791

Visioli, A., & Legnani, G. (2002). On the trajectory tracking control of industrial SCARA robot manipulators. *IEEE Transactions on Industrial Electronics*, *49*(1), 224–232. doi:10.1109/41.982266

Zheng, P., Sang, Z., Zhong, R. Y., Liu, Y., Liu, C., Mubarok, K., Yu, S., & Xu, X. (2018). Smart manufacturing systems for Industry 4.0: Conceptual framework, scenarios, and future perspectives. *Frontiers of Mechanical Engineering*, *13*(2), 137–150. doi:10.100711465-018-0499-5

ADDITIONAL READING

Chen, Z., Yuan, X., Ji, B., Wang, P., & Tian, H. (2014). undefined. *Energy Conversion and Management*, *84*, 390–404. doi:10.1016/j.enconman.2014.04.052

De Wit, C., & Praly, L. (2000). Adaptive eccentricity compensation. *IEEE Transactions on Control Systems Technology*, *8*(5), 757–766. doi:10.1109/87.865849

Deb, K., Pratap, A., Agarwal, S., & Meyarivan, T. (2002). A fast and elitist multiobjective genetic algorithm: NSGA-II. *IEEE Transactions on Evolutionary Computation*, *6*(2), 182–197. doi:10.1109/4235.996017

Hultmann Ayala, H. V., & Dos Santos Coelho, L. (2012). Tuning of PID controller based on a multi-objective genetic algorithm applied to a robotic manipulator. *Expert Systems with Applications*, *39*(10), 8968–8974. doi:10.1016/j.eswa.2012.02.027

Kumar, S., Saxena, R., & Singh, K. (2016). Fractional fourier transform and fractional-order calculus-based image edge detection. *Circuits, Systems, and Signal Processing*, *36*(4), 1493–1513. doi:10.100700034-016-0364-x

Malki, H., Li, H., & Chen, G. (1994). New design and stability analysis of fuzzy proportional-derivative control systems. *IEEE Transactions on Fuzzy Systems*, *2*(4), 245–254. doi:10.1109/91.324804

Pachauri, N., Singh, V., & Rani, A. (2017). Two degree of freedom PID based inferential control of continuous bioreactor for ethanol production. *ISA Transactions*, *68*, 235–250. doi:10.1016/j.isatra.2017.03.014 PMID:28351531

Pan, I., & Das, S. (2012). Chaotic multi-objective optimization based design of fractional order PIλDμ controller in AVR system. *International Journal of Electrical Power & Energy Systems*, *43*(1), 393–407. doi:10.1016/j.ijepes.2012.06.034

Sharma, R., Gaur, P., & Mittal, A. (2015). Performance analysis of two-degree of freedom fractional order PID controllers for robotic manipulator with payload. *ISA Transactions*, *58*, 279–291. doi:10.1016/j.isatra.2015.03.013 PMID:25896827

KEY TERMS AND DEFINITIONS

Genetic Algorithm: A natural selection-based strategy for addressing both constrained and unconstrained optimization problems, which is based on the process that drives biological evolution, is used to solve this type of problem.

Links: Essentially, it is a resisting body that is a component of the machine, linking other components that are in motion in relation to it.

Manipulators: It is a device that allows the operator to handle materials without having to make direct physical touch with them.

Chapter 15
Delineate Omnichannel Retailer and Consumer Engagement on Social Networks

Tania Mittal
Gurukula Kangri (Deemed), India

Pankaj Madan
https://orcid.org/0000-0002-4648-9863
Gurukula Kangri (Deemed), India

Kirti Sharma
Chandigarh University, India

Aditya Dhiman
Gurukula Kangri (Deemed), India

ABSTRACT

Customers are riding a wave of social media growth, transforming the customer's journey to purchase and aspire to go social. Social networking is the driving factor behind the evolution of retail and customer behavior. Today's retailers' widespread usage of social media as a marketing strategy has never been seen before. The omnichannel market has been addressed in Marketing 4.0 as a brand commitment approach where retailers incorporate omnichannel retail through social networks in the consumer purchasing route (5 A's: be aware, appeal, ask, act, and advocate). Omnichannel retailing convergence is a transition rather than a change that has a pronounced effect on consumers and retailers. The omnichannel market is a process of combining various platforms to provide a smooth and reliable consumer experience. This chapter discusses how technology serves as propulsion and gives a significant impetus to social networks for omni-retailing in the coming years in India. It also discusses how network integration differs depending on geography and product segment.

DOI: 10.4018/978-1-6684-4969-1.ch015

Copyright © 2022, IGI Global. Copying or distributing in print or electronic forms without written permission of IGI Global is prohibited.

1. INTRODUCTION

Consumer are riding a wave of digital technology. In future years, technology will act as propulsion to provide massive momentum to the retailing and marketing industry. Social networks are a group of digital platforms used to create and share content online. Various social media networks like Facebook are used to share news, exchange and micro-messaging services on Twitter, Photo and video sharing platforms such as Instagram, YouTube, Snapchat and professional networking sites like LinkedIn. Flipkart, Amazon, Myntra and, Ajio are among the significant e-commerce websites that are enticing new customers with social commerce, allowing consumers to click on photos and videos to buy items. Jio is a major retail player in India, connecting jio mart with Kirana stores and providing a solid omnichannel-tech platform that combines all customers, kiranas, and producers. (Tamal Nandi 2020). The mobile revolution has been created along with the growth of social media, the situation in which customers bring their entire social environment into their shopping experience. Social media is used to check the product rating, and customers can even reach the content creator for real information about the product. All videos, posts, and pictures will present people's satisfaction or dissatisfaction for the product. Some readers may remember the "beginnings" of social media when social media like Orkut and messenger were popular. These pages were the predecessors to Facebook, Instagram, Snapchat, and other social media platform that have progressed over the past years where images and videos have replaced text. The flourishing attractiveness of these social networks has prompted marketers to use it as a key marketing tool for communication.

1.1. Social Media Marketing as an Integral part of Selling and Purchase Path

Social media marketing refers to marketing communication techniques using social media. It promotes social commerce, enhances brand reputation through social media, helps companies create brands, and develops healthy customer relations. Social media represents a frontline for building long-term customer relationships and easy access to potential customers. It is essential for business leaders to use social media effectively and look for ways to better connect with customers by monetizing social media use. Customers demand direct links from businesses to their social media pages to remark promptly in real-time. But it raises additional issues because companies do not directly control a single social network but might seek to establish one-to-one interaction with the retailer through different marketing strategies like social listening.

1.2. Omnichannel Retailing through the Eyes of Retailers and Consumers

Transitioning between multichannel and omnichannel appears to be a natural yet essential trend in retail that many Multinational corporations are adopting. Therefore, the development of multichannel retail should be understood as omnichannel retail. The Latin word "Omni" signifies "all" or "all things". Growth in technical computing and virtual reality erodes the distinctions between conventional and online commerce. One of the most effective marketing tactics accessible to marketers today is omnichannel marketing. It's a marketing strategy that uses many channels to contact and engage customers, including social media, conventional media, the internet, and mobile phones. The omnichannel customer may also compare the same products across numerous websites and media before purchasing at the best price. For connected consumers, this opened up a new shopping path. "Collaborative management of various current channels and customer contact points to maximize customer experience and performance on all channels" (Verhoef, Kannan, and Inman 2015). "Omnichannel commerce" is being used by Reliance Retail, Aditya Birla Fashion & Retail, and Future Retail Limited. (Business world 2021). Social media posts usually let consumer compare it through website and consumer can swiftly browse through both. Grocery, Fashion, and general merchandise categories have the highest adoption among Indian retailers(Retailer 2021). Reliance Retail Ventures, Aditya Birla Fashion and Retail Limited, and OnePlus are among the firms that have implemented omnichannel selling. Ikea is also adopting an omnichannel approach target to reach 100 million people in India by 2022. Other than brands, many e-commerce platforms like Flipkart have launched '2GUD Local' to extend the benefits of e-commerce to traditional retail businesses. It would allow local companies - single brand or multi-brand shops to extend their digital presence for a more effective connection with their customers. This partnership will provide merchants a new sales channel and access to new regions for customer acquisition representing an all-important aspect of omnichannel retailing. Flipkart has also opened 20 locations across ten cities (ZeeBiz 2020).

1.3 Omnipresence on Social Media

All mobile, tabs, and desktop operating systems are integrated with social media (Facebook, Instagram, LinkedIn), making social media widespread and plentiful. It has stretched the network beyond particular platforms, making it omni-social. Through social media, consumers interact almost with every aspect of their lives, like work(LinkedIn), and snaps(Instagram) which make consumer decision-making path affected by social media in each stage. For example, one might get aware by watching their followed influencer on Instagram or Youtube or seeking the help of Facebook friends for a searching car of his choice. While the decision-making process is a spiral, consumers might skip all customer buying decisions and purchase products directly, which might differ from the traditional purchase path (Pele Cortizo-Burgess 2014). This trend will continue, making the word social media obsolete as its proliferation becomes the standard adoption for consumers, businesses, and artists in various industries.

2. PROBLEM STATEMENT AND HYPOTHESIS FORMULATION

Despite the exponential studies on social media marketing, new customer purchase path is yet to be explored. Marketers are still unsure about the shift and integration between the offline and online channels. The themes presented in this article are chosen to explain important use of social networking in omnichannel through the lenses of retailers, advertisers, consumers. Social media use in omnichannel retailing stirs up many questions like, how will interaction on social media affect people's purchase behavior of the different products? And for marketers, how can they strategically use social media in the spiral customer path of the connected consumer. Much previous research has discussed the application of the purchase path "AIDA" model, but 5A's customer path is yet to be addressed from a social media point of view. This section provides the result of the literature integration from which the research gap was identified wherein new customer path in omnichannel verse is tested.

H_{01}: There is no significant impact of gender on 'Aware' stage of omnichannel purchase path through social media

H_{02}: There is no significant impact of gender on 'Appeal' stage of omnichannel purchase path through social media

H_{03}: There is no significant impact of gender on 'Ask' stage of omnichannel purchase path through social media

H_{04}: There is no significant impact of gender on 'Act' stage of omnichannel purchase path through social media

H_{05}: There is no significant impact of gender on 'Advocate' stage of omnichannel purchase path through social media

3. MATERIALS AND METHODOLOGY

This chapter aims to comprehend the value of social media marketing in omnichannel commerce by looking at it from a societal perspective and through the eyes of the consumer. It is described in a manner that includes social media-aspired consumer purchasing pathways for omnichannel commerce. The chapter thoroughly examines previous research in social media marketing and omnichannel commerce. The papers were chosen from those published in scholarly journals between 2010 and 2020. This research looks at several critical unresolved issues regarding social media function in omni-marketing communications. For examining the hypothesis proposed, a survey questionnaire was adapted. The data was collected from 100 customers who purchased fashion apparel from social media within the last three months by using stratified random sampling in which strata are formed according to age group of respondents.

4. ANALYSIS

4.1. Omnichannel Customer Purchase Path

This path in Figure 1 is majorly given by (Kotler and Hermawan Kartajaya 2018), and here it is explained concerning social media marketing techniques

A. Aware

Customers' awareness of a brand is related to how well they know about its presence. The informational effect is most evident in the awareness phase when greater exposure to brand identifiers leads to more excellent brand recall. Two types of social media advertisements are owned and earned (Colicev, Kumar, and O'Connor 2019). Establishing brand awareness is the cornerstone of all branding and marketing activities. When exposed to brand identifiers, customers are more likely to remember and identify the brand while purchasing. With customers now spending so much time on social media, these channels have become essential for increasing brand awareness. The participatory element of social media significantly increases the opportunity for brand-related content. Viral marketing spreads content on social media like a virus and uses multiplication to reach hundreds, if not millions, of people. Exposure to them regularly increases brand awareness and recall. More precisely, the mere argument of the exhibition's impact shows that since all of the content is displayed in users' news sources, its very presence contributes to brand recognition. Users' interactions generate both good and bad brand content. However, regardless of the

Figure 1. Omnichannel customer purchase path

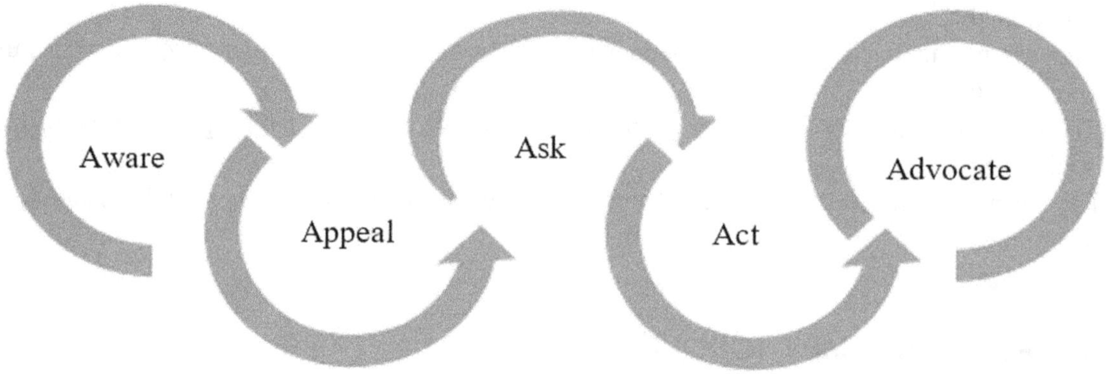

material, companies get greater exposure, impacting brand awareness (Wang and Kim 2017). Consumers come into touch with various companies and goods when they use social media daily by viewing, blogging, observing, reacting, ""Liking", and sharing. This sort of 's Consumer's Online Brand-Related Activities program reflects minimal participation and refers to customers who indirectly interact with the brand. The figure of likes and comments on posts is affected by videos and photographs. Content on social media is shared if it is exciting and informative, even if it promotes brand promotion. There is a higher no. of likes on the post with images and moderate text. Social media users often move through **three aspects when the material on the social network** is discussed. The first is content consumption, which involves consumer encounters with networks and online brand communities. Finding useful material related to internal social networks is difficult since information is dispersed and scattered on various platforms. Once the relevant information has been located, extra work is required to validate the quality of information, which is particularly important in the business sector. More recently, studies have focused on customers who "Like" products. The other two aspects are explained in the 3rd and 5th stages of the customer purchase path.

B. Appeal

Social media advertisement aims to persuade people to perform specific actions or change their attitudes about certain items or services. Social network advertisement appeals convey interests, motives, and identities or explain why customers should investigate or explore the offered items ((Kotler and Hermawan Kartajaya 2018). To retain user attention and create long-term memory for consumers, appealing brand pages and frequently made brand posts are required. Therefore, user involvement in the brand is an essential requirement. The level of user involvement through brand posts may be seen as a barometer of interaction efficacy since it reflects the post's popularity among brands. Posting on social media creates a memory about the brand in the user's mind. By giving new factual information, establishing emotional ties to brands, or providing instances of product use, advertisements may add to or alter the spokes of a brand memory. Memory either have rational or emotional appeal. A sensible appeal is described as stressing the product's simple terms, and Emotional appeals are described as methods of influencing a customer's mental state. Several items are available, each with its own set of features. Emotional responses to social media marketing are linked to long-term memory more strongly than reasoned answers. The narrative element of emotional advertising appeals adds to the vital link between emotion and brand memory, especially when contrasted with logical information processing. (Wagner, Baccarella, and Voigt 2017). Researchers have analyzed that there is implicit and explicit memory towards the ad. When ads are avoided Cognitively as a part of the vision screening, they form implicit memory. In contrast, explicit memory is formed when ads are directly seen, and attention is given to them. Recall and recognition are two aspects of clear memory that are likely to be greater if the ad is straight from a brand. After a delay, memory for the advertisement drops quicker than recall and recognition tests, with recall being lower than recognition.

C. Ask

Curiosity, as an emotion, drives consumers as explorers and discoverers. Consumers are typically interested as shoppers at this stage. A social media user is motivated to initiate the interaction by seeking information using social media and looking for a product or brand. Ghose, Ipeirotis, and Li (2014) focused on the interaction between search engines and social media. Google started incorporating various tweets and social network status updates in the search function and then developed its version of the Fb "Like" button, which would appear in search engine results. Chrome, Microsoft's search engine, also includes Facebook posts as results, illustrating how social media and search are intertwined. Other research identified that in comparison to Generation X, Generation Y has a stronger tendency for searching information online and seeking information on Facebook(Strutton, Taylor, and Thompson 2011). Consumers' contribution is a critical statistic for assessing the performance of social media marketing initiatives and has a substantial role in the acceptance of communication messages. As consumer decision process is a "goal-directed, problem-solving process". Customers may evaluate three aspects of a product to assess its quality: search characteristics, experience qualities, and credence characteristics (Schivinski, Christodoulides, and Dabrowski 2016) .Customers use social media platforms to develop and share the same information with their friends and families. Customers consider e-wom a strong base for creating trust since they view it devoid of commercial motives. Fashion brand customers use social media to share information and post material. These actions assist budget-conscious shoppers in locating a brand that best meets their desired price, quality, and brand value. Much prior research has depicted that social media marketing(SMM) activities, particularly e-WOM, increase brand recognition and spark consumers' interest in learning more about the business. Brands must focus on the three E's of WOM: engaging, equipping, and empowering their consumers. Brands would select the proper consumers in person to advocate for their goods or services, recruit them to participate, create a deal to incentivize them, follow consumers to check that they did support the brand, and last, figure out how to assess the worth of that customer's advocacy. This strengthened brand-customer connection, which results in higher client retention, is priceless. Because it transmits brand information to customers and helps them develop judgments about the brand and its goods, e-WOM is considered a socially created indicator of brand and product repute (El-Baz, Elseidi, and El-Maniaway 2018).

D. Act

This is the stage of the buying experience when the consumer buys the product. When contrasted to buying in brick-and-mortar shops and on standard merchant websites, shopping in a socially interactive environment facilitated by social media platforms gives a unique experience (Baethge, Klier, and

Klier 2016). Social commerce is an internet-based social network where people actively participate by marketing and selling products and services in online markets and communities (Esmaeili et al. 2015). E-commerce transactions conveyed with social media are known as a social business. Some people regard social commerce to be a subcategory of e-commerce. To be precise, it's a mix of e-commerce, e-marketing, supporting technology, and social media content. The development of Web 2.0 technology was a significant catalyst for the emergence of social commerce (SC). By 2025, social commerce in India's e-commerce industry (the US $ 38 billion in 2020) is projected to increase from 1 to 2 percent to 4-5 percent, where the industry's estimated to be $ 140 billion(Economic times 2020)

5. ADVOCATE

The third phase of content on a social network is the development of material related to the brand on social media. The customer takes on the roles of consumer, content developer, and brand advocate. Brand advocates are individuals whose impact may be seen in advice and recommendations. Advocates who help to co-create a brand's image and contribute to its positioning are known as presence. Brand advocates are true fans that may help promote community content that humanizes the brand and makes it more visible and relevant to other prospective buyers. The loyalty ladder concept looked at brand advocacy as a significant component, and it helped identify types of online brand advocates ranging from indifferent non-loyalists to active advocates (Harrigan and Miles 2014). On the other hand, self-proclaimed brand advocates make positive comments about the brand and defend it. It was identified that affective commitment is a persuasive driver to repurchase and customer advocacy towards the brand. According to active informants, enduring love and enthusiasm make them feel as if the brands are one-of-a-kind and irreplaceable (Kotler and Hermawan Kartajaya 2018). Brand supporters with high self-concept, representation, and self-esteem are the only ones with such links. The person might be a customer, contributor, and content developer for the same brand (Muntinga, Moorman, and Smit 2011).Similarly, a buyer may choose to contribute to one brand while consuming stuff from another. Baethge, Klier, and Klier (2016) have identified that Electronics & Computers, Tools, Beauty, Health & Grocery were the top three the major product categories consumers want to advocate for, followed by Clothing, Shoes, & Jewellery. It was also identified that consumers considered the "Sociality" of the products, i.e., having people with the same level of interest act as the main factor in deciding what items to share on social media sites. People share their ideas about social media brands is also because of "information" and "advice-seeking" factors. It also confirms that people consider information and advice-seeking essential when sharing products on social networks. Social media and online reviews provide the potential for brand advocacy. Here the following Figure 2 explain various touch point and strategies all through the purchase path.

5.1. Customer Engagement Techniques on Social Media

Social Commerce

Social media platforms are known as social commerce when used to promote, sell, and buy items and services. Social commerce is an emerging tool for manufacturers, where generation y and z customers purchasing things based on social media endorsement and others follow brands and trends on social media to keep up to date(Barnes 2014). About companies and products. Many electronic commerce com-

Figure 2. Customer's touchpoints and Retailers strategies throughout omnichannel purchase path

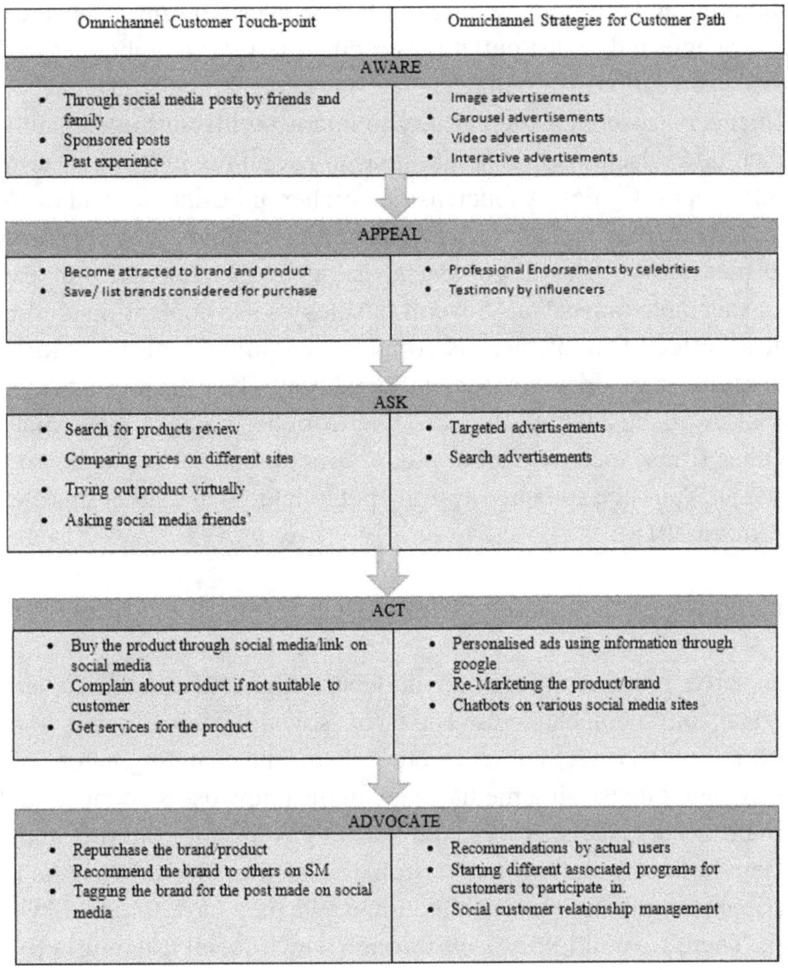

panies are making efforts to expand themselves on social networking sites and implement digitization. For example, through Facebook ads, the consumer can make purchases without going to a 'company's website. An amalgamation of social media and e-commerce help companies streamline their sales process. Social commerce is a new communication channel and transaction model for small to midsized businesses since it provides for more efficient online product discovery and more superficial connections with brands. User engagement is a top priority for brands and retailers. Social media networks like WhatsApp, Facebook, and Instagram, which have a combined user base of over 400 million, enable businesses to engage customers. More than a third of Internet users in India use social media to interact with companies and learn more about goods and services. (Ankur Pahwa 2021)

Content Marketing

Content marketing is used to achieve value and purpose differentiation in today's market, built on the relationship between consumers and the brand. It's a marketing strategy that entails producing and disseminating quality, relevant, and consistent online content for a specific target audience. Content production has gotten greater attention in marketing strategies as social media has become one of the most important digital marketing and communication aspects. Social networking celebrities, like "Influencers" are highlighted as a strategic and robust outlet for product marketing(Freberg et al. 2011). People who may influence attitudes and actions via online channels are social media influencers. What seems to be the key to these Influencers' success is their ability to interact with consumers and build trust. Companies of all sizes utilize it to raise brand recognition, acquire and retain loyal customers, and ultimately improve lucrative consumer activities. An increasing number of businesses and marketers have realized the power of content and begun to include content marketing methods in their promotional efforts. Five categories of metrics measure whether the content is visible (aware), relatable (appeal), searchable (ask), actionable (act), and shareable (advocate). Several businesses use content marketing and omnichannel shopping to significant effect. One of them is Amul, where all of topical creatives concentrate their ads according to the masses to address any societal condition. The ever-present Amul girl can be found in all of their material, as if she's telling the narrative from her point of view, making the brand even more personable. Other firms, such as Cadbury, have an omni-social presence on Facebook, Twitter, Instagram, Pinterest, and YouTube and have a strong potential to win market share via excellent content marketing. (Vinay Umarji 2016).

Social Listening

Social listening is an active process of watching, understanding, and reacting to various inputs through mediated, technological, and social channels. The term "social listening" refers to activities, tools, and approaches for gathering, analyzing, and interpreting data. The changing nature of communication in the digital environment and intensifying media usage impact how users connect, and social listening is no exception. The multifaceted character of social listening is used for internal and external communication situations where both corporations and customers listen to one another. As listeners, brands are being pushed in various natural and virtual directions, and they have to decide which messages they need to pay attention. There are multiple aspects through which social listening activities could be done, including qualitative and quantitative activities. Primary social media platform-based statistics like the reach of brands post, followers, time spent on the post, number of likes, and shares are basic quantitative activities in social listening. These metrics allow firms to observe changes in different business sectors over time and add value to the business. The act of social listening is actively ingesting and evaluating information. The availability of mobile technology and the existence of social media contribute to the building of social listening. People's behaviors have altered due to social media and mobile communication, including how they conduct conversations, form and sustain connections, and listen to others. In how individuals are impacted based on their online interactions, these social platforms function as tools among brands; therefore, listening to them becomes crucial (Stewart and Arnold 2018). Brands may monitor branded keywords and particular hashtag use using tools like Hoot Suite or Sprout Social. The Nike Service Twitter account, for example, is solely dedicated to reacting to customer service complaints, both individually and in terms of broader support patterns. These tailored interactions increase brand loyalty while also increasing the likelihood of people engaging in the first place. Social listening raises brand recognition, generates leads, locates online discussions to join, boosts engagement, and does competition research.

Social Customer Relationship Management

Customer relationship management is a business strategy concept supported by a technology platform, business rules, processes, and social features that create mutually beneficial value to both customer and company(Z. Wang and Kim 2017). Traditional Customer relation management methods are ill-equipped to deal with this new social media. Brand managers have used market research and retail audits to determine their customers and their spending on the purchase. Advertising, sales promotion, packaging, display, and other robust communication strategies influence customer behaviour. But it can't be customized to deal with individual consumers. The transition to Social CRM is more than a technological change. It is a philosophical and cultural movement. It is the process of connecting social data to current customer records for businesses to deliver new types of customer insight and context. Social CRM is a customer engagement approach that uses social media to generate trust and brand loyalty. Social CRM is how a business interacts with consumers conveniently and provides a personalized experience to keep consumers engaged, informed, interested, and amused. It blends conventional customer-facing activities with social media applications to engage customers in collaborative dialogues and strengthen customer relationships

5.2. Descriptive Analysis

The female sample made up 52%, and the male becomes 48% of the survey. When asked how many hours per week they spend on social media websites for shopping, most spend 3-4 hours. Here in the table 1 given below, the sample population were asked why they use social media, and the following were the results.

Table 1. Type of activity on social media.

Types of activity on Social Media	% of user's rate
1. To remain in contact with friends and family	36.8%
2. Expressing an opinion on social media through commenting or sharing posts	21.1%
3. Research products to buy	41.1%

5.3 Intrinsic Analysis

Table 2 shows that gender does not significantly impact the advocacy stage of omnichannel customer path on social media accepting $H_{5.}$ While all other hypotheses from H1 to H4 are rejected, it suggests that the first four stages, i.e. awareness, appeal, ask and act, have different impacts on men and women. Most men in the research accepted that they get aware of the product from their past purchases. In contrast, most of the female gave sponsored advertisements on social media as a source of their awareness, along with post from friends and family on SM. Similarly, only females agreed to the part where they make a list for the products on social media by saving different posts, while men did not agree to this touchpoint for the 'appeal" stage. In the third stage 'ask' men generally compared price on different social media sites and searched for online reviews, while females were more dependent on suggestions from social media friends who have use the product. In the fourth stage of the purchase path 'act' men's usually bought a product through link of e-commerce websionly, while females bought directly through social media and e-commerce websites. According to Levene statistics which show a significant variation of 0.019, 0.071 and 0.00 (below 0.005 for 5 percent meaning level) as the outcome of ANOVA may not be true for this component. Therefore, a test of homogeneity of variance is performed to test the hypothesis. As the significance values are much higher than required 0.05. The statistics and importance values suggest the null hypothesis is rejected i.e. H_1, H_2, H_3, H_4

Table 2. Impact of gender over omni-channel purchase path on social media

Test of Homogeneity of Variances				
	Levene Statistic	**df1**	**df2**	**Sig.**
Aware	5.735	1	98	.019
Appeal	3.338	1	98	.071
Ask	19.075	1	98	.000
Act	18.387	1	98	.000
Advocate	2.410	1	98	.124

IMPLEMENTATION AND FINDINGS

As we advance, we believe social media presence will be more normalized, and due attention would be given to increased challenges and competition in the Omni-market world. Companies used to follow multichannel retail and spend significant funds on online and offline sales channels separately. With the introduction of omnichannel retail and the growing popularity of social media platforms for market communication, the focus has shifted to connecting consumers with various touchpoints on social media platforms. Every business and organization should develop a cost-effective social media marketing strategy. After examining social media's role in omnichannel commerce and contemplating where it's going in consumer and retailer marketing, we've concluded that this is an area that's constantly evolving. The future of social media in marketing as part of the Omni-touchpoint strategy is both exciting and unpredictable. If nothing else, we must understand social media, which has become a culturally significant and dominating mode of communication. Because of the constant changes in customer behaviour, businesses must rapidly develop omnichannel marketing capabilities using social media. There is a significant difference over atleast four stages of the omnichannel purchase path on social media, which will help brands advertise their product accordingly. Females also prefer to buy products through social media while men like e-commerce websites. Retailers might focus on such results and improve their omni-presence on social media. The methods discussed in this article should assist companies in implementing omnichannel marketing to its full potential.

REFERENCES

Baethge, C., Klier, J., & Klier, M. (2016). Social Commerce—State-of-the-Art and Future Research Directions. *Electronic Markets*, *26*(3), 269–290. doi:10.100712525-016-0225-2

Barnes, N. G. (2014). Social Commerce Emerges As Big Brands Position Themselves to Turn ' Follows ', ' Likes ' and ' Pins ' into Sales. *American Journal of Management*, *14*(4), 11–18.

Bento, M., Martinez, L. M., & Martinez, L. F. (2018). Brand Engagement and Search for Brands on Social Media: Comparing Generations X and Y in Portugal. *Journal of Retailing and Consumer Services*, *43*(January), 234–241. doi:10.1016/j.jretconser.2018.04.003

Business World. (2021). Aditya Birla Fashion & Retail: Trendsetter. *Business World*. http://www.businessworld.in/article/Aditya-Birla-Fashion-Retail-Trendsetter/04-01-2019-165787/%09

Colicev, A., Kumar, A., & O'Connor, P. (2019). Modeling the Relationship between Firm and User Generated Content and the Stages of the Marketing Funnel. *International Journal of Research in Marketing*, *36*(1), 100–116. https://doi.org/10.1016/j.ijresmar.2018.09.005

Cortizo-Burgess, P. (2014). *The Traditional Purchase Funnel Is Kaput*. https://www.adweek.com/brand-marketing/traditional-purchase-funnel-kaput-156163/

Economic Times. (2020). Social Commerce in India Could Touch $7bn by 2025: RedSeer. *Economic Times*. https://economictimes.indiatimes.com/industry/services/retail/social-commerce-in-india-could-touch-7bn-by-2025-redseer/articleshow/79871583.cms?from=mdr

El-Baz, B. E.-S., Elseidi, R. I., & El-Maniaway, A. M. (2018). Influence of Electronic Word of Mouth (e-WOM) on Brand Credibility and Egyptian Consumers' Purchase Intentions. *International Journal of Online Marketing*, *8*(4), 1–14. https://doi.org/10.4018/ijom.2018100101

Esmaeili, L., Mutallebi, M., Mardani, S., & Seyyed, A. H. G. (2015). Studying the Affecting Factors on Trust in Social Commerce. *International Journal of Advanced Studies in Computer Science and Engineering IJASCSE*, *4*(6). https://arxiv.org/abs/1508.04048

Freberg, K., Graham, K., McGaughey, K., & Freberg, L. A. (2011). Who Are the Social Media Influencers? A Study of Public Perceptions of Personality. *Public Relations Review*, *37*(1), 90–92. https://doi.org/10.1016/j.pubrev.2010.11.001

Ghose, A., Ipeirotis, P. G., & Li, B. (2014). Examining the Impact of Ranking on Consumer Behavior and Search Engine Revenue. *Management Science*, *60*(7), 1632–1654. https://doi.org/10.1287/mnsc.2013.1828

Harrigan, P., & Miles, M. (2014). From E-CRM to s-CRM. Critical Factors Underpinning the Social CRM Activities of SMEs. *Small Enterprise Research*, *21*(1), 99–116. https://doi.org/10.1080/13215906.2014.11082079

IBEF Knowledge Centre. (2021). *India's Emerging Social Commerce Poised For Growth*. India Brand Equity Foundation.

Kumar, Greene, & Choi. (2017). Synergistic Effects of Social Media and Traditional Marketing on Brand Sales: Capturing the Time-Varying Effects. *J. of the Acad. Mark. Sci*, *45*, 268–88. doi:10.1007/s11747-016-0484-7

Lobschat, L., Osinga, E. C., & Reinartz, W. J. (2017). What Happens Online Stays Online? Segment-Specific Online and Offline Effects of Banner Advertisements. *JMR, Journal of Marketing Research*, 1–61.

Marolt, M., Pucihar, A., & Zimmermann, H.-D. (2015). Social CRM Adoption and Its Impact on Performance Outcomes: A Literature Review. *Organizacija, 48*(4), 260–71. doi:10.1515/orga-2015-0022

Muntinga, Moorman, & Smit. (2011). Introducing COBRAs: Exploring Motivations for Brand-Related Social Media Use. *International Journal of Advertising, 30*(1). doi:10.2501/IJA-30-1-013-046

Nandi, T. (2020). *RIL's JioMart to Convert Kirana Stores into Self-Service Stores*. Live Mint. https://www.livemint.com/companies/news/ril-s-jiomart-to-convert-kirana-

Pahwa, A. (2021). *How Social Commerce Is Helping India Move from Interaction to Transaction*. EY India. https://www.ey.com/en_in/e-commerce/how-social-commerce-is-helping-india-move-from-interaction-to-transaction

Redseer. (2019). *Omnichannel Adoption across Major Retail Categories in India*. Redseer. https://redseer.com/newsletters/omnichannel-adoption-across-major-retail-categories-in-india/

Retailer, I. (2021). *Online Fashion Industry Continues to Demonstrate Overall 51 Pc Growth in FY-21 & 66 Pc Growth on Brand Websites*. Indian Retailer. https://www.indianretailer.com/article/technology/digital-trends/online-fashion-industry-continues-to-demonstrate-overall-51-pc-growth-in-fy-21-66-pc-growth-on-brand-websites.a7096/

Sabate, F., Berbegal-Mirabent, J., Cañabate, A., & Lebherz, P. R. (2014). Factors Influencing Popularity of Branded Content in Facebook Fan Pages. *European Management Journal, 32*(6), 1001–1011. https://doi.org/10.1016/j.emj.2014.05.001

Safko, L. (2012). The Social Media Bible: Tactics, Tools, and Strategies for Business Success. Academic Press.

Strutton, D., Taylor, D. G., & Thompson, K. (2011). Investigating Generational Differences in E-WOM Behaviours for Advertising Purposes,Does X = Y? *International Journal of Advertising, 30*(4), 559–586. https://doi.org/10.2501/IJA-30-4-559-586

Umarji, V. (2016). *Amul to Launch Delivery Service via Online, Mobile App Ties up with Infibeam*. Tests Ahmedabad Market with Soft Launch.

Uzunoğlu, E., & Kip, S. M. (2014). Brand Communication through Digital Influencers: Leveraging Blogger Engagement. *International Journal of Information Management, 34*(5), 592–602. https://doi.org/10.1016/j.ijinfomgt.2014.04.007

Verhoef, Kannan, & Inman. (2015). From Multi-Channel Retailing to Omni-Channel Retailing. Introduction to the Special Issue on Multi-Channel Retailing. *Journal of Retailing, 91*(2), 174–81. doi:10.1016/j.jretai.2015.02.005

Wagner, T. F., Baccarella, C. V., & Voigt, K. I. (2017). Framing Social Media Communication: Investigating the Effects of Brand Post Appeals on User Interaction. *European Management Journal, 35*(5), 606–616. https://doi.org/10.1016/j.emj.2017.05.002

Wang, Z., & Kim, H. G. (2017). Can Social Media Marketing Improve Customer Relationship Capabilities and Firm Performance? Dynamic Capability Perspective. *Journal of Interactive Marketing, 39*, 15–26. https://doi.org/10.1016/j.intmar.2017.02.004

ZeeBiz. (2020). What Is Flipkart's '2GUD Local'? How Will It Help the Traditional Retail Business? *Zee Business*. https://www.zeebiz.com/small-business/news-what-is-flipkart-s-2gud-local-how-will-it-help-the-traditional-retail-business-142820

Compilation of References

Amazon. (2006b). *What is VPC.* http://aws. amazon/vpc

Amazon. (2006c). *Features of vpc.* http://aws.amazon/vpc-eips

AWS. (n.d.). *Elastic IP addresses.* https://docs.aws.amazon.com/AWSEC2/latest/UserGuide/elastic-ip-addresses-eip.html

Lu, Y., Lin, C., Lai, K., Tsai, M., Wu, Y., Chang, H., & Huang, K. (2019). Service Deployment and Scheduling for Improving Performance of Composite Cloud Services. *Computers and Electrical Engineering, 74*(1), 616-634.

Zia, Z., & Tian, X. (2013). A novel security private cloud solution. In *6th International Conference on Information Management, Innovation Management and Industrial Engineering*. IEEE.

Botran, L., & Alonso, M. (2014). Lozano: A Review of Auto Scaling Techniques for Elastic Applications in Cloud Environment. *Journal of Grid Computing, 12*(4), 559-592.

Mukhopadhyay, R., & Mukhopadhyay, I. (2016). Data encryption in virtual machine transfer over cloud network. In *IEEE 7th Annual Information Technology, Electronics and Mobile Communication Conference (IEMCON)*. IEEE. 10.1109/IEMCON.2016.7746078

Sun, C. (2012). Research of E-Commerce based on cloud computing. In *Advances in Computer Science and Information Engineering* (pp. 15–20). Springer. doi:10.1007/978-3-642-30223-7_3

Vinoth, S., Vemula, H. L., Haralayya, B., Mamgain, P., Hasan, M. F., & Naved, M. (2022). Application of cloud computing in banking and e-commerce and related security threats. *Materials Today: Proceedings, 51*, 2172–2175. doi:10.1016/j.matpr.2021.11.121

Bilgaiyan, S., Sagnika, S., & Das, M. (2014, February). Workflow scheduling in cloud computing environment using cat swarm optimization. In *2014 IEEE International Advance Computing Conference (IACC)* (pp. 680-685). IEEE. 10.1109/IAdCC.2014.6779406

Singh, S., Chaudhary, S., Sharma, V., Gupta, A., & Vatsa, M. (2021, October). Cloud Computing and E-Commerce Based Entrepreneurship. In *2021 2nd International Conference on Smart Electronics and Communication (ICOSEC)* (pp. 1468-1474). IEEE.

Parast, F. K., Sindhav, C., Nikam, S., Yekta, H. I., Kent, K. B., & Hakak, S. (2022). Cloud computing security: A survey of service-based models. *Computers & Security, 114*, 102580. doi:10.1016/j.cose.2021.102580

Almarabeh, T., & Majdalawi, Y. K. (2019). Cloud Computing of E-commerce. *Modern Applied Science, 13*(1), 27–35. doi:10.5539/mas.v13n1p27

Priya, Sathiya, C., & Kannan, K. (2019). *Resource Scheduling Algorithm with Load Balancing for Cloud Service Provisioning.* Elsevier.

Sontakke, V., Patil, P., Waghamare, S., Kulkarni, S., Saravanapriya, M., & Patil, N. (2015). *Survey on Dynamic Resource Allocation Strategy for Cloud Computing*. Elsevier.

Xcellhost. (2009). *Load balancing algorithms*. https://cloud/load-balancing-different-types-load-balancing-algorithms-cloud-computing

Winthrop, H. (1966). *The Mathematics of the Round-Robin*. Elsevier.

Kumari, P., & Kaur, P. (2018). A Survey of Fault Tolerance in Cloud Computing by Department of Computer Science & Information Technology. *Journal of King Saud University - Computer and Information Sciences, 5*(2), 1-18.

Ali, K., Mazen, A., & Hassanein, E. (2018). A Proposed Hybrid Model for Adopting Cloud Computing in E-government by Department of Information Systems. *Future Computing and Informatics Journal, 3*(2), 286-295.

5 blockchain healthcare use cases in digital health. (n.d.). https://stlpartners.com/articles/digital-health/5-blockchain-healthcare-use-cases/

Rana, M., Bilgaiyan, S., & Kar, U. (2014, July). A study on load balancing in cloud computing environment using evolutionary and swarm based algorithms. In *2014 international conference on control, instrumentation, communication and computational technologies (ICCICCT)* (pp. 245-250). IEEE.

Khan, N., Noraziah, A., Deris, M., & Ismail, E. (2011). CLOUD COMPUTING:Comparison of Various Features. In *Published in DEIS* (pp. 1–11). Springer.

Amazon. (n.d.). https://docs.aws.amazon.com/whitepapers/latest/aws-overview/introduction.html?pg=gs&sec=syj&refid=14a4002d-4936-4343-8211-b5a150ca592b

Citrix. (n.d.). https://www.citrix.com/en-in/solutions/app-delivery-and-security/load-balancing/what-is-load-balancing.html#:~:text=Load%20balancing%20is%20a%20core,responsiveness%20and%20prevent%20server%20overload

9 Characteristics of Well-Designed E-Commerce Websites. (n.d.). https://www.vandelaydesign.com/well-designed-ecommerce-websites/

Amazon. (2006a). *What is ec2*. http://aws. amazon/ec2

Abbad, M. (2018). Limitations and Usage of E-commerce in Developing Countries. *12th International Conference on Business, Social Sciences, Humanities and Education (BSSHE-18)*, 13-14. 10.17758/ERPUB.ED0318117

Abbasi, A. (2003). Intelligent feature selection for opinion classification. *Technology (Elmsford, N.Y.), 54*(14), 1269–1277.

Abbasi, A., Chen, H., & Salem, A. (2008). Sentiment analysis in multiple languages: Feature selection for opinion classification in web forums. *ACM Transactions on Information Systems, 26*(3), 1–34.

Abdelwahab, O., Bahgat, M., Lowrance, C. J., & Elmaghraby, A. (2015, December). Effect of training set size on SVM and Naive Bayes for Twitter sentiment analysis. In 2015 IEEE international symposium on signal processing and information technology (ISSPIT) (pp. 46-51). IEEE.

Abiodun, O. I., Jantan, A., Omolara, A. E., Dada, K. V., Mohamed, N. A. E., & Arshad, H. (2018). State-of-the-art in artificial neural network applications: A survey. *Heliyon, 4*(11), e00938. doi:10.1016/j.heliyon.2018.e00938

Aceto, G., Persico, V., & Pescape, A. (2020). Industry 4.0 and Health: Internet of Things, Big Data, and Cloud Computing for Healthcare 4.0. *Journal of Industrial Information Integration, 18*, 100129. doi:10.1016/j.jii.2020.100129

Acquire. (2022). *Top 7 Futuristic Ecommerce Technology Trends to Watch*. Retrieved from: https://acquire.io/blog/ecommerce-technology-trends/

Adadi, A., Lahmer, M., & Nasiri, S. (2021). Artificial Intelligence and COVID-19: A Systematic umbrella review and roads ahead. *Journal of King Saud University - Computer and Information Sciences.*

Aggarwal, A., & Travers, S. (2001). E-Commerce in Healthcare: Changing the Traditional Landscape. Springer.

Agrawal, R., Rajagopalan, S., Srikant, R., & Xu, Y. (2003, May). Mining newsgroups using networks arising from social behavior. In *Proceedings of the 12th international conference on World Wide Web* (pp. 529-535). Academic Press.

Ahmed, S. H., Albuquerque, V. H., Wei, W., & Wang, W. (2021). Guest Editorial AI and 5G Empowered Internet of Medical Things. *IEEE Journal of Biomedical and Health Informatics, 25*(10), 3688–3690. doi:10.1109/JBHI.2021.3108337

Ahsan, U., De Choudhury, M., & Essa, I. (2017, May). Towards using visual attributes to infer image sentiment of social events. In *2017 International Joint Conference on Neural Networks (IJCNN)* (pp. 1372-1379). IEEE.

Akar, E., & Nasir, V.A. (2015). A review of literature on consumers' online purchase intentions. *Journal of Customer Behaviour, 14*(3), 215-233. https://doi.org/ 14441 363 630837 doi:10.1362/147539215X

Akhmetova, Z., Baimukhanbetova, E., Belgozhakyzy, M., Alibaeva, A., & Tulebaeva, N. (2020). The development of e-commerce in modern conditions. *The 1st International Conference on Business Technology for Sustainable Environment System*, 159. 10.1051/e3sconf/202015904028

Akhter, S. H. (2003). Digital divide and purchase intention: Why demographic psychology matters. *Journal of Economic Psychology, 24*(3), 321–327. doi:10.1016/S0167-4870(02)00171-X

Alawneh, A., & Hattab, E. (2009). Importance of value system in business leveraging e-Technology. *International Arab Journal of e-Technology, 1*(2), 1-8.

Alawneh, A., & Hattab, E. (2007). E-Business Value Creation: An Exploratory Study. *Proceedings of the Seventh International Conference on Electronic Business*, 181-188.

Alcácer, V., & Cruz-Machado, V. (2019). Scanning the industry 4.0: A literature review on technologies for manufacturing systems. *Engineering Science and Technology, An International Journal, 22*(3), 899-919.

Alizadehyazdi, V., Bonthron, M., & Spenko, M. (2020). An Electrostatic/Gecko-Inspired Adhesives Soft Robotic Gripper. *IEEE Robotics and Automation Letters, 5*(3), 4679–4686. doi:10.1109/LRA.2020.3003773

Allen, P. J., Nissan, A., Picon, A. I., Kemeny, N., Dudrick, P., Ben-Porat, L., Espat, J., Stojadinovic, A., Cohen, A. M., Fong, Y., & Paty, P. B. (2005). Technical complications and durability of hepatic artery infusion pumps for unresectable colorectal liver metastases: An institutional experience of 544 consecutive cases. *Journal of the American College of Surgeons, 201*(1), 57–65. doi:10.1016/j.jamcollsurg.2005.03.019 PMID:15978444

Aman, S., & Szpakowicz, S. (2007, September). Identifying expressions of emotion in text. In *International Conference on Text, Speech and Dialogue* (pp. 196-205). Springer.

Amazon. (2020 December 18). Impact of COVID-19 on shopping behavior in India. *Amazonadvertising*. Retrieved from https://advertising.amazon.com/ blog/covid-19-impact-on-shopping-behavior-in-india

Amazon. (n.d.). *Amazon mechanical turk*. https://www.mturk.com/

Amin, S. U., & Hossain, M. S. (2021). Edge Intelligence and Internet of Things in Healthcare: A Survey. *IEEE Access: Practical Innovations, Open Solutions, 9*, 45–59. doi:10.1109/ACCESS.2020.3045115

Amit, B., & Steve, M. (2007). How to Plan E-Business Initiatives in Established Companies. *MIT Slogan Management Review, 49*(1), 11-22.

Anand, N. (2021). Effects of Demography on Opportunistic Product Return Behaviors in E-Commerce. *Honors Undergraduate Theses 924*. https://stars.library.ucf.edu/honorstheses/924

Anand, K. J., Niraj, R., Park, C. H., & Agarwal, M. K. (2018). The effect of relationship and transactional characteristics on customer retention in emerging online markets. *Journal of Business Research*, *92*, 25–35. doi:10.1016/j.jbusres.2018.07.007

Anand, N., Jain, P. A., Prabhu, S., Thomas, C., Bhat, A., Prathyusha, P. V., Bhat, S. U., Young, K., & Cherian, A. V. (2018). Internet Use Patterns, Internet Addiction, and Psychological Distress Among Engineering University Students: A Study from India. *Indian Journal of Psychological Medicine*, *40*(5), 458–467. doi:10.4103/IJPSYM.IJPSYM_135_18 PMID:30275622

Andrienko, O. (2020). *Ecommerce & consumer trends during coronavirus*. SEMrush Blog, Erişimadresi. https://www.semrush.com/blog/ecommerce-covid-19/

Anitha, T., & Gopu, G. (2021). Controlled mechanical ventilation for enhanced measurement in pressure and flow sensors. *Measurement: Sensors*, *16*, 100054.

Aranda-M, G., & Stewart, P. (2005). *Barriers to E-Business Adoption in construction international literature review*. https://www.researchgate.net/publication/27476067_Barriers_to_ebusiness_adoption_inconstruction_international_literature_review

Asif, S., & Wenhui, Y. (2020). Automatic detection of COVID-19 using X-ray images with deep convolutional neural networks and machine learning. medRxiv.

Avila, K., Sanmartin, P., Jabba, D., & Gomez, J. (2022). An analytical Survey of Attack Scenario Parameters on the Techniques of Attack Mitigation in WSN. *Wireless Personal Communications*, *122*(4), 3687–3718. doi:10.100711277-021-09107-6

Aydoğan, E., & Akcayol, M. A. (2016, August). A comprehensive survey for sentiment analysis tasks using machine learning techniques. In *2016 International Symposium on INnovations in Intelligent SysTems and Applications (INISTA)* (pp. 1-7). IEEE.

Ayo, C. K. (2006). The Prospects of e-Commerce Implementation in Nigeria. *Journal of Internet Banking and Commerce*, *11*(3), 68–75.

Ayush, A., Kumar, A., Jha, A., Sarkar, N., Moharana, S. C., & Das, H. (2019, May). Voice Controlled Automatic Dustbin with Garbage Level Sensing. In *2019 International Conference on Intelligent Computing and Control Systems (ICCS)* (pp. 450-453). IEEE. 10.1109/ICCS45141.2019.9065323

Baethge, C., Klier, J., & Klier, M. (2016). Social Commerce—State-of-the-Art and Future Research Directions. *Electronic Markets*, *26*(3), 269–290. doi:10.100712525-016-0225-2

Bansal, V. (2018). *Product Returns: Fashion e-comm firms like Flipkart, Myntra uncover fake product returns, Technology News, ETtech*. https://tech.economictimes.indiatimes.com/news/internet/fashion-e-comm-firms-like-flipkart-myntra-uncover-fake-product-returns/62533671

Banshwar, A., Sharma, N. K., Sharma, B. B., Sood, Y. R., & Shrivastava, R. (2018). Mixed GA-OPF based optimal procurement of energy and operating reserve in deregulated environment. *Journal of Intelligent & Fuzzy Systems*, *35*(5), 4963–4969. doi:10.3233/JIFS-169780

Bari, N., Qamar, U., & Khalid, A. (2021). *Efficient Contact Tracing for pandemics using blockchain*. Science Direct. doi:10.1016/j.imu.2021.100742

Barker, T. J., & Zabinsky, Z. B. (2008). Reverse logistics network design: A conceptual framework for decision making. *International Journal of Sustainable Engineering, 1*(4), 250–260. doi:10.1080/19397030802591196

Barnes, N. G. (2014). Social Commerce Emerges As Big Brands Position Themselves to Turn ' Follows ', ' Likes ' and ' Pins ' into Sales. *American Journal of Management, 14*(4), 11–18.

Bathrinath, S., Koshy, A. R., Bhalaji, K. A. R., & Koppiahraj, K. (2021). Identification of the critical activity in heat treatment process using TISM. *Materials Today: Proceedings, 39*(1), 60-65. doi:10.1016/j.matpr.2020.06.157

Behl, A., Dutta, P., Lessmann, S., Dwivedi, Y. K., & Kar, S. (2019). A Conceptual framework for the adoption of Big Data Analytics by e-commerce startups: A case-based approach. *Information Systems and e-Business Management, 17*(2-4), 285–318. doi:10.100710257-019-00452-5

Beites, N., Dias, M., Mendes, M. J. G. C., Carreira, F., Campos, F., & Calado, J. M. F. (2018). A gantry robot automatic positioning system using computational vision. *1st Iberic Conference on Theoretical and Experimental Mechanics and Materials/11th National Congress on Experimental Mechanics*, 1031–1042.

Benamara, F., Cesarano, C., Picariello, A., Recupero, D. R., & Subrahmanian, V. S. (2007). Sentiment analysis: Adjectives and adverbs are better than adjectives alone. *ICWSM, 7*, 203–206.

Bento, M., Martinez, L. M., & Martinez, L. F. (2018). Brand Engagement and Search for Brands on Social Media: Comparing Generations X and Y in Portugal. *Journal of Retailing and Consumer Services, 43*(January), 234–241. doi:10.1016/j.jretconser.2018.04.003

Bhagat, V. (2021). *The Role of Technology in Fostering E-commerce Business Growth.* TechTarget. Retrieved from: https://www.datasciencecentral.com/the-role-of-technology-in-fostering-e-commerce-business-growth/

Bhandari, V. B. (2010). Design of machine elements. Journal of the Franklin Institute, 256. doi:10.1016/0016-0032(53)90967-3

Bharadwaj, S. (2019). The War between Flipkart and Amazon India: A Study on Customer Perception. *International Journal of Research in Humanities, Arts and Literature, 7*(5), 391–402.

Bhargava, R., & Sharma, Y. (2017, January). MSATS: Multilingual sentiment analysis via text summarization. In *2017 7th International Conference on Cloud Computing, Data Science & Engineering-Confluence* (pp. 71-76). IEEE.

Bhargava, R., Sharma, Y., & Sharma, S. (2016, September). Sentiment analysis for mixed script indic sentences. In *2016 International conference on advances in computing, communications and informatics (ICACCI)* (pp. 524-529). IEEE.

Bhaskar, C., Ajay, B., & Ravi, S. C. (2020). Which economies showed the most digital progress in 2020? *Harvard Business Review.* Retrieved from https://hbr.org/2020/12/which-economies-showed-the-most-digital-progress-in-2020

Bhatia, A., Johnson, A., & Mason, T. M. (2019). Direct Drive Hands: Force-Motion Transparency in Gripper Design. *Robotics Science and Systems: Online Proceedings.* Advance online publication. doi:10.15607/RSS.2019.XV.053

Bickel, S., Brückner, M., & Scheffer, T. (2007, June). Discriminative learning for differing training and test distributions. In *Proceedings of the 24th international conference on Machine learning* (pp. 81-88). Academic Press.

Bigcommerce. (n.d.). *Artificial Intelligence in Ecommerce: How This Rapidly Evolving Tech Will Change the Online Storefront.* Retrieved from: https://www.bigcommerce.com/articles/ecommerce/ecommerce-ai/#benefits-of-using-artificial-intelligence-in-ecommerce-companies

Bigne, E., Ruiz, C., & Sanz, S. (2005). The Impact of Internet User Shopping Patterns and Demographics on Consumer Mobile Buying Behaviour. *Journal of Electronic Commerce Research, 6*(3), 193–209. www.amena.es

Bolu, A., & Korçak, Ö. (2021). Adaptive task planning for multi-robot smart warehouse. *IEEE Access: Practical Innovations, Open Solutions*, *9*, 27346–27358. doi:10.1109/ACCESS.2021.3058190

Bradley, M. M., & Lang, P. J. (1999). *Affective norms for English words (ANEW): Instruction manual and affective ratings* (Vol. 30). Technical report C-1, the center for research in psychophysiology, University of Florida.

Brahm, C. (2009). *E-Business and Commerce Strategic Thinking and Practice*. Houghton Mifflin.

Brown, E., Rodenberg, N., Amend, J., Mozeika, A., Steltz, E., Zakin, M. R., Lipson, H., & Jaeger, H. M. (2010). Universal robotic gripper based on the jamming of granular material. *Proceedings of the National Academy of Sciences of the United States of America*, *107*(44), 18809–18814. doi:10.1073/pnas.1003250107

Bulsara & Vaghela. (2020). Blockchain Technology for E-commerce Industry. *IJAST, 29*(5), 3793-3798.

Business World. (2021). Aditya Birla Fashion & Retail: Trendsetter. *Business World*. http://www.businessworld.in/article/Aditya-Birla-Fashion-Retail-Trendsetter/04-01-2019-165787/%09

Bux, H., Zhang, Z., & Ahmad, N. (2020). Promoting sustainability through corporate social responsibility implementation in the manufacturing industry: An empirical analysis of barriers using the ISM-MICMAC approach. *Corporate Social Responsibility and Environmental Management*, *27*(4), 1729–1748. doi:10.1002/csr.1920

Byrd, K., Mansurov, A., & Baysal, O. (2016, May). Mining twitter data for influenza detection and surveillance. In *Proceedings of the International Workshop on Software Engineering in Healthcare Systems* (pp. 43-49). Academic Press.

Cambria, E., Hussain, A., Havasi, C., Eckl, C., & Munro, J. (2010). Towards crowd validation of the UK national health service. *WebSci10*, 1-5.

Cambria, E., Speer, R., Havasi, C., & Hussain, A. (2010, November). Senticnet: A publicly available semantic resource for opinion mining. 2010 AAAI fall symposium series.

Cami, B. R., Hassanpour, H., & Mashayekhi, H. (2018). A content-based movie recommender system based on temporal user preferences. *Proceedings - 3rd Iranian Conference on Signal Processing and Intelligent Systems, ICSPIS 2017*, 121–125. https://doi.org/10.1109/ICSPIS.2017.8311601

Cardiovascular Pharmacology in Noncardiac Surgery. (2019). In L. P. Nguyen, & N. S. Gerstein, Essentials of Cardiac Anesthesia for Noncardiac Surgery (pp. 247-288). Elsevier.

Casino, F., Dasaklis, T. K., & Patsakis, C. (2019). A systematic literature review of blockchain-based applications: Current status, classification and open issues. *Telematics and Informatics*, *36*, 55–81. doi:10.1016/j.tele.2018.11.006

Chai, Y., Duan, Y., Ma, S., & Wang, J. (2018). New Digital Infrastructure, Cross-Border E-commerce and Global Vision of Creating Electronic World Trade Platform. *Global Trade and Customs Journal, 13*(4), 157–167.

Chakraborty, S., & Das, H. (2020, March). Performance Analysis of Feature Extraction Techniques for Medical Data Classification. In *International Conference on Emerging Trends and Advances in Electrical Engineering and Renewable Energy* (pp. 387-401). Springer.

Chalotra & Midha. (2017). Investigation of Amazon, Flipkart, Snapdeal, Jabong & Myntra: A Comparative Study. *Asia Pacific Journal of Research in Business Management*, *4*(9), 57–65.

Chamola, V., Hassija, V., Gupta, V., & Guizani, M. (2020). *A Comprehensive Review of the COVID-19 Pandemic and the Role of IoT, Drones, AI, Blockchain, and 5G in Managing Its Impact* (Vol. 8). IEEE.

Chan, E. Y., & Palmeira, M. (2021). Political ideology moderates consumer response to brand crisis apologies for data breach. *Computers in Human Behaviour, 121*. doi:10.1016/j.chb.2021.106801

Chanchaichujit, J., Tan, A. M., & Eaimkhong, S. (2019). An Introduction to Healthcare 4.0. In *Healthcare 4.0*. Palgrave Pivot. doi:10.1007/978-981-13-8114-0_1

Chandra & Sinha. (2013). Factors Affecting The Online Shopping Behaviour: A Study With Reference to Bhilai Durg. *International Journal of Advanced Research in Management and Social Sciences*, *2*(5).

Chang, H. H., & Meyerhoefer, C. D. (2021). COVID-19 and the Demand for Online Food Shopping Services: Empirical Evidence from TaiwanJEL Codes. *American Journal of Agricultural Economics*, *103*(2), 448–465. doi:10.1111/ajae.12170

Chatterjee, S. (2013). A Study of Demographic Variables Affecting Consumer Buying Behaviour with Reference to Synthetic Detergents. *Indian Journal of Marketing*, *43*(5), 58–63. doi:10.17010/ijom/2013/v43/i5/36387

Chatterji, S., Rahul, R. K., & Arora, A. (2015, July). A hybrid approach for identifying sentiments around aspects. In *2015 IEEE 2nd International Conference on Recent Trends in Information Systems (ReTIS)* (pp. 33-37). IEEE.

Chaudhari, B., & Borkar, S. (2020). Design considerations and network architectures for low-power wide-area networks. In *LPWAN Technologies for IoT and M2M Applications* (pp. 15–35). Academic Press. doi:10.1016/B978-0-12-818880-4.00002-8

Chavan, P., Neb, K., Shakya, R., & Ambekar, S. (2022). Role of Analytics in E-Commerce Supply Chain Management. In Changing face of e-commerce in Asia (pp. 187-203). Academic Press.

Che Azemin, M. Z., Hassan, R., Mohd Tamrin, M. I., & Md Ali, M. A. (2020). COVID-19 deep learning prediction model using publicly available radiologist-adjudicated chest X-ray images as training data: Preliminary findings. *International Journal of Biomedical Imaging*, *2020*, 2020. doi:10.1155/2020/8828855 PMID:32849861

Chen, C. C., & Tseng, Y. D. (2011). Quality evaluation of product reviews using an information quality framework. *Decision Support Systems*, *50*(4), 755–768.

Cheng, C. Y., Lu, M. Y., & Tsen, H. P. (2021). Predicting Online Consumer Transaction from Big Data: Influential Factors and Strategic Planning. *Wireless Communications and Mobile Computing*, *2021*, 1–9. Advance online publication. doi:10.1155/2021/8834713

Chenlo, J. M., & Losada, D. E. (2014). An empirical study of sentence features for subjectivity and polarity classification. *Information Sciences*, *280*, 275–288.

Chen, M., Sinha, A., Hu, K., & Shah, M. I. (2021). Impact of technological innovation on energy efficiency in industry 4.0 era: Moderation of shadow economy in sustainable development. *Technological Forecasting and Social Change*, *164*, 120521. doi:10.1016/j.techfore.2020.120521

Chen, Y. S., Chen, L. H., & Takama, Y. (2015, November). Proposal of lda-based sentiment visualization of hotel reviews. In *2015 IEEE International Conference on Data Mining Workshop (ICDMW)* (pp. 687-693). IEEE.

Chhabra, H., Mohan, V., Rani, A., & Singh, V. (2016). Multi objective PSO tuned fractional order PID control of robotic manipulator. The international symposium on intelligent systems technologies and applications. In *Advances in Signal Processing and Communication* (pp. 345–352). Springer.

Chhabra, H., Mohan, V., Rani, A., & Singh, V. (2020). Robust nonlinear fractional order fuzzy PD plus fuzzy I controller applied to robotic manipulator. *Neural Computing & Applications*, *32*(7), 2055–2079. doi:10.100700521-019-04074-3

Chiemeke, S. C., Evwiekpaefe, A., & Chete, F. (2006). The Adoption of Internet Banking in Nigeria: An Empirical Investigation. *Journal of Internet Banking and Commerce*, *11*(3), 33–49.

Chun, S. H. (2019). E-Commerce Liability and Security Breaches in Mobile Payment for e-Business Sustainability. *Sustainability, 11*(3), 715. doi:10.3390u11030715

Colicev, A., Kumar, A., & O'Connor, P. (2019). Modeling the Relationship between Firm and User Generated Content and the Stages of the Marketing Funnel. *International Journal of Research in Marketing, 36*(1), 100–116. https://doi.org/10.1016/j.ijresmar.2018.09.005

Consumer Returns in the Retail Industry. (2018). https://appriss.com/retail/wp-content/uploads/sites/4/2018/12/AR3018_2018-Customer-Returns-in-the-Retail-Industry_Digital.pdf

Coronavirus disease (COVID-19). (n.d.). https://www.who.int/health-topics/coronavirus#tab=tab_1

Coronavirus, COVID-19. (n.d.). https://my.clevelandclinic.org/health/diseases/21214-coronavirus-covid-19

Cortizo-Burgess, P. (2014). *The Traditional Purchase Funnel Is Kaput.* https://www.adweek.com/brand-marketing/traditional-purchase-funnel-kaput-156163/

Costa, H., Merschmann, L. H., Barth, F., & Benevenuto, F. (2014). Pollution, bad-mouthing, and local marketing: The underground of location-based social networks. *Information Sciences, 279*, 123–137.

Daft, R. L. (1982). Bureaucratic versus Nonbureaucratic Structure and the Process of Innovation and Change. In S. B. Bacharach (Ed.), *Research in the Sociology of Organizations* (pp. 129–166). JAI Press Inc.

Dai, X., & Prout, R. (2016, August). Unlocking Super Bowl insights: Weighted word embeddings for Twitter sentiment classification. In *Proceedings of the 3rd Multidisciplinary International Social Networks Conference on Social Informatics 2016, Data Science 2016* (pp. 1-6). Academic Press.

Daley, S. (2021, July 30). *How Using Blockchain in Healthcare Is Reviving the Industry's Capabilities.* Retrieved from BuiltIn: https://builtin.com/blockchain/blockchain-healthcare-applications-companies

Dannenberg, P., Fuchs, M., Riedler, T., & Wiedemann, C. (2020). Digital Transition by COVID-19 Pandemic? The German Food Online Retail. *Tijdschrift voor Economische en Sociale Geografie, 111*(3), 543–560. doi:10.1111/tesg.12453 PMID:32836487

Dansharif, A. R., Iyawa, G. E., Owoseni, A., & Iyawa, R. (2021). mHealth for Self-Management in Pregnancy: Perceptions of Women in Low-Resource Settings. *Procedia Computer Science, 181*, 738–745. doi:10.1016/j.procs.2021.01.226

Das, H., Naik, B., Behera, H. S., Jaiswal, S., Mahato, P., & Rout, M. (2020). Biomedical data analysis using the neuro-fuzzy model with post-feature reduction. *Journal of King Saud University-Computer and Information Sciences.*

Das, H., Jena, A. K., Nayak, J., Naik, B., & Behera, H. S. (2015). A novel PSO-based backpropagation learning-MLP (PSO-BP-MLP) for classification. In *Computational intelligence in data mining-volume 2* (pp. 461–471). Springer. doi:10.1007/978-81-322-2208-8_42

Das, H., Naik, B., & Behera, H. S. (2020). An experimental analysis of machine learning classification algorithms on biomedical data. In *Proceedings of the 2nd International Conference on Communication, Devices, and Computing* (pp. 525-539). Springer. 10.1007/978-981-15-0829-5_51

Das, H., Naik, B., & Behera, H. S. (2020). Medical disease analysis using neuro-fuzzy with feature extraction model for classification. *Informatics in Medicine Unlocked, 18*, 100288. doi:10.1016/j.imu.2019.100288

Dave, K., Lawrence, S., & Pennock, D. M. (2003, May). Mining the peanut gallery: Opinion extraction and semantic classification of product reviews. In *Proceedings of the 12th international conference on World Wide Web* (pp. 519-528). Academic Press.

David, W. (2001). *E-Commerce Strategy, Technologies and Applications*. McGraw Hill.

Davis, S., & Toney, L. (2020 July 29), How Coronavirus (COVID-19) Is Impacting Ecommerce. *ROI Revolution*. Retrieved from https://www.roirevolution.com/blog/2020/08/ coronavirus-and-ecommerce/

Deepak, H. (2020 March 25). Impact of COVID-19 on online shopping in India. *Economic Times*. Retrieved from https://retail.economictimes.indiatimes.com/re-tales/ mpact-of-covid-19-on-online-shopping-in-india/4115

Dey, N., Ashour, A. S., Kalia, H., Goswami, R. T., & Das, H. (Eds.). (2018). *Histopathological image analysis in medical decision making*. IGI Global.

Diaz, O., Kushibar, K., Osuala, R., Linardos, A., Garrucho, L., Igual, L., Radeva, P., Prior, F., Gkontra, P., & Lekadir, K. (2021). Data preparation for artificial intelligence in medical imaging: A comprehensive guide to open-access platforms and tools. *Physica Medica*, *83*, 25–37. doi:10.1016/j.ejmp.2021.02.007 PMID:33684723

Dodds, P. S., & Danforth, C. M. (2010). Measuring the happiness of large-scale written expression: Songs, blogs, and presidents. *Journal of Happiness Studies*, *11*(4), 441–456.

Dominici, A., Boncinelli, F., Gerini, F., & Marone, E. (2021). Determinants of online food purchasing: The impact of socio-demographic and situational factors. *Journal of Retailing and Consumer Services*, *60*, 102473. doi:10.1016/j.jretconser.2021.102473

Donta, P. K., Srirama, S. N., Amgoth, T., & Annavarapu, C. S. (2021). *Survey on recent advances in IoT application layer protocols and machine learning scope for research directions*. Digital Communications and Networks. doi:10.1016/j.dcan.2021.10.004

Duwairi, R. M., Marji, R., Sha'ban, N., & Rushaidat, S. (2014, April). Sentiment analysis in Arabic tweets. In *2014 5th international conference on information and communication systems (ICICS)* (pp. 1-6). IEEE.

Dwivedi, R., Mehrotra, D., & Chandra, S. (2022). Potential of Internet of Medical Things (IoMT) applications in building a smart healthcare system: A systematic review. *Journal of Oral Biology and Craniofacial Research*, *12*(2), 302–318. doi:10.1016/j.jobcr.2021.11.010 PMID:34926140

Earl, M. (2000). Evolving the E-Business. *Business Strategy Review*, 33–38.

Eben, O. (2003). *A Systematic Approach to E-Business Security*. University of New Brunswick, Canada, Faculty of Administration. http://ausweb.scu.edu.au/aw03/papers/otuteye/paper.html

E-commerce in India: Industry Overview, Market Size & Growth. (2021, December 17). *IBEF*. https://www.ibef.org/industry/ecommerce.aspx

Economic Times. (2020). Social Commerce in India Could Touch $7bn by 2025: RedSeer. *Economic Times*. https://economictimes.indiatimes.com/industry/services/retail/social-commerce-in-india-could-touch-7bn-by-2025-redseer/articleshow/79871583.cms?from=mdr

Efron, M., Marchionini, G., & Zhiang, J. (2003, October). Implications of the recursive representation problem for automatic concept identification in on-line governmental information. *Proceedings of the ASIST SIG-CR Workshop*.

El-Baz, B. E.-S., Elseidi, R. I., & El-Maniaway, A. M. (2018). Influence of Electronic Word of Mouth (e-WOM) on Brand Credibility and Egyptian Consumers' Purchase Intentions. *International Journal of Online Marketing*, *8*(4), 1–14. https://doi.org/10.4018/ijom.2018100101

Elijah, O., Rahman, T. A., Orikumhi, I., Leow, C. Y., & Hindia, M. N. (2018). An Overview of Internet of Things (IoT) and Data Analytics in Agriculture: Benefits and Challenges. *IEEE Internet of Things Journal, 5*(5), 3758–3773. doi:10.1109/JIOT.2018.2844296

Esmaeili, L., Mutallebi, M., Mardani, S., & Seyyed, A. H. G. (2015). Studying the Affecting Factors on Trust in Social Commerce. *International Journal of Advanced Studies in Computer Science and Engineering IJASCSE, 4*(6). https://arxiv.org/abs/1508.04048

Fachri, M. (2014). *Named entity recognition for Indonesian text using hidden Markov model*. Universitas Gadjah Mada.

Fang, Y. L., Qureshi, I., Sun, H. S., McCole, P., Ramsey, E., & Lim, K. H. (2014). Trust, satisfaction, and online repurchase intention: The moderating role of perceived effectiveness of e-commerce institutional mechanisms. *MIS Quarterly, 38*(2), 407. doi:10.25300/MISQ/2014/38.2.04

FAO. (2022). *FAO Cereal Supply and Demand Profile*. Retrieved from https://www.fao.org/worldfoodsituation/csdb/zh/

F-commerce in developing countries. Opportunities and challenges for small and medium sized enterprises. (2013). *World Trade Organization.* Retrieved from https://www.wto.org/english/res_e/booksp_e/ecom_brochure_e.pdf

Fei, Z., Liu, J., & Wu, G. (2004, September). Sentiment classification using phrase patterns. In *The Fourth International Conference onComputer and Information Technology, 2004. CIT'04.* (pp. 1147-1152). IEEE.

Ferrag, M., Shu, L., Djallel, H., & Choo, K.-K. (2021). Deep Learning-Based Intrusion Detection for Distributed Denial of Service Attack in Agriculture 4.0. *Electronics (Basel), 10*(11), 1257. doi:10.3390/electronics10111257

Foscht, T., Ernstreiter, K., Maloles, C. III, Sinha, I., & Swoboda, B. (2013). Retaining or returning?: Some insights for a better understanding of return behaviour. *International Journal of Retail & Distribution Management, 41*(2), 113–134. doi:10.1108/09590551311304310

Francis, S. K., & Syed, H. (2016). A Comparative study between Flipkart and Amazon India. *International Journal of Research in Regional Studies, Law, Social Sciences, Journalism and Management Practices, 1*(8), 3–11.

Freberg, K., Graham, K., McGaughey, K., & Freberg, L. A. (2011). Who Are the Social Media Influencers? A Study of Public Perceptions of Personality. *Public Relations Review, 37*(1), 90–92. https://doi.org/10.1016/j.pubrev.2010.11.001

Freeman, V., Chan, J., Levow, G. A., Wright, R., Ostendorf, M., & Zayats, V. (2014). Manipulating stance and involvement using collaborative tasks: An exploratory comparison. *Fifteenth Annual Conference of the International Speech Communication Association.*

Fu, Y., Yang, M., & Han, D. (2021). Interactive Marketing E-Commerce Recommendation System Driven by Big Data Technology. *Scientific Programming, 2021*, 1–11. Advance online publication. doi:10.1155/2021/3873059

Galhotra, B. (2019). Evolution of E-commerce in India: A Review and Its Future Scope. *Proceedings of the International Conference on Machine Learning, Big Data, Cloud and Parallel Computing: Trends, Prespectives and Prospects, COMITCon 2019*, 226–231. https://doi.org/10.1109/COMITCon.2019.8862252

Gamon, M., Aue, A., Corston-Oliver, S., & Ringger, E. (2005, September). Pulse: Mining customer opinions from free text. In International symposium on intelligent data analysis (pp. 121-132). Springer.

Ganguly, P. (2016). *E-commerce: E-commerce players in India bring down product returns this festive season, Technology News, ETtech.* https://tech.economictimes.indiatimes.com/news/internet/e-commerce-players-in-india-bring-down-product-returns-this-festive-season/55553507

García-Tadeo, Peram, Kumar, Vives, Sharma, & Manoharan. (2022). Comparing the impact of Internet of Things and cloud computing on organisational behavior: A survey. *Materials Today: Proceedings, 51*(8). https://doi.org/ doi:10.1016/j.matpr.2021.11.399

Gardas, B., Raut, R. D., & Narkhede, B. E. (2017). A state-of the-art survey of interpretive structural modelling methodologies and applications. *International Journal of Business Excellence, 11*(4), 505. doi:10.1504/IJBEX.2017.082576

Geng, R. R., Mills, J. K., & Yao, Z. Y. (2016). Design and analysis of a novel 3-DOF spatial parallel microgripper driven by LUMs. *Robotics and Computer-integrated Manufacturing, 42*, 147–155. doi:10.1016/j.rcim.2016.06.001

Ghag, K., & Shah, K. (2013, January). Comparative analysis of the techniques for sentiment analysis. In *2013 International Conference on Advances in Technology and Engineering (ICATE)* (pp. 1-7). IEEE.

Ghorbel, H., & Jacot, D. (2011). Sentiment analysis of French movie reviews. In *Advances in Distributed Agent-Based Retrieval Tools* (pp. 97–108). Springer.

Ghose, A., & Ipeirotis, P. G. (2010). Estimating the helpfulness and economic impact of product reviews: Mining text and reviewer characteristics. *IEEE Transactions on Knowledge and Data Engineering, 23*(10), 1498–1512.

Ghose, A., Ipeirotis, P. G., & Li, B. (2014). Examining the Impact of Ranking on Consumer Behavior and Search Engine Revenue. *Management Science, 60*(7), 1632–1654. https://doi.org/10.1287/mnsc.2013.1828

Ghosh, D. (2020). A Sentiment-Based Hotel Review Summarization. In *Emerging Technology in Modelling and Graphics* (pp. 39–44). Springer.

Gonçalves, P., Benevenuto, F., & Cha, M. (2013). *Panas-t: A pychometric scale for measuring sentiments on twitter.* arXiv preprint arXiv:1308.1857.

Gonçalves, P., Araújo, M., Benevenuto, F., & Cha, M. (2013, October). Comparing and combining sentiment analysis methods. In *Proceedings of the first ACM conference on Online social networks* (pp. 27-38). ACM.

Guo, M., Gealy, D. V., Liang, J., Mahler, J., Goncalves, A., McKinley, S., . . . Goldberg, K. (2017). Design of parallel-jaw gripper tip surfaces for robust grasping. *Proceedings - IEEE International Conference on Robotics and Automation*, 2831–2838. 10.1109/ICRA.2017.7989330

Hackbarth, G., & Kettinger, W. J. (2000). *Building an E-Business Strategy: Information Systems Management.* Taylor and Francis. Doi:10.1201/1078/43192.17.3.20000601/31243.10

Haleem, A., Javaid, M., Singh, R. P., & Suman, R. (2022). Medical 4.0 technologies for healthcare: Features, capabilities, and applications. *Internet of Things and Cyber-Physical Systems, 2*, 12–30. doi:10.1016/j.iotcps.2022.04.001

Haleem, A., Javaid, M., Singh, R. P., Suman, R., & Rab, S. (2021). *Blockchain technology applications in healthcare: An overview.* Science Direct.

Hanifah, R., Supangkat, S. H., & Purwarianti, A. (2014, September). Twitter information extraction for smart city. In *2014 International Conference on ICT For Smart Society (ICISS)* (pp. 295-299). IEEE.

Hao, N., Wang, H. H., & Zhou, Q. (2020). The impact of online grocery shopping on stockpile behavior in Covid-19. *China Agricultural Economic Review, 12*(3), 459–470. doi:10.1108/CAER-04-2020-0064

Haponik, A. (2021). *The best Machine Learning Use Cases in E-commerce.* Addepto. Retrieved from: https://addepto.com/best-machine-learning-use-cases-ecommerce/#:~:text=Machine%20Learning%20in%20e%2Dcommerce%20can%20be%20very%20helpful%20in,detect%20new%20demands%20and%20trends

Hariharan, S. (2021). User info linked to 18 crore's Domino's order leaked. *The Times of India.* Retrieved from https://timesofindia.indiatimes.com/business/india-business/user-info-linked-to-18-crore-dominos-orders-leaked/articleshow/82898118.cms

Harrigan, P., & Miles, M. (2014). From E-CRM to s-CRM. Critical Factors Underpinning the Social CRM Activities of SMEs. *Small Enterprise Research, 21*(1), 99–116. https://doi.org/10.1080/13215906.2014.11082079

Hartmann, M., Hashmi, U. S., & Imran, A. (2019). Edge computing in smart health care systems: Review, challenges, and research directions. *Transactions on Emerging Telecommunications Technologies.*

Hasanov, J., & Khalid, H. (2015). The Impact of Website Quality on Online Purchase Intention of Organic Food in Malaysia: A WebQual Model Approach. *Procedia Computer Science, 72*, 382–389. doi:10.1016/j.procs.2015.12.153

Healthcare E-Commerce Global Market Report 2021. (2021). https://www.prnewswire.com/news-releases/healthcare-e-commerce-global-market-report-2021-301451529.html

Hebi. (2015). *China's eight counties e-commerce model interpretation and inspiration two "Tongyu model"*. Retrieved from https://www.hebi.gov.cn/swj/741665/741688/1234529/index.html

Hebnews. (2014). *The "Qinghe model" has become one of the three typical Chinese e-commerce cluster development.* Retrieved from http://hebei.hebnews.cn/2014-10/22/content_4259183.htm

Herald, D. (2020 July 14). *Impact of COVID-19 on E-Commerce Business.* Retrieved from https://www.deccanherald.com/ brandspot/pr-spot/ impact-of- covid -19-on-e-commerce-business-861185.html

Hond, A. A., Leeuwenberg, A. M., Hooft, L., Kant, I. M., Nijman, S. W., Os, H. J., ... Chavannes, N. H. (2022). Guidelines and quality criteria for artificial intelligence-based prediction models in healthcare: A scoping review. *npj. Digital Medicine, 5*(2). PMID:35013569

Hong, Z., Hong, M., Wang, N., Ma, Y., Zhou, X., & Wang, W. (2022). A wearable-based posture recognition system with AI-assisted approach for healthcare IoT. *Future Generation Computer Systems, 127*, 286–296. doi:10.1016/j.future.2021.08.030

How fake COVID-19 vaccination certificates are adding fire to the pandemic. (n.d.). https://indianexpress.com/article/technology/tech-news-technology/how-fake-covid-19-vaccination-certificates-are-adding-fire-to-the-pandemic-7241485/

Hoyer, W. D., Kroschke, M., Schmitt, B., Kraume, K., & Shankar, V. (2020). Transforming the Customer Experience Through New Technologies. *Journal of Interactive Marketing, 51*, 57–71. doi:10.1016/j.intmar.2020.04.001

Hsiang, S., Kopp, R., Jina, A., Rising, J., Delgado, M., Mohan, S., Rasmussen, D. J., Muir-Wood, R., Wilson, P., Oppenheimer, M., Larsen, K., & Houser, T. (2017). Estimating economic damage from climate change in the United States. *Science, 356*(6345), 1362–1368. doi:10.1126cience.aal4369 PMID:28663496

Hsin Chang, H., & Wang, H. W. (2011). The moderating effect of customer perceived value on online shopping behaviour. *Online Information Review, 35*(3), 333–359. doi:10.1108/ 14684521111151414

Hsu, C., Chuan-Chuan Lin, J., & Chiang, H. (2013). The effects of blogger recommendations on customers' online shopping intentions. *Internet Research, 23*(1), 69–88. doi:10.1108/10662241311295782

Huang, L. (2015). *The impact of gender, age, price and cognitive dissonance on the e-commerce apparel product returns.* University of Groningen. Faculty of Economics and Business. https://feb.studenttheses.ub.rug.nl/14622/1/Thesis_s2659883.pdf

Huffman, J. (2018, July 09). *AI in healthcare: a six-step framework for getting the most out of your data*. Retrieved from https://www.philips.com/a-w/about/news/archive/blogs/innovation-matters/20180709-ai-in-healthcare-a-six-step-framework-for-getting-the-most-out-of-your-data.html

Hu, M., & Liu, B. (2004, August). Mining and summarizing customer reviews. In *Proceedings of the tenth ACM SIGKDD international conference on Knowledge discovery and data mining* (pp. 168-177). ACM.

Hussien, H. M., Yasin, S. M., Udzir, N. I., Ninggal, M. I., & Salman, S. (2021). Blockchain technology in the healthcare industry: Trends and opportunities. *Journal of Industrial Information Integration*, *22*, 100217. doi:10.1016/j.jii.2021.100217

IBEF Knowledge Centre. (2021). *India's Emerging Social Commerce Poised For Growth*. India Brand Equity Foundation.

Ilie, A. (2021). *Sensing Better Health: Complete Guide to Medical Sensors - Benefits and Applications*. Retrieved from Honeywell: https://sps.honeywell.com/us/en/support/blog/siot/complete-guide-to-medical-sensors-benefits-and-applications

Imran, S., Mahmood, T., Morshed, A., & Sellis, T. (2021). Big data analytics in healthcare – A systematic literature review and roadmap for practical implementation. *IEEE/CAA Journal of Automatica Sinica, 8*(1), 1-22.

Imtiaz, M. A. (2018). *E-Commerce Business Aims and Objectives*. Retrieved from https://www.ukessays.com/essays/ecommerce/ecommerce-business-aims-objectives-7791.php?vref=1

Indian E-commerce Industry Analysis. (2021). https://www.ibef.org/industry/ecommerce-presentation

IndustryWired. (2019). *How does technology impact on E-Commerce Industry?* IndustryWired. Retrieved from: https://industrywired.com/how-does-technology-impact-on-e-commerce-industry/

Ionescu, C. M. (2019). Computer-assisted Drug Delivery for General Anesthesia: Completing the Puzzle: Plenary Talk. *2019 IEEE 17th World Symposium on Applied Machine Intelligence and Informatics (SAMI)*, 13-16.

Jaffe, J. (2010). *Flip the funnel: how to use existing customers to gain new ones*. Wiley.Book.

Jain, S., Nehra, M., Kumar, R., Dilbaghi, N., Hu, T., Kumar, S., Kaushik, A., & Li, C.-Z. (2021). Internet of medical things (IoMT)-integrated biosensors for point-of-care testing of infectious diseases. *Biosensors & Bioelectronics*, *179*, 113074. doi:10.1016/j.bios.2021.113074 PMID:33596516

Jameela, A.-J., Nader, M., & Eman, A. (2020). Health 4.0: On the Way to Realizing the Healthcare of the Future. *IEEE Access: Practical Innovations, Open Solutions*, *8*, 211189–211210. doi:10.1109/ACCESS.2020.3038858 PMID:34976565

Jan, M. A., Cai, J., Gao, X.-C., Khan, F., Mastorakis, S., Usman, M., Alazab, M., & Watters, P. (2021). Security and blockchain convergence with Internet of Multimedia Things: Current trends, research challenges and future directions. *Journal of Network and Computer Applications*, *175*, 102918. doi:10.1016/j.jnca.2020.102918 PMID:34690484

Javaid, M., Haleem, A., Singh, R. P., & Suman, R. (2021). Substantial capabilities of robotics in enhancing industry 4.0 implementation. *Cognitive Robotics*, *1*, 58–75. doi:10.1016/j.cogr.2021.06.001

Jiang, H., Lin, Y., Luo, X., & Shao, T. (2022). Understanding the Selection of Cross-Border Import E-Commerce Platforms Through the DANP and TOPSIS Techniques: A Multi-Study Analysis. *Journal of Global Information Technology Management*, *25*(1), 26–53. doi:10.1080/1097198X.2021.2022397

Jiang, P., & Rosenbloom, B. (2005). Customer intention to return online: Price perception, attribute-level performance, and satisfaction unfolding over time. *European Journal of Marketing*, *39*(1–2), 150–174. doi:10.1108/03090560510572061

Johnson, J. (2022). *Internet usage worldwide- statistics and facts*. Retrieved from https://www.statista.com/topics/1145/internet-usage-worldwide/#topicHeader__wrapper

Jondhale, S. R., Mohan, V., Sharma, B. B., Lloret, J., & Athawale, S. V. (2022). Support Vector Regression for Mobile Target Localization in Indoor Environments. *Sensors (Basel)*, *22*(1), 358. doi:10.339022010358 PMID:35009896

Joseph, P. T. (2012). E-Commerce: An Indian Perspective (4th ed.). Eastern Economy Edition, PHI India.

Kakaria, T. C. (2021, December 31). An overview of E-commerce in 2021: Growth, hits, and misses. *Times of India*. https://timesofindia.indiatimes.com/blogs/voices/an-overview-of-e-commerce-in-2021-growth-hits-and-misses/

Kalakota, R., & Robinson, M. (1999). E-Business: Roadmap for success. Addison-Wesley.

Kamal, A. (2013). *Subjectivity classification using machine learning techniques for mining feature-opinion pairs from web opinion sources.* arXiv preprint arXiv:1312.6962.

Kamalul Ariffin, S., Mohan, T., & Goh, Y.-N. (2018). Influence of consumers' perceived risk on consumers' online purchase intention. *Journal of Research in Interactive Marketing*, *12*(3), 309–327. doi:10.1108/JRIM-11-2017-0100

Kamble, S. S., Gunasekaran, A., & Gawankar, S. A. (2020). Achieving sustainable performance in a data-driven agriculture supply chain: A review for research and applications. *International Journal of Production Economics*, *219*, 179–194. doi:10.1016/j.ijpe.2019.05.022

Kamilaris, A., Kartakoullis, A., & Prenafeta-Boldu, F. X. (2017). A review on the practice of big data analysis in agriculture. *Computers and Electronics in Agriculture*, *143*, 23–37. doi:10.1016/j.compag.2017.09.037

Kang, S., & Eltahir, E. A. B. (2018). North China Plain threatened by deadly heatwaves due to climate change and irrigation. *Nature Communications*, *9*(1), 2894. Advance online publication. doi:10.103841467-018-05252-y PMID:30065269

Kar, B., Tripathy, A., & Pathak, M. D. (2022). What Causes Product Returns in Online Purchases? A Review and Research Agenda. *Prabandhan: Indian Journal of Management*, *15*(4), 46–62. doi:10.17010/pijom/2022/v15i4/162837

Karjaluoto, H., & Mattila, M. (2002). Electronic Banking in Finland: Consumer Beliefs and Reactions to a New Delivery Channel. *Journal of Financial Services Marketing*, *6*(4), 346–361.

Kar, S. S., & Sahoo, S. K. (2009). Organised Retailing in India: Issues and Challenges. *Indian Journal of Marketing*, *39*(11), 10–14.

Kaur, K., & Kumar, Y. (2020). Swarm Intelligence and its applications towards Various Computing: A Systematic Review. *Proceedings of International Conference on Intelligent Engineering and Management, ICIEM 2020*, 57–62. https://doi.org/10.1109/ICIEM48762.2020.9160177

Kaur, A., Garg, R., & Gupta, P. (2021). Challenges facing AI and Big data for Resource-poor Healthcare System. *2021 Second International Conference on Electronics and Sustainable Communication Systems (ICESC)*, 1426-1433. 10.1109/ICESC51422.2021.9532955

Kaushik, C., & Mishra, A. (2014). Comparative analysis of sentiment analysis techniques. *ITSI Trans Electric Electron Eng (ITSI-TEEE)*, *2*(1).

Keelery, S. (2021). *India - internet users by age group 2020.* https://www.statista.com/statistics/751005/india-share-of-internet-users-by-age-group/

Kermany, D., Zhang, K., & Goldbaum, M. (2018). Labeled Optical Coherence Tomography (OCT) and Chest X-Ray Images for Classification. Mendeley Data, *2*. doi:10.17632/rscbjbr9sj.2

Khare, A., & Rakesh, S. (2011). Antecedents of Online Shopping Behavior in India: An Examination. *Journal of Internet Commerce*, *10*(4), 227–244. doi:10.1080/ 15332861. 2011.622691

Khurana, A. (2013, December 23). *8 Challenges for ecommerce in India*. Pitneybowes. https://www.pitneybowes.com/us/blog/8-challenges-ecommerce-india.html

Kincade, D. H., Giddings, V. L., & Chen-Yu, H. J. (1998). Impact of product-specific variables on consumers' post-consumption behaviour for apparel products: USA. *Journal of Consumer Studies & Home Economics*, *22*(2), 81–90. doi:10.1111/j.1470-6431.1998.tb00718.x

Klerkx, L., Jakku, E., & Labarthe, P. (2019). A review of social science on digital agriculture, smart farming and agriculture 4.0: New contributions and a future research agenda. *NJAS Wageningen Journal of Life Sciences*, *90-91*(1), 100315. doi:10.1016/j.njas.2019.100315

Koshal. (2011). *Difference Between Commerce and Business*. Retrieved from: https://www.differencebetween.com/difference-between-commerce-and-vs-business/

Koydemir, H. C., & Ozcan, A. (2018). Wearable and Implantable Sensors for Biomedical Applications. *Annual Review of Analytical Chemistry (Palo Alto, Calif.)*, *11*(1), 127–146. doi:10.1146/annurev-anchem-061417-125956 PMID:29490190

Krishna, V. (2020 May 21). Almost 50 pc Indians are stockpiling essentials, shopping online during COVID-19: Mintel. *Mintel's Consumer Tracker*. Retrieved from https:// yourstory.com/2020/05/mintel-consumer-tracker-indians-stockpiling-essentials-coronavirus/amp

Krishnan, M., Rajagopal, V., & Rathinasamy, S. (2018). Performance evaluation of sensor deployment using optimization techniques and scheduling approach for K-coverage in WSNs. *Wireless Networks*, *24*(3), 683–693. doi:10.100711276-016-1361-5

Kulis, B., Saenko, K., & Darrell, T. (2011, June). What you saw is not what you get: Domain adaptation using asymmetric kernel transforms. In *CVPR 2011* (pp. 1785–1792). IEEE.

Kumar & Dange. (2012). A Study of Factors Affecting Online Buying Behavior: A Conceptual Model. SSRN. https://dx.doi.org/ doi:10.2139/ssrn.2285350

Kumar, Greene, & Choi. (2017). Synergistic Effects of Social Media and Traditional Marketing on Brand Sales: Capturing the Time-Varying Effects. *J. of the Acad. Mark. Sci*, *45*, 268–88. doi:10.1007/s11747-016-0484-7

Kumar, S., Raut, D. R., Nayal, K., Kraus, S., Yadav, S. V., & Narkhede, E. B. (2021). To identify industry 4.0 and circular economy adoption barriers in the agriculture supply chain by using ISM-ANP. *Journal of Cleaner Production*, *293*. doi:10.1016/j.jclepro.2021.126023

Kumar, A., Razi, R., Singh, A., & Das, H. (2020, July). Res-VGG: A Novel Model for Plant Disease Detection by Fusing VGG16 and ResNet Models. In *International Conference on Machine Learning, Image Processing, Network Security and Data Sciences* (pp. 383-400). Springer. 10.1007/978-981-15-6318-8_32

Kumar, A., & Sharma, R. (2018). Linguistic Lyapunov reinforcement learning control for robotic manipulators. *Neurocomputing*, *272*, 84–95. doi:10.1016/j.neucom.2017.06.064

Kumari, A., Tanwar, S., Tyagi, S., & Kumar, N. (2018). Fog computing for Healthcare 4.0 environment: Opportunities and challenges. *Computers & Electrical Engineering*, *72*, 1–13. doi:10.1016/j.compeleceng.2018.08.015

Kumar, P., & Kanchan. (2019). Purchasing Criteria for Apparels among Indian Consumers. *Indian Journal of Marketing*, *49*(1), 48–60. doi:10.17010/ijom/2019/v49/i1/140606

Law, M., & Ng, M. (2016). *Age and gender differences: Understanding mature online users with the online purchase intention model*. doi:10.1080/21639159.2016.1174540

LeCun, Y., Bengio, Y., & Hinton, G. (2015). Deep learning. *Nature, 521*. Advance online publication. doi:10.1038/nature14539

Lee, D. H. (2015). An Alternative Explanation of Consumer Product Returns from the Postpurchase Dissonance and Ecological Marketing Perspectives. *Psychology and Marketing, 32*(1), 49–64. doi:10.1002/mar.20757

Lee, H., & Jeong, J. (2021). Mobile robot path optimization technique based on reinforcement learning algorithm in warehouse environment. *Applied Sciences (Basel, Switzerland), 11*(3), 1209. doi:10.3390/app11031209

Lee, S., & Choeh, J. Y. (2014). Predicting the helpfulness of online reviews using multilayer perceptron neural networks. *Expert Systems with Applications, 41*(6), 3041–3046.

Legnani, G., & Faglia, R. (1992). Harmonic drive transmissions: The effects of their elasticity, clearance and irregularity on the dynamic behaviour of an actual SCARA robot. *Robotica, 10*(4), 369–375. doi:10.1017/S0263574700008201

Lerttripinyo, T., Jatukannyaprateep, P., Prompoon, N., & Pattanothai, C. (2015, July). Accommodation recommendation system from user reviews based on feature-based weighted non-negative matrix factorization method. In *2015 12th International Joint Conference on Computer Science and Software Engineering (JCSSE)* (pp. 108-113). IEEE.

Levow, G. A., Freeman, V., Hrynkevich, A., Ostendorf, M., Wright, R., Chan, J., . . . Tran, T. (2014, December). Recognition of stance strength and polarity in spontaneous speech. In 2014 IEEE Spoken Language Technology Workshop (SLT) (pp. 236-241). IEEE.

Li, J., & Carayon, P. (2021). *Health Care 4.0: A Vision for Smart and Connected Health Care*. Academic Press.

Li, J. (2021). Artifcial intelligence hospital hardware system and clinical observation of molecular heparin sodium in hemodialysis patients. *Microprocessors and Microsystems, 81*, 103690. doi:10.1016/j.micpro.2020.103690

Li, K. (2022). SWOT analysis of e-commerce development of rural tourism farmers' professional cooperatives in the era of big data. *IET Communications, 16*(5), 592–603. doi:10.1049/cmu2.12358

Li, L., Su, F., Zhang, W., & Mao, J. Y. (2018). Digital transformation by SME entrepreneurs: A capability perspective. *Information Systems Journal, 28*(6), 1129–1157. doi:10.1111/isj.12153

Limberg, A. H. M. V., & Gemert-Pijnen, J. V. (2010). Towards innovative business modeling for sustainable eHealth applications. In *2010 Second International Conference on eHealth, Telemedicine, and Social Medicine*. IEEE.

Lin, Y., Zhu, T., Wu, H., Zhang, J., Wang, X., & Zhou, A. (2014, August). Towards online anti-opinion spam: Spotting fake reviews from the review sequence. In 2014 IEEE/ACM international conference on advances in social networks analysis and mining (ASONAM 2014) (pp. 261-264). IEEE.

Li, N., & Wu, D. D. (2010). Using text mining and sentiment analysis for online forums hotspot detection and forecast. *Decision Support Systems, 48*(2), 354–368.

Liquid Group to power UPI or acceptance in 10 Asian Markets. (2021). *National Payment Corporation of India*. Retrieved from https://www.npci.org.in/PDF/npci/press-releases/2021/NPCI-International-Press-Release-LIQUID-GROUP-TO-POWER-UPI-QR-ACCEPTANCE-IN-10-ASIAN-MARKETS.pdf

List of text emoticons: The ultimate resource. (n.d.). www.cool-smileys.com/text-emoticons

Liu, B. (2012). Sentiment analysis and opinion mining. *Synthesis Lectures on Human Language Technologies, 5*(1), 1-167.

Liu, Z., Dong, X., Guan, Y., & Yang, J. (2013, October). Reserved self-training: A semi-supervised sentiment classification method for chinese microblogs. In *Proceedings of the Sixth International Joint Conference on Natural Language Processing* (pp. 455-462). Academic Press.

Liu, X., Dou, Z., & Yang, W. (2021). Research on Influencing Factors of Cross Border E-Commerce Supply Chain Resilience Based on Integrated Fuzzy DEMATEL-ISM. *IEEE Access: Practical Innovations, Open Solutions*, *9*, 36140–36153. doi:10.1109/ACCESS.2021.3059867

Li, W., Liu, B. M., Liu, D., Ping, L. R., Wang, P., Luo, S., & Ni, W. (2019). Unified Fine-Grained Access Control for Personal Health Records in Cloud Computing. *IEEE Journal of Biomedical and Health Informatics*, *23*(3), 1278–1289. doi:10.1109/JBHI.2018.2850304 PMID:29994490

Li, Y. M., & Li, T. Y. (2013). Deriving market intelligence from microblogs. *Decision Support Systems*, *55*(1), 206–217.

Li, Y., Huang, T., & Chetwynd, D. G. (2018). An approach for smooth trajectory planning of high-speed pick-and-place parallel robots using quintic B-splines. *Mechanism and Machine Theory*, *126*, 479–490. doi:10.1016/j.mechmachtheory.2018.04.026

Li, Y., Xu, L., & Li, D. (2013). Examining relationships between the return policy, product quality, and pricing strategy in online direct selling. *International Journal of Production Economics*, *144*(2), 451–460. doi:10.1016/j.ijpe.2013.03.013

Lobschat, L., Osinga, E. C., & Reinartz, W. J. (2017). What Happens Online Stays Online? Segment-Specific Online and Offline Effects of Banner Advertisements. *JMR, Journal of Marketing Research*, 1–61.

Loebbecke, C., & Picot, A. (2015). Reflections on societal and business model transformation arising from digitization and big data analytics: A research agenda. *The Journal of Strategic Information Systems*, *24*(3), 149–157. doi:10.1016/j.jsis.2015.08.002

Lopes, J. M., Marrone, P., Pereira, S. L., & Dias, E. M. (2019). Health 4.0: Challenges for an Orderly and Inclusive Innovation. *IEEE Technology and Society Magazine*, *38*(3), 17–19. doi:10.1109/MTS.2019.2930265

López Seguí, F., Franch Parella, J., Gironès García, X., Mendioroz Peña, J., García Cuyàs, F., Adroher Mas, C., García-Altés, A., & Vidal-Alaball, J. (2020). A Cost-Minimization Analysis of a Medical Record-based, Store and Forward and Provider-to-provider Telemedicine Compared to Usual Care in Catalonia: More Agile and Efficient, Especially for Users. *International Journal of Environmental Research and Public Health*, *17*(6), 2008. doi:10.3390/ijerph17062008 PMID:32197434

Lopez, L. J., Garcia, A. R., & Aponte, G. P. (2019). Internet of things in healthcare monitoring to enhance acquisition performance of respiratory disorder sensors. *International Journal of Distributed Sensor Networks*, *15*(5).

Lu, K., & Liao, H. (2022). A survey of group decision making methods in Healthcare Industry 4.0: Bibliometrics, applications, and directions. *Applied Intelligence*. Advance online publication. doi:10.100710489-021-02909-y PMID:35002080

Lundervold, A. S., & Lundervold, A. (2019). An overview of deep learning in medical imaging focusing on MRI. *Zeitschrift für Medizinische Physik*, *29*(2), 102–127. doi:10.1016/j.zemedi.2018.11.002 PMID:30553609

Maas, A., Daly, R. E., Pham, P. T., Huang, D., Ng, A. Y., & Potts, C. (2011, June). Learning word vectors for sentiment analysis. In *Proceedings of the 49th annual meeting of the association for computational linguistics: Human language technologies* (pp. 142-150). Academic Press.

Maday, J. (n.d.). *The history of e-commerce: A long and winding road. The future of Customer Engagement and Experience*. Retrieved from: https://www.the-future-of-commerce.com/2020/01/30/history-of-e-commerce/

Madhav, C. (2016, April 28), Amazon pips Snapdeal to become India's 2nd largest online marketplace after Flipkart. *The Economic Times*. Retrieved from https://m.economictimes. com/industry/services/retail/amazon-pips-snapdeal-to-become-indias-2nd-largest-online-marketplace-after-flipkart/articleshow/52017176.cms

Madhav, C. (2017 January 20), Growth comes at a price for Flipkart, Amazon & Snapdeal. *The Economic Times*. Retrieved from https://economictimes.indiatimes.com /small- biz/startups/growth-comes-at-a-price-for-flipkart-amazon-snapdeal /articleshow /56674800.cms

Mahajan, H. B., Rashid, A. S., Junnarkar, A. A., Uke, N., Deshpande, S. D., Futane, P. R., Alkhayyat, A., & Alhayani, B. (2022). Integration of Healthcare 4.0 and blockchain into secure cloud-based electronic health records systems. *Applied Nanoscience*. Advance online publication. doi:10.100713204-021-02164-0 PMID:35136707

Makino, H. (2014). Development of the SCARA. *Journal of Robotics and Mechatronics*, *26*(1), 5–8. doi:10.20965/jrm.2014.p0005

Makkonen, M., Frank, L., & Kemppainen, T. (2021). The Effects of Consumer Demographics and Payment Method Preference on Product Return Frequency and Reasons in Online Shopping. In A. Pucihar, M. Kljajic Borstnar, R. Bons, H. Cripps, A. Sheombar, & D. Vidmar (Eds.), *Digital Support from Crisis to Progressive Change* (pp. 567–580). University of Maribor. doi:10.18690/978-961-286-385-9.2

Malhotra, N., Sahadev, S., & Purani, K. (2017). Psychological contract violation and customer intention to reuse online retailers: Exploring mediating and moderating mechanisms. *Journal of Business Research*, *75*(6), 17–28. doi:10.1016/j.jbusres.2017.01.013

Mamta, B. B., Li, K. -C., Leung, V. C., Psannis, K. E., & Yamaguchi, S. (2021). Blockchain-Assisted Secure Fine-Grained Searchable Encryption for a Cloud-Based Healthcare Cyber-Physical System. *IEEE/CAA Journal of Automatica Sinica, 8*(12), 1877-1890.

Markovic, S., Koporcic, N., Arslanagic-Kalajdzic, M., Kadic-Maglajlic, S., Bagherzadeh, M., & Islam, N. (2021). *Business-to-business open innovation: COVID-19 lessons for small and medium-sized enterprises from emerging markets*. Science Direct.

Marolt, M., Pucihar, A., & Zimmermann, H.-D. (2015). Social CRM Adoption and Its Impact on Performance Outcomes: A Literature Review. *Organizacija, 48*(4), 260–71. doi:10.1515/orga-2015-0022

Marr, B. (2016). A Short History of Machine Learning -- Every Manager Should Read. *Forbes*. Retrieved From: https://www.forbes.com/sites/bernardmarr/2016/02/19/a-short-history-of-machine-learning-every-manager-should-read/?sh=5d98c60815e7

Martinez-Dominguez, M., & Mora-Rivera, J. (2020). Internet adoption and usage patterns in rural Mexico. *Technology in Society*, *60*, 101226. Advance online publication. doi:10.1016/j.techsoc.2019.101226

Martín-Valdivia, M. T., Martínez-Cámara, E., Perea-Ortega, J. M., & Ureña-López, L. A. (2013). Sentiment polarity detection in Spanish reviews combining supervised and unsupervised approaches. *Expert Systems with Applications*, *40*(10), 3934–3942.

McKinsey & Company. (2021). *Why retail outperformers are pulling ahead*. Retrieved from https://www.mckinsey.com/industries/retail/our-insights/why-retail-outperformers-are-pulling-ahead

Medical Product Alert N°2/2021: Falsified COVID-19 Vaccine BNT162b2. (2021). https://www.who.int/news/item/26-03-2021-medical-product-alert-n-2-2021-falsified-covid-19-vaccine-bnt162b2

Mehta, N., Pandit, A., & Shukla, S. (2019). Transforming healthcare with big data analytics and artificial intelligence: A systematic mapping study. *Journal of Biomedical Informatics*, *100*, 103311. doi:10.1016/j.jbi.2019.103311 PMID:31629922

Meilatinova, N. (2021). Social commerce: Factors affecting customer repurchase and word-of-mouth intentions. *International Journal of Information Management*, *57*, 102300. doi:10.1016/j.ijinfomgt.2020.102300

Meiryani, Y. W. (2019). The Role of Information Technology in Ecommerce. *International Journal of Scientific & Technology Research, 8*(1). Retrieved from: https://www.ijstr.org/final-print/jan2019/The-Role-Of-Information-Technology-In-E-commerce.pdf

Mendo, F., & Fitzgerald, G. (2005). Theoretical Approaches to Study SMEs E-Business Progression. *CIT. Journal of Computing and Information Technology, 13*(02), 123–136.

Menezes, R. (2021 March 22). *Amazon beats Snapdeal on the ecommerce leaderboard, but is it the leader yet?* Retrieved from https:// indianonlineseller. com/ 2016/04/amazon-beats-snapdeal-on-the-ecommerce-leaderboard-but-is-it-the-leader-yet

Menon, C., Murphy, M., & Sitti, M. (2004). Gecko inspired surface climbing robots. *Proceedings - 2004 IEEE International Conference on Robotics and Biomimetics, IEEE ROBIO 2004*, 431–436. 10.1109/ROBIO.2004.1521817

Merhi, M. I. (2021). Multi-Country Analysis of E-commerce Adoption: The Impact of National Culture and Economic Development. *Pacific Asia Journal of the Association for Information Systems, 13*(3). https://aisel.aisnet.org/pajais/vol13/iss3/4

Miller, G. A. (1995). WordNet: A lexical database for English. *Communications of the ACM, 38*(11), 39–41.

Milong, L. (2011). The Analysis of Strengths and Weaknesses of Online-Shopping. In M. Dai (Ed.), *Innovative Computing and Information. ICCIC 2011. Communications in Computer and Information Science* (Vol. 231). Springer. doi:10.1007/ 978- 3-642 -23993-9_66

Ministry Of Commerce Of The People's Republic Of China. (2015). *Jilin Province on the promotion of e-commerce into rural areas in 2015 comprehensive demonstration project construction notice.* Retrieved from http://scjss.mofcom.gov.cn/article/jyjl/jyqc/201509/20150901117478.shtml

Ministry Of Commerce Of The People's Republic Of China. (2016). *The inspiration of "Tongyu model" to the development of e-commerce of agricultural products in China.* Retrieved from http://zys.mofcom.gov.cn/article/d/201605/20160501315059.shtml

Ministry Of Commerce Of The People's Republic Of China. (2017). *What changes are brought by "Internet+ ".* Retrieved from http://trb.mofcom.gov.cn/article/zuixindt/201701/20170102495621.shtml

Ministry Of Commerce Of The People's Republic Of China. (2020a). *China E-Commerce Report (2020).* Retrieved from http://scjss.mofcom.gov.cn/article/jyjl/jdzswn/202001/20200102932689.shtml

Ministry Of Commerce Of The People's Republic Of China. (2020b). *Lishui City, Zhejiang Province, actively explore the "Internet + green water and green mountains" to be a pioneer pioneer in the development of rural electric business.* Retrieved from https://dzswgf.mofcom.gov.cn/news/5/2021/9/1631698018580.html

Misic, V., & Zhao, J. (2006). E-Business Reference Models. In *Reference Modeling for Business Systems Analysis.* doi:10.4018/9781599040547

Misra, S., & Arivazhagan, D. (2017). Application of Design Thinking Techniques in Marketing of Fashion Apparel E - Commerce. *Indian Journal of Marketing, 47*(8), 18–30. doi:10.17010/ijom/2017/v47/i8/117430

Moghaddam, M., & Nof, S. Y. (2016). Parallelism of Pick-and-Place operations by multi-gripper robotic arms. *Robotics and Computer-integrated Manufacturing, 42*, 135–146. doi:10.1016/j.rcim.2016.06.004

Mohan, V., Chhabra, H., Rani, A., & Singh, V. (2019). An expert 2DOF fractional order fuzzy PID controller for nonlinear systems. *Neural Computing & Applications, 31*(8), 4253–4270. doi:10.100700521-017-3330-z

Mohan, V., Rani, A., & Singh, V. (2017). Robust adaptive fuzzy controller applied to double inverted pendulum. *Journal of Intelligent & Fuzzy Systems, 32*(5), 3669–3687. doi:10.3233/JIFS-169301

MSN messenger emoticons. (n.d.). http://messenger.msn.com/resource/emoticons.aspx

Mukhopadhyay, S. C., Tyagi, S. K., Suryadevara, N. K., Piuri, V., Scotti, F., & Zeadally, S. (2021). Artificial Intelligence-Based Sensors for Next Generation IoT Applications: A Review. *IEEE Sensors Journal, 21*(22), 24920–24932. doi:10.1109/JSEN.2021.3055618

Multidev Technologies. (2015). *10 E-commerce Functions Every E-tailer Needs*. Retail Management Software Blog. Retrieved from: https://multidev.com/blog/10-e-commerce-functions-every-e-tailer-needs-2/

Mungra, D., Agrawal, A., & Thakkar, A. (2020). A voting-based sentiment classification model. In *Intelligent Communication, Control and Devices* (pp. 551–558). Springer.

Muntinga, Moorman, & Smit. (2011). Introducing COBRAs: Exploring Motivations for Brand-Related Social Media Use. *International Journal of Advertising, 30*(1). doi:10.2501/IJA-30-1-013-046

Murali, M. V., Vishnu, T. G., & Victor, N. (2019). A Collaborative Filtering based Recommender System for Suggesting New Trends in Any Domain of Research. *2019 5th International Conference on Advanced Computing and Communication Systems, ICACCS 2019*, 550–553. https://doi.org/10.1109/ICACCS.2019.8728409

Mylavarapu, B. K. (2018). Collaborative Filtering and Artificial Neural Network Based Recommendation System for Advanced Applications. *Journal of Computer and Communications, 06*(12), 1–14. doi:10.4236/jcc.2018.612001

Nakamoto, S. (2008). *Bitcoin: A Peer-to-peer Electronic Cash System*. www.bitcoin.org

Nandi, T. (2020). *RIL's JioMart to Convert Kirana Stores into Self-Service Stores*. Live Mint. https://www.livemint.com/companies/news/ril-s-jiomart-to-convert-kirana-

Nandy, S., Adhikari, M., Chakraborty, S., Alkhayyat, A., & Kumar, N. (2022). IBoNN: Intelligent Agent-based Internet of Medical Things framework for detecting brain response from Electroencephalography signal using Bag-of-Neural Network. *Future Generation Computer Systems, 130*, 241–252. doi:10.1016/j.future.2021.12.019

Narin, A., Kaya, C., & Pamuk, Z. (2020). *Automatic detection of coronavirus disease (covid-19) using x-ray images and deep convolutional neural networks*. arXiv preprint arXiv:2003.10849.

Nasrin, S., Ghosh, P., Chowdhury, S. M., Abujar, S., & Hossain, S. A. (2020). Fraud detection of Facebook business page based on sentiment analysis. In *Proceedings of International Joint Conference on Computational Intelligence* (pp. 279-287). Springer.

Nasukawa, T., & Yi, J. (2003, October). Sentiment analysis: Capturing favorability using natural language processing. In *Proceedings of the 2nd international conference on Knowledge capture* (pp. 70-77). Academic Press.

Nawi, N. C., Mamun, A. Al, Hamsani, N. H. B., & Muhayiddin, M. N. (2019). Effect of Consumer Demographics and Risk Factors on Online Purchase Behaviour in Malaysia. *Societies, 9*(1), 10. doi:10.3390/soc9010010

Netscribes. (2018). *5 Emerging technology trends in e-commerce*. Netscribes. Retrieved from: https://www.netscribes.com/ecommerce-technology-trends/#:~:text=In%20fact%2C%20technology%20plays%20an,capabilities%20for%20e%2Dcommerce%20success

News, C. C. P. (2016). *Suichang Model Study - Service Driven County E-Commerce Development Model*. Retrieved from http://theory.people.com.cn/n1/2016/0804/c401815-28611279.html

Nguyen, D. H., de Leeuw, S., & Dullaert, W. E. H. (2018). Consumer Behaviour and Order Fulfilment in Online Retailing: A Systematic Review. *International Journal of Management Reviews*, *20*(2), 255–276. doi:10.1111/ijmr.12129

Ng, W. Y., Tan, T.-E., Movva, P. V. H., Fang, A. H. S., Yeo, K.-K., Ho, D., Foo, F. S. S., Xiao, Z., Sun, K., Wong, T. Y., Sia, A. T.-H., & Ting, D. S. W. (2021). Blockchain applications in health care for COVID-19 and beyond: A systematic review. *The Lancet. Digital Health*, *3*(12), e819–e829. doi:10.1016/S2589-7500(21)00210-7 PMID:34654686

Nie, P., Ma, W. L., & Sousa-Poza, A. (2021). The relationship between smartphone use and subjective well-being in rural China. *Electronic Commerce Research*, *21*(4), 983–1009. doi:10.100710660-020-09397-1

Nigam, A., Dewani, P. P., & Behl, A. (2020). Exploring Deal of the Day: An e-commerce strategy. *Benchmarking*, *27*(10), 2807–2830. doi:10.1108/BIJ-03-2020-0129

Nissen, A., & Krampe, C. (2021). Why he buys it and she doesn't - exploring self-reported and neural gender differences in the perception of e-commerce website. *Computers in Human Behavior*, *121*, 106809. doi:10.1016/j.chb.2021.106809

Nittala, R. (2015). Factors Influencing Online Shopping Behavior of Urban Consumers in India. *International Journal of Online Marketing*, *5*(1), 38–50. doi:10.4018/ IJOM.2015010103

Nizam, H., & Akın, S. S. (2014). Sosyal medyada makine öğrenmesi ile duygu analizinde dengeli ve dengesiz veri setlerinin performanslarının karşılaştırılması. *XIX. Türkiye'de İnternet Konferansı, 1*(6).

O'Connor, B., Balasubramanyan, R., Routledge, B. R., & Smith, N. A. (2010, May). From tweets to polls: Linking text sentiment to public opinion time series. *Fourth international AAAI conference on weblogs and social media.*

Odoom, J., Soglo, R. S., Danso, S. A., & Xiaofang, H. (2019). A Privacy-preserving Covid-19 Updatable Test Result and Vaccination Provenance based on Blockchain and Smart contract. In *2019 International Conference on Mechatronics, Remote Sensing, Information Systems and Industrial Information Technologies (ICMRSISIIT)*. IEEE.

OMG! Oxford English Dictionary grows a heart: Graphic symbol for love (and that exclamation) are added as words. (n.d.). tinyurl.com/klv36p

Omoniwa, B., Hussain, R., Javed, M. A., Bouk, S. H., & Malik, S. A. (2019). Fog/Edge Computing-Based IoT (FECIoT): Architecture, Applications, and Research Issues. *IEEE Internet of Things Journal*, *6*(3), 4118–4149. doi:10.1109/JIOT.2018.2875544

Ott, M., Cardie, C., & Hancock, J. T. (2013, June). Negative deceptive opinion spam. In *Proceedings of the 2013 conference of the North American chapter of the Association for Computational Linguistics: Human language technologies* (pp. 497-501). Academic Press.

Oustaloup, A., Levron, F., Mathieu, B., & Nanot, F. M. (2000). Frequency-band complex noninteger differentiator: Characterization and synthesis. *IEEE Transactions on Circuits and Systems. I, Fundamental Theory and Applications*, *47*(1), 25–39. doi:10.1109/81.817385

Owoputi, O., O'Connor, B., Dyer, C., Gimpel, K., Schneider, N., & Smith, N. A. (2013, June). Improved part-of-speech tagging for online conversational text with word clusters. In *Proceedings of the 2013 conference of the North American chapter of the association for computational linguistics: human language technologies* (pp. 380-390). Academic Press.

Oztemel, E., & Gursev, S. (2020). Literature review of Industry 4.0 and related technologies. *Journal of Intelligent Manufacturing*, *31*(1), 127–182. doi:10.100710845-018-1433-8

Padhy, S. K. (1992). On the dynamics of SCARA robot. *Robotics and Autonomous Systems*, *10*(1), 71–78. doi:10.1016/0921-8890(92)90016-R

Pahwa, A. (2021). *How Social Commerce Is Helping India Move from Interaction to Transaction.* EY India. https://www.ey.com/en_in/e-commerce/how-social-commerce-is-helping-india-move-from-interaction-to-transaction

Palmer, A. (2020September 29). How Amazon managed the coronavirus crisis and came out stronger. *CNBC Tech.* Retrieved from https://www.cnbc.com/2020/09/29/ how-amazon- managed-the-coronavirus-crisis-and-came-out-stronger.html

Pang, B., & Lee, L. (2004). *A sentimental education: Sentiment analysis using subjectivity summarization based on minimum cuts.* arXiv preprint cs/0409058.

Pang, B., Lee, L., & Vaithyanathan, S. (2002). *Thumbs up? Sentiment classification using machine learning techniques.* arXiv preprint cs/0205070.

Panigrahi, K. P., Das, H., Sahoo, A. K., & Moharana, S. C. (2020). Maize leaf disease detection and classification using machine learning algorithms. In Progress in Computing, Analytics, and Networking (pp. 659-669). Springer. doi:10.1007/978-981-15-2414-1_66

Panigrahi, K. P., Sahoo, A. K., & Das, H. (2020, June). A CNN Approach for Corn Leaves Disease Detection to support Digital Agricultural System. In *2020 4th International Conference on Trends in Electronics and Informatics (ICOEI)* (pp. 678-683). IEEE. 10.1109/ICOEI48184.2020.9142871

Panjwani, B., Singh, V., Rani, A., & Mohan, V. (2021a). Optimizing Drug Schedule for Cell-Cycle Specific Cancer Chemotherapy. In Soft Computing: Theories and Applications (pp. 71-81). Springer. doi:10.1007/978-981-16-1696-9_7

Panjwani, B., Mohan, V., Rani, A., & Singh, V. (2019). Optimal drug scheduling for cancer chemotherapy using two degree of freedom fractional order PID scheme. *Journal of Intelligent & Fuzzy Systems*, *36*(3), 2273–2284. doi:10.3233/JIFS-169938

Panjwani, B., Singh, V., Rani, A., & Mohan, V. (2021b). Optimum multi-drug regime for compartment model of tumour: Cell-cycle-specific dynamics in the presence of resistance. *Journal of Pharmacokinetics and Pharmacodynamics*, *48*(4), 543–562. doi:10.100710928-021-09749-w PMID:33751365

Pappas, Pateli, Giannakos, & Chrissikopoulos. (2014). Moderating effects of online shopping experience on customer satisfaction and repurchase intentions. *International Journal of Retail & Distribution Management*, *42*(3), 187–204. doi:10.1108/IJRDM-03-2012-0034

Park, J., Hyun, H., & Thavisay, T. (2021). A study of antecedents and outcomes of social media WOM towards luxury brand purchase intention. *Journal of Retailing and Consumer Services*, *58*, 102272. doi:10.1016/j.jretconser.2020.102272

Parmar, H., Khan, T., Tucci, F., Umer, R., & Carlone, P. (2021). Advanced robotics and additive manufacturing of composites: Towards a new era in Industry 4.0. *Materials and Manufacturing Processes*, 1–35.

Parviainen, J., & Rantala, J. (2022). Chatbot breakthrough in the 2020s? An ethical reflection on the trend of automated consultations in health care. *Medicine, Health Care, and Philosophy*, *25*(1), 61–71. doi:10.100711019-021-10049-w PMID:34480711

Pattanayak, R. M., Behera, H. S., & Panigrahi, S. (2021). A novel probabilistic intuitionistic fuzzy set-based model for high order fuzzy time series forecasting. *Engineering Applications of Artificial Intelligence*, *99*, 104136. doi:10.1016/j.engappai.2020.104136

Pattanayak, R. M., Panigrahi, S., & Behera, H. S. (2020). High-order fuzzy time series forecasting by using membership values along with Data and Support Vector Machine. *Arabian Journal for Science and Engineering*, *45*(12), 10311–10325. doi:10.100713369-020-04721-1

Paul, S., Riffat, M., Yasir, A., Mahim, M., Sharnali, B., Naheen, I., Rahman, A., & Kulkarni, A. (2021). Industry 4.0 Applications for Medical/Healthcare Services. *Journal of Sensor and Actuator Networks*, *10*(3), 43. doi:10.3390/jsan10030043

Peerzada, A. (2020 June 27). Covid-19 may lift India's e-commerce market to around $85 billion by 2024. *Business Standard.* Retrieved from https://www.business-standard.com/ article/economy-policy/despite-pandemic-india-s-e-commerce-expected-to-grow-three-fold-by-2028-120062402043_1.html

Pengnate, S. F., & Sarathy, R. (2017). An experimental investigation of the influence of website emotional design features on trust in unfamiliar online vendors. *Computers in Human Behavior*, *67*, 49–60. doi:10.1016/j.chb.2016.10.018

People.cn. (2020). *Zhejiang Lin'an pecan processing new model to help farmers increase income*. Retrieved from http://zj.people.com.cn/n2/2020/1023/c186806-34368234.html

Peral, J., Gallego, E., Gil, D., Tanniru, M., & Khambekar, P. (2020). Using Visualization to Build Transparency in a Healthcare Blockchain Application. *Sustainability*, *12*(17), 6768. doi:10.3390u12176768

Petersen, J. A., & Kumar, V. (2009). Are Product Returns a Necessary Evil? Antecedents and Consequences. *Journal of Marketing*, *73*(3), 35–51. doi:10.1509/jmkg.73.3.035

Pham, T. S. H., & Ahammad, M. F. (2017). Antecedents and consequences of online customer satisfaction: A holistic process perspective. *Technological Forecasting and Social Change*, *124*, 332–342. doi:10.1016/j.techfore.2017.04.003

Powers, T. L., & Jack, E. P. (2015). Understanding the causes of retail product returns. *International Journal of Retail & Distribution Management*, *43*(12), 1182–1202. doi:10.1108/IJRDM-02-2014-0023

Pradeep, K. (2020). Data Science and Deep Learning Applications in the e-Commerce Industry: A Survey. *Indian Journal of Computer Science and Engineering*, *11*(5). Advance online publication. doi:10.21817/indjcse/2020/v11i5/201105135

Prakash, V. J., & Nithya, D. L. (2014). *A survey on semi-supervised learning techniques.* arXiv preprint arXiv:1402.4645.

Pratama, T., & Cahyadi, A. T. (2020). Effects of User Interface and User Experience on application sale. *IOP Conference Series Material Science and Engineering*, 879(1). 10.1088/1757-899X/879/1/012133

Prathaban, B. P., Balasubramanian, R., & Kalpana, R. (2021). A Wearable ForeSeiz Headband for Forecasting Real-Time Epileptic Seizures. *IEEE Sensors Journal*, *21*(23), 26892–26901. doi:10.1109/JSEN.2021.3120307

Pujawan, I. N., & Bah, A. U. (2022, January). Supply chains under COVID-19 disruptions: Literature review and research agenda. In *Supply Chain Forum International Journal*, *23*(1), 81–95.

Putreve, S. (2003). Exploring the origins and information processing differences between men and women: Implications for advertisers. *Academy of Marketing Science Review*, *10*, 1–16.

Qu, Y., & Bao, X. (2019). Identification and Analysis of Influencing Factors of College Students' Degree of Learning Effort based in ISM. *Advances in Social Science, Education and Humanities Research,* Volume 340. *International Conference on Education Innovation and Economic Management.* 10.2991/iceiem-19.2019.43

Quasim, M. T., & Algarni, F. (2020). A Blockchain based Secured Healthcare Framework. *2020 International Conference on Computational Performance Evaluation (ComPE)*, 386-391. 10.1109/ComPE49325.2020.9200024

Rahmath, S., Hema, D., & Abdullah, K. (2011). In emerging economy: Indian consumer's perspective. International Arab Journal of e-Technology, *2*(1), 56–64.

Rajaretnam, J., & Sheth, N. J. (2017). *A Multi-Stage Model of Adoption of Online Buying in India.* doi:10.1080/08911762.2017.1369609

Rajesh, R. (2016). Forecasting Supply chain resilience performance using gray prediction. *Electronic Commerce Research and Applications, 20*, 42–58. doi:10.1016/j.elerap.2016.09.006

Rajput, S., & Singh, S. P. (2019). Identifying Industry 4.0 IOT enablers by integrated PCA-ISM-DEMATEL approach. *Management Decision, 57*(8), 1784–1817. doi:10.1108/MD-04-2018-0378

Ramanathan, V., & Meyyappan, T. (2019, January). Twitter text mining for sentiment analysis on people's feedback about oman tourism. In *2019 4th MEC International Conference on Big Data and Smart City (ICBDSC)* (pp. 1-5). IEEE.

Raman, P. (2014). Factors influencing women consumers' buying behavior towards online shopping in India. *Contemporary Management Research, 8*(2), 23–56.

Rasool, R. U., Ahmad, H. F., Rafique, W., Qayyum, A., & Qadir, J. (2022). Security and privacy of internet of medical things: A contemporary review in the age of surveillance, botnets, and adversarial ML. *Journal of Network and Computer Applications, 201*, 103332. doi:10.1016/j.jnca.2022.103332

Ravi, K., & Ravi, V. (2015). A survey on opinion mining and sentiment analysis: Tasks, approaches and applications. *Knowledge-Based Systems, 89*, 14–46.

Ray, P. P., Dash, D., & De, D. (2019). Edge computing for Internet of Things: A survey, e-healthcare case study and future direction. *Journal of Network and Computer Applications, 140*, 1–22. doi:10.1016/j.jnca.2019.05.005

Razzak, M. I., Naz, S., & Zaib, A. (2018). Deep learning for medical image processing: Overview, challenges and the future. *Classification in BioApps*, 323-350.

Reddy, P., Sharma, B., & Chaudhary, K. (2020). Measuring the digital competency of freshmen at a higher education institute. *Pacific Asia Conference on Information Systems Proceedings, 6*. https://aisel.aisnet.org/pacis2020/6

Reddy, P., Chaudhary, K., Sharma, B., & Chand, D. (2021). Contextualized game-based intervention for digital literacy for the Pacific Islands. *Education and Information Technologies, 26*(5), pp5535–pp5562. doi:10.100710639-021-10534-y PMID:33935574

Redseer. (2019). *Omnichannel Adoption across Major Retail Categories in India*. Redseer. https://redseer.com/newsletters/omnichannel-adoption-across-major-retail-categories-in-india/

Rehman, A., Naz, S., & Razzak, I. (2021). Leveraging big data analytics in healthcare enhancement: Trends, challenges and opportunities. *Multimedia Systems*. Advance online publication. doi:10.100700530-020-00736-8

Reina, A., Ferrante, E., & Valentini, G. (2021). Collective decision-making in living and artificial systems [editorial]. *Swarm Intelligence, 15*(1), 1–6. doi:10.100711721-021-00195-5

Retail Industry in India. (2021). https://www.investindia.gov.in/sector/retail-e-commerce

Retailer, I. (2021). *Online Fashion Industry Continues to Demonstrate Overall 51 Pc Growth in FY-21 & 66 Pc Growth on Brand Websites*. Indian Retailer. https://www.indianretailer.com/article/technology/digital-trends/online-fashion-industry-continues-to-demonstrate-overall-51-pc-growth-in-fy-21-66-pc-growth-on-brand-websites.a7096/

Ridzuan, F., & Zainon, W. M. (2019). A Review on Data Cleansing Methods for Big Data. *Procedia Computer Science, 161*, 731–738. doi:10.1016/j.procs.2019.11.177

Rout, J. K., Rout, M., & Das, H. (Eds.). (2020). *Machine Learning for Intelligent Decision Science*. Springer Singapore. doi:10.1007/978-981-15-3689-2

Rout, M., Jena, A. K., Rout, J. K., & Das, H. (2020). Teaching-learning optimization-based cascaded low-complexity neural network model for exchange rates forecasting. In *Smart Intelligent Computing and Applications* (pp. 635–645). Springer. doi:10.1007/978-981-13-9282-5_60

Rozario, K. (2021, July 13). E-Commerce In India Set To Reach $120 Billion In 2025, Says Report. *Forbes*. https://www.forbes.com/sites/kevinrozario/2021/07/13/e-commerce-in-india-set-to-reach-120-billion-in-2025-says-report/?sh=48af2f446119

Saarijärvi, H., Sutinen, U.-M., & Harris, L. C. (2017). Uncovering consumers' returning behaviour: A study of fashion e-commerce. *International Review of Retail, Distribution and Consumer Research*, *27*(3), 284–299. doi:10.1080/09593969.2017.1314863

Sabate, F., Berbegal-Mirabent, J., Cañabate, A., & Lebherz, P. R. (2014). Factors Influencing Popularity of Branded Content in Facebook Fan Pages. *European Management Journal*, *32*(6), 1001–1011. https://doi.org/10.1016/j.emj.2014.05.001

Saenko, K., Kulis, B., Fritz, M., & Darrell, T. (2010, September). Adapting visual category models to new domains. In *European conference on computer vision* (pp. 213-226). Springer.

Safko, L. (2012). The Social Media Bible: Tactics, Tools, and Strategies for Business Success. Academic Press.

Sagnika, S., Mishra, B. S. P., & Meher, S. K. (2020). Improved method of word embedding for efficient analysis of human sentiments. *Multimedia Tools and Applications*, *79*(43), 32389–32413.

Sagnika, S., Pattanaik, A., Mishra, B. S. P., & Meher, S. K. (2020). A Review on Multi-Lingual Sentiment Analysis by Machine Learning Methods. *Journal of Engineering Science & Technology Review*, *13*(2).

Sahoo, A. K., Mallik, S., Pradhan, C., Mishra, B. S. P., Barik, R. K., & Das, H. (2019). Intelligence-based health recommendation system using big data analytics. In *Big data analytics for intelligent healthcare management* (pp. 227–246). Academic Press. doi:10.1016/B978-0-12-818146-1.00009-X

Sahoo, A. K., Pradhan, C., & Das, H. (2020). Performance evaluation of different machine learning methods and deep-learning-based convolutional neural networks for health decision making. In *Nature-inspired computing for data science* (pp. 201–212). Springer. doi:10.1007/978-3-030-33820-6_8

Salema, M. I. G., Barbosa-Povoa, A. P., & Novais, A. Q. (2010). Simultaneous design and planning of supply chains with reverse flows: A generic modelling framework. *European Journal of Operational Research*, *203*(2), 336–349. doi:10.1016/j.ejor.2009.08.002

Samorani, M., Alptekinoglu, A., & Messinger, P. R. (2019). Product return episodes in retailing. *Service Science*, *11*(4), 263–278. doi:10.1287erv.2019.0250

Sarhan, A. M. (2020). Detection and Classification of Brain Tumor in MRI Images Using Wavelet Transform and Convolutional Neural Network. *Journal of Advances in Medicine and Medical Research*, 15–26. doi:10.9734/jammr/2020/v32i1230539

Sarkar, S., & Khare, A. (2017). Moderating effect of price perception on factors affecting attitude towards online shopping. *J Market Anal*, *5*, 68–80. doi:10.1057/ s41270-017 -0018-2

Scholten, K., & Schilder, S. (2015). The role of collaboration in supply chain resilience. *Supply Chain Management*, *20*(4), 471–484. doi:10.1108/SCM-11-2014-0386

Seo, J. Y., Yoon, S., & Vangelova, M. (2016). Shopping plans, buying motivations, and return policies: Impacts on product returns and purchase likelihoods. *Marketing Letters*, *27*(4), 645–659. doi:10.100711002-015-9381-y

Sequiera, R., Choudhury, M., Gupta, P., Rosso, P., Kumar, S., Banerjee, S., . . . Chakma, K. (2015, December). Overview of FIRE-2015 Shared Task on Mixed Script Information Retrieval. In FIRE workshops (Vol. 1587, pp. 19-25). Academic Press.

Seshadri, S. (2017). *An Introduction To E-Commerce Technology*. https://www.researchgate.net/publication/317277929_An_Introduction_To_E-Commerce_Technology

Seshadri, S. (2017). E-Commerce Technology Made Easy. *IJITR, 5*, 6183-6198. https://www.researchgate.net/publication/317278278_E-Commerce_Technology_Made_Easy

Sethuraman, S. C., Kompally, P., Mohanty, S. P., & Choppali, U. (2021). MyWear: A Novel Smart Garment for Automatic Continuous Vital Monitoring. *IEEE Transactions on Consumer Electronics*, *67*(3), 214–222. doi:10.1109/TCE.2021.3085888

Shaheen, S., El-Hajj, W., Hajj, H., & Elbassuoni, S. (2014, December). Emotion recognition from text based on automatically generated rules. In *2014 IEEE International Conference on Data Mining Workshop* (pp. 383-392). IEEE.

Sharma, A. (2011). Take-off of online marketing: Casting the next generation strategies. *Business Strategy Series*, *12*(4), 202–208. doi:10.1108/ 17515631111155160

Sharma, B. B., Banshwar, A., Pathak, M., Sharma, N. K., & Joshi, A. (2021). Microcontroller-based PID Temperature Controller Using Genetic Algorithms. In *Advances in Renewable Energy and Sustainable Environment* (pp. 277–283). Springer. doi:10.1007/978-981-15-5313-4_26

Sharma, K., & Doriya, R. (2021). Coordination of multi-robot path planning for warehouse application using smart approach for identifying destinations. *Intelligent Service Robotics*, *14*(2), 313–325. doi:10.100711370-021-00363-w

Sharma, N. K., Banshwar, A., Sharma, B. B., Sood, Y. R., & Shrivastava, R. (2018). Mixed GA-OPF based prioritized optimal location and rating of wind power generation in deregulated electricity market. *Journal of Intelligent & Fuzzy Systems*, *35*(5), 5071–5075. doi:10.3233/JIFS-169791

Sharma, N., Mangla, M., Mohanty, S. N., Gupta, D., Tiwari, P., Shorfuzzaman, M., & Rawashdeh, M. (2021). A smart ontology-based IoT framework for remote patient monitoring. *Biomedical Signal Processing and Control*, *68*, 102717. doi:10.1016/j.bspc.2021.102717

Sharma, S. K. (2015). Adoption of e-government services: The role of service quality dimensions and demographic variables. *Transforming Government: People, Process and Policy*, *9*(2), 207–222. doi:10.1108/TG-10-2014-0046/FULL/PDF

Shaw, N. (n.d.). *Ecommerce Machine Learning: AI's Role in the Future of Online Shopping*. BigCommerce. Retrieved from: https://www.bigcommerce.com/blog/ecommerce-machine-learning/

Shelly, S. (2016, October 6). Snapdeal slips against its two main rivals, Flipkart & Amazon. Can it get its mojo back? *The Economic Times*. Retrieved from https://economictimes. indiatimes. com/small-biz/startups/snapdeal-slips-against-its-two-main-rivals-flipkart-amazon-can-it-get-its-mojo-back/articleshow/54705032.cms

Shen, D., Wu, G., & Suk, H. I. (2017). Deep learning in medical image analysis. *Annual Review of Biomedical Engineering*, *19*(1), 221–248. doi:10.1146/annurev-bioeng-071516-044442 PMID:28301734

Siar, M., & Teshnehlab, M. (2019, October). Brain Tumor Detection Using Deep Neural Network and Machine Learning Algorithm. In *2019 9th International Conference on Computer and Knowledge Engineering (ICCKE)* (pp. 363-368). IEEE. 10.1109/ICCKE48569.2019.8964846

Singh, S. K., Paul, S., & Kumar, D. (2014). Sentiment analysis approaches on different data set domain: Survey. *International Journal of Database Theory and Application*, *7*(5), 39–50.

Singh, S., Firmin, S., & Chadhar, M. (2022). An interpretive study of stakeholders' privacy issues in blockchain: A healthcare context. *Australasian Computer Science Week, 2022*, 235–238. doi:10.1145/3511616.3513122

Sinha & Kim. (2012). Factor Affecting Indian Consumer's Online Buying Behavior. *Innovative Marketing*, *8*(2), 2012.

Sisodia, A., & Jindal, R. (2021). A meta-analysis of industry 4.0 design principles applied in the health sector. *Engineering Applications of Artificial Intelligence*, *104*, 104377. doi:10.1016/j.engappai.2021.104377

Sisodia, D. S., Bhandari, S., Reddy, N. K., & Pujahari, A. (2020). A comparative performance study of machine learning algorithms for sentiment analysis of movie viewers using open reviews. In *Performance Management of Integrated Systems and its Applications in Software Engineering* (pp. 107–117). Springer.

Smart Insights. (2020). *5 ways to use Augmented Reality in your marketing strategy*. Retrieved from: https://www.smartinsights.com/digital-marketing-platforms/augmented-reality/5-ways-to-use-augmented-reality-in-your-marketing-strategy/

Sobhaninia, Z., Rezaei, S., Noroozi, A., Ahmadi, M., Zarrabi, H., Karimi, N., . . . Samavi, S. (2018). *Brain tumor segmentation using deep learning by type-specific sorting of images.* arXiv preprint arXiv:1809.07786.

Sohani. (2009). *Technology and Banking Sector.* ICFAI University Press.

Song, X., Yang, S., Huang, Z., & Huang, T. (2019). The Application of Artificial Intelligence in Electronic Commerce. *Journal of Physics: Conference Series*, *1302*(3). Advance online publication. doi:10.1088/1742-6596/1302/3/032030

Speth, J., Morales, A., & Sanz, P. J. (2008). Vision-based grasp planning of 3D objects by extending 2D contour based algorithms. *2008 IEEE/RSJ International Conference on Intelligent Robots and Systems, IROS,* (3), 2240–2245. 10.1109/IROS.2008.4650632

Statista. (2020). *Frequently purchased online food products during the coronavirus (COVID-19) pandemic in India as of May 2020, by gender.* https://www.statista.com/statistics /1128411/india-coronavirus-frequent-online-products/

Strutton, D., Taylor, D. G., & Thompson, K. (2011). Investigating Generational Differences in E-WOM Behaviours for Advertising Purposes,Does X = Y? *International Journal of Advertising*, *30*(4), 559–586. https://doi.org/10.2501/IJA-30-4-559-586

Subramanian, G., & Thampy, A. S. (2021). Implementation of Blockchain Consortium to Prioritize Diabetes Patients' Healthcare in Pandemic Situations. *IEEE Access: Practical Innovations, Open Solutions*, *9*, 162459–162475. doi:10.1109/ACCESS.2021.3132302

Sun, Y., Lim, K. H., Jiang, C., Peng, J. Z., & Chen, X. (2010). Do males and females think in the same way? An empirical investigation on the gender differences in web advertising evaluation. *Computers in Human Behavior*, *26*(6), 1614–1624. doi:10.1016/j.chb.2010.06.009

Suresh, M., & Balajee, T. B. K. (2021). Modelling of factors influencing on the informal learning among school teachers: An ISM- MICMAC approach. *Materials Today: Proceedings*. doi:10.1016/j.matpr.2020.11.547

Suresh, A., Carmel, M. J., & Belinda, M. (2020). A Comprehensive Study of Hybrid Recommendation Systems for E-Commerce Applications Recommendation Systems for E-Commerce View project A Comprehensive Study of Hybrid Recommendation Systems for E-Commerce Applications. *International Journal of Advanced Science and Technology*, *29*(3), 4089–4101.

Sushil. (2012). Interpreting the Interpretive Structural Model. *Global Journal of Flexible Systems Management*, *13*, 87-106. https://doi.org/ doi:10.1007/s40171-012-0008-3

Syaifudin, Y., & Nurwidyantoro, A. (2016, July). Quotations identification from Indonesian online news using rule-based method. In *2016 International Seminar on Intelligent Technology and Its Applications (ISITIA)* (pp. 187-194). IEEE.

Tang, G., & Zeng, H. (2021). Evaluation of Tourism E-Commerce User Satisfaction. *Journal of Organizational and End User Computing*, *33*(5), 25–41. Advance online publication. doi:10.4018/JOEUC.20210901.oa2

Tang, H., Tan, S., & Cheng, X. (2009). A survey on sentiment detection of reviews. *Expert Systems with Applications*, *36*(7), 10760–10773. doi:10.1016/j.eswa.2009.02.063

Tausczik, Y. R., & Pennebaker, J. W. (2010). The psychological meaning of words: LIWC and computerized text analysis methods. *Journal of Language and Social Psychology*, *29*(1), 24–54.

Texnet. (2020). *What is the "Qinghe Model"? Come to the 27th China - Qinghe International Cashmere and Wool Products Fair to find out!* Retrieved from http://info.texnet.com.cn/detail-825672.html

Thakur, M. (n.d.). *E-commerce vs Traditional commerce*. EDUCBA. Retrieved from: https://www.educba.com/e-commerce-vs-traditional-commerce/

Thakur, R., & Srivastava, M. (2015). A study on the impact of consumer risk perception and innovativeness on online shopping in India. *International Journal of Retail & Distribution Management*, *43*(2), 148–166. doi:10.1108/IJRDM-06-2013-0128

The State Council Information Office Of The People's Republic Of China. (2021). *Poverty Alleviation: China's Experience and Contribution.* Retrieved from http://www.scio.gov.cn/zfbps/ndhf/44691/Document/1701663/1701663.htm

Thelwall, M. (2014). Heart and soul: Sentiment strength detection in the social web with sentistrength, 2017. *Cyberemotions: Collective emotions in cyberspace.*

Tian, L., Vakharia, A. J., Tan, Y., & Xu, Y. F. (2018). Marketplace, Reseller, or Hybrid: Strategic Analysis of an Emerging E-Commerce Model. *Production and Operations Management*, *27*(8), 1595–1610. doi:10.1111/poms.12885

Tortorella, G. L., Saurin, T. A., Fogliatto, F. S., Rosa, V. M., Tonetto, L. M., & Magrabi, F. (2021). Impacts of Healthcare 4.0 digital technologies on the resilience of hospitals. *Technological Forecasting and Social Change*, *166*, 120666. doi:10.1016/j.techfore.2021.120666

Treiblmaier, H., & Sillaber, C. (2021). *The impact of blockchain on e-commerce: A framework for salient research topics*. Science Direct.

Turney, P. D. (2002). *Thumbs up or thumbs down? Semantic orientation applied to unsupervised classification of reviews.* arXiv preprint cs/0212032.

Tutorials Point. (n.d.). *E-Commerce-Disadvantages*. Tutorials Point. Retrieved from: https://www.tutorialspoint.com/e_commerce/e_commerce_disadvantages.htm

Ulbrich, F., Christensen, T., & Stankus, L. (2010). Gender-specific on-line shopping preferences. *Electronic Commerce Research*, *11*(2), 181–199. doi:10.1007/s10660-010-9073-x

Ullal, M. S., Spulbar, C., Hawaldar, I. T., Popescu, V., & Birau, R. (2021). *The impact of online reviews on e-commerce sales in India: A case study.* doi:10.1080/1331677X.2020.1865179

Umarji, V. (2016). *Amul to Launch Delivery Service via Online, Mobile App Ties up with Infibeam.* Tests Ahmedabad Market with Soft Launch.

Uzunoğlu, E., & Kip, S. M. (2014). Brand Communication through Digital Influencers: Leveraging Blogger Engagement. *International Journal of Information Management*, *34*(5), 592–602. https://doi.org/10.1016/j.ijinfomgt.2014.04.007

Vahid-Araghi, O., & Golnaraghi, F. (2018). Friction-Induced Vibration in Lead Screw Drives. *Angewandte Chemie International Edition*, *6*(11), 951–952.

Vaitheeswaran. (2017). *Failing to Succeed: The Story of India's First E-Commerce Company.* Rupa Publications.

Variyar, M. (2018). *Amazon India: Amazon gets more product returns in India than any other markets, Technology News, ETtech.* https://tech.economictimes.indiatimes.com/news/internet/amazon-gets-more-product-returns-in-india-than-any-other-markets/66946547

Verhoef, Kannan, & Inman. (2015). From Multi-Channel Retailing to Omni-Channel Retailing. Introduction to the Special Issue on Multi-Channel Retailing. *Journal of Retailing, 91*(2), 174–81. doi:10.1016/j.jretai.2015.02.005

Verma, P., & Sood, S. K. (2018). Fog Assisted-IoT Enabled Patient Health Monitoring in Smart Homes. *IEEE Internet of Things Journal*, *5*(3), 1789–1796. doi:10.1109/JIOT.2018.2803201

Vishnuvarthan, R., Sakthivel, R., Bhanumathi, V., & Muralitharan, K. (2019). Energy-efficient data collection in strip-based wireless sensor networks with optimal speed mobile data collectors. *Computer Networks*, *156*, 33–40. doi:10.1016/j.comnet.2019.03.019

Visioli, A., & Legnani, G. (2002). On the trajectory tracking control of industrial SCARA robot manipulators. *IEEE Transactions on Industrial Electronics*, *49*(1), 224–232. doi:10.1109/41.982266

Wagner, G., Schramm-Klein, H., & Steinmann, S. (2020). Online retailing across e-channels and e-channel touchpoints: Empirical studies of consumer behavior in the multichannel e-commerce environment. *Journal of Business Research*, *107*, 256–270. doi:10.1016/j.jbusres.2018.10.048

Wagner, T. F., Baccarella, C. V., & Voigt, K. I. (2017). Framing Social Media Communication: Investigating the Effects of Brand Post Appeals on User Interaction. *European Management Journal*, *35*(5), 606–616. https://doi.org/10.1016/j.emj.2017.05.002

Wang, H., Can, D., Kazemzadeh, A., Bar, F., & Narayanan, S. (2012, July). A system for real-time twitter sentiment analysis of 2012 us presidential election cycle. In *Proceedings of the ACL 2012 system demonstrations* (pp. 115-120). Academic Press.

Wang, L., Wong, P. P. W., & Narayanan, E. A. (2019). *The demographic impact of consumer green purchase intention toward Green Hotel Selection in China.* doi:10.1177/1467358419848129

Wang, E., An, N., Gao, Z., Kiprop, E., & Geng, X. (2020). Consumer food stockpiling behavior and willingness to pay for food reserves in COVID-19. *Food Security*, *N0*(12), 739–747. doi:10.100712571-020-01092-1

Wang, L., Lin, Z. Q., & Wong, A. (2020). Covid-net: A tailored deep convolutional neural network design for detection of covid-19 cases from chest x-ray images. *Scientific Reports*, *10*(1), 1–12. doi:10.103841598-020-76550-z PMID:33177550

Wang, W. T., Wang, Y. S., & Liu, E. R. (2016). The stickiness intention of group-buying websites: The integration of the commitment-trust theory and e-commerce success model. *Information & Management*, *53*(5), 625–642. doi:10.1016/j.im.2016.01.006

Wang, Y., & Coe, N. M. (2021). Platform ecosystems and digital innovation in food retailing: Exploring the rise of Hema in China. *Geoforum*, *126*, 310–321. doi:10.1016/j.geoforum.2021.08.007

Wang, Z., & Kim, H. G. (2017). Can Social Media Marketing Improve Customer Relationship Capabilities and Firm Performance? Dynamic Capability Perspective. *Journal of Interactive Marketing*, *39*, 15–26. https://doi.org/10.1016/j.intmar.2017.02.004

Wankhade, N., & Kundu, G. K. (2020). Interpretive Structural Modelling (ISM) Methodology and its application in Supply Chain Research. *International Journal of Innovative Technology and Exploring Engineering, 9*(4), 1101-1109. https://doi.org/ doi:10.35940/ijitee.D1607.029420

Warfield, J. N. (1973a). Binary matrices in system modeling. *IEEE Transactions on Systems, Man, and Cybernetics, SMC-3*(5), 441–449. doi:10.1109/TSMC.1973.4309270

Watson, D., Clark, L. A., & Tellegen, A. (1988). Development and validation of brief measures of positive and negative affect: The PANAS scales. *Journal of Personality and Social Psychology, 54*(6), 1063.

What is Ecommerce? (n.d.). https://ecommerceguide.com/guides/what-is-ecommerce/

Whiteley. (2017). *E-Commerce: Strategy, Technologies and Applications.* McGraw Hill Education.

Williams, G., & Mahmoud, A. (2017, May). Analyzing, classifying, and interpreting emotions in software users' tweets. In *2017 IEEE/ACM 2nd International Workshop on Emotion Awareness in Software Engineering (SEmotion)* (pp. 2-7). IEEE.

Wiścicka-Fernando, M. (2021). The use of mobile technologies in online shopping during the Covid-19 pandemic - an empirical study. In *25th International Conference on Knowledge-Based and Intelligent Information & Engineering Systems.* Science Direct.

Wisetsri, W., Syam, E., Alanya-Beltran, J., Ramchandra Kulkarni, G., Vardhan Reddy, R. K., & Firdos Alam Sheikh, M. (2022). Assessing and comparing the role of information and communication technology (ICT) and supply chain management (SCM) and its impact on contribution of e-commerce. *Materials Today: Proceedings.* https://doi.org/ doi:10.1016/j.matpr.2021.12.429

Wudie, A. A. (2020). Analysis of Speeches by the Former President of the US, Barack Hussein Obama, Regarding the Middle East and Northern Africa. *International Journal of Translation, Interpretation, and Applied Linguistics, 2*(1), 20–32. Advance online publication. doi:10.4018/IJTIAL.2020010102

Xinhua. (2021). *"Lin'an Model" Promotes New Path of Rural Revitalization.* Retrieved from http://education.news.cn/2021-11/02/c_1211429647.htm

Xuan, H. N. T., & Le, A. C. (2012, November). *Linguistic features for subjectivity classification. In 2012 international conference on asian language processing.* IEEE.

Xu, L., & Sang, X. (2022). E-Commerce Online Shopping Platform Recommendation Model Based on Integrated Personalized Recommendation. *Scientific Programming, 2022.* Advance online publication. doi:10.1155/2022/4823828

Yadav, S. S., & Jadhav, S. M. (2019). Deep convolutional neural network-based medical image classification for disease diagnosis. *Journal of Big Data, 6*(1), 1–18. doi:10.118640537-019-0276-2

Yahoo messenger emoticons. (n.d.). http://messenger.yahoo.com/features/emoticons

Yan, R. N., Hyllegard, K. H., & Blaesi, L. F. (2012). Marketing eco-fashion: The influence of brand name and message explicitness. Journal of Marketing Communications, 18(2), 151-168. https://doi.org/ doi:10.1080/13527266.2010.490420

Yang, G., Pang, Z., Jamal Deen, M., Dong, M., Zhang, Y.-T., Lovell, N., & Rahmani, A. M. (2020, September). Homecare Robotic Systems for Healthcare 4.0: Visions and Enabling Technologies. *IEEE Journal of Biomedical and Health Informatics, 24*(9), 2535–2549. doi:10.1109/JBHI.2020.2990529 PMID:32340971

Yang, Z., Liang, B., & Ji, W. (2021). An Intelligent End–Edge–Cloud Architecture for Visual IoT-Assisted Healthcare Systems. *IEEE Internet of Things Journal, 8*(23), 16779–16786. doi:10.1109/JIOT.2021.3052778

Yao, L., Zhang, H., Zhang, M., Chen, X., Zhang, J., Huang, J., & Zhang, L. (2021). Application of artificial intelligence in renal disease. *Clinical eHealth, 4*, 54-61.

Yaqoob, I., Salah, K., Jayaraman, R., & Al-Hammadi, Y. (2021). Blockchain for healthcare data management: opportunities, challenges, and future recommendations. Springer.

Yaqoob, I., Salah, K., Jayaraman, R., & Al-Hammadi, Y. (2021). Blockchain for healthcare data management: Opportunities, challenges, and future recommendations. *Neural Computing & Applications*. Advance online publication. doi:10.100700521-020-05519-w

Yera, R., & Martínez, L. (2017). Fuzzy tools in recommender systems: A survey. *International Journal of Computational Intelligence Systems*, *10*(1), 776–803. doi:10.2991/ijcis.2017.10.1.52

Young Kim, E., & Kim, Y. (2004). Predicting online purchase intentions for clothing products. *European Journal of Marketing*, *38*(7), 883–897. doi:10.1108/03090560410539302

Young, S. (2022). AI in healthcare startups and special challenges. *Intelligence-Based Medicine*, *6*, 100050. doi:10.1016/j.ibmed.2022.100050

Yuan, X., Chen, J., Zhang, K., Wu, Y., & Yang, T. (2022). A Stable AI-Based Binary and Multiple Class Heart Disease Prediction Model for IoMT. *IEEE Transactions on Industrial Informatics*, *18*(3), 2032–2040. doi:10.1109/TII.2021.3098306

Zande, V. J. (n.d.). *What is e-commerce? Definition, benefits, examples. The Future of Customer Engagement and Experience*. Retrieved from: https://www.the-future-of-commerce.com/2020/01/19/what-is-e-commerce-definition-examples/

Zang, W., Zhou, C., Wang, X., & Guo, L. (2014, December). Topic Block: Mining User Inner Interests for Text and Link Analysis in Social Networks. In *2014 15th International Conference on Parallel and Distributed Computing, Applications and Technologies* (pp. 159-165). IEEE.

ZeeBiz. (2020). What Is Flipkart's '2GUD Local'? How Will It Help the Traditional Retail Business? *Zee Business*. https://www.zeebiz.com/small-business/news-what-is-flipkart-s-2gud-local-how-will-it-help-the-traditional-retail-business-142820

Zhang, B., Du, Z. J., Wang, B., & Wang, Z. H. (2019). Motivation and challenges for e-commerce in e-waste recycling under "Big data" context: A perspective from household willingness in China. *Technological Forecasting and Social Change*, *144*, 436–444. doi:10.1016/j.techfore.2018.03.001

Zhang, Q., Lu, J., & Jin, Y. (2021). Artificial intelligence in recommender systems. *Complex & Intelligent Systems*, *7*(1), 439–457. doi:10.100740747-020-00212-w

Zhang, W., Li, C., Ye, Y., Li, W., & Ngai, E. W. (2015). Dynamic business network analysis for correlated stock price movement prediction. *IEEE Intelligent Systems*, *30*(2), 26–33.

Zhang, Y., Sun, Y., Jin, R., Lin, K., & Liu, W. (2021). High-Performance Isolation Computing Technology for Smart IoT Healthcare in Cloud Environments. *IEEE Internet of Things Journal*, *8*(23), 16872–16879. doi:10.1109/JIOT.2021.3051742

Zheng, K., Zhang, Z. J., & Song, B. J. I. M. M. (2020). E-commerce logistics distribution mode in big-data context: A case analysis of JD. *COM*, *86*, 154–162. doi:10.1016/j.indmarman.2019.10.009

Zheng, P., Sang, Z., Zhong, R. Y., Liu, Y., Liu, C., Mubarok, K., Yu, S., & Xu, X. (2018). Smart manufacturing systems for Industry 4.0: Conceptual framework, scenarios, and future perspectives. *Frontiers of Mechanical Engineering*, *13*(2), 137–150. doi:10.100711465-018-0499-5

Zhou, W., Hinz, O., & Benlian, A. (2018). The impact of the package opening process on product returns. *Business Research, 11*(2), 279–308. doi:10.100740685-017-0055-x

Zhu, X., & Wang, D. (2019). Research on Blockchain Application for E-Commerce, Finance and Energy. In *ESMA 2018 IOP Conf. Series: Earth and Environmental Science*. IOP Publishing.

Zhuo, D., & Xiaoting, Z. (2010). An Empirical Study on Factors which Affect Consumers' Online Shopping Behavior. *2010 International Conference on E-Business and E-Government*, 2200-2203. doi: 10.1109/ICEE.2010.556

Zobrist, T. (2019). *Five e-commerce Functions You Should Be Doing Daily.* Retrieved from: https://www.zobristinc.com/five-e-commerce-functions-you-should-be-doing-daily/

Zou, J., Fekri, F., & McLaughlin, S. W. (2015, August). Mining streaming tweets for real-time event credibility prediction in twitter. In *Proceedings of the 2015 IEEE/ACM International Conference on Advances in Social Networks Analysis and Mining 2015* (pp. 1586-1589). IEEE.

About the Contributors

Himansu Das works as Associate Professor in the School of Computer Engineering, Kalinga Institute of Industrial Technology (KIIT), Deemed to be University, Bhubaneswar, India. He has received Ph.D. in Engineering degree from Veer Surendra Sai University of Technology (VSSUT), Odisha. He has received M.Tech degree in Computer Science and Engineering from the National Institute of Science and Technology, Odisha. He has also received B.Tech degree from the Institute of Technical Education and Research, Odisha, India. He has published several research papers in various international journals and has presented at conferences. He has also edited several books published by IGI Global, Springer, CRC press, and Elsevier. He has also served on many journals and conferences as editorial or reviewer board member. He is proficient in the field of Computer Science Engineering and served as an organizing chair, a publicity chair and acted as a member of the technical program committees of many national and international conferences. He is also associated with various educational and research societies such as IET, IACSIT, ISTE, UACEE, CSI, IAENG, and ISCA. His research interests include the field of Data Mining, Soft Computing, and Machine Learning. He has also more than twelve years of teaching and research experience in various engineering colleges and universities.

* * *

J. Badajena completed M.Tech in Information Technology from CET, Bhubaneswar in 2010. Research interests include wireless mesh network, mobile computing, distributed system, real-time system, programming language, data mining and data ware housing and embedded system, system programming.

Saurabh Bilgaiyan is currently working as an Assistant Professor in KIIT deemed to be University, Bhubaneswar, India since 2016. He has completed his Master's and Ph.D. in Computer Science Engineering from KIIT, Deemed to be University, Bhubaneswar, India in 2014 and 2018 respectively. Bachelor's degree of B.E. in Information Technology from B.I.R.T., Bhopal, India in 2012. Dr. Saurabh Bilgaiyan has published more than 44 research papers in various reputed International Journals, Conferences, and edited books. His area of interest includes soft computing, software engineering, cloud computing, image processing, and machine learning. He has reviewed various manuscripts in more than 25 International conferences and Journals including Soft Computing Springer, IEEE Access, IETE Journal of Research Taylor and Francis, Future Generation Computer System Elsevier, Concurrency and Computation: Practice and Experience Wiley, etc.

Jiai Chen is an independent researcher. Her research interests include business analysis, Chinese economy, and sustainability.

Aditya Dhiman is a Research Scholar in the Faculty of Management Studies, Gurukula Kangri (Deemed to be University), Haridwar. He has obtained her B.Com and MBA (Finance) from the HNBG and UTU respectively. He has also qualified NET in Management in year 2019.He has already published 2 articles in Scopus indexed journal and book.

Mahendra Kumar Gourisaria is presently working as an Assistant Professor in the School of Computer Engineering at KIIT University, Bhubaneswar, Odisha. He has received his Master degree in Computer Application from Indira Gandhi National Open University, New Delhi and M.Tech in Computer Science and Engineering from Biju Patnaik University of Technology - Rourkela. He is pursuing his Ph.D. from KIIT Deemed to be University. He has experience of more than 18 years in academia and 7 years in research. He has published more than 50 research papers in different international journals and conferences of repute. He has also served as the organizing committee members of various conferences and workshops. His area of research includes Cloud Computing, Machine Learning, Data Mining, Soft Computing, and Internet and Web Technology. He is a member of IAENG, UACEE, IEEE and a life member of ISTE, CSI, and ISCA.

Ritika Kapoor has 10 years of teaching experience. She has been taking classes of BCA students of GGSIPU. Currently, she is working as an Assistant Professor with Trinity Institute of Professional Studies, Dwarka (An affiliated college of GGSIPU). Her area of research is Big Data. She has co-authored a book on Fundamentals of Data Warehousing by Galgotia Publishing Company. She has attended various national and international conferences. She has authored a chapter on "Going Web or Mobile" on the New Digital Age: Reshaping Strategies for Business Organization and other on "Requirements Engineering technique for Data Warehouse using Information Packaging Methodology" in MERI Journal of Management and IT.

Brajaballav Kar is an Associate Professor of Production and Operations Management at the School of Management, KIIT University. His corporate experience included production, enterprise application design, implementation, and support. He takes up consulting engagements, training, and doctoral research projects in the areas of entrepreneurship, healthcare, and supply chain management. He is a life member of the Institution of Engineers of India and the Operational Research Society of India.

Kaveri Kar teaches Operating System and Computer System Architecture at Shri Shankaracharya Institute of Professional Management and Technology, Raipur under CSVTU Technical University, India. She has researched, published and taught in this area for more than 04 Years. She has published 10 papers in International journal and conferences. She is having Life Membership of Professional bodies like CSI. Currently, she is working with SSIPMT, Raipur as an Asst. Professor in Department of Computer Science & Engineering.

Satyaballav Kar is a mechanical engineer and master of business administration. He works as a Deputy General Manager of Steel Authority of India Limited, in the division of Central Marketing

Organisation. He is also a research scholar at GIET University, Rayagada, India. His research interest includes Agro-entrepreneurship, Supply Chain Management, and E-commerce.

Alisha Lakra has graduated with a degree of Mechanical Engineering from the College of Engineering and Technology, Bhubaneswar, India. Currently she is perusing her Master's Degree program in Manufacturing Processes and Systems, from KIIT Bhubaneswar, India. Her interest lies in the areas of e-commerce, supply chain management and sustainability.

Pankaj Madan is currently a Professor in the Faculty of Management Studies, Gurukula Kangri (Deemed to be University), Haridwar and Dean in Faculty of Engineering & Technology. He is Visiting Professor to Universities in China, Europe and Latin America. His research area includes operation management and data analytics. His literary contributions in Emerald, Taylor and Francis publications can be seen on scopus, researchgate.com or Google Scholar. He has authored more than ten books and conducted more than 500 workshops and training sessions.

S. Mageshwar is working asSelection Grade Assistant Professor at Mepco Schlenk Engineering College, Sivakasi, India. He has 26 years of Teaching experience. He has published 4 papers in Conferences. One copyright is granted to him. He is the Life Member of ISTE.

Bhabani Shankar Prasad Mishra is working as an Associate Professor in School of Computer Engineering at KIIT University, Bhubaneswar, Odisha since 2006. He has received his PhD degree in Computer Science from F.M. University, Balasore, Odisha in 2011. He completed his Post Doctoral Research from Soft Computing Laboratory, Yonsei University, Seoul, South Korea under the Technology Research Program for Brain Science through the National Research Foundation, Ministry of Education, Science & Technology, South Korea. His research interest includes Evolutionary Computation, Neural Networks, Pattern Recognition, Dataware housing and Mining, and Big Data. He has already published about 30 research papers in refereed journals and conferences, has published one book and edited two books in his credit. He is also acting as an editorial member of various journals.

Tania Mittal is a Research Scholar in the Faculty of Management Studies, Gurukula Kangri (Deemed to be University), Haridwar. She obtained her BCom(Hons) and MCom (Finance) from Delhi University and Panjab University respectively. She has also qualified NET in commerce in the year 2019. Two of her research paper is published in Web of science and UGC care list II.

S. Selva Nidhyananthan received his B.E degree in Electronics and Communication Engineering from Manonmanium Sundaranar University, Tirunelveli, in 1999, M.E. degree in Communication Systems from Anna University, Chennai, in 2005 and Ph.D degree in Speech Processing from Anna University, Chennai, in 2014. He has 20 years of teaching experience and he is currently working as Associate Professor in the department of Electronics and Communication Engineering at Mepco Schlenk Engineering College, Sivakasi, Tamil Nadu, India. He has published 2 patents and 3 copyrights are granted to him. He has published 100 papers in refereed Journals and Conferences. He has published 9 Book chapters. He has completed 1 sponsored R&D Project sponsored by DST, Govt. of India as Co-Investigator. His current research interest includes Signal Processing and Image Processing & Internet of Things. He is the

Editorial Board member of few refereed Journals. He is the Fellow Member of IETE and Life Member of ISTE and IAENG.

Wycliffe Nyaribo is a senior lecturer and currently the Dean School of Graduate Studies at KCA University Nairobi Kenya. Dr. Nyaribo holds a Ph.D. in Business Administration from MDS University Ajmer India. Dr. Nyaribo has been engaged in teaching research at the university level for the last eighteen years. His area of expertise is management with a special focus on human resource management. Dr. Nyaribo has authored many articles published in peer-review journals. He is a member of professional bodies both locally and internationally In addition to his research work, he has mentored and supervised many master's students. He has also attended and presented papers at international conferences globally. He is also a member of the editorial board of academic journals. Dr Nyaribos' professional mission is to work with a professional team in institutions of higher learning that will utilize his knowledge, skills, and abilities to make a difference in the life of students and the community at large while enhancing his personal growth in academic research and consultancy.

J. P. Patra teaches Artificial Intelligence, Analysis and Design of Algorithms, Cryptography and Network Security at Shri Shankaracharya Institute of Professional Management and Technology, Raipur under CSVTU Technical University, India. He has researched, published and taught in this area for more than 15 Years. He is known for his books Analysis and Design of Algorithms (ISBN-978-93-80674-53-7) and Performance Improvement of a Dynamic System Using Soft Computing Approaches (ISBN:978-3-659-82968-0) along with he has published 50 papers in International journal and conferences. He is Associated with IIT Bombay IIT Kharagpur as a Remote Centre Coordinator since 2012. He is on the editorial board and Reviewer Board of four leading international journals. In addition, he is on the Technical Committee Board for several International Conferences. He is having Life Membership of Professional bodies like CSI, ISTE also he is holding the post of Secretary of Raipur Chapter for Computer Society of India which is India's Largest Professional body for Computer Professionals. Currently, he is working with SSIPMT, Raipur as Professor and Head of Department of CSE.

Sohini Rudra is a 2021 mechanical engineering graduate with zeal towards inspecting, transforming, and modeling data and also with working experience in data analysis and strategy development from industry behemoths like Amazon, High Radius Corporation, and more. Her research areas are supply chain management, quality management and sustainability.

Sumitra Samal teaches Artificial Intelligence, Cryptography and Network Security at Shri Shankaracharya Institute of Professional Management and Technology, Raipur under CSVTU Technical University, India. She has researched, published and taught in this area for more than 10 Years. She has published 15 papers in International journal and conferences. She is having Life Membership of Professional bodies like CSI, ISTE. Currently, she is working with SSIPMT, Raipur as an Asst. Professor in Department of Computer Science & Engineering.

Michael Sampat is an independent researcher working in several interdisciplinary capacities. Current projects include books on business geography and mass media psychological conditioning.

Suchismita Satapathy is an Associate Professor in the School of Mechanical Sciences, KIIT University, Bhubaneswar, India. She has published more than 130 articles in national and international journals and conferences. She has also published many books and e-books for academic and research purpose. She has worked as a special issue editor in many journals, organizes national and international conference and FDP in school level. Her area of interest is production operation management, operation research, acoustics, Ergonomics, sustainability, supply chain management, etc. With more than 15 years of teaching and research experience, she has guided many PhD, MTech, and B.Tech students.

Bharat Bhushan Sharma earned a B.E. (Instrumentation & Control) from MDU, Rohtak, Haryana, an M.Tech. (Electrical Engineering (Instrumentation & Control) from DCRUST, Murthal, Haryana, and a Ph.D. (Electrical Engineering) from Jamia Millia Islamia, New Delhi. He has over eleven years of teaching and research experience in institutes of repute. He has published more than seventy papers in national and international journals and book chapters and has also reviewed research papers for reputed journals and conferences. He has six international innovation/design patents granted and five Indian patents published. He has delivered invited lectures and invited papers at conferences and workshops. His areas of research include electric drives, power quality, biomedical instrumentation, acoustics, automation, and industrial control.

Kirti Sharma is an Assistant Professor at UITHM Department, Chandigarh University, Mohali, Punjab. She has completed her PhD from Faculty of Management Studies, Gurukula Kangri (Deemed to be University), Haridwar. She was also an ICSSR Fellow. Her one research paper was published in Scopus-index journal and one in UGC-CARE listed journal. She obtained her BCom and MCom (Finance) from the HNB Garhwal University and Diploma of PGDBA from the Symbiosis, Pune. She also holds a National Certificate of Business Professional Programmer by doing 'O' level from NIELIT, formerly named as DOEACC Society.

Mukta Sharma has more than 17 years of teaching experience. She is currently associated as an Associate Professor & HOD-CS & IT with Trinity Institute of Professional Studies, Dwarka (An affiliated college of GGSIPU). She had taken classes for postgraduate (MCA, MBA, MS) and undergraduate students (BCA, BBA, BS) of varied universities like GGSIPU, DTU, Stratford, etc. Her area of research is Information Security, cryptography, E-Commerce, Software Engineering. To her credit, she has more than 25 research papers published both in national and international journals/conferences. She has authored several chapters with many renowned publications like IGI Global, USA, Springer, and Nova Publishers, USA. She has also written 3 textbooks in the computer science domain by Galgotia Publications, out of which 2 books are the reference book for GGSIPU MBA Syllabus.

Vinita Sharma is an academician with over 21 years of rich experience in teaching and training. Her area of interest is Information Technology with special expertise in the areas of Management Information Systems, e-Business, Machine Learning through Python, Data Analytics through R, Business Intelligence and Data Visualisation through Tableau and Power BI, Data modeling and data analysis through Advanced MS Excel. Dr. Sharma has various publications in Scopus and UGC CARE listed journals to her credit and presented various papers in prestigious National and International conferences.

Deepak Singhal is an assistant professor-II in the School of Mechanical Engineering of KIIT University, Bhubaneswar. He holds his a bachelor's degree in Mechanical engineering from Indian Institute of Information Technology (IIIT), Jabalpur. He completed his PhD in the area of Industrial engineering. His research interests include decision modelling, sustainability in supply chain. He has published the research papers in various reputed Journals like "International Journal of Production Research", "Resource, Conservation and Recycling", "Management Decision", "Sustainable Production and Consumption".

D. Suganya received her BE in ECE from Manonmanium Sundaranar University in 2004 and ME in Applied Electronics from Anna University Chennai in 2009. She has 12 years of Teaching experience. Her areas of interests include Digital Signal Processing, Embedded system Design. She is the Life Member of ISTE and IETE.

Shraddha Taunk teaches Computer Graphics and Database Management System at Shri Shankaracharya Institute of Professional Management and Technology, Raipur under CSVTU Technical University, India. She has researched, published and taught in this area for more than 06 Years. She has published 05 papers in International journal and conferences. Currently, she is working with SSIPMT, Raipur as an Asst. Professor in Department of Computer Science & Engineering.

Sushanta Tripathy is currently working as a Professor at the School of Mechanical Engineering in KIIT University, Bhubaneswar, Orissa, India. He has completed his PhD from the Department of Industrial Engineering and Management, Indian Institute of Technology, Kharagpur. He has over 30 years of teaching, research and industry experience in India and abroad. He has published more than 50 papers in international journals of high repute. He is also the editorial member of six reputed international journal. His major areas of interest include production operations management, multivariate analysis, service operations management, supply chain management and quality management. He is a Fellow of Institution of Engineers, India.

Poshan (Sam) Yu is a Lecturer in Accounting and Finance in the International Cooperative Education Program of Soochow University (China). He is also an External Professor of FinTech and Finance at SKEMA Business School (China), a Visiting Professor at Krirk University (Thailand) and a Visiting Researcher at the Australian Studies Centre of Shanghai University (China). Sam leads FasterCapital (Dubai, UAE) as a Regional Partner (China) and serves as a Startup Mentor for AIC RAISE (Coimbatore, India). His research interests include financial technology, regulatory technology, public-private partnerships, mergers and acquisitions, private equity, venture capital, start-ups, intellectual property, art finance, and China's "One Belt One Road" policy.

Index

G

H

I

L

M

N

O

P

R

S

U

V

W

Recommended Reference Books

IGI Global's reference books are available in three unique pricing formats: Print Only, E-Book Only, or Print + E-Book.

Shipping fees may apply.

www.igi-global.com

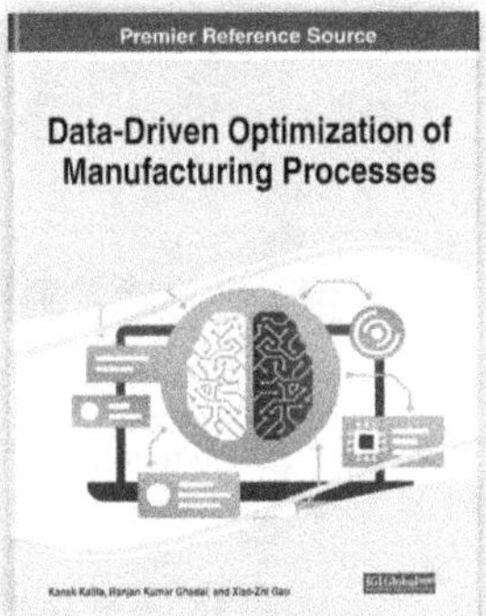

ISBN: 9781799872061
EISBN: 9781799872085
© 2021; 298 pp.
List Price: US$ **225**

ISBN: 9781799876113
EISBN: 9781799876120
© 2021; 210 pp.
List Price: US$ **225**

ISBN: 9781799847601
EISBN: 9781799847618
© 2021; 254 pp.
List Price: US$ **225**

ISBN: 9781799869924
EISBN: 9781799869948
© 2021; 522 pp.
List Price: US$ **295**

ISBN: 9781799843993
EISBN: 9781799844006
© 2021; 347 pp.
List Price: US$ **195**

ISBN: 9781799850625
EISBN: 9781799850632
© 2021; 367 pp.
List Price: US$ **215**

Do you want to stay current on the latest research trends, product announcements, news, and special offers?
Join IGI Global's mailing list to receive customized recommendations, exclusive discounts, and more.
Sign up at: **www.igi-global.com/newsletters.**

Publisher of Timely, Peer-Reviewed Inclusive Research Since 1988

IGI Global
PUBLISHER of TIMELY KNOWLEDGE

www.igi-global.com Sign up at www.igi-global.com/newsletters facebook.com/igiglobal twitter.com/igiglobal linkedin.com/igiglobal

Ensure Quality Research is Introduced to the Academic Community

Become an Evaluator for IGI Global Authored Book Projects

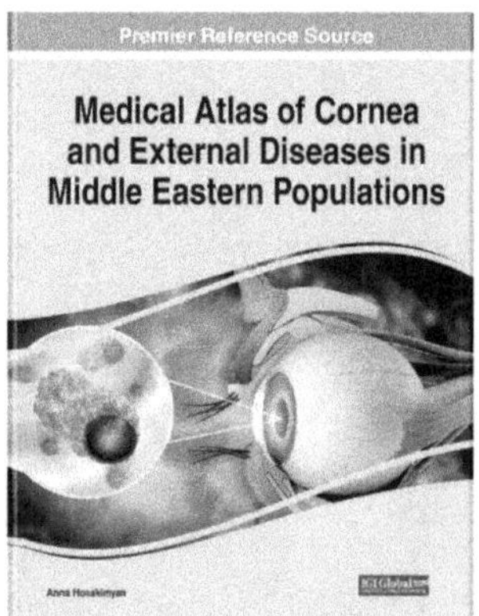

The overall success of an authored book project is dependent on quality and timely manuscript evaluations.

Applications and Inquiries may be sent to:
development@igi-global.com

Applicants must have a doctorate (or equivalent degree) as well as publishing, research, and reviewing experience. Authored Book Evaluators are appointed for one-year terms and are expected to complete at least three evaluations per term. Upon successful completion of this term, evaluators can be considered for an additional term.

If you have a colleague that may be interested in this opportunity, we encourage you to share this information with them.

Increase Your Manuscript's Chance of Acceptance

IGI Global Author Services

Copy Editing & Proofreading

Professional, native English language copy editors improve your manuscript's grammar, spelling, punctuation, terminology, semantics, consistency, flow, formatting, and more.

Scientific & Scholarly Editing

A Ph.D. level review for qualities such as originality and significance, interest to researchers, level of methodology and analysis, coverage of literature, organization, quality of writing, and strengths and weaknesses.

Figure, Table, Chart & Equation Conversions

Work with IGI Global's graphic designers before submission to enhance and design all figures and charts to IGI Global's specific standards for clarity.

- **Professional Service**
- **Quality Guarantee & Certificate**
- **Timeliness**
- **Affordable Pricing**

What Makes IGI Global Author Services Stand Apart?

Services/Offerings	IGI Global Author Services	Editage	Enago
Turnaround Time of Projects	*3-5 Business Days*	6-7 Busines Days	6-7 Busines Days
Pricing	Fraction of our Competitors' Cost	Up to **2x** Higher	Up to **3x** Higher

Learn More or Get Started Here:

For Questions, Contact IGI Global's Customer Service Team at cust@igi-global.com or 717-533-8845

IGI Global
PUBLISHER of TIMELY KNOWLEDGE
www.igi-global.com

6,600+ E-BOOKS. ADVANCED RESEARCH. INCLUSIVE & ACCESSIBLE.

IGI Global
PUBLISHER of TIMELY KNOWLEDGE

IGI Global e-Book Collection

- **Flexible Purchasing Options** (Perpetual, Subscription, EBA, etc.)
- Multi-Year Agreements with **No Price Increases** Guaranteed
- **No Additional Charge** for Multi-User Licensing
- No Maintenance, Hosting, or Archiving Fees
- Transformative **Open Access Options** Available

Request More Information, or Recommend the IGI Global e-Book Collection to Your Institution's Librarian

Among Titles Included in the IGI Global e-Book Collection

Research Anthology on Racial Equity, Identity, and Privilege (3 Vols.)
EISBN: 9781668445082
Price: US$ 895

Handbook of Research on Remote Work and Worker Well-Being in the Post-COVID-19 Era
EISBN: 9781799867562
Price: US$ 265

Research Anthology on Big Data Analytics, Architectures, and Applications (4 Vols.)
EISBN: 9781668436639
Price: US$ 1,950

Handbook of Research on Challenging Deficit Thinking for Exceptional Education Improvement
EISBN: 9781799888628
Price: US$ 265

Acquire & Open

When your library acquires an IGI Global e-Book and/or e-Journal Collection, your faculty's published work will be considered for immediate conversion to Open Access *(CC BY License)*, at no additional cost to the library or its faculty *(cost only applies to the e-Collection content being acquired)*, through our popular **Transformative Open Access (Read & Publish) Initiative.**

For More Information or to Request a Free Trial, Contact IGI Global's e-Collections Team: eresources@igi-global.com | 1-866-342-6657 ext. 100 | 717-533-8845 ext. 100

Have Your Work Published and Freely Accessible

Open Access Publishing

With the industry shifting from the more traditional publication models to an open access (OA) publication model, publishers are finding that OA publishing has many benefits that are awarded to authors and editors of published work.

Freely Share Your Research

Higher Discoverability & Citation Impact

Rigorous & Expedited Publishing Process

Increased Advancement & Collaboration

Acquire & Open

When your library acquires an IGI Global e-Book and/or e-Journal Collection, your faculty's published work will be considered for immediate conversion to Open Access *(CC BY License)*, at no additional cost to the library or its faculty *(cost only applies to the e-Collection content being acquired)*, through our popular **Transformative Open Access (Read & Publish) Initiative**.

Provide Up To **100%** OA APC or CPC Funding

Funding to Convert or Start a Journal to **Platinum OA**

Support for Funding an **OA Reference Book**

IGI Global publications are found in a number of prestigious indices, including Web of Science™, Scopus®, Compendex, and PsycINFO®. The selection criteria is very strict and to ensure that journals and books are accepted into the major indexes, IGI Global closely monitors publications against the criteria that the indexes provide to publishers.

WEB OF SCIENCE™ Compendex Scopus®

PsycINFO® IET Inspec

Learn More Here:

For Questions, Contact IGI Global's Open Access Team at openaccessadmin@igi-global.com

IGI Global
PUBLISHER of TIMELY KNOWLEDGE
www.igi-global.com

Are You Ready to

Publish Your Research?

IGI Global
PUBLISHER of TIMELY KNOWLEDGE

IGI Global offers book authorship and editorship opportunities across 11 subject areas, including business, computer science, education, science and engineering, social sciences, and more!

Benefits of Publishing with IGI Global:

- Free one-on-one editorial and promotional support.
- Expedited publishing timelines that can take your book from start to finish in less than one (1) year.
- Choose from a variety of formats, including Edited and Authored References, Handbooks of Research, Encyclopedias, and Research Insights.
- Utilize IGI Global's eEditorial Discovery® submission system in support of conducting the submission and double-blind peer review process.
- IGI Global maintains a strict adherence to ethical practices due in part to our full membership with the Committee on Publication Ethics (COPE).
- Indexing potential in prestigious indices such as Scopus®, Web of Science™, PsycINFO®, and ERIC – Education Resources Information Center.
- Ability to connect your ORCID iD to your IGI Global publications.
- Earn honorariums and royalties on your full book publications as well as complimentary copies and exclusive discounts.

Join Your Colleagues from Prestigious Institutions, Including:

Australian National University

Massachusetts Institute of Technology

Johns Hopkins University

Harvard University

Tsinghua University

Columbia University in the City of New York

Learn More at: www.igi-global.com/publish

or Contact IGI Global's Aquisitions Team at: acquisition@igi-global.com

Easily Identify, Acquire, and Utilize Published Peer-Reviewed Findings in Support of Your Current Research

IGI Global OnDemand

Purchase Individual IGI Global OnDemand Book Chapters and Journal Articles

For More Information:

www.igi-global.com/e-resources/ondemand/

Browse through 150,000+ Articles and Chapters!

Find specific research related to your current studies and projects that have been contributed by international researchers from prestigious institutions, including:

Massachusetts Institute of Technology

HARVARD UNIVERSITY

COLUMBIA UNIVERSITY IN THE CITY OF NEW YORK

Australian National University

- Accurate and Advanced Search
- Affordably Acquire Research
- Instantly Access Your Content
- Benefit from the InfoSci Platform Features

"It really provides an excellent entry into the research literature of the field. It presents a manageable number of highly relevant sources on topics of interest to a wide range of researchers. The sources are scholarly, but also accessible to 'practitioners'."

- Ms. Lisa Stimatz, MLS, University of North Carolina at Chapel Hill, USA

Interested in Additional Savings?

Subscribe to

IGI Global OnDemand *Plus*

Learn More

Acquire content from over 128,000+ research-focused book chapters and 33,000+ scholarly journal articles for as low as US$ 5 per article/chapter (original retail price for an article/chapter: US$ 37.50).

www.ingramcontent.com/pod-product-compliance
Lightning Source LLC
LaVergne TN
LVHW060414300926
849162LV00006B/1423